The McFarland Baseball Quotations Dictionary

THIRD EDITION

The McFarland Baseball Quotations Dictionary

THIRD EDITION

Compiled by David H. Nathan

McFarland & Company, Inc., Publishers
Jefferson, North Carolina, and London

LIBRARY OF CONGRESS CATALOGUING-IN-PUBLICATION DATA

The McFarland baseball quotations dictionary /
compiled by David H. Nathan.—3d ed.
p. cm.
Includes indexes.

ISBN 978-0-7864-4790-9
softcover : 50# alkaline paper ♾

1. Baseball players—United States—Quotations. 2. Sports personnel—United States—Quotations.
3. Baseball—United States—Quotations, maxims, etc. I. Nathan, David H., 1967–
GV707.B34 2011 796.357—dc22 2010047024

British Library cataloguing data are available

Manufactured in the United States of America

McFarland & Company, Inc., Publishers
Box 611, Jefferson, North Carolina 28640
www.mcfarlandpub.com

For all my students,
past, present and future,
who have taught me more than I've taught them.

And for my family,
who keep making it fun to head to the ballpark.

I can remember a reporter asking me for a quote, and I didn't know what a quote was. I thought it was some kind of soft drink.
—Joe DiMaggio, Hall of Fame outfielder.

What the hell do they need quotes for? They saw me play.
—Tommy Harper, Boston Red Sox outfielder.

Be on time. Bust your butt. Play smart. And have some laughs while you're at it.
—Whitey Herzog, upon his resignation as St. Louis Cardinals manager, 1990.

Contents

Individuals

Introduction

There's nothing quite like writing a book every decade to put your life into perspective.

For the first edition in 1991, I was the rookie author who had much to learn about baseball. I was single, living in Los Angeles, and writing the book on an old Apple computer. There was no internet, so everything was found in books and bound periodicals. When I was done, the 2,023 quotes fit neatly on a stack of small computer disks.

With the second edition in 2000, I buried myself researching in the Rice University Library where I sped through hundreds of spools of microfilm. I was married with two kids and two dogs. The book was written on an original iMac, and the 4,271 quotes all fit on a single CD.

Now I find myself a seasoned veteran. There are still a few players in the majors older than me, but not many, and not for long. Having been an English teacher since 1995, I'm a bit chagrined by some of the shoddy punctuation and grammar I used in earlier editions, and I've steadfastly endeavored to clean up my act this time around. I was originally aiming for 5,714 quotes (Nolan Ryan's career strikeout total), but I went a bit beyond that in the end. I still use magazines and books in my research, but the internet sure does help.

I have found that the web is both blessing and curse when it comes to researching quotations—there's lots of helpful information, but there are lots of errors, and quite often there's no context given to the quotes, which renders them either confusing or ineffective. Rather than just list the quotes randomly, I've tried my best to place them in useful chapters and within a framework that makes them relevant. Enjoy the ascriptions—they're the only opportunity I had to inject some trivia and humor to the proceedings.

Beyond the world of baseball lexicography, I've had the joy of coaching both my boys throughout Bellaire Little League (2000 National Little League World Series Champions). Whether it was on the Bulldogs, Cardinals, Owls, Storm, Mets, Red Bulls or Grasshoppers, the experience was worth all the effort and anxiety.

I have watched the Rice Owls make the NCAA baseball tournament every year since 1995, going to Omaha seven times, and culminating in the ultimate reward—winning the 2003 College World Series. Coming from Rice, where athletics was often ranked below computer science in terms of school priorities, this was a defining moment.

I saw the Houston Astros, after decades of futility, finally make the World Series in 2005. Yes, they were swept by the White Sox, but after all the lean years, the playoff disappointments, and the close calls, just hosting games in late October was an unmitigated thrill. (Albert Pujols's home run off Brad Lidge to win what should have been the clinching Game 5 of the NLCS notwithstanding.)

Looking back, I've attended the longest games in baseball history for each level of the playoffs. Division Series (2005, Game 4): Astros over Braves in 18 innings. League Championship Series (1986, Game 6): Mets over Astros in 16 innings. World Series (2005, Game 3): White Sox over Astros in 14 innings. Not bad for a franchise that doesn't have a storied history.

Those who have aided and abetted my love of the game have been thanked in previous editions of the book—I haven't forgotten about you all. Thanks for the 21st century include all the players, coaches and parents from Bellaire Little League (especially the "Brian" Trust), my friends and colleagues at St. John's School, the Sunday morning softball game and the Blue Horseshoe, and my proofreader and indexing assistant Hannah Potvin who "done splendid" without knowing much of anything about baseball.

I don't know if and when there will be a 4th edition of the book—unfortunately there aren't as many colorful and quotable characters in the game as there used to be, and my wife says I need to find another genre. In another ten years, my kids will be the same age I was when I compiled the first edition. Maybe they'll take over the franchise. Like the Astros' pitcher Joaquin Andujar said, "Youneverknow."

Aging Gracefully

1 I don't want to achieve immortality by making the Hall of Fame. I want to make immortality by not dying.—*Leo Durocher, manager and former All-Star shortstop. Durocher died in 1991 and was posthumously elected to the Hall of Fame by the Veterans Committee in 1994.*

2 Well, I used to look like this when I was young, and now I still do.—*Yogi Berra, Mets coach, on how he manages to stay looking young, 1970.*

3 Hey, you're only young once, but you can be immature forever.—*Larry Andersen, Astros reliever, 1988.*

4 A lot of people my age are dead at the present time.—*Casey Stengel, 73-year-old Mets manager, 1963.*

5 I was told by a very smart man a long time ago that talent always beats experience. Because by the time you get experience, the talent's gone.—*Pat Corrales, Phillies manager, 1982.*

6 The trouble with baseball is by the time you learn how to play it, you can't play it anymore.—*Frank Howard, former outfielder, 1976.*

7 If you think it's an advantage, it is. If the other team thinks it is, it's a bigger advantage. Actually, it means nothing.—*Jerry Reuss, Dodgers pitcher, on experience, 1980.*

8 They may OD on experience.—*Steve Stone, Cubs broadcaster, on the 1983 Philadelphia Phillies, known as the Wheeze Kids.*

9 You know how it is. If we win it, it's because we're a veteran team. If we lose it, it's because we're too old.—*Mike Schmidt, Phillies third baseman, on the Wheeze Kids who lost to Baltimore in the 1983 World Series.*

10 The Pilgrims didn't have any experience when they landed here. Hell, if experience was that important, we'd never have anybody walking on the moon.—*Doug Rader, former Astros third baseman, on being passed over as Padres manager due to lack of experience, 1981. Rader was eventually hired to manage the Rangers in 1983.*

11 Experience is a hard teacher because she gives the test first and the lesson afterwards.—*Vernon Law, Pirates pitcher.*

12 I'm still Reggie, but not so often.—*Reggie Jackson, 38-year-old Angels DH, 1984.*

13 I know I'm old, fat and ugly, but I'm still Ted Williams.—*Ted Williams, 65-year-old Hall of Fame outfielder, to a security guard at Fenway Park who didn't recognize him, 1983.*

14 The worst of this is that I no longer can see my penis when I stand up.—*Babe Ruth, Hall of Fame outfielder, on getting old and fat.*

15 Bruce Sutter has been around a while, and he's pretty old. He's 35 years old. That will give you an idea of how old he is.—*Ron Fairly, Giants broadcaster, on the Braves reliever, 1988.*

16 I didn't know whether to call him "Sir" or "Mister."—*Doug Sisk, Mets pitcher, on the return of 38-year-old pitcher Tom Seaver to New York, 1983.*

17 It seemed to me some skulking reprobate had moved the plate back at least five yards.—*Lefty Gomez, 33-year-old Yankees pitcher and seven-time All-Star, 1942. The next year, after pitching (and losing) one game for the Washington Senators, Gomez retired.*

18 In the '70s, I threw in the 90s; in the '90s, I throw in the 70s.—*Frank Tanana, 39-year-old Mets pitcher, on adjusting to life after losing his fastball, 1993.*

19 I can still throw it in the 70s. And I can throw it in the 80s if I don't want to comb my hair for a week.—*Bob Feller, 66-year-old Hall of Fame pitcher, 1985. Feller led the AL in strikeouts seven times.*

20 I see where Richard claims he throws 90 miles an hour. Maybe he does, providing he's throwing out of a car going 60.—*Bill Lee, Winter Haven Super Sox player-manager, on 39-year-old former Astros pitcher J.R. Richard, who was cut by the West Palm Beach Tropics of the short-lived Senior League, 1989.*

21 I think a 45-year-old man doing underwear commercials is even more amazing.—*Bob Matthews, sportswriter, on an attempted comeback by Hall of Fame pitcher Jim Palmer with the Orioles, 1990. When the comeback failed, Palmer went to the Baltimore broadcast booth.*

22 I didn't have a problem getting down on my knee, but I had a problem getting back up.—*Jim Palmer, 61-year-old Hall of Fame pitcher, on proposing marriage, 2007.*

23 When he gets down in a crouch, it sounds like a bowl of Rice Krispies.—*Greg Hibbard, White Sox pitcher, on 43-year-old catcher Carlton Fisk, 1991. Once Fisk broke Bob Boone's record for most games played at catcher in 1993, he was unceremoniously released by the White Sox.*

24 These guys are so old they're eligible for Meals on Wheels.—*Mickey Rivers, Rangers DH, on 36-year-old infielder Bill Stein and 37-year-old first baseman Larry Biittner, 1983.*

25 He's 33? What, in dog years?—*Darren Daulton, Phillies catcher, on free agent pitcher Fernando Valenzuela, 1994.*

26 If he's 33, then I'm the President of the Hair Club for Men.—*Larry Andersen, balding Phillies reliever, on the reported age of pitcher Fernando Valenzuela, 1994.*

27 I just want you to know one thing: When you get to be my age, there are no routine ground balls.—*Jim Fregosi, Rangers infielder and former Gold Glove shortstop (1967).*

28 This is one you can tell your grandchildren about—tomorrow.—*Ricky Horton, White Sox pitcher, on the 200th win by 39-year-old teammate Jerry Reuss, 1988. (Also attributed to Chisox pitcher Dave LaPoint.)*

29 I felt pretty good when I woke up this morning, but I got over it.—*Smokey Burgess, 40-year-old White Sox pinch hitter, on playing in his final season, 1967. Although he appeared in 77 games that season, Burgess never played an inning in the field. For his career, Burgess recorded 145 pinch hits.*

30 When I was a boy growing up in Cuba, Luis Tiant was a national hero. Now I'm 36 and he's 37.—*Tony Perez, Expos first baseman, on the Yankees pitcher, 1979.*

31 How old is Dad? The last time I checked, he was sixty-one. I'm fifty-three now. The way I've got it figured, in five years I'll be older than he is.—*Skip Caray, Braves broadcaster, on his father, Chicago Cubs broadcaster Harry Caray, 1992. The elder Caray was actually 72 at the time.*

32 Just think of it. Three generations of Carays broadcasting major league sports at the same time. It seems a mathematical impossibility. I must have been married when I was five years old.—*Harry Caray, Cubs broadcaster, on son Skip who broadcast for the Braves and grandson Chip, a broadcaster for the NBA's Orlando Magic, 1989.*

33 I have a grandfather who's 87 years old, and he hasn't had a hard-on for the last five years. If that Dr. Cowens can manipulate Catfish Hunter's arm and bring it back to life, I'm gonna have him play with my grandfather's dick.—*Lou Piniella, Yankees outfielder, 1978. Following surgery, Hunter went 2–9 in 1979 and retired. Piniella's grandfather presumably also stayed retired.*

34 It's amazing how fast you grow old in this game. At first you're the rookie right-hander; next season you're that promising right-hander; then suddenly you're the Old Man.—*Don Sutton, 32-year-old Dodgers pitcher, 1977. Sutton retired eleven years later and was inducted into the Hall of Fame in 1998.*

35 I just know it's an ugly rumor that you and I are the only two people left alive who saw Abner Doubleday throw the first pitch out.—*President Ronald Reagan to 44-year-old Mariners pitcher Gaylord Perry, 1983. Perry was* *the first player to win the Cy Young Award in both leagues: Cleveland in 1972 and San Diego in 1978.*

36 Say, Satch, tell me, was Abraham Lincoln a crouch hitter?—*Lefty Gomez, former Yankees pitcher, to Indians pitcher Satchel Paige. In 1948, Paige became baseball's oldest rookie at age 41 and helped Cleveland win the World Series over the Boston Braves.*

37 The goat ate the Bible with my birth certificate. That goat lived to be 27.—*Satchel Paige, Hall of Fame pitcher.*

38 Age is a question of mind over matter. If you don't mind, it doesn't matter.—*Satchel Paige, Hall of Fame pitcher.*

39 How old would you be if you didn't know how old you were?—*Satchel Paige, Hall of Fame pitcher.*

40 I'll be 35 this year, and I can only pitch as long as Satchel Paige. That gives me 35 more years.—*Tug McGraw, Phillies reliever, 1979.*

41 The game is too much fun to ever get too old to play it.—*Tug McGraw, Phillies reliever, who retired after the 1984 season at age 39.*

42 Our black players are so old they don't know how to high five.—*Lou Brock, Hall of Fame outfielder, on playing in an old-timers' game with fellow Hall of Famers Billy Williams, Ernie Banks and Willie McCovey.*

43 Oscar Gamble is so old that when he broke into the major leagues he was a Negro.—*Stan Williams, former pitcher.*

44 If this keeps up, by the end of the season I'll be an old man myself.—*Al Simmons, 26-year-old Philadelphia A's outfielder, on playing the outfield alongside 41-year-old Ty Cobb and 40-year-old Tris Speaker, 1928. In 1953, Simmons joined Cobb and Speaker in the Hall of Fame.*

45 All ballplayers should quit when it starts to feel as if all the baselines run uphill.—*Babe Ruth, Yankees outfielder. Ruth did not heed his words. After being released by the Yankees following the 1934 season, the 40-year-old Ruth hit .181 in 1935 for the abysmal Boston Braves before retiring.*

46 I remember one day in September when I was on second base and I looked home, and I said, "Boy, that's a long ways." And I knew it was time to go.—*Ted Williams, Hall of Fame outfielder, who retired at age 41 following the 1960 season in which he batted .316 and hit 29 home runs in 310 at-bats.*

47 You start chasing a ball, and your brain immediately commands your body to "Run forward! Bend! Scoop up the ball! Peg it to the infield!" Then your body says, "Who, me?"—*Joe DiMaggio, Yankees outfielder.*

48 I don't mind turning 50. It's just that at the beginning of the season I was 43.—*Hank Greenwald, San Francisco Giants broadcaster.*

49 He told me he thinks this is the last contract I have to do for him. He's told me that six times before.—*Dick Moss, agent, on his client, 44-year-old Rangers pitcher Nolan Ryan, 1991.*

50 Anyone who talks about me and Nolan in the same vein has mush for brains. The only comparison between me and Nolan is that we're both in our 40s.—*Rick Reuschel, Giants pitcher, 1989. The 40-year-old Reuschel won 17 games with a 2.94 ERA that season compared to Ryan's 16 wins with a 3.20 ERA.*

51 I guess I'm the only guy old enough to figure him out.—*Dave Winfield, 39-year-old Angels outfielder, on breaking up a no-hit bid by Rangers pitcher Nolan Ryan, 1991. Winfield had been 1 for 22 with 13 strikeouts in his career against Ryan before ruining his quest for an eighth no hitter in the eighth inning.*

52 I can remember my years with the Mets, just hoping that I'd get four years in so I'd qualify for my pension. That was my goal. Then, after I did that, I thought maybe I could hang on long enough to get ten years in.—*Nolan Ryan, Hall of Famer who pitched for 27 seasons and is the only player to have his uniform number retired by three teams (Angels, Astros, and Rangers).*

53 Nuts to being old. I'll try to manage as long as I don't have to take a pitcher out in a

wheelchair.—*Casey Stengel, Mets manager, 1965. Stengel managed the Mets until midway through the 1965 season when he broke his hip the day before his 75th birthday. Rather than use a wheelchair, Stengel retired.*

54 My wife doesn't like it. She says everyone thinks she's also 44.—*Tommy John, Yankees pitcher, asking sportswriters to avoid references to his age, 1987.*

55 Good Old Cy. Yeah, I think I pitched against him once in the Eastern League.—*Tommy John, Yankees pitcher, on tying a record with three errors in one inning on July 27, 1988, a feat first accomplished by New York Giants pitcher Cy Seymour in 1898.*

56 This guy is so old that the first time he had athlete's foot, he used Absorbine, Senior.—*Bob Costas, NBC broadcaster, on 45-year-old Yankees pitcher Tommy John, 1988.*

57 I'm so old I remember Preparation A.—*Jack McKeon, 73-year-old Marlins manager, 2004.*

58 When he came up with Cincinnati, the heavyweight champion was white.—*Al Oliver, Giants first baseman, on manager Frank Robinson, 1984. Robinson was Rookie of the Year in 1956 with the Reds and Rocky Marciano reigned with a perfect 49–0 record until his retirement at age 31 on April 27, 1956.*

59 He used to play with the Giants ... the New York Giants.—*Jose Cruz Jr., Blue Jays outfielder, on 37-year-old utility player Juan Samuel, 1998.*

60 I'm going to change my name to "Buck 65." That's all I read, "Jack Buck, 65."—*Jack Buck, 65, Cardinals broadcaster, 1990.*

61 What the hell do I need with a dental policy when I don't have half my teeth?—*Early Wynn, 65-year-old Hall of Fame pitcher, on the deductions from the baseball pension fund, 1985.*

62 Shortly after it happened I was in kind of a fog. I saw all these flowers, but I couldn't hear any music. I thought my wife had bought me a cheap funeral.—*Bob Uecker, broadcaster and former catcher, on waking up in the hospital after suffering a mild heart attack, 1989.*

63 You know a guy's getting old when the first thing he reads in *The Sporting News* is the obituaries.—*Tommy Lasorda, Dodgers manager, 1984.*

64 You'd think you'd have learned something in 20 years.—*George Brett, 40-year-old Royals DH, on hitting .285 in 1992. In 1974, his first full season, Brett hit .282.*

65 They're a little more serious. They don't want to go get a job.—*Pete Rose, Reds manager, explaining why he likes veteran players on his team, 1986.*

66 It's the same old story with him. It's youth, but that youth thing gets old after a while.—*Dick Pole, Giants pitching coach, on erratic 22-year-old pitcher Salomon Torres, 1994.*

67 Somebody will have to come out and take the uniform off me, and the guy who comes after it better bring help.—*Early Wynn, 40-year-old White Sox pitcher, 1960. Wynn tied for the AL lead with four shutouts that year. He retired in 1963 after recording his 300th win with Cleveland.*

68 They're going to retire my uniform—with me still in it.—*Steve Hovley, 26-year-old Oakland A's outfielder, 1971. Hovley retired in 1973.*

69 One wife and six kids.—*Jack Quinn, Brooklyn Dodgers pitcher, on why he was still pitching at age 47, 1931. Quinn made his final appearance at age 50 with Cincinnati and set records as the oldest player to win a game and to hit a home run.*

70 It's not how old you are, it's how old you feel. And I feel as old as any of those guys.—*Duane Kuiper, former infielder, on playing in old-timers' games at age 35, 1986.*

71 Baseball hasn't forgotten me. I go to a lot of old timers' games, and I haven't lost a thing. I sit in the bullpen and let people throw things at me. Just like old times.—*Bob Uecker, former catcher.*

72 I ain't what I used to be, but who the hell is?—*Dizzy Dean, Cardinals pitcher.*

73 In one day, I'm going to go from a very old law student to a very young baseball exec-

utive.—*Ed Lynch, 35-year-old former Mets pitcher, on graduating from the University of Miami Law School before taking over as director of minor league operations for the Padres, 1990. In 1994, Lynch was named GM of the Cubs.*

74 He doesn't celebrate birthdays anymore because he believes if you don't, you don't age. He doesn't celebrate Christmas anymore because all of these dates lend themselves to aging, and he doesn't want to age.—*Tim McCarver, broadcaster and former catcher, on 50-year-old Hall of Fame pitcher Steve Carlton, 1994.*

75 One day you can throw tomatoes through brick walls. The next day you can't dent a pane of glass with a rock. It hurts but you hang on, hoping it'll come back. Oh well, it's a helluva ride, the one on the way up.—*Dean Chance, Angels pitcher.*

76 Babe Ruth would be a good addition to the team right now. According to the local media, a 103-year-old slugger would fit in perfectly on an old team like ours.—*Kevin Malone, Orioles assistant GM, on the aging Orioles, 1998.*

77 I don't know how old Vic Davalillo and Manny Mota are, but someone told me they were both waiters at the Last Supper.—*Tommy Lasorda, Dodgers manager, 1977. Davalillo was 40 and Mota 39 years old.*

78 Pudge is so old they didn't have history class when he went to school.—*Steve Lyons, White Sox utility player, on 42-year-old catcher Carlton Fisk, 1990.*

79 The problem is, you can't take that many practice swings at my age because you're going to wear out parts that you need for pitching.—*Orel Hershiser, 39-year-old Giants pitcher, on breaking out of a hitting slump, 1998.*

80 Right now I can't find my glasses without my glasses.—*Art Howe, Oakland A's manager, on why he needed laser eye surgery, 1999.*

81 I'm 55 years old. I get up three times a night to go to the bathroom. The baby is on my schedule.—*Joe Torre, Yankees manager and new father, when asked if his new baby would upset his nightly routine, 1996.*

82 Not only will I be changing diapers at home, now I will be changing them in the clubhouse.—*Jim Eisenreich, 38-year-old Marlins outfielder and father of three young children, on all the youngsters with Florida's 1997 team.*

83 I'm in my pajamas by 4:30 P.M.—*Sparky Anderson, former manager, on retirement, 1996.*

84 I take it a decade at a time.—*Shirley Povich, 91-year-old baseball writer, on his secret to longevity, 1997.*

85 Time. I need more of it. Actually, I am the biggest shareholder of *Time*. I own *Time*. And now I'm running out of it.—*Ted Turner, Braves owner, 1997.*

86 The first thing I do in the morning is breathe on a mirror and hope it fogs up.—*Early Wynn, Hall of Fame pitcher, 1982.*

87 First you forget names; then you forget faces; then you forget to zip up your fly; and then you forget to unzip your fly.—*Branch Rickey, Hall of Fame executive, on the four stages of senility.*

88 You don't pitch with your birth certificate.—*Jim Bouton, Braves pitcher, on his comeback at age 38, 1978.*

89 At my age, I'm happy to be named the greatest living anything.—*Joe DiMaggio, Hall of Fame outfielder, on being named baseball's "greatest living player" at age 66, 1981.*

90 If I'd known I was going to grow this old, I'd have taken better care of myself.—*Cal Hubbard, umpire, 1979. (Also attributed to Mickey Mantle.)*

91 If you don't live to get old, you die young.—*James "Cool Papa" Bell, 84-year-old Hall of Famer, 1985.*

92 As you get older, you slow down and the infielders back up because they've got more time to throw you out at first. At the same time, you lose a little power, so the outfielders move in because you aren't hitting the ball so far. When they shake hands, you've had it.—*Paul Waner, Hall of Fame outfielder.*

93 There ought to be a rule that when the temperature drops below your age, you don't

have to play.—*Graig Nettles, Yankees third baseman, 1983.*

94 When you first sign that contract as a kid, they tell you your whole future is ahead of you. But they forget to tell you that your future stops at 35.—*Hal Jeffcoat, Cardinals pitcher, 1959.*

95 It's a mere moment in a man's life between an All-Star game and an old-timers' game.—*Vin Scully, broadcaster, 1980.*

96 I'd like to die of a heart attack on the pitcher's mound at 70 years of age.—*Gene Garber, Royals pitcher, 1988.*

97 I hope I die on the field. I hope when I walk to change the pitcher, I drop dead and that's it. I know my family would be so happy that it happened on the field. They wouldn't feel bad because that's what I've always wanted to do.—*Ozzie Guillen, White Sox manager, 2009.*

98 If I were a Tibetan priest and ate everything perfect, maybe I'd live to be 105. The way I'm going now, I'll probably only make it to 102. I'll give three years to beer.—*Bill Lee, Expos pitcher, 1979.*

99 Girls used to come up to me and say, "My sister loves you." Now they say, "My mother loves you."—*Lee Mazzilli, Mets outfielder, 1987.*

100 A couple of years ago they told me I was too young to be President and you were too old to be playing baseball. But we fooled them, and we're still fooling them.—*President John F. Kennedy, 45, to 41-year-old Cardinals first baseman Stan Musial at the 1962 All-Star Game.*

101 When you get older, you start looking funny in a uniform.—*Sandy Koufax, Hall of Fame pitcher, on turning down a full-time coaching position with the Los Angeles Dodgers.*

102 It's been 41 years between starts for him. If he's rested and ready to take the mound again, we want him on our team.—*Art Shamsky, Modi'in Miracle manager, on drafting 71-year-old Hall of Fame pitcher Sandy Koufax with the last pick in the inaugural draft of the Israel Baseball League, 2007.*

103 The great thing about baseball is when you're done, you'll only tell your grandchildren about the good things. If they ask me about 1989, I'll tell them I had amnesia.—*Sparky Anderson, Tigers manager. In 1989, the Tigers finished in last place, 59–103.*

104 When I was with Houston at the end of my career, Bob Gibson walked up to me one day when I was running in the outfield. He asked me why I didn't quit and said what a shame it was that I was ruining a great career and just trying to hang on. Years later I saw Gibson trying to do the same thing.—*Robin Roberts, Hall of Fame pitcher, who was 5–8 (4.82 ERA) in his final season, 1966. Gibson was 3–10 (5.04 ERA) in 1975.*

105 I've only been doing this fifty-four years. With a little experience, I might get better.—*Harry Caray, Cubs announcer, 1999.*

106 I'm only 32 in the Dominican Republic.—*Tim Raines, Marlins outfielder, on being 42 years old, 2002. Before the season, numerous Dominican players aged overnight following a closer inspection of their birth certificates.*

107 What's up? Did he have another birthday?—*Brad Ausmus, Astros catcher, on the media looking for shortstop Miguel Tejada, June 2008. Two months earlier, a report uncovered Tejada's birth certificate, which showed he was two years older than he claimed.*

108 Well, this is a real honor. And I'm glad I'm not dead like some of these guys.—*Larry Dierker, former Astros pitcher, announcer and manager, on having his No. 49 retired by the team, 2002. Two of the other five players so honored, Jim Umbricht and Don Wilson, had their numbers retired posthumously. The other living Astros were Nolan Ryan, Jose Cruz and Mike Scott (Jimmy Wynn, Jeff Bagwell and Craig Biggio were subsequently honored).*

109 The trick is growing up without growing old.—*Casey Stengel, Hall of Fame manager.*

110 *Steve Finley (Padres OF):* Rickey, you can sit anywhere you want. You've got tenure.

Rickey Henderson: Ten years? What are you talking about? Rickey got 16, 17 years.—*Con-*

versation as the Padres loaded onto a team bus, 1996.

111 I'm glad to see that young guy get in there.—*Jack McKeon, 74-year-old Marlins manager, on the election of 78-year-old Cardinal Joseph Ratzinger as the new pope, 2005.*

112 I don't know—there weren't too many of them living at that time.—*Yogi Berra, Hall of Famer, at his 80th birthday, when asked what he thought of 80-year-olds when he was young, 2005.*

113 I shook hands with Muhammad Ali recently. It took them 30 minutes to get us untangled.—*Jack Buck, Cardinals announcer, 2001. Both Ali and Buck suffered from Parkinson's disease.*

114 Based on his age and his pitching performance, President Barack Obama probably does not have a future in Major League Baseball when he leaves office. Then again, he is left-handed and nearly the same age as Jamie Moyer, so you never know.—*Jim Caple, sportswriter, on President Obama's ceremonial first pitch at the 2009 All-Star Game. In 2010, at 47 years old, Moyer became the oldest player ever to pitch a shutout.*

115 At a San Diego Padres game over the weekend, a 103-year-old man threw out the first pitch. I think that's great. Unfortunately, his entire arm went with it.—*Conan O'Brien, talk show host, 2009.*

116 How old is Madonna? Instead of A-Rod, maybe they should call him AARP-Rod.—*Jay Leno, talk show host, on rumors that Alex Rodriguez was having an extra-marital relationship with the 50-year-old Material Girl, 2008.*

117 With Bret Saberhagen and David Cone fighting for spots in the rotation, the Red Sox just might be the favorites to win the 1988 American League pennant.—*Tim Keown, sportswriter, on two aging pitchers, 2001. In his final season, Saberhagen (age 37) went 1–2 in three starts. Cone (age 38) fared better, going 9–7 in 25 starts.*

118 Almost anyone who was around to see the Yankees beat the Brooklyn Dodgers in 1956 now lives in Boca Raton, Fla.—*Bernie Lincicome, sportswriter, in preparation for the 2000 Yankees-Mets World Series, on whether New Yorkers would recall the last Subway Series.*

119 I've taken a lot of young players under my wing in 17 years, and my wings and feathers are gone.—*Tony Gwynn, 38-year-old Padres outfielder, 1998.*

120 Everybody on that team is dead but me. I guess I didn't get on base as often as the rest of them. Those fellas tired themselves out.—*Mark Koenig, shortstop for the 1927 New York Yankees, at the age of 87 in 1990.*

121 He is likely to be the only man in baseball history to collect a pension check and a salary check at the same time.—*Pitcher Eddie Fisher on reliever Hoyt Wilhelm, who pitched until he was 49 in 1972.*

122 When you reach the point when you're too slow to get out of the way, it's time to quit.—*Tom Brookens, Tigers third baseman, 1981.*

123 This is kind of odd. Earlier today he tested positive for cake.—*David Letterman, talk show host, on Barry Bonds celebrating his 44th birthday, 2008.*

Alibis, Excuses and Analysis

124 You must have an alibi to show why you lost. If you haven't one, you must fake one. Your self-confidence must be maintained. Always have that alibi. But keep it to yourself. That's where it belongs.—*Christy Mathewson, Hall of Fame pitcher.*

125 A string of alibis.—*Miller Huggins, Yankees manager, on what a player in a slump needs most.*

126 I think about the cosmic snowball theory. A few million years from now the sun

will burn out and lose its gravitational pull. The earth will turn into a giant snowball and be hurled through space. When that happens, it won't matter if I get this guy out.—*Bill Lee, Red Sox pitcher.*

127 I never blame myself when I'm not hitting. I just blame the bat, and if it keeps up, I change bats. After all, if I know it isn't my fault that I'm not hitting, how can I get mad at myself?—*Yogi Berra, Yankees catcher.*

128 It was pitching lousy.—*Rob Murphy, Red Sox reliever, on why he threw his glove into the stands during a game, 1990. Murphy finished the year 0–6 with a 6.32 ERA.*

129 My coordination was so bad, I had to pull my car off to the side of the road to blow the horn.—*Ellis Clary, Twins scout, on his playing days as an infielder with the 1923-1924 St. Louis Browns, 1985.*

130 My luck is so bad, if Mickey Mantle and I bought a cemetery, people would stop dying.—*Billy Martin, Yankees second baseman.*

131 I couldn't play when I played.—*Sparky Anderson, Tigers manager, on why he didn't participate in an old-timers' game, 1986. In 1959, his one and only pro season, Anderson hit .218 playing second base for the Phillies.*

132 We've been working on the basics because, basically, we've been having trouble with the basics.—*Bob Ojeda, Dodgers pitcher, 1992. Los Angeles finished the season in last place, 63–99.*

133 I feel my ability as a ballplayer is overshadowed by people saying: "Hey, look at that idiot at the plate."—*Mike "The Human Rain Delay" Hargrove, Indians first baseman, on his peculiar ritual of preparing for each pitch by taking three practice swings, digging in the batter's box with his left foot, adjusting his helmet, checking his uniform, tugging on his belt, and finally looking at the pitcher, 1981.*

134 I was calm in that situation and just let my abilities come out—what little abilities I have.—*Michael Jordan, Double A Birmingham Barons outfielder and former NBA MVP, on a bases-loaded, bottom-of-the-ninth situation in which he hit a grounder to third, 1994. The end result was a three-run throwing error and a 6–5 Birmingham victory.*

135 I'm glad I don't have a fourth pitch.—*Roger Mason, Giants pitcher, on giving up three straight home runs against San Diego to start a game, 1987.*

136 It's not a matter of the lively ball. It's my dead arm.—*Don Carman, Phillies pitcher, explaining the proliferation of home runs hit against him, 1987. Carman surrendered 34 homers that season.*

137 I was throwing up volleyballs today, and they were spiking them for kills.—*Erik Hanson, Mariners pitcher, 1990.*

138 I came out to ask if everything was all right, and Charlie said, "Yeah, everything's fine. I just stink."—*Rene Lachemann, Marlins manager, on pitcher Charlie Hough, 1994.*

139 We went almost five weeks into the season with five guys not hitting their weight, and none of them were fat guys.—*Pete Rose, Reds manager, 1987.*

140 We've put up more zeros than there were at Pearl Harbor.—*Rocky Bridges, Giants third base coach, 1985. The Giants scored only 556 runs, worst in the majors.*

141 When my father saw me play baseball, he got waivers from the rest of the family and traded me for a dog to be named later.—*Jack Buck, Cardinals broadcaster.*

142 The more I played with them the more I found out that no one there could take a joke—my batting average.—*Rocky Bridges, Vancouver Canadians manager, on playing two seasons with the Brooklyn Dodgers, 1987. As a rookie in 1951, Bridges hit .254, but he slumped to .196 the next season. Bridges bounced around the majors with six other teams before finding his niche as a minor league manager.*

143 It took us right out of the inning.—*George Bamberger, Brewers manager, on Milwaukee hitting into a triple play, 1980.*

144 I was an All-Star in Little League.—*Mike Gallego, Oakland A's shortstop, on being* *told the team had a former All-Star at every position except shortstop, 1990.*

145 I had tears in my eyes when I was doing the lineup. I can even hit in this lineup.—*Ozzie Guillen, White Sox manager, on his team's anemic offense, 2007.*

146 I feel like the fisherman who has made a record catch but has to throw the fish back.—*Felipe Alou, Expos manager, on having the best record in baseball before the cancellation of the 1994 season.*

147 I knew my days in Philadelphia were numbered. I went to the plate one night as a pinch hitter, and when I looked to the third-base coach for a sign, he turned his back.—*Bob Uecker, Brewers broadcaster and former Phillies catcher.*

148 I was going to make them forget Keith Hernandez. Then I was going to make them forget Bruce Sutter. As it turned out, the only person they wanted to forget in St. Louis was Neil Allen.—*Reliever Neil Allen on being sold to the Yankees, 1985. The Cardinals had acquired Allen in 1983 from the Mets for former MVP first baseman Keith Hernandez.*

149 I hope they don't put this season on the back of my baseball card. Maybe, they'll just put: "In Military Service."—*Bruce Sutter, Braves reliever, 1985. After leading the league in saves the previous season with St. Louis, Sutter's ERA skyrocketed his first year in Atlanta.*

150 The fans booed me when I came in. That's a first. Usually they boo me when I leave.—*Bob Stanley, Red Sox reliever, 1984.*

151 I think I hold the record for most games watched, career.—*Kurt Bevacqua, Padres utility player, 1984. Bevacqua played in the big leagues for 15 years, yet he appeared in only 970 games.*

152 I've been sitting on the bench so long, the kids are beginning to call me Judge.—*Gene Hermanski, Cubs outfielder, 1953. After hitting .150 in just 18 games, Hermanski was involved in a ten-player trade to Pittsburgh that included home run champion Ralph Kiner going to the Cubs. Hermanski hit only .177 for the Pirates before retiring.*

153 No one wants to admit it, but after a while as a backup you get afraid that playing regularly will expose the weakness that put you on the bench to begin with.—*Fran Healy, Yankees broadcaster and former catcher, 1980.*

154 We're like a hockey team. We play in shifts. And I'm still driving the Zamboni.—*Dave Collins, Reds outfielder.*

155 If it's not my 28 at-bats, they'll find some other excuse next year.—*John Marzano, Mariners backup catcher, on not making the 1996 All-Star team.*

156 Down in Atlanta, they have a guy they call "Prime Time." In San Diego, they call me "No Time."—*Dann Bilardello, Padres backup catcher, 1992. After hitting .121 for the season—and just .204 for his career—Bilardello was released.*

157 Alas, at 32 it's too late for Sanders to learn what Junior (Griffey) knew at 8 without knowing he knew it.—*Dave Kindred, sportswriter, on the arrival of outfielders Deion Sanders and Ken Griffey Jr. to Cincinnati, 2000. Sanders made his debut with three hits in one game ... and ten more the entire season to finish with a .173 average. Griffey made the All-Star team in 2000 before injuries curtailed his production with the Reds.*

158 Some people are so busy learning the tricks of the trade that they never learn the trade.—*Vern Law, Pirates pitcher, 1960.*

159 Well, I haven't seen him do anything except show up. He showed up well.—*Jim Riggleman, Cubs manager, when asked how second baseman Ryne Sandberg looked in spring training after a 16-month retirement, 1996. Sandberg hit just .244 that season and .264 in 1997 before retiring for good.*

160 He's kind of like a recovering emotionalist.—*Joe Maddon, Rays manager, on the inner struggles of pitcher Matt Garza, 2008.*

161 I'm so messed up. If I got 3,000 hits, I'd probably be thinking more about the 7,000 outs I've made.—*Jeff Bagwell, Astros first baseman, on not being able to enjoy getting his 1000th RBI, 2000. Bagwell finished his 15-year career with 2,314 hits.*

162 If you played in the World Series, people get the impression that you were somewhat more of an outstanding player than if you never did. You're put in a kind of special category if you were on a pennant-winning team.—*Ned Garver, former pitcher. The runner-up for the 1951 MVP, Garver never made the postseason in his 14-year career.*

163 Good is not good when better is expected.—*Vin Scully, Dodgers broadcaster.*

164 The only mistake I made in my whole baseball career was hitting .361 that one year (1961) because ever since then people have expected me to keep on doing it.—*Norm Cash, Tigers first baseman. After that career year in just his third full season, Cash never hit higher than .286.*

165 I know five reasons why he isn't going to—my wife and four children.—*Willie Miranda, Orioles shortstop, when told he might lose his job to a rookie, March 1958. Miranda hit .201 for the year and lost his job the following year when he hit .159.*

166 I had many years when I was not so successful as a ballplayer, as it is a game of skill.—*Casey Stengel, Yankees manager, 1958.*

167 I just pretend I'm back in my playing days with the bases loaded and two out.—*Steve Smith, Rangers coach, on how he hits pop-ups to the catchers during practice, 2003.*

168 He's thinking in French, and they're pitching to him in English.—*Fresco Thompson, Brooklyn Dodgers scout, on a trip to New Orleans during World War II to watch Paul Merrinow, a fast, defensively strong French-Canadian outfielder who had some problems hitting.*

169 Those four hitters combined for 454 strikeouts last year, which means—if nothing else—that the Rays should save a little money on air-conditioning.—*Peter Schmuck, sportswriter, on Tampa Bay acquiring Greg Vaughn and Vinny Castilla to join Jose Canseco and Fred McGriff, January 2000. The quartet only struck out 354 times as teammates that season, mostly due to injuries that limited Canseco and Castilla.*

170 I'm sick of hearing about J. Rodney Richard. We all know what he can do with his stuff., but what I'd like to see is what he could do with *my* stuff.—*Don Sutton, Dodgers pitcher. For five and a half seasons, Richard was the most feared pitcher in the NL—leading the league in strikeouts, walks and wild pitches—before a stroke ended his career midway through the 1980 season.*

171 The ball is smaller, the planets are in line, the hole in the ozone layer is bigger, and so is Juan Gonzalez.—*Terry Mulholland, Phillies pitcher, on why more home runs were being hit.*

172 This team makes your ulcers have a baby.—*Mark Grace, Cubs first baseman, on an extra-inning game during the peak of the pennant race, 1998. Chicago won the wild card by a game but got swept in the NLDS by Atlanta.*

173 If they moved that foul line 30 feet to the left, I'd make them forget Babe Ruth.—*Gene Freese, Reds third baseman.*

174 If we're gonna win, the players gotta play better, the coaches gotta coach better, the manager gotta manage better, and the owners gotta own better.—*George Scott, Brewers first baseman.*

175 I overslept.—*Outfielder Claudell Washington on why he was four days late to report to the White Sox after being traded by the Rangers for Bobby Bonds, May 1978.*

176 I was in St. Louis last year at the All-Star Game when he threw out the first pitch, and it's kind of like the same thing: 48 miles per hour and way outside the strike zone. But the sad part was, immediately afterward, the Mets signed him as their third starter.—*Bob Costas, broadcaster, on the ceremonial first pitch thrown by President Barack Obama, 2010.*

The All-Time Greats

177 The only thing Cy Young didn't win was the Cy Young Award.—*Joe Torre, Angels broadcaster, 1986. The award was first presented in 1956 to the best in baseball, and in 1967 one award was given in each league.*

178 While Honus was the best third baseman in the league, he was also the best first baseman, the best second baseman, the best shortstop, and the best outfielder. That was in fielding. And since he led the league in batting eight times between 1900 and 1911, you know that he was the best hitter, too.—*Tommy Leach, former Pirates infielder and teammate of Honus Wagner.*

179 We read that Johnson could strike out anybody he wanted to strike out and that Cobb never struck out. I could never figure out what happened when Walter Johnson pitched against Ty Cobb.—*James "Cool Papa" Bell, Hall of Fame outfielder, 1974. Johnson made his debut versus Ty Cobb and the Detroit Tigers on August 2, 1907.*

180 You can have the next one. It won't do me any good.—*Ray Chapman, Indians shortstop, to umpire Billy Evans as he walked away from the plate with a two-strike count against Walter Johnson, 1915.*

181 Crawford was a tremendous hitter. Hardly any pitchers which played against him is still alive. Half of 'em died of heart attacks.—*Casey Stengel, Yankees manager, on Tigers outfielder Sam Crawford, who was inducted into the Hall of Fame in 1957.*

182 Ty Cobb is a low-down, miserable excuse for a human being. He's also the greatest player I've ever seen.—*Sam Crawford, Tigers outfielder.*

183 When you talk about a comparison between me and Ty Cobb, all I can say is that from what I've heard and read, we were alike in two ways: we both hated to lose, and we'd both do anything to win.—*Pete Rose, Reds third baseman, 1977. Rose broke Cobb's career hit record on September 11, 1985.*

184 Cobb lived off the field as though he wished to live forever. He lived on the field as though it was his last day.—*Branch Rickey, Hall of Fame executive.*

185 About the best way to fool him is to get the ball up there faster than he can get his bat around.—*Walter Johnson, Washington Senators pitcher, on how to pitch to Ty Cobb.*

186 I don't want to say Maz doesn't belong in the Hall, but his career slugging percentage, .367, is the same as Ty Cobb's career batting average.—*Jim Armstrong, sportswriter, on the election of defensive-minded Pirates second baseman Bill Mazeroski, 2001. Technically, Cobb hit .366 for his career, but point taken.*

187 Cobb is a prick, but he sure can hit. God Almighty, that man can hit.—*Babe Ruth, Yankees outfielder, on Tigers outfielder Ty Cobb.*

188 All the lies about him are true.—*Joe Dugan, former Yankees third baseman, on Hall of Fame outfielder Babe Ruth.*

189 To understand him, you had to understand this: He wasn't human.—*Joe Dugan, Yankees third baseman, on teammate Babe Ruth.*

190 Babe Ruth ate and he slept around and he played baseball. Those were the three things he did in life.—*Herb Mitchelson, sportswriter.*

191 He hit 'em so high that everyone on the field thought he had a chance to get it. They'd all try to get under it to make the catch, and it looked like a union meeting.—*Casey Stengel, Hall of Fame manager, on Babe Ruth.*

192 If he hits a home run, he's gonna get the cheers, and if he strikes out, he's still gonna get the cheers. You were nothing out there when Ruth came up.—*Wes Ferrel, Yankees pitcher, on teammate Babe Ruth.*

193 Some 20 years ago, I stopped talking about the Babe for the simple reason that I realized that those who had never seen him didn't believe me.—*Tommy Holmes, former Boston Braves outfielder.*

194 Landis cleaned it up, and Babe Ruth glorified it.—*Tommy Henrich, former Yankees outfielder, on the contributions to baseball by Commissioner Kenesaw Mountain Landis and Yankees outfielder Babe Ruth.*

195 Ruth was the world's first hotdog. He was Charles Barkley plus Reggie Jackson squared.—*Scott Ostler, sportswriter, on Babe Ruth, 1993.*

196 You could be on the club ten years and he'd call you Kid. He couldn't remember anybody's name, so he called everybody Kid.—*Al Lopez, Hall of Fame catcher, on Babe Ruth.*

197 The more I see of Babe, the more he seems a figure out of mythology.—*Burt Whitman, sportswriter.*

198 Let's face it. I'm not a headline guy. I always knew that as long as I was following Babe to the plate, I could have gone up there and stood on my head. No one would have noticed the difference. When the Babe was through swinging, whether he hit one or fanned, nobody paid any attention to the next hitter. They all were talking about what the Babe had done.—*Lou Gehrig, Yankees first baseman.*

199 If Babe Ruth had been a soccer player, soccer would be our national pastime.—*Pete Rose, all-time hit leader, 1992.*

200 Sitting on the bench watching him pitch, I often forgot I was a ballplayer. I became a fan.—*Rube Miller, New York Giants pitcher, on teammate Christy Mathewson.*

201 Lou Gehrig was a guy who could really hit the ball, was dependable and seemed so durable that many of us thought he could have played forever.—*George Selkirk, former Yankees outfielder, on the Hall of Fame first baseman.*

202 Gehrig never learned that a ball player couldn't be good every day.—*Hank Gowdy, Boston Braves catcher.*

203 He was a symbol of indestructibility—a Gibraltar in cleats.—*Jim Murray, sportswriter, on Hall of Fame first baseman Lou Gehrig.*

204 I took the two most expensive aspirins in history.—*Wally Pipp, former Yankees first baseman, who sat out one game due to a headache and then became expendable when Lou Gehrig took his place in the lineup, 1925. Gehrig went on to play in every game for the next fourteen years, totaling 2,130 games.*

205 I once threw a sidearm spitter right into his belly, and he hit it into the upper deck. I may have got Waner out, but I never fooled him.—*Burleigh Grimes, Hall of Fame pitcher, on Pirates outfielder Paul Waner.*

206 "Poison" is Brooklynese for person. A fan in Ebbets Field is supposed to have complained, "Every time you look up, those Waner boys are on base. It's always the little poison on third and the big poison on foist."—*Red Smith, sportswriter, on how Paul and Lloyd Waner got the nicknames Big Poison and Little Poison.*

207 He had four passions and four only: he loved to fish, he loved the stuff that the vintners sell, he loved fires, and he loved to pitch ballgames. In about that order.—*Connie Mack, Philadelphia A's owner-manager, on pitcher Rube Waddell, whose contract with the A's featured a provision that he wouldn't eat animal crackers in bed. Ossie Schreckengost, his catcher and roommate, insisted on the agreement.*

208 He was at heart a gentle and generous man who loved to be admired. He found happiness in applause, in showing off, in playing tricks on his friends, in making love and vowing fidelity to a number of different women, in drinking in good company and without restraint, in riding fire engines, in leading parades, in fishing, in winning ball games, in wearing red neckties and brand-new clothes, and in talking about himself.—*Robert Smith, sportswriter, on Philadelphia A's pitcher Rube Waddell.*

209 When Waddell had control—and some sleep—he was unbeatable.—*Branch Rickey, Brooklyn Dodgers GM, on Hall of Fame pitcher Rube Waddell.*

210 He had more stuff than any pitcher I ever saw. He had everything but a sense of responsibility.—*Connie Mack, Philadelphia A's manager, on pitcher Rube Waddell.*

211 Jimmie Foxx wasn't scouted, he was trapped.—*Lefty Gomez, Yankees pitcher, on the Philadelphia A's first baseman, who hit 58 home runs in 1932.*

212 His motion was enough to give a batter nervous indigestion.—*Eddie Collins, Philadelphia A's second baseman, on the deliberate pitching style of teammate Eddie Plank.*

213 During the reign of Hubbell, first base itself is a Marathon route.—*Heywood Broun, sportswriter, on New York Giants pitcher Carl Hubbell.*

214 You trying to insult Hubbell? Coming up here with a bat in your hand.—*Gabby Hartnett, Cubs catcher, as Yankees pitcher Lefty Gomez approached the plate in the 1934 All-Star Game against Carl Hubble.*

215 As a ballplayer, Dean was a natural phenomenon, like the Grand Canyon or the Great Barrier Reef. Nobody ever taught him baseball and he never had to learn. He was just doing what came naturally.—*Red Smith, sportswriter, on Cardinals pitcher Dizzy Dean.*

216 If the roof fell in and Diz was sitting in the middle of the room, everybody else would be buried in the debris and a gumdrop would drop in his mouth.—*Leo Durocher, former manager, on Hall of Fame pitcher Dizzy Dean.*

217 Charlie Gehringer is in a rut. He hits .350 on opening day and stays there all season.—*Lefty Gomez, Yankees pitcher.*

218 He said "hello" opening day, "good-bye" closing day and, in between, hits .350.—*Mickey Cochrane, Tigers catcher-manager, on second baseman Charlie Gehringer, known as The Mechanical Man, 1935.*

219 I got a big charge out of seeing Ted Williams hit. Once in a while they let me try to field some of them, which sort of dimmed my enthusiasm.—*Rocky Bridges, former infielder and San Jose Bees manager, 1964.*

220 I guess the biggest thrill I had was crouching behind the plate, giving the signals when Ted Williams was the hitter. I didn't know whether to call the pitch or get his autograph.—*Joe Garagiola, broadcaster and former Cardinals catcher, on the 1946 World Series, 1974.*

221 Ted hit .400 without a helmet, and he will continue to be a great batter even if he decides to wear a derby hat at the plate.—*Casey Stengel, Yankees manager, on the reluctance of the Red Sox outfielder to wear a batting helmet, March 1958.*

222 I don't think Spahn will ever get into the Hall of Fame. He'll never stop pitching.—*Stan Musial, former Cardinals outfielder, on 44-year-old Mets pitcher Warren Spahn, 1965. Spahn was inducted into the HOF in 1973.*

223 First we'll use Spahn, then we'll use Sain
Then an off day followed by rain
Back will come Spahn followed by Sain
And followed we hope by two days of rain.
—*Gerald V. Hern, writer, 1948. The verse has been shorted to the maxim "Spahn and Sain and pray for rain." Boston Braves pitchers Warren Spahn and Johnny Sain played together from 1946 to 1951.*

224 Johnny Sain don't say much, but that don't matter much, because when you're out there on the mound, you got nobody to talk to.—*Casey Stengel, Yankees manager.*

225 DiMaggio even looks good striking out.—*Ted Williams, Red Sox outfielder, on Yankees outfielder Joe DiMaggio.*

226 He has a weakness for doubles.—*Bobo Newsome, Senators pitcher, on if Yankees outfielder Joe DiMaggio had any weaknesses.*

227 DiMaggio seldom showed emotion. One day, after striking out, he came into the dugout and kicked the ball bag. We all went, "Oooh." It hurt. He sat down and sweat popped out on his forehead and he clenched and unclenched his fists without ever saying a word. Everybody wanted to howl, but this was the god. You don't laugh at gods.—*Jerry Coleman, broadcaster and former Yankees second baseman, on Joe DiMaggio, 1972.*

228 I'm responsible for Joe DiMaggio's success. They never knew that he could go back on a ball until I pitched. All I ever saw was the back of his uniform. I wouldn't have known what he looked like, except we roomed together.—*Lefty Gomez, Yankees pitcher.*

229 It has been aptly said that while Ruth was the Home Run King, Gehrig was the Crown Prince. Joe DiMaggio must therefore have been heir apparent.—*Connie Mack, Philadelphia A's owner-manager.*

230 He was the greatest living ball player I've ever seen play.—*Yogi Berra, Hall of Fame catcher, on the death of Yankees legend Joe DiMaggio, March 8, 1999.*

231 He threw the ball as far from the bat and as close to the plate as possible.—*Casey Stengel, Hall of Fame manager, on Satchel Paige. After an illustrious career in the Negro Leagues, Paige became baseball's oldest rookie with the Indians in 1948. He went 6–1 with a 2.48 ERA to help the Tribe win the World Series over the Boston Braves.*

232 When [Satchel] Paige would up to pitch, he looked like a cross between Ichabod Crane and Rip Van Winkle. He was easy to imitate and funny to watch, unless you were the batter trying to hit against him.—*Al Hirshberg, sportswriter.*

233 He seemed to be doing everything wrong, yet everything came out right. He stopped everything behind the plate and hit everything in front of it.—*Mel Ott, New York Giants outfielder, on Yankees catcher Yogi Berra.*

234 Here stands baseball's perfect warrior. Here stands baseball's perfect knight.—*Ford Frick, baseball commissioner, on the retirement of Cardinals first baseman Stan Musial, 1963.*

235 They talk about Stan Musial being a great guy. What I want to know is, who wouldn't be a great guy with over thirty-six hundred hits? Show me a .200 hitter who's a great guy. That's what I want to see.—*Tommy Lasorda, Dodgers manager.*

236 It's ridiculous that we are gathered here tonight to honor a man who made more than 7,000 outs.—*Bob Prince, Pirates broadcaster, at Stan Musial's retirement dinner.*

237 You used to think if the score was 5–0, he'd hit a five-run homer.—*Slugger Reggie Jackson on Hall of Fame outfielder Willie Mays.*

238 Snider, Mantle and Mays—you could get a fat lip in any saloon by starting an argument as to which was best. One point was beyond argument, though. Willie was by all odds the most exciting.—*Red Smith, sportswriter.*

239 If he could cook, I'd marry him.—*Leo Durocher, New York Giants manager, on NL Rookie of the Year Willie Mays, 1951.*

240 I can't stand Mays. When he first came up from Minneapolis, he was something like 0 for 21 the first time I saw him. His first major league hit was a home run off me—and I'll never forgive myself. We might have gotten rid of Willie forever if I'd only struck him out.—*Warren Spahn, Boston Braves pitcher, on New York Giants outfielder Willie Mays, May 28, 1951. Mays finished his career with 660 home runs.*

241 I never saw a fucking ball go out of a fucking park so fucking fast in my fucking life.—*Leo Durocher, New York Giants manager, on the first career home run by outfielder Willie Mays, May 28, 1951. The blast off Warren Spahn cleared the left-field roof of the Polo Grounds.*

242 For the first sixty feet, it was a hell of a pitch.—*Warren Spahn, Milwaukee Braves pitcher, on surrendering the first career home run to Giants outfielder Willie Mays, May 28, 1951.*

243 I'm not sure what the hell charisma is, but I get the feeling it's Willie Mays.—*Ted Kluszewski, Reds first baseman.*

244 If I played that long, and got that good, they couldn't afford to pay me.—*Reggie Jackson, Oakland A's outfielder, on Braves outfielder Henry Aaron, 1974.*

245 It shows what you can accomplish if you stay up all night drinking whiskey all the time.—*Toots Shor, New York City restaurateur, on the Hall of Fame induction of former Yankees Whitey Ford and Mickey Mantle, 1974.*

246 No man in the history of baseball had as much power as Mickey Mantle. No man. You're not talking about ordinary power. Dave

Kingman has power, Willie Mays had power. Then when you're talking about Mickey Mantle—it's an altogether different level. Separates the men from the boys.—*Billy Martin, Yankees manager.*

247 He was the best one-legged player I ever saw play the game.—*Casey Stengel, former Yankees manager, on outfielder Mickey Mantle.*

248 When Mickey Mantle bunted with the wind blowing out in Crosley Field.—*Robin Roberts, Hall of Fame pitcher, when asked what his greatest All-Star Game thrill was, 1991.*

249 Without Ernie Banks, the Cubs would finish in Albuquerque.—*Jimmy Dykes, Indians manager.*

250 I don't think these people at Wrigley Field ever saw but two players they liked—Billy Williams and Ernie Banks. Billy never said anything, and Ernie always said the right thing.—*Fergie Jenkins, former Cubs pitcher.*

251 Ernie Banks is the only person who would have been happy to be here.—*Oscar Gamble, Yankees outfielder, during a mandatory off-day practice ordered by owner George Steinbrenner after a 13-inning loss, May 1982.*

252 There are two times in my life the hair on my arms has stood up: The first time I saw the ceiling of the Sistine Chapel and the first time I saw Sandy Koufax throw a fastball.—*Former Brooklyn Dodgers scout Al Campanis.*

253 What makes Sandy Koufax great is the same thing that made Walter Johnson great. The team behind him is the ghastliest scoring team in history. They pile up runs at the rate of one every nine innings. This is a little like making Rembrandt paint on the back of cigar boxes, giving Paderewski a piano with two octaves, Caruso singing with a high school chorus. With the Babe Ruth Yankees, Sandy Koufax would have been the first undefeated pitcher in history.—*Jim Murray, sportswriter.*

254 I can see how he won 25 games. What I don't understand is how he lost five.—*Yogi Berra, Yankees catcher, on Dodgers pitcher Sandy Koufax, 1963.*

255 A foul ball was a moral victory.—*Los Angeles Dodgers pitcher Don Sutton on pitching great Sandy Koufax.*

256 Lew would make coffee nervous.—*Fred Haney, Milwaukee Braves manager, on pitcher Lew Burdette, who was known for his constant fidgeting on the mound.*

257 Going over the hitters, it was decided that we should pitch Frank Robinson underground.—*Jim Bouton, Yankees pitcher, on the Orioles outfielder.*

258 He plays the bag like he came down from a higher league.—*Ed Hurley, umpire, on Orioles third baseman Brooks Robinson, 1958.*

259 Brooks never asked anyone to name a candy bar after him. In Baltimore, people name their children after him.—*Gordon Beard, sportswriter, on Orioles third baseman Brooks Robinson.*

260 Every time Bench throws, everybody in baseball drools.—*Harry Dalton, Orioles vice president, on Reds catcher Johnny Bench, 1970.*

261 If you pitch to him, he'll ruin baseball. He'd hit 80 home runs. There's no comparison between McCovey and anybody else in the league.—*Sparky Anderson, Reds manager, on Giants first baseman Willie McCovey, 1973.*

262 First, I found him hard to catch. Then, I found him hard to hit. And finally, I found it hard to manage him.—*Joe Torre, Braves manager, on pitcher Phil Niekro, 1984.*

263 He gets his hits in the present and lives in the past.—*Larry Merchant, sportswriter, on Pete Rose.*

264 Bob Gibson is the luckiest pitcher I ever saw. He always pitches when the other team doesn't score any runs.—*Tim McCarver, Cardinals catcher.*

265 The only people I ever felt intimidated by in my life were Bob Gibson and my daddy.—*Dusty Baker, Giants manager. Gibson's 1.12 ERA in 1968 ranks as the third lowest single season ever.*

266 Some people are only super stars statistically, but you are a .400 hitter as a person.

When I grow up, I want to be just like you.—*Joe Morgan, Astros second baseman, to Pirates first baseman Willie Stargell, 1980.*

267 One thing about Reggie, if he had something to say, he said it. What was on his lung was on his tongue.—*Robert Trimble, former high school gym teacher of Yankees outfielder Reggie Jackson.*

268 The thing about Reggie is that you know he's going to produce. And if he doesn't, he's going to talk enough to make people think he's going to produce.—*Catfish Hunter, Yankees pitcher, on teammate Reggie Jackson.*

269 The best thing about being a Yankee is getting to watch Reggie Jackson play every day. The worst thing about being a Yankee? Getting to watch Reggie Jackson play every day.—*Graig Nettles, Yankees third baseman.*

270 Reggie is a fascinating man. He has a sense of history, which so many athletes don't have. I think that's why he gets up for the big games. He has a sense of moment. Greatness against the odds is the thing. Anyone can be famous. Just by jumping out of one of these buildings you can be famous. To be *great* is a dimension of the authentic.—*The Rev. Jesse Jackson on how Yankees outfielder Reggie Jackson became known as Mr. October, 1977.*

271 Carew is the luckiest hitter I ever saw. When he hits the ball, there is no one there to field it.—*Gene Mauch, former Twins manager, on Hall of Fame in fielder Rod Carew, 1991. Carew retired with 3,053 base hits.*

272 Watching Carew bat is like watching Bulova make a watch, DeBeers cut a diamond.... Rod Carew doesn't make hits, he composes them.—*Jim Murray, sportswriter.*

273 Greaseball, greaseball, greaseball, that's all I throw him, and he still hits them. He's the only player in baseball who consistenly hits my grease. He sees the ball so well, I guess he can pick out the dry side.—*Gaylord Perry, Indians pitcher, on Twins second baseman Rod Carew.*

274 The difference between this guy and the rest of us is that when we get hot, we go up to .300. When he gets hot, he goes up to .500.—*Doug DeCinces, Angels third baseman, on California first baseman Rod Carew.*

275 When Rod Carew moved from second base to first base this year, I felt the same as Avis would feel if Hertz went into the hotel business.—*Bobby Grich, Orioles second baseman, on making the 1976 All-Star team.*

276 It just seemed fitting. When Rod Carew was inducted into baseball's Hall of Fame, Panamanian flags waved. When Ferguson Jenkins was inducted, Canadian flags were flown. When Gaylord Perry was inducted, it began to rain.—*George Owens, sportswriter, 1991.*

277 He's so good that blind people come to the park just to hear him pitch.—*Reggie Jackson, Yankees outfielder, on Reds pitcher Tom Seaver, 1977.*

278 *Reporter:* Would you rather face Jim Palmer or Tom Seaver?

Merv Rettenmund (Reds outfielder, 1974): That's like asking me if I'd rather be hung or go to the electric chair.

279 When Steve and I die, we are going to be buried in the same cemetery, 60-feet 6-inches apart.—*Tim McCarver, personal catcher for Phillies pitcher Steve Carlton, 1977.*

280 When you call a pitcher "Lefty" and everybody in both leagues knows who you mean, he must be pretty good.—*Clint Hurdle, Royals infielder, on pitcher Steve Carlton.*

281 The two best pitchers in the National League don't speak English—Fernando Valenzuela and Steve Carlton.—*Ernie Johnson, Braves broadcaster, 1983.*

282 Ryan's the only guy who put fear in me. Not because he could get me out, but because he could kill me. Every hitter likes fastballs like everybody likes ice cream. But you don't like it by the gallon. That's how you felt when Nolan was throwing fastballs by you. You just hoped to mix in a walk so you could have a good night and go 0 for 3.—*Reggie Jackson, Yankees outfielder, on Angels pitcher Nolan Ryan.*

283 You don't face Nolan Ryan without your rest. He's the only guy I go against that makes me go to bed before midnight.—*Reggie Jackson, Yankees outfielder.*

284 If I'm going to be struck out, that's the way to go. It may sound strange, but I actually enjoyed that. It was like a surgeon's knife—quick and painless.—*Reggie Smith, Dodgers outfielder, on being struck out by Astros pitcher Nolan Ryan, August 1980.*

285 A good night tonight is 0 for 4 and don't get hit in the head.—*Oscar Gamble, Indians DH, on facing Angels pitcher Nolan Ryan, 1973.*

286 He's baseball's exorcist—scares the devil out of you.—*Dick Sharon, Tigers outfielder, on Angels pitcher Nolan Ryan, 1974.*

287 He's not the best pitcher in baseball. Never has been. I'll say this: He's the most exciting .500 pitcher in baseball.—*Jim Fregosi, Angels manager, on Nolan Ryan, 1978.*

288 Everyone would like each other and no one would get a hit.—*Rance Mulliniks, Blue Jays infielder, when asked what baseball would be like if everyone was like Rangers pitcher Nolan Ryan, 1990.*

289 When he pitches, two things can happen: you can lose or be no-hit.—*Cito Gaston, Blue Jays manager, on playing against Rangers pitcher Nolan Ryan, 1991. Ryan recorded his seventh career no-hitter against the Blue Jays.*

290 He's the greatest arm ever to put on spikes.—*Whitey Herzog, Cardinals manager, on Astros pitcher Nolan Ryan, 1987.*

291 Houston used to be an R and R town—rest and rehabilitation. It's still an R and R town—Ryan and Richard—and that's not exactly rest and rehabilitation.—*Larry Bowa, Phillies shortstop, on Astros pitchers Nolan Ryan and J.R. Richard, 1980.*

292 I'm going to try to renegotiate my contract so I won't have to come to Houston. Can you imagine coming in for three days and seeing J.R. Richard and [Nolan] Ryan? They'll probably throw Joe Niekro in between just to break things up. One day we'll be swatting at butterflies and the next day trying to run that heat down.—*Willie Stargell, Pirates first baseman, 1979.*

293 I'm not going to say too much about it. He might end up being our governor one day, and I don't want him to raise my taxes.—*Scott Livingstone, Tigers infielder, on getting his first major league hit against Rangers pitcher Nolan Ryan, 1992.*

294 They shouldn't try to compare Dwight with Sandy Koufax or Nolan Ryan or anyone else because there is no comparison. They should be comparing the others to Dwight.—*Davey Johnson, Mets manager, on pitcher Dwight Gooden, 1984.*

295 Robin Yount in the first, Robin Yount in the fourth and Robin Yount in the seventh.—*Roger Clemens, Red Sox pitcher, on whom he considered the three most dangerous hitters in the game.*

296 George is getting to be such a monster that I'd hate to die in a car wreck with that guy. You'd be listed as: Others Killed.—*Clint Hurdle, Royals outfielder, on third baseman George Brett, 1981.*

297 The only way to pitch to him is way inside, so you force him to pull the ball. That way, the line drive won't hit you.—*Rudy May, Yankees pitcher, on pitching to Royals third baseman George Brett, 1980.*

298 A woman will be elected president before Wade Boggs is called out on strikes.—*George Brett, Royals first baseman, 1988.*

299 I think that when he comes to the plate, he should only get one swing.—*Greg Gagne, Twins shortstop, on Red Sox third baseman Wade Boggs.*

300 Eddie Murray's bronze bust in Cooperstown will chatter only slightly less than the man himself. The first line of text on the monument should read: He spoke rarely and carried a mighty bat.—*David Ginsburg, sportswriter.*

301 I'm a showboat. I grew up watching Rickey Henderson.—*Curtis Goodwin, Rockies outfielder, on his flashy home run trot, 1998.*

302 There are certain figures in American history who have passed into the realm of cultural mythology, as if reality could no longer contain their stories: Johnny Appleseed. Wild Bill Hickok. Davy Crockett. Rickey Henderson. They exist on the sometimes narrow margin between Fact and Fiction.—*Tom Verducci, sportswriter, 2003.*

303 Rickey is the modern-day Yogi Berra, only faster.—*Tom Verducci, sportswriter, 2003.*

304 I found his weakness. He can't slide into the wind.—*Ellis Clary, Blue Jays scout, on Cubs second baseman Ryne Sandberg, 1989.*

305 There's something about Nancy Kerrigan that reminds me of Ryne Sandberg, and something about Tonya Harding that reminds me of Lenny Dykstra.—*Ed Lynch, Mets executive, 1994.*

306 If he were playing in New York, there'd be a 5' 8" statue of him in Times Square.—*Andy MacPhail, Twins GM, on All-Star outfielder Kirby Puckett.*

307 He shouldn't have gone to high school. It took three years off his pension.—*Walt Weiss, Oakland A's shortstop, on 20-year-old Mariners outfielder Ken Griffey Jr., 1990.*

308 What does jelly do on peanut butter? That's what Junior means to us.—*Bill Plummer, Mariners manager, on outfielder Ken Griffey Jr., 1992.*

309 I wish they'd let us put on the mask and shin guards. Pitchers shouldn't be left out there alone with him.—*Dennis Martinez, Indians pitcher, on White Sox first baseman Frank Thomas, 1994. Thomas won back-to-back AL MVP Awards in 1993 and 1994. The only other first baseman to do so was Jimmie Foxx in 1932 and 1933.*

310 Maddux is like that little mouse that goes in the hole, out the hole. And you've got this cat with no patience who keeps running his head into the wall.—*Barry Bonds, Giants outfielder, on Braves pitcher Greg Maddux, 2000.*

311 He's like a tailor: a little off here, a little off there and you're done, take a seat.—*Vin Scully, Dodgers announcer, on Braves pitcher Tom Glavine.*

312 I'd like to have that feeling for one inning—to be able to do what he does with a baseball.—*Joe Kerrigan, Red Sox pitching coach, on Pedro Martinez, May 2000. Martinez won his third Cy Young Award in four years by going 18–6 with a 1.74 ERA and 284 strikeouts.*

313 I have no idea how they're doing it. When I'm chasing .400, I'm allowed to make outs. These guys get hits, and they're failures if they weren't home runs.—*Tony Gwynn, Padres outfielder, on Mark McGwire and Sammy Sosa's pursuit of Roger Maris's single-season home run record, 1998.*

314 He's not human. He doesn't count. Check his blood. Mac's an alien from the future who's come back to show us how to play the game.—*Jose Canseco, Oakland A's outfielder, on teammate Mark McGwire, 1997.*

315 Do people show up early to watch Michael Jordan shoot free throws? Do they show up at 10:20 A.M. to watch Steve Young loosen up his throwing arm? Does Tiger Woods draw crowds of thousands at the driving range?—*Tim Keown, sportswriter, on the crowds that arrived early at ballparks across the country in order to watch Mark McGwire take batting practice, 1998.*

316 I don't blame the fans. They wanted to see Mark hit. It's like paying to see Elvis and getting a garage band.—*John Mabry, Cardinals utility player, on filling in at first base one day in place of Mark McGwire, 1998.*

317 There are more reporters here than if Elvis found Jimmy Hoffa's body.—*John Mabry, Cardinals utility player, on the media coverage surrounding Mark McGwire, 1998.*

318 You pick up the newspaper, he's on the front page. He's on the front page of the Living section. He's on the front page of the Money section. They might as well change the name of the paper to the *St. Louis Post-McGwire.*—*Tom Lampkin, Cardinals catcher, on Mark McGwire mania, 1998.*

319 I saw something like this on TV when I

was a kid. I think they called themselves The Beatles.—*Tom Pagnozzi, Cardinals catcher, on 30,000 fans showing up in San Diego to watch Mark McGwire take batting practice, 1998.*

320 The best place to catch a baseball hit by McGwire is definitely not within the confines of the playing field or, sometimes even the entire park. Other players dial "1" for long distance. McGwire has to ask for an international operator.—*Thomas Boswell, sportswriter, on the prodigious home run clouts by Mark McGwire, 1998.*

321 When he singles, you feel like you've won.—*Terry Francona, Phillies manager, on Cubs outfielder Sammy Sosa, 1998.*

322 Roger Clemens going into the Baseball Hall of Fame as a New York Yankee is like George Harrison going into the Rock and Roll Hall of Fame as a Traveling Wilbury.—*Mike Bianchi, sportswriter, 2003. After becoming embroiled in a steroid controversy, it remains to be seen if Clemens gets into the Hall of Fame at all....*

323 He might be like Bugs Bunny someday. He might hit a ball and break it in half.—*Jose Rijo, Reds pitcher, on slugging outfielder Adam Dunn, 2002.*

324 He has the potential to be the next Babe Ruth, just without the vices.—*Wayne Graham, Rice University Head Coach, on former Rice player and Astros outfielder Lance Berkman, 2002.*

325 The kid throws too hard for us. He's too good for this league. I say we ban him from baseball.—*Tom Kelly, Twins manager, on Yankees reliever Mariano Rivera.*

326 Top Ten Perks of Being a Member of the National Baseball Hall of Fame

10. I get a ballpark frank for a reduced price of only $20.—*Lou Brock*

9. If I don't have the money for the Domino's kid, I hand him any old bat and say, "I used this to hit my 500th home run."—*Harmon Killebrew*

8. I once saw Earl Weaver naked.—*Brooks Robinson*

7. All the rosin you can eat.—*Ralph Kiner*

6. I'm not just a guy with a crazy mustache; I'm a Hall of Famer with a crazy mustache.—*Rollie Fingers*

5. I gotta do Hall of Fame stuff—perfect excuse to get out of plans the wife made.—*Bob Gibson*

4. I can run on the field shirtless and there ain't a damn thing you can do about it.—*Phil Niekro*

3. Get to appear on lame late night talk show.—*Bob Feller*

2. We're the only ones who can rebroadcast or retransmit an account of a game without the express written consent of Major League Baseball.—*Ozzie Smith*

1. One free swing at a costumed mascot of my choice.—*Gary Carter*

—*From* The Late Show with David Letterman, *July 23, 2003.*

Amazing Accomplishments and Records

Record Setters

327 Any minute, any day, some players may break a long-standing record. That's one of the fascinations about the game—the unexpected surprises.—*Connie Mack, former Philadelphia A's manager.*

328 You couldn't play on my Amazin' Mets without having held some kind of record, like one fella held the world's international all-time record for a pitcher getting hit on the ankles.—*Casey Stengel, former manager, 1967.*

329 I've never had a club record, except for car wrecks.—*Darren Daulton, Phillies catcher, on setting a team record for runs batted in by a catcher, 1992.*

330 I set records that will never be equaled. In fact, I hope 90 percent of them don't even

get printed.—*Bob Uecker, Brewers broadcaster and former catcher.*

331 It's like losing your goldfish. You know it wasn't going to last forever, but you just hate to see it go.—*Jim Deshaies, Astros broadcaster, on watching Astros pitcher Roy Oswalt break his team record of 12 wins by a rookie, 2001.*

332 You know, records are made to be broken. And I'm definitely breaking records. They're just the wrong damn records.—*Paul Janish, Reds shortstop, on giving up 11 total runs in two different mop-up pitching appearances—the most runs surrendered by a position player in 45 years, 2009.*

333 I wouldn't mind seeing someone erase my record of hitting into four triple plays.—*Brooks Robinson, Hall of Fame third baseman.*

334 Congratulations on breaking my home run record last night. I always thought the record would stand until it was broken. It couldn't have happened to a nicer guy. Best of luck the rest of the season, but take it easy on Dale (Berra) and the Pirates. Maybe we'll see you in October.—*Yogi Berra, Hall of Fame catcher, in a telegram to Reds catcher Johnny Bench who broke Berra's record for most career home runs by a catcher, July 16, 1980.*

335 It is interesting to see this 53-year-old man hustling down to first base on a pop fly. For some of our younger men, who are less enthusiastic, it made for an object lesson. One player objected to Minnie taking batting practice. That's understandable. You take Minnie at 53 hitting the ball into the left field stands, and here's a guy who can't get the ball to the warning track. I'd want to bar him, too. Beyond all that, on the other hand I wanted to see Minnie get a hit.—*Bill Veeck, White Sox owner, on bringing back former White Sox outfielder Minnie Minoso so he could become the oldest player to collect a base hit. As DH, Minoso singled on September 12, 1976. Veeck also brought Minoso back for two hitless at-bats in 1980.*

336 I don't think anyone will ever break this one, but I have no objection to someone tying it.—*Johnny Vander Meer, former Reds pitcher, on pitching back-to-back no-hitters in 1938.*

337 Those were the best pitches I ever heard.—*Mickey Stanley, Tigers outfielder, on striking out against Angels pitcher Nolan Ryan, July 15, 1973—Ryan's second no-hitter of the season.*

338 Why? It ain't gonna make any difference. I'm not going to hit Ryan anyway.—*Norm Cash, Tigers first baseman, on being sent back to the dugout for a bat after bringing a chair leg up to the plate to face Angles pitcher Nolan Ryan in the ninth inning of a no-hitter, July 15, 1973. Cash was right—it didn't matter—he popped out to short to end the game.*

339 Shoot, I don't get emotional about these things anymore.—*Nolan Ryan, Astros pitcher, on breaking Sandy Koufax's record by throwing his fifth career no-hitter, September 26, 1981. As a member of the Rangers, Ryan would toss two more no-hitters to extend his record.*

340 Of course, you'd like to get credit, but now that he's done it with seven different catchers, I think my cover is blown.—*Jeff Torborg, White Sox manager, on catching the first of Nolan Ryan's seven career no-hitters, 1991. As teammates with the Angels, Ryan and Torborg no-hit Kansas City on May 15, 1973. In his career, Torborg also caught a perfect game by Sandy Koufax and a no-hitter by Bill Singer.*

341 I'd like to thank all the umpires. If it wasn't for them, it wouldn't have been possible.—*Nolan Ryan, Astros pitcher, on setting the all-time walk record with 1,776 free passes, 1981. Ryan finished his career as baseball's all-time strikeout and walk leader.*

342 In the long history of organized baseball I stand unparalleled for putting Christianity into practice. And to prove I was not prejudiced, I served up home run balls to Negroes, Italians, Jews, Catholics alike. Race, creed, nationality made no difference to me.—*Robin Roberts, Phillies pitcher, on surrendering a record 46 home runs, 1956. Jose Lima (48) broke his NL record in 2000, and Bert Blyleven (50) eclipsed his major league record in 1986. Roberts held the career record for home runs allowed (505) until Jamie Moyer gave up his 506th in 2010.*

343 It means even more to me because I did it all with one team.—*Jim Thome, Indians first*

baseman, on tying the Indians team record with his 242nd home run, 2001.

344 Some people give their bodies to science; I give mine to baseball.—*Ron Hunt, Expos infielder, on getting hit by a pitch 50 times in one season (and 243 times in his career), 1971.*

345 It's not something I go around bragging about really. It really doesn't take a lot of talent to get hit by a pitch.—*Jerry Shelton, University of Alabama third baseman, on getting hit by a pitch a record 52 times in his collegiate career, 1993.*

346 My last year was Pete Rose's rookie year. By coincidence, my last game was against Cincinnati. I got two hits. And Pete Rose got three. He was gaining on me even then.—*Stan Musial, Hall of Fame outfielder, on Reds player-manager Pete Rose breaking his NL record of 3,630 hits, 1985.*

347 Hell, if I'da hit that many singles, I'da wore a dress.—*Mickey Mantle, Hall of Fame outfielder, on Reds player-manager Pete Rose breaking Ty Cobb's all-time hit record, 1985. Of Mantle's 2,415 hits, 39 percent went for extra bases (536 homers, 72 triples, and 344 doubles). Rose finished his career with 4,236 hits, 25 percent for extra bases.*

348 That's like a 10-year-old horse winning the Kentucky Derby.—*Dal Maxvill, Oakland A's infielder, on 35-year-old Cardinals outfielder Lou Brock stealing a record 118 bases, 1974.*

349 I don't want to be Babe Ruth. He was a great ballplayer. I'm not trying to replace him. The record is there and damn right I want to break it, but that isn't replacing Babe Ruth.—*Roger Maris, Yankees outfielder, responding to the pressure of his quest to break Babe Ruth's single-season home run record, 1961.*

350 It would be a shame if Ruth's record is broken by a .270 hitter.—*Rogers Hornsby, Hall of Famer, on Roger Maris's pursuit of the single-season home run record, 1961. Maris got the record with 61 homers while hitting .269 for the season.*

351 It would have been a helluva lot more fun if I had never hit those 61 home runs.—*Roger Maris, Yankees outfielder, on the 1961 season when he broke Babe Ruth's home run record.*

352 I don't care how many home runs Aaron or anyone else hits. They cannot replace the Babe. Lindbergh was the first man to fly nonstop across the Atlantic. Nobody remembers who was the second or third. So it is with the Babe.—*Claire Ruth, Babe Ruth's widow, on the prospect of Braves outfielder Hank Aaron breaking Babe Ruth's career home run record, 1973.*

353 If they want Hank Aaron to hit those home runs for the fans, why don't they let him go back to Milwaukee and do it?—*Bud Harrelson, Mets shortstop, on the planned benching of Braves outfielder Hank Aaron for all road games so he could break Babe Ruth's home run record in Atlanta, 1974. Commissioner Bowie Kuhn ordered the Braves to play Aaron on the road.*

354 It wasn't a bad pitch, but it wasn't good enough against Hank Aaron.—*Jack Billingham, Reds pitcher, on surrendering Aaron's 714th career home run.*

355 I thought tying the record would mean a great deal to me, but it seemed like just another homer. I guess if we had won, I would have felt like drinking champagne.—*Henry Aaron, Braves outfielder, on hitting his 714th home run in a 7–6 loss to Cincinnati, 1974.*

356 Aaron's 715th home run came in the fourth inning of the Braves' home opener with Los Angeles, off the Dodgers' Al Downing, a lefthander who had insisted doggedly before the game that for him this night would be "no different from any other." He was wrong, for now he joins a company that includes Tom Zachary (Babe Ruth's 60th home run in 1927), Tracy Stallard (Roger Maris' 61st in 1961) and Guy Bush (Ruth's 714th in 1935). They are destined to ride tandem through history with their assailants.—*Ron Fimrite, sportswriter, on Henry Aaron breaking Babe Ruth's career home run record at 9:07 P.M., April 8, 1974.*

357 I never say "seven-fifteen" anymore. I now say "quarter after seven."—*Al Downing, former Dodgers pitcher, on the 20th anniversary of surrendering Hank Aaron's 715th home run, April 1994.*

358 Since most of Aaron's homers went down the left-field foul line, I was surprised it

came to me. But it did. If I didn't catch it, I'd still have the stitches stamped on my forehead.—*Tom House, Braves reliever, on gloving Henry Aaron's 715th home run in the bullpen.*

359 I never want them to forget Babe Ruth. I just want them to remember Aaron.—*Henry Aaron at his Hall of Fame induction, 1982.*

360 Babe Ruth always will be Number One. Before I broke his record, it was the greatest of all. Then I broke it, and suddenly the greatest record is Joe DiMaggio's hitting streak.—*Henry Aaron, Hall of Fame outfielder, on breaking Babe Ruth's career home run record in 1974.*

361 If he does it, I hope 71 goes into McCovey Cove and some whale swallows it.—*Todd McFarlane, comic book publisher and owner of Mark McGwire's home run ball No. 70 (for which he paid $2.7 million) on if Barry Bonds could break the home run record, 2001. Bonds finished the season with 73 homers.*

362 Bonds' records must remain part of baseball's history. His hits happened. Erase them and there will be discrepancies in baseball's bookkeeping about the records of the pitchers who gave them up. George Orwell said that in totalitarian societies, yesterday's weather could be changed by decree. Baseball, indeed America, is not like that. Besides, the people who care about the record book—serious fans—will know how to read it. That may be Bonds' biggest worry.—*George Will, writer, May 2006.*

363 He's hit the home runs, so you have to give him credit, but he's not Babe Ruth. He never will be Babe Ruth, or Hank Aaron for that matter.—*Bob Feller, Hall of Fame pitcher, on Giants outfielder Barry Bonds, 2006.*

Milestones

364 Once he had that fifty-nine, that number sixty was sure as the setting sun. A more determined athlete than George Herman Ruth never lived.—*Paul Gallico, sportswriter, on Babe Ruth's record 60th home run, 1927.*

365 Heck, if I'd a known it was gonna be a famous record, I'da stuck it in his ear.—*Tom Zachary, former Washington Senators pitcher, on surrendering Babe Ruth's 60th home run in 1927.*

366 Sixty, count 'em, sixty. Let's see some other son-of-a-bitch match that.—*Babe Ruth, Yankees outfielder, after hitting his 60th home run of the season, September 30, 1927.*

367 Today's baseball numbers are funny numbers. When Babe Ruth hit 60 home runs in 1927, George Sisler finished second in the majors with 19. [Sammy] Sosa was second to [Barry] Bonds this season with 64.—*Rick Morrissey, sportswriter, 2001.*

368 When you talk about a name like Babe Ruth, I don't care if you beat him eating hamburgers, it's some kind of name.—*Larry Rothschild, Devil Rays manager, on third baseman Wade Boggs moving past Ruth into 33rd place on the career hit list, 1998.*

369 If I couldn't hit .400 all the way, I didn't deserve it.—*Ted Williams, Red Sox outfielder, on why he decided to play in a doubleheader on the final day of the 1941 season when he was batting .39955 (technically .400) to begin the day. Williams went 4 for 5 and then 2 for 3 to finish .406 for the season. No player has hit over .400 since.*

370 I hope somebody hits .400 soon. Then people can start pestering that guy with questions about the last guy to hit .400.—*Ted Williams, Hall of Fame outfielder, 1980. Rod Carew, George Brett and Tony Gwynn have all challenged, but Williams is still the last to accomplish the feat, hitting .406 in 1941.*

371 Last night the Chicago Cubs' Sammy Sosa became only the 13th player in history to hit 30 home runs and steal 30 bases in the same season. In a related story, last night the Mets' Chico Walker hit two really hard foul balls.—*David Letterman, talk show host, 1993. The Mets lost 103 games that season, aided by Walker's .225 average.*

372 I was in the 30–30 club at Tidewater—30 walks and 30 strikeouts.—*John Mitchell, Mets reliever, on his minor league credentials, 1989.*

373 He's already in the 1–1 club, and he's played only one game.—*John Wathan, Royals*

manager, on Oakland A's outfielder Jose Canseco, who hit one home run and stole one base in the season opener, 1989. Canseco became baseball's first 40–40 player in 1988. Barry Bonds (1996), Alex Rodriguez (1998) and Alfonso Soriano (2006) are the only other members of the 40–40 club.

374 Three hundred wins is nothing to spit at.—*Gaylord Perry, Mariners pitcher and noted spitball artist, 1982. Perry retired in 1983 with 314 victories, 15th on the all-time list.*

375 Do you think they'll stop the game for it?—*Brent Gates, Oakland A's second baseman, before closer Dennis Eckersley recorded his 300th save, May 25, 1995.*

376 I'm just glad to get off 399. It sounds like something you'd purchase at a discount store.—*Dave Winfield, Angels outfielder, on hitting his 400th home run, August 14, 1991. Winfield finished his Hall of Fame career with 465 homers.*

377 I know what it means to get close to 500. I gave up almost 500.—*Bert Blyleven, former pitcher, on Cubs outfielder Sammy Sosa closing in on 500 home runs, 2003. Blyleven surrendered 430 career homers while Sosa hit 609.*

378 I couldn't believe it. I looked around at the scoreboard to see if a Celtics score was on it.—*Bill Madlock, Tigers DH, on receiving a standing ovation at Fenway Park after collecting his 2,000th hit, 1987.*

379 You must remember, there wasn't much emphasis then on 3,000 hits. And to tell the truth, I didn't know how many hits I had when I quit.—*Sam Rice, Hall of Fame outfielder, on why he retired in 1934 with 2,987 hits.*

380 I was just in the right place at the right time.—*Cesar Geronimo, Reds outfielder, on being the 3,000th strikeout victim of both Bob Gibson and Nolan Ryan, 1980.*

381 It gave me no chance. He just blew it by me. But it's an honor. I'll have another paragraph in all the baseball books. I'm already in the books three or four times.—*Rickey Henderson, Oakland A's outfielder, on being Nolan Ryan's 5,000th strikeout victim, August 29, 1989.*

382 If Mayo Smith had come out to get me in the sixth inning, I wouldn't have given him the ball.—*Denny McLain, former Tigers pitcher, on his 31–6 record in 1968, which included 28 complete games. He remains the last pitcher to win at least 30 games in a season. In 1993, no team compiled as many complete games.*

Unforgettable Moments

383 It's like the Kennedy assassination. Everyone I see comes up and tells me where they were and what they were doing when Gibson hit that home run.—*Dennis Eckersley, Oakland A's reliever, on giving up a game-winning, pinch-hit home run to gimpy Dodgers outfielder Kirk Gibson in Game 1 of the 1988 World Series. The Dodgers upset the A's in five games.*

384 I actually didn't think too much about it at the time. We lost the game. Maybe if we had won, it would have meant more to me.—*Carl Hubble, Hall of Fame pitcher, on his performance in the 1934 All-Star Game in which he struck out five future Hall of Famers in succession: Babe Ruth, Lou Gehrig, Jimmie Foxx, Al Simmons and Joe Cronin.*

385 If I'd known that Paul was gonna throw a no-hitter, I'da thrown one, too.—*Dizzy Dean, Cardinals pitcher, after a double-header sweep over Brooklyn in which he threw a three-hitter and brother Paul Dean pitched a no-hitter, September 22, 1934.*

386 Branca throws. There's a long fly.... It's gonna be, I believe.... The Giants win the pennant! The Giants win the pennant! The Giants win the pennant! The Giants win the pennant! Bobby Thomson hits into the lower deck of the left-field bleachers! The Giants win the pennant, and they're going crazy! They're going crazy.—*Russ Hodges, announcer, calling Bobby Thomson's "Shot Heard Round the World," October 3, 1951. In the ninth inning of the deciding playoff game against the Brooklyn Dodgers, Thomson hit a home run off pitcher Ralph Branca that clinched the pennant for the Giants.*

387 Hollywood's most imaginative writers on an opium jag could not have scripted a more improbable windup of the season that started in April and had its finish today in the triumph of Bobby Thomson and the Giants.—*Shirley Povich, sportswriter, on Thomson's "Shot Heard Round the World," which defeated the Brooklyn Dodgers in a divisional playoff, 1951.*

388 Now it is done. Now the story ends. And there is no way to tell it. The art of fiction is dead. Reality has strangled invention. Only the utterly impossible, the inexpressibly fantastic, can ever be possible again.—*Red Smith, sportswriter, on Bobby Thomson's pennant-winning home run, 1951.*

389 The million-to-one shot came in. Hell froze over. A month of Sundays hit the calendar. Don Larsen today pitched a no-hit, no-run, no-man-reach-first game in a World Series.—*Shirley Povich, sportswriter, on a perfect game by Yankees pitcher Don Larsen against the Brooklyn Dodgers in Game 5 of the 1956 Series.*

390 The imperfect man pitched the perfect game yesterday.—*Dick Young, sportswriter, on Don Larsen's Game 5 World Series perfect game, 1956. With the Orioles in 1954, Larsen went 3–21.*

391 That might have been the best game you ever pitched.—*Yogi Berra, Yankees catcher, to Don Larsen after pitching a perfect game in the 1956 World Series.*

392 No, why should I?—*Don Larsen, Yankees pitcher, when asked if he ever tires of talking about his perfect game in the 1956 World Series.*

393 A pitcher does this once in a lifetime—once in baseball history—and we can't win the game for him.—*Bill Virdon, Pirates outfielder, on losing 1–0 in 13 innings to the Milwaukee Braves, after pitcher Harvey Haddix threw a perfect game for 12 innings, May 26, 1959.*

394 Forbes Field at this moment is an outdoor insane asylum.—*Jack Brickhouse, announcer, on Pirates second baseman Bill Mazeroski hitting a walk-off homer to defeat the Yankees in Game 7 of the 1960 World Series, October 13.*

395 If I'd known I was gonna pitch a no-hitter today, I would have gotten a haircut.—*Bo Belinski, Angels pitcher, on no-hitting Baltimore, May 5, 1962.*

396 I had two great thrills in the World Series: when I thought it was over and then when it actually was over.—*Sandy Koufax, Dodgers pitcher, on getting the final out in the 1963 World Series after second baseman Dick Tracewski dropped what would have been the final out. Koufax tossed two complete game victories in the sweep of the Yankees.*

397 Well, there goes the A's 113-game hitting streak.—*Jim Palmer, Orioles pitcher, after throwing a no-hitter against Oakland, August 13, 1969.*

398 Right now there are two very nervous people in the park: the pitcher and the official scorer.—*Lindsey Nelson, broadcaster, on Dodgers pitcher Jerry Reuss being seven outs away from a no-hitter, June 27, 1980. Reuss retired the remaining batters to secure the no-hitter.*

399 It couldn't have happened to a greater guy. Well, yes it could. It could have happened to me.—*Tommy Lasorda, Dodgers manager, on a no-hitter by Jerry Reuss, 1980.*

400 Tell Len I'm very proud of him; I hope he does better next time.—*Tokie Lockhart, grandmother of Indians pitcher Len Barker, when told her grandson had pitched a perfect game against the Blue Jays, May 15, 1981.*

401 You always dream of a no-hitter, and you dream of getting that last out and jumping up and down on the mound with all the guys in the infield. It just didn't work out that way.—*Andy Hawkins, Yankees pitcher, on losing to the White Sox, 4–0, despite pitching a no-hitter, July 1, 1990.*

402 Does a no-hitter against the Mets really count?—*Jim Donaghy, sportswriter, on a no-hitter by Astros pitcher Darryl Kile against the last-place Mets, 1993.*

403 What are the odds of throwing a no-hitter in Coors Field? About the same as traveling to the moon aboard a 1967 Volkswagen Bug.—*Jayson Stark, sportswriter, on Dodgers pitcher Hideo Nomo throwing a no-hitter against the Rockies in Denver, September 17, 1996.*

404 Hideo Nomo has pitched no-hitters at Coors Field and Camden Yards. Now he's ready for something easy like, say, memorizing

the New York City phone book.—*Jim Armstrong, sportswriter, 2001. Nomo threw his fist no-no as a Dodger on September 17, 1996, and his second came in his Red Sox debut, April 4, 2001.*

405 After the game Wells was pretty excited, as you can understand. He celebrated by retiring 27 Heinekens in a row.—*David Letterman, talk show host, on the perfect game thrown by Yankees pitcher David Wells against Minnesota on May 17, 1998.*

406 Does a perfect game against a team called the Isotopes really count?—*Tom FitzGerald, sportswriter, on a perfect game by Nashville Sounds pitcher John Wasdin, April 7, 2003. The Albuquerque Isotopes got their name from a team on* The Simpsons.

407 Touch 'em all, Joe. You'll never hit a bigger home run in your life.—*Tom Cheek, announcer, on Blue Jay outfielder Joe Carter hitting the World Series–clinching home run off Phillies reliever Mitch Williams, October 23, 1993.*

408 I'm not going to go home and commit suicide.... I wish I hadn't thrown it down and in to Carter. I was trying to keep the ball away from him. It was a mistake.... It ain't comin' back.... I can't replay it and win it.... I can't change this one, much as I'd like to, if only because my teammates busted their butts. I let 'em down.... But don't expect me to curl up and hide from people because I gave up a home run in the World Series. Life's a bitch. I could be digging ditches. I'm not.—*Mitch Williams, Phillies reliever, on life after surrendering the World Series–winning homer to Joe Carter, 1993.*

409 When the World Series was over, I got back here as fast as I could so I could get to my guns on my ranch. The people of Philly were looking to get even.—*Mitch Williams, Phillies reliever, on returning to his home in Hico, Texas, 1993.*

410 I'll be wearing a flak jacket, and we're going to borrow the Pope's bulletproof limousine.—*Reliever Mitch Williams, after being traded to Houston, on his return to Philadelphia for his wedding on December 26, 1993.*

411 When this streak started back in 1982, New York Yankees pitcher Steve Howe had only had two lifetime suspensions for drug abuse.—*David Letterman, talk show host, on Orioles shortstop Cal Ripken Jr. playing in over 2,000 consecutive games, 1994. Howe was suspended seven times in his career for a variety of drug- and alcohol-related infractions.*

412 When he stops breathing. Even then, we'll probably just wheel him out there and plant him at shortstop.—*Mike Mussina, Orioles pitcher, on when he thought shortstop Cal Ripken's consecutive game streak would end, 1994.*

413 I'll probably hear from God or Cal when it's time, and I'll probably hear it sooner from God.—*Davey Johnson, Orioles manager, on when third baseman Cal Ripken would end his consecutive game streak, 1997.*

414 You can't even do what he did on Nintendo. You can hit 65 home runs on Nintendo.—*Barry Larkin, Reds shortstop, comparing Cal Ripken's 2,632 consecutive games played streak versus the Sammy Sosa/Mark McGwire home run records, 1998.*

415 I was hoping for the Ripken thing.—*Ty Wigginton, Mets rookie third baseman, on being given a day off after starting the first 21 games of the 2003 season.*

416 Bill Buckner had a nineteen-game hitting streak going and always wore the same underwear. Of course, he had no friends.—*Lenny Randle, Cubs third baseman, 1980.*

417 Thirty-eight going for fifty-six! Sounds like Dolly Parton going through puberty.—*Johnny Carson, talk show host, after Reds third baseman Pete Rose hit in his 38th consecutive game, 1978.*

418 I wanted his streak to continue, but I wanted to get him out, too.—*Gene Garber, Braves reliever, on stopping Pete Rose's 44-game hitting streak, a dozen shy of Joe DiMaggio's all-time record, August 1, 1978.*

419 Hit in 56 straight games? Heck, it's the rare major-leaguer today who plays in 56 straight.—*Ken Rosenthal, sportswriter, on the magnitude of Joe DiMaggio's 1941 hitting streak, 1994.*

420 Did you know that if I got a hit tonight, I would have made $10,000? The Heinz

57 people wanted to make some deal.—*Joe DiMaggio, Yankees outfielder, on having his 56-game hitting streak snapped by Cleveland, July 17, 1941. DiMaggio promptly began a 16-game hitting streak the next day.*

Oddities

421 There's one record I hold: Most World Series on the most different teams for a right-handed third baseman who didn't switch hit and who never played for the Yankees.—*Heinie Groh, who played in the World Series with the Reds, New York Giants, and Pirates.*

422 I struck out the first eight batters I faced in a game, which is a record. I set the record for pickoff attempts to first base in a season, which I think is still standing. And I set the major league record for most at-bats without an extra-base hit (323), which I think still stands.—*Jim Deshaies, Astros broadcaster and former pitcher, on how he might have managed to have his name included on the 2000 Hall of Fame ballot. Deshaies received one vote; for his career he went 84–95.*

423 A lot of people say Maris hit 61 [home runs]. But I'm the only one who ran for a midget.—*Jim Delsing, former St. Louis Browns outfielder, on pinch-running for the 3'7" Eddie Gaedel, who walked on four pitches in his only major league at-bat, August 19, 1951.*

424 I won over 200 big league games, but no one remembers that. When they think of me, I'm the guy who killed Chapman with a fastball.—*Carl Mays, former Yankees pitcher, on the death of Cleveland Indians shortstop Ray Chapman, August 16, 1920—baseball's first and only on-field fatality in the major leagues.*

425 That was a maximization of a minimization of hits.—*Mike Macfarlane, Royals catcher, after beating the Oakland A's, 3–1, with only one base hit, 1992.*

426 I suppose you know why I took you out. You see the American League record for striking out is five times in one game, and I didn't want you to tie it in your very first game.—*Connie Mack, Philadelphia A's manager, to rookie second baseman Jimmy Dykes, 1918.*

427 I've always prided myself on not striking out four times in a game. And I still haven't.—*Scott Rolen, Phillies third baseman, on striking out five times against San Diego in one game, 1999.*

428 I carried up enough lumber to the plate to build a house today.—*Zach Wheat, Brooklyn Dodgers outfielder, on a 26-inning game against the Boston Braves, May 1, 1920. In the longest game in baseball history, Dodgers pitcher Leon Cadore and Braves pitcher Joe Oeschger both pitched the entire game until it was eventually called due to darkness, tied 1–1. Only three baseballs were used during the entire game.*

429 It was the most boring game of baseball I ever played.—*Chico Walker, Pawtucket Red Sox outfielder, on an eight-hour, 32-inning game against the Rochester Red Wings that was called at 4:09 A.M., tied 2–2, April, 18, 1981. The game was completed on June 23, with Pawtucket winning 3–2 in the bottom of the 33rd inning. Rochester center fielder Dallas Williams went 0-for-13 in the game.*

430 It was so long, I went on the 15-day disabled list before the game and was eligible to come off after it.—*Mickey Hatcher, Dodgers outfielder, on being placed on the DL just before the longest night game in history—22-innings in Houston that lasted seven hours and fourteen minutes, June 3, 1989.*

431 We had a beer on the first pitch, and by the end of the at-bat we were so drunk that we had to call a cab to take us home.—*Joey Cora, White Sox coach, on watching TV with manager Ozzie Guillen while his brother, Dodgers shortstop Alex Cora, had an 18-pitch, 14-minute at-bat that ended with a home run, 2004. Cora's at-bat was the longest in 15 years.*

432 [Johnny] Pesky missed the hit-and-run sign that many times.—*Dom DiMaggio, Red Sox outfielder, when asked how he managed to steal 15 bases in 1950. DiMaggio led the AL in stolen bases that year—the lowest total ever for a league leader.*

433 What's everyone blaming me for? Blame

Felix [Millan]. I wouldn't have hit into the double plays if he hadn't hit singles.—*Joe Torre, Mets third baseman, on hitting into a record-tying four double plays, July 21, 1975.*

434 Okay, all the outfielders into the training room for a neck rub.—*Frank Robinson, Orioles coach, after his players got whiplash watching Toronto hit a record ten home runs against Baltimore in one game, September 14, 1987.*

435 That was like a summer league softball game, and we won the keg of beer.—*Sean Casey, Reds first baseman, on defeating the Rockies, 24–12, at Coors Field, 1999.*

436 I don't think I've ever been involved in a game before where both teams are trying to sweep a series.—*Skip Caray, Braves broadcaster, on a rare one-game series between Atlanta and Cincinnati, 2001.*

437 It was like a slow-pitch softball game. I can't believe some of those balls that went out.—*Josh Barfield, Padres second baseman, after Jeff Kent, J.D. Drew, Russell Martin and Marlon Anderson of the Dodgers hit four straight home runs to tie a game in the bottom of the ninth, September 19, 2006. The Padres took a 10–9 lead in the tenth before Nomar Garciaparra hit a two-run, walk-off homer.*

438 You ever seen that monologue Steve Martin does where he has no control over his body? That's what the whole stadium looked like. I looked around after the fourth one, and it looked like 50,000 Steve Martins dancing.—*Rich Donnelly, Dodgers coach, on LA hitting four consecutive home runs against San Diego to start the ninth inning, September 19, 2006.*

439 We may be the only park that *starts* selling beer in the seventh inning.—*Rich Donnelly, Brewers coach, on playing four extra-inning games during a stretch of nine home games, 2004.*

440 A Rockies' pitcher is going to be the National League Rookie of the Year? That's like a stuntman winning an Oscar for best actor.—*Jim Armstrong, sportswriter, on Colorado pitcher Jason Jennings, who went 16–8, in 2002.*

441 In case you don't grasp the significance of this epochal event, allow me to offer some perspective. Beethoven wrote nine symphonies. Horn has one triple. Nolan Ryan has pitched seven no-hitters. Horn has one triple. There have been three *Godfather* movies, two World Wars and one Sam Horn triple.—*Mike Littwin, sportswriter, on Orioles first baseman Sam Horn hitting his first triple, 1992. Horn finished his eight-year career with that lone triple and no stolen bases.*

Big Games

442 I think there are going to be a lot of Reggies born in this town.—*Bill Lee, Red Sox pitcher, on Yankees outfielder Reggie Jackson hitting a record three home runs (off three different pitchers) in Game 6 of the 1977 World Series.*

443 You've got a better chance of winning the lottery.—*Mark McGwire, Cardinals first baseman, on teammate Fernando Tatis hitting two grand slams in the same inning against Dodgers pitcher Chan Ho Park, April 23, 1999.*

444 I had a good week today.—*Bob Horner, Braves first baseman, on hitting four home runs in one game, July 6, 1986. Atlanta lost the game 11–8 to Montreal.*

445 I'm sure glad the season is over.—*Luke Appling, 75-year-old Hall of Fame shortstop, on hitting a home run off Warren Spahn in an Old-Timers' Game, July 19, 1982. Remarkably, Appling hit only 45 homers in his 20-year career and had not swung a bat in two years before becoming the oldest player ever to hit a home run.*

446 He had the greatest day since Lizzy Borden went two-for-two in Fall River, Massachusetts.—*Arthur "Bugs" Baer, sportswriter, on Red Sox outfielder Smead Jolley going 4 for 4 in one game. A notoriously bad fielder, legend says Jolley once let a line drive go through his legs, bounce off the outfield wall, and roll back through his legs before making a wild throw to the infield to be charged with three errors on one play.*

447 The guy's been in the league two days, and he's hit two of the longest home runs I've ever seen. We're going to have to play him in the third deck and use a bungee cord.—*Lance Johnson, White Sox outfielder, on Blue Jays rookie*

outfielder Carlos Delgado hitting a 428-foot homer on opening day and then a 445-foot shot off a window of SkyDome's Hard Rock Cafe the next day, 1994. Delgado retired with 473 career homers.

448 The best achievement from a guy you thought retired in 1987.—*Keith Olbermann, sportscaster, on Dodgers utility player Cory Snyder hitting three home runs in one game, April 17, 1994.*

449 They may call me Mr. February.—*Rex Hudler, Angels utility player, on hitting a grand slam, a solo homer, and an RBI double in the first intrasquad game of spring training, 1996.*

450 I don't see myself telling stories about it in 10 years' time or 20 years' time because nobody in Australia knows who Randy Johnson is.—*Justin Huber, Padres outfielder and Aussie native, on hitting his first career home run off the Big Unit, 2008.*

451 It was like signing a guy to a 10-day contract in the NBA—and he comes in and scores 50.—*Jim Deshaies, Astros broadcaster, on catcher J.R. Towles, a September call-up, driving in eight runs against St. Louis, September 20, 2007.*

452 He hits it harder than me.—*Derek Jeter, Yankees shortstop, watching Prince Fielder hit during spring training—at twelve years old, 1997. Prince's father Cecil was the Yankees DH that season. Eight years later, Prince made his debut with the Brewers.*

453 I knew June was Pedro's favorite month, so I told him that in the U.S., June had 60 days. I'd see him in July and say, "Well, Pedro, it's June 52nd and I see you're still hot."—*Tommy Lasorda, Dodgers manager, on outfielder Pedro Guerrero, 1985.*

Anger and Intensity

454 I'll kill anyone that gets in my way.—*Ty Cobb, Tigers outfielder.*

455 You all done? You comfortable? Well, send for the groundskeeper and get a shovel ready 'cause that's where they're gonna bury you.—*Dizzy Dean, Cardinals pitcher, to any batter who tried to dig in against him in the batter's box.*

456 Son, what kind of pitch would you like to miss?—*Dizzy Dean, Cardinals pitcher, when he faced a new batter.*

457 Swing the bat, for Christ's sake. You're not a statue until you have pigeon shit on your shoulders.—*Bill Lee, Red Sox pitcher, to Tigers outfielder Al Kaline, after walking him on a close pitch, 1974.*

458 I didn't like the way he was looking at me.—*Ted Simmons, Cardinals catcher, on why he punched Cubs third baseman Bill Madlock.*

459 I'll take you and a player to be named later.—*Dick Radatz, 6'6" Expos pitcher, to 5'5" Pirates infielder Freddie Patek, during a bench-clearing brawl, 1969.*

460 Oh, hell, how did I get matched up with you?—*Pete O'Brien, Mariners first baseman, on being pitted against 6'5", 235-pound Brewers DH Dave Parker during a bench-clearing brawl, 1990.*

461 Okay, okay. You guys want me? The big guys come one at a time, and the little guys—you can come all at once.—*Frank Howard, 6'8", 275-pound Tigers outfielder, to some rowdy fans, 1973.*

462 The whole thing reminded me of the junior prom—not a lot of action; just a lot of guys standing around, watching what's going on.—*Dan Quisenberry, Royals reliever, on a bench-clearing brawl.*

463 *Cy Young (Red Sox pitcher):* It's too bad Sherman didn't do more to Georgia when he was down your way. He left too many corncobs lying around.

Ty Cobb (Tigers outfielder): I'm going to drive the next one down your throat and they can cart you off to the cemetery.

464 I'm coming down on the next pitch, Krauthead.—*Ty Cobb, Tigers outfielder, standing on first base, to Pirates shortstop Honus Wagner* *during the 1909 World Series. Wagner tagged Cobb out on the attempted steal of second and gave him a bloody lip in the process.*

465 I got hit enough times to have [Commissioner] Ford Frick's signature tattooed on my arms and body, but it t'warn't nuthin'. I just sat on the dugout steps and sharpened my spikes and went into second base. I sure as hell didn't say, "Excuse me cause I'm a-gonna slide." —*Enos "Country" Slaughter, former outfielder.*

466 Frank was not out to make friends but to knock someone on his tail.—*Brooks Robinson, Orioles third baseman, on outfielder Frank Robinson.*

467 Pitchers did me a favor when they knocked me down. It made me more determined. I wouldn't let that pitcher get me out. They say you can't hit if you're on your back. But I didn't hit on my back. I got up.—*Frank Robinson, former Orioles outfielder.*

468 I'm the designated punching bag.—*Rick Auerbach, Dodgers infielder, after fights with Tim Foley and Pete Rose, 1974.*

469 As of today, umpires are not breaking up any more fights. If they want to fight, let them kill each other.—*Joe West, umpire, August 29, 1990.*

470 You son of a bitch, you went for that outside ball! That pitch, that part of the plate belongs to me! If I ever make a mistake inside, all right, but the outside is mine, and don't you forget it.—*Bob Gibson, Cardinals pitcher, to Phillies first baseman Bill White, 1966.*

471 I'm always amazed when a pitcher becomes angry at a hitter for hitting a home run off him. When I strike out, I don't get angry at the pitcher, I get angry at myself.—*Willie Stargell, Pirates first baseman, 1971.*

472 Hank, it's me and you now. I'm going to throw you my best fastball right down the middle, and you're going to either hit it out of the park or not hit it out of the park. But there will be no more foul balls.—*Sandy Koufax, Dodgers pitcher, to Milwaukee Braves outfielder Henry Aaron, during a game in which Aaron fouled off a dozen full-count pitches, 1965. Next pitch, Aaron popped out.*

473 If you ever do that again, I'll cut you to pieces.—*Lou Brock, Cardinals outfielder, to Pirates second baseman Rennie Stennett, who stepped into the baseline during a stolen base attempt, 1974.*

474 Well, that's football.—*Ray Fosse, Indians catcher, on a collision at home plate with Reds outfielder Pete Rose in the 1970 All-Star Game. Rose scored the winning run and left Fosse with a fractured shoulder.*

475 If it had been me, I would have climbed up Barnett's back and bit his ear off. I would have Van Goghed him.—*Bill Lee, Red Sox pitcher, on a disputed call by umpire Larry Barnett in Game 3 of the 1975 World Series.*

476 So he likes tae kwon do. I like to hunt. I don't bring a shotgun out there.—*Tim Belcher, Angels pitcher, on Dodgers pitcher Chan Ho Park, who attempted a spin kick against Belcher during an on-field altercation, 1999.*

477 Stalling won't help. There's one more out to go and you're it.—*Dennis Eckersley, Indians pitcher, to Angels outfielder Gil Flores, before completing a no-hitter, May 30, 1977.*

478 Most guys would rather wear a hamburger suit in a lion's den than mess with me.—*Dave Parker, Reds outfielder, 1984.*

479 You ought to play it mean. They ought to hate you on the field.—*Whit Wyatt, Brooklyn Dodgers pitcher.*

480 The ballplayer who loses his head, who can't keep his cool, is worse than no ballplayer at all.—*Lou Gehrig, Yankees first baseman.*

481 Better cut it out, or I'll put on my old Yankee uniform and scare the shit out of you.—*Waite Hoyt, Pirates pitcher and former member of New York's "Murderer's Row" teams, to a disrespectful Cubs dugout the season after the Yankees swept the Cubs in the 1932 World Series.*

482 He's even-tempered. He comes to the ballpark mad and stays that way.—*Joe Garagiola, broadcaster, on feisty Red Sox shortstop Rick Burleson, 1980.*

483 It was no problem. I didn't talk to him on days he was mad, and he was mad all year long.—*Whitey Herzog, Cardinals manager, on how he got along with pitcher Joaquin Andujar, 1989.*

484 My wife wouldn't know me out there. If she ever came to the mound and talked to me, she'd divorce me. Hate is an ugly word, but I hate hitters.—*Goose Gossage, Yankees reliever, 1981.*

485 I pitch the way Lyle Alzado plays football.—*Goose Gossage, Padres reliever, on his aggressive pitching style, 1984.*

486 His stuff was nasty. But what you really noticed was that he pitched mean ... this man doesn't just want to get batters out, he wants to laugh at them.—*John Mayberry, Royals first baseman, on teammate Steve Busby.*

487 I like to feel nasty and grubby. I'm not out there to win a beauty contest. I'm out there to be mean and win, not make friends.—*Kirk Gibson, Tigers outfielder, 1984.*

488 Hate is a good thing, as long as you keep it under control. When it comes out anger, you lose.—*Al Hrabosky, Cardinals reliever, 1975.*

489 Wait a minute. If you want to stand on the mound, you'll have to ask me first. It's my mound.—*Al "The Mad Hungarian" Hrabosky, Cardinals reliever, to first baseman Joe Torre, 1974.*

490 When I'm on the road, my greatest ambition is to get a standing boo.—*Al Hrabosky, Royals reliever.*

491 I don't want to get to know the other guys too well. I might like them, and then I might not want to throw at them.—*Sal "The Barber" Maglie, New York Giants pitcher.*

492 I'm the man you just ran over. You hand me fifteen bucks, or I'll punch you in the eye. You ain't goin' to ruin my clothes and get away with it.—*Rube Waddell, Philadelphia A's pitcher, to a hit-and-run driver Waddell chased down.*

493 You should do everything possible to win, short of scratching the other guy's eyes out.—*Ken Aspromonte, Indians manager.*

494 He is like a terrier dog. He's going to get you, knock you down, bite you in the jugular and let you bleed to death.—*Bill Lee, Red Sox pitcher, on Cincinnati third baseman Pete Rose.*

495 I'm the kind of guy who doesn't let up. If I've got you bleeding in six or seven different places, I'll make sure you're bleeding in eight or nine.—*Dave Stewart, Oakland A's pitcher, 1990.*

496 I'm rapidly approaching the mentality of an ax murderer.—*John Felske, Phillies manager, 1985. Philadelphia finished the year 26 games out of first.*

497 We have a wonderful relationship with the Yankees. They like to beat our brains out, and we want to beat their brains out.—*Nelson Doubleday, Mets co-owner, 1988.*

498 What I really want to do is tear the whole stadium up, turn it upside down, run everybody out of the stands—just because I didn't get a hit.—*Bo Jackson, Royals outfielder, on why he breaks bats over his knee, 1990.*

499 If there weren't 15,000 people watching, I'd hit you over the head.—*Bob Gibson, Cardinals pitching coach, to a St. Louis pitcher during a visit to the mound.*

500 When I was in high school, I was called a hothead when I lost my temper. When I got to the major leagues, they called me competitive.—*Billy Martin, Tigers manager.*

501 Lots of people look up to Billy Martin. That's because he's just knocked them down.—*Jim Bouton, former Yankees pitcher, on the temperamental Oakland A's manager, 1980.*

502 Not many people know this, but a lot of the guys he beat up in his life were being held by somebody else.—*Jeff Torborg, White Sox manager, on fiery manager Billy Martin.*

503 Some people have a chip on their shoulder. Billy has a whole lumberyard.—*Jim Murray, sportswriter, on manager Billy Martin.*

504 I don't throw the first punch. I throw the second four.—*Billy Martin, Oakland A's manager.*

505 Playing for Billy Martin is like being married to him. Right now we're all sleeping on the couch.—*Matt Keough, A's pitcher.*

506 I'll give you a blank check now, and at the end of the season you just fill in my total fines.—*Billy Martin, Oakland A's manager, to AL President Lee MacPhail, 1981.*

507 *Stan Williams (Dodgers pitcher):* Hank, I'm sorry I hit you in the batting helmet.

Hank Aaron (Braves outfielder): Don't worry about it. Those things happen.

Stan Williams: No, you don't understand. I was trying to hit you in the neck.

508 Cobb would climb a mountain to take a punch at an echo.—*Arthur "Bugs" Baer, sportswriter, on Tigers outfielder Ty Cobb.*

509 Wasn't he the bigot, the drunk, the womanizer? Wasn't he the guy who darted into the stands one day to beat up a crippled heckler who had no hands to fight back? Wasn't he the guy who slashed infielders with his spikes, the Hall of Famer so despised that when he died, only two big-leaguers came to his funeral?—*Stan Hochman, sportswriter, on the release of the Ty Cobb postage stamp, 2000.*

510 It is highly doubtful that John McGraw ever won a fist fight. And it is without question that he never ducked one.—*Bill Klem, umpire, on the combative New York Giants manager.*

511 *George Barr (Umpire):* I shook my head. *(Indicating a ball.)*

Dizzy Dean (Cardinals pitcher): Oh no, you didn't. If you had, I'd have heard something rattle.

512 *George Magerkurth (Umpire):* I'll reach down and bite your head off.

Leo Durocher (Manager): If you do, you'll have more brains in your stomach than you've got in your head.

513 *Babe Ruth (after being called out on strikes):* There's 40,000 people here who know that last one was a ball, tomato head.

Babe Pinelli (Umpire): Maybe so, but mine is the only opinion that counts.

514 *Cleon Jones (Mets outfielder):* Can you get thrown out of a game for thinking?

Umpire: No.

Cleon Jones: Well, then, I think you're doing a lousy job.

515 Any ballplayers that played for me on either the Cardinals or Yankees could come to me if he were in need and I would give him a helping hand. I make only two exceptions: Carl Mays and Joe Bush. If they were in a gutter, I'd kick them.—*Manager Miller Huggins.*

516 To fit any more people in here, we would have had to have Kevin Brown come in and take out a wall.—*Bob Costas, broadcaster, on the size of the crowd at a roast for Don Zimmer, 2004. Brown broke his non-pitching hand in September when he punched a clubhouse wall after a Yankees loss to Baltimore.*

517 When I was in Double A with Earl [Weaver], he told me, "Son, you're never going to play in the big leagues—you've got too much of a temper." And I said, "Well, you're a heck of an example!"—*Lou Piniella, Devil Rays manager, 2004.*

518 What do I need to show fire for? I'm not a dragon.—*Lou Piniella, Cubs manager, on comments that he wasn't being fiery enough during a losing streak, 2009.*

519 I was going to kill Mitch, but they said I couldn't—it's illegal.—*John Kruk, Phillies first baseman, on a game that reliever Mitch Williams almost blew but eventually saved, 1993.*

520 Once again, my mother is very proud of me, and my wife and kids are creeping around in disguise.—*Phillip Wellman, Mississippi Braves manager, on having one of the most outrageous managerial meltdowns of all-time, 2007.*

521 ABC and ESPN, which are both owned by Disney, are combining forces to start a new reality show called *Extreme Makeover at the Ballpark.* You go to baseball game, you sit next to the Texas Rangers bullpen, and they give you a nose job with a folding chair.—*Jay Leno, talk show host, on an ugly incident in Oakland in which a brawl took place between members of the Rangers bullpen and Oakland fans, September 13, 2004. Reliever Frank Francisco was suspended for the remainder of the season after tossing a chair into the stands that struck a female fan.*

522 The breakdown: 18 pitchers, seven position players and eight guys to shag caps thrown by Lou Piniella.—*Bill Scheft, sportswriter, on the 33 non-roster players invited by the Tampa Bay Devil Rays to spring training, 2003.*

523 No one is mad any more. That's what the off-season is for. You go fishing, catch a bass, punch him six or eight times in the head and you're over it.—*Andy Van Slyke, Pirates outfielder, on coping with the disappointment of losing the 1991 NLCS to the Braves in seven games, 1992.*

524 If Early Wynn was pitching every day I was behind the plate, I'd rather join the Russian Army.—*Nestor Chylak, umpire, 1962.*

525 I've played a couple of hundred games of tic-tac-toe with my little daughter, and she hasn't beaten me yet. I've always had to win. I've got to win.—*Bob Gibson, Hall of Fame pitcher.*

526 Barry Bonds? I'll tell you what, if he hit a home run off (Bob) Gibson or (Don) Drysdale and stood and admired it, they'd knock that earring out of his ear the next time up.—*Umpire Doug Harvey.*

527 Dark throws stools; Hutch throws rooms.—*Ed Bailey, Giants catcher, comparing the temperament of San Francisco manager Alvin Dark and Cincinnati manager Fred Hutchinson.*

528 Son, it ain't the water cooler that's striking you out.—*Casey Stengel, Yankees manager, to rookie outfielder Mickey Mantle who was taking out his frustrations, 1952. Mantle led the league with 111 strikeouts.*

At the Stadium

529 In the seventh inning, they all get up and sing "Take Me Out to the Ballgame," and they're already there. It's a really stupid thing to say.—*Larry Andersen, Phillies reliever, 1993.*

530 I have discovered in 20 years of moving around a ball park, that the knowledge of the game is usually in inverse proportion to the price of the seats.—*Bill Veeck, White Sox owner.*

531 The guy with the biggest stomach will be the first to take off his shirt at a baseball game.—*Glenn Dickey, sportswriter, 1981.*

532 I'm not sure what it means, but whenever the ball is not in play, somebody grabs his crotch. —*Pamela Bouton, wife of former pitcher Jim Bouton, on attending her first baseball game, 1981.*

533 You had your choice: you could see the spitting, the groin pulling and the scratching—or you could go to the ball game.—*David Letterman, talk show host, on the dilemma of attending a Madonna concert in Philadelphia or Game 3 of the 1993 Phillies–Blue Jays World Series.*

534 There goes the hopes of Salt Lake City ever getting a major league baseball team.—*Jay Leno, talk show host, on the Utah Supreme Court ruling that grabbing one's crotch in public is against the law, 2001.*

535 The smaller the crowd, the less a baseball player scratches.—*Bernie Lincicome, sportswriter, 2001.*

536 The fine in Singapore for spitting in public is $500, which means Tony Phillips would use up a year's salary in one game.—*Joe Falls, sportswriter, on the Tigers utility player, 1994.*

537 A Southern League grounds crew consists of one old man and a rake.—*Jim Bouton, former All-Star pitcher.*

538 If you can't stand the heat, stay out of the Chicken.—*Ted Giannoulas, the famous San Diego Chicken, 1980.*

539 This is bad news. Earlier today, North Korea announced that they have the technology to create their own rally monkey.—*David Letterman, talk show host, 2002.*

540 THE GIANTS WELCOME THE CALIFORNIA SCHOOL FOR THE DEATH.—*Scoreboard message at Candlestick*

Park intended to welcome a group of hearing-impaired patrons, 1981.

541 Would the fans along the outfield please remove their clothes?—*Tex Rickart, Ebbets Field public address announcer, to fans using the outfield fence to hang their coats.*

542 A little boy has been found lost.—*Tex Rickart, Ebbets Field public address announcer.*

543 What is both surprising and delightful is that spectators are allowed, and even expected, to join in the vocal part of the game.... There is no reason why the field should not try to put the batsman off his stroke at the critical moment by neatly timed disparagements of his wife's fidelity and his mother's respectability.—*George Bernard Shaw (1856–1950), writer.*

544 Now she thinks that's how all games go. There's 55,000 people there and they jump and scream, there's a home run to end it, you catch the ball and go meet Kirby Puckett.—*Joe Reis, Twins fan, on his five-year-old daughter Michelle's first baseball game. Game 6 of the 1991 Minnesota-Atlanta World Series ended when her dad caught Puckett's game-winning, 12th-inning home run.*

545 As a nation we are dedicated to keeping physically fit—and parking as close to the stadium as possible.—*Bill Vaughan, columnist.*

546 It is interesting about people that leave early from ballgames. It's almost as if they came out to the ballgame to see if they can beat the traffic home.—*Lon Simmons, Oakland A's broadcaster.*

547 What it adds up to is that it is not baseball's responsibility to fit itself into our frantic society. It is, rather, society's responsibility to make itself worthy of baseball. I can never understand why anybody leaves the game early to beat the traffic. The purpose of baseball is to keep you from caring if you beat the traffic. —*Bill Vaughan, columnist.*

548 The atmosphere just ain't here. Softball games are more exciting than this.—*Kevin Mitchell, A's outfielder, on a spring training game, 1998.*

549 He bats for the drunk players.—*Anonymous six-year-old fan, explaining to his friends the responsibility of the designated hitter, 1999.*

550 How do they find all those kids with the initials B.B.?—*Valerie Walker, baseball fan, on the batboys, 1999.*

551 If you come out and watch the Pirates and Reds in 20-degree weather, something is not right with your life. I think you need to get yourself checked out.—*Deion Sanders, Reds outfielder, 1997.*

552 Watching a spring training game is as exciting as watching a tree form its annual ring.—*Jerry Izenberg, sportswriter.*

553 Yeah, I was in the show. I was in the show for 21 days once—the 21 greatest days of my life. You know, you never handle your luggage in the show; somebody else carries your bags. It was great. You hit white balls for batting practice, the ballparks are like cathedrals, the hotels all have room service, and the women all have long legs and brains.—*Kevin Costner (as Crash Davis) in Ron Shelton's* Bull Durham, *1988.*

554 The only way I'd worry about the weather is if it snows on our side of the field and not theirs.—*Tommy Lasorda, Dodgers manager.*

555 I love doubleheaders. That way I get to keep my uniform on longer.—*Tommy Lasorda, Dodgers manager.*

556 All baseball fans can be divided into two groups: those who come to batting practice and the others. Only those in the first category have much chance of amounting to anything.—*Thomas Boswell, writer.*

557 It's kind of freaky knowing you're diving into somebody's grandpa.—*Coco Crisp, Red Sox outfielder, on the decision to stop fans from spreading cremation ashes at Fenway Park, 2008.*

558 Now that is what you call long relief.—*Rich Donnelly, Brewers coach, on Indianapolis Indians outfielder Jeff Liefer, who got locked inside a dugout bathroom during a game, causing a 20-minute delay, 2004.*

559 I don't want to be remembered as the guy who got stuck in the bathroom. Hopefully, it will happen to someone else so it won't be

such a big deal.—*Jeff Liefer, Indianapolis Indians outfielder, 2004.*

560 Now batting, right defensive back, Eric Byrnes.—*Roy Steele, A's public address announcer, after the Oakland outfielder tackled a fan who had run onto the field, 2005.*

561 You know, there was a lot of good TV on this summer, and a lot of people missed their shows because they were watching a game and they kept stopping it. Every time you looked up, they were stopping the game. We had a guy ground out to second for the 48th time the other night. They even stopped the game for that.—*Rich Donnelly, Dodgers coach, on the many game interruptions to honor milestones, 2007.*

562 A great World Series reminds us that until October, baseball is for recreational use only.—*Bernie Lincicome, sportswriter, 2001.*

563 I'm waiting for the water bed.—*Russ Davis, Giants third baseman, on the delivery of a large reclining chair to star outfielder Barry Bonds in the San Francisco locker room, April 2000.*

Fan Reactions

564 I knew why they threw it at me. What I can't figure out is why they brought it to the ballpark in the first place.—*Joe Medwick, Cardinals outfielder, on being pelted by Tiger fans with lemons, tomatoes, and heads of lettuce during Game 7 of the 1934 World Series. St. Louis won the clincher, 11–0.*

565 Used to be the fans knew you were trying hard and that's all they cared about. Now, if you have a bad day, they want to behead you.—*Kirby Puckett, Twins outfielder, 1994.*

566 You meet a better class of fan around third base.—*Pete Rose, Reds third baseman, after moving from left field to the hot corner. During his career, Rose played several seasons at second base, right field, left field, third base, and first base.*

567 Eighteen men play a game of baseball and eighteen thousand watch them, and yet those who play are the only ones who have any official direction in the matter of rules and regulations. The eighteen thousand are allowed to run wild.—*Robert Benchley, humorist.*

568 One of the chief duties of the fan is to engage in arguments with the man behind him. This department has been allowed to run down fearfully.—*Robert Benchley, humorist.*

569 I'll know things get back to normal when they start booing me again.—*New York Mayor Rudy Giuliani, a fervent Yankees fan, on being cheered at Shea Stadium by Mets fans, October 2001.*

570 Here's what I want to know: Just how many beers do you have to drink to want Chad Kreuter's cap?—*Jim Armstrong, sportswriter, on an incident at Wrigley Field in which a fan ran onto the field and swiped the cap of the Dodgers catcher as he sitting in the bullpen, which led to a chase into the stands, a fight, and the eventual suspension of 19 Los Angeles players and coaches, May 17, 2000.*

571 I'd rather have them out at the park booing than at home kicking the television set or complaining that the movie was lousy.—*Earl Weaver, Orioles manager, on fan support, 1974.*

572 We Americans are a peculiar people. We are for the underdog no matter how much of a dog he is.—*Baseball commissioner Happy Chandler.*

573 All baseball fans are provincial. They don't want the best team to win, they want their team to win.—*Art Hill, sportswriter.*

574 Why certainly I'd like to have a fellow who hits a home run every time at bat, who strikes out every opposing hitter when he's pitching and who is always thinking about two innings ahead. The only trouble is to get him to put down his cup of beer, come down out of the stands and do those things.—*Danny Murtaugh, Pirates manager, 1974.*

575 My favorite part of major league baseball is when the drunken fan leans over the railing and interferes with the ball in play; that's what I'd like to see more of. I don't know how to facilitate more of that, but I'd like to see more of that.—*David Letterman, talk show host, 1990.*

576 A baseball fan has the digestive appara-

tus of a billy goat. He can—and does—devour any set of statistics with insatiable appetite and then muzzle hungrily for more.—*Arthur Daley, sportswriter.*

Singing

577 Most of us have such bad voices we respect the national anthem by not singing it.—*Sparky Anderson, Reds manager, on why players don't sing the national anthem, 1974.*

578 Where's the National Rifle Association when you need them?—*Ron Fairly, Giants broadcaster, while listening to a trumpeter of limited skill play the national anthem at Olympic Stadium, 1991.*

579 I don't mind if the Japanese buy the Mariners, just so long as they don't let Yoko Ono sing the national anthem at their games. —*Jay Leno, talk show host.*

580 If she didn't think she could do a good job, she would not have accepted Tom Werner's offer. She's probably in her shower right now warming up.—*Ron Seaver, Padres public relations director, on a request by owner Tom Werner that comedienne Roseanne Barr sing the national anthem before a Padres game, 1990. Roseanne's shrill rendition of the anthem, complete with crotch grabbing and spitting, became a public relations disaster.*

581 The Padres should stop playing. The fat lady has already sung.—*Neil J. Liss, announcer, on the singing of the national anthem by comedienne Roseanne Barr, July 25, 1990. The Padres were 15 games out of first place.*

Promotions

582 Giving away baseballs is a bad idea. Why not give them hand grenades.—*Bruce Froemming, umpire, after fans at Candlestick Park pelted players with promotional baseballs, 1993.*

583 It's a good thing it was Seat Cushion Night.—*Daryl Boston, White Sox outfielder, on diving into the stands to make a catch, 1987.*

584 I'm glad it wasn't Paperweight Night.—*Rich Donnelly, Pirates coach, after fans threw sticks onto the field during Flag Night, causing a 13-minute delay, 1995.*

585 They're just lucky it wasn't "Safe Sex" night.—*Bob Lacey, comedy writer, on a bench-clearing brawl between the Durham Bulls and the Winston-Salem Warthogs that took place on "Strike Out Domestic Violence" night at Durham Bulls Athletic Park, May 22, 1995.*

586 It was crazy. Hair was flying everywhere. I should have collected some in case I need a weave some day.—*Jay Buhner, Mariners outfielder, on watching 426 fans get their head shaved at Jay Buhner Haircut Night at the Kingdome, 1994. Everyone who received an ultra-short Buhner cut was rewarded with free tickets.*

587 I'd like to welcome everyone in the Coca-Cola Family Section. Remember, there's no alcohol, no smoking, no fun and you're not allowed to keep any foul balls you catch.—*Al Frechtman, St. Paul Saints public address announcer, 1994.*

588 Major league baseball has asked its players to stop tossing baseballs into the stands during games because fans fight over them and they get hurt. In fact, the Florida Marlins said that's why they never hit any home runs. It's a safety issue.—*Jay Leno, talk show host, 1999.*

589 It was the first time a game has ever been called on account of candy bars.—*Dick Schaap, sportswriter, after Yankees fans threw promotional Reggie Bars all over the field after a Reggie Jackson homer, causing a delay (but not a forfeit) April 13, 1978.*

590 I'm going to buy a ticket. I feel bad for the people donating the pizzas. They're probably going to go out of business.—*Ozzie Guillen, White Sox manager, on hearing that the Devil Rays were offering a promotion in which fans would win a free pizza if Chicago struck out 10 times, 2007.*

591 I didn't try too hard. I was afraid I'd get emotionally involved with the cow.—*Rocky Bridges, Phoenix Giants manager, on finishing second in a pregame cow milking contest, 1976.*

592 First guy in the dugout checks for alligators.—*Wayne Causey, Kansas City A's shortstop, on the promotional animals used by owner Charlie Finley, which included mules, monkeys and elephants.*

593 It's not very often you get to see the Lone Ranger and Toronto the same night.—*Bobby Bragan, Rangers administrative assistant, on a home game against the Blue Jays that also featured a promotional appearance by Clayton Moore, TV's original Lone Ranger, September 1981.*

594 There's a lesson to be drawn from the way the crowd went crazy on 10-Cent Beer Night in Cleveland: Mix baseball fans with dime beers and soon both will lose their heads.—*Charles Maher, writer, on the forfeiture of a game by Cleveland due to drunken fans storming the field and attacking the Texas Rangers and the umpires, June 4, 1974.*

Attendance

595 If the crowds get any smaller, they'll have to put fractions on the turnstiles.—*Mark Roth, Yankees traveling secretary.*

596 Our whole entire booster club was going to come tonight, but their van broke down.—*Dave Heaverlo, Oakland A's pitcher, on a game at the Oakland Coliseum that was attended by only 750 fans, September 18, 1979.*

597 What time can you get here?—*Bill Veeck, St. Louis Browns owner, to a fan who telephoned to ask what time the next Browns game would begin. Veeck bought the hapless Browns in 1951 and instituted publicity stunts that included sending midget Eddie Gaedel to pinch hit on August 18, 1951. Tired of his healthy disregard for authority, the other owners forced Veeck to sell the club to ownership in Baltimore, and thus the Browns became the Orioles in 1954.*

598 Sometimes you walk on the field and wonder if they've opened the gates.—*R.J. Reynolds, Pirates outfielder, on the attendance at Three Rivers Stadium, 1987.*

599 We sold an incredible amount of tickets for this game. I don't think it had anything to do with the 1,500 Frisbees we were giving out.—*Burl Yarbrough, Double A San Antonio Missions GM, on a rehabilitation appearance by Dodgers pitcher Orel Hershiser, 1991.*

600 It was the first time in history that everyone in the stands got a foul ball.—*Dave LaPoint, Giants pitcher, on a 1985 game at Candlestick Park attended by 1,632 fans.*

601 Both have been real nice.—*Bob Brenly, Giants catcher, when asked how the fans were treating the team, 1985.*

602 I was looking for my wife and counting the people. After I got to one, I didn't have to go a lot higher.—*Andy Stewart, Team Canada catcher, on attendance at an Olympic preliminary game against the Netherlands, August 17, 2004. Canada won 7–0 and advanced to the semifinal round in its first Olympic appearance.*

603 This is the only team in the big leagues with a WON'T CALL window. On your way to get a beer, it's not unusual to stumble upon two or three foul balls that nobody's gotten around to picking up. Mound meetings must be held at a whisper.—*Rick Reilly, sportswriter, on the woeful attendance in Montreal, 2001.*

604 It was so quiet you could hear the air conditioning running through the vents.—*Kevin Millar, Marlins outfielder, on a crowd of 2,887 in Montreal, September 19, 2001.*

605 Crowd? This isn't a crowd. It's a focus group.—*Fran Healy, Mets announcer, on the small crowds at Olympic Stadium, 2002.*

606 How many hot dogs do they precook for a game here? Five? It's quite interesting to be able to sit and watch nine innings of ball, then occasionally walk around and pick up balls that have been knocked into the stands.—*Bill Cosby, comedian, on Montreal, 2002.*

607 It's an honor to get booed by 30,000 fans in Boston. I was booed by 2,000 at Candlestick Park.—*Jack Clark, Red Sox DH, 1991.*

608 The fans are close and they can say anything they want to you ... and they do. I would tell you, but all you'd have is bleep, bleep,

bleep.—*Larry Walker, Cardinals outfielder, on fans at Fenway Park, 2004.*

609 I don't care what the fans think. All they are is character killers. They're jealous. When we go to Burger King or McDonald's, we don't yell at them if our burgers are not cooked right.—*Carlos Castillo, White Sox pitcher, 1999.*

610 Sometimes we'd look up from the dugout and say, "Gee, this would be a good day to paint the seats."—*Gerald Perry, Braves first baseman, on the small crowds at Atlanta–Fulton County Stadium, 1988.*

611 I didn't know if that was the attendance or the year Nolan Ryan was born.—*Mike Scott, Astros pitcher, on an attendance figure of 1938 that was displayed on the scoreboard in Atlanta, 1989. Ryan was actually born in 1947.*

612 He obviously wanted to take Laura someplace nice and quiet where they could be alone.—*Jerry St. James, San Diego disc jockey, on the husband of co-worker Laura Cain, who took her to a Padres game for her birthday, 1994.*

613 It's a partial sellout.—*Skip Caray, Braves broadcaster, on a crowd of 6,000 at Atlanta–Fulton County Stadium, 1990.*

614 The definition of a good seat in this ballpark is definitely changing.—*Jack Tyson, Braves ticket director, on the off-season demand for tickets following the Braves rise from last place in 1990 to NL Champions, 1991.*

615 When the one great scorer comes to mark against your name, it's not whether you won or lost but how many paid to see the game.—*Peter Bavasi, Blue Jays GM.*

Attitude Problems

616 He doesn't have an attitude problem. He doesn't have any.—*Ralph Kiner, Mets broadcaster, on outfielder Kevin McReynolds, 1988.*

617 You're wrong. Darryl Strawberry is not a dog. A dog is loyal and runs hard after balls.—*Tommy Lasorda, Dodgers manager, on his suspended outfielder, 1994. Strawberry later admitted to a substance abuse problem.*

618 How did I get along with Yastrzemski? Like everybody else. By that I mean nobody ever got along with Yastrzemski.—*Billy Herman, former Red Sox manager, on Hall of Fame outfielder Carl Yastrzemski.*

619 He's one of the biggest jerks in the game. He argued, almost begged, for strikes, which wouldn't have been so bad if he had actually thrown a few once in a while. He was wild. And dangerous, too. Dibble would throw at his own mother for a dime.—*Pam Postema, former minor league umpire, on Reds reliever Rob Dibble, 1992.*

620 I tell him something, and it goes in one ear, hits something hard and bounces back out.—*Davey Johnson, Reds manager, on reliever Rob Dibble, 1994.*

621 He would hold the lamp while his mother was cutting wood.—*Happy Chandler, baseball commissioner, on Brooklyn Dodgers manager Leo Durocher. Chandler suspended Durocher for the 1947 season as punishment for Durocher's reputed association with gamblers.*

622 You and Durocher are on a raft. A wave comes along and knocks him into the ocean. You dive in and save his life. A shark comes along and takes your leg. Next day, you and Leo start out even.—*Dick Young, sportswriter, on manager Leo Durocher.*

623 Leo never takes it out on me when he comes home to dinner after losing a game. He takes it out on the players before he leaves the park.—*Laraine Day, actress and wife of New York Giants manager Leo Durocher, 1950. Day became popular for her role as Nurse Mary Lamont on the* Dr. Kildare *TV series. She wrote a volume of memoirs entitled* Day with Giants (1952).

624 You know Earl. He's not happy unless

he's not happy.—*Elrod Hendricks, Orioles bullpen coach, on manager Earl Weaver.*

625 When the bastard dies, they'll have to hire pallbearers.—*Tom Haller, former umpire, on former Orioles manager Earl Weaver, 2007.*

626 Earl Weaver smokes too much and drinks too much. He has a voice that sounds like broken glass. He has a ferocious temper, especially with umpires, and doesn't know when to keep his mouth shut. He has never been accused of being a diplomat, and has never set out to win any popularity contests with his players. He is also one of the few baseball geniuses I have ever met.—*Reggie Jackson, Hall of Fame outfielder, who was managed by Weaver in 1976.*

627 I go back to 1965 with Reggie, but I guess I don't go back far enough to remember when he was shy.—*Rick Monday, Dodgers outfielder, on Yankees outfielder Reggie Jackson. Both players came up with the Kansas City Athletics.*

628 Lou Piniella argues on days ending with the letter "y."—*Ron Luciano, umpire, on the Yankees outfielder.*

629 "Sweet" refers to Lou's swing, not his personality.—*Phil Rizzuto, announcer, on Yankees outfielder "Sweet" Lou Piniella.*

630 They call him "Puff" because he's always provoking fights. Then when they start—puff—he's gone.—*Joe Garagiola, broadcaster, on Yankees third baseman Graig Nettles.*

631 Could be he's a nice guy when you get to know him, but why bother?—*Dizzy Dean, Cardinals pitcher, on New York Giants player-manger Bill Terry.*

632 It just goes to show, good bitching will beat good hitting anytime.—*Steve Simmons, sportswriter, on an argument between White Sox DH George Bell and manager Gene Lamont during the 1993 ALCS. Bell, who hit just .217 for the season, was benched during the loss to Toronto.*

633 If hits were words, he'd still be looking for his 200th hit.—*Bob Hertzel, sportswriter, on tight-lipped Dodgers first baseman Eddie Murray, 1989.*

634 Here's a guy who has spent his whole career as if he's auditioning for the lead in *The Marcel Marceau Story* and he ends up on a team where no one talks.—*Mike Littwin, sportswriter, on taciturn Mets first baseman Eddie Murray, 1992.*

635 Trading profanities with Tommy is like engaging in a dart duel with a porcupine.—*Scott Ostler, sportswriter, on Dodgers manager Tommy Lasorda, 1993.*

636 He's misunderstood. People don't have the realization of just how big a jerk he really is.—*Bob Waller, broadcaster, on former All-Star outfielder Dave Kingman, 1987. Due to his personality (and collusion by owners), Kingman was unable to find a team willing to sign him for the 1987 season even though he hit 35 home runs for Oakland in 1986.*

637 He's learning to say hello when it's time to say good-bye.—*Frank Graham, sportswriter, on how Yankees outfielder Bob Meusel began acting friendly late in his career.*

638 His affability quotient has improved greatly since he discovered he could make a living by being nice.—*George Vescey, sportswriter, on Hall of Fame outfielder Mickey Mantle, 1985.*

639 If he'd tip his cap once, he could be elected Mayor of Boston in five minutes.—*Eddie Collins, Hall of Fame second baseman, on Red Sox outfielder Ted Williams.*

640 He's as intense as the forest is green—except he doesn't have a change of seasons.—*Randy Wolf, Phillies pitcher, on manager Larry Bowa, 2003.*

641 Larry Bowa is a bleeping cancer on this club—K-A-N-C-E-R.—*Dallas Green, Phillies manager, on his All-Star shortstop.*

642 The problem is that he thinks the S and D on our shirts stands for Storm Davis.—*Larry Bowa, San Diego Padres manager, 1987.*

643 The year Billy roomed with me, I won the MVP. The year he roomed with Yogi Berra, he won the MVP, and the year he roomed with Mickey Mantle, Mickey won the MVP. Some bad influence, eh?—*Phil Rizzuto, former Yankees shortstop, on the June 15, 1957, eight-player trade*

that sent second baseman Billy Martin to the Kansas City A's, 1989.

644 He's the kind of guy you'd like to kill if he's playing for the other team, but you'd take ten of him on your side.—*Frank Lane, Indians GM, on second baseman Billy Martin, 1953 World Series MVP.*

645 I'm Billy's best friend, and I don't even like him.—*Whitey Ford, Hall of Fame pitcher, on former teammate Billy Martin, 1989.*

646 If you approach Billy Martin right, he's okay. I avoid him altogether.—*Ron Guidry, Yankees pitcher, on his manager.*

647 You have to remember, most of Billy Martin's boyhood friends are in San Quentin.—*Jerry Coleman, Padres broadcaster.*

648 Most of us would willingly endure slurs that would embarrass Andrew Dice Clay if they gave us $2 million to play centerfield for the Seattle Mariners.—*Alan Greenberg, sportswriter, on separate incidents in which Indians outfielder Albert Belle and Oakland A's outfielder Jose Canseco retaliated against verbally abusive fans, 1991.*

649 Play him, fine him, and play him again. —*Gene Mauch, Phillies manager, on how to manage third baseman Dick Allen.*

650 I dirty three uniforms in a day. He dirties three in a month.—*Pete Rose, Phillies first baseman, on Mets outfielder George Foster, 1982. Rose and Foster were teammates on Cincinnati's Big Red Machine from 1971 to 1978.*

651 I usually don't make a good first impression—or a good second impression. For that matter, I usually come across as a sack of manure.—*Doug Rader, Rangers manager, 1984.*

652 You have to remember one thing at all times when dealing with Barry: This is not an adult. This is a nine-year-old. He's a nine-year-old kid in the body of an extraordinary 28-year-old athlete. He's not a horrible guy, just a very immature person.—*Rick Cerone, Pirates executive, on Giants outfielder Barry Bonds, 1993.*

653 [Barry] Bonds is about as popular as high humidity. The media don't like him. The fans don't like him. A whole lot of players don't like him. I don't know about the clergy. I'm afraid to ask.—*Nick Canepa, sportswriter, 2001.*

654 Someday they'll be able to hold Bonds's funeral in a fitting room. When Bonds hit his 500th home run, in April, only one person came out of the dugout to greet him at the plate: the Giants' batgirl.—*Rick Reilly, sportswriter, August 2001.*

655 Bonds was born with a Silver Slugger in mouth, and life never taught him much perspective, humility or gratitude.—*Skip Bayless, sportswriter, on Barry Bonds, June 2002.*

656 If I've got baggage, he's got a whole set of Louis Vuitton.—*Milton Bradley, self-aware Rangers DH, on the challenge of any team signing free agent slugger Barry Bonds, July 2008.*

657 I want people to say Milton Bradley was a pretty good ballplayer and a pretty good person. Anybody who is going to stand between me and getting there, then they need to be eliminated.—*Milton Bradley, Dodgers outfielder, September 2005. In 11 seasons, the ill-tempered Bradley played for eight teams—and counting.*

658 He's a punk. He's putting all the blame on Jose when it's the whole team. Let them sweep us. I should have worn a red dress.—*Esther Canseco, wife of Oakland A's outfielder Jose Canseco, on manager Tony LaRussa benching Canseco for the fourth and final game of the 1990 World Series in which the Reds swept the heavily favored A's.*

659 They say happy cows give more milk, but they've basically told me I'm dog meat.—*Kirk Gibson, Royals outfielder, on being told he would be a platoon player, 1992. Gibson was traded to Pittsburgh during spring training the next year.*

660 Jack and I get along because he's as easygoing as I am obnoxious.—*Dick Williams, Padres manager, on GM Jack McKeon, 1984.*

661 This is a guy who likes to complain a lot about not playing, but that's what he does best—not play.—*Pat Gillick, Blue Jays GM, on Angels first baseman Mike Marshall, 1991.*

662 The more you hear what Steve has been saying lately, the more you realize how fortunate

America was that he refused to speak to the media all those years.—*John Steigerwald, sportswriter, on several bizarre comments made by pitcher Steve Carlton months before his Hall of Fame induction, 1994.*

663 When I was a little kid, teachers used to punish me by making me sign my name 100 times.—*Willie Wilson, Royals outfielder, on why he refused to sign autographs.*

664 You know what, kid? I'm sure it would. —*Albert Belle, Orioles outfielder, walking away from a youngster who had told Belle that an autograph would really make his day, 1999.*

665 They asked me if there was anything they could do for me. I asked if I could have a ball signed by Albert Belle. They said, "Wow, you really are a comedian!"—*Elayne Boosler, comedian, on throwing out a ceremonial first pitch in Cleveland, 1996.*

666 It's not easy being Albert Belle. So little time, so many people to offend.—*Tom Haudricourt, sportswriter, on the Indians outfielder, 1996.*

667 Yep, nothing says Christmas like a greedy, surly, carpet-bagging mercenary.—*Joe Knowles, sportswriter, on outfielder Albert Belle appearing on the cover of* Baseball Weekly *wearing a Santa cap, 1998. Belle utilized an escape clause in his contract to leave the White Sox and sign a five-year deal with the Orioles during the off-season.*

668 He developed some bad relationships with players that caused players to leave the team and players to lose respect for him. But I have nothing bad to say about the guy.—*Albert Belle, Indians outfielder, on the firing of manager Ray Miller, October 1999.*

669 He was a selfish churl who made his own bed of boos with 11 years of boorish, off-putting behavior, forfeiting any chance of his engendering more than token sympathy or goodwill now.—*John Eisenberg, sportswriter, on the retirement of Orioles outfielder Albert Belle, 2001.*

670 I loved him from 7 to 10 P.M., but he could take the joy out of a franchise. He was a fine player, but he never enjoyed his great fortune. It still bothers me to think a man so gifted could be so miserable.—*John Hart, Indians GM, on former Cleveland outfielder Albert Belle, 2001.*

671 Why shouldn't I tell the truth? I ain't trying to get no Pepsi commercial.—*Gary Sheffield, Yankees outfielder, on criticism he received for discussing team problems, August 2005.*

672 Many people are picking on Gary Sheffield, but we're talking about a fine ballplayer here. In fact, three cities have been named after him—Gary, Ind.; Sheffield, England; and Marblehead, Mass.—*Tom FitzGerlad, sportswriter, on the moody Dodgers outfielder, 2001.*

673 He comes off as a drill sergeant hell-bent on discipline. His smile is AWOL, and the look on his face resembles a man who just chugged a quart of motor oil.—*Dan Bickley, sportswriter, on Diamondbacks manager Buck Showalter, 1998.*

674 If I ain't startin', I ain't departin'.—*Garry Templeton, Cardinals shortstop, on being chosen as a reserve for the 1979 All-Star Game.*

675 Winning isn't as important as doing well individually. You can't take teamwork up to the front office to negotiate.—*Ken Landreaux, Dodgers outfielder, 1984.*

676 He's got a square jaw and a square head, and both match his personality. The way he thinks things should be is the way he has them. Period.—*Johnny Bench, Reds catcher, on Phillies first baseman Pete Rose, 1979. Rose and Bench were teammates with Cincinnati from 1967 to 1978.*

677 Pete Rose is the most likable arrogant person I've ever met.—*Mike Schmidt, Phillies third baseman, 1981.*

678 The guy's just not a friendly man. He eats nails and glass. He likes to swallow toads live.—*Lary Sorensen, Brewers pitcher, on pitcher Mike Caldwell, 1979.*

679 Why is it there are so many nice guys interested in baseball? Not me, I was a real bastard when I played.—*Burleigh Grimes, Hall of Fame pitcher. Old Stubblebeard was his nickname, given to him because he never shaved on the days he pitched. When the spitball was banned in 1920,*

Grimes was one of the few players given permission to continue throwing it.

680 Munson's not moody, he's just mean. When you're moody, you're nice sometimes.—*Sparky Lyle, Yankees reliever, on catcher Thurman Munson, 1978.*

681 He was one of those guys who worked very hard at refusing to let people think he was a nice fellow.—*Gabe Paul, Indians president, on Yankees catcher Thurman Munson, 1979.*

682 I'll be a terrible captain. I'm too belligerent. I cuss and swear at people. I yell at umpires, and maybe I'm a little too tough at home. I don't sign autographs like I should, and I haven't always been very good with writers.—*Catcher Thurman Munson on being named Yankees captain in 1976—the first player so honored since Lou Gehrig in 1939.*

683 I'm like Daffy Duck in the cartoons. I'm black, I've got big feet and I'm always bitching.—*Billy Sample, Rangers outfielder.*

684 I'm a hardheaded degenerate. If it wasn't for baseball, I might be a convict.—*David Wells, Yankees pitcher, 1998.*

685 We judge players on what they do on the field. If we wanted nice boys, we'd go on the church steps and pick up a nice collection.—*Gabe Paul, Yankees president, 1977.*

686 He was frank to the point of being cruel and subtle as a belch.—*Lee Allen, sportswriter, on St. Louis Browns manager Rogers Hornsby.*

687 The Yankees, too, are a family. A family like the Macbeths, the Borgias, and the Bordens of Fall River, Massachusetts.—*Ron Fimrite, sportswriter, October 1977.*

688 You've heard the old saying, "25 players, 25 cabs." But with the Astros it was 25 players, 30 cabs. You'd jump out of one cab and get into another one just in case they were following you.—*Todd Jones, Tigers closer, on his former team, March 1997.*

689 It has been said that Falk could curse for an hour and not repeat himself.—*Neal Farmer, sportswriter, on University of Texas baseball coach Bibb Falk (1940–1942, 1946–1967).*

690 Who's he?—*Rickey Henderson, Mets outfielder, when told that Mets hitting coach Tom Robson had been fired, 1999.*

691 I love the part where Rickey reports to camp a week late, and about noonish puts on his uniform and saunters out of the clubhouse, and if he sees his shadow that means there will be another six weeks of bitching about his contract.—*Scott Ostler, sportswriter, bemoaning a spring training without Rickey Henderson, February 2001. Rickey was eventually signed by San Diego.*

692 Can you imagine Rickey Henderson, who invented talking in the third person, at the lectern giving his induction speech at Cooperstown? "Today ... today ... today.... Rickey considers Rickey the luckiest dude on the face of the earth."—*Jim Armstrong, sportswriter, 2001. A humble Henderson was inducted to the Hall of Fame in 2009 and gave a speech that played against his often flamboyant reputation.*

693 Yes, he offended everyone.—*Felipe Alou, Giants manager, when asked if former catcher A.J. Pierzynski was more offensive-minded than new catcher Mike Matheny, 2005.*

694 I was actually talking to my wife about that because I thought maybe she had some input.—*Curt Schilling, Red Sox pitcher, on being named one of* GQ*'s 10 Most Hated Athletes, 2006.*

695 Nobody told me I was in competition. If there is competition, somebody better let me know. If there is competition, they better eliminate me out of the race and go ahead and do what they're going to do with me. I ain't never hit in spring training, and I never will. If it ain't settled with me out there, then they can trade me. I ain't going out there to hurt myself in spring training battling for a job. If it is, then I'm going into "Operation Shutdown." Tell them exactly what I said. I haven't competed for a job since 1991.—*Derek Bell, Pirates outfielder, on hearing he would have to compete for a job in spring training after a disastrous first season in Pittsburgh, March 18, 2002.*

696 Bell, who hit .172 in an injury-plagued 2001 season, might be better served by moving immediately to "Operation Shutup."—*Tom*

FitzGerald, sportswriter, on Pirates outfielder Derek Bell, who said he would perform "Operation Shutdown" rather than compete for a job, 2002. He didn't have to—Bell was released and the Pirates paid him $4.5 million not to play. Bell never played again in the majors and has since been arrested twice on drug-related charges.

697 Derek Bell becomes the ultimate Pirate: Lives on a boat and steals money—*Mark Madden, sportswriter, after the Pirates paid outfielder Derek Bell $4.5 million not to play for them in 2002.*

698 By reputation, which was formed through attitude, behavior and stupidity, Red Sox outfielder Carl Everett managed to accomplish last season the seemingly impossible. He surpassed John Rocker for the title of the worst human being in baseball.—*Randy Galloway, sportswriter, on the Texas Rangers off-season acquisition of Everett and Rocker, December 2001.*

699 Like you're going to get social action from a company that owns WCW wrestling and a baseball team that's been insulting Native Americans since 1912.—*Keith Olbermann, broadcaster, on protesters demanding the Atlanta Braves punish reliever John Rocker for his repeated incidents of insensitivity, February 2000.*

700 He slurred the first nine men he faced.—*Alan Ray, comedy writer, on Braves reliever John Rocker working his first game of spring training, 2000.*

701 Scott Rolen maintains the most even keel of any player in baseball. When he is going good, he appears to be miserable. And when he's going bad, he appears to be miserable.—*Bill Conlin, sportswriter, on the Phillies third baseman, May 2001.*

702 I hope to get up here and get yelled at sooner than later.—*Gordon Beckham, the No. 1 draft pick of the White Sox, on his timetable for being managed by Ozzie Guillen, 2008. Beckham made his major league debut on June 4, 2009.*

703 It's so easy to be negative. But I don't know of any situation that ever became better without a positive attitude. I just don't know how that happens. To go out and heap more pressure and more negativity on a group of people seems to invite what you had in the past.—*Joe Maddon, Devil Rays manager.*

704 Don't accuse me of not being happy just because I don't smile.—*Ken Griffey Jr., Reds outfielder, 2003.*

705 Frank Thomas could carry a baseball bat made of beef jerky and not get a pack of wild schnauzers to follow him.—*Rick Morrissey, sportswriter, on the lack of leadership shown by the White Sox DH, 2003.*

706 Make no mistake, the stink of Clemens hung over the Subway Series like a fog over a pumpkin patch. The man who just might be the greatest right-handed pitcher of the last half-century has the maturity of a child, the grace of a camel, the class of a mudhole.—*Rick Telander, sportswriter, on the behavior of Yankees pitcher Roger Clemens during the 2000 World Series.*

707 I don't want to mellow. I'd rather be known as a winner and a sore loser.—*Dick Williams, Red Sox manager, 1969.*

A Ballplayer's Life

708 Winning and losing is nothing. Going out and prowling the streets after the game is what I liked. You'd get half in the bag and wake up the next morning with a bird in your room—that's what baseball is all about.—*Bob Uecker, Brewers broadcaster and former catcher.*

709 People ask me what I do in winter when there's no baseball. I'll tell you what I do: I stare out the window and wait for spring.—*Rogers Hornsby, Cardinals second baseman.*

710 I never had a bad night in my life, but I've had a few bad mornings.—*Lefty Gomez, Hall of Fame pitcher.*

711 Ten-thirty? I'm not even done throwing

up at that hour.—*Jim Pagliaroni, Seattle Pilots catcher, on being told when to report for early batting practice, 1969.*

712 Jesus! Think of taking a ballplayer's nights away from him.—*Mike Donlin, New York Giants outfielder, on hearing that some minor league games were played at night.*

713 How to use your leisure time is the biggest problem of a ballplayer.—*Branch Rickey, Brooklyn Dodgers GM.*

714 On this club, if you go to sleep at night and wake up in the morning, you're considered strange.—*Sal Bando, A's third baseman, on the Oakland teams of the early '70s.*

715 In the daytime, you sat in the dugout and talked about women. At night, you went out with women and talked about baseball.—*Waite Hoyt, Hall of Fame pitcher.*

716 I think about baseball when I wake up in the morning. I think about it all day. And I dream about it at night. The only time I don't think about it is when I'm playing it.—*Carl Yastrzemski, Red Sox outfielder, 1978.*

717 One, I don't want anyone out-drinking me. Two, I don't want anyone to dress worse than me.—*Doug Rader, Rangers manager, on his two team rules, 1984.*

718 Open up a ballplayer's head and you know what you'll find? A lot of little broads and a jazz band.—*Mayo Smith, Tigers manager.*

719 *Bo Belinski (Angels pitcher):* I gotta go, or I'll miss bed check.

Mamie Van Doren (actress): I know, honey, I'm dancing as fast as I can.

720 Booze, broads and bullshit. If you got all that, what else do you need?—*Harry Caray, White Sox broadcaster, 1976.*

721 *Babe Ruth (Red Sox pitcher, 1919):* I don't want to pitch anymore.

Ed Barrow (Red Sox manager): How come?

Babe Ruth: I'm tired all the time.

Ed Barrow: Have you tried sleep?

722 The bad thing about big-league baseball is all the travel because all you can do in these big cities is shop. The good thing is you can afford it.—*Bobby Grich, Angels second baseman, 1985.*

723 You read seven papers and don't remember a thing. You drink 140 cups of coffee and go to the john after every thirtieth. Then maybe you go to a shopping mall and get lost. —*Jim Kern, Rangers reliever, on life in the big leagues, 1979.*

724 Players are the most helpless people in the world. If you told them to get to San Francisco by themselves, they might end up in Mexico City.—*Tom Yawkey, Red Sox owner.*

725 There are three types of baseball players: those who make things happen, those who watch it happen, and those who wonder what happens.—*Tommy Lasorda, Dodgers manager.*

726 Joe Altobelli tried to treat the players like men, but it's well known most ballplayers are a bunch of asses.—*Bill Madlock, Giants third baseman, on his manager, 1978.*

727 This life drives you crazy. I should know. It drove me crazy two years ago, and I never recovered.—*Jim Kern, Rangers reliever, 1979.*

728 Yeah, I was a little nutty. If there'd be some guy on a pogo stick with three girls around him, it would be me.—*Dave Rozema, former Tigers pitcher.*

729 If I get famous, I might get some endorsements for chain saws.—*Steve "Psycho" Lyons, White Sox utility player, 1987.*

730 This is Ralph Salvon. I'm not in my room, but I need wake up calls at 1, 3, 5, 7 and 9. I've got a severe eye infection and must take these drops every two hours. It's critical that I take them, or I may go blind.—*Moe Drabowsky, Orioles pitcher, to a hotel operator as part of a prank on team trainer Ralph Salvon.*

731 I'm not afraid of flying, I'm afraid of crashing.—*Charlie Hough, Rangers pitcher.*

732 I don't know how close it was, but the lady in 13D was having the chicken dinner.—*Jim Sundberg, Cubs catcher, on a near collision during a team flight, 1987.*

733 We're going down. We're going down

and I have a .300 lifetime average to take with me. Do you?—*Pete Rose, Reds left fielder, during a bumpy flight, to backup catcher Hal King.*

734 When they find the black box, it will confirm pilot error.—*Garry Maddox, Phillies outfielder, after seeing catcher Ozzie Virgil crash his $400 remote-controlled plane into the water, March 1985.*

735 It's the only time I've thrown up and passed out and had a good time.—*Travis Fryman, Tigers third baseman, on flying with the Blue Angels, 1996.*

736 Eighty percent of big-league ballplayers go out to the racetrack today. Sneak around in sunglasses. Other 20 percent ain't that holy. Just can't find anybody who'll give 'em free tickets.—*Rogers Hornsby, Cardinals second baseman.*

737 Players like rules. If they didn't have any rules, they wouldn't have anything to break.—*Lee Walls, Oakland A's coach.*

738 Rules are made to be broken, so there won't be any rules.—*Billy Herman, Pirates manager, 1947. In his first season as manager, Pittsburgh finished tied for last place. Herman was fired before the final game of the season.*

739 Don Baylor, the new manager of the Colorado Rockies, issued a no-facial-hair edict for his players. The Rockies are a very young team, though, and several of the players immediately shaved off their eyebrows.—*Scott Ostler, sportswriter, 1993.*

740 In Cincinnati, we were lucky we were allowed to have eyebrows.—*Dann Bilardello, Expos catcher, on playing for the Reds, 1986.*

741 Does this mean I have to shave my legs?—*Outfielder Andy Van Slyke when told there was a team policy prohibiting hair below the lip.*

742 You tell Marge to shave her St. Bernard, and I'll shave my mustache.—*Reliever Rollie Fingers on the Cincinnati Reds requirement that he shave his trademark handlebar mustache in order to receive an invitation to spring training, 1986. Fingers declined the invite from owner Marge Schott and retired with 341 career saves.*

743 The way he hits, he can show up in his underwear.—*George Steinbrenner, Yankees owner, on third baseman Wade Boggs. For his new player, Steinbrenner waived the team rule prohibiting facial hair, 1993.*

744 He doesn't have to march to the same drummer as long as he's in the same band.—*Dusty Baker, Giants manager, on outfielder Barry Bonds, who won his third MVP Award in four years after his first season with San Francisco, 1993.*

745 I'm just happy to be here. I'll take whatever they give me. If they took off my hat and shit in it, I'd put it right back on my head and say thanks.—*Jerry Stephenson, Seattle Pilots pitcher, 1969.*

746 If you stay around here long enough, you either go zany or become a monk. And monks aren't having too much fun these days.—*Ron Guidry, Yankees pitcher, 1988.*

747 Just stick your foot in the toilet and flush it.—*Tommy Lasorda, Dodgers manager, to a rookie who asked where the whirlpool was located.*

748 I'd love to, Bill, but I just had my shoes shined.—*Fresco Thompson, New York Giants infielder, on being asked by manager Bill Terry to pinch hit, 1934. That season, his last, Thompson recorded only one at-bat.*

749 I go out and do what we call, back home, slam dancing—go out and butt our heads and stuff like that.—*Charlie Kerfeld, Astros reliever, on how he spends his days off, 1987.*

750 Today's players like to play their stereos early because after the game their hair dryers cause static.—*Bob Lemon, Yankees manager, 1981.*

751 Always stand in the middle when you're having a group picture taken because that way they can't cut you out of it.—*Stan Musial, Hall of Fame outfielder.*

752 I ain't ever had a job. I just always played baseball.—*Satchel Paige, Hall of Fame pitcher, 1980.*

753 We hear the F-word all the time. I've had guys yell, "I was with your sister last night." I know that's not true. I don't have a sister.—*Mark Grace, Cubs first baseman, on verbal abuse from fans, 1996.*

754 I was pumping gas the other day and a guy came up to me to tell me what I'm doing wrong. I felt like saying, "Hey, I don't tell you how to put your lug nuts on."—*Chuck Finley, Angels pitcher, 1994.*

755 I am quite sure that statistics will show that the greatest number of successes have been scored by those who have led moderately dirty lives.—*W.O. McGeehan, sportswriter.*

756 When you can do it out there between the white lines, you can live any way you want.—*Denny McLain, Tigers pitcher. The hard-living McLain won the AL MVP and Cy Young Award in 1968 by recording 31 victories with a 1.96 ERA.*

757 The off-the-field stuff can kill you. It can absolutely destroy you.—*Denny McLain, former pitcher, 1976. In 1970, McLain was suspended three months for gambling. He later filed for bankruptcy, was suspended for gun possession, convicted of racketeering and smuggling cocaine, and served two separate stints in prison.*

758 A ballplayer is under contract for his ability on the field, not as a human being.—*Alex Johnson, Angels outfielder, 1970.*

759 I don't room with Babe. I room with his suitcase.—*Ping Bodie, Yankees outfielder, on Babe Ruth.*

760 The only thing Larsen fears is sleep.—*Jimmy Dykes, Orioles manager, on pitcher Don Larsen, 1954.*

761 Chuck Tanner used to have a bed check for me every night. No problem, my bed was always there.—*Bob Veale, former Pirates pitcher.*

762 The best way to avoid ballplayers is to go to a good restaurant.—*Tim McCarver, broadcaster and former catcher, 1987.*

763 Twenty-eight bars of Neutrogena soap is not an acceptable gift for your wife.—*Richard Griffin, Expos public-relations director, sharing his advice to the Houston Astros as they embarked on a 28-day, 26-game road trip, 1992. The Astros were unable to play home games at the Astrodome due to the 1992 Republican National Convention.*

764 Before we left Montreal, I went out and bought 25 pairs of underwear. I knew when I got down to my last pair, it would be time to go home—*Orlando Cabrera, Expos shortstop, on Montreal leaving for a 22-game, 25-day road trip, 2003.*

765 Like all players, I enjoy recognition. And I'm realistic: I know that the minute I quit playing, no one will care. I'm going to live it up while I can. A year after I have quit, I'll be forgotten.—*Al Hrabosky, Cardinals pitcher, 1975.*

766 If I had to leave the game, I'd surf all day and become a professional go-getter. My wife would go to work, and I'd go get 'er.—*Tim Flannery, Padres infielder, 1987.*

767 When I die, I want my tombstone to say, "Dodger Stadium was his address, but every ballpark was his home."—*Tommy Lasorda, Dodgers manager.*

768 I hate off days, 'cause I might get hit by a train.—*Pete Rose, Phillies first baseman.*

768 It doesn't take much to get me up for baseball. Once the national anthem plays, I get chills. I even know the words to it now.—*Pete Rose, Phillies first baseman, 1981.*

769 Too many people think an athlete's life can be an open book. You're supposed to be an example. Why do I have to be an example for your kid? You be an example for your kid.—*Bob Gibson, Cardinals pitcher, 1970.*

770 One thing about baseball—the dugout heaters only work when it's hot.—*Whitey Herzog, Cardinals manager, 1990.*

771 Baseball is a red-blooded sport for red-blooded men. It's no pink tea, and mollycoddles had better stay out.—*Ty Cobb, Tigers outfielder.*

772 Baseball is a lot like the Army; there aren't many individuals. About the only difference is that baseball players get to stay in nice hotels instead of barracks.—*Bill Lee, former pitcher.*

774 The kid doesn't chew tobacco, smoke, drink, curse or chase broads. I don't see how he can possibly make it.—*Richie Ashburn, Phillies outfielder, on a rookie.*

775 I notice guys don't want to shake hands with him. Everybody just gives him the fist.—*Dusty Baker, Cubs manager, on outfielder Moises Alou's admission that he urinates on his hands in order to make them harder, 2004.*

776 I hope he arouses the fire that's dormant in the innermost recesses of my soul. I plan to face him with the zeal of a challenger.—*Ichiro Suzuki (through an interpreter), Mariners outfielder, on facing Red Sox pitcher Diasuke Matsuzaka, April 2007.*

777 If they want me to play center field, I'll play center field. If they want me to park cars, I'll do that. At this point, I'll do whatever they want me to do, and that's my role.—*Kenny Lofton, Yankees outfielder and valet, 2003.*

778 She thought I was a drug dealer because I was young, had this big place, and didn't work during the day.—*Terry Mulholland, Indians pitcher, on his wife's first impression, 2003.*

779 I think I have already signed some scrap of paper for every man, woman and child in the United States. What do they do with all those scraps of paper with my signature on it?—*Vida Blue, Giants pitcher.*

780 When that gate shuts behind you, Randy Johnson don't have anything on a 700-pound steer.—*Herbert Perry, Devil Rays third baseman, on working during the off-season on his dairy farm, 2000.*

781 There is no way 25 men, whose livelihoods depend on records compiled on the field, can be kept happy in a game that calls for only nine players.—*Leonard Koppett, baseball historian.*

782 The bases were drunk, and I painted the black with my best yakker. But blue squeezed me, and I went full. I came back with my heater, but the stick flares one the other way and chalk flies for two bases. Three earnies! Next thing I know, skipper hooks me and I'm sipping suds with the clubby.—*Ed Lynch, Mets pitcher.*

Base Running

783 Speed is a great asset, but it's greater when it's combined with quickness—and there's a big difference.—*Ty Cobb, Hall of Fame outfielder, 1954.*

Strategy

784 Never trust a baserunner who's limping. Comes a base hit and you'll think he just got back from Lourdes.—*Joe Garagiola, broadcaster and former catcher, 1987.*

785 Base-stealing has fallen into limbo and the thrills that go with it are no more. But it'll return as surely as I'm writing these words.—*Ty Cobb, Hall of Fame outfielder, 1961.*

786 Lou Brock, along with Maury Wills, are probably the two players most responsible for the biggest change in the game over the last 15 years—the stolen base.—*Tom Seaver, Reds pitcher, 1987.*

787 It's impossible to steal more than 60 bases in one season without running foolishly.—*Maury Wills, Dodgers shortstop, 1962. Wills finished the year with a record 104 stolen bases.*

788 Frank Howard used to say that if I tried anything funny, like stealing home while he was up, he'd take my head off with his bat.—*Maury Wills, former Dodgers shortstop, on why he rarely attempted to steal home. In 1962, Wills stole 104 bases, breaking Ty Cobb's 1915 record of 96. The record stood until Lou Brock stole 118 in 1974. Rickey Henderson set the current record with 130 steals in 1982.*

789 You know you're always on the verge of disaster as a base stealer. If you're thrown out, you could be wiping out a potential rally. But you have to figure that you'll steal four out of five times. And if they catch you, well, then they owe you four.—*Lou Brock, Cardinals outfielder.*

790 If you aim to steal 30 or 40 bases a year, you do it by surprising the other side. But if your goal is 50 to 100 bases, the element of surprise doesn't matter. You go even though they know you're going to go. Then each steal becomes a contest, matching your skills against theirs.—*Lou Brock, Cardinals outfielder.*

791 When you steal a base, 99 percent of the time you steal on a pitcher. You actually never steal on a catcher.—*Hall of Fame outfielder Lou Brock.*

792 It's easier to pick off a fast runner than to pick off a lazy runner.—*Vin Scully, broadcaster.*

793 For me, stealing second is a lot easier after I've reached first.—*Enzo Hernandez, Padres shortstop, a career .224 hitter, 1973.*

794 The main quality a great third base coach must have is a fast runner.—*Rocky Bridges, Angels third base coach, 1971.*

795 Team speed, for Christ's sake, you get fuckin' goddamn little fleas on the fuckin' bases getting picked off trying to steal, getting thrown out, taking runs away from you. You get them big cocksuckers who can hit the fuckin' ball out of the fuckin' ballpark and you can't make any goddamn mistakes.—*Earl Weaver, Orioles manager, in response to a question from a fan on a Baltimore radio show as to why the Orioles did not get more team speed.*

On the Basepaths

796 The next time you hit another triple, please stop at second base.—*Connie Mack, Philadelphia A's manager, to second baseman Max Bishop, who was thrown out trying to stretch a double into a triple.*

797 It won't do any good, Casey. He missed second base, too.—*Cookie Lavagetto, Mets first base coach, to manager Casey Stengel, who was about to argue a call in which first baseman Marv Throneberry was called out on an apparent triple for failing to touch first base, June 17, 1962. Stengel added,* "I know damn well he didn't miss third because he's standing on it."

798 How could he be expected to remember where the bases were? He gets on so infrequently.—*Jack Lang, sportswriter, on Mets first baseman "Marvelous" Marv Throneberry, after he was called out on a triple for failing to touch first base, 1962.*

799 I couldn't resist. I never had a better jump on the pitcher.—*Lou Novikoff, Cubs outfielder, on why he tried to steal third base with two outs and the bases loaded.*

800 I had a lot of visitors, but no one went home. It was like a Monopoly game: No one would advance directly to Go. They were all stuck on some utility.—*Rich Donnelly, Pirates third base coach, on stranding 17 runners in a 6–4 loss to Philadelphia, 1994.*

801 We set the table, but no one ate.—*Johnny Oates, Rangers manager, on stranding 14 base runners in one game, 1996.*

802 Coaching third with a pitcher on base is like being a member of a bomb disposal squad. The thing can blow up in your face any moment.—*Rocky Bridges, Giants third base coach, 1985.*

803 I've never been to third, what do I do now?—*Pascual Perez, Expos pitcher, to third base coach Jackie Moore, 1988.*

804 Gomez, you must be crazy. It took you 13 years to get to third and now you want to ruin it.—*Art Fletcher, Yankees third base coach, in response to pitcher Lefty Gomez's request to steal home.*

805 Randy looked like Lurch rounding second and making third.—*Lou Piniella, Mariners manager, on 6'10" pitcher Randy Johnson, who reached base twice and scored a run in an interleague game, 1998.*

806 I hate being touched by other people. I'd

rather run away from them.—*Ichiro Suzuki, Mariners outfielder, on running out of the baseline to avoid a tag, September 2007.*

807 He got on first once this year and asked me whether to steal on the second pitch. The only trouble was there was already someone on second.—*Irv Noren, Oakland A's first base coach, on designated runner Herb Washington, 1974. Washington became the only man in baseball history to steal more than 30 bases and score over 30 runs without ever registering a plate appearance.*

808 He can hit, he can throw and he can run. He just needs to learn when.—*Don Zimmer, Cubs manager, on rookie outfielder Jerome Walton who was thrown out three times in one game, 1989.*

809 Hitting the ball was easy. Running around the bases was the tough part.—*Mickey Mantle, Hall of Fame outfielder.*

810 I can run. The hard part is stopping this body.—*Kent Hrbek, hefty Twins first baseman.*

Speedsters

811 When he runs, it's all downhill.—*Vin Scully, Dodgers announcer, on fleet-footed Dodgers outfielder Maury Wills.*

812 He was very bowlegged, and when he sped from first base to second on one of his 720 stolen bases, he looked like a hoop rolling down the baselines.—*Fred Lieb, sportswriter, on Hall of Fame shortstop Honus Wagner.*

813 I set a record in the Florida State League for stealing 74 bases in one season. Since I only got on base 18 times, I had to go like hell.—*Ellis Clary, Twins scout, 1985.*

814 I played some baseball in high school, so the game was not a total mystery to me. But I practiced for five days before I realized that I wasn't going to be asked to hit.—*Herb Washington, Oakland A's designated runner, 1975.*

815 He can run anytime he wants. I'm giving him the red light.—*Yogi Berra, Yankees manager, on outfielder Rickey Henderson, 1985.*

816 I don't have to steal bases. I steal bases because I want to.—*Lou Brock, Cardinals outfielder.*

817 It's like trying to keep water from going over the dam. You know what's coming, but you're powerless.—*Harry Parker, Mets pitcher, on what to do with speedy Lou Brock on base, 1974.*

818 I'm not a great runner, I'm no Joe Morgan, but I'm not bad for a white guy.—*Pete Rose, Reds third baseman.*

819 He's like a little kid in a train station. You turn your back on him and he's gone.—*Doc Medich, Brewers pitcher, on Oakland A's outfielder Rickey Henderson setting a record with his 119th stolen base of the season, 1982.*

820 I just figured out how to deal with Rickey at first base. Wind up real slow, then hope there's a close play at third.—*Steve McCatty, Oakland A's pitcher, on Yankees outfielder Rickey Henderson, 1983.*

821 When I was in those fastest-man competitions, those wide receivers would always chase me down, but I always had them over the first eight, 10 yards. I'll beat Carl Lewis over 10 yards.—*Rickey Henderson, all-time stolen base leader, 2001.*

822 No, he just got there in time.—*Yogi Berra, Yankees catcher, when asked if Joe DiMaggio was a fast runner.*

823 He is quick on the bases, but this is an attribute that is about as essential for catchers as neat handwriting.—*Roger Angel, sportswriter, on Mets catcher Choo Choo Coleman.*

824 Six bags. That's a season for me.—*Tim Wallach, Expos third baseman, on Atlanta outfielder Otis Nixon swiping six bases in one game, June 16, 1991. The record was tied by Eric Young in 1996 and Carl Crawford in 2009. Wallach stole 51 bases in his 17 big league seasons while Nixon swiped 620 in his career.*

Not So Fast

825 He's only seventeen and he runs like he's thirty.—*Casey Stengel, Mets manager, on rookie* *first baseman Ed Kranepool, 1962. In 18 seasons, Kranepool stole just 15 bases.*

826 He looks like a greyhound, but he runs like a bus.—*George Brett, Royals third baseman, on catcher Jamie Quirk.*

827 How can anyone who runs as slow as you pull a muscle?—*Pete Rose, Reds outfielder, to injured first baseman Tony Perez, 1974.*

828 I put weights on so when I run sprints I can see what it feels like to be Mike Scioscia.—*Mickey Hatcher, Dodgers utility player, on the slow-footed catcher, 1988.*

829 If he raced his pregnant wife, he'd finish third.—*Tommy Lasorda, Dodgers manager, on catcher Mike Scioscia, 1988.*

830 He had larceny in his heart, but his feet were honest.—*Bugs Baer, sportswriter, on a stolen base attempt by Yankees outfielder Ping Bodie.*

831 He is easily the slowest ballplayer since Ernie Lombardi was thrown out at first base trying to stretch a double into a single.—*Stanley Frank, sportswriter, on Indians shortstop Lou Boudreau.*

832 He couldn't outrace a snail, even with a head start.—*Arthur Daley, sportswriter, on New York Giants catcher Ernie Lombardi, who stole eight bases in 17 seasons.*

833 You have the sign to steal when you look in the dugout, and I jump up in the air and don't come down.—*Jim Leyland, Pirates manager, to catcher Junior Ortiz, 1989 Ortiz stole eight bases in 13 seasons.*

834 I run as hard as anyone, but not as fast.—*Boog Powell, Orioles first baseman, 1969.*

835 The wind always seems to be blowing against catchers when they are running.—*Joe Garagiola, broadcaster and former catcher.*

836 My reaction time is not good, and my running ability is not good. Sometimes they pick on my weaknesses.—*John Burkett, Giants pitcher, on getting thrown out at first base by Expos right fielder Larry Walker on an apparent single to right field, 1994.*

837 I have dreams where monsters are trying to catch me. I don't get away with my feet. I get away because I wake up.—*John Burkett, slow-footed Marlins pitcher, 1995.*

838 They told me to hit. Nobody said anything about running.—*Jimmy Key, Blue Jays pitcher, on batting in a spring training game and getting thrown out at first by an outfielder, 1992.*

839 To be honest, I don't know what the hit-and-run sign is, and I sure wouldn't be looking for it with Ashby running.—*Nolan Ryan, Astros pitcher, on missing a hit-and-run sign that led to catcher Alan Ashby stealing his first base in four years, 1986.*

840 I thought they'd stop the game and give me second base.—*Milt May, Astros catcher, on stealing his first base after five years in the majors, 1975. On May 4, 1975, May drove in Bob Watson for baseball's one-millionth run.*

841 I ran out there at full speed, but by the time I got there the fight was over.—*Charlie Hough, 46-year-old Marlins pitcher, on his involvement in a bench-clearing brawl against San Francisco, 1994.*

842 You can't be afraid to fail. I haven't been—because my whole career has been based on failure.—*Jeff Manto, Tigers third baseman, on stealing his first base in seven years, 1998.*

843 I'm trying to run the bases and score runs and don't want to feel like I've got a parachute on. I'm slow enough as it is.—*Kevin Brown, Padres pitcher, on refusing to wear a warm-up jacket on a cold night, 1998.*

844 Fielder's got one gear, easily mistaken for a home-run trot.—*Garth Woolsey, sportswriter, on first baseman/DH Cecil Fielder, who failed to make the Blue Jays in spring training, 1999.*

845 It replaced the Kentucky Derby as the most exciting two minutes in sport.—*Dave Baker, radio announcer, on the first career triple by Braves pitcher Greg Maddux, 1999.*

846 For me to get a triple, an outfielder would have to fall down, break an ankle or pull a muscle.—*Darrin Fletcher, Expos catcher, on needing a triple to hit for the cycle, 1996.*

847 Usually someone has to go on the DL for me to even get a triple.—*Robin Ventura, Dodgers first baseman, 2003. Ventura hit 14 triples in his 16-year career.*

848 I came around second and thought, "Oh no, I have to go to third." I was struggling and thought I would have a heart attack, but it would be a good heart attack.—*Eli Marrero, Cardinals catcher, on hitting a triple in the first game of the 1998 season.*

849 Two outfielders would have to fall down, and when they throw the ball in, the guy catching it has to lose it in the sun, and then I would need a generous call from the official scorer.—*Tony Clark, Tigers first baseman, on what it would take to hit an inside-the-park home run, 2001. Clark had just hit his first triple since 1997.*

850 For that to happen, I'd need both outfielders to collide and get carted off. And when the stretcher comes out, I figured I'd just be rounding third. And it would still be bang-bang.—*Mike Lowell, Marlins third baseman, on what it would take to hit an inside-the-park home run, 2003. Lowell had just hit his fist career triple after 2,041 at-bats without one.*

851 Now that I'm aware of it, I'm going for it. I'm just going to run until my hamstrings pop. I won't be sucking wind too bad, but they might have to get the stretcher out.—*Chili Davis, Yankees DH, on going almost 2,000 at-bats without a triple, June 1999. Davis did finally get that elusive triple before he retired at the end of the season.*

852 I don't ever remember stealing home before. Maybe in a previous life.—*Todd Helton, Rockies first baseman, on swiping home as part of a double steal, May 1998.*

853 I have only one speed, and it has never changed. That speed is very slow.—*Brooks Robinson, Orioles third baseman, 1973.*

854 Sometimes it seems like he's playing underwater.—*Vin Scully, Dodgers announcer, on slow-footed outfielder Bobby Bonilla, 1998.*

855 It was like Halley's Comet. You miss that, you won't see another for 75 years.—*Lenny Webster, Expos catcher, on his second career stolen base, July 9, 2000.*

856 I'm the first leadoff hitter in the history of baseball who has the stop sign.—*Matt Williams, Diamondbacks third baseman, on batting leadoff during a rehab stint with the El Paso Diablos, 2000. Williams was batting leadoff to get more swings.*

857 I can still hit, catch and throw. The running part of the game could be a problem.—*Gary Gaetti, 41-year-old third baseman, on the prospects of making the Red Sox as a free agent, 2000. Gaetti was unsuccessful in his quest for a 20th season and later became a hitting instructor.*

858 More like a blinking yellow.—*Ryan Howard, burly Phillies first baseman, on whether or not he would have the green light after stealing the first base of his career, 2007.*

859 I've never been to second base.—*Don Carman, Phillies pitcher, on why he got picked off second base following just his second career base hit, 1987. Carman began his career 0 for 48.*

860 If Frank [Thomas] gets a base hit, it takes five hits to score him.—*Ozzie Guillen, White Sox manager, on the Oakland A's DH, September 2006.*

861 The only way you can do that is by breaking into the equipment room.—*Pete Rose, Phillies first baseman, to teammate Greg Luzinski who claimed he could steal 20 bases, 1980. Bull never stole more than eight bases in one season.*

862 I used to shave before games. And once Reitz was up at the plate, and he hit the ball, and by the time he got to first base I had to shave again.—*Manager Whitey Herzog on Cardinals third baseman Ken Reitz, 1980.*

863 I won two blue ribbons at a Kiwanis track meet as a fifth-grader. I won the 50 and the 100, and I did it in street shoes. That just shows how slow our whole town was.—*Gary Varsho, Pirates outfielder, 1991. Varsho stole a career-high nine bases that season.*

Sliding

864 I couldn't. I carry my cigars in my back pocket, and I was afraid I'd break them.—

Jimmy Dykes, Philadelphia A's infielder, on why he didn't attempt to slide on a close play.

865 That wasn't a slide. I just couldn't stand up anymore.—*Gary Varsho, Pirates outfielder, on the completion of a not-so-graceful inside-the-park home run, 1992.*

866 The only rule I got is if you slide, get up.—*Bill Lee, Winter Haven Super Sox player-manager of the Senior League, 1989.*

867 I think it's smarter to slide head first. I'd rather have an arm spiked than an ankle—plus you get your picture in the paper.—*Pete Rose, Reds third baseman, 1976.*

868 For me, going into a base was like driving 20 mph and jumping out of the car.—*Willie Wilson, former stolen base leader, 2009.*

Conditioning

869 To run a marathon? Probably not. To play baseball? The bases aren't that far apart.—*John Kruk, Phillies first baseman, when asked if he was in shape, 1993.*

870 A baseball player's idea of a successful triathlon is being able to run to third base without paramedics.—*Alan Greenberg, sportswriter, 1993.*

871 Soccer players run virtually nonstop for 90 minutes despite searing temperatures that sometimes reach 120 degrees. Baseball players beat out an infield grounder and complain that there's no beer in the clubhouse.—*Mike Penner, sportswriter, 1994.*

872 I've never seen an athlete get to first base hyperventilating. Even a poker player should be able to run 90 feet without hyperventilating. I thought I was going to have to revive him. I told him, "I know CPR, but I'm not going to perform it on you."—*Andy Van Slyke, Tigers first base coach, on pitcher Jeremy Bonderman being winded after beating out an infield single for his first major league hit, 2007.*

Baseball Fans of Note

873 I watch a lot of baseball on radio.—*Gerald R. Ford, former President of the United States, 1978.*

874 I've had a lifelong ambition to be a professional baseball player, but nobody would sign me.—*Gerald R. Ford, 38th President of the United States.*

875 Bennet Cerf, my deceased publisher, always sensed that there was something about him I didn't like, something that kept us from being good friends. He finally asked me what it was, and I told him I could never be comfortable with anyone who was a Yankee fan, which he was. I told him I thought there was something fundamentally sick about being affiliated with the Yankees.—*James Michener, writer.*

876 Anyone who is a lifetime Philadelphia Phillies fan acquires a sense of tragedy.—*James Michener, Pulitzer Prize-winning author and Phillies fan, 1996.*

877 Baseball is the greatest of American games.... A day seldom passes when I do not read the sporting pages of the newspapers. In this way I keep a close tab on the two major leagues, and there was one time when I could name the players of every club in both leagues.—*Thomas Edison, inventor, 1927.*

878 When we played softball, I'd steal second, then feel guilty and go back.—*Woody Allen, stand-up comic and filmmaker. Concerning his baseball prowess, Allen said he once got upset and tried to throw his glove on the ground—and missed.*

879 I love baseball. You know it doesn't have to mean anything, it's just very beautiful to watch.—*Woody Allen, writer/actor/director, from* Zelig, *1983.*

880 The only man I idolize more than myself is Henry Aaron.—*Muhammad Ali, former heavyweight boxing champion.*

881 Joe DiMaggio was the best I ever saw. He made it look so effortless. If Joe played in Fenway Park in Boston, he would have hit 1,000 homers.—*Secretary of State Henry Kissinger, 1975.*

882 I like the fact that it's a non-polluting industry with no tall buildings.—*Jimmy Buffett, singer-songwriter, on becoming a minority owner of the Fort Meyers Miracle, 1989.*

883 The Twins are my favorite team for obvious reasons.—*Morganna Roberts, baseball's "Kissing Bandit," whose measurements were listed as 60–23–39.*

884 The best show on television is Red Sox baseball. Everything else sucks.—*Stephen King, writer and Red Sox fan, 1982. Following the 2004 season, King published* Faithful: Two Diehard Boston Red Sox Fans Chronicle the Historic 2004 Season.

885 I hold no public office. I can't even get you Red Sox tickets. Of course, you wouldn't want them.—*Paul Tsongas, Democratic presidential candidate and former Massachusetts Congressman, 1992.*

886 Last year, more Americans went to symphonies than went to baseball games. This may be viewed as an alarming statistic, but I think that both baseball and the country will endure.—*President John F. Kennedy at a White House concert by the National High School Symphony Orchestra, August 6, 1962.*

887 Joe DiMaggio's 56-game hitting streak is still the greatest streak of all time in sports, and no matter how many points I score, I will never match that feat.—*Wayne Gretzky, Edmonton Oilers center, 1984.*

888 The only thing on television that isn't going to give you a headache is baseball.—*Emmylou Harris, country music singer, 1993.*

889 She was smart, beautiful, independent and could explain the infield fly rule. What else could a guy want?—*Charlie Pride, country music singer and former Birmingham Black Barons pitcher, on his wife Rozene, 1994.*

890 Baseball without fans is like Jayne Mansfield without a sweater.... That can be taken two ways, can't it?—*Vice President Richard M. Nixon at a New York Baseball Writers' dinner, 1958.*

891 This isn't a guy that shows up at season openers to take bows and get his picture in the paper and has to have his secretary of state tell him where first base is. This man knows baseball.—*Dick Young, sportswriter, on President Richard Nixon.*

892 The Senators were never very good, but not much has changed in Washington. The senators they have there still aren't very good.—*Richard M. Nixon, 37th President of the United States, 1992.*

893 I helped put Dwight in the majors, and he helped put me in football.—*Jay Schroeder, Washington Redskins quarterback, on a minor league encounter with future Mets pitcher Dwight Gooden, 1985. Before opting for the NFL, Schroeder spent four years as a catcher/outfielder in the Toronto minor league system.*

894 I was an outstanding ballplayer, but I pulled a hamstring when I was four, and it took me 31 years to recover.—*Danny Kaye, entertainer and co-owner of the Mariners from 1977 to 1981.*

895 I play baseball in Malibu. Once I hit the ball all the way to the backyard of my neighbor, Neil Diamond.—*Pia Zadora, entertainer and minority owner of the Portland Beavers of the Pacific Coast League, 1986.*

896 They say you never forget your first love. Well, as a little kid, I hated broccoli, but I loved baseball.—*George Bush, 41st President of the United States, 1993.*

897 All I ever wanted to be president of was the American League.—*A. Bartlett Giamatti, on being named President of Yale University, 1977. Giamatti became National League President in 1986 and commissioner in 1989.*

898 A lot of players bring tapes and CDs to

the park. Deion brings the actual artist.—*Jim Bowden, Reds GM, on outfielder Deion Sanders bringing rap music star Hammer to a game, 1994. By 1996, Hammer was bankrupt and owed his good friend Deion a reported $500,000.*

899 I don't look like John Kruk. He looks like me. I was here first.—*Meat Loaf, rock musician, on the loaf-like Phillies first baseman, 1994. Meat Loaf's classic 1977 song "Paradise by the Dashboard Light" featured Yankees broadcaster Phil Rizzuto doing play-by-play.*

900 If it weren't for baseball, many kids wouldn't know what a millionaire looked like.—*Phyllis Diller, comic.*

901 He pitched all that time with that team behind him? Well, he sure deserves more than a raise. He ought to bargain for a piece of the ballpark.—*Jimmy Hoffa, Teamsters President, on Mets pitcher Roger Craig throwing 223 innings and losing 18 straight games, 1963. Craig finished the season with a 5–22 record.*

902 The decline of Western civilization started when the Dodgers and Giants moved. —*Frank Layden, Utah Jazz basketball coach and Brooklyn native, 1985.*

903 I burst into tears. The Yankees. I would never do that, if I was a Dodger. It's morally reprehensible.—*Actress Winona Ryder on her favorite player, second baseman Steve Sax, signing with the Yankees after eight seasons in Los Angeles, 1989.*

904 You get so nervous when you're on the mound. You have to calm yourself down. Now I know why pitchers talk to themselves out there.—*Joan Jett, rock musician and Baltimore fan, on pitching in an Orioles fantasy camp game, 1991.*

905 It was weird. I had to stand with my back to the crowd because the flag was in center field. My butt was facing the players. I thought to myself, "I should have jogged more."—*Comedian Elayne Boosler on singing the national anthem at a Mariners game, 1992.*

906 We're the only stadium act that's not on strike.—*Mick Jagger, lead singer of the Rolling Stones, on touring the U.S. during the 1994 baseball strike.*

907 In Freehold [N.J.], all my buddies were Yankee fans. We listened to them on the radio—when we weren't listening to Elvis and the Beatles.—*Bruce Springsteen, rock musician, 1998.*

908 He has power potential from both sides —and he can sing the anthem. But I don't think we can afford the $30 million a week he makes. —*Ed Wade, Phillies GM, on country music star Garth Brooks taking batting practice with the team and homering from both sides of the plate, 1998. Brooks played in spring training with the Padres in 1999 and the Mets in 2000.*

909 When he comes to the plate, he ought to wear a protective cup over his vocal cords.—*Lou Piniella, Mariners manager, on his hitting advice to country music star and Padres spring training utility player Garth Brooks, 1999.*

910 He starts into the hitting area slow, then slows it down more.—*Merv Rettenmund, Braves hitting coach, evaluating the swing of country music star Garth Brooks during spring training, 2000.*

911 I'm just a singer, not some magical baseball genie who can make or break someone's game.—*Singer Mariah Carey on her seemingly positive influence on the performance of boyfriend and Yankees shortstop Derek Jeter, 1998.*

912 He's a hunk, and I don't even like that word. Women like guys who have a big presence but sort of play it down. It's very appealing.—*Kim Basinger, actress, on Yankees shortstop Derek Jeter, 1999.*

913 He has the heart of a poet trapped inside an insanely gorgeous body.—*Madonna, entertainer, on Yankees third baseman—and alleged lover—Alex Rodriguez, 2008.*

914 I'm moon-eyed goofy for Brad Ausmus. So, I'm ready for my pathetic, girlie, dweebie, wimp, horrible pitch, and I looked up and there he was, and I just wanted to drop the ball and jump on him.—*Diane Sawyer, host of* Good Morning America, *on her encounter with the Astros catcher before throwing out the ceremonial first pitch, April 30, 2002.*

915 One way to liven up a boring game would

be to have the players dress like their mascots. Then you could have the Pirates chasing Indians around the bases. It would make it a little more like Vegas.—*Susan Sarandon, actress and star of* Bull Durham, *1998.*

916 You cannot root for any team that plays on plastic grass or under a roof. The biorhythms get jammed amidst all those petroleum byproducts. Domed stadia are a symbol of the violation of the ozone layer.—*Susan Sarandon, actress, 1998.*

917 I do not want to hear about saving trees. Any tree in America would gladly give its life for the glory of a day at home plate.—*Rep. Richard H. Durbin (D-Ill.), July 26, 1989.*

918 I am not disputing that she's a Yankee fan, but I have been to Yankee Stadium maybe a thousand times in my life, and I've yet to see Hillary Clinton there.—*Rudy Giuliani, New York City mayor, on the First Lady's claim that she was a New York fan despite previously professing her allegiance to the Chicago Cubs, 1999.*

919 He should have bought tickets when I was pitching.—*Chuck Finley, Angels pitcher, on actor Charlie Sheen buying out all the tickets in left field of Anaheim Stadium in hopes of catching a home run ball, 1996. Sheen came up empty despite having the entire section to himself.*

920 Hey, Appier, pitch faster! By the time you get done, my clothes will be out of style!—*Chi Chi Rodriguez, pro golf legend, to Royals pitcher Kevin Appier, 1996.*

921 There have only been two geniuses in the world—Willie Mays and Willie Shakespeare. But, dahling, I think you'd better put Shakespeare first.—*Tallulah Bankhead, actress, 1962.*

922 They will have to wait a few minutes till I get my turn at bat.—*Abraham Lincoln on being informed of his nomination as president.*

923 I see by the Journal you are playing baseball and that you play well. I am pleased with this. I like to have my boys enjoy and practice all athletic sports and games.... But I am a little afraid ... that overexertion and excitement in playing baseball will injure your hearing.... If you find there is any injury you ought to resolve to play only for a limited time—say an hour or an hour and a half on the same day.—*Rutherford B. Hayes, 19th President of the United States, in a letter to his son, June 3, 1870.*

924 Father and all of us regarded baseball as a mollycoddle game. Tennis, football, lacrosse, boxing, polo, yes: they are violent which appealed to us. But baseball? Father wouldn't watch it, not even at Harvard.—*Alice Roosevelt Longworth, daughter of President Theodore Roosevelt, 1961.*

925 I never saw a game without taking sides and never want to see one. There is the soul of the game.—*Warren G. Harding, 29th President of the United States.*

926 I honestly feel that it would be best for the country to keep baseball going. There will be fewer people unemployed and everybody will work longer hours and harder than ever before, and that means they ought to have a chance for recreation and for taking their minds off their work even more than before.—*President Franklin D. Roosevelt in a letter to baseball commissioner Kenesaw Mountain Landis, 1941. The decision cleared the way for baseball to continue play during World War II.*

927 May the sun never set on American baseball.—*President Harry S Truman on the 75th anniversary of baseball, February 2, 1951.*

928 When I was a boy growing up in Kansas, a friend of mine and I went fishing, and as we sat there in the warmth of a summer afternoon on a river bank we talked about what we wanted to be when we grew up. I told him I wanted to be a real major league baseball player, a genuine professional like Honus Wagner. My friend said he wanted to be President of the United States. Neither of us got our wish.—*Dwight D. Eisenhower, 34th President of the United States.*

929 Not making the baseball team at West Point was one of the greatest disappointments of my life, maybe the greatest.—*Dwight D. Eisenhower, 34th President of the United States.*

930 Every member of our baseball team at

West Point became a general: this proves the value of team sports.—*General Omar Bradley.*

931 It is wonderful to be here, to be able to hear the baseball against the bat, ball against glove, the call of the vendor, and be able to boo the umpire.—*General Douglas MacArthur on his return to the United States after World War II, 1946.*

932 I take a national view of the American League and an American view of the National League.—*Vice President Hubert H. Humphrey on which league he preferred, 1967.*

933 I do all I can for them. I even pray for them each night. I hope the Supreme Court doesn't declare that unconstitutional.—*Vice President Lyndon B. Johnson on the Washington Senators.*

934 Hotter 'n hell, ain't it, Prez?—*Babe Ruth, Yankees outfielder, to President Calvin Coolidge.*

935 A baseball game is twice as much fun if you're seeing it on the company's time.—*William C. Feather, publisher.*

936 That's baseball, and it's my game. Y'know, you take your worries to the game, and you leave 'em there. You yell like crazy for your guys. It's good for your lungs, gives you a lift, and nobody calls the cops. Pretty girls, lots of 'em.—*Humphrey Bogart, actor.*

937 If it's properly done (not aimed at anyone or anyone's shoes) it's part of the charm. It's a terribly baseballly thing to do.—*Judith Martin, aka Miss Manners, on the fine art of spitting, October 1993.*

938 I don't know the rules of baseball. I know if you hit it far, you got to go run. Then another one catches.—*Svetlana Kuznetsova, tennis player, 2007.*

939 It's only been in the last two years that I stopped calling the bullpen "the pigpen."—*Azra Shafi-Scagliarini, psychic consultant for A's first baseman Jason Giambi, 2000.*

940 Baseball is the only major sport that appears backwards in a mirror.—*George Carlin, comedian, 1997.*

941 He never complained about his team's bad luck or bad talent, never stopped playing the game with joy, never stopped giving his all, never lost his proud demeanor, and never acted like anything but a winner. He was a symbol of the Cub fan's undiminishing resilience. If he could be happy to come to the park each afternoon, then so could we.—*Actor Joe Mantegna on Hall of Famer Ernie Banks, 2002. Mantegna also wrote the play* Bleacher Bums (1977).

942 I felt like my bubble-gum card collection had come to life.—*Actor James Garner on speaking at a sports dinner.*

943 One thing I do well is hit fly balls. There's nothing quite like being able to hit towering flies. It's not like writing Beethoven's Ninth, but it's definitely in the top two.—*Charles M. Schulz, cartoonist, 1985.*

944 Big news for New York last night—the Yankees are going to the World Series. They're playing the Phillies, from Philadelphia. Of course, I hate the Yankees and the Phillies. I'm a Mets fan. So for me, last night was like coming home and catching your wife *&#ing the Yankees and the Phillies.—*Jon Stewart, talk show host, October 26, 2009.*

Baseball 101: The Fundamentals

945 Now there's three things you can do in a baseball game: you can win or you can lose or it can rain.—*Casey Stengel, Hall of Fame manager.*

946 Baseball is simple but never easy.—*Roger Angell, sportswriter.*

947 Baseball is a game of inches.—*Branch Rickey, Hall of Fame executive.*

948 Whoever wants to know the heart and mind of America had better learn baseball, the rules and realities of the game.—*Jacques*

Barzun, Columbia University philosophy professor.

949 Baseball is the only field of endeavor where a man can succeed three times out of ten and be considered a good performer.—*Ted Williams, Red Sox outfielder.*

950 Close don't count in baseball. Close only counts in horseshoes and hand grenades.—*Frank Robinson, Hall of Fame outfielder.*

951 There are five things you can do in baseball—run, throw, catch, hit and hit with power.-—*Leo Durocher, Brooklyn Dodgers manager.*

952 There's sunshine, fresh air and the team's behind us. So, let's play two.—*Ernie Banks, former Cubs infielder, at his Hall of Fame induction, 1977.*

953 Baseball gives you every chance to be great. Then it puts every pressure on you to prove that you haven't got what it takes. It never takes away that chance, and it never eases up on the pressure.—*Joe Garagiola, broadcaster and former Major League catcher.*

954 Nearly every boy builds a shrine to some baseball hero, and before that shrine a candle always burns.—*Kenesaw Mountain Landis, baseball commissioner.*

955 You got to get 27 outs to win.—*Casey Stengel, Yankees manager.*

956 If you don't get on first, you can't score a run.—*Enos Slaughter, Cardinals outfielder.*

957 They still can't steal first base.—*Phil Rizzuto, broadcaster and former Yankees shortstop.*

958 Luck is the residue of design.—*Branch Rickey, Hall of Fame executive.*

959 Luck is the residue of luck.—*Scott Ostler, sportswriter.*

960 Luck is the by-product of busting your fanny.—*Don Sutton, Dodgers pitcher.*

961 I'd rather be lucky than good.—*Lefty Gomez, Yankees pitcher.*

962 Most one-run games are lost, not won. —*Gene Mauch, Phillies manager.*

963 You gotta believe!—*Tug McGraw, Mets reliever, 1973.*

964 Who's on first, What's on second, I Don't Know's on third.—*Bud Abbott to Lou Costello, as part of their classic vaudeville routine, 1939.*

965 You gotta be a man to play baseball for a living, but you gotta have a lot of little boy in you, too.—*Roy Campanella, Brooklyn Dodgers catcher.*

966 It's not the boy in the fight ... but the fight in the boy.—*Happy Chandler, baseball commissioner.*

967 A good professional athlete must have the love of a little boy. And the good players feel the kind of love for the game that they did when they were Little Leaguers.—*Tom Seaver, Mets pitcher.*

968 Baseball is a fun game. It beats working for a living.—*Phil Linz, Yankees infielder.*

969 When they start the game, they don't yell, "Work Ball." They say, "Play Ball."—*Willie Stargell, Pirates first baseman, 1981.*

970 If you're not having fun in baseball, you miss the point of everything.—*Chris Chambliss, Yankees first baseman.*

971 Baseball has got to be fun, because if it is not fun, it's a long time to be in agony.—*Tom Trebelhorn, Brewers manager, 1989.*

972 Spring is a time of year when the ground thaws, trees bud, the income tax falls due—and everybody wins the pennant.—*Jim Murray, sportswriter.*

973 Sometimes you take baseball so seriously you miss out on the fun of the game.—*Rick Dempsey, Orioles catcher, 1977.*

974 You always get a special kick on opening day, no matter how many you go through. You look forward to it like a birthday party when you're a kid. You think something wonderful is going to happen.—*Joe DiMaggio, Yankees outfielder.*

975 A baseball game is simply a nervous breakdown divided into nine innings.—*Earl Wilson, writer.*

976 The great thing about baseball is that there's a crisis every day.—*Gabe Paul, Indians president.*

977 In baseball, it's not what you did for me yesterday that counts. It's what you're doing for me today.—*Ernie Banks, Cubs shortstop, 1961.*

978 The beauty and joy of baseball is not having to explain it.—*Chuck Shriver, Cubs publicist, 1974.*

979 You can't tell the players without a scorecard.—*Harry M. Stevens, concessionaire.*

980 It may be that baseball is, under close analysis, pointless. What seems apparent to me is that close analysis is pointless. The game is there. It is the best game there is. That's all I need to know.—*Art Hill, sportswriter.*

981 Baseball was made for kids, and grownups only screw it up.—*Bob Lemon, Hall of Fame pitcher.*

982 Like driving, the name of the game is to get home safe.—*Tommy Lasorda, Dodgers coach, 1976.*

983 Baseball gives every American boy a chance to excel. Not just to be as good as someone else, but to be better. This is the nature of man and the name of the game.—*Ted Williams, Hall of Fame outfielder.*

984 Give a boy a bat and a ball and a place to play and you'll have a good citizen.—*Joe McCarthy, Yankees manager.*

985 If you rush in and out of the clubhouse, you rush in and out of baseball.—*Pee Wee Reese, Hall of Fame shortstop.*

986 Baseball is a game where a curve is an optical illusion, a screwball can be a pitch or a person, stealing is legal and you can spit anywhere you like except in the umpire's eye or on the ball.—*Jim Murray, sportswriter.*

987 Thou shalt not steal. I mean defensively. On offense, indeed thou shall steal and thou must.—*Branch Rickey, Brooklyn Dodgers GM.*

988 Prefer the errors of enthusiasm to the complacency of wisdom.—*Branch Rickey, Hall of Fame executive.*

989 Baseball is a peculiar profession, possibly the only one which capitalized a boyhood pleasure, unfits the athlete for any other career, keeps him young in mind and spirit, and then rejects him as too old before he has yet attained the prime of life.—*Gerald Beaumont, writer.*

990 Baseball and malaria keep coming back. —*Gene Mauch, Angels manager.*

991 Baseball can survive anything.—*Bill Terry, New York Giants manager.*

992 Baseball is a lot like life. The line drives are caught, the squibbers go for base hits. It's an unfair game.—*Rod Kanehl, Mets utility player. On July 9, 1962, Hot Rod hit the first grand slam in the history of the Mets.*

993 The only real happiness a ballplayer has is when he is playing a ball game and accomplishes something he didn't think he could do.—*Ring Lardner, sportswriter.*

994 It's tomorrow that counts. So you worry all the time. It never ends. Lord, baseball is a worrying thing.—*Stan Coveleski, Indians pitcher. The spitball legend won 215 career games and was elected to the Hall of Fame in 1969.*

995 You know why it's the most unique game in the world? Because it ameliorates the classic polarization between self-motivated individuals and collective ideology.—*Ernie Banks, Cubs shortstop, on baseball.*

996 The only thing that's certain is that they'll play the national anthem before every game.—*Rick Monday, Dodgers outfielder, 1984.*

997 I don't care how long you've been around, you'll never see it all.—*Bob Lemon, White Sox manager, 1977.*

998 Say this much for big league baseball—it is beyond question the greatest conversation piece ever invented in America.—*Bruce Catton, historian.*

999 This ain't a football game. We do this every day.—*Earl Weaver, Orioles manager.*

1000 In baseball, you don't know nothing.—*Yogi Berra, Hall of Fame catcher.*

1001 In baseball you're supposed to sit on your ass, spit tobacco and nod at stupid things.—*Bill Lee, Red Sox pitcher.*

1002 A ballplayer's got to be kept hungry to become a big leaguer. That's why no boy from a rich family ever made it to the big leagues.—*Joe DiMaggio, Hall of Fame outfielder.*

1003 Because there is always some kid who may be seeing me for the first or last time. I owe him my best.—*Joe DiMaggio, Yankees outfielder, on why he played so hard every game.*

1004 General Doubleday is the Santa Claus of baseball. He actually existed, a West Point graduate and career soldier who won two brevets for bravery during the Civil War and wound up as a major general of volunteers; but his actual connection with the game of baseball is somewhat like Santa Claus' connection with Christmas, indecipherable but unbreakable.—*Bruce Catton, historian.*

1005 The only thing Abner Doubleday ever started was the Civil War.—*Branch Rickey, baseball executive, dismissing the theory that Doubleday invented baseball. As a Union officer in the Civil War, Doubleday fired the first shot in defense of Fort Sumter on April 12, 1861.*

1006 Ain't no man can avoid being average, but there ain't no man got to be common.—*Satchel Paige, Hall of Fame pitcher.*

1007 Ability gets you to the majors, mentality keeps you there.—*Willie Stargell, Pirates first baseman.*

1008 Making the majors is not as hard as staying there, staying interested day after day. It's like being married. The hardest part is to stay married.—*Henry Aaron, Braves outfielder, 1974.*

1009 Work like you don't need the money. Love like you've never been hurt. Dance like nobody's watching.—*Satchel Paige, Hall of Fame pitcher.*

1010 Correct thinkers think that "baseball trivia" is an oxymoron: nothing about baseball is trivial.—*George Will, columnist, 1990.*

1011 With those who don't give a damn about baseball, I can only sympathize. I do not resent them. I am even willing to concede that many of them are physically clean, good to their mothers and in favor of world peace. But while the game is on, I can't think of anything to say to them.—*Art Hill, sportswriter.*

1012 The game has a cleanness. If you do a good job, the numbers say so. You don't have to ask anyone or play politics. You don't have to wait for the reviews.—*Sandy Koufax, Hall of Fame pitcher.*

1013 Baseball is a game, yes. It is also a business. But what it most truly is, is disguised combat. For all its gentility, its almost leisurely pace, baseball is violence under wraps.—*Willie Mays, Hall of Fame outfielder.*

1014 No game in the world is as tidy and dramatically neat as baseball, with cause and effect, crime and punishment, motive and result, so cleanly defined.—*Paul Gallico, sportswriter.*

1015 Baseball has no penalties at all. A home run is a home run. You cheer. In football, on a score, you look for flags. If there's one, who's it on? When can we cheer? Football acts can be repealed. Baseball acts stand forever.—*Thomas Boswell, sportswriter. 1987. This was Reason No. 49 from "Why Is Baseball So Much Better than Football?"*

1016 No matter how many errors you make, no matter how many times you strike out, keep hustling. That way you'll at least look like a ballplayer.—*Tony Kubek Sr. to his son, Yankees rookie Tony Kubek who was named the 1957 AL Rookie of the Year.*

1017 I don't know anything about ballet, but I wish people would watch baseball the way ballet fans watch the dance—not to see who wins but to see how well each player performs his part.—*Mike Marshall, Dodgers reliever. In 1974, Marshall set the record by pitching in 106 games—no other pitcher ever appeared in relief more than 90 times in a season.*

1018 I think a baseball field must be the most beautiful thing in the world. It's so honest and precise. And we play on it. Every star gets humbled. Every mediocre player has a great moment.—*Lowell Cohn, sportswriter, 1981.*

1019 If asked where baseball stood amid such notions as country, family, love, honor, art, and religion, we might say derisively, "Just a game." But, under oath, I'd abandon some of those Big Six before I'd give up baseball.—*Thomas Boswell, writer.*

1020 Baseball to me is still the national pastime because it is a summer game. I feel that almost all Americans are summer people; that summer is what they think of when they think of their childhood. I think it stirs up an incredible emotion within people.—*Steve Busby, Kansas City Royals pitcher.*

1021 Baseball is a matter of razor-edge precision. It's not a game of inches like you hear people say. It's a game of hundredths of inches.—*Rube Bressler, Brooklyn Dodgers outfielder.*

1022 A king may be a king because his father was, but a ballplayer is a major leaguer only so long as his averages show he is.—*Jim Murray, sportswriter.*

1023 You have to be lucky and stay healthy. And since my retirement, I've decided you have to be pretty darn good, too.—*Stan Musial, Hall of Fame outfielder, 1972.*

1024 *Satchel Paige on* How to Stay Young:

1. Avoid fried meats which angry up the blood.
2. If your stomach disputes you, lie down and pacify it with cool thoughts.
3. Keep the juices flowing by jangling around gently as you move.
4. Go very lightly on the vices, such as carrying on in society. The social ramble ain't restful.
5. Avoid running at all times.
6. Don't look back. Something might be gaining on you.

Batter Up

1025 Happiness is going 2-for-5 and seeing your average drop.—*Richie Hebner, Pirates infielder.*

The Fundamentals

1026 Keep your eye clear and hit 'em where they ain't.—*Wee Willie Keeler, Orioles outfielder, 1898.*

1027 Every great hitter works on the theory that the pitcher is more afraid of him than he is of the pitcher.—*Ty Cobb, Tigers outfielder.*

1028 I have observed that baseball is not unlike war, and when you get right down to it, we batters are the heavy artillery.—*Ty Cobb, Tigers outfielder.*

1029 Batting is a continual problem that you solve in detail over and over but never thoroughly master.—*Ty Cobb, Philadelphia A's outfielder, 1927.*

1030 You have to keep your eye on the ball.—*Joe Sewell, Indians shortstop, who struck out only 114 times in 8,329 plate appearances over 14 seasons.*

1031 In my opinion, baseball is the hardest sport to play. To narrow it down further, hitting a baseball is the single most difficult thing there is in sports. It takes more skill to hit a baseball than it does to do anything else.—*Ted Williams, Hall of Fame outfielder, 1967.*

1032 No one can see the ball hit the bat because it's physically impossible to focus your eyes that way. However, when I hit the ball especially hard, I could smell the leather start to burn as it struck the wooden bat.—*Ted Williams, Hall of Fame outfielder.*

1033 See the ball, hit the ball, run like hell.

—*Tony Gwynn, Padres outfielder, on his hitting strategy.*

1034 When you see the ball, you have a better idea where it is.—*Jeff Torborg, White Sox manager.*

1035 How hard is hitting? You ever walk into a pitch-black room full of furniture that you've never been in before and try to walk through it without bumping into anything? Well, it's harder than that.—*Ted Kluszewski, Reds first baseman. In 1955, Big Klu set a modern NL record by scoring a run in 17 consecutive games.*

1036 Those who hit for average—and those who hit for damage.—*Fresco Thompson, Los Angeles Dodgers GM, on the two types of hitters.*

1037 You hit .320 and they say you don't know anything about hitting. You hit .210 and they make you a hitting coach.—*George Foster, former All-Star outfielder and 1977 NL MVP, 1991.*

1038 I got released because I couldn't hit. Then they signed me as a hitting instructor.—*Mike Jorgensen, Cardinals coach, 1986. Jorgensen hit .196 the previous season with St. Louis.*

1039 When I'm hitting, the ball comes up to the plate like a basketball. You can see the stitches and the writing on the ball. When you're not hitting, you don't see anything.—*Rod Carew, Angels first baseman, 1979.*

1040 When you're hitting, the ball looks like a grapefruit. When you're not, it looks like a black-eyed pea.—*George Scott, Red Sox first baseman.*

1041 You can't really explain it. Sometimes the ball looks like a beach ball. And then there's the exact opposite of that, where it looks like an aspirin coming out of a shotgun.—*Jason Bay, Red Sox outfielder, 2009.*

1042 I don't always swing at strikes. I swing at the ball when it looks big.—*Moose Skowron, Yankees first baseman.*

1043 If I'm hitting, I can hit anyone. If not, my 12-year-old son can get me out.—*Willie Stargell, Pirates first baseman, 1979.*

1044 It's only a hitch when you're in a slump. When you're hitting the ball, it's called rhythm.—*Eddie Matthews, Braves third baseman.*

1045 It's all right to have a hitch in your swing, but when you have a flaw in your hitch, you're in trouble.—*Leon Wagner, Giants outfielder, 1969.*

1046 It's not the bat that counts. It's the guy who's wheeling it.—*Paul Waner, Pirates outfielder.*

1047 Nobody should hit .200. Anybody should hit .250.—*Charlie Lau, Yankees hitting instructor, 1979.*

1048 Any big-league starter who hits .200 shouldn't be where he is. He ought to be waiting outside the gate to get in the park.—*Satchel Paige, Hall of Fame pitcher, 1972.*

1049 Everybody tries to make hitting a science, which it is. But you can't treat it like a science; you have to treat it like an art.—*George Brett, Royals first baseman, 1988.*

1050 The secret of hitting is physical relaxation, mental concentration—and don't hit the fly ball to center.—*Stan Musial, Hall of Fame outfielder.*

1051 There's no skill involved. Just go up there and swing at the ball.—*Joe DiMaggio, Yankees outfielder.*

1052 All I can tell 'em is pick a good one and sock it. I get back to the dugout, and they ask me what it was I hit, and I tell 'em I don't know except it looked good.—*Babe Ruth, Yankees outfielder.*

1053 Every strike brings me closer to the next home run.—*Babe Ruth, Yankees outfielder.*

1054 Don't forget to swing hard, in case you hit the ball.—*Woodie Held, Indians infielder.*

1055 Gentlemen, swinging a bat is a great tonic, a fine exercise. It strengthens the diaphragm. Besides, you may hit the ball.—*Billy Southworth, Boston Braves manager.*

1056 The sign of a good hitter is when you look for it, get it, and send it.—*Brooks Robinson, Orioles third baseman.*

1057 My approach is see something I like and attack it.—*Dave Parker, Pirates outfielder.*

1058 Think about each pitch like you think about women, then select one which is particularly appealing.—*Tommy Lasorda, Spokane Indians manager, 1970.*

1059 The art of hitting is the art of getting your pitch to hit.—*Bobby Brown, Yankees outfielder.*

1060 If you don't swing at bad pitches, they have to throw you a good one.—*Gates Brown, Tigers hitting coach.*

1061 There is only one legitimate trick to pinch-hitting, and that's knowing the pitcher's best pitch when the count is 3-and-2. All the rest is a crapshoot.—*Earl Weaver, Orioles manager.*

1062 It's like chopping down a tree. You don't warm up. You got work to do and you do it.—*Dick Allen, White Sox first baseman, on pinch-hitting, 1973.*

1063 Pressure? Well, it ain't hittin' in 44 straight games 'cause I've done that and it was fun. The playoffs are pressure.—*Pete Rose, Phillies first baseman, 1980.*

1064 Sex is great and playing the trumpet is out of sight, but there is no greater thrill than hitting a baseball.—*Carmen Fanzone, Cubs infielder, 1973.*

1065 The pitcher has got only a ball. I've got a bat. So the percentage of weapons is in my favor, and I let the fellow with the ball do the fretting.—*Hank Aaron, Hall of Famer.*

1066 You hit a four-ounce baseball with a 35-ounce bat and there's going to be some damage.—*George Foster, Reds outfielder, 1979.*

1067 Guys who can field you can shake out of any old tree. Give me a guy who can hit.—*Rogers Hornsby, St. Louis Browns manager.*

1068 Every time I stepped up to the plate with a bat in my hands, I felt sorry for them.—*Rogers Hornsby, Hall of Fame infielder, on pitchers.*

1069 I don't make speeches. I let my bat speak for me in the summertime.—*Honus Wagner, Pirates shortstop, 1909.*

1070 You don't always make an out. Sometimes the pitcher gets you out.—*Carl Yastrzemski, Red Sox outfielder.*

1071 Make believe every lefty is a righty.—*Tim McCarver, Cardinals catcher, on how to hit left-handed pitching, 1964.*

1072 You have to swing like a man. A walk won't get you off the island.—*Rafael Ramirez, Braves shortstop, on why so few players from the Dominican Republic will take a base on balls, 1987.*

1073 My mother used to pitch to me, and my father would shag balls. If I hit one up the middle, close to my mother, I'd have some extra chores to do. My mother was instrumental in making me a pull hitter.—*Eddie Matthews in his Hall of Fame induction speech, 1978.*

1074 A baseball swing is a very finely tuned instrument. It is repetition, and more repetition, then a little more after that.—*Reggie Jackson, Oakland A's outfielder.*

1075 If I had my career to play over, one thing I'd do differently is swing more. Those 1,200 walks I got, nobody remembers them.—*Pee Wee Reese, former Brooklyn Dodgers shortstop.*

1076 All I want out of life is that when I walk down the street folks will say, "There goes the greatest hitter who ever lived."—*Ted Williams, Red Sox outfielder, 1939.*

1077 If he can hit .350, we figured he could see.—*Harley Duncan, Missouri drivers' license bureau official, on why he waived the eye test for Royals third baseman George Brett, 1985.*

1078 This doesn't mean I'm in a zone for good. I was in a zone. I just hope it's not the no-parking zone.—*Andy Van Slyke, Pirates outfielder, on going 10 for 12 in a weekend series to break a prolonged slump, 1994. During the series, Van Slyke got eight consecutive hits in a doubleheader, falling one shy of tying the record set by New York Giants first baseman Bill Terry in 1929.*

1079 They don't just beat you up. They put you in a trunk and drive you away somewhere.—*Joe Torre, Yankees manager, on the prodigious offense of the Cleveland Indians, 1999.*

1080 One club will watch your delivery and say, "Oh, boy, here comes a fastball," and they jump on it. Others say, "Oh, boy, here comes a change-up." The Pirates just say, "Oh, boy, here comes a baseball."—*Don Sutton, Dodgers pitcher, 1973.*

1081 I think they're going to start pitching around the whole lineup to face me.—*Ozzie Guillen, White Sox shortstop, on the Chicago lineup that included Albert Belle, Frank Thomas, Robin Ventura and Harold Baines, 1997.*

1082 When Manny takes a pitch, it's either a wild pitch or paralysis set in.—*Joe Brown, Pirates GM, on catcher Manny Sanguillen, who recorded 632 plate appearances with only 21 walks, 1974.*

1083 I'm a free swinger. They can put the strike zone wherever—on third base, in left field. It doesn't matter to me.—*Vladimir Guerrero, Expos outfielder, on the proposed higher strike zone, 2001. Although known to swing at just about anything, Guerrero never struck out more than 95 times in a season.*

1084 Some hitters try and hit the ball where it's pitched. Ralph Garr hits the ball if it's pitched.—*Clyde King, Braves manager, 1975.*

1085 He swings and swings and swings. Someday a pitcher with a good move is going to throw over to first base—and Frank Howard is going to swing at it.—*Pete Reiser, Dodgers coach, on the Senators outfielder, 1969.*

1086 If Rod Carew has two strikes on him and fouls off five pitches and then takes the sixth down the middle, I'm calling it a ball.—*Ron Luciano, umpire.*

1087 Nobody's gone after Reds with this much vigor since Joe McCarthy.—*Jeff Blair, sportswriter, on Expos third baseman Shane Andrews, who hit .471 (16 for 36) with six homers and 21 RBI against Cincinnati in August, 1996.*

The Bad

1088 Everybody's talking about the ball being juiced. The balls I've been hitting have had prune juice in them.—*Andy Van Slyke, Pirates outfielder, 1994.*

1089 Can you believe it? They sent me a whole shipment of bats and not one set of instructions.—*Steve Lake, Cubs catcher, 1985. Lake hit .151 for the season.*

1090 It's easy to hit .300 with your swing. Try doing it with mine.—*Dave Valle, Mariners catcher, to outfielder Ken Griffey Jr., 1993.*

1091 Why are you asking me? Do my grounders to second look a little harder?—*Kent Hrbek, Twins first baseman, when asked if he thought the baseballs were juiced, 1994.*

1092 Sure I screwed up that sacrifice bunt. But look at it this way, I'm a better bunter than a billion Chinese. Those poor suckers can't bunt at all.—*John Lowenstein, Orioles outfielder, 1981.*

1093 I experimented with corking my bat until I realized all those bloop hits I was getting were turning into routine fly balls.—*Jim Sundberg, Rangers broadcaster and former All-Star catcher, 1994.*

1094 It would have been embarrassing to die on national television, and besides, you can't hit when you're dead.—*John Kruk, Phillies first baseman, on facing Mariners pitcher Randy Johnson in the 1993 All-Star Game. After a Johnson fastball sailed over his head, Kruk waved at the next three pitches as quickly as he could and retreated to the safety of the dugout.*

1095 He could speak eight languages, but he couldn't hit in any of them.—*Ted Lyons, White Sox pitcher, on polyglot catcher Moe Berg.*

1096 He looks like Zorro out there. Swish, swish.—*Lou Piniella, Mariners manager, on utility player Andy Sheets, 1996.*

1097 The only thing bothering him as a hitter is making contact.—*Ralph Kiner, Mets broadcaster, on rookie catcher Todd Hundley, 1992.*

1098 His nickname is Rambo, but he hits like

Brigitte Nielsen.—*Harry Caray, Cubs broadcaster, on Pirates utility man Mike Diaz, 1987*

1099 Before the game they told me I looked like Babe Ruth. Then, in my bat against Don Carman, I looked like Dr. Ruth.—*John Kruk, Padres outfielder.*

1100 Why did Barry Bonds take his dad with him to pick up a new car? Because Barry can't drive in anything in October.—*Dave Ailes, sportswriter, on the inability of the Pirates outfielder to drive in runs during Pittsburgh's three consecutive NLCS losses, 1992. In 20 NLCS games, Bonds collected three RBI for the Pirates.*

1101 The Angels couldn't break a chandelier if they held batting practice in a hotel lobby.—*Bill Lee, Red Sox pitcher, on California's weak offense.*

1102 We can't knock the fuzz off peaches.—*Joe Frazer, Mets manager, 1976.*

1103 It was unbelievable in Chicago. You felt like you had to pitch a shutout to tie.—*Goose Gossage on his days with the anemic White Sox. After leading the majors in saves in 1975, Gossage was converted to a starter and went 9–17 in 1976. He returned to the bullpen for good, saved 310 career games, and was inducted into the Hall of Fame in 2008.*

1104 He has reacted worse to sunlight than Count Dracula.—*Bob Hertzel, sportswriter, on Pirates second baseman Jose Lind's .190 batting average during day games, 1989.*

1105 All I'd have to do is make my head look like a slider, and he'd miss it.—*Jim Colborn, Brewers pitcher, on Tigers third baseman Aurelio Rodriguez, who threatened to break a bat over Colborn's head following a bean ball incident.*

1106 DiMaggio, who popped out in his first four at-bats, could have done all his hitting in a chimney.—*Arthur "Bugs" Baer, sportswriter, on Yankees outfielder Joe DiMaggio, 1950.*

1107 I've been telling people I've been hitting a lot of sacrifice flies. There just hasn't been anybody on base.—*Denny Hocking, Twins shortstop, 1996.*

1108 What are they going to do if I don't get a hit? Bench me?—*Bill Nahorodny, seldom-used Braves infielder, on getting a pinch hit, 1981.*

1109 The first thing I look for in the Sunday papers is to see who's below the Mendoza Line. —*George Brett, Royals third baseman, on weak-hitting infielder Mario Mendoza. The Mendoza Line became the established term for hitting .200, even though Mendoza hit .215 for his career.*

1110 I could field as long as I can remember, but hitting has been a struggle all my life.—*Brooks Robinson, Orioles third baseman, a lifetime .267 hitter.*

1111 My bat was so slow today that one time a fly lit on it when I swung.—*Frank Robinson, Angels DH, 1973.*

1112 Nick took two third strikes—proving he's in mid-season form.—*Al Lopez, White Sox manager, on outfielder Dave Nicholson striking out looking twice in a spring training game, 1963. That season Nicholson struck out 175 times in just 449 at bats.*

1113 Until he allows the pitcher to actually let go of the ball before he takes a whack at it, he's going to struggle.—*Clint Hurdle, Rockies manager, on shortstop Juan Uribe, July 2002. Uribe finished the season hitting .240 with 120 strikeouts.*

1114 You know, this game's not very much fun when you're only hitting .247.—*Reggie Jackson, Angels outfielder.*

1115 I had a manager one time who told 'em I had the quickest bat in baseball. I looked at him like he was crazy. He said, "You can get the bat out of the rack and make an out and get it back in the rack quicker than anybody in baseball."—*Grady Little, Red Sox manager and career .207 hitter in the minors, 2002.*

The Ugly: Pitchers at the Plate

1116 I was so bad I never broke a bat until last year. Then I was backing out of the garage. —*Lefty Gomez, Yankees pitcher.*

1117 I was the worst hitter you ever saw. You know, last year, I underwent open heart surgery. They performed a triple bypass. I told the doctor it was the first triple I'd ever had in my life.—*Lefty Gomez, Hall of Fame pitcher, 1979.*

1118 Don't ask me what the pitch was. It could have been a fastball down the pipe. With a bat in my hands, I couldn't tell a curve from a Cuban palm ball. I do recall that only one of my eyes was closed when I swung.—*Lefty Gomez, Yankees pitcher, on getting the first hit in All-Star Game competition, July 6, 1933.*

1119 I'm seeing the ball real good. I just can't hit it.—*Don Carman, Phillies pitcher, 1988. For his career, Carman hit .057 (12 for 209).*

1120 I start swinging when the pitcher gets the sign.—*Charlie Hough, 46-year-old Marlins pitcher, on his secret to getting three hits in his first four at-bats of 1994.*

1121 I've always said I'm an athlete trapped inside a pitcher's body.—*Mark Portugal, Giants pitcher, on collecting two hits in one inning, 1994. Portugal hit .354 for the season and won the Silver Slugger Award.*

1122 I'm shooting to have a higher batting average than ERA.—*Jose Rijo, Reds pitcher, on hitting .232 with a 2.73 ERA in August 1993. His average went up (.268) and his ERA dropped (2.48) as Rijo finished fifth in the Cy Young voting.*

1123 I've never hit 1.000 before. I think I can do it, too, if I can keep my stroke going—and not get any more at-bats.—*Mitch Williams, Phillies reliever, on getting a hit in his first at-bat of the year, July 2, 1993. Wild Thing maintained his perfect average for the season but hit just .188 for his career (3 for 16).*

1124 I know Koufax's weakness. He can't hit.—*Whitey Ford, Yankees pitcher, on Dodgers pitcher Sandy Koufax, a career .097 hitter.*

1125 I had Rick Burleson's bat. I had Buddy Bell's gloves. I had Tom Paciorek's helmet. All I needed was somebody's swing.—*Dave Steib, Blue Jays pitcher, on unexpectedly having to bat in the 1981 All-Star Game, August 7. For his career, Steib went 0 for 13.*

1126 Mel Ott did it and it worked for him. Of course, I'm not sure I pick up the correct foot.—*Reliever Dan Quisenberry, on why he lifted his foot when batting.*

1127 He's not afraid of the ball. He can't hit a hog in a ditch, but he's not afraid.—*Jim Leyland, Tigers manager, on the hitting prowess of pitcher Nate Robertson, 2006.*

1128 The bottom line is entertaining the fans, and watching some of out pitchers hit is pretty funny.—*Tom Kelly, Twins manager.*

1129 You know you're pitching well when the batters look as bad as you do at the plate.—*Duke Snider, Expos coach, to his pitchers, 1975.*

1130 Usually the manager wants his players to get a hit. I cheer for him not to get a hit because then he will have to run the bases.—*Ozzie Guillen, White Sox manager, on having pitcher Jose Contreras bat during interleague games. Thru 2010, Contreras was hitless in 29 at-bats.*

1131 He's such a bad hitter, sometimes someone pinch hits for him in batting practice.—*Jim Leyland, Pirates manager, on pitcher Jeff Robinson.*

1132 Most pitchers ought to have "For Display Purposes Only" on their bat.—*Joe Garagiola, broadcaster.*

Battle of the Sexes

1133 I like going to games with my wife. It is an interesting experience. I also like not going with my wife.—*Arnold Hano, sportswriter.*

1134 *Joan Lasorda:* I think you love baseball more than you love me.

Tommy Lasorda (Dodgers manager): Yeah, but I love you more than I love football and basketball.

1135 My wife, she takes half of everything I make. I give up six runs, three are charged to her.—*Jose Rijo, Reds pitcher, 1991. Rijo and his wife Rosie (daughter of Hall of Fame pitcher Juan Marichel) were in the midst of a divorce.*

1136 There was never any question about his courage. He proved it by getting married four times.—*Jack Brickhouse, broadcaster, on former Cardinals outfielder Enos Slaughter.*

1137 I know a baseball star who wouldn't report the theft of his wife's credit cards because the thief spends less than she does.—*Joe Garagiola, broadcaster.*

1138 He's a hell of a competitor. He plays baseball the way my wife shops.—*Tommy Lasorda, Dodgers manager, on outfielder Kirk Gibson, 1988. Gibson won the NL MVP that season.*

1139 I'm a four-wheel-drive pickup kind of guy. So is my wife.—*Mike Greenwell, Red Sox outfielder, 2005.*

1140 That Knight's a lucky guy. He has a wife who makes a million dollars a year. Mine spends that.—*Pete Rose, Reds manager, on Tigers first baseman Ray Knight, who was married to LPGA golfer Nancy Lopez, 1988.*

1141 I'm going to have a hard time finding room for it in our trophy case. Nancy's are all over the place. I've got four or five, I think.—*Ray Knight, Mets third baseman, on his World Series MVP Award, 1986.*

1142 I married George for better or worse, but not for lunch.—*Hazel Weiss, wife of former Yankees executive George Weiss, on having her husband around the house all day, 1961. Weiss got back to work in 1962 when he became the first GM of the expansion New York Mets.*

1143 Marriage is a great institution—to a lot of women.—*Ron Luciano, former umpire, 1980.*

1144 I promised that if we ever fussed, I would go outside. Fifty-seven years in the open air does wonders for a man's health.—*Happy Chandler, baseball commissioner, on his wedding vow.*

1145 He's a slob. A total slob. He doesn't clean. He doesn't know we have a place for dirty clothes. He just figures they go on the floor next to the bed. Miraculously they get clean. He doesn't know the front end of the dishwasher opens. He eats between three and five in the morning. When I get up, I see a line of stuff, from the refrigerator to the living room. It's like a little trail.—*Joanne Dibble, wife of Reds reliever Rob Dibble, on life at home with her husband, 1994.*

1146 I'm glad I didn't burn your toast this morning.—*Krys Hobson, wife of Red Sox manager Butch Hobson, following a game in which he was ejected for taking a swing at an umpire, 1994.*

1147 Say what you want about major league baseball, at least it is not a bastion of male chauvinism. Cincy owner Marge Schott has been given every opportunity to make as many stupid mistakes as her male counterparts, and she has taken full advantage.—*Blackie Sherrod, sportswriter, 1992.*

1148 If a woman has her Ph.D. in Physics, has mastered in quantum theory, plays flawless Chopin, was once a cheerleader, and is now married to a man who plays baseball, she will forever be "former cheerleader married to star athlete."—*Maryanne Ellison Simmons, wife of catcher Ted Simmons.*

1149 Before the women's movement, was Mike Sharperson known as Mike Sharperman?—*Bob Hertzel, sportswriter, 1991.*

1150 The next time I marry it'll be a man, and with my luck he'll get pregnant.—*Joe Pepitone, thrice divorced former All-Star first baseman.*

1151 It's got to be better than rooming with Joe Page.—*Joe DiMaggio, former Yankees outfielder, on his marriage to movie star Marilyn Monroe, 1954.*

1152 *Marilyn Monroe (returning from a USO tour of Korea):* Oh Joe, you've never heard such cheering.

Joe DiMaggio: Yes, Marilyn, I have.

1153 It proves that no man can be a success in two national pastimes.—*Oscar Levant, sportswriter, on the separation of former Yankees outfielder Joe DiMaggio and actress Marilyn Monroe after just nine months of marriage.*

1154 I was born under pressure. My mom

wanted a girl.—*Lee Smith, Cardinals reliever, 1990.*

1155 It's like your wife. If you want something from her, you butter her up.—*Cliff Johnson, Cubs catcher, on why he sometimes kissed his bat, 1980.*

1156 I've had marriages that didn't last that long.—*Skip Caray, Braves broadcaster, on a 4-hour, 11-inning game, 1993.*

1157 She'll get mad because, with the zip code, there's more writing on the outside of the envelope than on the inside.—*Rocky Bridges, Cardinals second baseman, on sending a letter to his wife Mary.*

1158 I went to an all-boys high school, but I'm making up for it now.—*Frank Tanana, Angels pitcher, 1975.*

1159 She gave me a $5 bill and a white shirt, and she told me not to change either one of them.—*Mickey McDermott, former Red Sox pitcher, on his wife Betty sending him out for the evening.*

1160 I asked her, "How'd you like to be married to a major league manager?" And she said, "What, is Tommy Lasorda getting a divorce?"—*John Wathan, informing his wife that he had been named manager of the Royals, 1987.*

1161 I'm no major feminist, but I do believe that if we women could sit at the table, there would be no war because we'd get things done, so we could get to the nail salon sooner. We have more important things to take care of.—*Morganna Roberts, baseball's "Kissing Bandit," during the 1994 baseball strike.*

1162 That's too bad for me. He blows enough hot air as it is.—*Carmen Franco, wife of Indians shortstop Julio Franco, when told her husband wanted to take saxophone lessons, 1987.*

1163 I looked up the definition of "star." It said it's a self-contained mass of gas. I'm not arguing.—*Pat Brickhouse, wife of former Cubs broadcaster Jack Brickhouse, 1991.*

1164 It was too bad I wasn't a second baseman; then I'd probably have seen a lot more of my husband.—*Karolyn Rose, on her ex-husband Pete Rose, 1981.*

1165 I was served with divorce papers and a paternity suit and went 17-for-28.—*Pete Rose, Reds player-manager, 1987.*

1166 Hey, just give her a million bucks, and tell her to hit the road.—*Pete Rose, Philadelphia Phillies first baseman, on how to end a marriage.*

1167 Maybe I should get divorced every day. I'd be broke, but I'd be in the Hall of Fame. —*Keith Hernandez, Mets first baseman, on collecting two home runs and seven RBI the day after finalizing his divorce, 1988.*

1168 Two years ago I retired from baseball to be closer to my family. Last October, my wife left me.—*Jerry Grote, Royals catcher, on why he came out of retirement, 1981.*

1169 No. 1 is baseball. No. 2 is basketball. No. 3 is hockey. No. 4 is football. No. 5 is girlfriends.—*Chan Ho Park, Dodgers pitcher, listing his five favorite things, 1994.*

1170 I feel I've stayed with Mike Cuellar longer than I did my first wife. At least, I've given him more chances.—*Earl Weaver, Orioles manager. Cuellar slipped to 4–13 in 1976 after winning the Cy Young Award the previous season.*

1171 For most ballplayers, all getting married means is that now they have to hide their date books.—*Don Kowet, sportswriter, 1974.*

1172 No one is a pull hitter in the first year of marriage.—*Walker Cooper, Cardinals catcher, 1945.*

1173 *Eddie Lopat (Yankees pitcher):* Know what the penalty is for bigamy?
Yogi Berra (Yankees catcher): Dunno.
Eddie Lopat: Two mothers-in-law.

1174 I was just wondering: Does Padre outfielder Al Martin get twice as many courtesy seats in the "wives section" at all Padre home games?—*Jerry Perisho, comedy writer, on outfielder Al Martin, who married a woman in Las Vegas while already being married, 2000.*

1175 You'd think after 11 years in the majors

you'd know better, but you still do it. You know how if you've been married 20 years, and you know what ticks your wife off, and you know you shouldn't do it, but sometimes you still do it anyway? It's like that.—*Andy Van Slyke, Pirates outfielder, after getting thrown out at home attempting an inside-the-park home run, 1994.*

1176 We try to live good, clean lives, but whether or not we do is for our wives to judge.—*Bob Dernier, Cubs outfielder.*

1177 I didn't want to interrupt her.—*Whitey Herzog, former manager, on why he didn't speak to his wife during their first year of marriage, 1998.*

1178 Alimony is like buying oats for a dead horse.—*Arthur "Bugs" Baer, sportswriter.*

1179 I never realized how short a month was until I started paying alimony.—*Harry Caray, Cubs broadcaster.*

1180 I'm so sick and tired of lawyers that I don't care anymore. Let all the women go in. Personally, I'm opposed to it. I believe our players have a right to their privacy.—*Jim Campbell, Tigers GM, on a court order allowing female reporters into locker rooms, 1979.*

1181 It doesn't make any difference. They don't ask any dumber questions than the guys do.—*Jim Fregosi, Angels manager, on the decision to allow female reporters into the locker rooms, 1979.*

1182 Sure, women sportswriters look when they're in the clubhouse. Read their stories. How else do you explain a capital letter in the middle of a word?—*Bob Uecker, broadcaster.*

1183 I don't talk to people when I'm naked, especially women, unless they're on top of me or I'm on top of them.—*Jack Morris, Tigers pitcher, to sportswriter Jennifer Frey, August 1990.*

1184 I think it would be great if a woman played major league baseball—especially if her locker were next to mine.—*Johnny Bench, Reds catcher, 1974.*

1185 They'll certainly do something for a uniform that a male athlete can't.—*Bill Veeck, White Sox owner, on female ballplayers, 1976.*

1186 NOW (The National Organization of Women) is such a blowhard organization. They are a bunch of lesbians. Their focus has nothing to do with women's rights. It has everything to do with women wanting to be men.—*Bob Knepper, Astros pitcher, 1988.*

1187 This is not an occupation a woman should be in. In God's society, woman was created in a role of submission to the husband. It's not that woman is inferior, but I don't believe woman should be in a leadership role.—*Bob Knepper, Astros pitcher, on minor league umpire Pam Postema, 1988.*

1188 This is one of the class guys in the game. And he has a great wife—if there is such a thing as a great wife.—*Ralph Kiner, Mets broadcaster.*

1189 This club is a lot of fun, like my wife, but there's no profit in either one.—*Ray Kroc, Padres owner, 1978.*

1190 I think whores got a lot more class than some straight broads. You know where you stand with them.—*Bo Belinsky, Angels pitcher. During his brief career, Belinsky dated Hollywood starlets Ann-Margret, Tina Louise, Connie Stevens and Mamie Van Doren.*

1191 The players disliked Bo so much he had to catch his own pop flies.—*Mamie Van Doren, actress, on her ex-husband and former pitcher, Bo Belinsky, 1973.*

1192 I needed her like Custer needed Indians.—*Bo Belinsky, former pitcher, on actress Mamie Van Doren.*

1193 In a way an umpire is like a woman. He makes quick decisions, never reverses them, and doesn't think you're safe when you're out.—*Larry Goetz, umpire.*

1194 I went three days without a hit, and my wife refused to cook me dinner. When I didn't get a hit the fourth day, she gave her tickets away. I guess if I ever go a week without a hit, I'll be sleeping in a tent in the backyard.—*Al Oliver, Rangers outfielder, 1979.*

1195 We've been married twenty-eight years, and we still go out dining and dancing three times a week. She goes on Mondays, Wednesdays and Fridays; I go on Tuesdays, Thursdays and Saturdays.—*Tommy Lasorda, Dodgers manager.*

1196 If a woman has to choose between catching a fly ball and saving an infant's life, she will choose to save the infant's life without even considering if there are men on base.—*Dave Barry, humorist.*

1197 Every time that I have ever tried to help a woman out, I have been incarcerated.—*Jose Canseco, former AL MVP, appearing on* The Surreal Life, *a TV reality show, 2006.*

1198 People say I'm a gold digger, but do you see me wearing gold? No. I'm wearing diamonds.—*Anna Benson, wife of Mets pitcher Kris Benson, 2006.*

1199 It's better than my wedding ring. You can always get wedding rings.—*Johnny Damon, Red Sox outfielder, on receiving his 2004 World Series ring.*

1200 Indians catchers now have four signs to flash [Chuck] Finley: fastball, curve, changeup and "Look Out! It's your wife!"—*Paul Giles, comedy writer, on the Indians pitcher who missed his first start of the season after his wife, actress Tawny Kitaen, was charged with spousal abuse for kicking and scratching him in the car, April 2002.*

1201 The Cardinals traded for veteran lefty Chuck Finley. Not to be outdone, the Reds acquired the only person who can hit him—Tawny Kitaen.—*Bill Scheft, writer, July 2002.*

1202 It's all bull. It's a typical custody battle. I can't believe she left out the cross-dressing.—*Chuck Finley, Indians pitcher, on wild charges brought by his estranged wife, Tawny Kitaen, that included Finley abusing alcohol, marijuana and steroids, May 2002.*

1203 It was the shortest honeymoon in history not involving someone named Zsa Zsa.—*Tom FitzGerald, sportswriter, on New York Mets fans booing high-priced free agent pitcher Tom Glavine during an Opening Day loss to the Cubs, 2003. For the season, Glavine made $11 million and went 9–14 with a 4.52 ERA.*

1204 My wife wanted a big diamond.—*Mookie Wilson, Mets outfielder, on why he got married on a baseball field.*

1205 All I remember about my wedding day in 1967 is that the Cubs lost a doubleheader.—*George Will, columnist.*

1206 I married my wife on her birthday to cut down on expenses.—*Rocky Bridges, San Jose Bees, 1964.*

1207 If she gets the money, let her pitch.—*Bugs Raymond, New York Giants pitcher, on manager John McGraw having Raymond's paychecks sent directly to his wife so he wouldn't spend the money on alcohol, 1909.*

1208 No need to worry about my arm. I carried my wife's bags through the airport.—*Jay Howell, Dodgers reliever, when asked if his arm was healthy.*

1209 Darryl Strawberry's ex-wife is suing him for non-support. Could the Yankees' lineup be far behind?—*Jerry Perisho, comedy writer, on the embattled slugger who played in just 32 games for New York, 1995.*

1210 Money and women. They're the two strongest things in the world. The things you do for a woman you wouldn't do for anything else. Same with money.—*Satchel Paige, Kansas City Monarchs pitcher.*

The Broadcast Booth

1211 Good afternoon ladies and gentlemen. Welcome to the first telecast of a sporting event. I'm not sure what it is we're doing here, but I certainly hope it turns out well for you people who are watching.—*Bill Stern, broadcaster, during the first televised baseball game between Columbia University and Princeton, 1939.*

1212 Baseball was designed for American television—15 seconds of action and three-minute breaks for commercials.—*Bogdan Chruscicki, Polish radio announcer.*

1213 Isn't it odd that in the communications field you seem to have the biggest breakdown in communications of any business?—*Mel Allen, Hall of Fame broadcaster.*

1214 I really believe it's a sickness in this country that so many millions of people have nothing better to do than watch a sports event on television.—*Red Barber, Hall of Fame broadcaster, 1981.*

1215 Never start a broadcast on an empty stomach or a full bladder.—*Red Barber, Brooklyn Dodgers broadcaster.*

1216 On a ball hit to right field, Vin wanted to say, "There's a hot shot hit to right," but it didn't come out that way. He quickly learned that you don't use *shot* and *hit* in the same sentence if you have to say it fast.—*Joe Garagiola, broadcaster, on his* Game of the Week *partner, Vin Scully.*

1217 Baseball is the blessed silence that comes between Dick Vitale and John Madden.—*Bernie Lincicome, sportswriter, on the animated basketball and football broadcasters, 1993.*

1218 I've never been fired from radio.—*Jack Buck, Cardinals broadcaster, when asked the difference between working on television and radio, 1993.*

1219 When Dean did not have at his disposal a word suitable for the occasion, he simply invented one.—*Jack Clarke, sportswriter, on the unique syntax utilized by Hall of Fame pitcher-turned-broadcaster Dizzy Dean.*

1220 Spart is pretty much like gumption or fight. Like the Spart of St. Louis, that plane Lindbergh flowed to Europe.—*Dizzy Dean, announcer.*

1221 Radio Announcing I Have Did.—*Name of a lecture given by Dizzy Dean at Southern Methodist University.*

1222 Old Diz knows the King's English. And not only that, I also know the Queen is English.—*Dizzy Dean, announcer, defending his unique use of grammar.*

1223 It don't make no difference how you say it, just say it in a way that makes sense. Did you ever meet anybody in your life who didn't know what "ain't" means?—*Dizzy Dean, broadcaster.*

1224 A lot of folks that ain't saying ain't ain't eatin'.—*Dizzy Dean, broadcaster.*

1225 I imagine myself as the broadcaster for a Cubs–White Sox World Series—a Series that would last seven games, with the final game going extra innings before being suspended because of darkness at Wrigley Field.—*Jack Brickhouse, former Cubs broadcaster, on his fantasy.*

1226 I heard that doctors revived a man after he was dead for nearly five minutes. When they asked what it was like being dead, he said it was like listening to Yankees' radio announcer Phil Rizzuto during a rain delay.—*David Letterman, TV talk show host.*

1227 If you ever worked with Rizzuto, you'd know my motivation. How would you like to work 18 years with a guy who still doesn't know your first name?—*Bill White, former broadcaster, on why he gave up announcing Yankees games with Phil Rizzuto to become president of the National League, 1989.*

1228 Hey microphone face, are you ever going to stop talking?—*Oscar the Grouch, professional curmudgeon, to broadcaster Tim McCarver during an appearance on* Sesame Street, *1992.*

1229 If [Tim] McCarver sat next to me in first class, I'd downgrade to coach quicker than you could say "honey-roasted peanuts."—*Norman Chad, sportswriter, 1998.*

1230 The Cubs continue to make the effort to improve by trading for Phillies' second baseman Mickey Morandini. Best of all, Harry Caray gets plenty of time to begin practicing assorted mispronunciations.—*Joe Knowles, sportswriter, on an off-season acquisition by Chicago, 1997.*

1231 I love Harry, but I don't want to go on the air and have him introduce me as Michael Jackson.—*Michael Jordan, Chicago Bulls All-Star, on his reluctance to visit with Cubs broadcaster Harry Caray on the air.*

1232 I really love baseball. The guys and the game. And I love the challenge of describing things. The only thing I hate—and I know you have to be realistic and pay the bills in this life—is the loneliness of the road.—*Vin Scully, Los Angeles Dodgers broadcaster.*

1233 The Washington Senators and the New York Giants must have played a doubleheader this afternoon—the game I saw and the game Graham McNamee announced.—*Ring Lardner, sportswriter, on a game during the 1924 World Series.*

1234 What do I think of Howard Cosell? I have tried very hard to like Howard. And I have failed.—*Red Smith, sportswriter.*

1235 The Russians have a weapon that can wipe out 280 million Americans. That puts them exactly 10 years behind Howard Cosell. —*Red Smith, sportswriter, 1979.*

1236 Howard calls a good game, it's just not the same one you're watching.—*Gene Autry, Angels owner.*

1237 More than anyone I know he sucks the oxygen out of a room.—*David Halberstam, writer, on broadcaster Howard Cosell, 1984.*

1238 I tell it like it is. Cosell tells it like Roone Arledge wants it told.—*Harry Caray, Cubs broadcaster.*

1239 When the action is at its peak, you should shut up and let the scene tell the story. But some people like Cosell feel a need to be part of the moment and can't stay quiet.—*Tony Kubek, broadcaster, 1985.*

1240 Sometimes egos get the best of you, and broadcasters talk too much. I call it the Cosell syndrome. Jerkocracy, if you will.—*Tony Kubek, NBC broadcaster, on sportscaster Howard Cosell, 1985.*

1241 He's a tremendous ham, a cartoon-like character. He comes across that way on television, too. He's the same way if you're eating dinner with him—he broadcasts the meal.—*Woody Allen, comedian, on Howard Cosell, 1971.*

1242 Why are we honoring this man? Have we run out of human beings?—*Milton Berle, comedian, at a roast for Howard Cosell.*

1243 Arrogant, pompous, vain, cruel, verbose, show off. I have been called all of these. Of course, I am.—*Howard Cosell, broadcaster, 1973.*

1244 There are two professions that one can be hired at with little experience. One is prostitution. The other is sportscasting. Too frequently, they become the same.—*Howard Cosell, broadcaster, 1978.*

1245 If a young guy asked me for advice on how to get into broadcasting, I'd say, "Hit .350 or win the Heisman."—*Skip Caray, Braves broadcaster. Caray forgot to mention that it never hurts to have a relative in the business.*

1246 Like his father Harry, Skip Caray is a first-rate baseball announcer. I used to think it was a genetic thing. But then I heard Skip's son, Chip, do play-by-play on an Atlanta Braves telecast on TBS. Either the boy was adopted or I was wrong.—*Bruce Keidan, sportswriter, 1991. Chip became the voice of the Cubs after the death of his grandfather Harry in 1998.*

1247 It was unbelievable. The ultimate example of someone having no clue what television is about and not caring. When I asked him to talk about a particular pitcher who'd come into the game, his response was, "Who's he?"—*Al Michaels, broadcaster, on a guest appearance by Tigers pitcher Mark "The Bird" Fidrych as color commentator, 1978.*

1248 I'd like to be sort of like Lou Boudreau. He does a good job of recapping the play before it happens.—*Johnny Logan, former shortstop, on becoming an announcer, 1973.*

1249 The first time Sparky Anderson saw a microphone, he thought it was for milking.—*Johnny Bench, Reds catcher, on the short broadcasting stint of his former manager.*

1250 Ted Kluszewski was on third. Somebody like Odrowski on second, maybe Timowitz on first. Boy was I sweatin', hopin' nobody'd get a hit and I wouldn't have to call all those names.—*Dizzy Dean, broadcaster and Hall of Fame pitcher.*

1251 Interviews were the hardest thing for me at first. I felt so damn funny asking players questions when I already know the answers.—*Don Drysdale, Angels broadcaster, on making the transition from player to broadcaster, 1972.*

1252 He talks great—particularly great for a guy who spent most of his life with two fingers in his mouth.—*Gene Mauch, Twins manager, on former Dodgers pitcher Don Drysdale, 1977.*

Live ... and on the Air

1253 Last night I neglected to mention something that bears repeating.—*Ron Fairly, San Francisco Giants broadcaster and former All-Star outfielder–first baseman.*

1254 He fakes a bluff.—*Ron Fairly, Giants broadcaster.*

1255 That's another example of the lack of speed the Giants have—or don't have.—*Ron Fairly, Giants broadcaster, 1988.*

1256 Harrah makes the play. That isn't Harrah. Who is that down there? The third baseman makes the play.—*Ron Fairly, Angels broadcaster.*

1257 Leon Wagner hits a fly ball deep to right.... Will it be fair? Will it be foul? ... It is.—*Herb Score, Indians broadcaster and 1955 Rookie of the Year.*

1258 There's a two-hopper to Eddie Leon, who catches it on the first bounce.—*Herb Score, broadcaster.*

1259 Swing and a miss, called third strike on poor Joe Azcue.—*Herb Score, broadcaster.*

1260 Coming in to pitch is Mike Moore, who is 6-foot-1 and 212 years old.—*Herb Score, Indians broadcaster, 1997.*

1261 Well, the Giants just got a taste of the medicine they've been enjoying all day.—*Mike Shannon, Cardinals broadcaster.*

1262 The bases are f.o.b.—full of Brooklyns.—*Red Barber, Brooklyn Dodgers announcer.*

1263 Now the Dodgers have broken it wide open.—*Rick Monday, Dodgers broadcaster and former All-Star outfielder, on a two-run double that gave the Dodgers a 16–2 lead over Pittsburgh, 1994.*

1264 It was raining so hard three people were injured by buckets.—*Lon Simmons, Oakland A's broadcaster, 1978.*

1265 It's a beautiful day for a night game.—*Frankie Frisch, broadcaster and Hall of Fame second baseman.*

1266 Every statue in New York is smiling right now.—*Ernie Johnson, Braves broadcaster, on outfielder Dion James hitting a bird with a fly ball at Shea Stadium, 1987.*

1267 This is his first major league debut.—*Steve Stone, Cubs broadcaster, on Giants pitcher William VanLandingham, 1994. The rookie pitcher set a record by having the longest full name in major league history.*

1268 There've been times when they've had hits from time to time, but they weren't timely hits at the right time.—*Gary Carter, Marlins broadcaster and former All-Star catcher, 1993.*

1269 You hear those footprints, don't you?—*Billy Martin, Yankees broadcaster and former manager, on a near-collision between a shortstop and an outfielder, 1986.*

1270 They've had some standing-room seats on sale.—*Don Drysdale, Dodgers broadcaster and Hall of Fame pitcher.*

1271 The Houston Astros are the youngest team in the National League if you judge by age.—*Don Drysdale, broadcaster, 1979.*

1272 Forbes Field at this moment is an outdoor insane asylum.—*Jack Brickhouse, broadcaster, after Pirates catcher Hal Smith hit a three-run homer to give Pittsburgh a 9–7 lead over the Yankees in the eighth inning of Game 7 of the 1960 World Series. The Yankees would tie the score in the top of the ninth, setting up Bill Mazeroski's game-winning home run in the bottom of the ninth.*

1273 That ball took a bad hop in the air.—*Phil Rizzuto, Yankees broadcaster and former All-Star shortstop.*

1274 *Phil Rizzuto:* What a nice-looking young lady. She reminds me of that old song, "A Pretty Girl Is Like a Memory."

Bill White: Scooter, I think that's "Melody."

Phil Rizzuto: Really? How do you know her name is Melody?

1275 A high fly, and while it's in the air, happy birthday to Daphne Lapizana. She turns 18 today.—*Phil Rizzuto, Yankees broadcaster, calling the final out of the 1990 regular season.*

1276 *Phil Rizzuto:* There's a foul ball smashed into the Yankee dugout. Boy, I hope that's not Guidry who got in the way.

Frank Messer: Scooter, uh, Guidry is on the mound.

Phil Rizzuto: You know, Frank, you're right.

1277 And that ball is out of here. No, it's not. Yes, it is. What happened?—*Phil Rizzuto, Yankees broadcaster, on a long fly ball that was caught, 1993.*

1278 *Phil Rizzuto (on radio):* Reggie's home run has gone clear out of the stadium.

Bill White: Actually, Scooter, that ball landed in the seats.

Phil Rizzuto: It doesn't matter, they can't see it at home.

1279 Swung on. That's gone ... if it stays fair ... it doesn't ... and it wouldn't have been gone anyway.—*Phil Rizzuto, Yankees broadcaster, 1988.*

1280 Two balls, two strikes, two runs in for the Yankees. Jammed him. That went pretty far for a jam job. A home run. Oh! It went ... holy cow! I don't ... it jammed him. A home run. I ... the old eyes are gone! Holy cow! I'm going home. I've got to get my eyes examined.—*Phil Rizzuto, Yankees broadcaster.*

1281 With this eye of mine, a normal human being would be in the hospital. I've had four specialists work on my foot.... Not my foot. My eye.—*Phil Rizzuto, Yankees broadcaster.*

1282 Well, hi everybody, and welcome to New York Yankee baseball. I'm Bill White...—*Phil Rizzuto, Yankees broadcaster.*

1283 Nolan Ryan is pitching a lot better now that he has his curve ball straightened out.—*Joe Garagiola, broadcaster.*

1284 He's a 6-foot-4-inch, 224-year-old pitcher.—*Harry Caray, Cubs broadcaster, on Marlins reliever Robb Nen, 1994.*

1285 Grounder to Duncan, to Morris, for an unassisted 4–3 double play.—*Joe Nuxhall, Reds broadcaster, 1990.*

1286 That was a complicated play, fans. So we're going to run that down again for you sports fans scoring in bed.—*Bob Kelly, broadcaster.*

1287 That play went 5–4–3 if you're scoring at home—or even if you're watching by yourself.—*Keith Olbermann, broadcaster, 1994.*

1288 Holy Cow!—*Harry Caray, Hall of Fame broadcaster.*

1289 How 'bout that, sports fans?—*Mel Allen, Hall of Fame broadcaster.*

1290 We don't care who wins—as long as it's the Cubs.—*Bert Wilson, Cubs broadcaster.*

1291 He's been a former outfielder most of his career.—*Ross Porter, broadcaster.*

1292 Hi, Curt Gowdy, I'm everybody.—*Curt Gowdy, broadcaster.*

1293 He was originally born in Chicago.—*Curt Gowdy, broadcaster, on Dodgers first baseman Wes Parker, 1966.*

1294 And at the game's end, it's National League 6, American League 4. That score again is American League 6, National League 4.—*Curt Gowdy at the 1971 All-Star Game, July 13. For the record, the AL did win the game, 6-4.*

1295 Luis Tiant comes from everywhere except between his legs.—*Curt Gowdy, broadcaster.*

1296 The Cardinals stole three bases successfully.—*Bob Starr, broadcaster, 1978.*

1297 And Jackson will score easily on that one.—*Al Helfer, broadcaster, on a home run that scored Oakland A's outfielder Reggie Jackson from third base.*

1298 The groan is audible. It can also be heard.—*Harry Caray, broadcaster, during the 1968 World Series.*

1299 *Harry Caray:* Mike Marshall went back to LA to get cocaine for his foot.
Steve Stone: That's novocaine, Harry.

1300 Winfield robbed Armas of at least a home run.—*Bill White, broadcaster, during the 1981 ALCS.*

1301 It's playable—if it stays in play.—*Steve Zabriskie, broadcaster.*

1302 I see in the game in Minnesota that Terry Felton has relieved himself on the mound in the second inning.—*Fred White, broadcaster, looking at an erroneous report that had Felton starting and coming in to relieve, 1982.*

1303 It's another record for the Duke! He's the first person ever to hit his 400th home run on color television.—*Lindsey Nelson, broadcaster, on Mets outfielder Duke Snider, 1963.*

1304 We're having an earth...—*Al Michaels, ABC broadcaster, as an earthquake struck the San Francisco Bay Area before Game 3 of the 1989 World Series, October 17.*

1305 White Sox fans may remember Alan Bannister, who was with the White Sox. When he was with Arizona State, he went with the college All-Star team to Japan, and the Japanese do not slide going into second, and he wound up hitting a Japanese baserunner between the eyes, and in fact killed him. Here's the 2–1 pitch—it's low, a ball...—*Lorn Brown, broadcaster.*

1306 You know, in a few months I'm going to be out of work, and I thought I might as well audition.—*President Ronald Reagan during a television broadcast with his old employer WGN, 1988.*

1307 His prodigious resume had one noticeable blank. He never broadcast a perfect game. But he broadcast thousands of games perfectly.—*Dave Enders, sportswriter, on the retirement of Tigers announcer Ernie Harwell, 2002.*

1308 The reason we call that pitch up and in is because the arms are attached to the shoulder.—*Tim McCarver, announcer.*

1309 That pitch wasn't down and in, that pitch was down and up.—*Tim McCarver, announcer, 2006*

1310 Well, David Eckstein, like most of us, has 20 digits. Ten fingers. Ten toes.—*Tim McCarver, announcer, 2006.*

1311 Watch (Phillies catcher) Darren Daulton use his mitt like a glove.—*Tim McCarver, announcer, 1993.*

1312 One thing about ground balls. They don't go out of the ball park.—*Tim McCarver, announcer, 2004.*

1313 I think Tim Wakefield would even say tonight that Tim Wakefield got to Tim Wakefield tonight.—*Tim McCarver, announcer, during Game 1 of the 2004 World Series, October 23. Wakefield gave up five runs in 3.2 innings while walking five and hitting a batter.*

1314 You don't realize how easy this game is until you get up in that broadcasting booth.—*Mickey Mantle, Hall of Fame outfielder.*

1315 Jose Canseco leads off the third inning with a grand slam.—*John Gordon, Twins announcer.*

1316 Isn't that cute? He kisses her on the strikes, and she kisses him on the balls.—*Curt Gowdy, announcer, on an overly affectionate couple in the stands. (Also attributed to Dizzy Dean.)*

1317 *Howard Cosell*: Ueck, you don't have to get so truculent. You do know what truculent means.
Bob Uecker: Of course, Howard. If you had a truck and I borrowed it, it would be a truck you lent.

1318 Hello, everybody, and welcome to Two Rivers Stadium.—*Hank Greenwald, Giants announcer, after being told to shorten his pregame comments.*

1319 Tom Griffin will be facing the heart of the order. Well, maybe not the heart, maybe the kidneys.—*Hank Greenwald, Giants announcer.*

1320 Let's check the scoreboard, brought to you by Subway sandwiches.... It's still there. —*Hank Greenwald, Giants announcer, during a day game when no other games were taking place.*

1321 How many double plays can the Astros hit into with men on base?—*Bill Worrell, Astros announcer.*

1322 The batter is standing calmly and confidentially at the plate.—*Dizzy Dean, announcer and Hall of Fame pitcher.*

1323 The score is nothing to nothing and nobody's winning.—*Dizzy Dean, announcer.*

1324 He slud into third.—*Dizzy Dean, announcer.*

1325 *Pee Wee Reese:* Diz, you've watched this pitcher out there for four innings, and he's doing a great job. What would you say he's been throwing out there?

Dizzy Dean: Well, Pee Wee, I've been watching him for four innings and I believe that's a baseball he's throwin'.

1326 I've just been informed that the fat lady is the Queen of Holland.—*Dizzy Dean, St. Louis Browns announcer, on Queen Juliana of the Netherlands, who was attending the game.*

1327 The Yankees, as I told you later, are in a slump.—*Dizzy Dean, announcer and Hall of Fame pitcher.*

1328 I don't know how our folks come off callin' this the "Game of the Week." There's a much better game—Dodgers and Giants—over on NBC.—*Dizzy Dean, CBS announcer.*

1329 I can't tell you why there's a delay, but stick your head out of the window and you'll know why.—*Dizzy Dean, announcer, during a rain delay. Due to wartime regulations, radio announcers were not allowed to comment upon the weather for fear of aiding the enemy.*

1330 Don't fail to miss tomorrow's game.—*Dizzy Dean, announcer.*

Jerry Coleman: Padres Announcer and Former Yankees Second Baseman

1331 Hi folks, I'm Johnny Grubb. No I'm not. This is Jerry Coleman.

1332 After five full innings, we're still where we started the day: Padres 2, Phillies 2.

1333 And Kansas City is at Chicago tonight, or is that Chicago at Kansas City? Well, no matter, Kansas City leads in the eighth, four to four.

1334 Ozzie Smith just made another play that I've never seen anyone else make before, and I've seen him make it more than anyone else ever has.

1335 There's somebody warming up in the bullpen, but he's obscured by his number.

1336 Next up is Fernando Gonzalez, who is not playing tonight.—*1979.*

1337 Rich Folkers is throwing up in the bullpen.

1338 Larry Lintz steals second standing up. He slid, but he didn't have to.

1339 Johnny Grubb slides into second with a stand-up double.

1340 (Johnny) Grubb goes back. He's under the warning track. He makes the catch.

1341 There's a fly ball deep to center field. (Dave) Winfield is going back, back.... He hits his head against the wall. It's rolling toward second base.

1342 They throw (Dave) Winfield out at second, but he's safe.

1343 We're all sad to see Glenn Beckert leave. Before he goes, though, I hope he stops by so we can kiss him good-bye. He's that kind of guy.—*1975.*

1344 There's a hard shot to (Johnny) LeMaster, and he throws (Bill) Madlock into the dugout.

1345 (Willie) McCovey swings and misses, and it's fouled back.

1346 On the mound is Randy Jones, the left-hander with the Karl Marx hairdo.

1347 Willie Davis is not as young as he used to be.

1348 Young Frank Pastore may have just pitched the biggest victory of 1979, maybe the biggest victory of the year.

1349 Whenever you get an inflamed tendon you've got a problem. Okay, here's the next pitch to Gene Tendon.—*On a pitch to Padres catcher Gene Tenace.*

1350 We now pause ten stations for a minute identification.

1351 The Phillies beat the Cubs today in the doubleheader. That puts another keg in the Cubs' coffin.

1352 The ex-left-hander Dave Roberts will be going for Houston.

1353 With one out here in the first, Dave Roberts looks a lot better than the last time he pitched against the Padres.

1354 If Rose's streak were still intact, with that single to left, the fans would be throwing babies out of the upper deck.—*1978.*

1355 Enos Cabell started out here with the Astros. And before that he was with the Orioles.

1356 Gaylord Perry and Willie McCovey should know each other like a book. They've been ex-teammates for years now.

1357 The Phillies scored two runs in the fourth, but the Braves countered with one run in the second.—*1993.*

1358 You never want to come right down the middle on 3-and-0, no matter what the count.—*1989.*

1359 Over the course of a season, a miscue will cost you more games than a good play.—*1989.*

1360 George Hendrick simply lost that sun-blown pop-up.

1361 The big ballpark can do it all.

1362 You can't throw a curveball to Tim Wallach. He's been killing the Padres for 15 years on that pitch. For Wallach, that's number.... Wait a minute! What am I doing! That's Eric Karros.—*1994.*

1363 The sky is so clear today you can see all the way to Missouri.—*On a game from Royals Stadium in Kansas City, Missouri, 1987.*

1364 We've got an absolutely perfect day here at Desert Sun Stadium and we're told it's going to be even more perfect tomorrow.—*During spring training.*

1365 If Pete Rose brings the Reds in [first place], they ought to bronze him and put him in concrete.—*On the Cincinnati player-manager, 1985. The Reds finished second behind Los Angeles.*

1366 (John) D'Acquisto has a blister on the index hand of his pitching finger.

1367 Kevin Brown fires, and the bunt is taken by the pitcher for a strike.—*1998.*

1368 A day without newspapers is like walking around without your pants on.

1369 All the Padres need is a fly ball in the air.

1370 The first pitch to Tucker Ashford is grounded into left field. No, wait a minute. It's ball one. Low and outside.—*1977.*

1371 Well, it looks like the All-Star balloting is about over, especially in the National and American Leagues.

1372 At the end of six innings of play, it's Montreal 5, Expos 3.

1373 Mike Caldwell, the Padres' right-handed southpaw, will pitch tonight.

1374 Hector Torrez, how can you communicate with Enzo Hernandez when he speaks Spanish and you speak Mexican?

1375 Billy Almon has all of his in-laws and outlaws here this afternoon.

1376 Gonzo leaps like a giraffe and grabs it.

1377 Our hats go off to drug abusers everywhere.

1378 That noise in my earphones knocked my nose off and I had to pick it up and find it.

1379 There's a soft liner which is caught by the second baseman. And the ball game is over—for this inning.—*1997.*

1380 There's a long fly left centerfield—he got all of that one—it's to the wall, at the wall, and that ball is caught—no, I mean he dropped it—wait a minute, he caught it! That was the best play Greg Vaughn made of his life!

1381 Larry Moffett is six-three, 190. Last year he was six-six.

1382 He can be lethal death.

1383 Davis fouls out to third in fair territory.

1384 There's a shot up the alley. Oh, it's just foul.

1385 Turner pulls into second with a sun-blown double.

1386 Ron Guidry is not very big, maybe 140 pounds, but he has an arm like a lion.

1387 You might want to put this in the back of your craw and think about it.

1388 Sometimes you lose your concentration—but it's part of the game.

1389 I sure hope you're staying alive for the upcoming Dodgers series.

1390 He leaped up to make one of those diving stops only he can make.—*On third baseman Graig Nettles.*

1391 [Sammy] Sosa's a triple threat—run, throw, field, hit, hit for power.—*1997*

1392 Sunday is Senior Citizens' Day. And if you want to become a senior citizen, just call the Padre ticket office.

1393 [Steve] Boros is not with the team today because he's attending his daughter's funeral. Oh, wait, it's her wedding.—*1986.*

1394 You walk into the locker room, and you see players with their ripping muscles and stomachs you could wash your clothes in.

1395 Gene Richards swings—the ball bounces foul and hits him in the head. No harm done.

1396 Thomas is racing for it, but McCovey is there and can't get his glove to it. That play shows the inexperience, not on Thomas' part, but on the part of Willie McC ... well, not on McCovey's part either.

1397 [Manny] Sanguillen is totally unpredictable to pitch to because he's so unpredictable.

1398 Bob Davis is wearing his hair differently this year, short and with curls like Randy Jones wears; I think you call it a Frisbee.

1399 They've taken the foot off Johnny Grubb. Uh, they've taken the shoe off Johnny Grubb.

1400 Tony Taylor was one of the first acquisitions that the Phillies made when they reconstructed their team. They got him from Philadelphia.

1401 I've made a couple of mistakes I'd like to do over.—*1980.*

The Bullpen

1402 I've come to the conclusion that the two most important things in life are good friends and a good bullpen.—*Bob Lemon, Yankees manager, 1981.*

1403 A sense of humor and a good bullpen. —*Whitey Herzog, Royals manager, on what makes a good manager, 1979.*

1404 The intelligence of any manager is magnified in proportion to the failure of the other team's bullpen.—*Bernie Lincicome, sportswriter, 1992.*

1405 That's the best part of it.—*Jim Brosnan, Reds reliever, when asked if the bullpen offers a poor view of the game.*

1406 There are a lot of things that go through your head when you're coming in to relieve in a trouble spot, and one of them is, "Should I spike myself?"—*Lefty Gomez, Yankees pitcher. Gomez won 189 games, primarily as a starter; however, he saved nine games early in his career.*

1407 I took the ball from Greg and I said, "Th-th-th-thanks."—*Larry Andersen, Padres reliever, on manager Greg Riddoch placing him in a ninth-inning, bases-loaded, no-out, one-run-lead situation, 1991. Andersen got the save.*

1408 One of the ways to get some extra time so your bullpen can get ready is to fake a legitimate injury.—*Tony Kubek, broadcaster and former Yankees shortstop.*

1409 He's pressing because he's trying too hard.—*Jim Lefebvre, Cubs manager, on reliever Randy Myers blowing five consecutive save opportunities, 1993. Myers recovered to register an NL record 53 saves for the season.*

1410 A manager uses a relief pitcher like a six-shooter—he fires until it's empty and then takes the gun and throws it at the villain.—*Dan Quisenberry Royals reliever, 1986.*

1411 You can't be thinking about too many things. Relief pitchers have to get into a zone of their own. I just hope I'm stupid enough.—*Dan Quisenberry Royals reliever.*

1412 We're parasites. We live off the people who spend two hours on the field.—*Dan Quisenberry on relief pitchers.*

1413 I want to thank all the pitchers who couldn't go nine innings, and manager Dick Howser, who wouldn't let them.—*Dan Quisenberry, Royals reliever, on winning the AL Fireman of the Year Award with a league-leading 35 saves, 1982.*

1414 I'm just a garbage man. I come in and clean up other people's messes.—*Dan Quisenberry, Cardinals reliever, 1989. Quiz retired the following season with 240 career saves.*

1415 In the bullpen, there's no definite mood. Anything goes down there as long as you remember three basic rules: No women are allowed, don't do crossword puzzles in the open, and hide the food.—*Dan Quisenberry, Royals reliever, 1983.*

1416 When the bullpen phone rings, we just jump up and run in circles. It's like musical chairs when the music ends—whoever doesn't have a seat will go in to pitch.—*Dan Quisenberry, Cardinals reliever, on manager Whitey Herzog's frequent use of the pen, 1989.*

1417 I can't trade myself. I can't release myself. I can only be like a St. Bernard and just hang.—*Dan Quisenberry, Royals reliever, on his reduced role with the team, 1988. Quiz was traded to St. Louis later that season.*

1418 Long relief is like being a plumber. Some days it's okay, but when thirty septic tanks back up, it's no fun at all.—*George Frazier, Cubs reliever.*

1419 We call ourselves bottom feeders. The whole world under-appreciates middle relievers. Everyone looks at the lineup, the starting pitchers and maybe the closer.... We pride ourselves on being the plankton of the baseball world.—*Jeff Zimmerman, Rangers pitcher, on the role of the middle reliever, 1999. Zimmerman gained the rare distinction of being named to the 1999 All-Star Team as a middle reliever and finished third in Rookie of the Year voting.*

1420 Relief pitching is the penthouse or the warehouse. Sometimes you throw three average pitches and get three outs. Then you throw ten good ones, but two or three bad ones, and you end up like I did tonight.—*Jim Kaat, Yankees pitcher, on losing in relief, 1980. Kaat was a starting pitcher his first 21 seasons before moving to the bullpen his final four years.*

1421 It was the first time in a year-and-a-half reporters had talked to me. That's how you know a middle reliever is getting traded.—*Reliever John Habyan on being traded from the Cardinals to the Angels, July 9, 1995.*

1422 I don't have to get dressed until the third inning.—*Tom Waddell, Indians reliever, on the advantage of being a closer, 1985.*

1423 It's the first time I've ever been used for

long relief.—*Dave Smith, Astros reliever, after being urinated on by a Mets fan at Shea Stadium, 1986.*

1424 At least they had all their off-days on the same day.—*Joe Torre, Cardinals manager, on his relief pitching in a 15–5 loss to Houston, 1994. Later that season, the St. Louis bullpen failed to hold an 11–0 lead against the Astros and lost 15–12.*

1425 A lot of guys have that many all by themselves.—*Yogi Berra, Mets manager, on the 14 games saved by his bullpen for the entire 1974 season. Harry Parker, who had a 4–12 record, led the Mets with four saves.*

1426 I think our relievers are a lot like peanut butter and jelly. We're better as a group than we are separately.—*Tom Niedenfuer, Dodgers reliever.*

1427 The only thing wrong with our pitchers is they all have to pitch on the same night.—*Don Osborn, Pirates coach.*

1428 Any more changes and they would have needed a new set of tires for the bullpen car.—*Chuck Cottier, Mariners manager, on a 13–10 win over Milwaukee in which the Brewers used 10 pitchers, 1985.*

1429 At least I didn't have to pay for the calls.—*Art Kusnyer, Oakland A's bullpen coach, on using eight pitchers in one game, five of them in the span of eight pitches, 1994.*

1430 I sure didn't hit any spots. The only spot I hit was the middle of Cabrera's bat.—*Rod Brewer, Cardinals first baseman, on an emergency relief appearance in which he surrendered five runs, including a grand slam to Braves utility player Francisco Cabrera, 1993.*

1431 We've found the perfect short man.—*Dave Smith, Cubs reliever, on 5'7" outfielder Doug Dascenzo, who pitched two perfect innings of relief against Los Angeles, 1991. For the season, Dascenzo made three relief appearances, pitching four innings, allowing two hits, two walks and getting two strikeouts without surrendering an earned run.*

1432 Reynolds just isn't effective going on 1000 days' rest.—*Ray Miller, Pirates pitching coach, on Astros infielder Craig Reynolds getting hit hard in his first emergency relief appearance in three years, 1989.*

1433 We heard someone yelling at us from the second deck. We looked up and they said, "Hey, can you get Uncle Ed's teeth?" Sure enough, the man's dentures had fallen out into the bullpen. Still had pizza on them.—*Bob Patterson, Pirates reliever, 1992.*

1434 It always seems when you get up to warm somebody up, there's only about 1,500 fans in the whole ballpark. But there's always some big fat guy in a white T-shirt, about 310 pounds, who stands right behind the pitcher, eating something and watching him pitch.—*Gary Allenson, Red Sox bullpen coach, 1993.*

1435 I'm a short reliever, and to your relief, I'm being short—I'm finished.—*Gregg Olson, Orioles reliever, speaking at a sports banquet, 1990.*

1436 I'm salad today. I'm just tossing it up there.—*Dennis Eckersley, Oakland A's reliever, to manager Tony LaRussa.*

1437 Your closer is always your favorite player. He's the only guy that if he has a good day, you're guaranteed a win. Your center fielder can hit four home runs, and you might lose. Your starting pitcher can pitch a shutout and not win. Your closer has a good day, he's your favorite player.—*Tony LaRussa, Cardinals manager, 1996.*

1438 The relief pitcher is the one man on a team that can make a manager look like a genius.—*Berdie Tebbetts, Reds manager.*

1439 I think I did a great set-up job. I set up Johnny [Franco] for a save.—*Toby Borland, Mets reliever, on walking the only two batters he faced to start the ninth inning, which allowed Franco to enter the game in a save situation, 1997.*

1440 I told him I wasn't tired. He told me, "No, but the outfielders sure are."—*Jim Kern, Rangers reliever, on being removed from a game, 1979.*

1441 The bullpen is a nice place to visit, but I wouldn't want to live there.—*Bill Singer, Angels pitcher, 1975.*

1442 What they start, I finish.—*Rollie Fingers, Oakland A's reliever.*

1443 Some people say you have to be crazy to be a relief pitcher. Well, I was crazy before I became one.—*Sparky Lyle, Rangers reliever, 1980.*

1444 Why pitch nine innings when you can become just as famous pitching two?—*Sparky Lyle, Rangers reliever, 1980.*

1445 When you go to an opera, you anticipate the tenor at the end. Instead, I'm like some guy who knows the words but can't sing. He just climbs up on stage and finishes the show.—*Doug Jones, Indians reliever, 1990.*

1446 The ultimate reliever would be a Tibetan monk. Standing on the mound, he would raise his hand and direct the ball over the plate simply by using mind over matter.—*Bill Lee, former pitcher.*

1447 We had a very scientific system of bringing in relief pitchers. We used the first one who answered the phone.—*Chuck Estrada, former Rangers pitching coach, 1974.*

1448 Usually we sit in the bullpen and listen to Vin Scully announce the Los Angeles Dodgers games.—*Mark Schaeffer, Padres reliever, 1972.*

1449 Watching Pat Corrales signal for a reliever is like watching a guy with no money in his pocket reach for a restaurant check, desperately hoping somebody will come along and save him.—*Moss Klien, sportswriter, on the Indians bullpen, 1987.*

1450 A lot of them are ashamed to tell their parents what they do. The only nice thing about it is that you get to wear a uniform like everybody else.—*Jim Bouton, former pitcher, on long relievers, 1981.*

1451 *Earl Weaver:* [Before Game 6 of the 1971 World Series] I want you to be ready. Be ready to warm up around the eighth inning.

Dave Leonhard: I'm honored you're contemplating using me in a World Series game.

Weaver: I ain't using you. I just want [Jim] Palmer to see you warming up so he can pitch better.

1452 The difference between relief pitching when I did it and today is simple: there's too much of it. It's one of those cases where more is not necessarily better.—*Bob Feller, Hall of Fame pitcher.*

1453 If I were a commissioner, I'd petition for eight-inning games.—*Lou Piniella, Mariners manager, on his atrocious bullpen, September 1997. Despite the late-inning struggles, Seattle won the AL West but lost in the Division Series to the Orioles.*

1454 Look at Goose. He's 6-foot-4 and most of it is fat. He pitches maybe an inning a week, and for that they pay him a million dollars a year. You know what? He's worth it.—*Rudy May, Yankees pitcher, on closer Goose Gossage.*

1455 I was mowing my lawn during the baseball strike. I got the front yard done and about half the back, and then I kept waiting for Goose Gossage to come out and finish it for me.—*Tommy John, Yankees pitcher, 1981.*

1456 Here is how we're going to run tonight's show. I'm going to be hosting for eight commercials, and then we bring in Mariano Rivera.—*David Letterman, talk show host, 2009.*

1457 I get the ball, I throw the ball and then I take a shower.—*Mariano Rivera, Yankees closer, on his job description.*

1458 There's not much to do but put the voice mail on the phone—*Chad Durbin, Phillies reliever, on what it's like in the bullpen whenever Roy Halladay starts, 2010.*

The Business Section

1459 Baseball is too much of a sport to be a business and too much of a business to be a sport.—*Phillip Wrigley, Cubs owner.*

1460 Baseball isn't a business; it's more like a disease.—*Walter O'Malley, Dodgers owner.*

1461 Is baseball a business? If it isn't, General Motors is a sport.—*Jim Murray, sportswriter.*

1462 We are constitutionally opposed to the creation of young sports millionaires.—*John Fetzer, Tigers owner, 1978.*

1463 For a hundred years the owners screwed the players. For 25 years the players have screwed the owners. They've got 75 years to go.—*Jim Bouton, former pitcher.*

1464 I'm going to write a book—*How to Make a Small Fortune in Baseball.* You start with a large fortune.—*Ruly Carpenter, Phillies president, 1976.*

1465 It's the only industry where owners try to outdo each other every season by announcing who lost the most money.—*Bill Lankhof, sportswriter, on baseball, October 2002.*

1466 Gee, should I believe a magazine that spends 365 days a year researching finances or a guy with zero credibility?—*Denny Hocking, Twins infielder, on a report in* Forbes *that said 20 of the 30 major league teams made money in 2001 compared to a report from Commissioner Bud Selig that said most teams were financially ailing, 2002.*

1467 Let's just say that if I had to choose between putting my trust with the Gambino crime family or a group of MLB team owners, I'd be eating fagioli every night of the week.—*Norman Chad, sportswriter, on the claim that owners lost $232 million, April 2002.*

1468 I have a hard time believing athletes are overpriced. If an owner is losing money, give it up. It's a business. I have trouble figuring out why owners would stay in if they're losing money.—*Reggie Jackson, Hall of Fame outfielder.*

1469 You keep the salary, I'll take the cut.—*Lefty Gomez, Yankees pitcher, to owner Jacob Ruppert who wanted Gomez to take a $12,500 salary cut (from $20,000 to $7,500), 1935.*

1470 Either you give me what I demand, or I'll take what you're offering.—*Joe Torre, Cardinals third baseman, on his contract demands after winning the 1971 NL MVP.*

1471 I got a million dollars worth of free advice and a very small raise.—*Eddie Stanky, Brooklyn Dodgers second baseman, on contract negotiations with GM Branch Rickey, 1945.*

1472 He told me it was too much money, to take it back and reconsider. We came back and offered $5,000 less, and he signed.—*Paul Snyder, Braves scout, on signing Dale Murphy as their top draft pick, 1974. Murphy was signed as a catcher before becoming a two-time MVP outfielder.*

1473 That kind of bothered my dad at the time, because he didn't have that kind of money to pay out. But eventually he scraped it up.—*Bob Uecker, former catcher, on signing with the Milwaukee Braves for $3,000.*

1474 My father looked at the check and then told the scout, "Throw in another hundred and you can take the rest of the family."—*Joe Dugan, former third baseman, on receiving a $500 contract.*

1475 I don't worry about hitting as much as I do about other things in life, like money.—*Willie McGee, Giants outfielder, 1994.*

1476 The will to win is worthless if you don't get paid for it.—*Reggie Jackson, Yankees outfielder, 1981.*

1477 He wants Texas back.—*Tommy Lasorda, Dodgers manager, on the contract demands of Mexican-born pitcher Fernando Valenzuela, 1981.*

1478 All last year we tried to teach him English, and the only word he learned was "million."—*Tommy Lasorda, Dodgers manager, on the contract holdout of pitcher Fernando Valenzuela, 1982. The Mexican-born Valenzuela won the Cy Young and Rookie of the Year in 1981, and in 1983 he became the first player awarded $1 million in salary arbitration.*

1479 Fernando Valenzuela now makes one million dollars a year. Three years ago, Valenzuela's alarm clock was a rooster.—*Tommy Lasorda, Dodgers manager.*

1480 I pay that much for a backup shortstop. —*Drayton McLane, Astros owner, on learning the highest paid college and university presidents make about $500,000 a year, 1993.*

1481 I believe there are certain things that cannot be bought: loyalty, friendship, health, love and an American League pennant.—*Edward Bennett Williams, Orioles owner.*

1482 There are two classes of people whose wealth is always exaggerated by the great public. They are actors and ballplayers.—*King Kelly, White Sox catcher, 1880s.*

1483 In the movies, the stars get all the money. The others get scale.—*Walter Matthau, actor, on the key difference between Hollywood salaries and baseball salaries, 1990. Matthau played Coach Morris Buttermaker in* The Bad News Bears *(1976).*

1484 People don't blink when Paul Newman gets paid millions to make a movie, or Frank Sinatra to sing. Why not a ballplayer? It's like a lot of other professions. The money is just there.—*Ray Boone, Tigers infielder.*

1485 I don't think Johnny Carson got a lot of hate mail when he signed for $5 million. Bruce Sutter probably did. Why? Well, Johnny's a lot funnier than Bruce. I mean, Bruce is a wonderful guy, but his Karnak is weak.—*Steve Stone, Orioles pitcher, 1980.*

1486 Jimmy Connors plays two tennis matches and winds up with $850,000, and Muhammad Ali fights one bout and winds up with five million bucks. Me, I play 190 games—if you count exhibitions—and I'm overpaid!—*Johnny Bench, Reds catcher.*

1487 People say we should be paying our nurses more. I agree, but don't blame Don Mattingly because we're not paying our nurses more.—*George Will, columnist, 1990.*

1488 Do you know why the .213-hitting shortstop of the Pirates who drove in 11 runs in 122 games last year doesn't want to be President of the United States? Because he doesn't want to take a pay cut.—*Gene Collier, sportswriter, comparing Rafael Belliard's $225,000 salary to George Bush's $200,000, 1989.*

1489 How can there be a recession in America when Rafael Belliard earns $450,000 a year?—*Bob Hertzel, sportswriter, 1991.*

1490 Come January 2001, the salary of the president of the United States will double to $400,000, which means that finally, the person with arguably the most important job in the world will earn roughly what the Pirates pay Keith Osik to catch as infrequently as possible.—*Gene Collier, sportswriter, 2000.*

1491 That's like Al Capone speaking out for gun control.—*Blackie Sherrod, sportswriter, on comments by Braves owner Ted Turner that baseball salaries are too high, 1986.*

1492 That's more than the Clinton administration is going to spend on arms.—*Don McMillan, comedian, on the $64.5 million in contracts for Braves pitchers Greg Maddux, Tom Glavine and John Smoltz, 1993.*

1493 I don't know whether I signed him or he signed me.—*Alva Bradley, Indians president, on pitcher Bob Feller's $32,500 contract, 1940.*

1494 We were gold dust twins. Tim got the gold, I got the dust.—*Phil Gagliano, Cardinals utility player, on catcher Tim McCarver who signed with St. Louis for a $75,000 bonus, 1959.*

1495 I'll be making more than Jimmy Carter, but not as much as Billy Carter.—*Ron Guidry, Yankees pitcher, on his new contract.*

1496 Ballplayers and deer hunters are alike. They both want the big bucks.—*Larry Doughty, Pirates GM, 1990.*

1497 *Walter Briggs (Tigers owner):* You're asking for too much money. When I was your age, I had two children and was making twenty-five dollars a week.

Hank Greenberg (Tigers first baseman): That's why I'm asking for so much now. When I'm your age, I could have two children and be making twenty-five dollars a week.

1498 It has options through the year 2020 or until the last *Rocky* movie is made.—*Reliever Dan Quisenberry on his contract with the Giants, 1990. Quisenberry retired that season after five appearances and the release of* Rocky V. *Quisenberry died in 1998, before the release of* Rocky Balboa *in 2006, which remains the final Rocky film—for now...*

1499 It's kind of discouraging to realize I'm the lowest-paid member of the Yale class of '56.—*Ken MacKenzie, Mets pitcher, 1962. Manager Casey Stengel responded to MacKenzie's complaint by noting that he also had the highest ERA of any Yale graduate.*

1500 The front office will make up his salary on one good weekend. They can make up my salary with a rainout.—*Danny Frisella, Mets reliever, on the acquisition of outfielder Willie Mays from the San Francisco Giants for $50,000, 1972.*

1501 I'd like to go home to San Diego or Los Angeles/Anaheim, but I'll play in New York, Chicago, Africa, wherever the money is.—*Barry Bonds, Pirates outfielder, 1992. Bonds signed a six-year, $43.75-million contract with San Francisco.*

1502 I got here a couple of days early, but I'm anxious for the workouts to begin. I need the meal money.—*Bill Haas, Mets pitcher, on reporting early to spring training, 1964. Haas never made it to the majors.*

1503 My biggest problem in the big leagues is that I can't figure out how to spend $43 a day in meal money.—*Andy Van Slyke, Cardinals outfielder, 1983.*

1504 Nobody ever gives you meal money in real life.—*Phil Niekro, Braves pitcher.*

1505 I lose money on the golf course in the morning, and I lose money in the afternoon taking my wife shopping, then I go to the dog track at night and lose some more.—*Earl Weaver, former Orioles manager, on his retirement, 1984.*

1506 If they're losing $798,000, they might as well make it $799,000 and give me another $1,000.—*Alan Gallagher, San Francisco Giants third baseman, on his contract demands. Known as "Dirty Al," his given name was Alan Mitchell Edward George Patrick Henry Gallagher.*

1507 The truth was, I would have played for nothing. Of course, I never told Connie that.—*Lefty Grove, former Philadelphia A's pitcher, on team owner and manager Connie Mack.*

1508 I don't have a contract problem. The only problem with mine is where to put the decimal point.—*Orel Hershiser, Dodgers pitcher, 1986.*

1509 I'm not going to ask for more money; I'll just wait and let them come and insist I take a raise.—*Bo Belinsky, Angels pitcher, after starting his rookie season 5–0 with a no-hitter, 1962.*

1510 I haven't invested my money yet. No CDs, IRAs, annuities. I don't want my money to mature before I do.—*Eric Hillman, Mets pitcher, 1994.*

1511 If Tom Paciorek will guarantee his performance, we will guarantee his contract.—*George Argyros, Mariners owner.*

1512 I know if they make me an offer like that, I'm asking them to pass me the pen or, at least, prick my finger and I'll sign in blood. —*Andy Van Slyke, Pirates outfielder, on teammate Bobby Bonilla rejecting a four-year, $15.5-million contract, 1991.*

1513 For Brewer general manager Sal Bando, giving in to that clause must have been like agreeing to not eat seal blubber for Lent.—*Peter Gammons, sportswriter, on an incentive clause in DH Brian Harper's contract that would pay him $50,000 if he won a Gold Glove Award, 1994.*

1514 Mickey Mantle wanted to bet me $10,000 he could beat me in a race. I told him, "Mickey, I don't make $10,000."—*Pedro Ramos, former All-Star pitcher. Ramos, who led the AL* *in losses four straight years (1958–1961), was frequently used as a pinch runner and hit 15 home runs in his career.*

1515 If I were the White Sox, I'd reassign Error Jordan to a new minor-league team every other week.—*Woody Woodburn, sportswriter, on outfielder Michael Jordan who bought a new bus for the Double-A Birmingham Barons, 1994.*

1516 Some sad news. Former major league outfielder Ethan Allen has passed away at the age of 89. The timing is awful because he just signed a two-year, $4-million deal to play for the Mets.—*David Letterman, talk show host, 1993.*

1517 When will all the madness finally end? Hopefully, right after the first $1-million-a-year Baltimore Sun baseball writer.—*Peter Schmuck,* Baltimore Sun *baseball writer, 1990.*

1518 She is now.—*Chuck Tanner, Pirates manager, when asked if his aunt, Alyce Bartberger, who won $2.5 million in the Pennsylvania lottery, was his favorite aunt, 1984.*

1519 *Stan Williams (Reds coach, 1990):* There are utility players sitting on the bench today who make more money in one year than I have made in my 35-year career—including coaching, World Series shares, everything.

Lou Piniella (Reds manager): And you were still overpaid.

1520 Terry, you can ask for more money in the winter and do less in the summer than any ballplayer I know.—*John McGraw, New York Giants manager, to first baseman Bill Terry.*

1521 Any company that invests in the Chicago Cubs has a view of the future we cannot even begin to comprehend.—*Jeff MacNelly, cartoonist, on the sale of the Cubs to the* Chicago Tribune, *1982.*

1522 Any day a club owner doesn't like the club or is losing money, all he has to do is look for someone else with a ton of money and a ton of ego, sell it to him for a big profit, take the capital gains and go live on a mountain.—*Bob Feller, Hall of Fame pitcher, 1985.*

1523 My position is that while the players don't deserve all that money, the owners don't deserve it even more.—*Jim Bouton, former All-Star pitcher, 1993.*

1524 Sure it's nice to win, but there is only one thing that's important to me, and that's the money that we're going to get, win or lose. It's a business with me, and I refuse to lie to all the Little Leaguers and try to con them. I don't love baseball, I like it. And to me baseball means money, and that's all I care about.—*Vida Blue, Oakland A's pitcher.*

1525 I enjoyed the coaching part, but I'm the first to say I'm doing it for the money. You hear people say it's not about the money? That's bull. I'm doing it for the money.—*John Kruk on quitting his coaching position in the Phillies organization to take a job as a television analyst, 2001.*

1526 My goal is to take the club to arbitration when I'm 50—and win. That is unless they sign me to a long-term contract when I'm 49.—*Jerry Koosman, 42-year-old Phillies pitcher, 1985.*

1527 Whose lifetime, yours or mine?—*Whitey Herzog, Cardinals manager, on being offered a lifetime contract by 85-year-old owner Augie Busch, 1984.*

1528 I think for me, $84 million would have to be for 168 years, and I don't know if I can give that kind of service time. My kids would have to work for the Twins, too.—*Mike Trombley, Twins reliever, on catcher Mike Piazza turning down an $84-million contract from the Dodgers, 1998.*

1529 Ninety-one million dollars is an awful lot of money, but don't kid yourself. For Mr. Piazza, this is not an easy paycheck. This man, for the next seven years, has to attend every single Mets game.—*David Letterman, talk show host, on the contract signed by Mets catcher Mike Piazza, 1998.*

1530 Let me give you an idea how much money that is, because it's hard for people to break that down to an hourly wage. By the time he gets a sign from his brain to scratch his groin, he's made $1,600.—*Jay Leno, talk* *show host, on Mariners outfielder Ken Griffey Jr's, $8.5-million-per-year contract, 1996.*

1531 Dutchman, some friends of mine are starting a company they think will do well. It's a drink, and the stock is selling for something like a quarter a share. I'm going to buy some, and if you have any spare money lying around, give it a try.—*Ty Cobb, Tigers outfielder, advising Yankees third baseman Fritz Maisel to invest in Coca-Cola. Maisel ignored the tip that helped make Cobb a millionaire.*

1532 I was in Vietnam. A big payroll doesn't always win.—*Sandy Alderson, Oakland A's president, on his low-budget team winning a series over the high-priced Orioles, 1998.*

1533 No court in the world can make a Gene Autry or a George Steinbrenner give a player three million dollars. The courts cocked the gun. It's the owners who pulled the trigger.—*Ruly Carpenter, Phillies president, on the skyrocketing salaries paid by the owners due to free agency.*

1534 There are exceptions, but mainly these guys don't care where they play. Wave a few extra million in their face and they will live on the moon.—*Johnny Oates, Rangers manager, on free agency, 1999.*

1535 I don't understand this. I don't mind the little Nike swoosh or whatever that is, but I wouldn't want to see players wearing so many ads they look like race car drivers.—*Jerry Reinsdorf, White Sox owner, on the possibility of advertising being sold on uniforms, 1999.*

1536 Money chasing is the great American game. Professional baseball is based on money chasing.—*John B. Sheridan, sportswriter. 1922.*

1537 Baseball is a public trust, not merely a money-making industry.—*Ford Frick, baseball commissioner.*

1538 Champions cost money.—*Connie Mack, Philadelphia A's owner. Mack sold off the players on his 1915 and 1923 teams because salaries were too high.*

1539 We live by the Golden Rule. Those who have the gold make the rules.—*Buzzie Bavasi, baseball executive.*

1540 There's a lot more future in hamburgers than in baseball.—*Ray Kroc, Padres owner and founder of McDonald's.*

1541 Oakland has now increased its payroll to the point that it now ranks third in the Bay Area among all McDonald's franchises.—*Sandy Alderson, major league baseball executive vice president of operations, on the financially challenged A's, 2000.*

1542 Once Montreal has to pay its players more than minimum wage, it drops out of the bidding. That's the only team in major league baseball where taking a job at Burger King is considered a lateral move.—*Tony Kornheiser, sportswriter, 1997.*

1543 Ninety percent I'll spend on good times, women and Irish whiskey. The other ten percent I'll probably waste.—*Tug McGraw, Phillies reliever, on how he intended to spend his $75,000 salary, 1975.*

1544 I had a better year than he did.—*Babe Ruth, Yankees outfielder, when asked if he felt guilty about making $5,000 more than President Herbert Hoover, 1930.*

1545 Wives of ballplayers, when they teach their children their prayers, should instruct them to say: "God bless Mommy, God bless Daddy, God bless Babe Ruth. Babe Ruth has upped daddy's paycheck by fifteen to forty percent."—*Waite Hoyt, Yankees pitcher.*

1546 Stan and I get along very well. He goes his way and I go mine. Stan goes to the deposit window, and I go to the credit department.—*Charley James, Cardinals outfielder, on outfielder Stan Musial, 1963.*

1547 You know, they say money talks. But the only thing it ever says to me is good-bye.—*Paul Waner, Pirates outfielder.*

1548 Making money is easy; knowing what to do with it becomes a problem.—*Ring Lardner, sportswriter.*

1549 I had a problem with money. I couldn't hold on to any.—*Willie Davis, Dodgers outfielder.*

1550 The more money you have, the more

problems you have. I never knew I had so many relatives.—*Don Baylor, Angels outfielder, 1980.*

1551 The only thing I like about money is that it brings a grin to mom's face. It's not that she cares so much about it, it's just that she thought I would wind up busted.—*Dick Allen, White Sox first baseman, 1973.*

1552 With the money I'm making, I should be playing two positions.—*Pete Rose, Reds third baseman, 1977.*

1553 With all the money I make now, I don't get my uniform any less dirty than when I was nine years old. The only difference is that my mother used to wash it.—*Pete Rose, Phillies first baseman.*

1554 Playing baseball for a living is like having a license to steal.—*All-Star Pete Rose.*

1555 Pete doesn't count his money anymore. He weighs it.—*Stan Musial, Hall of Fame outfielder, on Phillies first baseman Pete Rose, 1981.*

1556 Remember when I used to say I wanted to be the first $100,000 singles hitter? This year I paid over $100,000 in state taxes.—*Pete Rose, Reds manager, 1987.*

1557 What you've got to have in baseball is pitching, speed and money.—*Ted Turner, Braves owner, 1981.*

1558 I read where he was embarrassed by the $4.5 million Atlanta offered. I didn't want to add to his embarrassment.—*Tom Grieve, Rangers GM, on free agent first baseman Bob Horner, 1987.*

1559 My objective right now, of course, is money. I want money because I want the titles that go underneath—leader, professional, man and winner. Henry Aaron is the best ballplayer around today. He's got all those things, and I want them, too.—*Reggie Jackson, Oakland A's outfielder, on being named 1973 AL MVP.*

1560 I'll probably get a million more than I should, but I didn't make the rules. I'm just taking advantage of them.—*Reggie Jackson, Orioles outfielder, on becoming a free agent, 1976.*

1561 Most people can't afford to live where I live, and that's why I live there.—*Reggie Jackson, Angels outfielder.*

1562 Money let's you live better. It doesn't make you play better.—*Reggie Jackson, Angels broadcaster, 1990.*

1563 George Steinbrenner is going to have to make me a millionaire, too, so I can speak to all my players on the same level.—*Billy Martin, Yankees manager, 1977.*

1564 I hear he's so rich he bought his dog a boy.—*Billy Gardner, Twins manager, on new owner Carl Pohlard, 1984.*

1565 I'm proud of them and happy they don't have to work for a living.—*Phil Niekro Sr., father of Braves pitcher Phil and Astros pitcher Joe, 1979.*

1566 You can't get rich sitting on the bench—but I'm giving it a try.—*Phil Linz, Yankees infielder.*

1567 I get $1,000 for every old-timer game. By playing seven times a year, I make as much playing baseball as I did in 1951 as a rookie.—*Minnie Minoso, former White Sox outfielder, 1990.*

1568 If I made a million dollars, I would come in at six in the morning, sweep the stands, wash the uniforms, clean out the offices, manage the team and play the game.—*Duke Snider, Hall of Fame outfielder, 1980.*

1569 We're still about two Cadillacs apart.—*Ken Holtzman, Cubs pitcher, on negotiations for a new contract, 1968.*

1570 If I were sitting down with George Steinbrenner and, based on what Dave Winfield got for his statistics, I'd have to say, "George, you and I are about to become partners."—*Joe DiMaggio, Hall of Fame outfielder, on what kind of salary he would command if he were playing in 1981.*

1571 A Yankee pitcher should never hold out because he might be traded, and then he would have to pitch against them.—*Waite Hoyt, Yankees pitcher.*

1572 When you're walking to the bank with

that World Series check every November, you don't want to leave. There were no Yankees saying play me or trade me.—*Hank Bauer, former Yankees outfielder.*

1573 Players no longer have to be dedicated because performance doesn't always dictate what the salary will be. If a player doesn't have to have a super year to collect a big salary, the motivating factor is missing.—*Frank Robinson, Orioles coach, 1979.*

1574 It's like going to an auction, seeing an old moose head and buying it on the spur of the moment. Then, when you get it home, it looks hideous and you wonder why you bought it. I don't want to denigrate the players in this year's draft, but I think a lot of teams bought a lot of ugly moose heads.—*Harry Dalton, Brewers GM, on the free agent draft, 1979.*

1575 I'm glad I didn't get a bonus. I think you're supposed to get paid after you do your job.—*Bob Feller, Hall of Fame pitcher.*

1576 I knew I was in trouble when the arbitrator asked what we meant by such symbols as IP, BB and ERA.—*Greg Minton, Giants reliever, 1986.*

1577 If I do something nobody's ever done, who can they compare me to in arbitration?—*Barry Bonds, Pirates outfielder, on becoming the first player ever to hit .300, drive in 100 runs, score 100 runs, hit 30 home runs, and steal 50 bases in a single season, 1990.*

1578 No problem. I was either going to wake up rich or richer.—*Mike Norris, Oakland A's pitcher, on accepting a $325,000 contract through salary arbitration instead of the $450,000 he was seeking, 1981.*

1579 For him to say there are no hard feelings is like Brutus telling Julius Caesar there are no hard feelings after he stabbed him.—*George Steinbrenner, Yankees owner, on catcher Rick Cerone winning a salary arbitration case against the club, 1981.*

1580 I want to pitch my way right into arbitration.—*Joe Decker, Twins pitcher, 1975.*

1581 Isn't it amazing that we're worth so much on the trading block and worth so little when we talk salary with the general manager?—*Jim Kern, Indians reliever, 1978.*

1582 Right now, 10 percent of the baseball players are making all the money. The rest are jealous.—*Joe Burke, Royals GM, 1979.*

1583 The first principle of contract negotiation is don't remind them of what you did in the past; tell them what you're going to do in the future.—*Stan Musial, Cardinals first baseman.*

1584 All I'm asking for is what I want.—*Rickey Henderson, all-time stolen base leader.*

1585 I don't mind paying a player, but I don't want to pay for his funeral.—*Pat Gillick, Blue Jays executive, on a demand for a three-year contract by 39-year-old DH Rico Carty, 1979. Toronto declined and Carty retired.*

1586 I'm the most loyal player money can buy.—*Don Sutton, free agent pitcher, 1980.*

1587 Wherever I go, the pitchers' salaries increase so much there's nothing left for me.—*Johnny Sain, White Sox pitching coach, 1973.*

1588 A well-paid slave is a slave nonetheless.—*Curt Flood, All-Star outfielder, on challenging baseball's reserve clause, 1969.*

1589 Before all this free agency came into being, a lot of fellows playing ball said we were "slaves." Well, what are you doing when you go through free agency? You're selling yourself as if you were a slave. That doesn't interest me at all.—*Rod Carew, Twins first baseman, 1978.*

1590 The concept of the reserve clause seems to be that it's sort of slavery. I don't know many slaves getting $150,000 for six months' work. Is anybody who voluntarily enters the slavery system really suffering? I don't think so.—*Walter O'Malley, Dodgers owner, 1976.*

1591 In Mexico, you get 100 pesos meal money. That's four American dollars a day. In the big leagues, you have to tip that much a day.—*Vic Davallio, Dodgers outfielder, 1978.*

1592 Not much money, but I no want to work, so I play baseball.—*Mario Soto, Reds* *pitcher, on signing for $1,000 in the Dominican Republic, 1977.*

1593 One dollar back home buys five beers. People will look at me like a rich man.—*Andres Galarraga, Expos first baseman, on his home town of Caracas, Venezuela, 1988.*

1594 AIG has assets over $1 trillion.... Has anybody ever had $1 trillion and still failed? OK, besides the New York Yankees.—*Jay Leno, talk show host, 2008.*

1595 Some of the Astros' promotions next season at Enron Field reflect a trend to cut costs for the troubled energy company—Flashlight Doubleheaders.—*Alan Ray, comedy writer, on the collapse of Enron, 2001. Enron Field was renamed Astros Field for the 2002 season before Minute Maid bought the naming rights.*

1596 You can have money stacked to the ceiling, but the size of your funeral is still going to depend on the weather.—*Chuck Tanner, Pirates manager, 1978.*

1597 Who says there's an unemployment problem in this country? Just take the five percent unemployed and give them a baseball stat to follow.—*Andy Van Slyke, Pirates outfielder.*

1598 People think we make $3 million and $4 million a year. They don't realize that most of us only make $500,000.—*Pete Incaviglia, Rangers outfielder, 1990.*

1599 The hitter asks the owner to give him a big raise so he can go somewhere he's never been, and the owner says, "You mean third base?"—*Henny Youngman, comedian.*

1600 If they want to pay me like Mike Gallego, I'll play like Gallego.—*Rickey Henderson, Athletics outfielder, on the light-hitting Oakland second baseman.*

1601 Gas is up and so am I.—*Manny Ramirez, free agent outfielder, when asked about his value on the open market after helping the Dodgers get to the playoffs, 2008. Manny eventually re-upped with Los Angeles for $45 million over two years.*

1602 With the price of gas these days, I would have preferred they'd gone to Tiffany's—*Joe Maddon, Rays manager, on having his debit card stolen and used to buy gas, 2008.*

1603 Investing is like batting in baseball, except that you get as many pitches as you want and you never have to swing. Wait for the home run ball before investing.—*Warren Buffett, billionaire and minority owner of the Triple-A Omaha Royals.*

1604 I am loath to criticize my fellow geniuses, and not all of the clubs participated in the orgy. But some of the guys are going to rue the day they paid out so much money in long-term contracts.... Some of these guys are lucky to be playing baseball, let alone signing million-dollar contracts.—*John Moores, Padres owner, on free agent contracts of over $1 billion.*

1605 Alex Rodriguez gets a $100,000 bonus for being a starter on the American League All-Star Team. What, exactly, are the Texas Rangers paying him $25.2 million a season to do?—*Ron Cook, sportswriter, 2001. Rodriguez made the All-Star squad 12 times from 1996 to 2009, failing to make the team in 1999 and 2009.*

1606 That's rough. But I'll take the boos for $25 million.—*Milton Bradley, Athletics outfielder, on hearing that Yankees third baseman Alex Rodriguez gets booed at Yankee Stadium, 2006.*

1607 It was a dollar well spent.—*Terry Mulholland, Twins pitcher, on having his contract purchased for a buck, 2004. Mulholland went 5–9 for Minnesota.*

1608 Coaches are getting together to buy time shares in it.—*Grady Little, Red Sox manager, on pitcher John Burkett trying to sell his 2000 Porsche 911 Turbo for $96,500, 2003.*

1609 Twelve million dollars in Tennessee? He might as well be Donald Trump.... That's a lot of generic-brand beer and a lot of NASCAR tickets. You know how many lures you can buy at Wal-Mart with $12 million?—*Todd Jones, Tigers reliever, on the contract that former teammate Jamie Walker signed with the Orioles in the offseason, 2007.*

1610 No, my name is Mike.—*Mike Hampton, Braves pitcher, when asked by a student at* *his old elementary school if he was rich, 2003. Hampton made $9.5 million the previous season with Colorado.*

1611 It's like smokers suing the cigarette companies or the obese people suing McDonald's. Nobody forced them to overspend.—*Mike Piazza, Mets catcher, on owners blaming players for making them spend too much money, 2002.*

1612 Bud Selig says the players' greed is killing us. That's a little like the customer saying of the lap dancer, "She just won't leave me alone."—*Mitch Albom, sportswriter, 2001.*

1613 My best year was 1965, when I made $21,000—and $17,000 of that came from selling other players' equipment.—*Bob Uecker, broadcaster.*

1614 I hear a player say, "How can I be paid $5 million less than Player B?" My response to this is, "How can you make $11 million more than Willie Mays?"—*Todd Zeile, Mets first baseman, 2001.*

1615 The main thing is to have an owner with a billion dollars.—*Chipper Jones, Braves third baseman, on the secret of success, 2001.*

1616 I thought the Yankees did well—given their financial constraints.—*Terry Mulholland, facetious Twins pitcher, on losing to New York in the 2004 Divisional Series.*

1617 It used to be, people would ask me for $10. Now they ask for $40,000.—*Torii Hunter, Twins outfielder, on how life as changed since signing a $34-million contract, 2003.*

1618 What's breathtaking this time is the majestic size of the blunder the Rangers have pulled. At least when they blunder, they supersize it, Texas style. This takes the French off the hook for the Louisiana Purchase.—*Thomas Boswell, writer, on the signing of Alex Rodriguez for $252 million.*

1619 If Alex Rodriguez had just been given a quarter of a billion to play for the Cubs or Sox, would fans be lamenting baseball's financial ruin? No, they would be counting the days until spring training.—*Skip Bayless, sportswriter, 2000.*

1620 We've never been in that position. We wouldn't know how to operate. I mean, do we get him a corsage?—*Billy Beane, Athletics GM, on why his small-market franchise didn't court free agent Alex Rodriguez, 2000.*

1621 George Steinbrenner says the Rangers hurt baseball by giving A-Rod all that money. That's rich! Steinbrenner giving lessons in fiscal prudence! [...] That's like Darryl Strawberry advising players on how to avoid drugs and alcohol.—*Scott Ostler, sportswriter, on the 10-year, $252-million contract given to shortstop Alex Rodriguez, 2001. Steinbrenner traded Alfonso Soriano to Texas for A-Rod before the 2004 season (although the Rangers did agree to pay $67 million of the remaining $179 million left on the contract). After the 2007 season, the Yankees finalized a new 10-year, $275 million contract for Rodriguez ... plus incentives.*

1622 Do I feel stupid. I only asked the Indians for two Greyhound bus tickets a year and a hot dog stand in front of Jacobs Field.—*David Segui, free agent first baseman, on the perks negotiated into the Alex Rodriguez contract, 2000. He eventually signed a 4-year, $28-million deal with Baltimore. And for all that money, the Orioles got multiple DL stints, 18 homers, and 97 RBI—total.*

1623 The New York Yankees lead all teams with a record payroll of $126 million, with the Boston Red Sox coming in second at $108 million. A Red Sox official defended his payroll, saying: "You have to spend money to come close to winning, then slip back, then appear to win again, then ultimately choke and dash the hopes of millions of fans."—*Jon Stewart, comedian, 2002.*

1624 If I get this job, we'll stay in Five-Star hotels. If I don't, we'll stay in youth hostels.—*Pete Mackanin, Reds interim manager, on a trip to Europe with his wife that he planned for the 2007 offseason. The Reds hired Dusty Baker to manage in 2008 and Mackanin became Phillies bench coach in 2009.*

1625 You know, after seeing them in the playoffs all these years, I've got to admit it. These Yankees play the game like it's meant to be played by players other teams can't afford.—*Jim Armstrong, sportswriter, 2001.*

1626 In a collect call to FoxSports.com, a Devil Ray spokesperson said the report was completely inaccurate.—*Randy Hill, sportswriter, on reports that Tampa Bay might not have enough money to cover payroll costs, 2001.*

1627 This just in—the New York Yankees have purchased Peru.—*Jerry Greene, sportswriter, 2000.*

1628 Because the Mets and Yankees don't have to travel to another city for the World Series, they're saving about $200,000 each. Which in stadium dollars amounts to two hot dogs and four beers.—*Conan O'Brien, talk show host, 2000.*

1629 They make money the old-fashioned way: They let Jose gamble with it.—*Keith Olbermann, broadcaster, on Canseco Financial Group, a mortgage and financial investments firm run by the Devil Rays DH, 2000.*

1630 Lou Gehrig's farewell-speech jersey has sold for $400,000, which makes the buyer The Looniest Man on the Face of the Earth.—*Greg Cote, sportswriter, December 1999.*

1631 You can no longer buy a beat-up Bronco from a beat-up Bronco.—*Scott Ostler, sportswriter, on Florida Marlins owner Wayne Huizenga buying all of John Elway's car dealerships, 1997.*

1632 People ask me why we didn't sign David Cone. Heck, we can't even afford an ice cream cone.—*Jim Leyland, Pirates manager, on his financially strapped team, 1995.*

1633 It's possible to spend money anywhere in the world if you put your mind to it, something I proved conclusively by running up huge debts in Cincinnati.—*Leo Durocher, former Reds shortstop (1930–1933).*

1634 I went back to Philly to talk contract with Mr. Nugent. My hotel and food cost me more while I was there negotiating than the raise I got.—*Kirby Higbe, pitcher, on Phillies owner Gerald Nugent who owned the team from 1931 to 1942.*

1635 Fans are mad at us because we make so much money, then they throw money at us—quarters, nickels. Why? Throw me a tax audit. Throw me your electric bill.—*Andy Van Slyke, Pirates outfielder.*

1636 These guys are so rich I'm surprised they don't play the game on horseback. And in pith helmets. It's got to be easy to strike out a guy worried about the federal re-discount rate.—*Jim Murray, sportswriter, 1980.*

1637 Maybe he'll pay for some cab rides.—*Paul Assenmacher, Cubs reliever, on second baseman Ryne Sandberg, who had just signed a $7-million contract, 1992.*

1638 I don't fine players. These days if I fine a $4-million player $400, he's liable to tip me $200.—*Jim Leyland, Marlins manager.*

1639 The financial careers of most professional athletes can be summed up in these words: short and sweet—but mostly short.—*Willie Mays, Mets outfielder, 1972.*

Agents

1640 A complete ballplayer today is one who can hit, field, run, throw and pick the right agent.—*Bob Lurie, Giants owner, 1981.*

1641 These days baseball is different. You come to spring training, you get your legs ready, your arm loose, your agent ready, your lawyer lined up.—*Dave Winfield, Yankees outfielder.*

1642 When they smile, blood drips off their teeth.—*Ted Turner, Braves owner, on agents.*

1643 They have an argument with their wives, they've got to call their agent to settle it.—*John McMullen, Astros owner, on ballplayers, 1990.*

1644 I don't need an agent. Why should I give somebody 10 percent when I do all the work?—*Mark "The Bird" Fidrych, Tigers pitcher, 1977.*

1645 After all those years, I felt like I owed him the benefit of the doubt. It turns out he got all the benefit, and I got the doubt.—*Joe*

Oliver, Reds catcher, on why he didn't fire his agent even though his salary went down each year, 1997.

1646 This deal indicates that major league baseball is healthy, Kevin Mitchell is wealthy and the Giants are wise.—*Joe Sroba, agent, after inking a four-year, $15-million contract extension for his client, 1990.*

1647 We had statistics showing he was the third-best pitcher in the league. They had a chart showing he was the sixth-best pitcher on the Red Sox.—*Bob Woolf, agent, on negotiating a contract for Red Sox reliever Bob Stanley.*

1648 Not that agent Scott Boras' 65-page testament to Alex Rodriguez's greatness is syrupy or anything, but it begins, "He was born in a hospital, but it was near a manger."—*Jim Armstrong, sportswriter, 2000.*

1649 McGwire walks away from a $30 million, two-year contract extension—while his agent walks away from a new Porsche and a summer home in East Hampton.—*Craig Kilborn, talk show host, on the retirement of Cardinals first baseman Mark McGwire, November 2001.*

Strike!

1650 The owners and the players are well-matched antagonists. Both are so greedy and self-serving that neither group can evoke much sympathetic support in the outside world.—*Arthur Daley, sportswriter, before the 1972 players' strike.*

1651 This strike was never for the Hank Aarons, Carl Yastrzemskis or Willie Mayses. It was for the four-year players who pass up college, spend three to five years to make the majors and have a career ruined by a dead arm or leg.—*Howard Cosell, broadcaster, on the 1972 players' strike.*

1652 Money is not the issue. The real issue is the owners' attempt to punish the players for having the audacity not to crawl.—*Marvin Miller, executive director of the players' association, on the 1972 players' strike.*

1653 Never in the history of baseball have so many refused to play for so much.—*Frank Cashen, Orioles executive, on the high number of player holdouts, 1972.*

1654 The handwriting is on the wall, but these athletes can't read.—*Charlie Finley, Oakland A's owner, during the 1976 labor dispute.*

1655 I think it's basically like any labor problem; nobody talks about it until the last minute. If it's trash, you wait until the stink gets too bad. If it's coal, you wait until black lung disease sets in. If it's nuclear energy, you wait until Joan Baez shows up.—*Dan Quisenberry, Royals reliever, on the 1981 strike.*

1656 Sport and business go together like oysters and chocolate sauce. That is to say, not very palatably.—*Joseph Epstein, writer, on the 1981 baseball strike.*

1657 O, Sovereign Owners and Princely Players, masters of amortization, tax shelters, bonuses and deferred compensation, go back to work. You have been entrusted with the serious work of play, and your season of responsibility has come.—*A. Bartlett Giamatti, President of Yale University, on the 1981 baseball strike.*

1658 Americans are being bombarded with television reruns and old movies. Divorce rates are soaring as husbands and wives are being forced to pay attention to each other.—*New York Senator Alphonse D'Amato on why he introduced a Senate resolution calling for an end to the 1981 baseball strike.*

1659 Everyone is losing in this strike, whether it's the fans, the players, the owners and even the nation as a whole. When you get right down to it, the really sad thing is that no one is winning.—*Ken Griffey, Reds outfielder, on the 50-day baseball strike of 1981.*

1660 If Bowie Kuhn were alive today, this strike would never have occurred.—*Peter Gammons, sportswriter, 1981. Kuhn was commissioner at the time.*

1661 You can only watch boxing and rugby on ESPN for so long.—*Willie Wilson, Royals outfielder, on predicting the fans would return after the 1985 strike, which was resolved after two days.*

1662 I am not a romantic. I don't think you can be, in my position. Unlike many people, I don't think American culture will collapse if baseball collapses.—*Donald Fehr, negotiator for the baseball players union, 1990.*

1663 Let me get this straight. The owners are about to shut down baseball when it's more prosperous than it's even been, and the players are the ones who have to get their urine tested? —*Ron Darling, Mets pitcher, on the eve of the 1990 lockout.*

1664 I'm the kind of player they're trying to weed out.—*Jack Morris, Indians pitcher, on baseball's labor situation, 1994. Morris was released two days before the strike.*

1665 I'm rich. What am I supposed to do, hide it?—*Lou Whitaker, Tigers second baseman, on arriving in a stretch limo for a players' union meeting during the 1994 baseball strike.*

1666 There's a better chance of the United States returning to a monarchy.—*Agent Tom Reich on the likelihood of players accepting a salary cap, 1994.*

1667 The two things people like about August are baseball and no Congress. Somehow I think we got this wrong.—*Vice President Al Gore on the baseball strike and the passage of the Crime Bill, 1994.*

1668 We're committed. Or about to be committed.—*Bob Klaus, vice president of Ohio radio station WJMP, which played "Take Me Out to the Ballgame" nonstop during the 1994 baseball strike.*

1669 We're just in a situation where we picked a bad year to have a good year.—*Ken Griffey Jr., Mariners outfielder, on how tremendous seasons by he and White Sox first baseman Frank Thomas were jeopardized by the baseball strike, 1994. The Big Hurt won the AL MVP over Griffey in the strike-shortened season.*

1670 I don't think there's going to be a work stoppage. I don't think anybody's that dumb. If they do walk out, make sure it's September 11. Be symbolic. Let [Players Union Head] Donald Fehr drive the plane right into the building, if that's what they want to do.—*Jim Bowden, Reds GM, 2002. The Reds later released a statement apologizing for Bowden's poor choice of metaphor.*

Crossing the White Line

1671 I do not recall one instance where baseball has allowed either race, creed or color to enter into its selection of players.—*John Heydler, NL president, 1933.*

1672 Get that nigger off the field.—*Cap Anson, Chicago White Stockings player-manager, on Toledo (Northwestern League) catcher Moses Fleetwood Walker, 1882.*

1673 Baseball is biding its time and waiting for the social change which is inevitable. Times are changing.—*Ford Frick, NL president.*

1674 I have seen many Negro players who should be in the major leagues. There is no room in baseball for discrimination. It is our national pastime and a game for all.—*Lou Gehrig, Yankees first baseman.*

1675 If managers were given permission, there'd be a mad rush to sign up Negroes.—*Gabby Hartnett, Cubs manager, 1940.*

1676 There's a couple of million dollars' worth of talent on the loose, ready for the big leagues, yet unsigned by any major league. Only one thing is keeping them out of the big leagues, the pigmentation of their skin.—*Shirley Povich, sportswriter, 1941.*

1677 There is no rule, formal or informal, or any understanding—unwritten, sub-terranean, or sub-anything—against the hiring of Negro players by the teams of organized ball.—*Kenesaw Mountain Landis, baseball commissioner, 1942.*

1678 The greatest untapped reservoir of raw

material in the history of our game is the black race.—*Branch Rickey, Brooklyn Dodgers GM, on signing Jackie Robinson, 1946.*

1679 I had to get a man who would carry the burden on the field. I needed a man to carry the badge of martyrdom. The press had to accept him. He had to stimulate a good reaction of the Negro race itself, for an unfortunate one might have solidified the antagonism of other colors. And I had to consider the man's teammates.—*Branch Rickey, Brooklyn Dodgers GM, on the criteria for choosing Jackie Robinson to be the first black player in the major leagues.*

1680 *Jackie Robinson:* Are you looking for a Negro who is afraid to fight back?

Branch Rickey: No. I'm looking for a ballplayer with the guts enough not to fight back.

1681 The Negro Leagues are doing all right, and Negro players should be developed and then remain as stars. This thing won't work out.—*Rogers Hornsby, Hall of Fame infielder, on the signing of Jackie Robinson.*

1682 I do not mind public criticism. That sort of thing has not changed any program I thought was good.—*Branch Rickey, Dodgers GM.*

1683 I used to tell Jackie sometimes when they were throwing at him, "Jackie, they aren't throwing at you because you are black. They are throwing at you because they don't like you."—*Pee Wee Reese, Hall of Fame shortstop, on teammate Jackie Robinson.*

1684 It was probably the only day in history that a black man ran from a white mob with love instead of lynching on its mind.—*Sam Martin, sportswriter, on the crowd that chased Montreal Royals second baseman Jackie Robinson after winning the minor league championship, 1946.*

1685 Robinson will not make the major leagues. He is a thousand-to-one shot at best. The Negro players simply don't have the brains or the skill.—*Jimmy Powers, sportswriter, 1946.*

1686 The only people who seemed to recognize that giving Robinson a chance was right, or even fair, were Rickey and me, and believe me I had to do a lot of talking to make sure the other owners didn't do something really stupid. Some actually wanted me to throw Rickey, great as he was, out of the game.—*Happy Chandler, former baseball commissioner.*

1687 I told Mr. Rickey that someday I was going to have to meet my maker, and if He asked me why I didn't let that boy play and I said it was because he was black, that might not be a satisfactory answer.—*Happy Chandler on Jackie Robinson, 1947.*

1688 Honey, if you come out to Ebbets Field today, you won't have any trouble recognizing me. My number is 42.—*Jackie Robinson, Brooklyn Dodgers first baseman, to his wife Rachel, before his first ballgame, 1947.*

1689 I don't care if the guy is yellow or black or if he has stripes like a fucking zebra. I'm the manager of this team, and I say he plays.—*Leo Durocher, Brooklyn Dodgers manager, on the arrival of Jackie Robinson, 1947.*

1690 I'm not putting my team on the same field with that nigger.—*Connie Mack, Philadelphia A's owner-manager, on having to play an exhibition game against the Brooklyn Dodgers and Jackie Robinson, 1947. The teams played as scheduled.*

1691 I do not care if half the league strikes. Those who do will encounter quick retribution. All will be suspended, and I don't care if it wrecks the National League for five years. This is the United States of America, and one citizen has as much right to play as another.—*Ford Frick, NL president, in a statement directed to members of the Cardinals who threatened to strike because of Jackie Robinson, 1947.*

1692 As long as the Pittsburgh club hasn't signed a Negro, there's no need for me to worry.—*Spud Davis, Pirates catcher.*

1693 We were all white.—*Richie Ashburn, former outfielder for the 1950 NL Champion Phillies, when asked why the team never won another pennant, 1984.*

1694 Before that black son of a bitch accuses

us of being prejudiced, he should learn how to hit an Indian.—*Casey Stengel, Yankees manager, after Brooklyn Dodgers second baseman Jackie Robinson struck out three times on nine pitches against Allie Reynolds in the 1952 World Series.*

1695 His bunts, his steals and his fake bunts and fake steals humiliated a legion of visiting players. He bore the burden of a pioneer and the weight made him strong. If one can be certain of anything in baseball, it is that we shall not look upon his like again.—*Roger Kahn, sportswriter, on Hall of Fame second baseman Jackie Robinson.*

1696 I had to fight hard against loneliness, abuse and the knowledge that any mistake I made would be magnified because I was the only black man out there. Many people resented my impatience and honesty, but I never cared about acceptance as much as I cared about respect.—*Jackie Robinson, Hall of Famer, 1972.*

1697 When I finally get a nigger, I get the only one who can't run.—*Casey Stengel, Yankees manager, on Elston Howard, the first African American to play for New York, 1955.*

1698 Every time I look at my pocketbook, I see Jackie Robinson.—*Willie Mays, Hall of Fame outfielder.*

1699 The only change is that baseball has turned Paige from a second-class citizen into a second-class immortal.—*Satchel Paige on being named to the Hall of Fame's new wing for players from the Negro Leagues, 1971.*

1700 People say it's a shame he never pitched against the best. But who's to say he didn't?—*Negro League star Buck O'Neil at the funeral of Hall of Fame pitcher Satchel Paige, 1982.*

1701 If they ever let him play ball in a small place like Ebbets Field or old Fenway Park, Josh Gibson would have forced baseball to rewrite the rules. He was, at the minimum, two Yogi Berras.—*Bill Veeck, White Sox owner.*

1702 Wake up, Dad, you've just made it in.—*Josh Gibson Jr., on his late father's induction to the Hall of Fame, 1972.*

1703 Baseball is very big with my people. It figures. It's the only time we can get to shake a bat at a white man without starting a riot.—*Dick Gregory, social activist and comedian, 1962.*

1704 I don't think there ever will be a black manager in the major leagues. Baseball's attitudes haven't changed since Jackie Robinson first signed in 1946.—*Bill White, broadcaster and former first baseman, 1974. Frank Robinson was hired as player-manager by the Indians later that year, and White became the first African-American president of the NL in 1989.*

1705 I don't think baseball should be exceptionally proud of this day. It's been long overdue.—*Bowie Kuhn, baseball commissioner, on the hiring of Frank Robinson by the Indians as baseball's first African-American manager, 1974.*

1706 If I had one wish in the world today, it would be that Jackie Robinson could be here to see this happen.—*Frank Robinson on being named manager of the Indians, October 3, 1974. Jackie Robinson died in 1972.*

1707 It's nice to come into town and be referred to as the manager of the Cleveland Indians instead of as the first black manager.—*Frank Robinson, Indians manager, 1975.*

1708 I think a lot of teams are afraid that if they fire their manager, someone is going to make them hire a black one.—*Bob Gibson, Hall of Fame pitcher, noting that no managers had been fired midway through the 1987 season. Frank Robinson returned to managing with Baltimore in 1988 and Cito Gaston was hired by Toronto in 1989.*

1709 I don't want to take anything away from Dr. King. He was a close personal friend of mine. But through baseball, Jackie did more to tear down segregation in hotels and sports arenas than any other man. Nobody will ever do more, because it won't ever be necessary again.—*Don Newcombe, former pitcher, on Jackie Robinson, 1976.*

1710 At the time, I didn't know baseball from ping-pong. We had been told every day of our lives a lie: That we couldn't make it. This showed that regardless of skin color, ethnicity, and all the things that determine a person's worth, all of us have the capacity to reach out for the stars. He did.—*Bishop Desmond Tutu on Jackie Robinson, 1997.*

1711 We have trouble because we have so many Negro and Spanish-speaking ballplayers on this team. They are just not able to perform up to the white ballplayers when it comes to mental alertness.—*Alvin Dark, Giants manager, on the 1964 team that featured future Hall of Famers Willie Mays, Orlando Cepeda, Willie McCovey, and Juan Marichal.*

1712 I'll tell you why we came to Minnesota. It was when I found out you only had fifteen thousand blacks here. Black people don't go to ballgames, but they'll fill up a wrassling ring and put up such a chant it'll scare you to death.... We came here because you've got good, hard-working white people here.—*Calvin Griffith, Twins owner, on why he moved the franchise in 1960 from Washington, D.C., to Minneapolis, October 1, 1978.*

1713 It's hard to say, because of the color situation. Every player we have outside [Doug] Frobel is black. We might have to trade for a white player. You can't play nine blacks, I don't think. I don't think you can play nine blacks in any big city.—*Howie Haak, Pirates scout, May 17, 1982.*

1714 I'm not saying it's a racial thing, but that seems to be the case in sports these days. When a ballclub can, they replace a George Foster or a Mookie Wilson with a more popular white player.—*George Foster, Yankees outfielder, 1986.*

1715 It's just that they may not have some of the necessities to be a manager. I don't know. How many quarterbacks are there? How many pitchers?—*Al Campanis, Dodgers executive, on blacks in the majors, April 6, 1987. Campanis was fired two days later.*

1716 Having Dick Kraft as your community relations person is like having Attila the Hun on your community's welcome wagon.—*Fernando Ferrer, Bronx Borough president, after the Yankees vice president of community affairs likened the youth of the Bronx to monkeys, 1994. Kraft resigned days later, citing health problems.*

1717 I'd like to be a minority owner—no pun intended—after I retire.—*Reggie Jackson, Angels outfielder.*

1718 When Henry came up, I heard fans yell, "Hit that nigger. Hit that nigger." Henry hit the ball up against the clock. The next time he came up, they said "Walk him, walk him."—*Herb Aaron, father of Milwaukee Braves outfielder Henry Aaron.*

1719 I've taken a lot of crap from a lot of people. Probably more than anybody in the history of this sport. I know Hank [Aaron] and Jackie [Robinson] took a good deal of crap, but I guarantee it wasn't for six years. I just keep thinking: How much am I supposed to take?—*John Rocker, former reliever.*

1720 The only difference between me and those other great Yankees is my skin color.—*Reggie Jackson, Hall of Fame outfielder.*

1721 After Jackie Robinson, the most important black in baseball history is Reggie Jackson. I really mean that.—*Reggie Jackson, Hall of Fame outfielder.*

1722 If a Latin player or even an American Negro is sick, they say it is all in the head. Felipe Alou once went to his team doctor and the doctor said, "You don't have anything." So he went to a private doctor and the doctor said, "You have a broken foot."—*Roberto Clemente, Pirates outfielder.*

1723 I don't see why you reporters keep confusing Brooks and me. Can't you see we wear different numbers.—*Frank Robinson, Orioles outfielder, on teammate Brooks Robinson.*

1724 I am pleased that God make my skin black, but I wish He had made it thicker.—*Curt Flood, former outfielder, on challenging baseball's reserve clause, 1969.*

1725 Baseball put me in multiracial situations at a very early age. It was there that I realized that we will not fulfill our ideal until we can see deeper than skin color to the individual.—*Senator Bill Bradley, former NBA star, 2002.*

Defense

1726 Catching the ball is a pleasure; knowing what to do with it is a business.—*Tommy Henrich, Yankees outfielder.*

1727 The phrase "off with the crack of the bat," while romantic, is really meaningless, since the outfielder should be in motion long before he hears the sound of the ball meeting the bat.—*Joe DiMaggio, Hall of Fame outfielder.*

1728 What's a baseball fundamental? It's any baseball act that is so simple that the man in the stands thinks, "I could do that. Why can't those big leaguers?"—*Ken Singleton, Orioles outfielder, 1980.*

1729 A great catch is like watching the pretty girls go by—the last one you see is always the prettiest.—*Bob Gibson, Cardinals pitcher, 1964.*

1730 The way to get a ball past Honus is to hit it eight feet over his head.—*John McGraw, New York Giants manager, on Pirates shortstop Honus Wagner.*

1731 In the beginning, I used to make one terrible play a game. Then I got so I'd make one a week, and finally I'd pull a bad one about once a month. Now I'm trying to keep it down to one a season.—*Lou Gehrig, Yankees first baseman.*

1732 Willie Mays and his glove: where triples go to die.—*Fresco Thompson, Dodgers executive.*

1733 I didn't know whether to shit or go blind.—*Harvey Kuenn, Giants outfielder, on witnessing center fielder Willie Mays make an over-the-shoulder catch.*

1734 Harvey Kuenn gave it an honest pursuit, but the only center fielder who could have caught it, hit it.—*Bob Stevens, sportswriter, on Willie Mays hitting a triple in the All-Star Game, July 7, 1959.*

1735 Wertz hit the ball a long way. But it was to straight center in the Polo Grounds, and you could hit 'em a long way.... I turned my back and ran, looked over my shoulder once to gauge the flight of the ball, then kept running. I caught it the way a football end catches a long leading pass. Then I spun and threw.—*Willie Mays, Hall of Fame outfielder, on "The Catch," which was made in Game 1 of the 1954 World Series, September 19. Mays robbed Indians first baseman Vic Wertz of an extra-base hit.*

1736 But the throw! What an astonishing throw to make all other throws ever before it, even the four Mays himself had made during fielding practice, appear the flings of teenage girls. This was the throw of a giant, the throw of a howitzer made human.—*Arnold Hano, sportswriter, on the throw that followed "The Catch" by Willie Mays to complete a double play in the 1954 World Series.*

1737 Mays threw so many base runners out he may lead the entire Giants infield in assists. He should play in handcuffs to even things up a bit.—*Jim Murray, sportswriter, on Willie Mays.*

1738 I can't very well tell my batters don't hit it to him. Wherever they hit it, he's there anyway.—*Gil Hodges, Mets manager, on Giants outfielder Willie Mays.*

1739 There is nobody who ever played second base like he did. Ever. I had the hardest job in baseball for 10 years. I had to back him up on every play, and he never let a ball get through. But I still had to back him up.—*Bill Virdon, former Pirates outfielder, on Hall of Fame second baseman Bill Mazeroski, 2001.*

1740 I'm beginning to see Brooks in my sleep. If I dropped this paper plate, he'd pick it up on one hop and throw me out at first.—*Sparky Anderson, Reds manager, on the outstanding defensive plays made by third baseman Brooks Robinson in the 1970 World Series.*

1741 He can throw his glove out there and it will start ten double plays by itself.—*Sparky Anderson, Reds manager, on Orioles third base-*

man Brooks Robinson after the 1970 World Series.

1742 He's not at his locker yet, but four guys are over there interviewing his glove.—*Rex Barney, broadcaster, on reporters looking to interview Orioles third baseman Brooks Robinson during the 1970 World Series.*

1743 Look, I like hitting fourth and I like the good batting average, but what I do every day behind the plate is a lot more important because it touches so many more people and so many more aspects of the game.—*Thurman Munson, Yankees catcher.*

1744 He plays like he's on a mini-trampoline or wearing helium kangaroo shorts.—*Andy Van Slyke, Pirates outfielder, on Cardinals Gold Glove shortstop Ozzie Smith.*

1745 I want to thank Bert for giving up all those 400-foot fly balls so I could go way back and make those catches that helped get me elected.—*Hall of Fame inductee Kirby Puckett, on former Minnesota teammate Bert Blyleven, 2001.*

1746 Most people don't understand catchers. For example, Jerry Grote is a catcher who hits. Johnny Bench is a hitter who catches. There is a big difference.—*Joe Torre, Mets infielder, 1975.*

1747 He's the only defensive catcher in baseball who can't catch.—*Casey Stengel, Mets manager, on catcher Chris Cannizzaro, 1963.*

1748 He calls for the curve ball too much. He can't hit it, so he figures nobody else can.—*Casey Stengel, Mets manager, on catcher Chris Cannizzaro.*

1749 Has anybody ever satisfactorily explained why the bad hop is always the last one? —*Hank Greenwald, Giants broadcaster.*

1750 When a fielder gets a pitcher into trouble, the pitcher has to pitch himself out of a slump he isn't in.—*Casey Stengel, Hall of Fame manager.*

1751 Watching Yogi Berra play third base is like watching a man trying to put up a tent in a windstorm.—*Red Smith, sportswriter, on the Yankees experimenting with their catcher at third, 1954.*

1752 I'll tell you why he's a good hitter. He's a good hitter because he hates the ball, and when the pitcher throws the ball, he wants to hurt it. In fact, he hates the ball so much that when he's in the outfield and they hit one towards him, he won't go near it.—*Casey Stengel, Yankees manager, on outfielder Lou Skizas, 1956.*

1753 Some right fielders have rifles for arms, but he had a howitzer.—*Tim McCarver, Cardinals catcher, on Pirates outfielder Roberto Clemente.*

1754 His only limitation is his ability to move around.—*Joe Torre, Cardinals manager, on first baseman-outfielder Pedro Guerrero, 1992.*

1755 Pepe Mangual can drop anything he gets his hands on.—*Jack Lang, sportswriter, on the Mets outfielder, 1976.*

1756 He is improving in the outfield. To be sure, he hasn't caught a ball yet, but he's getting closer to them.—*Gordon Cobbledick, sportswriter, on Orioles outfielder Dave Nicholson. A pure power hitter, Nicholson has the distinction of being the easiest player to strike out—averaging one for every 2.48 at-bats. In 1964, while playing for the White Sox, Nicholson hit the longest home run ever recorded—573 feet.*

1757 Jorge Orta never got acquainted with his glove, never met a ground ball he liked.—*Paul Richards, White Sox manager, on his outfielder-third baseman, 1976.*

1758 You won't make any errors. You don't get to a ball until it stops rolling.—*Joe Lovitto, Rangers outfielder, in response to a statement by teammate Jeff Burroughs that one of his goals was to win a Gold Glove; however, Burroughs did win AL MVP in 1974.*

1759 He was no intellectual giant, but he understood better than anybody the rule that says you can't be charged with an error if you don't touch the ball. And so he assiduously avoided touching anything that looked difficult.—*Edward Bennett Williams, Orioles president, on former White Sox first baseman Zeke Bonura. Because he rarely attempted to field his position,*

Bonura led AL first basemen in fielding percentage in 1936.

1760 This has got to be the worst first baseman who ever lived. He doesn't wave at balls, he salutes them.—*Jimmy Dykes, White Sox manager, on Zeke Bonura.*

1761 Any time you see a fielder get under a ball and pound his glove—even in Little League—you know he's going to catch it. I have seen Rhodes pound his glove and have the ball fall 20 feet behind him.—*Leo Durocher, New York Giants manager, on outfielder Dusty Rhodes.*

1762 He did not always catch fly balls on the top of his head, but he could do it in a pinch. He never tripled into a triple play, but he once doubled into a double play, which is the next best thing.—*John Lardner, sportswriter, on Brooklyn Dodgers outfielder Babe Herman.*

1763 Never once did I get hit on the head by a fly ball. Once or twice on the shoulder maybe, but never on the head.—*Babe Herman, Brooklyn outfielder, on his defense.*

1764 If I put him in the line-up every day, he can hit .400, if he sets his mind to it. But he'll lose the club two to three games a week with his glove.—*Otto Miller, Brooklyn Dodgers coach, on outfielder Babe Herman. Miller also managed Herman with the Atlanta Crackers in 1923.*

1765 *Babe Herman (Brooklyn outfielder, 1931):* It's a helluva note to dress with a .250 hitter.

Fresco Thompson (Dodgers infielder): How do you think I feel dressing with a .250 fielder?

1766 He wore a glove for only one reason: It was a league custom. The glove would last a minimum of six years because it rarely made contact with the ball.—*Fresco Thompson, Brooklyn Dodgers executive (and 1931 Dodgers teammate), on outfielder Babe Herman, who led the league in errors at first base in 1927 and the outfield in 1928.*

1767 I've seen better hands on a clock.—*Mel Durslag, sportswriter, on watching Dodgers shortstop Bill Russell commit five errors in one doubleheader.*

1768 When you field a ball, it sounds like Big Ben at one o'clock—bong!—*Rollie Fingers, Oakland A's reliever, to outfielder Reggie Jackson.*

1769 Our fielders have to catch a lot of balls—or at least deflect them to someone who can.—*Dan Quisenberry, Royals reliever, 1984.*

1770 Soccer players play the ball off their shins, thighs, ankles, knees, chests, hips, shoulders, and heads. When he plays left field for the Phillies, so does Pete Incaviglia.—*Mike Penner, sportswriter, 1994.*

1771 He has a glove contract with U.S. Steel.—*Charlie Hough, Rangers pitcher, on outfielder Pete Incaviglia, who led AL outfielders in errors, 1986.*

1772 Gross currently leads the American League in fielding balls with his face.—*Thomas Boswell, writer, on Orioles third baseman Wayne Gross, 1985.*

1773 I hope Stuart doesn't think that means him.—*Danny Murtaugh, Pirates manager, on error-prone first baseman Dick "Dr. Strangeglove" Stuart, following a public address announcement stating that anyone interfering with a ball in play would be ejected from the stadium.*

1774 Errors are part of my image. One night in Pittsburgh, thirty thousand fans gave me a standing ovation when I caught a hot dog wrapper on the fly.—*Dick Stuart, former first baseman.*

1775 He has trouble with the thrown ball. —*Charlie Manuel, Charlotte Knights manager, on the defensive liability of DH Sam Horn, who occasionally tried to play first base, 1994.*

1776 Our goal is to get him through one game without having to use his batting helmet in the outfield.—*Nick Leyva, Phillies manager, on rookie outfielder Wes Chamberlain, 1991.*

1777 You've got to hang onto the ball. We have doctors, we have plastic surgeons, but we can't replace outs.—*Sparky Anderson, Tigers manager, to outfielder Billy Bean, who dropped a fly ball after colliding with the outfield wall, 1988.*

1778 The game is supposed to be: you pitch it, you hit it, you catch it. The game was never meant to be: you pitch it, you hit it and then you catch up with it later.—*Sparky Anderson, Tigers manager, on the team's defense, or lack thereof, 1993.*

1779 They made more mistakes than Ross Perot's barber.—*Chris Myers, broadcaster, on the Mets making six errors in one game, 1994.*

1780 They should have called a welder.—*Richie Ashburn, Phillies broadcaster, on seeing the glove of Mets first baseman Dave Kingman getting fixed, 1982.*

1781 I didn't know if he was playing baseball or soccer.—*Lou Piniella, Seattle Mariners manager, on second baseman Rich Amaral, 1994.*

1782 [Mark] Koenig got a hit on a ground ball that would have been an easy out for any first baseman that was not so much of a recluse as Joe Harris.—*Ring Lardner, sportswriter, on the defense during the Yankees sweep of the Pittsburgh Pirates in the 1927 World Series.*

1783 Some players have warning track power. Foster has warning track defense. As soon as his foot hits the warning track, he stops.—*Ray Shore, Phillies scout, on Mets outfielder George Foster, 1984.*

1784 If you prefer baseball in slow motion, don't miss George Foster chasing a double into the left-field corner.—*Charles Bricker, sportswriter.*

1785 I look at a guy like George Foster and I think, if I'm a bad fielder, where does that place him?—*Jack Clark, Giants outfielder, 1982.*

1786 He reacted to the ball with the speed of a sedated hippo.—*Lowell Cohn, sportswriter, on Giants outfielder Jack Clark.*

1787 The toughest part about playing left field is staying awake.—*Carlton Fisk, White Sox catcher, on being converted to an outfielder, 1986. Fisk played 31 games in the outfield before returning to catcher full-time the next season.*

1788 In center field you've got too much time to think about everything but baseball.—*Joe Pepitone, Yankees outfielder, who later split time between the outfield and first base.*

1789 At 30, Moreland has run out of positions to misplay.—*Bill Conlin, sportswriter, on Cubs outfielder Keith Moreland, who also played at least a dozen games at third base, first base and catcher, 1986.*

1790 It will come on *Wide World of Sports* right after the guy who falls off the ski slope.—*Alan Knicely, Cardinals catcher, on a play in which he was hit on the head after missing a popup, 1986.*

1791 Tonight I'm going to sleep in my crouch. —*Sandy Alomar Jr., Indians catcher, on playing all 19 innings in a 7–5 loss to Boston, 1992.*

1792 They had a better defense at Pearl Harbor.—*Andy Van Slyke, Pirates outfielder, on Pittsburgh's league-worst defense, 1989.*

1793 When he punched Keith Hernandez in spring training last season, it was the only time Darryl Strawberry hit the cutoff man all year.—*Steve Wulf, sportswriter, on the troubled Mets outfielder, 1989.*

1794 Having Marv Throneberry play for your team is like having Willie Sutton play for your bank.—*Jimmy Breslin, columnist, on the Mets first baseman, 1962.*

1795 He was a genius at turning victory into defeat, a puller of boners, a wondrously bad judge of which base to throw to, a juggler of grounders, and a dropper of pop flies. He was not simply a Met; he was *the* Mets.—*Lindsey Nelson, Mets broadcaster, on first baseman Marv Throneberry.*

1796 We were going to give you a cake, but we thought you'd drop it.—*Richie Ashburn, Mets outfielder, to Marv Throneberry on his 29th birthday, 1962.*

1797 Is it okay if I wear a chest protector and shin guards under my uniform?—*John Russell, Phillies outfielder, after making two errors in one game at first base, 1985.*

1798 I used to look out and see [Ralph] Kiner practicing his batting stroke, [Hank] Sauer chewing tobacco and [Frankie] Baumholtz taking oxygen.—*Joe Garagiola, broadcaster and former Cubs catcher, on Chicago's 1954 outfield.*

1799 As a pinch-hitter, if you're 1-for-4, you're doing your job. Defensively, they won't let you go 1-for-4. I've tried it.—*Alan Bannister, Rangers utility player, 1985. As the starting shortstop for the White Sox in 1977, Bannister led the majors with 40 errors.*

1800 I am not going to close my eyes this year when I go after pop-ups.—*Paul Casanova, Washington Senators catcher.*

1801 Al's was an aerodynamic pirouette. Mine was brutal stupidity.—*Turner Ward, Pirates outfielder, comparing a diving catch by teammate Al Martin to a catch made by Ward in which he crashed through a wooden outfield fence, 1998.*

1802 It played Pinball Wizard with my legs. It lit up all my bones and won a free game.—*Dan Quisenberry, Royals reliever, on being hit by a Wade Boggs line drive.*

1803 Sometimes it seems like he's playing underwater.—*Vin Scully, Dodgers broadcaster, on Los Angeles third baseman Bobby Bonilla, 1998.*

1804 I owe him a lot. Nobody would know how good I was at digging balls out of the dirt if it wasn't for him and all those bad throws.—*Mark Grace, Cubs first baseman, on shortstop Shawon Dunston. In 1986, Dunston not only led the NL in errors, but also in putouts, assists, double plays, and total chances per game.*

1805 The CIA is looking into acquiring the services of Cubs shortstop Shawon Dunston. They believe he could overthrow Nicaragua.—*Mark Maxham, sportswriter, 1989.*

1806 Richard just picked up a hot-dog wrapper at shortstop. It's the first thing he's picked up all night.—*Harry Caray, White Sox broadcaster, on an error-filled game by Lee "Bee Bee" Richard, 1971.*

1807 You miss a ball like that in Little League and you throw your glove down and start crying.—*Paul O'Neill, Yankees outfielder, on a three-base error, 1997.*

1808 I thought I had it. I was twisting around like this. It grazed my glove, hit me on the head, and bounced over. I'll be on ESPN for about a month.—*Jose Canseco, Rangers outfielder, on a ball hit by Indians corner infielder Carlos Martinez that bounced off his head and over the fence for a home run, May 26, 1993. Thanks to YouTube, this blooper will be played every day until the end of time.*

1809 The World Cup is coming to Dallas. Jose was just practicing.—*Jeff Huson, Rangers infielder, on a fly ball that bounced off outfielder Jose Canseco's head and over the wall for a home run, May 26, 1993.*

1810 Don't hit it to me.—*Jose Canseco, Red Sox outfielder, on how to improve the team's defense, 1996.*

1811 If I'd played all of my career in the outfield, I'd have 500 homers and 600 errors.—*Jose Canseco, Devil Rays DH, 1999.*

1812 What did he win, five Gold Gloves? I don't think I have five of anything, not even shoes.—*Greg Norton, White Sox third baseman, on comparisons to former Chicago third baseman Robin Ventura, who was playing for the Mets, 1999.*

1813 One year I led the National League in errors. They named a vitamin after me that year—One-a-Day.—*Roy Smalley, former Cubs shortstop, 1961.*

1814 I look up in the stands, and I see them miss balls, too.—*Devon White, Marlins outfielder, on being booed after dropping a fly ball, 1996.*

1815 They're going to have to put a bell around one of those guys' necks.—*Larry Haney, Brewers coach, on Angels outfielders Brian Downing and Gary Pettis, who collided twice in four days, 1986.*

1816 Errors are part of the game, but Abner Doubleday was a jerk for inventing them.—*Billy Ripken, Orioles second baseman, 1988.*

1817 If nobody ever screwed up, why would baseball be worth watching?—*Darryl Motley, Royals outfielder, 1985.*

1818 He should concentrate on the routine out. He makes too many senseless errors. He has that little gong that goes off, saying: "Hey, this time I'll do something different." That's when I swallow my tobacco.—*Charlie Fox, Giants manager, on second baseman Tito Fuentes, 1973.*

1819 First, I pray to God that nobody hits the ball to me. Then, I pray to God nobody hits the ball to Steve Sax.—*Pedro Guerrero, Dodgers third baseman, 1984.*

1820 What was I supposed to say? Glad you got over Watergate?—*Steve Sax, Yankees second baseman, on former President Richard Nixon, who commented that he was glad Sax had overcome his throwing problems.*

1821 The only way I'm going to get a Gold Glove is with a can of spray paint.—*Reggie Jackson, Angels DH, 1986.*

1822 If I won a Gold Glove, that thing might sit in front of my house bronzed.—*Bobby Bonilla, Pirates third baseman, on making 32 errors, 1988.*

1823 The only problem I have in the outfield is with fly balls.—*Carmelo Martinez, Padres outfielder, 1984.*

1824 I can't play perfect every day.—*Teddy Martinez, Mets shortstop, on making five errors in five games, 1974.*

1825 After he was switched from the outfield to third base, he hated for fellows to bunt to him. He was the only ballplayer I ever knew who threw at the runner instead of the base.—*Rip Collins, former Cardinals first baseman, on Pepper Martin, 1965.*

1826 Bobby Brown reminds me of a fellow who's been hitting for 12 years and fielding one.—*Casey Stengel, Yankees manager, on his third baseman, 1952.*

1827 After one of his tosses almost killed a peanut vendor in the twenty-sixth row, the coaches handed him an outfielder's glove.—*Bill Lee, Red Sox pitcher, on infielder Juan Beniquez.*

1828 Claudell Washington plays the outfield like he's trying to catch grenades.—*Reggie Jackson, Oakland A's outfielder.*

1829 If you hit Polonia 100 fly balls, you could make a movie out of it—*Catch-22.*—*Dennis Lamp, Yankees pitcher, on outfielder Luis Polonia, 1989.*

1830 Nick Etten's glove fields better with Nick Etten out of it.—*Joe Trimble, sportswriter, on the Yankees first baseman, 1945.*

1831 I lost it in the sun.—*Billy Loes, Brooklyn Dodgers pitcher, on missing a routine ground ball in the Game 6 of the 1952 World Series, October 6.*

1832 I can't remember the last time I missed a ground ball. I'll remember that one.—*Bill Buckner, Red Sox first baseman, on his error in Game 6 of the 1986 World Series, October 25.*

1833 I heard Billy Buckner tried to commit suicide over the winter. He stepped in front of a car, but it went through his legs.—*Billy Gardner, Royals manager, 1987.*

1834 Would Bill Buckner have ridden a horse around Shea Stadium had the Red Sox won in '86, or would it have slipped through his legs?—*Mark Whicker, sportswriter, on seeing Yankees third baseman Wade Boggs celebrate winning the 1996 World Series on horseback.*

1835 If I knew it was worth that much after I missed it, I would've run after it.—*Bill Buckner, former Red Sox first baseman, after the ball that went through his legs in Game 6 of the 1986 World Series was sold for $93,500 in 1998.*

1836 They want me to play third base like Brooks Robinson, but I think I'll play it more like Mel Brooks.—*Tim Flannery, Padres infielder, 1986.*

1837 Fresh acquisition Todd Zeile plays third base less like Brooks Robinson of the Orioles and more like Mrs. Robinson of "The Graduate." He couldn't catch a fish if it jumped into the boat.—*Woody Paige, sportswriter, April 2002.*

1838 With Bobby Bonds in right field and three first basemen, I might as well donate my gloves to charity.—*Ron Blomberg, Yankees DH, 1975.*

1839 Listen, punk, the next time Cobb comes to bat and lays a bunt down along the third-base line, never mind trying to throw him out at any base. Just grab the damned ball and run back to third base and try to cut him off there.—*Joe Cantillion, Washington Senators manager, to third baseman Jimmy Smith, 1909. In two previous at-bats, Smith made errors on bunts by Ty Cobb, who wound up on third base both times.*

1840 How could he lose the ball in the sun? He's from Mexico.—*Harry Caray, announcer, on a miscue by White Sox outfielder Jorge Orta.*

1841 I'm not in a rut. I'm in a ravine with Teflon-coated sides.—*Desi Relaford, Phillies shortstop, on his defensive problems, 2000.*

1842 Look at that stupid throw by Knoblauch. He actually hit an old lady in the face. Wait a minute! That's my mom.—*Keith Olbermann, broadcaster, on an errant toss by Yankees second baseman Chuck Knoblauch, 2000.*

1843 In Minneapolis, fans throw golf balls, hot dogs and beer cups at Yankee left fielder Chuck Knoblauch, a former Twin. In a bizarre, yet touching tribute to Knoblauch, all the throws miss.—*Scott Ostler, sportswriter, 2001. Knoblauch's throwing woes got so bad that New York moved him from second base to the outfield.*

1844 I could field the ball all right, but on the throw I couldn't hit the first baseman or anything near him—*John McGraw, New York Giants manager, on his days as a minor league infielder. McGraw once made nine errors in one game.*

1845 Amazing strength, amazing power—he can grind the dust out of the bat. He will be great, super, even wonderful. Now if he can only learn to catch a fly ball.—*Casey Stengel, Mets manager, on outfielder Ron Swoboda, who made 11 errors in 1965.*

1846 It's not that Reggie is a bad outfielder. He just has trouble judging the ball and picking it up.—*Billy Martin, Yankees manager, on Reggie Jackson.*

1847 I was playing it like Willie Wilson, but I forgot that I'm in Clint Hurdle's body.—*Clint Hurdle, Royals outfielder.*

1848 I did my job. The ball didn't do its job.—*Coco Crisp, Indians outfielder, on dropping a fly ball in the 2004 season opener.*

1849 I find it more and more difficult to stop myself from yelling "Mayday" every time a ball heads Roger Cedeno's way.—*Mike Lupica, sportswriter, on the Mets centerfielder, 2003.*

1850 Watching him chase a pop fly down the first-base line is like watching an aircraft carrier trying to make a U-turn.—*Jerry Perisho, comedy writer, on Mets first baseman Mo Vaughn, 2003. After a disappointing first season in New York in 2002, a knee injury in 2003 ended his career. In 2004, he had the second highest salary ($17+ million) even though he never played.*

1851 Choo Choo is the fastest catcher in the league at running after passed balls.—*Casey Stengel, Mets manager, on Choo Choo Coleman. In 1963, Coleman totaled 15 errors and 11 passed balls in 91 games.*

1852 If I did anything funny on the ball field, it was strictly accidental. Like the way I played third base. Some people thought it was hilarious, but I was on the level all the time.—*Rocky Bridges, former infielder, coach and manager.*

1853 First of all, it's way over on the other side of the field.—*David Justice on making the transition from right field to left field with the Indians, 1997.*

1854 It's like if you go to another country and they drive on the left side of the road. I can do it, but I might make a couple of mistakes.—*David Justice, Indians outfielder, on moving from right field to left field once again, 2000.*

1855 Don is a triple-threat player. He can run, hit and lob.—*Merv Rettenmund, Orioles outfielder, on teammate Don Baylor, who played much of his career as a designated hitter.*

1856 He'd be in a fog out in the field, filling his mind with heroic visions of Wags the hitter, Wags the home run king. Every now and then, balls would whistle by to break the tranquility, and he would generously misplay them into bigger hits.—*Jack Zanger, sportswriter, on Angels outfielder Leon "Daddy Wags" Wagner.*

1857 Defensively the Red Sox are a lot like Stonehenge. They are old, they don't move, and no one is certain why they are positioned the way they are.—*Dan Shaughnessy, sportswriter, June 1993.*

1858 Don't worry, son, if they were trying to steal center field, you would've had them every time.—*Charles Murphy, father of Braves catcher Dale Murphy. After years of substandard defense, Atlanta shifted Murphy to the outfield in 1980 where he became a seven-time All-Star and back-to-back MVP (1982–1983).*

1859 I think they put me in center field because that's as far from home plate they could put me and still keep me in the same county.—*Dale Murphy, Braves outfielder, on his transition from catcher, 1985.*

1860 I couldn't help but laugh at that one. I've dodged line drives before, but never a throw from a catcher.—*Tom Candiotti, Dodgers pitcher, on getting hit by a throw from Mike Piazza, 1993.*

1861 No matter where he was stationed in the field, Rudy York always played the same position. He played bat.—*Red Smith, sportswriter, on the Tigers first baseman (1934–1945).*

1862 Pete Reiser busted more fences than busted him—though the margin wasn't very big.—*Charles Einstein, sportswriter, on the Brooklyn Dodgers outfielder. After leading the NL in hitting as a rookie in 1941, Reiser's promising career was hindered by numerous collisions with the outfield wall.*

1863 If he flies out to me out there, how do you score it?—*Craig Biggio, Astros second baseman, on moving to left-center field to give the Astros four outfielders against Cardinals slugger Mark McGwire, 1999. From an official scoring standpoint, even if Biggio had made a catch against the fence, it is scored F4 (fly out to second base).*

1864 I can play anywhere in the infield as long as the darned ball doesn't come to me.—*Kirby Puckett, Twins outfielder, on playing second base, third base, and shortstop during an extra inning game, September 1999.*

1865 When you have hands as bad as mine, one hand is better than two.—*Ken Harrelson, former outfielder, on why he used one hand instead of two when catching fly balls, 1979.*

1866 Is your name Elmer? Every time I look at a Reds box score I see E Concepcion.—*Larry Bowa, Phillies shortstop, to his Reds counterpart, Dave Concepcion.*

1867 I fought the wall and the wall won.—*Dimitri Young, Reds outfielder, on almost making a great play against the fence, May 1999.*

1868 Oscar Gamble hits as if he were worth his $450,000 salary, but plays the field as if he were carrying the full bulging amount in his uniform.—*Pete Axthelm, sportswriter.*

1869 Clomping around in the outfield, he catches hell from crowds more than he catches anything else.—*Ron Smith, sportswriter, on outfielder Frank Howard.*

1870 Because you're a .399 fielder.—*Billy Southworth, Cardinals manager, to .400-hitting rookie outfielder Don Padgett, on why he was sitting the bench despite his lofty batting average, 1937. Padgett finished the season hitting .314 and then hit .399 in part-time duty in 1939.*

1871 On turf the ball comes to me and says, "Catch me." On grass it says, "Look out, sucker."—*Greg Pryor, Kansas City infielder, 1985.*

1872 Let's put it this way—pigeons have been roosting on him for two years.—*Vin Scully, Dodgers announcer, on the range of Los Angeles third baseman Ron Cey.*

1873 Show me a guy who can handle a pitching staff, and I'll show you a guy hitting .210.—*Joe Garagiola, former catcher and career .257 hitter.*

1874 I look at it this way—suppose those thirty pitches had been balls? Then I would have had no errors in 1979.—*George Brett, Hall of Fame third baseman.*

1875 You don't get a hell of a lot of practice. It's not easy to find guys who'll come out early before games and run into you.—*Mike Scioscia, Dodgers catcher, on how he became so good at blocking the plate.*

The Disabled List

1876 Andre Dawson has a bruised knee and is listed day-to-day.... Aren't we all?—*Vin Scully, Dodgers broadcaster, on the Cubs outfielder, 1991.*

1877 For you readers of English descent, I'll be back in a fortnight.—*Joe Magrane, Cardinals pitcher, on being placed on the 15-day disabled list, 1987.*

1878 He gets hurt running into a strong wind. —*Hugh Alexander, Cubs scout, on oft-injured Dodgers outfielder Eric Davis, 1992.*

1879 Some bad news for Red Sox fans: Roger Clemens is on the disabled list with a groin pull. If you ever watch baseball players, I'm sure you realize this is probably a self-inflicted injury.—*Jay Leno, talk show host, 1993.*

1880 Fractured, hell! The damn thing's broke.—*Dizzy Dean, Cardinals pitcher, when told by a team doctor that a line drive fractured his toe in the 1937 All-Star Game.*

1881 It's only puffy when it's swollen.—*Charlie Hough, White Sox pitcher, on a broken finger, 1986.*

1882 Getting hurt hurt him.—*Yogi Berra, Yankees manager, on pitcher Shane Rawley, 1984.*

1883 The Braves' Bob Horner is on the disabled list more often than eggs are on a grocery list.—*Dick Young, sportswriter, on the Braves third baseman.*

1884 I've been healthy my whole career except for a few nagging injuries the last few years. —*Mike Smith, Reds reliever.*

1885 There's nothing wrong with his shoulder except some pain—and pain don't hurt you. —*Sparky Anderson, Tigers manager, on an injury to shortstop Alan Trammell, 1989.*

1886 It feels good unless I breathe, sneeze, cough or bend over.—*Mike Schmidt, Phillies third baseman, on playing with a cracked rib, 1987.*

1887 Bob Uecker (former catcher, 1984): I made a major contribution to the Cardinals' pennant drive in 1964—I came down with hepatitis.

Johnny Carson (talk show host): How did you catch it?

Bob Uecker: The trainer injected me with it.

1888 If You Don't Let Me Play—I'll Take My Ball And Go Home.—*T-shirt worn by Phillies first baseman John Kruk following the preseason removal of a cancerous testicle, 1994.*

1889 He hurt his arm when he cut off his toe while mowing the lawn.—*Ralph Kiner, Mets broadcaster, on former Phillies pitcher Curt Simmons.*

1890 It wasn't my arm. It was my forearm.—*Joaquin Andujar, Astros pitcher, when asked about an old injury, 1988.*

1891 I won't be in the lineup for a few days, anyway.—*Sixto Lezcano, Pirates outfielder, when asked if a sore arm would keep him from playing for a few days, 1985.*

1892 [Bruce] Benedict may not be hurt as much as he really is.—*Jerry Coleman, Padres broadcaster.*

1893 [Rey] Sanchez is hurt—but he's okay.—*Harry Caray, Cubs broadcaster, 1994.*

1894 *Nurse*: So you're the famous pitcher. You know, I never cared much for baseball.

Leon Cadore (former Brooklyn pitcher, 1958): That's your prerogative, nurse. I never cared much for hospitals either.

1895 From the way Denny is shaking his head, he's either got an injured shoulder or a gnat in his eye.—*Jerry Coleman, Padres broadcaster, on pitcher John Denny.*

1896 My bad shoulder feels good, but my good shoulder feels bad.—*Roberto Clemente, Pirates outfielder.*

1897 I was a little numb. I started calling Chico Lind "Mommy."—*Mike Macfarlane, Royals catcher, on getting hit in the head by a bat, 1994.*

1898 I kept looking for little guys and grabbing big ones.... Finally, two of them took my legs and made a wish.—*Rick Camp, Braves pitcher, on suffering a pulled groin muscle during a bench-clearing brawl with San Diego, 1984.*

1899 That's great. I didn't know how to dance before the surgery.—*Charlie Hough, Rangers pitcher, when told by a doctor that he would be able to dance two weeks after knee surgery, 1984.*

1900 I had three things going for me tonight—sinker, slider and bone chips.—*Joe Magrane, Cardinals pitcher, 1988.*

1901 The Yankees wondered if Henderson's hamstring was more ham than string.—*Dave Anderson, sportswriter, on outfielder Rickey Henderson, 1987.*

1902 I have no corns, bunions or ingrown toenails, and my feet never smell. I just change my socks every six months and spray for termites once a year.—*Rip Sewell, former All-Star pitcher, on his two artificial legs, 1986.*

1903 Suffering is overrated. It doesn't teach you anything.—*Bill Veeck, White Sox owner, on his wooden leg.*

1904 Your attempt at suicide fully understood. Deepest sympathy you didn't succeed.—*Frankie Frisch, Pirates manager, in a telegram to Boston Braves manager Casey Stengel, 1943. Stengel was hospitalized after being hit by a car.*

1905 We were doing a hit and run. I ran, and he hit me.—*Dave Magadan, Marlins third baseman, on getting hit on the foot by outfielder Matias Carrillo during batting practice, 1994.*

1906 I have a pulled pride muscle.—*Earl Weaver, Orioles manager, on retiring after finishing his final season in last place, 1986.*

1907 Sometimes when he gets hit by a pitch, I'm almost embarrassed to ask him about it. By the time he gets back to the dugout, the bruise is gone.—*Richie Bancells, Orioles trainer, on the durability of shortstop Cal Ripken Jr., 1992.*

1908 It's not as bad as it sounds. Cal Ripken gets to use him for spare parts.—*Bill Scheft, comedy writer, on a career-ending hip injury to Orioles outfielder Albert Belle, 2001.*

1909 Injuries are part of the game. Without them, I wouldn't have a job.—*Gene Gieselmann, Cardinals trainer, 1987.*

1910 There was no way to cover up the McDowell incident since he bled all over the salad.—*Frank Luksa, sportswriter, on Rangers outfielder Oddibe McDowell, who sliced open his finger with a knife at a team luncheon, 1993.*

1911 This can't be true, can it? It's April, right? He's played one game, right? Talk about durability. Was this guy built in Detroit? Heck, the cherry blossoms outlasted him this year.—*Mike Littwin, sportswriter, on oft-injured Orioles first baseman Glenn Davis, 1992.*

1912 Question: Why did the Bay Area go after both Darryl Strawberry and the LA Raiders? Answer: They hoped to get 16 games out of each of them.—*Mike Downey, sportswriter, 1994. The frequently injured Strawberry was signed by the Giants after being released by the Dodgers and played in just 29 games.*

1913 We've got to get Jacob training wheels.—*Kevin Mitchell, Reds outfielder, after teammate Jacob Brumfield was injured in a bicycling accident, 1993.*

1914 Pete had one failing—he never knew where the walls were.—*Cookie Lavagetto, Brooklyn Dodgers third baseman, on outfielder Pete Reiser, who was carried off the field eleven times after collisions with the walls. After crashing into the center field wall in Ebbets Field in 1947, he was given his last rites. Reiser's misfortune is credited with the implementation of warning tracks at all stadiums.*

1915 Now I'm using everything on it: Ice, lotions, electricity, baby oil and guacamole sauce.—*Omar Vizquel, Indians shortstop, on the many treatments for his sore shoulder, 1996.*

1916 He was a cholesterol expert. He removed the fat from my wallet.—*Ellis Clary, Twins scout, on his former doctor, 1985.*

1917 You get a little tired of people telling you how lucky you are. Luck is having the ball miss you by a foot.—*Matt Keough, Angels pitcher, on getting hit in the head by a foul ball and being listed in critical condition, 1992.*

1918 That's what happens when you don't wear a helmet.—*Charlie Hough, Rangers pitcher, after a seagull was accidentally killed by a throw during spring training, 1982.*

1919 This is one of the freakiest injuries I've ever seen. And a bit annoying, because I had to look up a number later.—*John Adam, Brewers trainer, on pitcher Steve Sparks, who dislocated his shoulder in an attempt to rip a telephone book in half, 1994.*

1921 The trouble with having your jaw wired is that you can never tell when you're sleepy. You can't yawn.—*Rocky Bridges, San Jose Bees manager, on getting hit in the jaw by Tigers pitcher Frank Lary midway through the 1958 season, 1964.*

1922 My groin has no comment.—*Al Leiter, Marlins pitcher, when asked about an injury, 1997.*

1923 It's better to have an orthopedic procedure named after you than a proctological surgery. "Tommy John hemorrhoid surgery" doesn't sound quite as good as "Tommy John elbow surgery."—*Tommy John, former pitcher, on the ligament transplant surgery that bears his name, 1997. John pitched for 26 seasons, 14 of which preceded the experimental procedure.*

1924 When they operated on my arm, I asked them to put in a Koufax fastball. They did, but it was a Mrs. Koufax fastball.—*Tommy John, Dodgers pitcher, 1978.*

1925 They put a hamstring from my leg into my arm. So I don't know whether to call it a leg or an arm, but I will race anybody on my hands.—*Kent Mercker, Reds reliever, on his Tommy John surgery, 2007.*

1926 I was going to feed my bone to my dog so we could bond.—*Mike Cather, Braves reliever, on having a three-inch piece of rib removed, 1999.*

1927 I've had so many X-rays that my pitches might take on a subtle glow.—*Joe Magrane, oft-injured Cardinals pitcher, 1987.*

1928 You never know with these psychosomatic injuries. You have to take your time with them.—*Jim Palmer, Orioles pitcher, on when he would pitch again.*

1929 Suddenly I'm in favor of aluminum bats.—*Steve Yeager, Dodgers catcher, on being wounded in the neck by a broken bat while standing in the on-deck circle, September 6, 1976. Because of the incident, Yeager invented the chin strap for catchers that became a standard part of the tools of ignorance.*

1930 All we can do is put our best foot forward and try not to sprain it.—*Kevin Young, Pirates first baseman, on the team having 13 players on the disabled list, 1999.*

1931 The trouble with some pitchers these days is that they don't know the difference between an ache and a pain. One needs work and the other needs rest.—*Mayo Smith, Tigers manager, 1970.*

1932 It looks like a groin injury, but Fisk will stick it out.—*Ken Coleman, broadcaster, on an injury to Red Sox catcher Carlton Fisk.*

1933 I don't think it will affect Fisk's mobility. Electrical storms might be a problem.—*Jeff Torborg, White Sox manager, on a metal plate in catcher Carlton Fisk's broken right hand, May 1989.*

1934 We've got more MRIs than RBIs on this team.—*Jack McKeon, Reds manager, 2000.*

1935 I'm going to start thumb wrestling.—*Rick Aguilera, Cubs reliever, on how he plans to rehabilitate his broken thumb, September 2000.*

1936 I feel like a shrimp cocktail, I've spent so much time on ice.—*Mike Piazza, Mets catcher, on the treatment of his pulled hamstring, 2002.*

1937 I knew I was in trouble when they had to call a proctologist to set my thumb.—*Rick Dempsey, Orioles catcher, after blocking home plate against Royals outfielder Bo Jackson.*

1938 The last thing you want to do is go down in the history of the All-Star Game competition as the only injury sustained during the team picture.—*Cal Ripken, Orioles shortstop, on having his nose broken by White Sox reliever Roberto Hernandez, who had momentarily lost his balance stepping off a riser, July 10, 1996.*

1938 My *real* story is I hit my head on the rim during a charity slam dunk contest.—*Chris Dickerson, Reds outfielder, on being knocked out after running into a revolving glass door at a Pittsburgh hotel, 2009.*

1939 I guess that's what I get for making fun of guys who go on the DL for burning their faces in suntan booths.—*Ryan Dempster, Cubs pitcher, on breaking a toe by hopping over the dugout fence to celebrate a Chicago win, 2009.*

1940 It was a serious situation. I pray for his buttocks and his family.—*Jim Bowden, Washington Nationals GM, on a procedure to remove an abscess from the backside of pitcher Jesus Colome, 2007.*

1941 The doctor recommended surgery.... From what I understand, if somebody in 1793 had it, they amputated.—*Joe Girardi, Yankees manager, on the torn foot ligament of reliever Brian Bruney, 2008.*

1942 So Giant second baseman Jeff Kent sustained a broken wrist while washing his truck. At least he wasn't doing something really dangerous like, say, brushing his teeth.—*Jim Armstrong, sportswriter, 2002.*

1943 People are having fun with it, but it's not funny to me.... When you make fun of someone washing his truck, that's sad.—*Jeff Kent, Giants second baseman, on allegedly injuring his wrist while washing his truck, 2002. It was later discovered that Kent suffered the injury while riding a motorcycle—a violation of his contract.*

1944 I'm telling you the truth. I wasn't riding a motorcycle or washing my car.—*Mark Grace, Diamondbacks first baseman, explaining that he broke his toe on a clubhouse couch, July 2002.*

1945 Former San Diego Padre star Tony Gwynn was hired by ESPN. As he was reviewing his contract, Gwynn pulled a hamstring hustling from the first paragraph to the second.—*Jerry Perisho, comedy writer, 2002.*

1946 He said he broke it in two places; I, of course, told him to stay out of those two places.—*Steve Stone, announcer, on Reds pitcher Jose Rijo's broken ankle, 1991.*

1947 He made enough money off me to buy a boat; he better be happy for me.—*Jose Rijo, Reds pitcher, on receiving a congratulatory telegram from Dr. James Andrews, who performed five elbow surgeries to get Rijo back to the big leagues, 2002.*

1948 I didn't want Dr. [Frank] Jobe building a swimming pool with my knee.—*Pitcher Steve Howe on choosing not to undergo a procedure with the famed orthopedic surgeon.*

1949 I'm tired of handing a lineup card to an umpire with Whiteout on it.—*Bob Boone, Reds manager, on his injury-plagued team, 2001.*

1950 My nose was running like an Olympic sprinter.—*Dmitri Young, Tigers first baseman, on playing sick, 2004.*

1951 My heart got quiet, but my underwear didn't.—*Tony LaRussa, Cardinals manager, on an injury scare involving superstar first baseman Albert Pujols on a slide into second base, June 2009.*

1952 David Justice, slight hamstring pull. In baseballese, Justice tweaked a hammie. Sounds almost like a fun injury, doesn't it? "What did you do over the weekend? Went up to the lake, drank some beer, did some fishin', tweaked a hammie."—*Scott Ostler, sportswriter, 2002.*

1953 They're calling it cramps—surgery on Thursday.—*Jerry Manuel, Mets manager, joking about the status of outfielder Gary Sheffield, who came out of a game with an injury, July 17, 2009. New York placed 18 players on the DL for the season.*

1954 Next time I am going to use plastic.—*Carlos Gonzalez, Rockies outfielder, on accidentally grabbing a knife while doing the dishes and winding up on the DL, August 2009.*

1955 It was a good thing he wasn't given a chain saw.—*Michael Ventre, sportswriter, on Cardinals catcher Mike Matheny, who cut two tendons and a nerve in his right ring finger while holding a hunting knife, October 2000.*

1956 I'm kind of the horse, and he's the jockey. It depends on how he wants to whip me ... but I don't want to be glue in the near future.—*Bret Saberhagen, Red Sox pitcher, on pitching in pain at GM Dan Duquette's request, September 2000. Saberhagen was not asked to saddle up that season and was put out to pasture after just three starts in 2001.*

1957 Kerry Wood has been the most celebrated invalid since the Venus de Milo.—*Bernie Lincicome, sportswriter, on the oft-injured Cubs pitcher, 2000. After winning the NL Rookie of the Year in 1998, Wood missed all of 1999 after undergoing Tommy John surgery and resurrected his career as a reliever.*

1958 It's lucky it didn't hit me in a worse area.—*Norm Charlton, Phillies reliever, on getting hit in the head by a line drive, 1995.*

1959 He's taken on more ice than the *Titanic.*—*Larry Andersen, Phillies announcer, on pitcher Steve Ontiveros spending 1,220 days on the DL for myriad injuries, March 1998. From 1985 thru 2000, Ontiveros won just 34 games.*

1960 Right now, I can spit farther than I can throw.—*Randy Velarde, Angels second baseman, on suffering from a sprained ligament in his throwing arm that would cost him the entire season, March 1997.*

1961 That guy has had more physical examinations than the astronauts.—*Birdie Tebbetts, Milwaukee Braves manager, on catcher Del Crandall, March 1962.*

1962 Our problem right now is we have too many pitchers on the 15-day Pavano.—*Mike Mussina, Yankees pitcher, taking a shot at oft-injured teammate Carl Pavano, April 2007.*

1963 The Yankees are pretty strong, but they are weak on the disabled list. That's why they picked up Butch Hobson, so they could put him on the disabled list.—*Hank Greenwald, broadcaster, on the 1982 trade that send Hobson from California to New York.*

1964 I knew it would ruin my arm, but one year of 25–7 is worth five of 15–15.—*Steve Stone, Cubs broadcaster, on throwing curveballs over half the time during his 1980 Cy Young Award season with the Orioles. After an injury-plagued 1981 season, Stone retired and became an announcer.*

Elixirs and Pharmaceuticals

1965 It was straight whiskey. I never drank lemonade at that hour in my life.—*Mike "King" Kelly, Chicago White Stockings catcher, to manager Albert Spalding, who had accused Kelly of drinking lemonade at 3 A.M.*

1966 It depends on the length of the game. —*Mike "King" Kelly, Chicago White Stockings catcher, when asked if he drank during ballgames, 1880s.*

1967 Read about your case of Amnesia. Must be a new brand.—*Babe Ruth, Yankees outfielder, in a telegram to pitcher Waite Hoyt, who was hospitalized with a case of "amnesia."*

1968 The Babe would sit there and drink a fifth of whiskey while we played. The next day, he'd hit the ball nine miles and I'd still be drunk from inhaling the fumes.—*Ben Chapman, former Yankees outfielder, on playing cards with teammates Babe Ruth, Dusty Cooke and Lou Gehrig.*

1969 *Joe Dugan (former Yankees infielder):* I'd give a hundred dollars for a cold beer.

Waite Hoyt (former Yankees pitcher): So would the Babe.—*As pallbearers at Babe Ruth's funeral, 1948.*

1970 I never eat before a game. I always eat after the game. I have my couple of martinis, a couple of Budweisers and a couple of Grand Marniers, and by the time I get home I'm feeling pretty good.—*Harry Caray, Cubs broadcaster, 1994.*

1971 Bud Light.—*Chris Carpenter, Cardinals pitcher, when asked to name his favorite pitcher, 2006.*

1972 He's not a high-ball pitcher. He's a highball drinker.—*Lee Elia, Cubs manager, on pitcher Bill Caudill, 1981.*

1973 No, the fast highball.—*Gene Mauch, Phillies manager, when asked if third baseman Dick Allen had a weakness for the high fastball.*

1974 In his salad days, Sam McDowell drank more highballs than he pitched.—*Bucky Walters, former All-Star pitcher.*

1975 The doctor told me I can't run for the rest of the season. And I can only drink Chivas Regal.—*Jamie Easterly, Indians pitcher, explaining to manager Pat Corrales a prescription given by the team doctor for treating a rash, 1985.*

1976 When I played for Doug Rader, we weren't allowed to leave the clubhouse until all the beer was gone.—*Tim Flannery, Padres infielder.*

1977 I don't want anybody in bed by midnight. Everybody is to go out tonight and get loaded.—*Chuck Dressen, Brooklyn Dodgers manager, on dealing with a long losing streak.*

1978 Drinking is not a spectator sport.—*Jim Brosnan, Reds reliever.*

1979 If any of my players don't take a drink now and then, they'll be gone. You don't play this game on gingersnaps.—*Manager Leo Durocher.*

1980 A drunk is a pitcher who's lost his fastball. A confirmed drunk is a pitcher with a sore arm. An incurable drunk is a pitcher who hasn't won a game.—*Leo Durocher, former manager, 1975.*

1981 Anybody that can't get drunk by midnight ain't trying.—*Toots Shor, New York restaurateur and baseball fan.*

1982 You couldn't disprove his story by the way he smelled.—*Branch Rickey, Cardinals GM, on the claim by pitcher Flint Rhem that he had been kidnapped and forced to drink large quantities of liquor in a hotel room, 1930.*

1983 It was the closest thing to baseball I could find.—*Syd O'Brien, former Angels infielder, on why he became a liquor distributor.*

1984 I decided to get out when my bartender was driving a Caddy and I was driving a Chevy. —*Billy Gardner, Royals manager, on why he no longer owns a bar, 1987.*

1985 I made a vow in church when I was a kid that I would not drink until I was eighteen. I've made up for it since.—*Billy Martin, Oakland A's manager, 1980.*

1986 It's not that Billy drinks a lot. It's just that he fights a lot when he drinks a little.—*Dick Young, sportswriter, on manager Billy Martin.*

1987 He's got a good heart—but I can't say much for his liver.—*Whitey Ford, Hall of Fame pitcher, on former Yankees manager Billy Martin, 1989.*

1988 It's the worst decision since the Cubs traded Lou Brock for Ernie Broglio.—*Jerry Pritkin, Cubs fan, on a decision to ban beer sales in the Wrigley Field bleachers, 1988.*

1989 He was built along the lines of a beer keg and not unfamiliar with its contents.—*Shirley Povich, sportswriter, on Cubs outfielder Hack Wilson.*

1990 Hack Wilson usually played in the outfield, but I'd put him at first base because he wouldn't have as far to stagger to the dugout.—*Mike Royko, sportswriter.*

1991 I guess, Skip, that proves that if you drink, you'll never get worms.—*Hack Wilson, Cubs outfielder, after manager Joe McCarthy demonstrated how a worm would die when dropped into a bottle of Prohibition-era liquor, 1926. Wilson battled alcohol his entire career, but he still managed to set an untouchable record in 1930 with 191 runs batted in. His 56 home runs that season were tops in the NL until 1998.*

1992 I never played drunk; hungover yes, but never drunk.—*Hack Wilson, Cubs outfielder.*

1993 I liked starting because you got three days to drink and one day to recover. Relieving you had to pick your spots.—*Former pitcher Bill Lee, 2002.*

1994 The hitters tell me my fastball looks faster when they're still a little hung over.—

Brian Bannister, Royals pitcher, on why he has more success in day games, 2008.

1995 No thanks, I don't drink.—*Jeff Stone, Phillies outfielder, when asked if he wanted a shrimp cocktail, 1985.*

1996 Hey, I really like your beer.—*Dave LaPoint, Pirates reliever, to Vice President George Bush, 1988.*

1997 Whitey Herzog will need a fifth after the fourth.—*Al Michaels, broadcaster, on the Cardinals manager during the 1987 World Series. St. Louis lost the first two games to the Twins after allowing a total of 13 runs to score in the fourth inning. The Twins won the Series in seven games.*

1998 Everybody who roomed with Mickey said he took five years off their careers.—*Waite Hoyt, Yankees pitcher, on outfielder Mickey Mantle.*

1999 He likes to drink. I hope I don't have to go out with him. I'm going to have a clause in my contract that says I don't have to go out and drink with him.—*Ichiro Suzuki, Mariners outfielder, on his relationship with Mariners reliever Kazuhiro Sasaki, 2000. Suzuki's translator added, "That's a joke." Sasaki had just been named AL Rookie of the Year.*

2000 When I came over here, I always heard it was a stronger league, with amphetamines all over the clubhouse, but all I found was Michelob Dry.—*Reliever Dan Quisenberry on moving from the Royals to the Cardinals, 1988.*

2001 I'm not going into another unless they use plastic cups.—*Kevin Mitchell, Reds outfielder, on a barroom incident in which he was hit above the eye by a beer bottle thrown by a woman, 1994.*

2002 I loved Venezuela. The fans loved me down there. Down there, beers are $3 for 24. Gas is 11 cents a gallon. If you like to drink beer and drive, it's great.—*Bill "Spaceman" Lee, former All-Star pitcher, on the Venezuelan Winter League, 1985.*

2003 I went all spring without taking a shower in our room. First day in camp, Steve [Bilko] hired a bellhop to keep the bathtub filled with ice and beer. He'd close the bathroom door; sit on the toilet drinking beer with hot water running over the ice. It was like a steam room. He thought he was sweating off all the beer he was drinking.—*Buck Rodgers, Angels manager, recalling his first spring training as a rookie catcher with California, 1961.*

2004 The Cardinals had a Foster Brooks night—five doubles.—*Don Sutton, Braves broadcaster, 1994.*

2005 I see both of them coming back, but coming back to what? None of us come back to what we were. And in the case of these two guys, they weren't what they were when they left.—*Mookie Wilson, former Mets outfielder, on Giants outfielder Darryl Strawberry and Mets pitcher Dwight Gooden, 1994. Strawberry acknowledged a substance abuse problem, was released by the Dodgers, and was subsequently signed by the Giants. Gooden tested positive for cocaine use and was suspended for 60 days.*

2006 He got two bases, and I'll get a urine test.—*Steve Howe, Yankees reliever, on making a throwing error on a ball hit by Brewers catcher Dave Nilsson, 1992. Howe had served five previous drug-related suspensions and would serve two more.*

2007 I don't do stimulants. I don't do anything to alter the physiological condition of my body. It's running perfect on 82% body fat.—*Doug Rader, Rangers manager.*

2008 Johnson is the tallest left-hander to pitch for the Expos, but not the highest. Bill Lee was the highest.—*Richard Griffin, Expos director of public relations, on 6'10" rookie pitcher Randy Johnson, 1988.*

2009 Amphetamines improved my performance about five percent. Unfortunately, in my particular case that wasn't enough.—*Jim Bouton, former All-Star pitcher.*

2010 Police have arrested the man who was pictured throwing snowballs at Giants Stadium. If convicted, he may face six months in jail and a $1,000 fine. If it turns out he was under the influence of alcohol or drugs, he'll be signed by the Yankees.—*David Letterman, talk show host.*

2011 John Kruk now owns a bar in Keyser, W.Va., called Third Base. Why third base, when he was a first baseman? It's the last place you stop on your way home.—*Peter Gammons, sportswriter, 1998.*

2012 He passed the bar exam and there were times when I hardly passed a bar.—*Jim Leyland, Pirates manager, on Oakland A's manager Tony LaRussa, 1990.*

2013 I did pass the bar. But as some might say, I haven't passed one since.—*Mel Allen, lawyer-turned-Hall of Fame broadcaster, 1995.*

2014 At a New York Yankees game earlier today, the umpire had to go out to the mound to break up an AA meeting.—*David Letterman, talk show host, 1996.*

2015 I drink after wins. I drink after losses. I drink after rainouts.—*Bob Lemon, Yankees manager, 1978.*

2016 I had my bad days in the field, but I didn't take them home with me. I left them in a bar along the way.—*Bob Lemon, former Yankees pitcher, at his Hall of Fame induction, 1976.*

2017 I met my wife in a New York bar. We had a lot in common. We were both from California and we were both drunk.—*Tug McGraw, Phillies reliever, 1979.*

2018 We're in such a slump that even the ones that are drinkin' aren't hittin'.—*Casey Stengel, Mets manager, 1962.*

2019 Look at him. He doesn't drink, he doesn't smoke, he doesn't chew, he doesn't stay out late and he still can't hit.—*Casey Stengel, Yankees manager, on second baseman Bobby Richardson.*

2020 Casey [Stengel] once told us that he didn't mind you going out with your own roommate. But he didn't want four or five of us going out together because that way everybody would want to buy one round and by the end of the night we'd all be gassed.—*Ed Kranepool, Mets first baseman, 1973.*

2021 They say some of my stars drink whiskey, but I have found that the ones who drink milkshakes don't win many ball games.—*Casey Stengel, Yankees manager.*

2022 One place I won't allow my players to drink is at the hotel where we're staying. That's where I do my drinking.—*Hank Bauer, Oakland A's manager, 1968.*

2023 There is much less drinking now than there was before 1927, because I quit drinking on May 24, 1927.—*Walter "Rabbit" Maranville, former shortstop.*

2024 Avoid the hellish booze that makes a man's brain a mud puddle.—*Billy Sunday, evangelist and former White Sox outfielder.*

2025 Jack Daniel's stock doesn't drop when I'm flying between baseball games.—*Rusty Staub, Tigers DH, on his fear of flying, 1979.*

2026 I see three baseballs, but I only swing at the middle one.—*Paul Waner, Pirates outfielder, on how to play after drinking.*

2027 He had to be a graceful player because he could slide without breaking the bottle on his hip.—*Casey Stengel, Yankees manager, on Pirates outfielder Paul Waner.*

2028 Paul Waner was always sipping from a Coke bottle in the dugout. One day, while he was batting, a new batboy snuck a long swig. The kid woke up with a crashing hangover.—*Mike Royko, columnist.*

2029 I could put away three cases of beer a night. Now I can't handle that much. If I have only 15 beers, I'm totally gone.—*Dickie Noles, Cubs pitcher.*

2030 Most of the time you send them a bottle of Dom Perignon when they win their first game. But our kids are so young, you send a can of Ovaltine.—*Jim Leyland, Marlins manager, on his pitching staff, 1998.*

2031 Bugs [Raymond] drank a lot, you know, and sometimes it seemed the more he drank the better he pitched. They used to say he didn't spit on the ball; he blew his breath on it and the ball came up drunk.—*Hall of Fame pitcher Rube Marquard on Bugs Raymond, whose career was cut* *short due to alcohol abuse—he was killed in a bar brawl in 1912.*

2032 If I had done everything that everybody said I'd done, I'd have cirrhosis of the liver, be a junkie and have 45 children. In other words, I'd be dead.—*Bobby Bonds, Cubs outfielder, 1981.*

2033 Using pot is a way to let you down slowly from a ballgame. It's made players a lot less alcoholic.—*Bill Lee, former pitcher.*

2034 I don't know. I never smoked AstroTurf.—*Tug McGraw, Mets reliever, when asked if he preferred grass or artificial turf, 1974.*

2035 Every time I fail to smoke a cigarette between innings, the opposition will score.—*Earl Weaver, Orioles manager.*

2036 You would think the lung would have only so much capacity for smoke for a guy in his 60s. He's got great genetics. If I come up with lung cancer in the next five years, I am suing Jim Leyland for secondhand smoke.—*Andy Van Slyke, Tigers coach, October 2006.*

2037 I'll give them up when we get 10 games over. But I'll start smoking them again when we get to 11 games over .500.—*Jack McKeon, Reds manager, on his promise to stop smoking cigars, 1999.*

2038 You know it's bad when your three-year-old holds up a water bottle and asks if Daddy spit in this before she drinks.—*Josh Hamilton, Rangers outfielder, on why he quit using chewing tobacco, 2009.*

2039 The other day they asked me about mandatory drug testing. I said I believed in drug testing a long time ago. All through the sixties I tested everything.—*Bill Lee, former pitcher.*

2040 I hate needles.—*Bob Kearney, Mariners catcher, on why he objected to drug testing.*

2041 If someone saw me in the shower, they'd never think I was on the juice.—*Jason Schmidt, Giants pitcher.*

2042 Let me start by telling you this: I have never used steroids. Period. I don't know how to say it any more clearly than that. Never.—*Rafael Palmeiro, Orioles first baseman, in his opening statement to Congress, March 17, 2005. On August 1, he was suspended ten days for testing positive for stanozolol, and in 2007 his name appeared on the Mitchell Report for using performance-enhancing drugs earlier in his career.*

2043 You can't just go out and buy a championship ring ... well, unless Dwight Gooden runs out of coke.—*Adam Carolla, comedian, on the Yankees trading for shortstop Alex Rodriguez in February 2004.*

2044 I should have a third ear coming out of my forehead.—*Roger Clemens, seven-time Cy Young Award winner, on why he couldn't have taken steroids, 2008.*

2045 The stronger you get, the more relaxed you get. You feel good. You just let it fly. If you don't feel good, you try so hard to make something happen. You grip the bat harder and swing harder and that's when you tighten up. But you get that edge when you feel strong. That's the way I felt. I felt strong, like I could just try to meet the ball and—wham!—it's going to go 1,000 mph. Man, I felt good. I'd think, Damn, this pitcher's in trouble and I'd crush the ball 450 feet with almost no effort. It's all about getting an edge.—*Ken Caminiti, former third baseman, 2002.*

2046 I would say there are only a couple of guys on a team that don't take greenies before a game. One or two guys. That's called going out there naked. And you hear it all the time from teammates, "You're not going to play naked, are you?" And even the guys who are against greenies may be taking diet pills or popping 25 caffeine pills and they're up there with their hands shaking. So how good is that? This game is so whacked out that guys will take anything to get an edge. You got a pill that will make me feel better? Let me have it.—*Ken Caminiti, 1996 NL MVP, 2002.*

2047 The thing that disturbs me most about Ken Caminiti's steroid revelations ... is that the Orioles' .248 team batting average last season might have actually been inflated.—*Dan Daly, sportswriter, 2002.*

2048 I take steroids to get bigger, stronger and faster on the keyboard.—*Tony Kornheiser, sportswriter, 2002.*

2049 Imagine that. The media creating a story, not covering it. To wit: A San Francisco newspaper guy saying on Fox TV that Barry Bonds may be on steroids. Sorry, but you don't say a guy could be doing 'roids, then take off your mike and go have a cold one with the boys. Reporters are accountable, just like players.—*Jim Armstrong, sportswriter, 2001—the season Bonds finished with 73 home runs.*

2050 The sports question people ask me most is, "Can you get me tickets?" But a close second is, "Do you think Barry does steroids?"—*Scott Ostler, sportswriter, on Giants outfielder Barry Bonds, July 2002.*

2051 The People for the Ethical Treatment of Animals [PETA] is leaning on Barry Bonds to give up his gig as a pitchman for KFC Popcorn Chicken. PETA says those chickens are pumped up on harmful steroids. The chickens indignantly denied using 'roids. They insist their unusual size is a product of hard work in the weight room.—*Scott Ostler, sportswriter, 2002.*

2052 I never asked Greg [Anderson]. When he said it was flaxseed oil, I just said, whatever.—*Barry Bonds, Giants outfielder, in his Grand Jury testimony on why he never questioned what his personal trainer was giving him, December 4, 2003.*

2053 According to media reports, which are never wrong, Barry Bonds' hat size grew by two sizes last year. Medical experts say that kind of skull expansion for a 37-year-old man can only happen if he is taking steroids, or he's paid $18 million and allowed exclusive use of three lockers, a lounge chair, a television and a personal trainer and French chef in the clubhouse.—*David Whitley, sportswriter, June 2002.*

2054 Before the union agrees to drug testing, Donald Fehr says he needs "tangible proof" of steroid use. What does he want—Barry Bonds batting with a syringe sticking out of his arm and a voice deeper than Lou Rawls?—*Mike Bianchi, sportswriter, June 2002.*

2055 You guys better hurry up and ask me quick because one more Bloody Mary and you're not going to understand anything I say. —*Lou Piniella, Cubs manager, to reporters at the annual Cubs Convention, 2008.*

2056 You get a ten-game suspension for steroids and a six-game suspension for milk.—*Brad Penny, Dodgers pitcher, on the suspension given to a Marlins batboy who threw up after trying to win a $500 bet by drinking a gallon of milk, 2005.*

2057 It's the Bong-Puffer card. It's the first baseball card with its own estimated street value.—*Keith Olbermann, broadcaster, on a 2003 Topps baseball card featuring pitching prospects Jung Bong and Brandon Puffer.*

2058 The key is to hit the cup.—*Josh Paul, Devil Rays catcher, on taking a drug test, 2007.*

2059 Sure I eat what I advertise. Sure I eat Wheaties for breakfast. A good bowl of Wheaties with bourbon can't be beat.—*Dizzy Dean, broadcaster and Hall of Fame pitcher.*

2060 I knew they weren't going to strike. Last Wednesday, I saw Martha Stewart buying stock in steroids.—*Jay Leno, talk show host, September 2002.*

2061 Playing on this team and seeing what is happening around me, I feel that something is beginning to fall apart. But, if I was not in this situation, and I was objectively watching what just happened this week, I would probably be drinking a lot of beers and booing. Usually, I enjoy Japanese beer, but given the situation, if I was objectively watching the game, I wouldn't care if it was Japanese beer, American beer or beer from Papua New Guinea. —*Ichiro Suzuki, Mariners outfielder, on the abysmal start of the 2008 season.*

2062 Who would do the testing? Will results be kept private? Or will they be leaked to the media? What about false positives? You think it's going to be confidential? I laugh at that.—*Nomar Garciaparra, Red Sox shortstop, on drug testing in baseball, 2002. Turns out, Nomar was right—many of the names of those who tested positive for steroids were leaked to the media.*

2063 After batting practice or right before the game, Mark [McGwire] and I would duck into a stall in the men's room, load up our syringes, and inject ourselves. I always injected myself, because I had practiced enough to know just what I was doing, but often I would inject Mark as well.—*Jose Canseco, 1988 AL MVP, on his days in Oakland as part of the Bash Brothers, 2005.*

2064 I'm not here to talk about the past.—*Retired slugger Mark McGwire, dodging questions about his steroid use at a Congressional hearing, March 17, 2005.*

2065 Unless Manny Ramirez delivers triplets in November, I'm not buying his story.—*Bob Costas, broadcaster, on the Dodgers slugger who explained that the reason he tested positive for taking a female hormone (one that is often used in conjunction with steroids) was for a "personal health issue." Ramirez was suspended 50 games, 2009.*

2066 Manny Ramirez is being suspended for 50 games for taking a banned substance believed to be a woman's fertility drug. While some people are calling it a suspension, Manny's calling it maternity leave.—*Jay Leno, talk show host, 2009.*

2067 Manny Ramirez is playing for a Triple-A minor league baseball team while he serves out his suspension for using female fertility drugs. So far, Manny's gone hitless. But in Manny's defense, it *is* that time of month.—*David Letterman, talk show host, 2009.*

Farewell Addresses

2068 You can only milk a cow so long, then you're left holding the pail.—*Henry Aaron, Brewers DH, on his retirement, 1976. Aaron hit .229 with ten home runs in his final season.*

2069 Us ballplayers do things backward. First we play, then we retire and go to work.—*Charlie Gehringer, Hall of Fame second baseman.*

2070 Nobody is going to retire gracefully anymore. To get them to retire nowadays, you have to pour gasoline on them and set fire to the uniform and peel it off.—*Bob Feller, Hall of Fame pitcher, 1987.*

2071 The league will be a little drier now, folks.—*Gaylord Perry, renowned spitballing pitcher, on his retirement, 1983.*

2072 In one day, I went from a negative presence to a man with a great past.—*Jim Palmer, Orioles pitcher, on his retirement, 1984. Palmer went 0–3 in his final season.*

2073 I got tired of ducking line drives and backing up home plate.—*Bob Miller, Mets reliever, on his retirement, 1974.*

2074 When you have a brother who's an umpire and you're still only hitting .200, it's time to get out.—*Tom Haller, Tigers catcher, on his retirement, 1973. Tom's brother Bill Haller was an AL umpire.*

2075 I'm doing what every retired Floridian does: Play golf, watch the sunset, wait for the mailman, and drive slowly.—*Joe Sambito on retiring as a Red Sox reliever, 1988.*

2076 Like a steam bath. Once you get used to it, it's not so hot.—*Blackie Sherrod, sportswriter, when asked what retirement was like, 2003.*

2077 You get older. I mean, how many bases do you want to back up? I got to the point where I knew the third-base coaches and the on-deck hitters better than I knew my teammates.—*Dan Quisenberry, Giants reliever, on his retirement, 1990.*

2078 Every day was Christmas. Sometimes I didn't like the packages, but I loved opening the presents.—*Dan Quisenberry, Giants reliever, on announcing his retirement, 1990.*

2079 I'll go home and be Mr. Mom. My two boys are about to start baseball. I'll go out and boo 'em.—*Goose Gossage, Yankees pitcher, on his release, 1989. Gossage sat out the 1990 season before coming out of retirement and pitching four more seasons. He was inducted into the Hall of Fame in 2008.*

2080 Baseball is the best. But it's like everything else, I guess, some players for you, some against you. I'm a tough guy, a gambler on horses, a slave driver and in general a disgrace to the game. I wish I knew why. I only wanted to win.—*Rogers Hornsby, following his final season in baseball as manager of the Reds, 1953.*

2081 I'm not quitting because I'm too old. I'm quitting because I think the people want me to.—*Connie Mack, 88-year-old Philadelphia A's owner-manager, on his retirement after 50 years as manager, 1950. The A's finished 52–102 in Mack's final season.*

2082 I'd die within two weeks if I ever left baseball.—*Connie Mack, Philadelphia A's owner, on selling the team, 1954. Mack died fifteen months later, February 8, 1956. Mack holds the career managerial record for most games (7,755), victories (3,731) and losses (3,948).*

2083 I never saw a ball hit so hard.... He was fat and old, but he still had that great swing.—*Guy Bush, Pirates pitcher, on surrendering the final home run to Boston Braves outfielder Babe Ruth, May 25, 1935.*

2084 You know, this baseball game of ours comes up from the youth. That means the boys. And after you've been a boy, and grow up to know how to play ball, then you come to the boys you see representing themselves today in our national pastime. The only real game in the world, I think, is baseball. As a rule, some people think if you give them a football or a baseball or something like that, naturally they're athletes right away. But you can't do that in baseball. You've got to start from way down, at the bottom, when you're six or seven years old. You can't wait until you're fifteen or sixteen. You've got to let it grow up with you, and if you're successful and you try hard enough, you're bound to come out on top, just like these boys have come out on top now. There's been so many lovely things said about me, I'm glad I had the opportunity to thank everybody. Thank you.—*Babe Ruth in his farewell address at Yankee Stadium, June 13, 1948.*

2085 I no longer have it, and when baseball is no longer fun, it is no longer a game.—*Joe DiMaggio, Yankees outfielder, on announcing his retirement, 1951. DiMaggio, a career .325 batter, hit .263 in his last season.*

2086 I'm 49 and I want to live to be 50.—*Eddie Sawyer, Phillies manager, on retiring after winning the first game of the season, 1960. He was replaced by rookie manager Gene Mauch.*

2087 It hasn't been a labor of love for Ted this year; it's just been labor.—*Jack Fadden, Red Sox trainer, before Ted Williams' last game, September 26, 1960.*

2088 And now Boston knows how England felt when it lost India.—*Edward Linn, sportswriter, on the retirement of Red Sox outfielder Ted Williams, 1960. Williams, at age 41, hit .316 with 29 home runs in his final season.*

2089 People don't know it, but Ted Williams and I had a lot in common. We both hit home runs in our last major league at-bats. The only difference was he knew it was his last. I was released the next day.—*Richie Hebner, Red Sox coach, 1991. Hebner's 18-year career ended with the Cubs in 1985.*

2090 If you had one good arm and one bad arm and somebody said you could buy back the use of your bad arm, I think you'd do it. In a sense, that's what I'm doing.—*Sandy Koufax, Dodgers pitcher, on his retirement due to arthritis of his pitching arm, 1966. In his final season, Koufax won the Cy Young by going 27–9 with a 1.73 ERA. During the last five years of his career, Koufax went 111–34 with 1,444 strikeouts and five consecutive ERA titles.*

2091 I had one foot in the grave and the other on a banana peel.—*Wes Westrum, Mets manager, on his retirement, 1967.*

2092 I finally came to the conclusion it's time for me to go fishing.—*Tigers manager Ralph Houk announcing his retirement, September 22, 1978.*

2093 I was actually dreading playing another

season. I just can't play any more and I know it.—*Mickey Mantle, Yankees outfielder, on announcing his retirement, March 1, 1969. Mantle hit .237 with 18 home runs in 1968.*

2094 But god-damn, to think you're a .300 hitter and end up at .237 in your last season, then find yourself looking at a lifetime .298 average—it made me want to cry.—*Mickey Mantle, Hall of Fame outfielder, on his final season in 1968.*

2095 I want to be remembered as a ballplayer who gave all he had to give.—*Roberto Clemente, Pirates outfielder, 1972. Clemente collected his 3,000th hit in the final game of the season and was killed on New Year's Eve when his plane, which was transporting emergency supplies for earthquake victims, crashed en route to Managua, Nicaragua.*

2096 I look at the kids over here and the way they're playing and the way they're fighting for themselves, and that says one thing to me: "Willie, say goodbye to America."—*Willie Mays, Mets outfielder, in his farewell address at Shea Stadium, September 25, 1973. Mays, at age 42, hit .211 his final season.*

2097 It's like crying for your mother after she's gone. You cry because you love her. I cried, I guess, because I loved baseball and I knew I had to leave her.—*Willie Mays on his retirement from the Mets, 1973.*

2098 When you're 21 you're a prospect. When you're 30, you're a suspect.—*Jim McGlothlin, pitcher, on being released by the White Sox, 1974.*

2099 Youth movements are great when you're part of them.—*Rick Monday, Dodgers outfielder, on his release, June 22, 1984. At age 38, Monday hit .191 in his final season.*

2100 Baseball is both the greatest and worst thing that ever happened to me. Not because people asked too much of me, but because I asked too much of myself. As it turned out, my talent was a curse. The curse was the way I handled it and didn't handle it.—*Sam McDowell, Pirates pitcher, on his retirement, 1975.*

2101 There's a conspiracy among the clubs. Nobody's hiring 37-year-old players who can't hit.—*Mike Jorgensen, veteran first baseman and career .243 hitter, on not getting a contract after 17 seasons in the big leagues, 1986.*

2102 You're always surprised when somebody tells you you are retiring, I guess.—*Robin Yount, 36-year-old Brewers outfielder, on reports that GM Sal Bando said Yount would retire following the 1992 season. The two-time AL MVP ultimately retired after the 1993 season.*

2103 I guess this is one of the few times when you get to see your own last rites.—*Steve Stone on his retirement at age 34, one year after winning the AL Cy Young Award, 1981.*

2104 I'm mad at Hank Aaron for deciding to play one more season. I threw him his last home run and thought I would be remembered forever. Now I'll have to throw him another.—*Bill Lee, Red Sox pitcher, 1976.*

2105 I've been fortunate enough to have a long career. I really can't imagine how it could've been better. But it's over now, and time for something else.—*Brooks Robinson, Orioles third baseman, on his retirement, August 21, 1977. Robinson hit .211 in his final season.*

2106 Fifty years from now, I'll be just three inches of type in a record book.—*Brooks Robinson, Orioles third baseman, on his retirement, 1977.*

2107 The Yankees lost more class on the weekend than George Steinbrenner could buy in 10 years.—*Red Smith, sportswriter, on the death of former Yankees catcher and coach Elston Howard, December 14, 1980.*

2108 I'll never be considered one of the all-time greats, maybe not even one of the all-time goods. But I'm one of the all-time survivors.—*Jim Kaat, Cardinals pitcher, on his retirement at age 44, 1983. Kaat won 283 games and 16 Gold Gloves.*

2109 I've always done what was best for the club. Like this week, when I retired.—*Reliever Kent Tekulve on retiring from the Reds, 1989.*

2110 They broke it to me gently. The manager came up to me before a game and said they didn't allow visitors in the clubhouse.—

Bob Uecker, former catcher, on being released, 1976.

2111 I knew when my career was over. In 1965, my baseball card came out with no picture.—*Bob Uecker, former catcher.*

2112 As I walked back to the dugout after striking out, I looked into the stands and saw my wife and kids booing me.—*Fran Healy, Yankees catcher, on knowing when it was time to retire, 1978.*

2113 Somewhere along the line, I couldn't raise hell as much as I used to. Couldn't have those eight drinks of Jack Daniel's and play the next day.—*Lou Piniella, Yankees outfielder, on his retirement, 1984.*

2114 Venezuela had three million people without jobs. Now they've got 3,000,001.—*Infielder Ozzie Guillen on being released by the Devil Rays, 2001. Ozzie made it back to the Show as manager of the White Sox in 2004.*

2115 Joe, I'm out of the lineup. I'm just not doing the team any good.—*Lou Gehrig, Yankees first baseman, to manager Joe McCarthy, May 2, 1939, which ended Gehrig's consecutive games played streak at 2,130.*

2116 Fans, for the past two weeks you have been reading about a bad break I got. Yet today I consider myself the luckiest man on the face of this earth.—*Lou Gehrig, addressing the Yankee Stadium crowd on Lou Gehrig Appreciation Day, July 4, 1939. Gehrig suffered from a rare neuromuscular disease, amyotrophic lateral sclerosis, which became known as Lou Gehrig's disease. It ultimately claimed his life June 2, 1941.*

2117 I never knew how someone dying could say he was the luckiest man in the world. But now I understand.—*Mickey Mantle in his farewell address at Yankee Stadium, June, 1969.*

2118 You spend a good piece of your life gripping a baseball and in the end it turns out that it was the other way around all the time.—*Jim Bouton, Astros pitcher, 1970.*

Food Fights and Weighty Issues

2119 A hot dog at the ballgame beats roast beef at the Ritz.—*Humphrey Bogart, actor.*

2120 Are you excited about baseball being back? I love it. I mean the leather, the pine tar, the rosin—and that's just the hot dogs.—*David Letterman, talk show host, 2003.*

2121 If I get sprayed with meat, I'm suing SkyDome. I don't think they considered the whole vegetarian thing. What if I had my mouth open and a piece of hot dog landed in my mouth? I can't even walk by a hot dog stand without gagging. Imagine being sprayed by wiener shrapnel. I would have died.—*Sarah Higginson, vegetarian fan, after an ill-fated promotion in which a Hot Dog Blaster, intended to deliver dogs to fans, was more powerful than expected and showered the crowd with little bits of franks and buns, May 2000.*

2122 Ballplayers who are first into the dining room are usually last in the averages.—*Jimmy Cannon, sportswriter.*

2123 Mr. President, I was on a diet for 25 years. Now that I'm making some money, I'm making sure I eat enough to make up for the lean years.—*Dizzy Dean, broadcaster and Hall of Fame pitcher, when asked by President Dwight D. Eisenhower how he came to weigh almost 300 pounds.*

2124 We spelled poor with only one "o" because we ate the other one.—*Mel Hall, Indians outfielder, on his family, 1986.*

2125 Krukie doesn't lead anything but the stampede to the buffet table.—*Mitch Williams, Phillies reliever, when asked if first baseman John Kruk was a team leader, 1993.*

2126 Don't worry, I can always put the weight back on.—*John Kruk, Phillies first base-*

man, on concerns that his weight loss might adversely affect his performance.

2127 With the money I'll make with my new contract, it won't matter. I'll be able to afford liposuction.—*Kirby Puckett, Twins outfielder, on concerns that his weight gain might affect his performance, 1992.*

2128 I'm superstitious, and every night after I got a hit, I ate Chinese food and drank tequila. I had to stop hitting or die.—*Tim Flannery, Padres infielder, on a long hitting streak, 1987.*

2129 It's kind of pathetic to think a lunch can get you hits in a baseball game, but that's how mental this game is.—*Lee Stevens, Rangers DH, on baseball superstitions, 1998.*

2130 Scallions are the greatest cure for a batting slump ever invented.—*Babe Ruth, Yankees outfielder.*

2131 He's the only guy I know who gets paid to eat and diet.—*Jim Leyland, Pirates manager, on Cubs manager Don Zimmer, who made commercials for both Popeye's Chicken and the Nutri/System weight-loss plan, 1989.*

2132 I'd think it would be a little tough eating right now. They should eat all that food and then puke. That would be the appropriate thing to do.—*Toby Harrah, Rangers manager, on the team eating after a 13–0 defeat, 1992.*

2133 I kept craving Mexican food. One time, I woke up in the middle of the night and I was staring at a giant chicken taco. It was a nightmare.—*Terry Forster, Braves reliever, on the off-season diet that helped him lose almost 50 pounds, 1984.*

2134 I could no longer fit on my baseball card. —*Kent Hrbek, Twins first baseman, on why he started a diet.*

2135 She's poisoning the world with her hamburgers.—*Goose Gossage, Padres reliever, on Joan Kroc who owned the team and McDonald's, 1986.*

2136 He spent seven dollars at McDonald's for lunch, and equipment manager Charlie Samuels believes it to be a Met record. McDowell holds all the fast-food records on the team and should be a top candidate for the Rolaids Relief Award.—*Steve Marcus, sportswriter, on Mets reliever Roger McDowell, 1986.*

2137 I knew it would be beer or Ding Dongs, I just didn't know which.—*Mitch Williams, Phillies reliever, on trading first baseman John Kruk two cases of beer for Kruk's uniform No. 28, 1991.*

2138 Speaking of food, up steps Rick Reuschel.—*Hank Greenwald, Giants broadcaster, following a commercial break for a supermarket, 1990. The San Francisco pitcher was conservatively listed at 230 pounds.*

2139 I picked up a little Spanish, at least. When I went out to eat, I learned how to say "Whopper con queso" and "McNuggets de pollo." Stuff like that.—*Paul Faries, Padres infielder, on playing winter ball in Puerto Rico, 1992.*

2140 I've heard him use three English words —food, beer and light beer.—*Mike Scioscia, Dodgers catcher, on pitcher Fernando Valenzuela, 1981.*

2141 They should chew the gum that comes with baseball cards. And then they should also eat the cards. Bubblegum cards are very good in a little leaguer's diet.—*Doug Rader, Astros third baseman, on his advice to young ballplayers, 1971. Rader also cautioned kids not to eat the cards of players with bad statistics.*

2142 Of the day.—*Ken Landreaux, Dodgers outfielder, when asked by manager Tommy Lasorda what kind of soup was being served in the clubhouse.*

2143 The bread is wet and the meat loaf is dry. Am I in jail or what?—*Dave Winfield, Yankees outfielder, on a postgame spread, 1986.*

2144 That's for birds to eat. I'm afraid my players might start molting or going to the bathroom on newspapers.—*Rocky Bridges, Vancouver Canadians manager, on players eating sunflower seeds instead of chewing tobacco, 1987.*

2145 I prefer fast food.—*Rocky Bridges, Giants coach, when a waiter suggested escargot as an appetizer, 1985.*

2146 Walt Alston would order corn on the cob in a Paris restaurant.—*Jim Murray, sportswriter, on the Dodgers manager.*

2147 If I stop chewing, okay. Now I'm going to eat a ton of sunflower seeds and gain 50 pounds and die of a heart attack.—*John Wockenfuss, Carolina Mudcats manager, on the ban of tobacco products in the minor leagues, 1993.*

2148 All these guys eating wheat germ and granola ... maybe they should mix in some nachos and chili dogs.—*Rich Donnelly, Pirates coach, 1992.*

2149 One of the security guards gave us a list of things we couldn't eat—meat, potatoes, salad, water, fish, chicken and Mexican food. So that pretty much boiled the things we could eat down to Pringles and Oreos.—*Rich Donnelly, Rockies coach, on the precautions taken during an opening series trip to Monterey, Mexico, 1999.*

2150 When we lose, I eat. When we win, I eat. I also eat when we're rained out.—*Tommy Lasorda, Dodgers manager.*

2151 I'll have some french fries, but no potatoes because I'm on a diet.—*Yogi Berra, Astros coach, 1986.*

2152 Get me a diet Tab.—*Yogi Berra, Hall of Fame catcher.*

2153 You have to have a sense of humor to eat there. The food tastes funny.—*Jack Buck, Cardinals broadcaster, on the press box food at Atlanta–Fulton County Stadium.*

2154 Anyone who would eat a chicken dog would pay scalper's prices to a USFL game.—*Bob Costas, broadcaster, on chicken dogs being sold at some ballparks, 1984.*

2155 *Boots Poffenberger (Tigers pitcher, 1937):* I'll have the breakfast of champions.

Room service waiter: Cereal?

Boots Poffenberger: Hell no. Two fried eggs and a bottle of beer.

2156 Negotiators should be locked in a room with no windows and air conditioning, and should be fed baked beans, fried cheese, hard-boiled eggs and chocolate kisses. In eight hours, they'd be pleading, "Play Ball!"—*James Traficant, U.S. Representative (D-Ohio), on his suggestion to resolve the 1994 baseball strike. In 2002, Traficant was expelled from Congress and jailed seven years for a variety of charges including taking bribes and racketeering.*

2157 Yankee pitcher David Wells is learning a hard baseball reality: "Three steaks and you're gout."—*Roger Brigham, sportswriter, on Wells' preseason bout with gout, 1997.*

2158 Have you heard about the David Wells diet? You get to eat everything but your words. Those you blame on somebody else.—*Wallace Matthews, sportswriter, on the outspoken, portly White Sox pitcher, 2001.*

2159 The deal will be complete following a physical, which has been delayed in order to assemble enough people to lift Wells onto the scales.—*Ken Rudolph, broadcaster, on the Yankees finalizing the free agent signing of pitcher David Wells, January 2002.*

2160 I always look at it this way, I'm fat and you're ugly. But I can diet.—*David Wells, White Sox pitcher, 2001.*

2161 Did you ever see a monkey with a cramp? —*Bill "Spaceman" Lee, Expos pitcher, on his new banana diet.*

2162 After four days you're hallucinating, and after a week you want to go out and find a grapefruit farmer and blow his head off.—*Frank Robinson, Orioles coach, on a grapefruit diet that helped him lose 22 pounds, 1980.*

2163 You mix two jiggers of scotch to one jigger of Metrecal. So far I've lost five pounds and my driver's license.—*Rocky Bridges, Phoenix Giants manager, on his new diet drink, 1975.*

2164 Ever notice the vampires when they see a crucifix? That's the way I am when I see scales.—*Tommy Lasorda, Dodgers manager, 1986.*

2165 A lot of times I quit eating, not because I was full, but because my arms were tired. I was bending at the elbow. I teach them to bend at the wrist.—*Tommy Lasorda, Hall of Fame manager, on how to eat at a buffet, 2001.*

2166 For every enemy I make, I make 40

friends. And a lot of them are restaurant owners.—*Tommy Lasorda, Dodgers manager.*

2167 I eat fish, baked potatoes, a lot of vegetables and fruits, and I drink eight glasses of water a day. I've drunk enough water to float a ship.—*Tommy Lasorda, Dodgers manager, on his diet, 1989.*

2168 What do you think, that I'm going to the electric chair or that Tommy Lasorda is managing the Reds?—*Jack McKeon, Reds manager, on seeing three plates of food left for him in his office after a game, 1998.*

2169 He has license plates that say, "Honk if you have groceries."—*Steve Stone, Cubs broadcaster, on Dodgers manager Tommy Lasorda, 1987.*

2170 Tommy's the only manager in the major leagues who uses a fork for a letter opener.—*Rick Monday, Dodgers outfielder, on Tommy Lasorda.*

2171 Tommy will eat anything, as long as you pay for it.—*Joe Torre on Dodgers manager Tommy Lasorda.*

2172 He donated one of his old uniforms to the homeless. They made it into a tent and it sleeps a family of 12.—*Frank Sinatra, entertainer, at a celebrity roast for Dodgers manager Tommy Lasorda, 1989.*

2173 Having dinner with Tommy Lasorda is like pitching a game in the big leagues. Afterwards you need three days' rest.—*Joe Garagiola, broadcaster, 1986.*

2174 His stomach used to rumble in the outfield if the other team had a big inning.—*Jim Murray, sportswriter, on Yankees outfielder Babe Ruth.*

2175 If you cut that big slob in half, most of the concessions at Yankee stadium would come pouring out.—*Waite Hoyt, Yankees pitcher, on outfielder Babe Ruth.*

2176 I've seen him order everything on the menu except, "Thank you for dining with us."—*Jerry Royster, Braves infielder, on outfielder Dale Murphy, 1983.*

2177 Yeah, you're a vegetarian, all right. What do you eat? Palm Trees? Redwoods?—*John Candelaria, Pirates pitcher, to outfielder Dave Parker, 1982.*

2178 I'm a light eater. When it gets light, I start eating.—*Tommy John, Yankees pitcher.*

2179 I always eat frog legs before I pitch. It makes my fastball jump.—*Rick Rice, Orioles minor league pitcher.*

2180 I'll have a pie à la mode with ice cream. —*Johnny Logan, Milwaukee Braves shortstop.*

2181 I didn't eat breakfast this morning. Why? Number one, I ain't got no maid. Number two, I ain't got no wife anymore, and number three, I can't cook.—*Willie Mays, Giants outfielder, 1962.*

2182 All the fat guys look at me and say to their wives, "See? There's a fat guy doing okay. Bring me another beer."—*Mickey Lolich, Tigers pitcher, 1971.*

2183 The fatter you get, the faster you get in perpetual motion. I'd come off the mound to field a bunt and just let my weight propel me.—*Mickey Lolich, portly Tigers pitcher.*

2184 Lots of guys have a good belly and a bad arm, but I've got a bad belly and a good arm.—*Mickey Lolich, Tigers pitcher.*

2185 I have to be careful about eating all the fattening foods they serve. I have to watch my playing weight. But the problem there is that I don't know what my playing weight is. I never play.—*Joe Lis, Indians outfielder, 1976.*

2186 My mother must have sent them my baby picture; that was the last time I weighed 175.—*Charlie Kerfeld, Astros reliever, on being listed on his baseball card as 5'11" and 175 lbs, when he was really 6'6" and 245 lbs.*

2187 I've only been intimidated by one thing in my life, and it's not human. It's a scale.—*Charlie Kerfeld, Astros reliever, 1986.*

2188 So I'm watching the game last night and they're talking about the New York Yankees having one of the strongest benches in baseball. And I'm thinking, well, they'd have to have a strong bench to support Don Zimmer and Cecil Fielder.—*David Letterman, talk show host, 1996.*

2189 Did you watch the Macy's Thanksgiving Day parade? The Fat Albert balloon springs a leak and at the last minute was replaced by Yankee first baseman Cecil Fielder.—*David Letterman, talk show host, 1996.*

2190 The fattest man in professional sports—a fat tub of goo.—*David Letterman, talk show host, on Braves reliever Terry Forster.*

2191 A waist is a terrible thing to mind.—*Terry Forster, Braves reliever, 1985.*

2192 I won't have my bodyguard, and there will be more food for everybody.—*Tippy Martinez, Orioles pitcher, explaining how the trade of 300-pound pitcher Tim Stoddard to Oakland would affect the team, 1984.*

2193 If I pulled up in front of a restaurant and he came out to park my car, I'd eat someplace else.—*Bob Brenly, Giants catcher, on reliever Juan Berenguer, 1986.*

2194 He makes a great hitting background.—*Richie Ashburn, Phillies announcer, on noticing that 300-pound John McSherry was umpiring second base, May 1987. McSherry's weight may have been closer to 400 pounds and was a factor in a fatal heart attack suffered before the opening game of the 1996 season.*

2195 I've got three seats for you at my show tonight: One for you, one for your wife and one for your stomach.—*Don Rickles, comedian, to Boston Red Sox manager Don Zimmer.*

2196 His heart is as big as his stomach.—*Roger Craig, Giants manager, on 225-pound pitcher Don Robinson, 1990.*

2197 Like they say, it ain't over till the fat guy swings.—*Darren Daulton, Phillies catcher, on first baseman John Kruk, 1992.*

2198 He looks like a guy who went to a fantasy camp and decided to stay.—*Don Sutton, Braves broadcaster, on beefy Phillies first baseman-outfielder John Kruk, 1991.*

2199 I think any great performer or athlete has to have a little bit of a gut to be great.—*Lance Berkman, Astros first baseman.*

2200 He'd walk into the clubhouse and could barely squeeze into his pants. Once when we were playing the California Angels, he borrowed 20 bucks from Haywood Sullivan to go sightseeing. I didn't realize that you could sightsee in grocery stores, but when Scott returned several hours later, he'd gained seven pounds.—*Dick Williams, former Red Sox manager, on hefty first baseman George Scott.*

2201 I was worried about the horse.—*John Harrington, Red Sox CEO, when asked if he was worried about the safety of first baseman Mo Vaughn riding a horse during the celebration for the Red Sox clinching the AL East, September 1995.*

2202 To endorse this sandwich is not really the message I want to send the club. You can't even eat one side. You have to take it home and eat it for a week.—*Mo Vaughn, weighty Mets first baseman, on the Mo-Licious Sandwich at the Carnegie Deli, a creation designed to welcome Vaughn to the Big Apple, 2002.*

2203 Mo Vaughn of the Mets ripped former teammate Troy Percival and his former team, the Angels, in a tirade that included 35 expletives. The Mets looked on the bright side, however, pointing out that the more time Mo spends spewing four-letter words, the less time he spends eating.—*Michael Ventre, sportswriter, April 2002.*

2204 If [Mo] Vaughn weighed in at 275 pounds [his listed weight] last season, so did Rhode Island.—*Mike Lupica, sportswriter, on the Mets first baseman, November 2002.*

2205 Our steroids were white beans, corn bread and pig's feet.—*Sidney Bunch, former Birmingham Black Barons outfielder, 2005.*

2206 I've started taking food orally again.—*Larry Lucchino, Red Sox president, a few days after Boston lost the ALCS to the Yankees, 2003.*

2207 Now that the Dodgers have added some popular new concessions, like Krispy Kreme doughnuts, King Taco and Subway, fans are hoping they'll add one more item—Maalox.—*Earl Hochman, comedy writer, on the new food choices at Dodger Stadium, 2000.*

2208 Sure, Bobby Bonilla signed a minor league deal with the Braves, but don't expect him to land in the minors. From the looks of him, he'd never make it on minor league meal money.—*Jim Armstrong, sportswriter, 2000. Bonilla did make the Braves, hitting .255 in a reserve role.*

2209 He's never been 220 before. Not since he was five.—*Buddy Bell, Tigers manager, on outfielder Pete Incaviglia arriving for spring training 40 pounds lighter, 1998. In just 20 games with the Tigers and Astros, Incaviglia hit .100 before retiring.*

2210 My kids will love 'em to play in. They're better than refrigerator boxes.—*Rick Stowe, Reds equipment manager, on the size 50 uniform pants purchased from a sporting goods store for Calvin Pickering, 2001. When the Reds acquired the 297-pound first baseman from Baltimore, they didn't have any pants to fit him. Days later, the Red Sox claimed Pickering off waivers, thus making the pants expendable. When asked how much Pickering really weighed, Reds GM Jim Bowden quipped, "Somewhere under 500 pounds."*

2211 You know, Roger, if you get more at-bats this year, you'll have a chance at baseball immortality. You might become the first guy in history to hit his weight and lead the league in batting.—*Ted Simmons, Cardinals catcher, to seldom-used first baseman Roger Freed, during spring training 1978.*

2212 He's the only man who could pitch in 90-degree weather and still gain weight.—*Harry Dorish, Astros coach, on pitcher Jack Lamabe, 1965.*

2213 Charlie is old, he'll blow away; and Bibby is the largest man in North America.—*Doug Rader, Rangers manager, explaining why he bumped scheduled starter Charlie Hough in favor of 250-pound pitcher Jim Bibby on a windy day in Toronto, 1984.*

2214 We had catfish today in the restaurant, and announcer Wayne Hagin said he wouldn't eat anything named after a pitcher.—*Lon Simmons, announcer.*

2215 I think one of the requirements for being a DH is weighing at least 200 pounds, so maybe if I was that heavy I would do it. [But] the day I weigh 200 pounds is the day I'm inside a coffin.—*Ichiro Suzuki, 36-year-old Mariners outfielder, on the possibility of moving to DH when he turned 40, 2009.*

Golf, or How I Spent My Off Day

2216 Baseball reveals character; golf exposes it.—*Ernie Banks, Hall of Famer.*

2217 I was three over—one over a house, one over a patio and one over a swimming pool.—*George Brett, Royals first baseman, on his performance in the Bob Hope Classic golf tournament, 1991.*

2218 When I hit a ball I want someone else to go chase it.—*Rogers Hornsby, Hall of Fame second baseman, on his preference of baseball to golf.*

2219 I never like to golf in the morning and get involved in a ball game at night. I don't like to think twice in the same day.—*Yogi Berra, Yankees catcher.*

2220 Sometimes when I look down at that little white ball, I just wish it was moving.—*Dusty Baker, Giants hitting coach, 1991.*

2221 Last time I played a golf match, I lost 20 balls. I lost one on every hole, one on the 19th hole and one in a ball washer.—*Bob Feller, Hall of Fame pitcher.*

2222 I hit one that far once. And I still bogeyed the hole.—*Ron Fairly, Expos broadcaster, on a mammoth home run by Phillies third baseman Mike Schmidt.*

2223 Sometimes I wonder if we're a baseball team or members of the PGA Tour.—*Casey Candaele, Astros utility player, on the number of golf bags brought on team flights, 1992.*

2224 Spring training should last one day. We'd have the team golf outing and head north.—*John Kruk, Phillies first baseman, 1993.*

2225 Women were outdriving me.—*Ralph Houk, Red Sox manager, on why he left the golf courses in Florida and returned to baseball, 1981.*

2226 Gaylord Perry had the only thing harder to hit than a golf ball.—*Johnny Bench, Hall of Fame catcher.*

2227 Going for a strikeout is like showing off your drive in golf. They pay off on how you putt. I like to save my strikeouts for when I need them.—*Gaylord Perry, Rangers pitcher, 1976.*

2228 If Ueberroth's secretary ever tells you he'll call back after nine, find out if that means nine o'clock or nine holes.—*Phil Mushnick, sportswriter, on baseball commissioner Peter Ueberroth, 1988.*

2229 I tell myself Jack Nicklaus probably has a lousy curveball.—*Bob Walk, Pirates pitcher, on dealing with his golf limitations, 1992.*

2230 The pay is great and the only way you can get hurt playing golf is getting struck by lightning.—*Ted Williams, Rangers manager and Hall of Fame outfielder, 1972.*

2231 From what I saw out there, the players were to the game of golf what the *Exxon Valdez* was to shrimp.—*Mike Scioscia, Dodgers catcher, at a celebrity golf tournament, 1989.*

2232 I'm going to retire at 40, practice for 10 years, then join the Senior golf tour when I turn 50.—*Albert Belle, Indians outfielder, 1994.*

2233 My conscience hurt me. I hate to play golf when I should be working, so the only thing to do was quit working.—*Jim Umbricht, Houston Colt .45s pitcher, on quitting his off-season job as a team ticket salesman, 1963.*

2234 Because I married a rich husband. Now I can miss a $5,000 putt and not worry about the money.—*Nancy Lopez, LPGA golfer and wife of Astros first baseman Ray Knight, on why she doesn't feel any pressure on tour, 1984.*

2235 If it weren't for the money, I'd retire and go caddie for my wife.—*Ray Knight, Mets third baseman, on his wife Nancy Lopez, 1986. Following his retirement in 1988, Knight became his wife's tour caddie.*

2236 He's still caddying for me. He carries the bag from the trunk of the car to the golf course.—*Nancy Lopez, LPGA golfer, on firing husband Ray Knight as her tour caddie, 1990.*

2237 I want to win here, stand on the 18th green and say, "I'm going to the World Series."—*Larry Nelson, PGA golfer and Braves fan, on playing in the Walt Disney Classic while the Braves and Twins played in the 1991 World Series.*

2238 Tension was stepping on the first tee, playing for $20 when you know damn well you have only $10 in your pocket.—*Denny McLain, 1968 AL Cy Young winner and MVP, on making a living after baseball as a golf hustler, 1985.*

2239 I think my skills are at that level. Plus, Birmingham has some nice golf courses.—*Michael Jordan, former Chicago Bulls guard, on being assigned to the Double-A White Sox affiliate, 1994.*

2240 An average guy who works at IBM can become a 10 handicap, but an average guy at IBM can't play baseball. In baseball, Michael is an average guy.—*Andy Van Slyke, Pirates outfielder, on the attempt by basketball star Michael Jordan to become an outfielder for the White Sox, 1994.*

2241 Baseball is ridiculous. You've got an outfielder standing out there picking his nose and catching three fly balls a day and hitting .220, and he's making $1.9 million a year.—*Mark Calcavecchia, PGA golfer, 1989.*

2242 You can't call it a sport. You don't run, jump; you don't shoot, you don't pass. All you have to do is buy some clothes that don't match.—*Steve Sax, Dodgers second baseman, on golf.*

2243 I've hit many balls into the drink in my time. It's usually with seven-irons and five-irons.—*Mark Grace, Cubs first baseman, on being the first player to hit a home run into the swimming pool at the Bank One Ballpark in Phoenix, 1998.*

2244 I saw a splash. It was reminiscent of one of my golf shots.—*Terry Bevington, White Sox manager, on seeing first baseman Frank Thomas hit a home run into the waterfall at Royals Stadium, July 1995.*

2245 Anybody. Please make some noise.—*Ken Griffey Jr., Mariners outfielder, on the deafening silence before a putt at a celebrity golf tournament, 1999.*

2246 You're *supposed* to hit fly balls in this game.—*Jeff Maggert, PGA golfer, to his struggling pro-am partner, Indians outfielder Kenny Lofton, 1996.*

2247 How about Tiger Woods? You see how far he hit that ball? The only way he could have hit it farther is if one of the Cubs pitchers were pitching to him.—*Jay Leno, talk show host, 1997.*

2248 I was a 10-handicap at 10 [years old], and I won the 10-and-under division at a pro-am tournament at Candlewood Country Club in Southern California. I beat Tiger Woods by five strokes—but he was only 6 at the time.—*Gregg Zaun, Tigers catcher, 2000. Zaun's uncle is former catcher Rick Dempsey.*

2249 Ninety percent of putts that are short don't go in.—*Yogi Berra, Hall of Fame catcher.*

2250 I suddenly had a lot of friends in the clubhouse. Guys are coming up to me and telling me they're part Irish. With Carlos Lee, I kind of doubt it.—*Paul Konerko, White Sox DH, after he won a trip for four to Ireland by making a hole-in-one shot at a benefit golf tournament, 2000.*

2251 Okay, I'm positive my shot is going into the water.—*Yogi Berra, Hall of Fame catcher, when told to "think positively" during a game of golf.*

2252 That's great news. Now, when you hit a drive into the ocean, it doesn't cost you a stroke. It's just a foul ball.—*Jerry Perisho, comedy writer, on former baseball commissioner Peter Ueberroth being part of a group that purchased the Pebble Beach golf course, June 1999.*

2253 I couldn't get my golf clubs in the Ferrari.—*Livan Hernandez, Marlins pitcher, on trading in his yellow Ferrari for a black Mercedes, 1998.*

2254 The last time I batted was in Little League, and that's the speed he was throwing.—*Paul Azinger, PGA golfer, on tour pro Phil Mickelson's pitching tryout with the Toledo Mud Hens, September 2003.*

2255 I know that people who have seen me out on the course find it mighty hard to believe that golf's my hobby. Actually, it's not a hobby. It's an ordeal. I'd do much better if they'd build golf courses in a circle. You see, I have this slice.—*Rocky Bridges, San Jose Bees manager, 1964.*

2256 Too bad there aren't water hazards in baseball like there are in golf. We could lose all the balls and go home.—*Lon Simmons, announcer.*

2257 I wanted to shoot in the 80s, so I walked off the course with five holes to go.—*Tom Brookens, Detroit Tigers coach, after a round of golf during spring training, 2010.*

2258 It took me 17 years to get 3,000 hits. I did it in one afternoon on the golf course.—*Henry Aaron, Braves first baseman-outfielder, 1971.*

Home Runs

2259 I have only one superstition. I make sure I touch all bases when I hit a home run.—*Babe Ruth, Yankees outfielder.*

2260 There is something uniquely American in hitting one out of the park.—*Dick Young, sportswriter.*

2261 The fans would rather see me hit one homer to right than three doubles to left.—

Babe Ruth, Yankees outfielder. Ruth finished his career with 714 home runs. Before Ruth, the career home run record was 136 by 19th century Hall of Famer Roger Connor.

2262 Before the season, we took a survey of the fans and found out they want to see home runs more than anything else. So we went out to build a pitching staff to oblige them.—*Clark Griffith Jr., Twins executive.*

2263 Home run hitters drive Cadillacs; singles hitters drive Fords.—*Ralph Kiner, Pirates outfielder. Kiner led the NL in home runs his first seven seasons.*

2264 A homer a day will boost my pay.—*Josh Gibson, Negro League catcher, who purportedly hit more than 800 career home runs.*

2265 Taters, that's where the money is.—*Reggie Jackson, Yankees outfielder, who retired with 563 home runs, 13th on the all-time list.*

2266 No one can tell you how to hit home runs. You either have the natural strength and reflexes, or you don't.—*Hank Greenberg, Tigers outfielder, who had 183 RBI in 1937 and hit 58 home runs in 1938.*

2267 As far as I can tell, there is no correlation between running the mile and hitting a home run.—*Harmon Killebrew, Royals DH, 1975, who retired fifth on the all-time homer list with 573 (11th as of 2010).*

2268 It's a lot more fun running around the bases than going to first and stopping.—*George Brett, Royals third baseman, 1977. In his Hall of Fame career, Brett hit 317 home runs.*

2269 I'd rather hit home runs. You don't have to run as hard.—*Dave Kingman, Cubs outfielder, who finished with 442 home runs yet failed to garner even 1% of the vote for his only year (1992) on the Hall of Fame ballot. His .236 career batting average and surly personality probably didn't help his cause.*

2270 I've hit over 300 of these. I deserve the opportunity to run them out any way I want to.—*Dave Parker, Oakland A's DH, on his leisurely home run trot, 1989. Parker retired in 1991 with 339 homers.*

2271 I'd like to get four singles in a game, but a home run is easier on the legs.—*Rob Deer, Tigers outfielder, 1992. In his ten-year career, Deer led the AL in strikeouts four times.*

2272 As I remember, the bases were loaded. —*Garry Maddox, Phillies outfielder, recalling his first grand slam, 1979.*

2273 I didn't know it was a grand slam until I rounded third and saw three people waiting to greet me.—*Mike Pagliarulo, Yankees third baseman.*

2274 You don't get your first home run too often.—*Rick Wrona, Cubs catcher, 1989.*

2275 It's like scoring your first touchdown.—*Brian Jordan, Cardinals outfielder and Atlanta Falcons safety, on breaking an 0-for-19 slump by hitting his first career home run, 1992. Jordan had never scored a touchdown as an NFL player.*

2276 It seems impossible to go a decade without a home run, but Rafael Belliard somehow went from May 5, 1987 to Sept. 26, 1997 between homers (1,869 at bats). In between, 40,653 homers were hit by everyone else and 379 just by Mark McGwire.—*Jayson Stark, sportswriter, 2000.*

2277 What's one home run? If you hit one, they are just going to want you to hit two.—*Mick Kelleher, Tigers infielder, on not hitting a home run in ten seasons, 1981. Kelleher logged 1,081 at-bats without ever hitting a homer.*

2278 It really wasn't very dramatic. No little boy in the hospital asked me to hit one. I didn't promise it to my kid for his birthday, and my wife will be too shocked to appreciate it. I hit it for me.—*Rocky Bridges, Angels infielder, on hitting his first home run in two years, 1961. Bridges retired at the end of the season with just 16 homers in his 11-year career.*

2279 I thought as I got to second, "Did I touch first?"—*Dave Van Gorder, Reds catcher, on his first career home run, 1985.*

2280 I wanted to go into my home run trot, but I realized I didn't have one.—*Jim Essian, White Sox catcher, 1977. During nine seasons Essian hit 33 home runs.*

2281 I really hit ten, but I want the ones in batting practice too.—*Grady Little, Red Sox manager, on hitting two home runs in six minor league seasons, 2002.*

2282 When I got to second base, I didn't know whether to continue or to stop and apologize to the pitcher.—*Sandy Koufax, Dodgers pitcher, on hitting a grand slam, 1963. Koufax, a career .097 hitter, swatted only one other homer in his career.*

2283 Where I'm trying to hit the ball, the turf ain't got nothing to do with it. If I hit a ball in the turf, it's a mistake.—*Reggie Jackson, Oakland A's DH, on whether he preferred playing on turf or natural grass, 1987.*

2284 It was nothing for me to hit two home runs and punch out three times. That was a Reggie day—a hat trick and a couple of bombs. —*Slugger Reggie Jackson.*

2285 It was an insurance run, so I hit it to the Prudential Building.—*Reggie Jackson, Yankees outfielder, on hitting a home run in Boston.*

2286 The homers he has hit against us would be homers in any park, including Yellowstone.—*Paul Richards, former manager and executive, on Hall of Fame outfielder Harmon Killebrew, 1984.*

2287 Sammy's ball would have been out of most national parks. Not National League parks. National parks.—*Buck Showalter, Diamondbacks manager, on a 479-foot spring training home run by Cubs outfielder Sammy Sosa, 1998.*

2288 Anything that goes that far in the air ought to have a stewardess on it.—*Paul Splittorf, Royals pitcher, on a tremendous home run by third baseman George Brett.*

2289 When Neil Armstrong first set foot on the moon, he and all the space scientists were puzzled by an unidentifiable white object. I knew immediately what it was. That was a home-run ball hit off me in 1937 by Jimmie Foxx.—*Lefty Gomez, Hall of Fame pitcher, 1978.*

2290 That thing had to stop in Albuquerque to refuel.—*Larry Walker, Rockies outfielder, on a 529-foot home run by first baseman Andres Galarraga, 1996*

2291 Your basic George Foster home run—it probably would have killed four people and broken three seats.—*Ed Ott, Pirates catcher, on the Reds outfielder, October 1979.*

2292 You know how the fans in the left field stands will gather and wait for the home run ball to come down? Well, he hit the ball so hard they scattered.—*Frank LaCorte, Astros reliever, on Atlanta Braves third baseman Bob Horner, 1981.*

2293 That ball went farther than I ever went on vacation as a kid.—*Gene Gieselmann, Cardinals trainer, on a 470-foot spring training home run by Rangers outfielder Juan Gonzalez, 1994.*

2294 Baseball is a game of inches. The Bull just put 4,800 of them together.—*Tim McCarver, Phillies catcher, on a home run by outfielder Greg Luzinski, 1977.*

2295 There have been a plethora of guys to hit it up there, but that was the plethorest.—*Chuck Pool, Marlins publicist, on an upper-deck home run at Joe Robbie Stadium by Reds outfielder Kevin Mitchell, 1994.*

2296 They need to start changing the measurement system for him. Using feet is getting too ridiculous. Quarter-miles would be nice.—*Doug Glanville, Phillies outfielder, on the gargantuan home runs by Cardinals first baseman Mark McGwire, 1998.*

2297 That guy hits home runs so far that they should only count the ones he hits into the second or third decks. If he hits 'em in the lower deck, they should be ground rule doubles.—*Eddie Taubensee, Reds catcher, on Cardinals first baseman Mark McGwire, 1997.*

2298 I hit them off scoreboards. Mark hits them over scoreboards.—*Ken Griffey Jr., Mariners outfielder, on Oakland A's first baseman Mark McGwire, 1997.*

2299 These stadiums are like Little League to him.—*Dennis Eckersley, Cardinals reliever, on first baseman Mark McGwire, who was traded mid-season from Oakland to St. Louis, 1997.*

2300 How feared is this man? They even pitched around him in a home-run derby.—*Jayson Stark, sportswriter, on Mark McGwire not getting many good pitches to swing at during the All-Star Game home run hitting contest, 1998.*

2301 You can't put anything of value where he can reach it. If it's in the park, he's going to break it.—*Rich Donnelly, Rockies coach, on a 507-foot home run by Mark McGwire that knocked out a light panel on the Shea Stadium scoreboard, September 1999.*

2302 The best place to catch a baseball hit by McGwire is definitely not within the confines of the playing field, or sometimes even the ballpark. Other players dial '1' for long distance. McGwire has to ask for an international operator.—*Thomas Boswell, sportswriter, on Cardinals first baseman Mark McGwire.*

2303 Some of our guys would have to pick up the ball and hit it three times to get it that far.—*Steve McCatty, Oakland A's pitcher, on a 450-foot homer by Mariners first baseman Bruce Bochte, 1980.*

2304 It sounded like a cannon. Not as loud, but very crispy.—*Sandy Guerrero, Brewers minor league hitting coach, on giving up a 503-foot homer to Milwaukee first baseman Prince Fielder during the 2009 Home Run Derby.*

2305 Buck hit a home run so far off Bob Feller that it cleared the fence, the bleachers, a row of houses, and hit a big old water tower out there. It rained in that town for five weeks.—*Negro League star Ted "Double Duty" Radcliffe on first baseman Buck Leonard.*

2306 If it goes 500 feet off me, I'm as amazed as he is.—*Rob Dibble, Reds reliever, on why he doesn't mind if a batter stands and admires a home run, 1990.*

2307 The only thing that bothers me is that it takes them so long to run around the bases. I just wish that when a guy hits one, he could walk straight back to the dugout.—*Gary Nolan, Reds pitcher, on home runs, 1976.*

2308 Nearly every sports hero who has a superiority complex has come by it honestly. Home run hitters are criticized for standing at home plate and admiring their work. When Michelangelo finished a ceiling, did he toss aside his brush and trot quickly out of the building?—*Scott Ostler, sportswriter, 2002.*

2309 I had some friends here from North Carolina, and they'd never seen a home run, so I gave them a couple—*Catfish Hunter, Oakland A's pitcher, on surrendering two home runs in the 1974 World Series against Los Angeles.*

2310 It's pretty bad when your family asks for passes to the game and wants to sit in the left-field bleachers.—*Bert Blyleven, Twins pitcher, 1987, who was on pace to break his own 1986 record of 50 home runs surrendered in a season. Blyleven gave up a mere 46 homers in 1987, good for second on the single-season lis. For his career, he finished seventh with 413 home runs allowed.*

2311 When you get that nice celebration coming into the dugout and you're getting your ass hammered by guys—there's no better feeling than to have that done.—*Matt Stairs, Phillies outfielder, on hitting a two-run homer in Game 4 of the 2008 NLCS against the Dodgers, October 13, 2008.*

2312 The greatest thrill in the world is to end the game with a home run and watch everybody walk off the field while you're running the bases on air.—*Al Rosen, Indians third baseman.*

2313 I got to third base and I was looking for someone to hand the baton to.—*Doug Strange, Expos utility player, on hitting an inside-the-park home run, 1997.*

2314 You do that in the regular season and it's crazy because the whole team is out there to meet you at the plate. In the spring it's just like, "Sweet. No extra innings. We're outta here."—*Travis Lee, Diamondbacks first baseman, on hitting a walk-off homer in spring training, 1999.*

2315 I called my mom after the game because it was her anniversary and told her the home run was for her. I had to because I didn't send her a card. I got bailed out.—*Cliff Floyd, Marlins outfielder, 2000.*

2316 He does have big-time power. Unfortunately, he showed most of it in batting practice.—*Jim Leyland, Tigers manager, on backup outfielder Alexis Gomez hitting a home run in Game 2 of the 2006 ALCS.*

2317 There were only two Bash Brothers (Mark McGwire and Jose Canseco), and one's in Boston now. Maybe I can be a Bash Stepchild.—*Scott Brosius, Oakland A's third baseman, who had 10 homers, after suggestions that he was ready to become a Bash Brother.*

2318 It's OK with me, I guess—as long as I hit 85 homers.—*Adam Dunn, Nationals outfielder, when told that no player had ever hit more home runs that his team had wins, 2009. On July 20, Dunn had 24 dingers and Washington had 26 wins. Dunn finished the year with 38 homers while the Nationals won 59 games.*

2319 I never thought home runs were all that exciting. I still think the triple is the most exciting thing in baseball. To me, a triple is like a guy taking the ball on his 1-yard line and running 99 yards for a touchdown.—*Hank Aaron, Milwaukee Braves outfielder.*

2320 I don't know why people like the home run so much. A home run is over as soon as it starts.... The triple is the most exciting play of the game. A triple is like meeting a woman who excites you, spending the evening talking and getting more excited, then taking her home. It drags on and on. You're never sure how it's going to turn out.—*George Foster, Reds outfielder, 1978.*

2321 The most exciting hit in baseball is the triple.... You usually have two or three men handling the ball; and, if everything fits together, the runner is flagged down on a close play. On doubles and triples, several men must contribute. On a home run, one man does it all.—*Harry Walker, Astros manager.*

2322 A guy who strikes out as much as I do had better lead in something.—*Mike Schmidt, Phillies third baseman, after leading the majors in home runs and whiffs each season from 1974 to 1976.*

2323 It was a low fastball. It just happened to be right where I was swinging.—*Alan Ashby, Astros catcher, on how he hit a home run, 1981.*

2324 No, I was thinking wild pitch.—*Elrod Hendricks, Orioles catcher, when asked if he was thinking about hitting a homer before he cracked a game-winning, three-run dinger, August 1975.*

2325 Chicks who dig home runs aren't the ones who appeal to me. I think there's sexiness in infield hits because they require technique. I'd rather impress the chicks with my technique than with my brute strength. Then, every now and then, just to show I can do that, too, I might flirt a little by hitting one out.—*Ichiro Suzuki, Mariners outfielder, August 2009. In his first nine major league seasons, Ichiro had 2,030 hits, 84 of which were homers.*

2326 That's from the outhouse to the penthouse right there.—*Scott Hatteberg, Red Sox catcher, on hitting a grand slam the at-bat after hitting into a triple play versus Texas, August 6, 2001.*

2327 Mickey tried to hit every one like they didn't count under 400 feet.—*Manager Casey Stengel on Yankees outfielder Mickey Mantle.*

2328 Whenever I'm tempted to grouse about the hype surrounding another Sammy Sosa-Mark McGwire home run chase, I remind myself that it could be Albert Belle and Juan Gonzalez.—*Michael Ventre, sportswriter, September 1999.*

2329 He hits the ball too far to hit singles. You could take one of his hits and cut it up and make 10 singles. Right now the ballparks are just too small for him. So he can't hit a single.—*Mike Krukow, Giants broadcaster, on Barry Bonds hitting so many homers and so few singles, May 2001. Bonds finished the season with 49 singles, 32 doubles, 2 triples, and 73 homers.*

2330 *Sportswriter:* You hit only two home runs all last year, and already you've hit seven this year. What's the difference?

Alex Johnson (Reds outfielder, 1969): Five.

2331 You hit home runs by not trying to hit home runs. I know that doesn't sound right, and it won't read right, but that's the way it is.—*Hitting coach Charlie Lau.*

Hyperbolic Praise

2332 Two-thirds of the earth is covered by water; the other one-third is covered by Garry Maddox.—*Ralph Kiner, Mets broadcaster, 1978.*

2333 One time he hit a line drive right past my ear. I turned around and saw the ball hit his ass sliding into second.—*Satchel Paige, Negro league pitcher, on outfielder James "Cool Papa" Bell.*

2334 Cool Papa Bell was so fast he could get out of bed, turn out the light across the room and be back in bed under the covers before the lights went out.—*Josh Gibson, Negro League catcher.*

2335 This kid runs so fast in the outfield, he doesn't bend a blade of grass.—*Casey Stengel, Yankees manager, on outfielder Mickey Mantle.*

2336 Trying to sneak a pitch past Hank Aaron is like trying to sneak a sunrise past a rooster.—*Joe Adcock, Milwaukee Braves infielder. (Also attributed to Philadelphia A's pitcher Curt Simmons.)*

2337 Trying to hit him is like trying to eat Jell-O with chopsticks. Once in a while you might get a piece, but most of the time you go hungry.—*Bobby Murcer, Cubs outfielder, on Braves knuckleball pitcher Phil Niekro.*

2338 It's like attempting to strike a cotton ball in a tornado.—*Paul O'Neill, Yankees outfielder, on hitting the knuckleball of Red Sox pitcher Tim Wakefield, 1999.*

2339 Trying to hit Carl Hubbell's screwball was like a guy trying to hit fungoes out of a well.—*Frankie Frisch, Cardinals manager, on the New York Giants pitcher and two-time MVP.*

2340 He could throw the ball by you so fast you never knew whether you swung under it or over it.—*Smoky Joe Wood, Red Sox pitcher, on Washington Senators pitcher Walter Johnson. Wood was also an accomplished batter (.283 career average) and would platoon in right field when he wasn't pitching.*

2341 Sandy's fastball was so fast, some batters would start to swing as he was on his way to the mound.—*Jim Murray, sportswriter, on Hall of Fame pitcher Sandy Koufax.*

2342 Either he throws the fastest ball I've ever seen, or I'm going blind.—*Richie Ashburn, Phillies outfielder, on Dodgers pitcher Sandy Koufax.*

2343 Sometimes I hit him like I used to hit Sandy Koufax, and that's like drinking coffee with a fork.—*Willie Stargell, Pirates first baseman, on Phillies pitcher Steve Carlton, 1972.*

2344 He could throw a lamb chop past a wolf.—*Bugs Baer, sportswriter, on Philadelphia A's pitcher Lefty Grove.*

2345 He could throw a cream puff through a battleship.—*Johnny Frederick, Brooklyn Dodgers outfielder, on pitcher Dazzy Vance.*

2346 He is quite strong enough to throw a soft-boiled egg through a battleship.—*Blackie Sherrod, sportswriter, on Dodgers pitcher Don Drysdale, 1961.*

2347 He throws so hard he could start a forest fire.—*Willie Stargell, Pirates first baseman, on Astros pitcher J.R. Richard, 1975.*

2348 Nobody throws harder than Nolan Ryan. Not even God.—*George Scott, Red Sox first baseman, 1978.*

2349 [Don] Gullett's the only guy who can throw a baseball through a car wash and not get the ball wet.—*Pete Rose, Reds outfielder, 1970.*

2350 He could throw strikes at midnight.—*Billy Herman, Hall of Fame second baseman, on Hall of Fame pitcher Carl Hubble.*

2351 It's like someone throwing a chainsaw to the plate, and I'm supposed to hit it with my bat.—*Tony Gwynn, Padres outfielder, on Dodgers pitcher Kevin Brown, 1999.*

2352 He could recognize a great player from the window of a moving train.—*Jim Murray, sportswriter, on Hall of Fame executive Branch Rickey.*

2353 He once hit a ball between my legs so hard that my center fielder caught it on the fly backing up against the wall.—*Dizzy Dean, Hall of Fame pitcher, on Hall of Fame first baseman Bill Terry, 1973.*

2354 Charley Gehringer could hit me in a tunnel at midnight with the lights out.—*Lefty Gomez, Hall of Fame pitcher, 1980.*

2355 The nice thing about Cedeno is that he can play all three outfield positions—at the same time.—*Gene Mauch, Expos manager, on Astros outfielder Cesar Cedeno, 1974.*

2356 If Satch and I were pitching on the same team, we'd cinch the pennant by July 4 and go fishing until the World Series.—*Dizzy Dean, Cardinals pitcher, on Pittsburgh Crawfords pitcher Satchel Paige, 1934.*

2357 It starts out like a baseball, and when it gets to the plate, it looks like a marble.—*Hack Wilson, Cubs outfielder, on facing Satchel Paige.*

2358 It got so I could nip frosting off a cake with my fastball.—*Satchel Paige, Hall of Fame pitcher.*

2359 He could have knocked a gnat off a hitter's nose.—*Bob Skinner, Pirates outfielder, on pitcher Harvey Haddix.*

2360 The man has only one weakness. He can hit a ball 450 feet left-handed, but can hit it only 420 feet right-handed.—*Mike LaValliere, Pirates catcher, on third baseman Bobby Bonilla, 1988.*

2361 Richie Allen is so strong he has arms like legs.—*Gene Mauch, Expos manager, 1974.*

2362 I was such a dangerous hitter, I even got intentional walks in batting practice.—*Casey Stengel, Hall of Fame manager, on his playing days, 1967.*

2363 If someone threw him a resin bag, he'd get a double.—*Gene Mauch, Angels manager, on Mariners outfielder Tom Paciorek, 1981.*

2364 That guy could hit from an operating table.—*Vic Wertz, Twins first baseman, on oft-injured Yankees outfielder Mickey Mantle, 1963.*

2365 George Brett could get good wood on an aspirin.—*Jim Frey, Royals manager.*

2366 He could hit buckshot with barbed wire. —*Jim Frey, Royals manager, on third baseman George Brett.*

2367 If God had him no balls and two strikes, he'd still get a hit.—*Steve Palermo, umpire, on Royals DH George Brett, 1992.*

2368 When Hal is on, the only way to get him out is to pitch him an invisible ball. Then again, he'd probably hit that, too, and the fielders wouldn't be able to find it.—*Kevin Mitchell, Reds outfielder, on first baseman Hal Morris, 1994.*

2369 Rod Carew could get more hits with a soup bone than I could get with a rack full of bats.—*Steve Brye, Twins outfielder, on the 1967 AL Rookie of the Year.*

2370 He's the only guy I know who can go 4-for-3.—*Alan Bannister, White Sox infielder, on Angels first baseman Rod Carew, 1979.*

2371 He is so hot, he could shoot a gun off in the air and kill a fish.—*Bernard Gilkey, Diamondbacks outfielder, on teammate Luis Gonzalez who was hitting .396 and logged a 30-game hitting streak, 1999. With that amazing start, Gonzo made his first All-Star team.*

2372 He is hitting so well he could single off a dandruff flake. Throw him an acorn at 90 mph, and it's off the wall or out of the park.—*Frank Luksa, sportswriter, on Rangers first baseman Rafael Palmeiro, who was such a good hitter that he won a Gold Glove despite playing only 28 games at first base, 1999.*

2373 He hits the ball so hard, the guy in the on deck circle can score.—*Mike Stanley, Red Sox catcher, on first baseman Mo Vaughn, 1997.*

2374 He's the only guy I know who can drive in three runs with nobody on base.—*Mark McLemore, Rangers second baseman, on teammate Juan Gonzalez, who won the 1996 and 1998 AL MVP.*

2375 He has a strike zone the size of Hitler's heart.—*Jim Murray, sportswriter, on Oakland A's outfielder Rickey Henderson.*

2376 Trying to hit the ball through the Baltimore infield was like trying to throw a hamburger through a brick wall.—*Mayo Smith, former Tigers manager, on the Orioles infield of 1969: third baseman Brooks Robinson, shortstop Mark Belanger, second baseman Davey Johnson and first baseman Boog Powell. All but Powell won a Gold Glove that season.*

2377 The Giants without Rusie would be like *Hamlet* without the Melancholy Dane.—*O.P. Caylor, sportswriter and former Red Stockings manager, on New York Giants pitcher Amos Rusie, 1894.*

2378 If you pitched inside to him, he'd tear a hand off the third baseman; and if you pitched him outside, he'd knock down your second baseman.—*Ed Walsh, White Sox pitcher, on Indians second baseman Nap Lajoie. Walsh was the last 40-game winner, going 40–15 in 1908.*

2379 His fastball looked about the size of a watermelon seed, and it hissed at you as it passed.—*Ty Cobb, Tigers outfielder, on Washington Senators pitcher Walter Johnson.*

2380 He could have hit .300 with a fountain pen.—*Joe Garagiola, broadcaster, on Hall of Famer Stan Musial.*

2381 Once [Stan] Musial timed your fastball, your infielders were in jeopardy.—*Warren Spahn, Milwaukee Braves pitcher.*

2382 He hit line drives that put the opposition in jeopardy. And I don't mean infielders, I mean outfielders.—*Ossie Bluege, Senators farm director, on Washington third baseman Harmon Killebrew, whom he scouted and signed.*

2383 As a batter, his only weakness is a wild pitch.—*Bill Rigney, Giants manager, on outfielder Willie Mays.*

2384 The last time Willie Mays dropped a pop fly he had a rattle in one hand and a bonnet on his head.—*Jim Murray, sportswriter.*

2385 Does Pete hustle? Before the All-Star Game he came into the clubhouse and took off his shoes, and they ran another mile without him.—*Hank Aaron, Braves outfielder, on Reds All-Star Pete Rose.*

2386 I never saw anything like it. He doesn't just hit pitchers, he takes away their dignity.—*Don Sutton, Dodgers pitcher, on Pirates first baseman Willie Stargell.*

2387 He's so good, I even worry about him in the winter.—*Ted Williams, Red Sox outfielder, on Yankees pitcher Bob Lemon.*

2388 Never in Seattle's 25 years in the major leagues has there been a hitter who can get mothers to pause before fixing dinner, fathers to halt channel surfing, and ballpark patrons to scurry back from beer lines, just to witness an infield grounder.—*Art Thiel, sportswriter, on the arrival of Mariners outfielder Ichiro Suzuki, May 2001.*

2389 You could make a strike zone shaped like a triangle, and with both those guys, it wouldn't matter. I'd be willing to bet they'd find a way to be successful.—*John Schuerholz, Braves GM, on Atlanta pitchers Greg Maddux and Tom Glavine, 2001.*

2390 He's such a good, all–American kid. You want to stand next to him in a rainstorm because you know lightning won't hit him.—*Ron Fairly, Angels broadcaster, on first baseman Wally Joyner.*

2391 I know I couldn't have done it. I'd rather have been in a ring with 15 pit bulls and no clothes on.—*Clyde Wright, former Angels pitcher, on watching his son, Indians pitcher Jaret Wright, beat the Yankees in the Division Series, October 2, 1997.*

2392 If Ortiz were any more comfortable at the plate, he'd bring a chaise lounge, a pitcher of pina coladas and a couple of Cuban cigars with him to the batter's box.—*Mike Vaccaro, sportswriter, on Red Sox DH David Ortiz, 2006. Big Papi finished in the top five of the MVP voting every year from 2003 to 2007.*

2393 He has muscles in his hair.—*Lefty Gomez, Yankees pitcher, on Philadelphia A's first baseman Jimmie Foxx.*

2394 Even his perspiration has muscles.—

Jimmie Foxx, former All-Star first baseman, on Reds first baseman Ted Kluszewski.

2395 He hit a popup against us one day that went so high, all nine guys on our team called for it.—*Rich Donnelly, Marlins coach, on Cardinals first baseman Mark McGwire, 1998.*

2396 Batting against Don Drysdale is the same as making a date with a dentist.—*Dick Groat, Pirates shortstop.*

2397 That guy could hit me in the middle of the night, blindfolded and with two broken feet to boot.—*Hall of Fame pitcher Bob Feller on Yankees outfielder Tommy Henrich.*

2398 Their only weakness is they can't hit balls rolled under the plate.—*Cubs manager Charlie Grimm on Pittsburgh outfielders Paul and Lloyd Waner.*

2399 Slapping a rattlesnake across the face with the back of your hand is safer than trying to fool Henry Aaron.—*Claude Osteen, Astros pitcher, 1974.*

Insults

2400 Joe, when they list all the great catchers, you'll be there listening.—*Casey Stengel, Hall of Fame manager, to former catcher Joe Garagiola.*

2401 Call me anything, call me motherfucker, but don't call me Durocher. A Durocher is the lowest form of living matter.—*Harry Wendlestedt, umpire, on Astros manager Leo Durocher, 1973.*

2402 Leo Durocher is a man with an infantile capacity for immediately making a bad thing worse.—*Branch Rickey, Brooklyn Dodgers GM.*

2403 It took the United States 35 years to get revenge for Pearl Harbor.—*Vin Scully, Dodgers broadcaster, on Leo Durocher being hired as manager of the Taiheio Club Lions of the Japanese Pacific League, 1976. Durocher retired due to illness before the season began.*

2404 Run a team? He couldn't run a tollbooth. —*Sal Bando, Oakland A's third baseman, on manager Alvin Dark.*

2405 I did not call Johnson an idiot. Someone else did and I just agreed.—*Jim Palmer, Orioles pitcher, on not being named to the 1976 All-Star team by Red Sox manager Darrell Johnson. Palmer went on to win the AL Cy Young Award and Johnson was fired after the All-Star break.*

2406 He's the only man I know Dale Carnegie would hit in the mouth.—*Bill Veeck, White Sox owner, on Dodgers owner Walter O'Malley, 1973.*

2407 Today I told my little girl I was going to the ballpark, and she asked, "What for?"—*Dave Anderson, Dodgers infielder, 1987.*

2408 So all those people booing wouldn't know you were my father.—*Shirlee Anderson on why she booed her father, manager Sparky Anderson, who hit .218 as a second baseman for the Phillies in 1959, his only season in the majors as a player.*

2409 Sparky Anderson has a slight impediment of speech. Every once in a while, he stops to take a breath.—*Milton Richman, sportswriter, on the Tigers manager, 1984.*

2410 I like playing for Dick. But once I get out of the game, I'm going to run him over with a car.—*Tim Flannery, Padres second baseman, on Mariners manager Dick Williams, 1987.*

2411 Playing for Dick Williams is like being the chef for Moammar Kadafi.—*Kurt Bevacqua, former utility player, on his former manager, 1986.*

2412 Tommy Lasorda's curve had as much hang time as a Ray Guy punt.—*Rocky Bridges, Giants coach, on the Dodgers manager, 1985. In a brief career with the Brooklyn Dodgers and Kansas City A's, Lasorda compiled a 0–4 record with a 6.52 ERA.*

2413 Tommy really has a one-track mind, and the traffic on it is very light. He's one guy who has a sixth sense, but there's no evidence of the other five.—*Steve Garvey, Padres first baseman, on Dodgers manager Tommy Lasorda, 1985.*

2414 You could plant two thousand rows of corn with the fertilizer he spreads around.—*Joe Garagiola, broadcaster, on Dodgers manager Tommy Lasorda, 1977.*

2415 This guy's a problem. He's obstinate. An insecure man. Not a very good manager. I don't think he's a good leader.—*Peter Angelos, Orioles owner, on Baltimore manager Johnny Oates, 1994. Despite finishing in second place, Oates was fired after the season.*

2416 Congratulations, you've managed to get one more man out than a dead man could. —*Ron Perranoski, Dodgers pitching coach, on a visit to the mound to see pitcher Jerry Reuss.*

2417 Sit down, Paul. We ain't giving up yet. —*Leo Durocher, Cubs manager, to infielder Paul Popovich, who was getting off the bench to enter a game that Chicago was losing, 1966.*

2418 I wish I could buy you for what you're really worth and sell you for what you think you're worth.—*Mickey Mantle, Yankees outfielder, to teammate Joe Pepitone.*

2419 Vince is the only player I ever saw who could strike out three times in one game and not be embarrassed. He'd walk into the clubhouse whistling. Everybody would be feeling sorry for him, but Vince always thought he was doing good.—*Casey Stengel, Boston Braves manager, on outfielder Vince DiMaggio, 1938. That season DiMaggio hit .228 and struck out a league-leading 134 times. The next closest player in either league had 101 strikeouts.*

2420 The one thing that has kept Jack Perconte from being a good major leaguer is performance.—*Del Crandall, Mariners manager, on his second baseman, 1984. Perconte was a three-time minor league All-Star who hit .270 with only two home runs in the majors.*

2421 Ladies and gentlemen, I suffer with you. I've never seen such stupid baseball playing in my life.—*Ray Kroc, Padres owner, during San Diego's home-opening loss to Houston 9–1, 1974. The comments were made over the stadium's public address system.*

2422 If it's true we learn by our mistakes, then Jim Frey will be the best manager ever.—*Ron Luciano, broadcaster and former umpire.*

2423 Jim Frey has the emotional intensity of a comatose eggplant.—*Bill James, baseball analyst, on the Royals manager, 1980.*

2424 The evidence suggests he couldn't identify Babe Ruth in a lineup with Alice Cooper, Billy Carter and Morris, the finicky cat.—*Dave Kindred, sportswriter, on Angels GM Harry Dalton, 1977.*

2425 *Radio announcer:* Billy, next to being on my show, what has been your biggest thrill?

Billy Martin (Yankees manager): Getting off your show.

2426 Pardon me, but I have to go. Someone important just came in.—*Toots Shor, New York City restaurateur, to Sir Alexander Fleming, the Nobel Prize–winning discoverer of penicillin, on seeing New York Giants manager Mel Ott enter his restaurant.*

2427 All these women flocked around Bubby. I said, "What about me?" One said, "I want to smell cologne, not Ben-Gay."—*Jim Leyland, Pirates manager, on attending a local sports banquet with Pittsburgh Steelers quarterback Bubby Brister, 1990.*

2428 I'm where I belong, he's where he belongs.—*Ozzie Guillen, Braves shortstop, on his former White Sox manager Terry Bevington, who was managing the Triple-A Syracuse SkyChiefs, 1998.*

2429 Roger Clemens was blessed with a $31-million arm and a pea-sized brain.—*Mike Barnicle, columnist, on Clemens leaving Boston to sign with the Blue Jays, 1996.*

2430 If Gabe Paul was running a hospital, I'd invest in a mortuary.—*Bill James, baseball analyst, on the former executive.*

2431 What's he ever done for the game? He's basically a glorified flag football player who can run.—*Curt Schilling, Phillies pitcher, on Cincinnati Reds outfielder and Dallas Cowboys cornerback Deion Sanders, June 1997. After the season, "Prime Time" left baseball to focus full-time on his other sport.*

2432 Deion is truly one of a kind. He plays two professional sports and doesn't hit in either one.—*Jerry Perisho, comedy writer, on Cincinnati Reds outfielder Deion Sanders, 2001. After last playing baseball full-time in 1997, Prime Time attempted a comeback four years later but only hit .173 for the season. He retired from the NFL in 2000.*

2433 One's a born liar and the other's convicted.—*Billy Martin, Yankees manager, on outfielder Reggie Jackson and owner George Steinbrenner, 1978.*

2434 The man knows nothing about pitching or pitchers. He's a lifetime .230 hitter who's been beaned three times. He hates pitchers. We will never see eye-to-eye.—*Ferguson Jenkins, Red Sox pitcher, on manager Don Zimmer.*

2435 The next thing you know they'll be voting in Charlie McCarthy. He's a dummy, too, you know. All he ever did, for goodness sake, was saw logs. Why, he slept longer in office than ... Rip Van Winkle.—*Happy Chandler, former commissioner, on the election of his successor, Ford Frick, to the Hall of Fame, 1970.*

2436 We're given a choice. We can either run around the field three times or around Tommy Lasorda once.—*Steve Sax, Dodgers second baseman, on spring training workouts, 1984.*

2437 Every year Tommy offers $50,000 to the family of the unknown soldier.—*Don Sutton, Astros pitcher, on Dodgers manager Tommy Lasorda, 1981.*

2438 When he asks for the bar tab, his arm shrinks six inches.—*Tommy Lasorda, Dodgers manager, on Yankees manager Billy Martin, 1978.*

2439 That midget can barely see over the top of the dugout steps, and he claims he can see the pitches. He blames every loss on the players, the umpires or the ground conditions. He's 500-and-0 in his little mind. He's a good manager, but as a person he stinks.—*Marty Springstead, umpire, on Orioles manager Earl Weaver, 1978.*

2440 The best way to test a Timex watch would be to strap it to his tongue.—*Marty Springstead, umpire, on Orioles manager Earl Weaver.*

2441 Earl Weaver is the Son of Sam of baseball. He has no respect for law and order.—*Jim Evans, umpire, 1979.*

2442 Weaver is like a nightmare that keeps coming back. To me, he is the Ayatollah of the '80s.—*Nick Bremigan, umpire, on manager Earl Weaver, 1985.*

2443 I never saw him do anything funny. No, I take it back. I once saw him slip and fall coming out of the dugout. That was funny.—*Larry Barnett, umpire, on Orioles manager Earl Weaver.*

2444 He'd be the first one dressed and on home to his momma.—*Pete Sheehy, Yankees clubhouse attendant, on the devotion of Yankees first baseman Lou Gehrig to his mother.*

2445 They didn't get along. Gehrig thought Ruth was a big-mouth and Ruth thought Gehrig was cheap. They were both right.—*Tony Lazzeri, former Yankees second baseman.*

2446 Jerry Lumpe looks like the best player in the world until you put him in the lineup.—*Casey Stengel, Yankees manager, on his second baseman.*

2447 Mike Ivie is a $40-million airport with a $30 control tower.—*Rick Monday, Dodgers outfielder, 1981.*

2448 The only thing Reggie can do better than me on the field is talk.—*Rod Carew, Twins first baseman, on Yankees outfielder Reggie Jackson, 1978.*

2449 Reggie's really a good guy. He'd give you the shirt off his back. Of course, he'd call a press conference to announce it.—*Catfish Hunter, Yankees pitcher, on outfielder Reggie Jackson.*

2450 There isn't enough mustard in the world to cover that hot dog.—*Darold Knowles, Oakland A's reliever, on teammate Reggie Jackson.*

2451 When you unwrap a Reggie Bar, it tells you how good it is.—*Catfish Hunter, Yankees pitcher, 1979.*

2452 It's the only candy bar that tastes like a hot dog.—*Dave Anderson, sportswriter, on the Reggie Bar.*

2453 Reggie's whole life is based on the unreal world of baseball. He has no stable family, no great business knowledge. His friends are those who tell him how good he is.—*Thurman Munson, Yankees catcher, on teammate Reggie Jackson, 1978.*

2454 Reggie Jackson couldn't shine Willie Mays' shoes. He never hit .300, he's a butcher in the outfield and he's got a big mouth. What does he make, $8,000 a week? I wouldn't pay him $8 a week. He's a bum.—*Leo Durocher, former manager, 1980.*

2455 He's an "I" man. He's all for himself. It takes a team to win, not one man. One time he held a team meeting and rapped the guys for not getting on base enough so he could drive in runs.—*Don Money, Brewers second baseman, on former teammate George Scott, 1977.*

2456 He's good, but I don't think there's anyone in the world who's as good as he thinks he is.—*Gene Mauch, Angels manager, on Blue Jays pitcher Dave Steib.*

2457 Hey, Catfish, I know how Steinbrenner can get back all the money he paid you. All he has to do is sell insurance to the people sitting in the right-field seats when you pitch.—*Lou Piniella, Yankees outfielder, to newly acquired pitcher Catfish Hunter, 1975.*

2458 I just thought you might like to know that I passed a kennel on the way to the game and your mother is all right.—*Ralph Houk, Yankees manager, to umpire Bill Klem.*

2459 He's got the personality of a tree trunk. —*John Sterns, Mets catcher, on Oakland A's DH Dave Kingman, 1984.*

2460 Kingman was more of an idiot savant than a baseball player. He was an abominable fielder. He never hit for average, mostly because he couldn't distinguish between a ball and a strike.—*Bruce Keidan, sportswriter, on former outfielder-first baseman Dave Kingman, 1991.*

2461 Haven't they suffered enough?—*Beano Cook, football broadcaster, on hearing that Commissioner Bowie Kuhn presented all the freed Iran hostages with a lifetime major league baseball pass, 1981.*

2462 What's the difference between Tim McCarver and appendicitis? Appendicitis is covered by most health plans.—*Norman Chad, sportswriter.*

2463 I try to keep my distance from it. I don't want to catch anything. That thing has been passed around more often than Paris Hilton.—*Theo Epstein, Red Sox GM, on the 2004 World Series trophy.*

2464 I don't mind catching your fastball at all. Naturally, I'd want to have a glove on in case you might be having an especially good day.—*Cardinals catcher Gene Green to pitcher Jim Brosnan.*

2465 At the end of this season they're gonna tear this place down. The way you're pitchin', that right-field section will be gone already.—*Mets manager Casey Stengel to Tracy Stallard on the fate of the Polo Grounds, 1963. The old home of the New York Giants was the temporary home of the Mets for their first two seasons before Shea Stadium opened.*

2466 If they really wanted to punish us, they would have made you play two games.—*Ken Griffey Jr., Mariners outfielder, to backup catcher John Marzano, who was suspended two games for getting into a fight.*

2467 You take a team with 25 assholes and I'll show you a pennant. I'll show you the New York Yankees.—*Bill Lee, Red Sox pitcher.*

2468 That's not showing your emotions. That's being an idiot.—*Larry Bowa, Phillies manager, on the behavior of Braves closer John Rocker, 2001. Rocker was traded midseason to Cleveland.*

2469 He knew absolutely nothing about pitching. What he knew about pitching you could put in the head of a pin in the boldest print in the world and still have room for the Constitution.—*Ralph Branca, former Brooklyn Dodgers pitcher, on manager Charlie Dressen and the collapse of the 1951 Dodgers, 2001. Branca served up baseball's most famous home run when New York Giants outfielder Bobby Thomson hit the game-winner in the 1951 playoff.*

2470 A mockery? A mockery is his last four movies.—*Lou Merloni, Red Sox infielder, on actor Ben Affleck who, during a 2002 interview, criticized Merloni for saying that the team made a "mockery" of his career by sending him to the minors so often.*

2471 Matt Damon made you what you are, Slick.—*Trot Nixon, Red Sox outfielder, to actor Ben Affleck who had ripped Nixon for his anemic .114 average against lefties, 2002.*

2472 If [Kevin] Kennedy worked as a sideline reporter during the creation of the world, he'd ask God if he had any plans for the weekend.—*Norman Chad, sportswriter, on the television analyst and former manager, 2001.*

2473 You had a great career, Tim. Too bad you didn't realize it was over a couple of years sooner.—*Richie Ashburn, broadcaster and Hall of Fame outfielder, to his announcing partner Tim McCarver.*

2474 You think it's a coincidence you can't spell "Valentine" without the letters in "evil?" When Marilyn Manson sings about Bobby Valentine, you can play it backward and clearly hear, "The New York Mets are managed by the Antichrist."—*Dan LeBatard, sportswriter, on Marlins outfielder Cliff Floyd not being named to the 2001 NL All-Star team by the Mets manager.*

2475 There's no love lost between us. You ever watch a Mets game? Who do they show, always? [...] He knows where the cameras are. One day I was pitching against the Mets and he gets thrown out and tries to come back in disguise. What a loser. Just go to the office and go have a beer and watch it on TV.—*David Wells, White Sox pitcher, on Mets skipper Bobby Valentine, 2001.*

2476 Giving [Terry] Francona three more years is like giving Saddam Hussein the Nobel Peace Prize the day after the Republican Guard invaded Kuwait.—*Bill Conlin, sportswriter, 1999. While Francona got run out of Philly after finishing last in 2000, he led the Red Sox to two World Series championships in his first four years in Boston.*

2477 Billy Martin is a mouse studying to be a rat.—*John Schulian, sportswriter, on the combative manager.*

2478 You're the Sultan of Squat because you spend so much time on the bench.—*Merv Rettenmund, Orioles outfielder, to reserve infielder Larry Brown, 1973.*

2479 That's scary. The only thing worse would be if they cloned Joe Oliver.—*Hal Morris, Reds first baseman, on learning of sheep cloning in Scotland, February 1997.*

2480 My mother always taught me that if the only thing you have to say is "Screw Dave Samson," then don't say anything at all. So I'm not going to say anything at all.—*Bill Bavasi, Mariners GM, after Marlins president David Samson criticized the $90-million extension that Seattle gave to outfielder Ichiro Suzuki—"I would say it's the end of the world as we know it," July 2007.*

Intelligence

2481 I never tried to outsmart nobody, it was easier to outdummy them.—*Dizzy Dean, Hall of Fame pitcher.*

2482 LaRussa is a very bright man. He's a lawyer in the off-season, although that doesn't necessarily mean he's smart.—*Peter Bavasi, Indians president, on White Sox manager Tony LaRussa.*

2483 There isn't a single ex-pitcher managing in the majors. The consensus is that they're dumb. Maybe, on the other hand, they're too smart.—*Edwin Pope, sportswriter, 1973.*

2484 He didn't sound like a baseball player. He said things like "Nevertheless," and "If, in fact."—*Dan Quisenberry, Royals reliever, on Brewers catcher Ted Simmons.*

2485 I think most ballplayers read the sports pages, but I'm sorry to say that in most cases that's all they read.—*Ted Simmons, Cardinals catcher.*

2486 You're only as smart as your ERA.—*Jim Bouton, former All-Star pitcher.*

2487 Never think. It can only hurt the ballclub.—*Rod Dedeaux, University of Southern California coach.*

2488 When you start thinkin' is when you get your ass beat.—*Sparky Lyle, Yankees reliever.*

2489 The less time you spend thinking about it, the less trouble you'll get into. I think the game's more intelligent than most of the guys playing it.—*Jeff Russell, Rangers reliever, 1990.*

2490 Trying to think with me is a mismatch. Most of the time *I* don't know where the pitch is going.—*Sam McDowell, Indians pitcher.*

2491 The first catcher to make no sense in two languages.—*Dan Barreiro, sportswriter, on Twins catcher Junior Ortiz, 1992.*

2492 The doctor asked me the day of the week, and I said, "Friday." Then he asked me who was President of the United States. I said, "Hell, I didn't know that before I hit my head."—*Don Zimmer, Cubs coach, on an accident in which he fell off an exercise machine and was knocked unconscious, 1986.*

2493 Here's how smart Pete is. When they had that big power blackout in New York, Pete was stranded for 13 hours on an escalator.—*Joe Nuxhall, Reds broadcaster, on manager Pete Rose.*

2494 In high school, his history teacher asked the class to write down the nine greatest Americans, but Rose could only think of eight. When asked why just eight, Rose replied, "I can't think of a third baseman."—*Joe Nuxhall, Reds broadcaster, on manager Pete Rose.*

2495 I also read *The Lou Gehrig Story*. I did a report on it in the sixth grade, the seventh grade, the eighth grade, and I eventually got an A on it in the ninth grade.—*Pete Rose, Reds player-manager, 1985.*

2496 You have to give Pete credit for what he's accomplished. He never went to college, and the only book he ever read was *The Pete Rose Story*.—*Karolyn Rose, ex-wife, 1981.*

2497 I wish there was some way I could have gotten a college education. I'm thinking about buying a college, though.—*Pete Rose, Reds manager, 1988.*

2498 He is a complex character. He graduated with a triple major from Rice University, one of the most respected schools in the southwest: political science, religion and physical education. He also hunts alligators.—*Blaine Newnham, sportswriter, on Mariners reliever Norm Charlton, 1993.*

2499 If I can't talk you out of it and I can't preach you out of it, I'll beat you out of it.—*Norm Charlton, Phillies reliever, on the practical application of his political science, religion and physical education triple major from Rice, May 1995.*

2500 Dibble's in his own world. And from what I understand, Myers is in his own world, too. Now they can be on their own planets together.—*John Franco, Mets reliever, on the Reds bullpen of Rob Dibble and Randy Myers, 1989. Franco was traded by Cincinnati to New York for Myers.*

2501 Not if I had to have his brains too.—*Bob Ojeda, Mets pitcher, when asked if he would like to have the fastball of reliever Randy Myers, 1989.*

2502 I think most players don't know Cy Young was a pitcher. I think most players think Cy Young is just the name of an award.—*Buck Rodgers, Expos manager, 1991.*

2503 Next to the catcher, the third baseman has to be the dumbest guy out there. You can't have any brains to take those shots all day.—*Dave Edler, Mariners third baseman, 1981.*

2504 I spent years attempting to master a

number of foreign languages and what happens? I turn out to be a catcher and am reduced to sign language.—*Moe Berg, catcher.*

2505 I understand, Moe, that you are in counter-intelligence, which, I assume, means you are against intelligence.—*Red Smith, sportswriter, to catcher Moe Berg, who also worked as a spy for the Office of Strategic Services.*

2506 I'd have Bill Clinton take an IQ test, and I'd have Dan Quayle score it.—*Andy Van Slyke, Pirates outfielder, on what he would do if he ruled the world, 1992.*

2507 The guy who did it has to be the stupidest person in the world. If he's so smart now that he can fire him after just 44 games, he had to be dumb to hire him.—*Sparky Anderson, Tigers manager, on the firing of manager Tony Perez by Reds GM Jim Bowden, 1993.*

2508 He was a big, overgrown kid, that's all he was. I don't think he read any books. He didn't know the difference between Robin Hood and Cock Robin. He was just interested in girls, drinking and eating.—*Mark Koenig, former Yankees shortstop, on teammate Babe Ruth.*

2509 What ocean is that?—*John Kruk, Padres rookie outfielder, on seeing Lake Michigan for the first time on a road trip to Chicago, 1986.*

2510 Now, Paris is France. But London, that's just London, right?—*Lenny Dykstra, Phillies outfielder, during an off-season trip to Europe, 1993.*

2511 He once asked me if Beirut was named after that baseball player who hit home runs.—*Ray Page, teacher at St. Anthony High School, Jersey City, NJ, on former student and Sacramento Kings point guard Bobby Hurley, 1994.*

2512 It puzzles me how they know what corners are good for filling stations. Just how did these fellows know there was oil and gas under here?—*Dizzy Dean, former Cardinals pitcher.*

2513 Gee, that's too bad. I guess I didn't know him. What league was he in?—*Pete Browning, Louisville Colonels outfielder, on the death of President James Garfield, 1881.*

2514 I remember him. Short guy, mustache, played third base for Pittsburgh.—*Jackie Moore, Blue Jays coach, when told economist John Kenneth Galbraith was on their team flight.*

2515 How can I play baseball if I'm stupid? If I was stupid I wouldn't have pitched in the World Series. I'd be playing ball in Mexico or Yugoslavia or on Pluto.—*Joaquin Andujar, Cardinals pitcher.*

2516 He just flies in for about 3½ hours a day, checks us Earthlings out and goes on his way.—*Don Baylor, Rockies manager, on outfielder Dante Bichette, 1994.*

2517 Pascual not only talks to the ball, he talks to the rosin bag, the grass, planes going overhead and, once in a while, he even talks to his catcher and manager.—*Buck Rodgers, Expos manager, on pitcher Pascual Perez, 1988.*

2518 How could it be mental? I don't have a college education.—*Steve Farr, Royals reliever, on an elbow injury, 1987.*

2519 When you have dumb people working for you, don't have them work a whole day. Let them work half a day, and then they only screw up half as much.—*Paul Richards, major league executive.*

2520 When you play with dumb players, you have to think dumb.—*Joe Ferguson, Dodgers catcher, 1980.*

2521 You're supposed to be the smartest guy on this ball club. I wanted to see what you'd do with the ball under these circumstances.—*Lefty Gomez, Yankees pitcher, to second baseman Tony Lazzeri, on why Gomez threw a ball to him instead of shortstop Frank Crosetti who was covering second base.*

2522 If you think long, you think wrong.—*Jim Kaat, former All-Star pitcher.*

2523 When a pitcher works fast, he has less time to think, which is a good thing.—*Ray Miller, Pirates pitching coach, 1994.*

2524 The Indians don't pay me to think. Computer analysts think. Stock brokers think. Baseball players do not.—*Mel Hall, Indians outfielder, 1988.*

2525 Well, an elephant never forgets. Not that I'm an elephant.—*Johnny Logan, Milwaukee Braves shortstop, 1959.*

2526 I don't know anything about chemistry. I flunked it in high school.—*Jesse Barfield, Yankees outfielder, when asked about the chemistry of his former team, the Blue Jays, 1989.*

2527 Yeah, and we're missing a little geography and arithmetic around here, too.—*Whitey Herzog, Cardinals manager, on his team's poor chemistry.*

2528 Three guys like that in your lineup, they're dangerous and they know they're dangerous. They might as well put a machine gun on 'em and send 'em to Ruwaiti. That's how much confidence they've got.—*Kevin Mitchell, Reds outfielder, on the San Francisco trio of Barry Bonds, Matt Williams and Darryl Strawberry, 1994.*

2529 I didn't learn nothing. I'll never take that long of a flight again.—*Kevin Mitchell, Red Sox outfielder, on what he learned playing the previous season for the Fukuoka Daiei Hawks in Japan, 1996.*

2530 I wouldn't want to get that smart—at least not that quickly.—*Davey Johnson, former Mets manager, on why he would not become a broadcaster, 1990.*

2531 Watching Tom Lasorda manage against Gene Mauch would be too much fun to bear. The best dumb manager against the worst smart manager.—*Thomas Boswell, sportswriter, 1985.*

2532 Some of the owners in baseball, if they had a brain, they'd be idiots.—*Charlie Finley, former Oakland A's owner, 1990.*

2533 I've never gone 0-for-6 before ... well, maybe the first six questions of a test.—*Andy Van Slyke, Pirates outfielder, 1989.*

2534 Professor, this is the first time I've ever set foot on a college campus in my life. As a matter of fact, I had a little trouble with grade school. Why, when I was promoted to the second grade, I was so nervous I didn't dare shave for a couple of days.—*Dusty Rhodes, New York Giants outfielder, after a speech at the University of Alabama.*

2535 The older you get in baseball the smarter you get. The trouble with some players is that by the time they get smart their career is over.—*Preston Gomez, Astros manager, 1974. Houston finished the season 81–81, the only time in seven seasons that a team managed by Gomez did not finish in last place.*

2536 You get smart only when you begin getting old.—*Allie Reynolds, Yankees pitcher.*

2537 It's what you learn after you know it all that counts.—*Earl Weaver, Orioles manager, 1968.*

2538 You learn 'em English and I'll learn 'em baseball.—*Dizzy Dean, St. Louis Browns broadcaster, after the St. Louis Board of Education circulated a petition against Dean's misuse of the English language.*

2539 Joe was always into books, anything to get an edge. Sometimes it was like a philosophy class. "If a tree falls in New York, will Todd Zeile hit the curve ball?" Stuff like that.—*Darrin Fletcher, Expos catcher, on former pitching coach Joe Kerrigan who went to the Red Sox, 1997.*

2540 To think of all the hours I wasted in hotel rooms, watching TV, when I could have been taking correspondence courses. I might be a doctor by now.—*Mookie Wilson, former Mets outfielder, on returning to school after 19 years to earn his degree from Mercy College, 1996.*

2541 It's a big word and I don't know any big words.—*Garrett Stephenson, Phillies pitcher, on what doctors told him was wrong with his injured knee, 1997.*

2542 Lou has three rules for us—to be on time, play heads up, and, uh, I forget the third. —*Todd Benzinger, Reds first baseman, on manager Lou Piniella, 1990.*

2543 Right now I have the three C's: comfortable, confident, and seeing the ball well.—*Jay Buhner, Mariners outfielder, 1997.*

2544 Because the track coach was the biology teacher, and I had trouble with biology. I'm not crazy.—*Claudell Washington, White Sox outfielder, on why he ran track in high school, 1979.*

2545 I tell every kid I talk to that they should make sure they get a college education before signing a pro contract. You don't have to know anything to get a college degree. But if you've got one, people think you're intelligent.—*Calvin Griffith, Twins owner.*

2546 I may be dumb, but I'm not stupid.—*Ted Turner, Braves owner.*

2547 Reggie's got an IQ of 160? Out of what? A thousand?—*Mickey Rivers, Yankees outfielder, on teammate Reggie Jackson, 1978.*

2548 You're so dumb you don't even know how to spell IQ.—*Carlos May, former Yankees DH, to outfielder Mickey Rivers, 1978.*

2549 Rivers' full name was John Milton Rivers. He may well be the only person named for John Milton who has never heard of John Milton.—*Roger Kahn, sportswriter, on Mickey Rivers.*

2550 I took a little English, a little math, some science, a few hubcaps and some wheel covers.—*Gates Brown, Tigers coach, on what he took in high school, 1984.*

2551 I majored in eligibility.—*Tim Laudner, Twins catcher, on playing at the University of Missouri, 1982.*

2552 In my sophomore year, I had more complete games than credits.—*Mike Flanagan, Orioles pitcher.*

2553 I'm not the brightest guy in the world. If my dad hadn't been principal of my high school, I never would have graduated.—*Andy Van Slyke, Cardinals outfielder.*

2554 I only went to the third grade because my father only went to the fourth, and I didn't want to pass him.—*Dizzy Dean, Hall of Fame pitcher, 1973.*

2555 People don't understand what history's about.—*Marty Perez, Braves shortstop, 1974.*

2556 I think too much on the mound sometimes, and I get brain cramps.—*Britt Burns, White Sox pitcher.*

2557 I don't understand the questions of things he can answer.—*Ed Lynch, Mets pitcher, on teammate and former Yale student Ron Darling, 1984.*

2558 Baseball players are smarter than football players. How often do you see a baseball team penalized for too many men on the field?—*Jim Bouton, former pitcher, 1988.*

2559 The definition of a smart player is someone who can't play.—*Cal McLish, Brewers scout.*

2560 A full mind is an empty bat.—*Branch Rickey, Cardinals GM.*

2561 I never heard of Gehrig before I came here. And I always thought Babe Ruth was a cartoon character. I really did. I mean, I wasn't born until 1961, and I grew up in Indiana.—*Don Mattingly, Yankees first baseman, 1985.*

2562 I know some people think I'm stupid, but my parents didn't raise no dummies. Hey, there are different kinds of intelligence. Albert Einstein was bad in English. Of course, Einstein was a German.—*Bob Kearney, Mariners catcher, 1985.*

2563 I believe there were no dinosaurs. I've never seen one. I've never seen a Tyrannosaurus Rex. How do you know those bones are millions of years old? Stuff you can't prove, I don't believe. Like men walking on the moon. Half of what you hear, I don't believe—actually 95 percent of what I hear. It's just me—I have to witness it. I don't believe someone got out of a ship up there.—*Carl Everett, Red Sox outfielder, 2000.*

2564 The Bible never says anything about dinosaurs. You can't say there were dinosaurs when you never saw them. Somebody actually saw Adam and Eve. No one ever saw a Tyrannosaurus Rex.—*Carl Everett, White Sox outfielder.*

2565 The sun has been there for 500, 600 years.—*Mike Cameron, Mets outfielder, after teammate Carlos Beltran lost a ball in the sun, August 1, 2005.*

2566 Therapy can be a good thing; it can be therapeutic.—*Alex Rodriguez, Yankees third baseman, 2005.*

2567 If you throw at someone's head, it's very dangerous, because in the head is the brain.—*Ivan Rodriguez, Tigers catcher, 2006.*

2568 You know how Tommy Lasorda says he bleeds Dodger blue? I bleed Met whatever-colors-they-are.—*John Franco, Mets reliever, 2001.*

2569 I only had a high school education and believe me, I had to cheat to get that.—*Sparky Anderson, Tigers manager.*

2570 Hitting your first grand slam is a thrill. I'll always remember this.... [Reminded that he had hit a grand slam two years earlier] ... You're right, I guess I forgot about that one.—*Steve Balboni, Royals first baseman.*

2571 Hey, Pedro, how do you say "adios" in Spanish?—*Clay Carroll, Reds pitcher, to teammate Pedro Borbon.*

2572 I don't speak Spanish. C'est la vie.—*Bob Kearney, Mariners catcher, on being benched whenever a Hispanic pitcher started, 1987.*

2573 There are so many Latin players, we're going to have to get a Latin instructor up here.—*Phil Rizzuto, Yankees broadcaster, during a spring training game against the Expos, 1989.*

2574 Q: What's the capital of Argentina?

Jim Gantner (Milwaukee Brewers infielder): Buenos Días.

2575 I wasn't big on school. When someone asked me how I liked school, I said closed.—*Yogi Berra, Hall of Fame catcher, on receiving an honorary doctorate from Roger Williams University in Bristol, Rhode Island, May 19, 2001.*

2576 I went to see him about three times, and then he went to see a psychiatrist.—*Mitch Williams, Phillies reliever, seeing a hypnotherapist after surrendering the winning home run in the 1993 World Series.*

2577 If they did, I don't remember it.—*Manny Ramirez, Red Sox outfielder, when asked if his former team, the Cleveland Indians, had him tested for attention-deficit disorder, 2001.*

2578 Only in America!—*Yogi Berra, Hall of Fame catcher, on hearing that a Jewish mayor had been elected in Dublin ... which is in Ireland.*

2579 Were you born that way?—*Jesse Rogers, Cubs radio announcer, during an interview with closer Antonio Alfonseca, who has six fingers on each hand, April 2002.*

2580 We don't know a lot, but so far it's working for us. I'm young and dumb, and I want to keep it that way as long as I can.—*Taylor Tankersley, 23-year-old Marlins reliever, on the early success of the team's young pitching staff, 2006.*

2581 If Brad [Lidge] had spent as much time studying in school as he does in fantasy football, he would have been a straight-A student.—*Brad Ausmus, Astros catcher, 2004.*

2582 How's your dad?—*Bruce "Cousin Brucie" Morrow, radio disc jockey, at a charity telethon to Roberto Clemente Jr., 2004. Clemente's namesake father died in a plane crash that was transporting emergency supplies to earthquake victims in Nicaragua on New Year's Eve, 1972.*

2583 We've had guys go to the Astrodome, where they don't even play games anymore. We've had guys go to Shea Stadium when we were playing at Yankee Stadium. You realize we haven't got the smartest group of guys.—*Doug Mientkiewicz, Twins first baseman, after three teammates went to Berkeley instead of Oakland before Game 1 of the Division Series, 2002.*

2584 I haven't really researched the topic. I know it's been done. I remember the first Austin Powers movie.—*Mike Piazza, Mets catcher, on cryogenics, 2002.*

2585 The sooner you fall behind, the more time you have to catch up.—*Sam Ogden, writer.*

2586 That's what happens when you build a ballpark on the ocean.—*Dennis "Oil Can" Boyd, Red Sox pitcher, on a postponement in Cleveland due to fog.*

2587 After Alex Rodriguez donated $3.9 million to the University of Miami and then announced he would start attending classes there, think there's a professor there who'll give him a B?—*Dwight Perry, sportswriter, October 2002.*

2588 I wish I had 10 pitchers with Bo Belinsky's stuff and none with his head.—*Gene Mauch, Angels manager.*

2589 If you put his brain in a blue jay, it would fly backwards.—*Al Nipper, former Cubs pitcher, on rookie reliever Mitch Williams, 1989.*

2590 The elevator hasn't stopped on his floor for years, but now he has company.—*Bob Verdi, sportswriter, on reliever Mitch Williams joining the free-spirited Phillies, 1993.*

2591 I know how to spell *lasagna.*—*Mike Hargrove, former manager, on his qualifications to serve as Italy's bench coach in the 2009 World Baseball Classic.*

2592 Randy Johnson will talk to you if you get there early enough but will not make sense no matter how long you stay.—*Jim Armstrong, sportswriter, on the Diamondbacks pitcher, 2001.*

2593 I don't even remember where I was in 1969. I've been on so many teams, I don't remember where I'm at half the time.—*Don Zimmer, Yankees coach, 2000.*

2594 When I'm on the mound, I'm thinking all the time. It may not be about baseball but, believe me, I'm thinking.—*Gene Host, Tigers pitcher, on charges that he wasn't thinking enough on the mound, 1956.*

2595 Ask him the time and he'll tell you how to make a watch.—*Bob Lemon, Yankees manager, on pitcher Tommy John, 1981.*

2596 He can run, hit, throw, and field. The only thing Willie Davis has never been able to do is think.—*Buzzie Bavasi, Dodgers executive, on the speedy Dodgers outfielder.*

2597 [A.J.'s] the smart one. Intelligence skips a generation, like male-pattern baldness. A.J. will be bald and smart, like his granddad. A.J.'s son will be stupid, but he'll have a giant Afro.—*Andy Van Slyke, former all-star outfielder, on his oldest son, 2005. Van Slyke joined the Tigers as first base coach in 2006.*

2598 Hell, if the game was half as complicated as some of these writers make out it is, a lot of us boys from the farm would never have been able to make a living at it.—*Bucky Walters, Reds pitcher.*

2599 I have nothing against Cleveland, but I'd rather have been traded somewhere in the United States.—*Outfielder Leon Wagner on being traded from the Angels to the Indians after the 1963 season.*

2600 It has to be someone who can read, and that eliminates a lot of these guys.—*Casey Candaele, Astros utility player, on finding a successor for the club's kangaroo court "district attorney" Ken Oberkfell, who was released, July 1991.*

2601 I'm going to Radio Shack to buy one of those headsets like the broadcasters use. It seems as soon as you put them on, you get 100 times smarter.—*Nick Leyva, Phillies manager.*

2602 I ain't afraid to tell the world that it don't take school stuff to help a fella play ball.—*"Shoeless" Joe Jackson, White Sox outfielder.*

2603 He never remembered a sign or forgot a newspaperman's name.—*Leo Durocher, former Cubs manager, on Hall of Famer Ernie Banks, 1976.*

2604 If you don't think too good, don't think too much.—*Ted Williams, Hall of Fame outfielder.*

2605 Slow thinkers are part of the game too. Some of these slow thinkers can hit a ball a long way.—*Alvin Dark, Indians manager, 1968.*

2606 Remember, half the lies they tell about the Dodgers aren't true.—*Walter O'Malley, Dodgers owner.*

2607 Baseball is the most intellectual game because most of the action goes on in your head. —*Henry Kissinger, former Secretary of State.*

2608 I never use a big word when a diminutive word would suffice.—*Pete Mackanin, Phillies bench coach, 2010.*

Law and Order: MLB

2609 The sports section needs a crime page. —*Mike Lupica, sportswriter.*

2610 If you know how to cheat, start now.—*Earl Weaver, Orioles manager, to struggling pitcher Ross Grimsley.*

2611 You have to give him credit. He's only 20 years old. Most guys don't start cheating until later in their careers.—*Mark Grace, Cubs first baseman, on Diamondbacks rookie pitcher Byung-Hyun Kim being ejected for having a foreign substance, June 9, 1999.*

2612 The tradition of professional baseball always has been agreeably free of chivalry. The rule is, "Do anything you can get away with."—*Heywood Broun, sportswriter.*

2613 *Joe Falls (sportswriter):* What's your favorite number?

Gates Brown (Tigers outfielder): The one I wore as a kid. Number 5081782.

2614 Nolan Ryan recorded his 5,000th strikeout on a 96-mph fastball. It's ironic it was against the A's, since that's the same speed Jose Canseco drives his car through a school zone. —*Mark Patrick, broadcaster, 1989.*

2615 Jose Canseco is already three weeks behind in bad publicity.—*Buddy Baron, Cincinnati radio announcer, on the spring training lockout, 1990.*

2616 Jose continues to grow with each year and each arrest.—*Sandy Alderson, Oakland A's GM, when asked if outfielder Jose Canseco was maturing, 1992.*

2617 Now that Jose is in Texas, I'll be expecting him to hit 60 home runs—and drive 55.—*Texas Governor Ann Richards after outfielder Jose Canseco was traded from the Oakland A's to the Rangers, 1992.*

2618 If you're a real baseball purist like me, you know the season doesn't really begin until Jose Canseco gets arrested.—*David Letterman, talk show host, on the Rangers DH, 1994.*

2619 How does somebody flunk a drug test while under house arrest? That's like being arrested for drunk driving while cutting the lawn on your riding mower.—*Alex Kaseberg, comedy writer, June 2003. Canseco was arrested for testing positive for steroids, a violation of his probation.*

2620 If Jose Canseco keeps getting arrested, he may soon get his wish. In no time at all, he could be back in a lineup.—*Jim Greene, comedy writer, June 2003.*

2621 The last time I smiled so much was for a jury.—*Pascual Perez, Braves pitcher, on winning four games in a row. After the 1983 season, Perez spent time in a Dominican jail on drug charges.*

2622 That's the first time I got a letter from [NL President] Bill White where I didn't have to pay a fine.—*John Kruk, Phillies first baseman-outfielder, on being named to the All-Star team, 1991.*

2623 Mr. Kuhn told Willie Mays to get out of baseball. I would like to offer the same advice to Mr. Kuhn.—*Frank Sinatra, entertainer, after baseball commissioner Bowie Kuhn suspended Hall of Fame outfielder Willie Mays from baseball for accepting a position at Bally's Park Place Casino in Atlantic City, 1979. Kuhn's successor, Peter Ueberroth, overturned the suspension in 1985.*

2624 You don't want to get thrown out of your favorite bar, much less banned from baseball.—*Mickey Mantle, Hall of Fame outfielder, after his suspension from baseball was overturned by Commissioner Peter Ueberroth, 1985. Commissioner Bowie Kuhn suspended Mantle in 1983 for taking a job as a greeter at the Claridge Resort and Casino in Atlantic City.*

2625 I dreamt I died and went to heaven. I'm waiting at the Pearly Gates and St. Peter asked who I was. I answered "Mickey Mantle." And he said, "Oh, good, God wants to talk to you." So I go in and God says, "Because of the life you led on earth we can't let you stay here. But before you go, would you sign these six dozen baseballs?"—*Mickey Mantle, Hall of Fame outfielder, 1987.*

2626 They never wrote about how much I won.—*Lenny Dykstra, Phillies outfielder, after his gambling debts of $78,000 were publicized, 1991.*

2627 The last time the Bees were in Reno, I lost the bus and two outfielders, but I won a shortstop and a bat.—*Rocky Bridges, San Jose Bees manager, 1964.*

2628 If I did everything they said I did, I'd be in a jar at the Harvard Medical School.—*Bo Belinsky, former pitcher, on his reported lifestyle.*

2629 The principal dragged us back to school and whipped us with a paddle that had holes in it. I'd been married for over a year, and here I was getting a spanking.—*Jim Davenport, Giants manager and former All-Star third baseman, on getting caught skipping high school in order to visit the pool hall, 1985.*

2630 Yeah, in prison.—*Mel Hall, Yankees outfielder, when asked if he ever thought he'd be wearing pinstripes, 1989.*

2631 It's not like we were in the car plotting, like, to blow up a plane or anything.—*Eric Davis, Dodgers outfielder, on what transpired in the car before Mets outfielder Vince Coleman tossed fireworks towards a crowd of fans outside Dodger Stadium, 1993.*

2632 On July 4, wherever we are, you're going to room with me.—*Hal McRae, Royals manager, to newly acquired free agent outfielder Vince Coleman, 1994. Coleman was suspended by the Mets in 1993 for tossing fireworks from a car in front of Dodger Stadium.*

2633 *Elderly Criminal:* I'll be dead before I serve that sentence, Your Honor. I'm a sick man. I can't do five years.

Judge Kenesaw Mountain Landis (future baseball commissioner): You can try, can't you?

2634 Anyone who can prove she actually spent four seasons on the road watching nothing but Red Sox games should be good for $12 million in damages for mental anguish, easily, even if she never went back to the hotel.—*John Robertson, sportswriter, on Margo Adams filing a lawsuit against Red Sox third baseman Wade Boggs, 1988. Boggs and Adams ended their affair with a $500,000 out-of-court settlement.*

2635 He was known to play night games no matter what it said on the schedule.—*Vic Ziegel, sportswriter, on Yankees outfielder Joe Pepitone. In the 1980's, Pepitone was arrested on gun and drug charges and spent time in prison.*

2636 Joe Pepitone, the once-upon-a-time Yankees first baseman, didn't mind it when a guy in a bar reminded him he's a "washed-up nobody" a couple of times. When he kept at it, 50-year-old Joe, out on a promotional gig for the Yanks, began duking it out and reportedly held his own, taking on three brothers, all in their 20's. The subsequent arrest isn't going to look good on his résumé, though.—*Phil Jackman, sportswriter, 1992.*

2637 If he's convicted, he'll be re-signed by the Yankees.—*David Letterman, talk show host, on the arrest of 55-year-old former Yankees first baseman Joe Pepitone on drunk driving charges, 1995. Pepitone, who served four months in prison in 1988 on drug charges, pleaded guilty.*

2638 I went to jail. I looked like one of those savings-and-loan guys leaving the jailhouse.—*Dave Winfield, Angels outfielder, on his August 4, 1983, arrest in Toronto for "cruelty and causing unnecessary suffering to animals" when he killed a seagull with a throw, 1991.*

2639 They say he hit the gull on purpose. They wouldn't say that if they'd seen the throws he'd been making all year. It's the first time he's hit the cutoff man all year.—*Billy Martin, Yankees manager, defending outfielder Dave Winfield who was arrested and charged with intentionally killing a seagull in Toronto, 1983.*

2640 If his mommy and his wife haven't heard from him, why should I?—*Eric Davis, Tigers outfielder, when asked if he knew the whereabouts of his friend, Dodgers outfielder Darryl Strawberry, who failed to show up for the team's final exhibition game of 1994. Strawberry turned up the next day, admitted a substance abuse problem, and began rehab. He was released by the Dodgers May 25 and subsequently signed with San Francisco.*

2641 Either way, he'll get to meet Darryl Strawberry.—*Jay Leno, talk show host, on Senator George Mitchell trying to decide between a possible career as a Supreme Court Justice or baseball commissioner, 1994. Mitchell turned down both options and entered into the business world, although he did lead an investigation into steroid use in baseball in 2006.*

2642 Do you think they'll change Yankee Stadium's nickname to "The Halfway House That Ruth Built"?—*Bob Lacey, comedy writer, on the possibility that New York would sign troubled former teammates Darryl Strawberry and Dwight Gooden, May 1995. The Yankees signed Strawberry the next month and Gooden in 1996.*

2643 My life is going in the right direction. —*Darryl Strawberry, former All-Star outfielder, on being sentenced to 18 months in prison as a result of six probation violations, 2002.*

2644 Just 0.3 grams of coke were found on Darryl Strawberry's person, but that probably means 0.7 were *in* his person.—*Bud Geracie, sportswriter, on the arrest of the Yankees outfielder on charges of drug possession and solicitation of a prostitute, 1999. Strawberry was placed on "administrative leave" before being suspended for 120 days.*

2645 I bought this very rare item—a tax form signed by Darryl Strawberry. This is the hottest thing out there now.—*Billy Crystal, comedian, 1995.*

2646 Darryl Strawberry collected his 3,000th arrest, for reckless driving and leaving the scene of an accident. He was sentenced to two years house arrest. He asked if he could serve it at Whitney Houston's house.—*Jay Leno, talk show host, September 2000.*

2647 If I'd paid $7,000 for a tree, I'd have at least gotten the wood for my fireplace.—*Dave Parker, Reds outfielder, on teammate Cesar Cedeno, who pleaded no-contest to a charge of intoxication and running his car into a tree, resulting in a $7,000 fine, 1985.*

2648 I've got "For Steal" signs on all three. I leave the keys in the ignition, and no one takes them.—*Doug Rader, Angels manager, on his three cars, each with over 100,000 miles, 1989.*

2649 I must be getting smarter, I finally punched something that couldn't sue me.—*Billy Martin, Oakland A's manager, after punching a wall and breaking a finger, 1982.*

2650 I was driving to Yankee Stadium and a state trooper stopped me. I told him, "I'm Billy Gardner, I play for the Yankees, and I'm in a hurry." The guy said, "Okay, I'll hurry up and write you a ticket."—*Billy Gardner, Twins manager and former Yankees third baseman.*

2651 Either he was out very late, or he was out very early.—*Casey Stengel, Yankees manager, on pitcher Don Larsen, who drove his car into a telephone pole during spring training, 1956.*

2652 Anybody who can find something to do in St. Petersburg at five in the morning deserves a medal, not a fine.—*Casey Stengel, Yankees manager, when asked if pitcher Don Larsen would be fined for wrecking his car during spring training, 1956.*

2653 *Cop:* Your driver's license says you wear glasses. Why aren't you wearing them?

Phil Linz (Yankees infielder): I got contacts.

Cop: I don't care who you know, you still have to wear glasses when you drive.

2654 If this had to happen to Steve, I'm glad it was as a private citizen and not as a member of the New York Yankees.—*Bob Watson, Yankees GM, on pitcher Steve Howe getting arrested for carrying a loaded gun onto an airplane the day after being released by New York, 1996.*

2655 This is your last chance, and I'm not talking about one of those Major League Baseball Steve Howe kind of last chances.—*Leslie Nielsen (as Lt. Frank Drebin) to Tanya Peters (played by Anna Nicole Smith) in* Naked Gun 33 ⅓ *(1994). Howe was suspended seven times, including the entire 1984 season.*

2656 It's the first time in history that a Yankee player has ever sat in the front of a police car.—*Jay Leno, talk show host, on former Yankees outfielder Stan Jefferson becoming a New York police officer, 1998.*

2657 It may sound incredible, but they seemed more interested in the ball game.—*Wilfred Denno, warden of Sing Sing prison, on the reaction of death row inmates to the abolition of capital punishment in New York, 1965.*

2658 Never stand on the outside looking in, unless it's jail.—*Spike Hennessey, baseball scout, 1932.*

2659 The fan-friendly White Sox signed convicted wife beater Wil Cordero to a one-year contract for $1 million. But they hope to soften their image by naming Lorena Bobbitt as the new bat girl.—*Steve Rosenberg, sportswriter, 1998.*

2660 Who says baseball players aren't heroes. Earlier today, Baltimore second baseman Roberto Alomar visited a little kid in the hospital and promised the kid that he'd spit on two umpires.—*David Letterman, talk show host, September 1996. Alomar spat in the face of umpire John Hirschbeck during a heated argument over a called third strike, and he was suspended the first five games of the 1997 season. Despite publicly apologizing and later befriending Hirschbeck, the backlash against Alomar may have played a part in Alomar not making the Hall of Fame in 2010, his first year of eligibility.*

2661 The fine was more than I expectorated. —*Frenchy Bordagaray, Brooklyn Dodgers outfielder, on being fined $50 and suspended for 60 days after spitting at an umpire.*

2662 Not nearly enough.—*Duane Ward, Rangers reliever, when asked by a police officer how much he'd had to drink, 1997. Two days after this spring training incident, Ward was released by Texas.*

2663 As a former baseball player, I find this is not unlike minor league training camps—living together, eating together and a bed-time curfew.—*Orlando Cepeda, former outfielder/first baseman, on serving a five-year jail sentence for importing and possessing illegal drugs, 1978.*

2664 I don't know how you get to where I am from where I was 17 years ago.—*Denny McLain, former Cy Young Award winner, on being sentenced to 23 years in prison for racketeering, extortion and drug dealing, 1985.*

2665 The Rose lawyers were better. They knew when to shut up.—*Fay Vincent, baseball commissioner, on the legal counsel for George Steinbrenner, 1990. Vincent suspended Steinbrenner for life after the Yankees owner paid a gambler $40,000 to dig up dirt on his own player, outfielder Dave Winfield. Steinbrenner's ban was overturned in 1993.*

2666 I think his being kicked out of baseball is really bad for American business and human relations because we have now lost a symbol of how not to do things.—*Jim Bouton, writer and former Yankees pitcher, on the banishment of New York owner George Steinbrenner, 1990.*

2667 Regardless of the verdict of juries, no player that throws a ball game, no player that undertakes or promises to throw a ball game, no player that sits in conference with a bunch of crooked players and gamblers where the ways and means of throwing games are planned and discussed and does not promptly tell his club about it, will ever play professional baseball.—*Kenesaw Mountain Landis, baseball commissioner, on his banishment of eight White Sox players involved in the 1919 World Series betting scandal—despite their acquittal in a Chicago trial, 1920.*

2668 Say it ain't so, Joe.—*Anonymous young boy to White Sox outfielder "Shoeless" Joe Jackson as he left a Chicago courthouse during the "Black Sox" betting scandal, 1920.*

2669 Benedict Arnolds! Betrayers of American boyhood. Not to mention American Girlhood and American Womanhood and American Hoodhood.—*Nelson Algren, writer, on the 1919 Chicago Black Sox.*

2670 I have played a crooked game and I have lost.—*Eddie Cicotte, White Sox pitcher, after being banished from baseball, 1920.*

2671 Cops 4—Mets 0.—*T-shirt in Houston following the arrest of Mets players Tim Teufel, Ron Darling, Bob Ojeda and Rick Aguilera at a local nightclub, 1986.*

2672 Foremost, we must recognize that there are two people here: Pete Rose the living legend, the all-time hit leader and the idol of millions, and Pete Rose the individual, who appears today convicted of cheating on his taxes. Today we are not dealing with the legend. History and the tincture of time will decide his place among the all-time greats of baseball. With regard to Pete Rose, the individual, he has broken the law, admitted his guilt and stands ready to pay the penalty.—*Arthur Spiegel, U.S. District Judge, on sentencing Pete Rose to five months in prison for income tax fraud, 1990.*

2673 The matter of Mr. Rose is now closed. Let no one think that it did not hurt baseball. The hurt will pass, however, as the great glory of the game asserts itself and a resilient institution goes forward. Let it also be clear that no individual is superior to the game.—*A. Bartlett Giamatti, baseball commissioner, on the lifetime banishment of Pete Rose due to gambling, August 24, 1989.*

2674 If Pete Rose bets on prison softball games, will he be barred from jail for life?—*Jay Leno, comedian, 1990.*

2675 I'd be willing to bet you, if I was a betting man, that I have never bet on baseball.—*Pete Rose, Reds manager, 1989. Baseball commissioner A. Bartlett Giamatti decided otherwise, suspending Rose from baseball for life. Rose steadfastly denied any wrongdoing even though he accepted the suspension, which also prevents his election to the Hall of Fame. In 2004, Rose finally admitted to betting on baseball.*

2676 Thanks for not playing "Jailhouse Rock." —*Pete Rose to band leader Doc Severinsen after being introduced as a guest on the* Tonight Show, *1991.*

2677 Cincinnati is the only National League team not to win a division title in the 1980's. Things have a way of evening out, however. Pete Rose is the only NL manager who has ever hit a Pick-Six.—*Mike Hlas, sportswriter, 1989.*

2678 If Pete Rose were still managing, Service would have guaranteed himself a job.—*Peter Gammons, sportswriter, on Reds reliever Scott Service who made $56,000 by twice winning the Fantasy Five in the Florida Lotto in one week, 1997.*

2679 Pete Rose failed to make the Canadian Baseball Hall of Fame because he wasn't listed on 75% of the selectors' ballots. Rumor has it that Pete's day wasn't a total loss, though. He had the under.—*Dwight Perry, sportswriter, 2003. Rose was nominated due to the half season he played with the Expos in 1984.*

2680 Although the baseball that Pete Rose hit for a double for his 4000th base hit sold recently for an auction price of $39,422, Rose was laying 2–1 odds that it would go for at least $50,000.—*Earl Hochman, sportswriter, 2000.*

2681 It's bad for me because I've never been in jail that long.—*Rafael Furcal, Braves shortstop, on his 21-day jail sentence for a parole violation, 2004.*

2682 This, of course, can in some way hurt his career as a professional ballplayer.—*Jose Luis Tamayo, defense attorney for pitcher Ugueth Urbina, on his client being charged with attempted murder in Venezuela, 2005. Urbina, the only player ever with the initials UUU, was sentenced to 14 years in prison in 2007.*

2683 He's been very talkative. But it is usually under oath.—*Sandy Alderson, Oakland A's GM, on surly slugger Albert Belle, who had a litany of run-ins with the law, February 1997.*

2684 At night time, you just try to keep him out of jail.—*David Cone, Yankees pitcher, on hitting the town with teammate David Wells.*

2685 I like to give pedicures to ballboys.—*David Letterman's Top Ten List: Joe Niekro's Excuses, August 6, 1987. The Twins knuckleball pitcher was caught throwing a nail file from his back pocket during an inspection by umpires, resulting in a 10-game suspension.*

2686 The Yankees have changed their signs. When the third base coach wants the batter to take, he holds up a photo of Ruben Rivera.—*Alan Ray, comedy writer, on a spring training incident in which outfielder Ruben Rivera was released after he stole shortstop Derek Jeter's glove, 2002.*

2687 I plead the eighth.—*Terry Francona, Red Sox manager, on who was tougher to handle,* *his 14-year-old daughter or outfielder Manny Ramirez, 2008. Manny was traded to the Dodgers in July while Francona's daughter stayed with the home team.*

2688 Another example of how knowledgeable the New York baseball fans are: The guy who sucker-punched David Wells escalated the beef by insulting Wells' dead mother. Those fans know the players and their families!—*Scott Ostler, sportswriter, on a brawl involving the Yankees pitcher outside a New York diner, September 2002.*

2689 It gives new meaning to the baseball phrase "sliding into home."—*Jerry Perisho, comedy writer, on Rockies pitcher John Thomson being arrested after his Corvette skidded into a house during spring training in Tucson, 2000. After going 1–10 with an 8.04 ERA in 1999, the new decade didn't get off to a much better start—Thomson stayed in the minors for the 2000 season.*

2690 Actually, when you think about it, baseball has a lot in common with the O. J. [Simpson] trial. Attendance is down in both, they both feature spoiled millionaires, and in both cases somebody's going to walk.—*Jay Leno, talk show host, July 1997.*

2691 But Phillips, who has a long history as a quality leadoff man, will get picked up by somebody. The vice squad, probably.—*Steve Rosenbloom, sportswriter, on Angels utility player Tony Phillips not being offered a contract extension following his arrest for cocaine possession, 1997. Toronto signed Phillips on July 1, 1998.*

2692 Miguel Sanchez claims he was intentionally hit, while Gibson's lawyers are expected to argue that the former pitcher was merely painting the blacktop, trying to establish the inside half of the lane.—*Dwight Perry, sportswriter, on a road rage incident involving Hall of Famer Bob Gibson, 2003.*

2693 Cheating in baseball is just like hot dogs, french fries and cold Cokes.—*Manager Billy Martin.*

The Lighter Side of Baseball

2694 A sense of humor is a saving grace. It saves people from the sin of pride because humor involves a sense of proportion and the power of seeing yourself from outside.—*George Will, columnist.*

2695 Baseball is a circus, and as is the case in many a circus, the clowns and the sideshows are frequently more interesting than the big stuff in the main tent.—*W.O. McGeehan, sportswriter.*

2696 There are things you can do when you have talent that are colorful. If you do them without talent, they're bush.—*Gabe Paul, Indians president.*

2697 Playing baseball is much easier if everyone thinks you're an off-the-wall babbling idiot.—*Jim Kern, Rangers reliever, 1980.*

2698 The good Lord was good to me. He gave me a strong body, a good right arm and a weak mind.—*Dizzy Dean at his Hall of Fame induction, 1953.*

2699 They X-rayed my head and didn't find anything.—*Dizzy Dean, Cardinals pitcher, after being hit in the head during the 1934 World Series.*

2700 The last time they checked me for cork, they X-rayed my head.—*Mickey Hatcher, Rangers coach and former utility player, 1994.*

2701 He's the first guy ever to make the major leagues on one brain cell.—*Roy Smalley, Twins shortstop, on utility player Mickey Hatcher, 1980.*

2702 That ball had a hit in it, so I want it to get back in the ball bag with the rest of the balls there. Maybe next time it'll learn some sense and come out as a pop-up next time.—*Mark "The Bird" Fidrych, Tigers pitcher, on why he always returns a ball after an opposing batter gets a hit, 1976.*

2703 Sometimes I get lazy and let the dishes stack up. But they don't stack too high. I've only got four dishes.—*Mark Fidrych, Tigers pitcher, 1976.*

2704 When cerebral processes enter into sports, you start screwing up. It's like the Constitution, which says separate church and state. You have to separate mind and body.—*Bill Lee, Red Sox pitcher.*

2705 They have a lot of germs over there, and since everyone over there is so small, I got them first.—*Bill Lee, Red Sox pitcher, on why he cut short a trip to China, 1976.*

2706 Thirty-two pounds per square inch at sea level.—*Bill Lee, Expos pitcher, on how much pressure he felt on the mound, 1980.*

2707 There is no way an ordinary mortal can evaluate everything Bill Lee tells in a short period. I need time to put it into the computer.—*John McHale, Expos owner, 1979.*

2708 On a scale of 1 to 10 for flakiness, Bill is about a 10 and I'm a 3. I was a freshman at USC when Bill was a senior. I used to hang around with him so people would think I'm normal.—*Tom House, Red Sox reliever, on teammate Bill Lee, 1976.*

2709 If he played for me, I wouldn't handle him with a strong arm; I'd handle him with a straightjacket like the rest of the nuts.—*Billy Martin, Yankees manager, on Red Sox pitcher Bill Lee.*

2710 I have no trouble with the twelve inches between my elbow and my palm. It's the seven inches between my ears that's bent.—*Tug McGraw, Phillies reliever.*

2711 Tug McGraw has got about forty-eight cards in his deck.—*Tom Seaver, Mets pitcher.*

2712 Some guys have grace under pressure, some have dignity, but Tug McGraw has flake under pressure.—*Joe Garagiola, broadcaster.*

2713 I talk to Tug McGraw in the bullpen all the time. Neither of us has an elevator that goes to the top floor, so mostly we talk from the waist down.—*Al Holland, Phillies reliever.*

2714 We don't have any corked bats; we only have corked heads.—*Pat Corrales, Indians manager.*

2715 If you act like you know what you're doing, you can do anything you want—except maybe perform neural surgery.—*John Lowenstein, Orioles outfielder, 1981.*

2716 They should move first base back one step to eliminate all those close plays.—*John Lowenstein, Orioles outfielder, 1984.*

2717 Baseball players are the weirdest of all. I think it's all that organ music.—*Peter Gent, writer.*

2718 Harmon [Killebrew] told me never to chew gum at the plate. He said it makes your eyeballs bounce up and down.—*Charlie Manuel, Indians coach, 1988.*

2719 The Angels are the first team I've ever been on where I feel I belong. They're all nuts, too.—*Jimmy Piersall, Angels outfielder, 1965.*

2720 Spread the diaper in the position of the diamond with you at bat. Then fold second base down to home and set the baby on the pitcher's mound. Put first base and third together, bring up home plate and pin the three together. Of course, in case of rain, you gotta call the game and start all over again.—*Jimmy Piersall, former outfielder and father of nine, on how to diaper a baby, 1968.*

2721 He showed them it was a game, so they locked him up.—*Abbie Hoffman, political activist, on outfielder Jimmy Piersall, who was temporarily committed to a mental institution.*

2722 I plead guilty to assigning Jay Johnstone and Jim Piersall as roommates. It was an easy decision. I didn't want to screw up two rooms.—*Bill Rigney, Angels manager, 1967.*

2723 Jay Johnstone is all right. Everybody else is just nuts.—*Danny Ozark, Phillies manager, 1977.*

2724 The most amazing thing I've ever seen was Jay Johnstone, in uniform, in line at a concession stand in Dodger Stadium after a game had already started.—*Fred Claire, Dodgers GM, 1987.*

2725 My wife of 24 years never saw me perform. She thought I was an airline pilot.—*Max Patkin, The Clown Prince of Baseball, 1980.*

2726 Why did you cross the road?—*Skip Caray, Braves broadcaster, on being introduced to the San Diego Chicken, 1982.*

2727 Who knows? They've got a broadcasters wing, they've got a players wing. Maybe one day they'll have a chicken wing.—*Ted Giannoulas, the man inside The Famous Chicken, on his chances of making it into the Hall of Fame, 1993.*

2728 Just call me poultry in motion.—*Ted Giannoulas, The Famous Chicken.*

2729 I've seen the future, and it is much like the present, only longer.—*Dan Quisenberry, Royals reliever.*

2730 I'm looking forward to putting on my glasses with the fake nose so I can walk around and be a normal person.—*Dan Quisenberry, Royals reliever, after the 1980 World Series.*

2731 You clowns can go on *What's My Line?* in full uniforms and stump the panel.—*Billy Meyer, Pirates manager, to his players who lost 112 games, 1952.*

2732 There is no room in baseball for a clown. —*Chuck Dressen, Milwaukee Braves manager, on sending catcher Bob Uecker to the minors, 1961.*

2733 Between me and my roommate, we've hit 400 major league home runs.—*Bob Uecker, Milwaukee Braves catcher, on third baseman Eddie Mathews, 1963. Uecker hit 14 career home runs while Mathews finished with 512.*

2734 The highlight of my career? Oh, I'd say that was in 1967 in St. Louis. I walked with the bases loaded to drive in the winning run in an intersquad game in spring training.—*Bob Uecker, broadcaster and former Cardinals catcher, 1980.*

2735 I remember one time I'm batting against the Dodgers in Milwaukee. They lead, 2–1, it's the bottom of the ninth, bases loaded, two out and the pitcher has a full count on me. I look over to the Dodger dugout and they're all in street clothes.—*Bob Uecker, broadcaster, 1980.*

2736 Gene Mauch was my favorite manager. He'd say to me, "Grab a bat and stop this rally." —*Bob Uecker, broadcaster, 1981.*

2737 Sporting goods companies pay me not to endorse their products.—*Bob Uecker, former catcher.*

2738 I have so many splinters from sitting on the bench that if somebody struck a match, I might catch fire.—*Bill Grabarkewitz, Dodgers infielder, 1972.*

2739 Tell her that I'm alive and well and not pitching in Pittsburgh.—*Luke Walker, Pirates pitcher, in a message to his mother, 1969.*

2740 It beats shoveling dog stuff. I did that in high school. This is better and I get paid more. I like watching games; I've got a good seat.—*Bill Buckner, Cubs first baseman, on sitting the bench, 1984.*

2741 I'm being showcased on the bench. They have me sitting where people can see me. —*Ron Gardenhire, Mets infielder, 1983.*

2742 I don't have anything to be embarrassed about, but it's embarrassing that I did it. When I got back to the bench, girls were waving money at me.—*Steve "Psycho" Lyons, White Sox utility player, on dropping his pants to brush away some dirt after sliding head-first into first base, 1990.*

2743 This winter I'm working out every day, throwing at a wall. I'm 11-and-0 against the wall.—*Pitcher Jim Bouton on an attempted comeback, 1977. Bouton returned briefly with the Braves in 1978.*

2744 I could be a candidate for comeback-of-the-year honors. The problem is that I've never been any place to come back to.—*Clay Dalrymple, Phillies catcher, 1968.*

2745 *Ron Fraser (U.S. Olympic baseball coach, 1991):* You must believe in free speech.

Tommy Lasorda (Dodgers manager): Sure, I believe in free speech.

Fraser: That's good, because you're going to give one.

2746 I can hit any pitcher alive—if he'll stand still.—*Richie Scheinblum, Royals outfielder, 1972.*

2747 I'm so poor I can't even pay attention.—*Ron Kittle, Yankees DH, 1987.*

2748 One good thing about cold weather is that you can ice your arm while you're pitching.—*Jeff Parrett, Cardinals reliever, 1996.*

2749 Roses are red
Violets are blue.
I'm a schizophrenic
And so am I.
—*Larry Andersen, Astros reliever, 1989.*

2750 One time I was going for a ground ball and a rabbit ran across my path. In the confusion I picked up the rabbit and fired it to first base. I got the runner by a hare.—*Honus Wagner, Pirates shortstop.*

2751 A doctor tells Cubs first baseman Dee Fondy that his heart is too small and advises him to drink absinthe. When Fondy asks why he should drink the stuff, the doctor says, "Absinthe makes the heart grow, Fondy."—*Dave Kindred, sportswriter.*

2752 I've got a new invention. It's a revolving bowl for tired goldfish.—*Lefty Gomez, Hall of Fame pitcher.*

2753 I was so skinny that until I was 23, I never cast a shadow.—*Lefty Gomez, Hall of Fame pitcher.*

2754 So far I've played right, left and first base and I'm Polish. Does that make me a utility pole?—*Frank Kostro, Twins utility player, 1968.*

2755 It wasn't a high fly. It wasn't a low fly or a line drive, either. It was more of a medfly. —*Andy Van Slyke, Pirates outfielder, 1990.*

2756 Herndon seems to be bothered by insects at the plate. I don't know what species it is. Maybe it's an infield fly.—*Hank Greenwald, Giants broadcaster, 1981.*

2757 Is he the guy they named the cookie after? Wee Willie Keebler?—*George Brett, Royals first baseman, on being told he tied Willie Keeler for 20th place on the career list with 2,955 base hits, 1992.*

2758 If you're a baseball player and you come out of a game with only one single to your credit, it should be said that you hit for the unicycle.—*Michael Ventre, sportswriter, 1994.*

2759 Dedmon, don't wear plaid.—*Ted Turner, Braves owner, after seeing reliever Jeff Dedmon wearing a plaid jacket, 1984.*

2760 Is that called "dustin" Hoffman?—*Joe Torre, announcer, on a brush-back pitch thrown at Angels infielder Glenn Hoffman, May 1989.*

2761 He's turned his life around. He used to be depressed and miserable. Now he's miserable and depressed.—*Harry Kalas, Phillies broadcaster, on outfielder Garry Maddox, 1981.*

2762 He's writing a book: *The Summer of 4 to 3.*—*Clint Hurdle, Mets infielder, on teammate Howard Johnson, who grounded out to second base four times in one game, 1985.*

2763 It takes him an hour and a half to watch *60 Minutes.*—*Donald Davidson, Astros executive, on methodical pitcher Joe Niekro, 1981.*

2764 I have an Alka-Seltzer bat. You know, "Plop, plop, fizz, fizz." When the pitchers see me walking up there they say, "Oh, what a relief it is."—*Andy Van Slyke, Pirates outfielder, 1989.*

2765 All my problems are behind me.—*George Brett, Royals third baseman, on suffering from hemorrhoids during the 1980 World Series.*

2766 An hour after the game you want to go out and play them again.—*Rocky Bridges, minor league manager, on playing an exhibition game against a Japanese team.*

2767 Tell them I used to manage the Reds.—*Sparky Anderson, Tigers manager, to an interpreter for the visiting coaches of the Soviet National baseball team, 1988.*

2768 My wife bought me a tie for $135. For $135, it should tie itself.—*Wally Backman, Mets second baseman, 1988.*

2769 I kiss them on the cheek because I hate chewing tobacco. And when the cops are chasing you, you don't have time to find out if a guy is chewing bubble gum or tobacco.—*Morganna Roberts, baseball's Kissing Bandit.*

2770 And so they escorted her off the field, two a breast.—*Si Burick, sportswriter, on the removal of Morganna from a game.*

2771 How can a guy win a game if you don't give him any runs?—*Bo Belinsky, Angles pitcher, after losing a game 15–0.*

2772 Raise the urinals.—*Darrel Chaney, Atlanta shortstop, on how management could keep the Braves on their toes.*

2773 You have two hemispheres in your brain —a left side and a right side. The left side controls the right side of your body, and the right controls the left half. It's a fact. Therefore, left-handers are the only people in their right minds. —*Bill Lee, Red Sox pitcher.*

2774 I don't personify the typical left-hander. I try to hang out with as many right-handers as I can.—*Tom Martin, Mets reliever, 2001.*

2775 They have crooked arms. They throw crooked, they walk crooked, and they think crooked. They even wear their clothes crooked. You have to figure they're a little crazy.—*Al Schacht, Senators pitcher, on lefthanders.*

2776 Lefthanders have more enthusiasm for life. They sleep on the wrong side of the bed and their head gets more stagnant on that side.—*Casey Stengel, Hall of Fame manager.*

2777 There ain't a left-hander in the world who can run a straight line. It's the gravitational pull on the axis of the earth that gets 'em.—*Ray Miller, Pirates pitching coach.*

2778 Just because I'm left-handed and quotable doesn't mean I'm from another planet.—*Joe Magrane, Cardinals pitcher.*

2779 It was so cold at Yankee Stadium, throwing out the first pitch was Ted Williams.—*David Letterman, talk show host, April 2003. Williams died in 2002 and was cryogenically frozen.*

2780 When scientists find a way to bring the well-preserved dead back to life, how cool will this matchup be: King Tut pitching to Ted Williams.—*Scott Ostler, sportswriter, 2003.*

2781 Ted Williams' daughter wants to cremate him, and his son wants to freeze him. [Commissioner] Bud Selig stepped in and declared it a tie—and said they'd stuff him.—*David Letterman, talk show host, 2002.*

2782 The son of Ted Williams wants to freeze Ted's body to save his DNA. But the daughter says that is against Ted's wishes. The son wants to freeze him, the daughter wants to cremate him, and Anna Nicole Smith wants to marry him.—*Jay Leno, talk show host, 2002.*

2783 From *The Late Show with David Letterman:* Top Ten Things I'd Like to Get Off My Chest Now That I'm in the Baseball Hall of Fame:

10. Once, after I hit a grand slam, I kissed the umpire on the mouth.—*Paul Molitor.*

9. In case there's any confusion, when I die, please don't freeze me.—*Dennis Eckersley.*

8. On July 17, 1984, I told the manager I pulled a hamstring and I went to see *Ghostbusters.*—*Paul Molitor.*

7. Thank God I was never a Devil Ray.—*Dennis Eckersley.*

6. I joined a gym so I can continue to shower with men.—*Paul Molitor.*

5. Forget all that stuff during contract negotiations—I was seriously overpaid.—*Dennis Eckersley.*

4. I traded my 1993 World Series ring for two front-row tickets to a Jethro Tull concert.—*Paul Molitor.*

3. Once a guy made a joke about the mustache, so I beat him to death with a fungo bat.—*Dennis Eckersley.*

2. During difficult times in my life, I rebroadcast or retransmitted games without the express written consent of Major League Baseball.—*Paul Molitor..*

1. Earlier today, I married Brittany Spears. —*Paul Molitor and Dennis Eckersley.*

2784 Listen, people are always saying, "Rickey says Rickey." But it's been blown way out of proportion. People might catch me, when they know I'm ticked off, saying, "Rickey, what the heck are you doing, Rickey?" They say, "Darn, Rickey, what are you saying Rickey for? Why don't you just say, I?" But I never did. I always said, "Rickey," and it became something for people to joke about.—*Rickey Henderson, the all-time stolen base leader and the original master of referencing oneself in the third person.*

2785 This is Rickey calling on behalf of Rickey. Rickey wants to play baseball.—*Outfielder Rickey Henderson in a phone message to Padres GM Kevin Towers, offering his services, 2001.*

2786 I think Colon disappeared. I think immigration is looking for him. I worry about Colon because Colon was a big-time Michael Jackson fan. He might see the TV and cry all day long. He maybe is in L.A. at his funeral because I can't find him.—*Ozzie Guillen, White Sox manager, on pitcher Bartolo Colon, who went missing during a minor league rehab assignment in Charlotte, June 2009.*

2787 He's like that guy in *Seinfeld*, the close talker. You think Casey's going to lick your face.—*Phil Nevin, Padres third baseman, on Reds first baseman Sean Casey's tendency to talk with opposing baserunners, August 2002.*

2788 In baseball there are Deviants and there are Goofballs. You cannot live with the former, but you almost always try to live with the latter.—*Bob Ryan, sportswriter, 2002.*

2789 Actually, I thought there were about three of them. If there had been three, that would have meant we were in some other galaxy. So I'm pretty sure there was actually only one. I thought I had gone to Jupiter or something.—*Doug Glanville, Phillies outfielder, on losing three fly balls in the sun and then wondering if there had been more than one sun in the sky, 2001.*

2790 I'm sure if this had happened back in the year 1300 or so, people would go, "I don't know what all the commotion is about. People lose their head all the time."—*Doug Glanville, Phillies outfielder, on the theft of the Phillie Phanatic's head during spring training, 2004.*

2791 When I met him, he was kind of a human being that you would never meet in Japan. So whenever I was around him, I almost felt like I was witnessing a creature, not a human being.—*Ichiro Suzuki, Mariners outfielder, on former teammate Bret Boone, 2008.*

2792 Hey, Pulpo, give me six!—*Jim Leyland, Marlins manager, to reliever Antonio Alfonseca (aka El Pulpo), who was born with six fingers on each hand (and six toes per foot).*

2793 It was ridiculous how hot it was. You start seeing oases out there. I know I saw an oasis. It looked like a giant cheesecake. And it had eyes. I was really losing it.—*Doug Glanville, Phillies outfielder, on temperatures reaching 160 degrees on the artificial turf at Veterans Stadium, July 1999.*

2794 I always check the weather. I'm a big weather guy. I either want to be a meteorologist or an American Gladiator when I retire. —*Brian Giles, Pirates outfielder, 1999.*

2795 A Pennsylvania woman purchased baseball player Ty Cobb's dentures for $7,475 through a Sotheby's auction. She said she always wanted a little plaque of a Hall of Famer. —*Jerry Perisho, comedy writer, 1999.*

2796 I could run for governor of Idaho.—*Dave Bresnahan, Williamsport Bills backup catcher, on a trick play in which he sculpted a potato to look like a baseball and then made a wild throw with it to lure a runner home and apply the tag with the real ball, August 28 1987. The umpires allowed the runner to score, Bresnahan was fined by his manager, and then the Cleveland Indians released him from his contract.*

2797 Lou Gehrig had to play in 2,130 consecutive games and hit .340 for his number to be retired, and all I had to do was bat .140 and throw a potato.—*Dave Bresnahan, former Williamsport Bills catcher, on having his No. 59 retired following the notoriety he received for deceiving a runner with a potato, 1988.*

2798 Don't bet on the A's.—*Connie Mack, Philadelphia A's owner, to a cab driver who asked him for a tip.*

2799 Some things strike me as funny, as strange. *I'm* one of those things.—*Charlie Hough, Marlins pitcher, on still playing at 45 years old, 1993.*

2800 Boredom is having to listen to someone talk about themselves when I want to talk about me.—*Tom Paciorek, All-Star outfielder.*

2801 Children have been conceived and born during a Mike Hargrove at-bat.—*Norm Hitzges, broadcaster, 1990. Hargrove's lengthy preparation before every pitch earned him the nickname The Human Rain Delay.*

The Literate View

Authors and Baseball

2802 Nothing flatters me more than to have it assumed that I could write prose—unless it be to have it assumed that I once pitched a baseball with distinction.—*Robert Frost, poet.*

2803 Poets are like baseball pitchers. Both have their moments. The intervals are the tough things.—*Robert Frost, poet.*

2804 Some baseball is the fate of us all. For my part I am never more at home in America than at a baseball game ... in beautiful weather ... and my side winning. Beyond this, I know not. And dare not.—*Robert Frost, poet, 1956.*

2805 Every boy likes baseball, and if he doesn't, he's not a boy.—*Zane Grey, writer, 1909.*

2806 Baseball is the very symbol, the outward and visible expression of the drive and push and rush and struggle of the raging, tearing, booming nineteenth century.—*Mark Twain, humorist, April 8, 1889.*

2807 To be an American and unable to play baseball is comparable to being a Polynesian and unable to swim. It's an impossible situation.—*John Cheever, writer, 1953.*

2808 Writing a column is easy. All you do every day is sit down to a typewriter, open a vein and bleed.—*Red Smith, sportswriter, 1976.*

2809 Baseball is the best sport for a writer to cover, because it's daily. It's ongoing. You have to fill the need, write the daily soap opera. —*Peter Gammons, sportswriter.*

2810 I have a theory—the larger the ball, the less writing about the sport. There are superb books about golf, very good books about baseball, not many good books about football and very few good books about basketball. There are no books about beachballs.—*George Plimpton, writer, 1982.*

2811 Football is violence and cold weather and sex and college rye. Horse racing is animated roulette. Boxing is smoky halls and kidneys battered until they bleed. Tennis and golf are best played, not watched. Basketball, hockey and track meets are action upon action, climax upon climax, until the onlooker's responses become deadened. Baseball is for the leisurely afternoons of summer and for the unchanging dreams.—*Roger Kahn, sportswriter.*

2812 There is only one perfect time in sports, apart from individual knockouts and no-hitters. That is the never-never land of spring training when every man is Alice, and the looking glass is there for all to step through.—*Robert Ruark, writer.*

2813 Opera in English is, in the main, just about as sensible as baseball in Italian.—*H.L. Mencken, journalist.*

2814 I know of no subject, save perhaps baseball, on which the average American newspaper discourses without unfailing sense and understanding.—*H.L. Mencken, journalist.*

2815 When a man asks you to come and see baseball played twice, it sets you to asking yourself why you went to see it played once.—*George Bernard Shaw, playwright, 1930.*

2816 Who is this Baby Ruth? And what does she do?—*George Bernard Shaw, playwright, 1930.*

2817 Baseball has the great advantage over cricket of being sooner ended.—*George Bernard Shaw, playwright, 1930.*

2818 I don't think I can be expected to take seriously any game which takes less than three days to reach its conclusion.—*British playwright Tom Stoppard, comparing baseball to cricket.*

2819 England and America should scrap cricket and baseball and come up with a new game that they both can play. Like baseball, for example.—*Robert Benchley, humorist.*

2820 The majority of American males put themselves to sleep by striking out the batting order of the New York Yankees.—*James Thurber, humorist.*

2821 Love America and hate baseball? Hate America and love Baseball? Neither is possible, except in the abstract.—*John Krich, writer, 1989.*

2822 Baseball is a skilled game. It's America's game—it, and high taxes.—*Will Rogers, humorist.*

2823 America became a great nation under baseball. And began to decline the moment it took up a lot of poor substitutes.—*Will Rogers, humorist.*

2824 It breaks your heart. It is designed to break your heart. The game begins in the spring, when everything else begins again, and it blossoms in the summer, filling the afternoons and evenings, and then as soon as the chill rains come, it stops and leaves you to face the fall alone.—*A. Bartlett Giamatti, President of Yale University and future National League president and baseball commissioner.*

2825 These are the saddest of possible words—
Tinker to Evers to Chance.
Trio of Bear Cubs and fleeter than birds—
Tinker to Evers to Chance.
Ruthlessly pricking our gonfalon bubble,
Making a Giant hit into a double,
Words that are weighty with nothing but trouble—
"Tinker to Evers to Chance."

—*Franklin P. Adams, columnist, 1910. Cubs shortstop Joe Tinker, second baseman Johnny Evers, and first baseman Frank Chance were all enshrined in the Hall of Fame, due in no small part to their fame from this poem.*

2826 There was ease in Casey's manner as he stepped into his place;
There was pride in Casey's bearing and a smile on Casey's face.
And when, responding to the cheers, he lightly doffed his hat,
No stranger in the crowd could doubt 'twas Casey at the bat....

Oh, somewhere in this favored land the sun is shining bright;
The band is playing somewhere, and somewhere hearts are light,
And somewhere men are laughing, and somewhere children shout;
But there is no joy in Mudville—mighty Casey has struck out.

—*Ernest L. Thayer, writer, from "Casey at the Bat," 1888.*

2827 The idea staggered me. I remembered of course that the World's Series had been fixed in 1919 but if I had thought of it all I would have thought of it as a thing that merely happened, the end of some inevitable chain. It never occurred to me that one man could start to play with the faith of fifty million people—with the single-mindedness of a burglar blowing a safe.—*F. Scott Fitzgerald, writer, from* The Great Gatsby.

2828 I'm forever blowing ballgames,
Pretty ballgames in the air.
I come from Chi
I hardly try
Just go to bat and fade and die;
Fortune's coming my way,
That's why I don't care.
I'm forever blowing ballgames
And the gamblers treat us fair.

—*Ring Lardner, sportswriter, in a parody of the song "I'm Forever Blowing Bubbles," after learning that the White Sox threw the 1919 World Series.*

2829 I see great things in baseball. It's our game—the American game. It will take our people out-of-doors, fill them with oxygen, give them a larger physical stoicism. Tend to relieve us from being a nervous, dyspeptic set. Repair these losses, and be a blessing to us.—*Walt Whitman, poet and pitcher for the Cosmic All-Stars.*

2830 Is it the rule that the fellow who pitches the ball aims to pitch it in such a way the batter cannot hit it? Gives it a twist—what not—so it slides off, or won't be struck fairly?—*Walt Whitman, poet, 1889.*

2831 Take me out to the ball game,
Take me out to the park—
Buy me some peanuts and cracker jack,
I don't care if I never come back.
Let me root, root, root for the home team,
If they don't win it's a shame.
For it's one, two, three strikes, "You're out!"
At the old ball game.
—*Jack Norworth, lyricist, 1908.*

2832 Mathewson pitched against Cincinnati yesterday. Another way of putting it is that Cincinnati lost a game of baseball. The first statement means the same as the second.—*Damon Runyon, writer.*

2833 My eyes are very misty
As I pen these lines to Christy;
O, my heart is full of heaviness today.
May the flowers ne'er wither, Matty,
On your grave at Cincinnati,
Which you've chosen for your final fade-away.
—*Ring Lardner, sportswriter, on the decision of New York Giants pitcher Christy Mathewson to retire as a player in order to manage the Reds, 1916.*

2834 The ball is not hurled about rudely, but introduced to the bat through proper channels at a society function. And one does not steal bases like a commoner; one sends word ahead to the next base by messenger, requesting permission to approach at the base's leisure. Of course, what the bat cannot reveal is that though he loves the ball desperately, he has sworn an oath of loyalty to the glove to whom the ball was promised. So the bat must pretend he hates the ball, swatting at it, though he wishes nothing more than to profess his undying affection, but he can't, he mustn't, he shan't! And so, the bat must retreat to the gardens of his estate and ... pine.—*Stephen Colbert, talk show host, imagining how Jane Austen might have written about baseball, November 13, 2008. Austen referenced baseball in her 1817 novel* Northanger Abbey.

2835 Your arm is gone; your legs likewise,
But not your eyes, Mize, not your eyes.
—*Dan Parker, sportswriter, on Yankees infielder Johnny Mize, 1950.*

2836 If you're a singer, you lose your voice. A baseball player loses his arm. A writer gets more knowledge, and if he's good, the older he gets the better he writes.—*Mickey Spillane, crime novelist.*

2837 A baseball park is the one place where a man's wife doesn't mind his getting excited over somebody else's curves.—*Brendan Francis, Irish writer.*

2838 "I would like to take the great DiMaggio fishing," the old man said. "They say his father was a fisherman. Maybe he was as poor as we are and would understand."—*Ernest Hemingway, writer, from* The Old Man and the Sea.

2839 They can't yank a novelist like they can a pitcher. A novelist has to go the full nine, even if it kills him.—*Ernest Hemingway, writer.*

2840 A damned good poet and a fair critic; but he can kiss my ass as a man and he never hit a ball out of the infield in his life.—*Ernest Hemingway, writer and journalist, on fellow writer T.S. Eliot, 1950.*

2841 With vim and verve he walloped the curve from Texas to Duluth,
Which is no small task, and I beg to ask:
Was there ever a guy like Ruth?
—*John Kieran, sportswriter, 1927.*

2842 Baseball is a game dominated by vital ghosts; it's a fraternity, like no other we have of the active and the no longer so, the living and the dead.—*Richard Gilman, theater critic, 2005.*

2843 All literary men are Red Sox fans. To be a Yankee fan in literary society is to endanger your life.—*John Cheever, novelist, 1978.*

2844 Baseball would be a better game if more third basemen got hit in the mouth by line drives.—*Dan Jenkins, sportswriter.*

2845 Tom Seaver is the only one who comes to mind. But I do know that Steve Boros reads.

—*W.P. Kinsella, author of* Shoeless Joe, *when asked if there were any literate baseball players.*

2846 I never thought about being a writer as I grew up; a writer wasn't something to be. An outfielder was something to be. Most of what I know about style I learned from Roberto Clemente.—*John Sayles, writer and motion picture director* (Eight Men Out).

2847 I became a sportswriter because, back in my days at *Time* magazine, I was the only one in the building who could spell Yastrzemski.—*Jim Murray, sportswriter, 1986.*

2848 Writing a column is like riding a tiger. You don't want to stay on, but you don't want to get off either.—*Jim Murray, sportswriter, 1961.*

2849 Ninety feet between the bases is the nearest thing to perfection that man has yet achieved.—*Red Smith, sportswriter.*

2850 Nothing on earth is more depressing than an old baseball writer.—*Ring Lardner, sportswriter.*

2851 I'm going to be a writer like Ring Lardner or somebody—that's if things don't work out first with the Yankees, or the Cubs, or the Red Sox, or maybe possibly the Tigers.... If I get down to the St. Louis Browns, then I'll definitely be a writer.—*Playwright Neil Simon from* Brighton Beach Memoirs, *1984.*

2852 Center field is like some observation post, a kind of control tower, where you are able to see everything and everyone, to understand what's happening the instant it happens.... Oh, to be a center fielder, a center fielder —and nothing more.—*Novelist Philip Roth from* Portnoy's Complaint, *1969.*

2853 Baseball was a kind of secular church that reached into every class and region of the nation and bound us together in common concerns, loyalties, rituals, enthusiasms, and antagonisms. Baseball made me understand what patriotism was about, at its best.—*Philip Roth, author of* The Great American Novel, *1973.*

2854 I've been trying to write a book and listen to the Braves games at the same time. The Braves are delaying the completion of my book. —*Jimmy Carter, 39th President of the United States.*

2855 I find baseball fascinating. It strikes me as a native American ballet—a totally different dance form. Nearly every move in baseball—the windup, the pitch, the motion of the infielders—is different from other games. Next to the triple play, baseball's double play is the most exciting and graceful thing in sports.—*Alistair Cooke, journalist.*

2856 Baseball is an allegorical play about America, a poetic, complex, and subtle play of courage, fear, good luck, mistakes, patience about fate, and sober self-esteem.—*Saul Steinberg, illustrator.*

2857 The reason I have always loved baseball so much is that it has been not merely the "great national game," but really a part of the whole weather of our lives, of the thing that is our own of the whole fabric, the million memories of America.—*Tom Wolfe, journalist.*

2858 Nearly everyone's son wants to be a baseball player. Why not? What other profession could he choose where he can slide around in the dirt, never work when it rains and spit whenever he wants?—*Erma Bombeck, humorist, 1993.*

2859 Is there anything that can tell more about an American summer than, say, the smell of the wooden bleachers in a small town baseball park, that resinous, sultry and exciting smell of old dry wood?—*Thomas Wolfe, writer.*

2860 Two events are supremely beautiful: the strikeout and the home run. Each is a difficult and unlikely thing flawlessly achieved before your eyes.—*William Saroyan, writer and playwright, August 1954.*

2861 The worst fault of baseball—and it is an unpardonable fault in any game that pretends to be a spectacle—is that it is not lively. For vivacity I would compare baseball with chess or billiards. It is somewhat less exciting than a spelling bee.—*Louis Graves, writer, 1916.*

2862 Baseball is the favorite American sport because it's so slow. Any idiot can follow it. And just about any idiot can play it.—*Gene*

Vidal, aviation pioneer and father of Gore Vidal, 1973.

2863 I think baseball is a wretched game.... I call it one of the worst games, although I know it is called the American national game.—*Charles William Eliot, President of Harvard, 1880s.*

2864 Rooting for the Yankees is like rooting for U.S. Steel.—*Red Smith, sportswriter, 1951.*

2865 The charm of baseball is that, dull as it may be on the field, it is endlessly fascinating as a rehash.—*Jim Murray, sportswriter.*

2866 Baseball is dull only to those with dull minds.—*Red Smith, sportswriter.*

2867 I think there are only three things America will be known for 2,000 years from now when they study this civilization: the Constitution, jazz music, and baseball.—*Gerald Early, essayist.*

2868 Baseball will always remain a symbol of the era of the hot mommas, jazz babies ... and the fast buck.—*Marshall McLuhan, television critic, 1967.*

2869 Though I like the various forms of football in the world, I don't think they begin to compare with these two great Anglo-Saxon ball games for sophisticated elegance and symbolism. Baseball and cricket are beautiful and highly stylized medieval war substitutes, chess made flesh, a mixture of proud chivalry and base —in both senses—greed. With football we are back to the monotonous clashing armor of the brontosaurus.—*John Fowles, British author.*

2870 Yes, it's Dean, Dean, Dean
He's a beggar with a bullet through your spleen,
Though at times some bat has flayed you,
by the Texas sun that made you,
you're a better man than bats are, Dizzy Dean.
—*Grantland Rice, sportswriter, with apologies to Rudyard Kipling.*

2871 Baseball is reassuring. It makes me feel as if the world is not going to blow up.—*Sharon Olds, poet, 1987.*

2872 The whole history of baseball has the quality of mythology.—*Bernard Malamud, author of* The Natural.

2873 Whenever I took a swing they would howl with laughter, as if I'd dropped my pants in a burlesque house.—*Donald Hall, United States poet laureate, on taking batting practice with the Pirates in 1973.*

2874 The basic difference between a sportswriter and a sports-talker is that one wishes he could write the Great American novel and the other wishes he could read it.—*Bernie Lincicome, sportswriter, 2002.*

2875 I am a natural-born sportswriter. I have a knack for it, a God-given talent. After I learned it was possible to sleep late and still get paid for it, I never did anything else.—*Hunter S. Thompson, gonzo journalist, 2001.*

2876 There is magic in the moment, for when I open my eyes and see my sons in the place where my father once sat, I feel an invisible bond between our three generations, an anchor of loyalty linking my sons to the grandfather whose face they never saw but whose person they have already come to know through this most timeless of all sports, baseball.—*Doris Kearns Goodwin, writer, 1994.*

2877 What's important is that baseball, after twenty-eight years of artificial turf and expansion and the designated hitter and drugs and free agency and thousand-dollar bubble gum cards, is still a gift given by fathers to sons.—*Michael Chabon, writer, 1991.*

2878 Some say our national pastime is baseball. Not me. It's gossip.—*Erma Bombeck, humorist.*

2879 Assign Yogi Berra to Cape Canaveral; he could handle any missile.—*Poet Marianne Moore.*

2880 Shooting gives me a good feeling [...]. It is faster than baseball and you are out on one strike.—*Ernest Hemingway, American author.*

2881 Baseball is a game played by idiots for morons.—*F. Scott Fitzgerald, American author.*

2882 Every baseball carries with it the history of the game, in a mysterious way that you don't find in football or tennis or basketball. People have scrambled over baseballs, fought over baseballs, and the wonderful mystery of the Bobby Thomson home-run ball is in part what prompted me to write *Underworld*. If we knew who had that baseball, it's possible I never would have begun work on the novel.—*Don DeLillo, American author, 1998.*

2883 Basically I am a low-culture person. I prefer watching baseball with a beer and some meatballs.—*Woody Allen, writer and filmmaker.*

2884 The collapse of the 1964 Phillies ruined our lives. There has never been any point in continuing. Like the tormented characters in *Waiting for Godot*, we merely go on because we have no choice but to go on. But we're not enjoying any of this. Inside, we are dead.—*Joe Queenan, writer, 1996.*

2885 Baseball, because of its continuity over the space of America and the time of America, is a place where memory gathers.—*Donald Hall, poet.*

2886 Progress always involves risks. You can't steal second base and keep your foot on first.—*Frederick B. Wilcox, writer.*

2887 Like a feather caught in a vortex, Williams ran around the square of bases at the center of our beseeching screaming. He ran as he always ran out home runs—hurriedly, unsmiling, head down, as if our praise were a storm of rain to get out of. He didn't tip his cap. Though we thumped, wept, and chanted "We want Ted" for minutes after, he hid in the dugout, he did not come back. Our noise for some seconds passed beyond excitement into a kind of immense open anguish, a wailing, a cry to be saved. But immortality is nontransferable. The papers said that the other players, and even the umpires on the field, begged him to come out and acknowledge us in some way, but he never had and did not now. Gods do not answer letters.—*John Updike, author, on Red Sox outfielder Ted Williams hitting a home run in his final career at-bat, September 28, 1960.*

Ballplayers and Writing

2888 If TV executives ever got Hemingway's *The Old Man and the Sea*, they'd say: "Ernie, we love you. But the part about the fishing is boring. And the man is too old. He should have a girlfriend."—*Jim Bouton, former All-Star pitcher and author of* Ball Four.

2889 What paper do you write for, Ernie?—*Yogi Berra, Yankees catcher, on being introduced to Ernest Hemingway.*

2890 If you run across any words you don't understand, whatever you do, don't ask your mother to explain them.—*Andy Armour, eleven-year-old fan, on loaning a friend a copy of Jim Bouton's book,* Ball Four.

2891 I thought if I ever got to be famous or great I'd write a book about it. Unfortunately, I couldn't wait any longer.—*Jim Bouton, writer and Astros pitcher, on the release of* Ball Four, *1970.*

2892 Fuck you, Shakespeare!—*Pete Rose, Reds outfielder, to Astros pitcher Jim Bouton, following the publication of Bouton's tell-all book,* Ball Four, *1970.*

2893 Baseball is the bellybutton of society. Straighten out baseball and you'll straighten out the rest of the world.—*Bill Lee, former All-Star pitcher and co-author (with Dick Lally) of* The Wrong Stuff.

2894 It would be four pages long without the expletives.—*Wally Backman, former infielder, on Phillies outfielder Lenny Dykstra's book (with Marty Noble)* Nails, *1993.*

2895 You won't find a single four-letter word in there. I don't go for that bullshit.—*Bob Feller, Hall of Fame pitcher, on his 1947 autobiography* Strikeout Story.

2896 I didn't put stuff like that in my book. Of course, I didn't sell many books.—*Lou Piniella, Yankees GM and co-author (with Maury Allen) of* Sweet Lou, *on outfielder Dave Winfield's controversial book* Winfield: A Player's Life *(with Tom Parker), 1988.*

2897 It would be called *I Hate the Game But*

I Love Drinking Beer.—Kent Hrbek, Twins first baseman, on his proposed biography. The title was in reference to teammate Kirby Puckett's book I Love This Game!

2898 I read the book, and when I woke up the next day, I beat the hell out of my pillow.—*Lefty Gomez, Hall of Fame pitcher, on Yankee manager Billy Martin's autobiography (with Peter Golenbock)* No. 1, *1981.*

2899 Before he writes a book, he's got to read one.—*Dallas Green, Yankees manager, on outfielder Rickey Henderson, 1989. Before the season was over, Henderson was traded to Oakland and Green was fired. In 1992, Henderson (with John Shea) wrote* Off Base: Confessions of a Thief.

2900 Sparky's the only guy I know who's written more books than he has read.—*Ernie Harwell, Hall of Fame broadcaster, on former manager Sparky Anderson's third book (with Dan Ewald),* They Call Me Sparky, *1998.*

2901 I'm supposed to be writin' a book, and I can hardly read.—*Mark "The Bird" Fidrych, Tigers rookie pitcher, 1976.*

2902 If I ever decide to do a book, I've already got the title—*The Bases Were Loaded and So Was I.—Jim Fregosi, Rangers infielder, 1977.*

2903 How'd your book come out?—*Yogi Berra, Yankees rookie catcher, to third baseman Bobby Brown after Yogi had just read a comic book while Brown, who was also a medical student, was reading* Gray's Anatomy, *1946.*

2904 I don't know. I haven't read it yet.—*Yogi Berra, Astros coach, when asked by broadcaster Milo Hamilton what his new book* Yogi: It Ain't Over *was about, 1989.*

2905 I'm just writing down a lot of things that go through my mind, so there will probably be a lot of blank pages.—*Doug Rader, Rangers manager, on writing his autobiography.*

2906 This isn't easy, but I'll try to stay within myself and take it one paragraph at a time.—*Cito Gaston, Blue Jays manager, in a commencement speech at the University of Toronto where he received an honorary Doctor of Laws degree, 1994.*

2907 I said that if I ever had to be stranded on a desert island—with a man—he would be the man.—*Vin Scully, Dodgers broadcaster, at the memorial service for sportswriter Jim Murray, 1998.*

2908 Strike one was the call from the man in blue
And four pitches later, it was three and two.
Now everything rode on the very next pitch,
Would Eric stay a poor man or suddenly rich?
Then, the crack of the bat and a line drive to right.
The back of Joe Rudi's uniform was the only thing in sight.
Then the roar of the crowd was a deafening scream.
...Ah, then Eric fell out of bed;
It was only a dream.
—*Eric Soderholm, White Sox third baseman, 1977.*

2909 I read one good book, *JFK—The Man and the Airport.—Joe Magrane, Cardinals pitcher, on how he spent his time on the disabled list, 1987.*

2910 Hey, sports fans, put that $29 book back in your pants. I've obtained publishing rights to the Reader's Digest condensed version of David Wells' new book. Here it is, in its entirety: "I'm drunk, I'm fat, I'm stupid, I'm lazy, I'm disloyal. I'm gossipy, but I can throw hard, so I'm rich and famous. Burp."—*Scott Ostler, sportswriter, on* Perfect I'm Not, *2003.*

2911 It's always good to go home, in spite of what Thomas Wolfe may have said.—*Joe Maddon, Rays manager, after a 2–9 road trip, September 2009.*

2912 Speech and me don't even get along sometimes.—*Rickey Henderson on why he sought assistance for his Hall of Fame induction speech, August 2009.*

2913 One of them had me dead already.—*Mark Koenig, former New York shortstop, on not trusting books written about the 1927 Yankees.*

Logic Problems

2914 The longer something illogical doesn't happen, the more likely it is to happen eventually.—*Tom House, Rangers pitching coach, 1990.*

2915 My favorite word in English is "youneverknow."—*Joaquin Andujar, Astros pitcher.*

2916 You can't worry if it's cold. You can't worry if it's hot. You can only worry if you get sick. Because if you don't get well, you die.—*Joaquin Andujar, Cardinals pitcher.*

2917 Ninety percent of the game is half mental.—*Jim Wohlford, Royals outfielder, 1977. (Also attributed to Yogi Berra.)*

2918 I've been doing my best not to think about it, but by trying so hard not to think about it, I can't help thinking about it.—*Paul Zuvella, Yankees shortstop, on a batting slump, 1986.*

2919 I'm trying not to put too much pressure on myself, but I think I'm overcompensating. I'm putting too much pressure on myself not to put too much pressure on myself.—*Dann Bilardello, Pirates catcher, 1990.*

2920 In order to do what we've done, we have to keep doing what we've done in the past.—*Earl Weaver, Orioles manager, 1979.*

2921 The Yankees are only interested in one thing, and I don't know what that is.—*Luis Polonia, Yankees outfielder, on being traded to the Angels, 1990.*

2922 When you're not winning, it's tough to win.—*Tony LaRussa, Oakland A's manager, 1987.*

2923 Understanding is something you'll never truly understand.—*Sparky Anderson, Tigers manager, 1994.*

2924 Whatever is going to happen is going to happen when it happens, regardless of what happens.—*Mike LaValliere, Pirates catcher.*

2925 All that we have been told is to be ready for spring training, to treat everything like we will have spring training, but be prepared that there won't be spring training. That's what I'm doing.—*Mike LaValliere, Pirates catcher, on the possibility of a spring training lockout, 1990.*

2926 If the Expos come up with an offer I can't refuse, I wouldn't turn it down.—*Gary Carter, Expos catcher.*

2927 There's no doubt about it, but you can never be sure.—*Lou Piniella, Yankees manager, when asked if pitcher Rick Rhoden would make his next start, 1987.*

2928 Frankly, I'd prefer someplace else.—*Babe Herman, Brooklyn Dodgers outfielder-first baseman, on an offer by owner Charles Ebbets for Herman to take a trip around the world.*

2929 We told him to learn from the past, but forget about it.—*Lou Piniella, Reds manager, on infielder Chris Brown, 1990.*

2930 It went quickly, but it was like an eternity.—*Dave Winfield, Angels outfielder, on his ten-year stint with the Yankees, 1991.*

2931 Bench me or keep me.—*Chico Salmon, Indians utility player.*

2932 Bench me or trade me.—*George Thomas, Red Sox outfielder.*

2933 What was the name of that dog on *Rin Tin Tin*?—*Mickey Rivers, Angles outfielder.*

2934 The wind was blowing east to west, so it must have gone backwards in time.—*Mickey Rivers, former Yankees outfielder, on Bucky Dent's game-winning homer in a one-game playoff to clinch the 1978 AL East over Boston.*

2935 I play bingo, but I don't play bingo. Which is not to say I'm not a bingo player, just that I'm not a bingo player—*Mickey Rivers on playing (or not playing?) bingo, 1989.*

2936 Right now I feel I've got my feet on the ground as far as my head is concerned.—*Bo Belinsky, Angels pitcher.*

2937 It's not because the Mariners have a bad pitching staff, because they don't. It's not because I see the ball well here, because I don't. It's not because I'm swinging great, because I'm not. You figure it out.—*Roy Smalley, Twins infielder, when asked why he hits so well in the Seattle Kingdome.*

2938 Brooks is not a fast man, but his arms and legs move very quickly.—*Curt Gowdy, broadcaster, on Orioles third baseman Brooks Robinson. In his 23-year Hall of Fame career, Robinson stole just 28 bases.*

2939 I wore my right contact on my left eye and my left contact on my right eye. When I thought a pitch was down and in, it was really up and away. And when I thought a pitch was up and away, it was really down and in.—*Junior Ortiz, Indians catcher, 1992.*

2940 It was the first time I'd seen Charlie since the funeral.—*George Brett, Royals third baseman, on viewing a video of hitting instructor Charlie Lau, 1985. Lau died on March 18, 1984.*

2941 The game was closer than the score indicated.—*Dizzy Dean, Cardinals pitcher, after a 1–0 game.*

2942 One-run games can go either way, and most of the time they do.—*Lance Berkman, Astros first baseman.*

2943 There must be some reason we're the only ones facing the other way.—*Jeff Torborg on catchers.*

2944 I wasn't any good at baseball. I never played it.—*George Steinbrenner, Yankees owner.*

2945 Now it's just a forgotten memory.—*Dave Boswell, Twins pitcher, on a fist-fight with manager Billy Martin, 1969.*

2946 I think computers are useful, I just don't use them.—*Sparky Anderson, Tigers manager.*

2947 We lost because what was real didn't happen.—*Sparky Anderson, Tigers manager, on a game in which many hard-hit balls were slowed down by a strong wind.*

2948 The only thing I'm doing different is I'm not doing anything different.—*Tony Gwynn, Padres outfielder, on his improved hitting with men in scoring position, 1991.*

2949 I'm not in midseason form, but it's not midseason yet, either. I guess that's why they call it midseason form. That's the form you're supposed to be in at midseason.—*Kent Tekulve, Pirates reliever, 1984.*

2950 Sometimes I look on Roy as my nephew, but sometimes only as my sister's son.—*Gene Mauch, Twins manager, on the erratic play of Twins infielder Roy Smalley.*

2951 I've heard about the sophomore jinx. But I plan to ignore it. I'm going straight to my junior year.—*Joe Charboneau, Indians outfielder, on winning the 1980 AL Rookie of the Year Award. After hitting .208 in 1981, Charboneau was sent to the minors. 1982 wasn't much better for Super Joe, who hit .214 with only nine RBI. By 1983 he was out of pro ball after the Buffalo Bisons released him for making obscene gestures to fans.*

2952 Where do you buy that stuff?—*Jerry Willard, Oakland A's catcher, to a trainer who suggested he gargle with warm water, 1987.*

2953 He tells me to drink lemon juice after a hot bath, but I can never finish drinking the bath.—*Bob Uecker, broadcaster, on his doctor's prescription for treating a cold.*

2954 Did you trade me to Houston?—*Jose DeLeon, Pirates pitcher, to manager Jim Leyland who had told DeLeon he would have to pitch inside, 1986.*

2955 You have to have stable individuals to have emotions. So we're not emotionally spent at all.—*Jim Fregosi, Phillies manager, when asked if his team was "emotionally drained" after beating the Braves in the 1993 NLCS.*

2956 What's a player supposed to do? Try less?—*Howard Johnson, Mets third baseman, on a comment by manager Bud Harrelson that Johnson was trying too hard, 1991.*

2957 I'm going to play with harder nonchalance this year.—*Jackie Brandt, Orioles outfielder. Many consider Brandt the original baseball flake. One of his teammates once noted,* "Things seem to flake off his mind and disappear."

2958 Wish—To end all the killing in the

world. Hobbies—Hunting & Fishing.—*Bryan Harvey, Angels reliever, in his team biography.*

2959 The movie or the airport?—*Roger McDowell, Dodgers reliever, when asked if he had seen* JFK, *1992.*

2960 McEnaney, get that damned dog inside.—*Vern Rapp, Indianapolis Indians manager, to pitcher Will McEnaney who would sometimes walk an imaginary dog outside the dugout. McEnaney made it to the Reds in 1974 and saved Game 7 of the 1975 World Series against Boston.*

2961 What was he doing with Miss Saigon?—*Buck Showalter, Yankees manager, on hearing GM Gene Michael had gone to Broadway.*

2962 What I liked about him is that he's scared, but he's not afraid.—*Sparky Anderson, Tigers manager, on rookie pitcher Rusty Meacham, 1991.*

2963 You look at a player being brave. He's afraid, or he wouldn't be brave. If he isn't afraid, he's stupid.—*Joe Torre, Braves manager.*

2964 I don't know if "fear" is the right word. You have to anticipate the hit. You have to stay stationary. You have to know who is coming.... I guess fear is the right word.—*Rick Cerone, Mets catcher, on preparing for a collision at home plate, 1991.*

2965 Incentive clauses give you, well, incentive.—*Ernie Whitt, Blue Jays catcher, 1987.*

2966 I hope the change doesn't change things. —*John Montefusco, Yankees pitcher, on Billy Martin replacing Yogi Berra as manager, 1985.*

2967 *Fernando Valenzuela (Dodgers pitcher, 1981):* It's a great honor to win this award just as it was a great honor to win.... What's his name?

Jaime Jarrin (interpreter): The Cy Young Award.

2968 I think everybody gets caught up in superstitions. But I don't put much stock in them—knock on wood.—*Jim Deshaies, Twins pitcher, on why he ignored superstitions during a no-hitter by Scott Erickson, April 27, 1994.*

2969 It's bad luck to be superstitious.—*Dave Coggin, Phillies pitcher, on changing shirts every inning, 2001.*

2970 I don't believe in superstitions. They're bad luck.—*Bobby Valentine, Mets manager, on pitcher Shawn Estes losing a no-hit bid (he finished with a one-hit shutout) shortly after the Shea Stadium scoreboard informed fans of the four no-hitters Estes threw in high school, 2002.*

2971 We need to capture the fresh senior baseball fan.—*Rick Horrow, Senior Professional Baseball Association president, on learning that 80 percent of the fans were repeat visitors, 1990.*

2972 I'm a baseball player.—*Ryan Thompson, Mets rookie outfielder, when asked what kind of player he was, 1993.*

2973 A slick way to outfigure a person is to get him figuring you figure he's figuring you're figuring he'll figure you aren't really figuring what you want him to figure you figure.—*Whitey Herzog, Cardinals manager.*

2974 And that's what makes the game of baseball so great. The expected is always happening when it's least expected and vice versa.—*Al Helfer, broadcaster.*

2975 Now this guy is a first ball hitter. He'll either swing at the first pitch or he'll take it.—*Rusty Staub, Houston Colt .45s first baseman, to pitcher Hal Woodeshick*

2976 I guess they'll be getting a lot of take signs.—*Edgar Martinez, Mariners DH, when a Seattle split squad arrived for a spring training game without any bats, 1998.*

2977 All they do is watch games.—*Marge Schott, Reds owner, on scouts.*

2978 What are we going to do in a game? The only thing he knows is "Good Morning." He says "Good Morning" 24 times a day.—*Alberto Castillo, Mets catcher, on Japanese pitcher Koichi Taniguchi, 1997.*

2979 If we don't finish ahead of the Reds, it won't be because we get beat but just because we run out of time.—*Steve Yeager, Dodgers catcher, 1977.*

2980 The game is played with a round bat and a round ball, the players run around the bases, and what goes around comes around.—*Frank Wills, Blue Jays pitcher, 1989.*

2981 It's a round ball and a round bat and you got to hit the ball square.—*Joe Schultz, Seattle Pilots manager, 1969.*

2982 Good pitching will beat good hitting any time, and vice versa.—*Bob Veale, Pirates pitcher, 1966. (Also attributed to Casey Stengel.)*

2983 All you've got to do is prove you can do what you can do.—*Del Unser, Expos outfielder, 1977.*

2984 You can't be proud of what you don't do. —*Birdie Tebbetts, Indians manager, 1963.*

2985 You can never have too much talent. Even the 1927 Yankees didn't win every year.—*Buzzie Bavasi, Angels GM.*

2986 The only reason we're 7–0 is because we won all seven of our games.—*Dave Garcia, Indians manager, 1979.*

2987 One less hit and he would have had a no-hitter.—*Harry Dalton, Angels GM, on a one-hitter by Nolan Ryan, 1972.*

2988 When you get no runs it's hard to win. —*Del Crandall, Milwaukee Brewers manager, 1975.*

2989 We're going to hang our heads high.—*Harvey Kuenn, Brewers manager, after a loss to St. Louis in the 1982 World Series.*

2990 You can lead a horse to water, but you can't stick his head in it.—*Paul Owens, Phillies manager, 1983.*

2991 I throw as hard as I can, when I think that I have to throw as hard as I can.—*Walter Johnson, Washington Senators pitcher.*

2992 When I wake up in the morning, I pray I am still asleep.—*Roberto Clemente, Pirates outfielder.*

2993 He really jumped on it. He hit that ball a lot farther than it went.—*Curt Young, Oakland A's pitcher, on a home run by Yankees outfielder Rickey Henderson, 1986.*

2994 All right, everyone line up alphabetically according to your height.—*Casey Stengel, Mets manager, during spring training, 1962.*

2995 *Reporter:* Bill, how would you characterize the World Series so far?
Bill Lee (Red Sox pitcher, 1975): Tied.

2996 Baseball is the only sport I know that when you're on offense, the other team controls the ball.—*Ken Harrelson, White Sox GM.*

2997 I never look toward the past.—*Ron Blomberg, Yankees DH, 1974.*

2998 Since I'm only 25, I figure my future is ahead of me.—*Barry Foote, Phillies catcher, 1977.*

2999 It could permanently hurt a batter for a long time.—*Pete Rose, Reds third baseman, on the brushback pitch.*

3000 They shouldn't throw at me. I'm the father of five or six kids.—*Tito Fuentes, Giants second baseman, 1974.*

3001 The best thing about baseball is that you can do something about yesterday tomorrow.—*Manny Trillo, Phillies second baseman.*

3002 Nobody ever heard of great teams before they became great.—*Ted Turner, Braves owner.*

3003 I don't get upset over things I can't control, because if I can't control them there's no sense in getting upset. And I don't get upset over things I can't control, because if I can't control them there's no sense in getting upset. —*Mickey Rivers, Yankees outfielder.*

3004 You're never gonna get hurt falling out of bed if you sleep on the floor.—*Al Campanis, Dodgers executive, 1974.*

3005 Mike Anderson's limitations are limitless.—*Danny Ozark, Phillies manager, on his outfielder, 1975.*

3006 His reputation preceded him before he got there.—*Don Mattingly, Yankees first baseman, on facing pitcher Dwight Gooden in a spring training game, 1989.*

3007 We've got a problem here. Luis Tiant wants to use the bathroom, and it says no foreign objects in the toilet.—*Graig Nettles, Yan-*

kees third baseman, on the dilemma facing the Cuban-born pitcher on a team flight, 1979.

3008 I know 1,000 times more about this game than you, and what I know I can't explain. —*Bob Boone, Royals manager, to reporters.*

3009 Yankee pitchers have had great success this year against (Orlando) Cabrera when they get him out. —*Tim McCarver, announcer, during the 2004 ALCS.*

3010 National League pitchers pitch (Jim) Edmonds up and in. That is his strength and his weakness. —*Tim McCarver, announcer, 2004.*

3011 I have not had second thoughts. I skipped right past second and have had third, fourth, fifth, and so on. —*Gabe Kapler, outfielder, on his decision to leave the Red Sox to play the 2005 season in Japan. After struggling through 38 games, Kapler was waived by the Yomiyuri Giants and re-signed by the Red Sox.*

3012 I jump rope 300 times without stopping. If I stop, I just keep going. —*Ernie Harwell, 82-year-old Tigers announcer, on his workout ritual, 2000.*

3013 One-run baseball games always make great doorstops of the second-guessers who love to throw open the gates and charge headlong into the land of 20–20 hindsight. —*Brian Hewitt, sportswriter.*

3014 The Mets had gotten their leadoff batter on base only once this inning. —*Jayson Starke, sportswriter.*

3015 I was nearly an orphan myself. I had only one mother and one father. —*Joe Dugan, Yankees third baseman.*

3016 I'd have to say, looking back, this is the high point of my career. —*Kelly Paris, Cardinals infielder, on scoring the winning run in his first game, 1982.* Really *looking back, after playing parts of six seasons in the majors while scoring only 20 runs and driving in 14, that first run scored might really have been the high point of his career.*

3017 If you didn't know he had been cut on, you wouldn't know he had been cut on. —*Tony Muser, Royals manager, on the first spring training appearance of pitcher Mac Suzuki, who had off-season shoulder surgery, March 2001.*

3018 If I'm going to use Wil [Cordero], I've got to start using him. —*Charlie Manuel, Indians manager, 2001.*

3019 When Russell [Branyan] is striking out, he's missing the ball a lot. —*Charlie Manuel, Indians manager, 2001.*

3020 Sometimes people don't see what they are seeing. —*Charlie Manuel, Indians manager, 2001.*

3021 It's just one of those things that didn't happen. —*Tim Wakefield, Red Sox pitcher, on losing a no-hitter in the ninth inning against Tampa Bay, 2001.*

3022 He was more serious, where in the past he had the tendency to be not serious enough when it hurt him. —*Birdie Tebbetts, Reds manager, on catcher Ed Bailey, 1956.*

3023 The better he gets, the better he's going to be. —*Kirby Puckett, Hall of Fame outfielder, on Twins outfielder Torii Hunter, 2002.*

3024 I don't want to say this is no big deal, but it's no big deal. —*Marcus Giles, Braves second baseman, on a loss to the Giants, 2005.*

3025 At the end of the day, the sun comes up and I still have a job. —*Joba Chamberlain, Yankees pitcher, after a rough outing, July 5, 2009.*

3026 It'll be anywhere from Sunday to Sunday—but I doubt it'll be Sunday. —*Jack McKeon, Marlins manager, on when pitcher Josh Beckett would come off the disabled list, 2004.*

3027 It's a place where men become children—and children never forget as men. —*Jason Giambi, Yankees first baseman, on playing in the final season for Yankee Stadium, 2008.*

3028 We couldn't believe he was still available. —*Bob Fontaine, Angels scouting director, after Anaheim chose Darin Erstad with the first pick overall in the amateur draft, 1995.*

3029 He looks much better than he did last year in big league camp, and he wasn't even in big league camp last year. —*Rick Peterson, A's* *pitching coach, on pitcher Tim Hudson, March 2000.*

3030 We had our father-son game the other day. Our guys thought they were supposed to call their fathers to come in for the game.—*Rich Donnelly, Pittsburgh coach, on the youthful 1995 Pirates.*

3031 I never have trouble remembering the things I can remember, but I have trouble remembering the things I've forgotten.—*Jerry Coleman, Padres broadcaster.*

3032 The X-rays came back negative? *All* X-rays are negative.—*Lon Simmons, announcer.*

3033 *Jim Dickson* (Houston pitcher): Open the sliding glass door and let in some fresh air—and the screen, too.

John Bateman (Houston catcher) What for? The air can come through the screen!

Dickson: I know, but it gets all chopped up!

3034 Baseball is probably more physical of the two mentally.—*Bo Jackson, two-sport star, on the difference between football and baseball.*

Gems from Larry Andersen (Former Houston Astros Reliever)

3035 All I want is to have less to do, to have more time to do it in and to get paid more for not getting it done.

3036 What do they call a coffee break at the Lipton Tea Company?

3037 What do they ship Styrofoam in when they ship it?

3038 How do you explain counter-clockwise to someone with a digital watch?

3039 I dropped some spot remover on my dog, now he's gone.

3040 How come fat chance and slim chance mean the same thing?

3041 I can't tell if I'm in a groove or a rut.

3042 When you see a fly on the ceiling, was it flying upside down all the time, or was it flying right-side up and flipped over at the last possible second?

3043 If Americans throw rice at weddings, do Chinese throw hot dogs at Chinese weddings?

3044 Why is it always raining cats and dogs? Why doesn't it ever rain yaks and wildebeests?

3045 Was Robin Hood's mother known as Mother Hood?

3046 How do you know when you run out of invisible ink?

3047 Why does sour cream have an expiration date?

3048 *When asked to explain his unique world-view, Andersen replied:* If you spend ten years in the minors, like I did, you have to have a sense of humor.

Looks Aren't Everything

Size Matters

3049 He's either a short ballplayer or a tall midget.—*Bill Veeck, St. Louis Browns owner, on Yankees shortstop Phil Rizzuto.*

3050 Kid, you're too small. You ought to go out and shine shoes.—*Casey Stengel, Brooklyn Dodgers manager, to shortstop Phil Rizzuto after a tryout, 1936.*

3051 Freddie Patek is the only guy in the major leagues who needs a life preserver to go into the whirlpool bath.—*Jim Murray, sportswriter, on the not-so-tall shortstop.*

3052 Fred Patek was so small when he was born that his father passed out cigar butts.—*Joey Adams, comedy writer.*

3053 Well, you know how Earl is. Can you imagine going through life without seeing a parade?—*Ron Luciano, umpire, on diminutive Orioles manager Earl Weaver.*

3054 Old Hoss? At 5-foot-9 and 168 pounds, he's more like a little pony.—*Tim McCarver, broadcaster, on Hall of Fame pitcher Old Hoss Radbourn. As a pitcher for the Providence Grays in 1884, Radbourn won 60 of his 73 starts, all complete games.*

3055 I can't put you in a Giants uniform—you'd look like a Giant midget.—*Charlie Fox, Giants scout, to Cincinnati high school ballplayer Pete Rose.*

3056 Andy is the only electrician I know who has to use a ladder to put in a floor plug.—*Charlie Grimm, Cubs first baseman, on 5'6" Cardinals third baseman Andy High, who ran an electrical supply shop in the off-season.*

3057 We have baked potatoes back in North Carolina that are bigger than him.—*Greg Booker, Padres pitcher, on second baseman Bip Roberts, 1986.*

3058 I was worried about seeing him at Wrigley Field above the grass.—*Jim Fregosi, Phillies manager, on 5'5" outfielder Ricky Otero, 1996.*

3059 I didn't know they made those things life-sized.—*Brad Henderson, Cardinals assistant trainer, on a bobblehead of second baseman Fernando Vina, July 3, 2002.*

3060 He's so skinny the only place he could have won a college letter is Indiana.—*Pete Rose, Reds outfielder, on pitcher Wayne Granger, 1970.*

3061 He's as thin as the center field foul pole.—*Jay Randolph, broadcaster, on Pirates reliever Kent Tekulve, 1979.*

3062 He looks like he got here on a raft.—*Vin Scully, Dodgers announcer, on 6'5", 180-pound Mets pitcher Pat Zachary.*

3063 The first time I saw him in a uniform, I thought it was two guys standing next to each other.—*Tommy Jones, Memphis Chicks manager, on outfielder Bo Jackson, 1986.*

3064 Maybe they should see if his body is corked.—*Howard Johnson, Mets third baseman, on Royals outfielder Bo Jackson, August 1989.*

3065 He doesn't have a pickoff move. He just reaches out and tags the runners.—*Rich Donnelly, Pirates coach, on 6'10" Mets pitcher Eric Hillman, 1992.*

3066 That head's so big, if he wore a Malcolm X hat, helicopters would land on it.—*Eric Hillman, Mets pitcher, on public relations director Jay Horowitz, 1993.*

3067 Now you take Ernie Lombardi who's a big man and has a big nose and you take [Billy] Martin who's a little man and has a bigger nose. How do you figure it?—*Casey Stengel, Yankees manager.*

3068 When Richard finishes his delivery, he's so close to you that you can smell his breath. —*Richie Hebner, Phillies first baseman, on 6'8" Astros pitcher J.R. Richard, 1978.*

3069 The pitch was over the head of anyone else, but with Randy, it was right over the knees.—*Steve Avery, Reds pitcher, on surrendering a hit to 6'10" Diamondbacks pitcher Randy Johnson, 1999.*

3070 If Boog Powell held out his right arm, he'd be a railroad crossing.—*Joe Garagiola, broadcaster.*

3071 If you took those two legs and barbecued them, you'd have enough to feed a family for a month.—*Larry Bowa, Cubs shortstop, on White Sox outfielder Greg Luzinski, 1982.*

3072 The first time I saw him, I thought he fell out of a Wheaties box.—*Joe Garagiola, broadcaster, on outfielder Rick Reichardt.*

3073 I'll tell you what. This kid is going to be something. Just look at him. He's built like a Greek goddess.—*Sparky Anderson, Detroit Tigers manager, on Oakland A's outfielder Jose Canseco, who later admitted to steroid use throughout his career.*

3074 Mark McGwire's arms are bigger than my legs.—*Harmon Killebrew, Hall of Fame outfielder, on the Cardinals first baseman.*

3075 I'm a little past the stage of "Wow, look how big he is." But he's remarkably bigger than everybody else.—*Randy Wolf, Phillies pitcher, on striking out 6'5" Cardinals first* *baseman Mark McGwire three times in one game, 2000.*

3076 If you put Willie Mays and Mickey Mantle next to Mark McGwire, they'd look like his grandkids.—*Alex Rodriguez, Mariners shortstop, 1998.*

3077 He's Godzilla.—*Masato Yoshii, Mets pitcher, on Mark McGwire, 1998.*

3078 She has your eyes and Barry Bonds' head.—*David Letterman, talk show host, on one of the Top Ten Signs Your Baby is Too Fat, 2007.*

3079 I'm 5' 6" and a strapping 150, and unlike some people, I came by all of it naturally.—*Bob Costas, broadcaster, responding to Giants outfielder Barry Bonds who referred to Costas as "that little midget man who absolutely knows jack shit about baseball," 2007.*

3080 The boy's got talent and desire, but he ain't got no neck.—*John McGraw, New York Giants manager, on Cubs outfielder Hack Wilson, who was a physical oddity—he wore a size 18 shirt collar and size 6 shoes.*

3081 The only juicing Ryan has ever done is apple or orange. Anyone who knows us can tell you he is the smallest boy in the family.—*Chris Howard, brother of 6'4", 230-pound Phillies first baseman Ryan Howard, 2006. In his first five years in the league, Howard won the Rookie of the Year and Most Valuable Player and finished in the top five for MVP voting the other three years.*

You Ain't Got No Alibi

3082 So I'm ugly. So what? I never saw anyone hit with his face.—*Yogi Berra, Yankees catcher.*

3083 I don't think we're the oldest battery, but we're certainly the ugliest.—*Yogi Berra, on being called out of retirement for two games by the Mets to catch for Warren Spahn, 1965.*

3084 You scare people—you could be anything in the jungle but the hunter.—*Luis Tiant, Red Sox pitcher, to Brewers outfielder Gorman Thomas.*

3085 He's got the kind of face, if he came home with your daughter, you'd disown them both.—*Bob Verdi, sportswriter, on Brewers DH Gorman Thomas.*

3086 I'm old, I'm fat, I'm bald, I'm ugly, I have a plate in my head, and I have this team to manage.—*Don Zimmer, Rangers manager, 1982. Zimmer was fired after Texas began the season 38–58.*

3087 Don Zimmer has a face like a blocked punt.—*Joe Garagiola, broadcaster.*

3088 McDonough's a fine one to be criticizing another guy's appearance. He has a face that looks like someone put out a forest fire with a screwdriver.—*Roger Clemens, Blue Jays pitcher, on a statement by sportswriter Will McDonough that Red Sox first baseman Mo Vaughn looked out of shape, 1997.*

3089 Why does Donald Fehr always look like he just drank half a quart of bad milk?—*Mark Kriegel, sportswriter, on the baseball players' union negotiator, 1994.*

3090 He always looks like his team has just hit into a game-ending triple play.—*Leonard Koppett, sportswriter, on Reds manager Fred Hutchinson.*

3091 Wearing dark glasses and open shirts and looking slightly bloated, Pete Rose is beginning to take on the look of an Elvis Presley impersonator.—*Dan Shaughnessy, sportswriter, 1988.*

3092 I was so ugly that when my father first saw me, he thought I had already gone ten rounds with Joe Louis.—*Champ Summers, utility player, on how he got his nickname.*

3093 I hate the kid's guts. He's tall, good-looking, in shape and single.—*Skip Caray, Braves broadcaster, on his son Chip, 1989.*

3094 Don't get carried away. All it means is that you're ugly.—*Mike Greenwell, Red Sox outfielder, to infielder John Valentin, who was often told he looked like Greenwell, 1993.*

3095 I found out there are a lot of ugly people out there.—*Eddie Murray, Orioles first baseman, on wearing glasses for the first time, 1986.*

3096 The Giants hired a psychiatrist last year. After he'd talked to Frank for a while, he told him, "You're crazy." Frank said he wanted a second opinion. The psychiatrist said, "Okay, you're ugly, too."—*Joe Morgan, Oakland A's second baseman, on Giants manager Frank Robinson, 1984.*

3097 In all the years I played, he was the only guy who ever scared me. And he was on my team.—*Ron Fairly, former Dodgers first baseman, on former Dodgers reliever Stan Williams.*

3098 I dreamt I was in heaven and Phil Seghi was there with the ugliest girl I ever saw. I asked St. Peter, "How come?" He said, "Phil lived a bad life and he's being punished." Then I saw Gabe Paul with Bo Derek. I said to St. Peter, "Gabe must have lived a good life." He said, "No, he's Bo Derek's punishment."—*Rick Sutcliffe, Indians pitcher, on the two Cleveland executives, 1984.*

3099 When you're 5-feet-8, a little overweight and wear glasses, you can go easily unnoticed.—*Jim Frey, Cubs manager, 1984.*

3100 What's Albert Einstein doing here?—*Kevin Mitchell, Reds outfielder, on seeing* Today Show *movie critic Gene Shalit in the Cincinnati clubhouse during spring training, 1994.*

3101 They tell us for months that their swimsuit issue is coming out, but then they put Marge Schott on the cover and they give us no warning at all.—*Bob Golic, broadcaster and former NFL player, on* Sports Illustrated, *1996.*

3102 We were set to shoot some pictures at her house and she comes out wearing a lime-green teddy. I've seen Marge Schott in a lime-green teddy, so I'm not afraid to die.—*Rick Reilly, sportswriter, on the Reds owner, 2002.*

3103 The ugliest guy I ever saw was Danny Napoleon. He was so ugly that when you walked by, your clothes would wrinkle.—*Mickey Rivers, Yankees outfielder.*

3104 I've got a face made for radio.—*Ron Luciano, former umpire, on his short career as a television broadcaster, 1984.*

3105 I'm a handsome, debonair, easygoing six-footer. Anyway, that's what I told them at the Braille Institute.—*Rocky Bridges, San Jose Bees manager, 1964.*

3106 If I ever get married, all the beautiful women will be happy and all the ugly, fat ones will be pissed.—*Charlie Kerfeld, Astros reliever, 1986.*

3107 It cost $34,000, but it just doesn't look like me. I keep saying that one of these nights I'm going to get a few buddies and grab that thing and throw it in the river.—*Stan Musial, former Cardinals outfielder, on his statue in front of Busch Stadium, 1971.*

3108 Hank Bauer had a face that was once described as "looking like a clenched fist."—*Maury Allen, sportswriter.*

3109 Bob Lemon's face always looks as if it spent the night in a snow bank.—*Lowell Cohn, sportswriter.*

3110 I'm bald. I have a big nose. I've been released five times. I have a thick skin. I'll make it.—*Terry Francona, Phillies manager, on criticism from fans and the media, 2000. Francona was fired at the end of the season but found redemption as manager of the Red Sox in 2004.*

3111 A chunky, unshaven hobo who ran the bases like a berserk locomotive, slept in the raw, and swore at pitchers in his sleep.—*Lee Allen, sportswriter, on Cardinals third baseman Pepper Martin, 1961.*

3112 He looked like he was falling apart when he ran. Looked like he was coming apart when he threw. His stance at the plate was ridiculous; he really looked less like a ball player than anyone I'd ever seen. It was a crazy thing. The only thing that made him look sensational was the results.—*Robin Roberts, Phillies pitcher, on Pirates outfielder Roberto Clemente.*

3113 We went from a team where no one could get a date to guys getting married and having kids. I didn't think some would ever get married. We've got some ugly guys on this team.—*John Boles, Marlins manager, on seven players who got married during the off-season, 2001.*

3114 I've seen him in the shower, and I wouldn't call him the Greek god of anything.—*Terry Francona, Red Sox manager, on third baseman Kevin Youkilis, nicknamed the "Greek God of Walks," April 2004.*

3115 How many games was it before they told you about the mask?—*Hank Greenwald, announcer, to fellow broadcaster and former catcher Ken Dito.*

3116 It's better looking than I am. You can't see any of the wrinkles or gray hair.—*Larry Dierker, Astros manager, on his bobblehead, 2001.*

Hair Today

3117 I wanted to go out and kiss the guy, but he never shaves, and I could have hurt myself.—*Mickey Hatcher, Dodgers utility player, on the game-winning home run by outfielder Kirk Gibson in Game 1 of the 1988 World Series.*

3118 Where'd you get that haircut, in a pet shop?—*Norm Cash, Tigers first baseman, to Yankees catcher Thurman Munson.*

3119 I cover up everything I can.—*Joe Torre, Angels broadcaster and 1971 NL MVP, on why he calls his hair style "Watergate," 1989.*

3120 I don't care if they call me "baldie" and "chrome dome." God took an eraser and brushed my head clean. I'd rather be bald on top than bald inside.—*Joe Garagiola, broadcaster, 1975.*

3121 I look 10 years younger. Now, I've got 10 more years to pitch.—*Gaylord Perry, Indians pitcher, after getting a hair transplant, 1975. Perry ultimately retired in 1983.*

3122 How can I intimidate batters if I look like a goddamn golf pro?—*Al Hrabosky, Cardinals pitcher, on a decision by manager Vern Rapp to prohibit facial hair, 1977.*

3123 Some people are really ugly without facial hair, and I'm one of them. Now, we can hide behind beards and mustaches.—*Dimitri Young, Reds outfielder, on the lifting of the long-standing Cincinnati ban on facial hair, 1999.*

3124 I've got to get a dress for him. He reminds me of you-know-who, Rodman.—*Marge Schott, Reds owner, on an orange-yellow dye job by outfielder Dimitri Young that resembled NBA star Dennis Rodman, 1999.*

3125 Gorman Thomas looks like he could grate cheese with his beard stubble.—*Scott Ostler, sportswriter.*

3126 *David Letterman (talk show host, 1988):* Would you rather have a career-threatening injury or Whitey Herzog's haircut?

David Cone (Mets pitcher): I think I'd rather blow out my knee.

3127 The nation's first drive-through barber shop must be in Milwaukee. How else to explain Bud Selig's haircut?—*Dave Kindred, sportswriter, 2002.*

3128 The hair's too long. Their beards are too evident. They're a grubby-looking bunch of caterwaulers.—*Bill Werber, baseball's oldest living major leaguer, on modern ballplayers, July 2008. Werber played third base for five teams over 11 seasons; he passed away in 2009 at 100 years old.*

Clothing and Accessories

3129 I was raised to believe that men wearing earrings are fruity.—*Marge Schott, Reds owner, defending her statement that "only fruits wear earrings," 1994.*

3130 I'm not going to wear one, even though my wife has some nice ones in her jewelry box. It would be hard for a pitcher to take a catcher seriously when he is wearing an earring.—*Ed Taubensee, Reds catcher, 2000.*

3131 I've got plenty of room. I've got a big butt.—*Mike Maksudian, Cubs catcher, when asked if he would add a tattoo of his new team to his posterior along with tattoos of his previous teams—the Blue Jays and Twins, 1994.*

3132 I got tired of pulling out my wallet and showing everyone my pictures.—*David Wells, Orioles pitcher, on why he got a tattoo of his son Brandon on his right arm, 1996.*

3133 What's that, a Mr. T starter set?—*Mike Diaz, Pirates utility player, on the numerous gold chains worn by pitcher Vicente Palacios, 1987.*

3134 Me carrying a briefcase is like a hog wearing earrings.—*Sparky Anderson, Tigers manager, 1979.*

3135 I wasn't that upset because the tux looked like Jimy had slept in it.—*Gerry Hunsicker, Astros GM, on whether he was worried about being upstaged by new manager Jimy Williams who wore a tuxedo to an informal baseball dinner, 2002.*

3136 When I first met J.P. [Ricardi], I thought, "Smooth cat—smooth-lookin' cat. He looks like a pimp back in his day."—*Orlando Hudson, Blue Jays second baseman, on the fashion sense of his GM, 2002. The day after making the statements, Hudson was optioned to the minors.*

3137 He's a dull, boring potato farmer from Long Island who just happened to be a great ballplayer. But he was the worst dresser in organized baseball. He made Inspector Clouseau look like a candidate for Mr. Blackwell's list of best-dressed men. He had the same London Fog raincoat during his entire career. We'd throw it in trashcans all around the league, and somehow it mysteriously made its way back.—*Bill Lee, Red Sox pitcher, on Hall of Fame outfielder Carl Yastrzemski.*

3138 I've found that you don't need to wear a tie if you can hit.—*Ted Williams, Red Sox outfielder.*

Uniforms

3139 We've got to change these things. We need to start looking like a ballclub, instead of like jailbirds. We look like Taco Bell.—*Garry Templeton, Padres shortstop, on the San Diego uniforms, 1990.*

3140 Instead of looking like the American flag, I look like a taco.—*Steve Garvey, Padres first baseman, on the difference between his new brown-and-yellow San Diego uniform and his old Dodgers uniform, 1982.*

3141 They look like a jar of mustard.—*Norm Miller, Astros outfielder, on the bright yellow uniforms of the Padres, 1972.*

3142 What difference does the uniform make? You don't hit with it.—*Yogi Berra on becoming a coach for the Houston Astros, 1986.*

3143 It makes them look like grasshoppers. —*Ralph Houk, Yankees manager, on the green-and-gold uniforms of the Kansas City A's, 1963.*

3144 I feel like a massive blood clot.—*Boog Powell, Indians first baseman, on Cleveland's bright red uniforms, 1975.*

3145 They look like Hawaiian softball uniforms.—*Charlie Hough, Dodgers pitcher, on the Astros rainbow-striped uniforms, 1975.*

3146 We never knew what we were going to look like. One day, we'd look like bumblebees. The next day, you couldn't see us. Then we'd look like a bunch of taxicabs running around the field.—*Phil Garner, Astros third baseman, on the gold-and-black uniform combinations worn by the Pirates in the Seventies, 1987.*

3147 I'm not going to wear short pants unless they let me wear a halter top, too.—*Jack Brohamer, White Sox second baseman, on the old-style Chicago uniforms, complete with Bermuda shorts, 1976.*

3148 At least they have better-looking uniforms. The White Sox's uniforms were great if you like softball.—*Ron Kittle, Yankees DH, after being traded from Chicago, 1986.*

3149 I look like a big apricot.—*Dusty Baker, Giants manager, on wearing San Francisco's bright orange 1970's retro uniforms, 1999.*

3150 A century of baseball uniform research and design, trial and error, innovation and experimentation, and you get a uniform that looks like it was painted by Earl Scheib.—*Scott Ostler, sportswriter, on the bright teal uniforms chosen by the expansion Florida Marlins, 1993.*

3151 Sorry, Miami, but this is one ugly fish. If you left it outside overnight, even the cats wouldn't go near it.—*Rick Folstad, sportswriter, on Billy Marlin, Florida's new mascot, 1993.*

3152 Instead of one or two guys looking like idiots, now we'll all look like idiots together.—*John Flaherty, Devil Rays catcher, on manager Hal McRae's new dress code requiring players to wear their uniform pants short enough to show at least four inches of their stirrups, 2002.*

3153 All of the old dirt was on Lenny Dykstra's uniform.—*Frank Coppenbarger, Phillies clubhouse attendant, on having new dirt delivered to Veterans Stadium, 1990.*

3154 He manages to get dirty playing on an artificial surface by the third inning.—*Joe Torre, Cardinals manager, on first baseman Gregg Jefferies, 1994.*

Losses, Losing and Losers

Individuals

3155 If a tie is like kissing your sister, losing is like kissing your grandmother with her teeth out.—*George Brett, Royals third baseman, 1986.*

3156 If at first you don't succeed, failure may be your thing.—*Larry Andersen, Astros reliever, 1989.*

3157 Some days you tame the tiger. And some days the tiger has you for lunch.—*Tug McGraw, Phillies reliever, 1980.*

3158 The sun don't shine on the same dog's ass all the time.—*Catfish Hunter, Yankees pitcher, after losing Game 2 of the 1977 World Series, October 12.*

3159 Show me a good loser in professional sports and I'll show you an idiot. Show me a sportsman and I'll show you a player I'm looking to trade.—*Leo Durocher, Brooklyn Dodgers manager.*

3160 Nice guys finish last.—*Leo Durocher, Brooklyn Dodgers manager, 1946. Although apocryphal, this quotation has been attributed to Durocher. (See #5529 for what Durocher actually said.)*

3161 There are no worse consequences than losing.—*Gene Michael, Yankees GM.*

3162 Without losers where would the winners be?—*Casey Stengel, Hall of Fame manager.*

3163 You gotta lose 'em some time. When you do, lose 'em right.—*Casey Stengel, Hall of Fame manager.*

3164 When you're a winner you're always happy, but if you're happy as a loser, you'll always be a loser.—*Mark "The Bird" Fidrych, Tigers pitcher.*

3165 I can deal with the losses. It's the losing I can't handle.—*Tom Runnels, Expos manager, 1991.*

3166 I'm not emotionally suited for any occupation in which you are hailed as a success if you lose "only" 62 times in a year.—*Edward Bennett Williams, Orioles owner.*

3167 I don't mind getting beaten, but I hate to lose.—*Reggie Jackson, Yankees outfielder, 1977.*

3168 You can pitch a gem and lose, but you can't lose when you win.—*Eric Show, Padres pitcher. Show surrendered Pete Rose's record-setting hit No. 4,139 on September 11, 1985.*

3169 I should have stood in bed.—*Joe Jacobs, boxing promoter, after leaving his sickbed to see a 1935 World Series game between the Cubs and Tigers. Detroit won, but Jacobs bet on Chicago.*

3170 Baseball is like a poker game. Nobody wants to quit when he's losing. Nobody wants you to quit when you're ahead.—*Jackie Robinson, Brooklyn Dodgers second baseman.*

3171 You know, they say when it rains it pours. But this is drowning.—*Tim Belcher, Tigers pitcher, on his 0–5 start, 1994. For the strike-shortened season, Belcher led the league with 15 losses.*

3172 It's like Noah's wife told him. She said, "Noah, honey, it's going to stop raining one of these days."—*Mike Krukow, Cubs pitcher, on being the losing pitcher in a 21–3 loss to St. Louis, 1977. Krukow finished his rookie season 8–14.*

3173 You know your team's not in the race when guys are growing beards for the duck hunting season.—*Steve Boros, Oakland A's manager.*

3174 Show me a team in last place, and I'll show you a death watch.—*Eddie Einhorn, White Sox owner.*

3175 Sitting on the bench for a team that loses 99 games—that's as close to the bottom of the barrel as you can get.—*Todd Benzinger, Giants first baseman, on sitting the bench for the hapless 1992 Los Angeles Dodgers (63–99), 1993.*

3176 It's stupid to stay six years in baseball and get out with nothing. All I can say is, "I've been in the big leagues and I've played with the Mets." I don't think you can get far in life saying that.—*Randy Tate, former Mets pitcher, on retiring from the minor leagues, 1977. Tate went 5–13 in 1975—his only major league season —and had a 34–62 record in the minors.*

3177 My back hurts, I can't play golf, my ballclub is horrible, and in the seventh inning a seagull pooped on me and ruined my shirt.—*Bill Giles, Phillies president, 1992.*

3178 On my tombstone, just write, "The sorest loser that ever lived."—*Earl Weaver, Orioles manager, 1986. Weaver never had a losing season as O's manager until he came out of retirement to manage the 1986 team that finished 73–89, dead last in the AL East, after which he retired for good.*

3179 There should be a new way to record standings in this league. One column for wins, one for losses and one for gifts.—*Gene Mauch, Phillies manager. In 1964, with two weeks remaining and a 6-game lead, the Phillies lost ten games in a row, finishing a game behind the eventual World Series champion St. Louis Cardinals.*

3180 I have an amazing ability to forget things, if people would only let me.—*Gene Mauch, Angels manager, on coping with many tough losses, the latest of which was the 1986 ALCS in which California was one pitch away from victory in Game 5 but ultimately lost to Boston in seven games. Mauch never won a pennant in his 26 years of managing.*

3181 [Don] Gullett's going to the Hall of Fame, but I'm going to the Eliot Lounge.—*Bill Lee, Red Sox pitcher, after losing Game 7 of the 1975 World Series to Cincinnati.*

3182 I've come away with nothing. No, I've come away with less than nothing because I've got a loss.—*Kevin Appier, Royals pitcher, on being 0–1 in three starts despite an 0.86 ERA, 1992. Appier finished the season 15–8 with a 2.46 ERA.*

3183 I could make him millions—*Butch Henry, Expos pitcher, on Phillies third baseman Dave Hollins, who was 12-for-15 in his career against Henry with five home runs, 1994.*

3184 I didn't want to strike out, but if I didn't, the fans would have felt cheated.—*Ron Swoboda, Mets outfielder, on striking out five times in one game, 1969.*

3185 I guess he didn't get off to such a good start.—*Buddy Groom, Tigers pitcher, on being told in 1992 that Washington Senators rookie pitcher Bob Groom had a 19-game losing streak in 1909. Buddy recorded his first win in 1995—after 77 career appearances. Braves pitcher Ed Olwine (1986–1988) holds the all-time record for appearances without a win (80).*

3186 Dallas Green has been starting Anthony Young to enhance his chances of breaking his losing streak, which would make a lot of sense if Green could figure a way for Young to pitch against the Mets rather than for them.—*Ray Ratto, sportswriter, 1993. Young set an unenviable record by losing 27 consecutive games over the 1992–1993 seasons.*

3187 Maybe two Young Awards should be presented each year—the Cy for the best pitcher and the Anthony for the worst.—*Allan Malamud, sportswriter, on Mets pitcher Anthony Young, whose record 27-game losing streak ended on July 28, 1993, against the expansion Marlins.*

3188 On that day for that kid, giving up a double was a moral victory.—*J. Walter Morris, Texarkana shortstop, on a teammate who pitched all of a 51–3 loss to Corsicana, June 15, 1902.*

3189 There was a game where I decided to change pitchers. I walked to the mound and held out my hand for the ball. The kid on the mound hesitated and said, "Please, Coach, let me face this next guy. Last time he was up I struck him out." That's true, son, I told him, but if you just think back, the last time he was up was in this same inning.—*Walter Rabb, University of North Carolina coach, 1962.*

3190 Even my wife thinks I stink.—*Eric Nolte, Padres pitcher, after giving up seven runs in 1 ⅔ innings, 1991. Nolte finished the season with a 10.22 ERA.*

3191 Losing streaks are funny. If you lose at the beginning, you got off to a bad start. If you lose in the middle of the season, you're in a slump. If you lose at the end, you're choking.—*Gene Mauch, Expos manager, 1973.*

3192 *Duane Kuiper (Giants broadcaster, 1988):* It doesn't hurt as much when you get beat as it does when you beat yourself.

Ron Fairly (Giants broadcaster): I know what you're saying. In other words, what you're saying is that you can get beat, and then on the other hand, you can beat yourself.

3193 You can learn a little from victory. You can learn everything from defeat.—*Christy Mathewson, Hall of Fame pitcher.*

3194 The greatest feeling in the world is to win a major league game. The second-greatest feeling is to lose a major league game.—*Chuck Tanner, Pirates manager, 1985. Tanner experienced the greatest feeling in the world 1,352 times.*

3195 It's not whether you win or lose, it's how you play the game.—*Grantland Rice, sportswriter.*

3196 Grantland Rice, the great sportswriter, once said, "It's not whether you win or lose, it's how you play the game." Well, Grantland Rice can go to hell as far as I'm concerned.—*Gene Autry, Angels owner, 1981.*

3197 It's like being on the beach with the girl of your dreams. Then Godzilla steps in and messes up the whole mood.—*Robert Person, Phillies pitcher, on taking a one-hitter and a 3–0 lead into the ninth against the Dodgers—and eventually losing the game, 1999.*

3198 I like the game. I like the grind. It sucks losing, but it's still fun playing. I'd rather play and lose than not play.—*Greg Maddux, Padres pitcher, July 2008. In his final season (8–13 between San Diego and the Dodgers), Maddux's streak of 20 straight seasons with at least 12 wins came to an end.*

3199 I'm not going to jump off the roof. Besides, I live in a one-story house, so it would look pretty stupid.—*Greg Cadaret, Yankees pitcher, after New York went 71–91 in 1991 and finished in fifth in the AL East, 1992.*

3200 Do you think that three months into any of Christopher Columbus' trips anybody asked him if the next three months are the most important? Heck, surviving the first month was pretty important, too. If they sank the first month, the last five months weren't very important.—*Andy Van Slyke, Pirates outfielder, 1991.*

3201 I lost 24 games my first year with the Mets. You've got to be a pretty good pitcher to lose that many. What manager is going to let you go out there that often?—*Roger Craig, Albuquerque Dodgers manager, 1968.*

3202 When you're eight games behind, it feels like eight miles; when you're eight games in front, it's like eight inches.—*Ron Santo, Cubs third baseman.*

3203 There's only one difference between a game in May and a game in September. You lose in September, there's less time to get it back.—*Roberto Clemente, Pirates outfielder.*

3204 It's a good thing we won one game, or I'd be eating my heart out. As it is, I'm only eating my left ventricle.—*Ron Swoboda, Mets outfielder, on splitting a doubleheader, 1969.*

Teams

American League East

3205 I like to call the American League East the Fortune 500—because they are spending a fortune and playing .500.—*Syd Thrift, former GM, 1990.*

American League West

3206 In the American League West, where clubs are lucky if all 24 players get their shoes on the proper feet, it's no sweat if you stink for 80 or 100 games.—*Thomas Boswell, sportswriter, 1986.*

3207 The AL West race is like the Hotel California: You can check out any time you like, but you can never leave.—*Scott Ostler, sportswriter, 1994.*

3208 If the American League West was a fish, it would be wrapped in newspaper.—*John Eisenberg, sportswriter, 1993.*

Arizona Diamondbacks

3209 We're caught in a vortex of horseshit right now, and it's just sucking us right down. I can't figure out how to make it stop.—*Bob Brenly, Diamondbacks manager, on the 2004 season in which Arizona lost 111 games.*

Atlanta Braves

3210 They're a shelter all right. A bomb shelter.—*Ted Turner, Atlanta owner, when asked if the Braves were a tax shelter, 1979.*

3211 This losing streak is bad for the fans, no doubt, but look at it this way: We're making a lot of people happy in other cities.—*Ted Turner, Braves owner, on his team that finished 61–101, 1977.*

3212 Go Braves ... and Take the Falcons With You.—*Bumper sticker in Atlanta, 1990. The Braves finished in last place (65–97) before rebounding to win 14 consecutive division titles.*

3213 The Atlanta Braves are in last place, where they have been for the last four years. I wonder if they signed a lease?—*Hank Greenwald, Giants announcer, 1979.*

Baltimore Orioles

3214 Baseball was an exhibition sport at the Olympics this year—sort of like it was in Baltimore.—*David Letterman, talk show host, on the Orioles losing the first 21 games of the 1988 season.*

3215 To hell with the Gipper. Let's win one for me.—*Frank Robinson, Orioles manager, on the season-opening 21-game losing streak, 1988. The previous record for losses to begin a season was 13. The O's finished 54–107.*

3216 We're so bad right now that for us back-to-back home runs means one today and another one tomorrow.—*Earl Weaver, Orioles manager.*

3217 With the Orioles, it's an old story. In their case, a very old story. The average Orioles player is about 33, which might explain why the team already looks like it's running out of steam. When you go in their clubhouse, the only wonder is why left-hander Jesse Orosco isn't there anymore. He fits the O's profile: old and overpriced. Just like last year. And the year before.—*Jon Heyman, sportswriter, 2000. From 1998 to 2009, the O's never won more than 79 games. Orosco left Baltimore at age 42 and pitched until 2003 at 46 years old.*

3218 The last time I was on a team that gave up 30, I was playing high school football. Our secondary defense was terrible that night.—*Kevin Millar, Orioles first baseman, on losing 30–3 to the Rangers, August 22, 2007.*

3219 Do you say, "OK, guys, let's hit four grand slams—and we'll only be losing by 11?"—*Kevin Millar, Orioles first baseman, on trying to find a way to motivate his team during a 30–3 loss to the Rangers, August 22, 2007.*

3220 Maybe we need to cut the head off a monkey or something to switch it up. I think it's usually a chicken, but I'm thinking maybe a monkey would work. But that's animal cruelty. I wouldn't do that.—*Jay Payton, Orioles outfielder, on losing 13 straight Sunday games, 2008.*

Boston Red Sox

3221 Baseball isn't a life-and-death matter, but the Red Sox are.—*Mike Barnicle, columnist, 1978.*

3222 At my stupidest, I was never as stupid as

the Boston Red Sox.—*Ted Turner, Braves owner, 1981.*

3223 Since then, there have been 15 U.S. Presidents and seven Popes. Mickey Mouse was only a gleam in Walt Disney's eye in 1918, freeze-dried coffee didn't exist, World War I hadn't been numbered and McDonald's had not sold a single hamburger.—*Stephen Williams, writer, on the changing world since the Red Sox won their last World Series in 1918.*

3224 The Red Sox Magic Number: 911—*T-shirt in Boston, 1992.*

3225 We were doing all right until the defensive backs started falling down on the crossing patterns.—*Charlie Moss, Red Sox trainer, on a 21–2 loss to the Twins, 1994.*

3226 Our pain isn't as bad as you might think. Dead bodies don't suffer.—*Bill Lee, Red Sox pitcher, on losing six late-season games to the Yankees, 1978.*

3227 I'd hate to be on a team that goes down in history with the '64 Phillies and the '67 Arabs. —*Bill Lee, Expos pitcher, on leaving the '78 Red Sox, who blew a 14-game lead to the New York Yankees and then lost a one-game playoff, 1979.*

3228 The only other thing the Red Sox have on ice indefinitely, besides Ted Williams, is their bottle of World Series victory champagne.—*David Letterman, talk show host, 2002.*

3229 The Red Sox killed my father and now they're coming after me—*Marty Nolan, Boston journalist.*

3230 The Red Sox truly are the boys of summer; it's always been the fall that's given them trouble.—*Dan Shaughnessy, sportswriter.*

3231 What can I say? I just tip my hat and call the Yankees my daddy.—*Pedro Martinez, Red Sox pitcher, on losing to New York, 2004.*

3232 In Massachusetts, scientists have created the first human clone. The bad thing is that in 30 years, the clone will still be depressed because the Boston Red Sox will still have not won a World Series.—*Craig Kilborn, talk show host, 2004.*

3233 An almost inexorable baseball law: A Red Sox ship with a single leak will always find a way to sink.... No team is worshipped with such a perverse sense of fatality.—*Thomas Boswell, writer, 1982.*

3234 Maybe I've got Red Sox cancer, the kind everybody beats.—*Thomas Speers (aka Butch from the Cape), Boston sports fan, on his medical prognosis, 2001. Alas, Speers succumbed to the disease three years before the Sox won the World Series.*

Brooklyn Dodgers

3235 You may glory in a team triumphant, but you fall in love with a team in defeat.—*Roger Kahn, sportswriter, on the Brooklyn Dodgers.*

3236 Playing those Dodgers is like shooting quail on the ground. But I'm glad there's no law against it.—*Charlie Keller, Yankees outfielder, after New York defeated Brooklyn in the 1941 World Series.*

3237 Overconfidence may cost the Dodgers sixth place.—*Edward T. Murphy, sportswriter, on the Brooklyn teams of the 1930s. From 1933 to 1938 the Dodgers never finished higher than fifth.*

California/Anaheim/ Los Angeles Angels

3238 Now I know why they call them Angels. No matter what the pitcher throws, they never hit back.—*Don Riley, sportswriter, on California and their league-worst .246 average, 1975.*

3239 They're like the American League All-Star team, and that's the problem. The American League All-Star team always loses.—*Dan Quisenberry, Royals reliever, on the 1982 Angels. California lost the ALCS to Milwaukee in five games despite the presence of All-Stars Rod Carew, Fred Lynn, Reggie Jackson and Don Baylor.*

Chicago Cubs

3240 I don't think either team is capable of winning.—*Warren Brown, sportswriter, on the 1945 Cubs-Tigers World Series. The 1945 season was played without most of the best players of the era due to military service in World War II. Detroit won the series in seven games.*

3241 The only bad thing about being released by the Cubs is they made me keep my season tickets.—*Ken Reitz, former Cubs third baseman, 1982.*

3242 One thing you learn as a Cubs fan: when you bought your ticket, you could bank on seeing the bottom of the ninth inning.—*Joe Garagiola, broadcaster and former Cubs catcher.*

3243 CUB FEVER—CATCH IT ... AND DIE.—*T-shirt in Chicago.*

3244 One thing about the Chicago Bears. When their season starts, it takes some of the heat off the Cubs.—*Bill Madlock, Cubs third baseman, 1975.*

3245 The Cubs are into their thirty-sixth rebuilding year.—*Joe Goddard, sportswriter, 1981.*

3246 There's nothing wrong with this team that more pitching, more fielding and more hitting couldn't help.—*Bill Buckner, Cubs first baseman, 1981.*

3247 I don't know why we bought the Cubs. We already had a perfectly good company softball team.—*Bob Verdi,* Chicago Tribune *sportswriter, after the Tribune Company purchased the team, 1981. The Tribune Company sold the Cubs to the Ricketts family in 2009 for roughly $900 million.*

3248 What does a mama bear on the pill have in common with the World Series? No Cubs. —*Harry Caray, Cubs broadcaster, 1989.*

3249 With 11 managers in 11 years, the Cubs might have concluded by now that this is not a solution. This is like rotating the tires on a hand cart.—*Bernie Lincicome, sportswriter, 1993.*

3250 Yesterday a boatload of Haitian refugees landed in Miami. They got on a plane, flew to Chicago—and beat the Cubs, 6–3.—*David Letterman, talk show host, 1994.*

3251 We look like monkeys trying to play football.—*Tom Trebelhorn, Cubs manager, on the 0–12 start at Wrigley Field, 1994.*

3252 This could be likened to a masochistic daydream or waiting for root canal. It's not a lot of fun.—*Tom Trebelhorn, Cubs manager, on his team's terrible start, 1994. Trebelhorn was fired after the season.*

3253 Cubs Bumper-Stickers Removed Here. —*Sign at a Chicago gas station, 1994.*

3254 Phil Donahue says he'll go to the Supreme Court for the right to televise an execution on his show. And he says if they won't let him, he'll do the next best thing and show a Chicago Cubs game.—*David Letterman, talk show host, 1994.*

3255 Good news from the IRS if you are a Cubs fan. They say if you are a Cubs fan, you can deduct the entire new year as a total loss.—*Jay Leno, talk show host, on the Cubs starting the 1997 season with 14 consecutive losses, finishing 68–94.*

3256 I've never been on a team where winning the second game of the season meant so much. I guess it's part of being a Cub.—*Scott Servais, Cubs catcher, on not starting the season with a 14-game losing streak like they did the previous season, April 1998.*

3257 A lot of good ballgames on tomorrow, but we're going to be right here with the Cubs and Mets.—*Thom Brennaman, Cubs broadcaster, 1993.*

3258 The last time the Chicago Cubs won a World Series, Teddy Roosevelt was President, Babe Ruth was 13 years old, Henry Ford had just rolled his first Model-T off the assembly line and there was no euphoria on talk shows—because no one had invented radios yet. Now that, friends, is what you call a drought.—*Jayson Stark, sportswriter, 1998.*

3259 It's amazing to think that since five years after the first airplane, this club hasn't won a World Series.—*Ed Lynch, Cubs GM, 1998.*

3260 Any team can have a bad century.—*Tom Trebelhorn, Cubs manager. The Cubs haven't won a World Series since 1908 or appeared in the series since 1945. (Also attributed to Ernie Banks.)*

3261 The nation of Sri Lanka, competing in Sydney, won its first medal in 52 years. Doing well every 52 years [...] that pretty much marks them as the Chicago Cubs of the Olympic Village.—*Jerry Perisho, comedy writer, on the 2000 Summer Olympics in Australia.*

3262 When the crunch came, the Cubs swallowed their tongues, and New York in its greed, had another championship. Since that season, I have made a point of seeing the movie *Fail Safe* every time it is on TV, because the movie ends with New York being nuked.—*Mike Royko, columnist, on the collapse of the Cubs in 1969, which paved the way for the improbable postseason run of the Miracle Mets.*

3263 This has been the remarkable thing about the fans in Chicago, they keep drawing an average of a million-three a year, and, when the season's over and they've won their usual 71 games, you feel that those fans deserve a medal.—*Harry Caray, Cubs announcer.*

3264 To say that both teams have come up short of expectations is like saying Mike Tyson has come up short of sainthood.—*Rick Morrissey, sportswriter, on the disappointing 2002 season for both the Cubs and White Sox.*

3265 It has been 42 seasons since either the White Sox or Cubs went to the World Series, and 84 since either of them won a Series championship. Heck, we've thrown one since we've won one.—*Phil Rogers, sportswriter, 2002. The White Sox ended one record for futility by winning the 2005 World Series while the Cubs continue to find new ways to come up short.*

3266 I played on some bad teams, man. We would have been contracted before the All-Star break.—*Ernie Banks, Mr. Cub, on the proposed contraction of the Twins and Expos, 2001.*

3267 How do you think that makes the Chicago Cubs feel? The last time they won the World Series (1908), Arizona was still a territory (1912).—*Jay Leno, talk show host, on the Diamondbacks winning the 2001 World Series in just their fourth year of existence.*

3268 In our case, since I've been here.... I'm not 100 percent sure of this, but I think a lot of our one-run losses, we've been down more than one run and come back and got within a run, you know what I'm saying?—*Bruce Kimm, Cubs manager, 2002.*

3269 At times like these I am always reminded of Frank Lloyd Wright complaining that doctors get to bury their mistakes while an architect can only plant vines. Wright had to be a Cub fan.—*Bernie Lincicome, sportswriter, on another losing season in Chicago, 2000.*

3270 Other than getting drunk and stealing opposing players' hats, he's the only reason to go to Wrigley Field.—*Gerry Callahan, sportswriter, on Cubs outfielder Sammy Sosa, June 2000. Sosa hit 50 home runs while the Cubs lost 97 games—last in the NL Central.*

3271 Since 1946, the Cubs have had two problems: They put too few runs on the scoreboard and the other guys put too many. So what is the new management improving? The scoreboard.—*George Will, writer, 1998.*

3272 What's the problem? There's nothing illegal about selling customers a product designed to fail. The Chicago Cubs do it every year. Are they going to jail?—*Stephen Colbert, talk show host, on the Goldman Sachs financial scandal, 2010.*

Chicago White Sox

3273 If there was a league in this nation that that team could have won in, it has not been brought to my attention. And that includes Little League.—*Paul Richards, baseball executive, on managing the 1976 White Sox (64–97).*

3274 Since 1919, no one has ever had to pay a Chicago baseball team to lose.—*Scott Simon, sportswriter, 1991.*

3275 I grew up in an age when we used to pray the White Sox and Cubs would merge so Chicago would have only one bad team.—*Tom Dreesen, comedian, 1988.*

3276 Things were so bad in Chicago last summer that by the fifth inning we were selling hot dogs to go.—*Ken Brett, White Sox pitcher, 1977.*

3277 Bullfrog Bill Dietrich was a symbol of the White Sox frustration. He had a 7–15 record one year and actually held out because it was a good year for him. The fans would watch him shake off two signs from the catcher and break up. They knew he had only two pitches—slow curve and wild fast ball.—*Jean Shepherd, writer and actor.*

3278 That's 12 hours of my life I wasted, and I'm never going to get it back.—*Ozzie Guillen, White Sox manager, on watching his team lose a doubleheader to the Red Sox by a combined score of 21–4, 2007.*

3279 Being a White Sox fan meant measuring victory in terms of defeat. A 6–5 defeat was a good day. A big rally was Wally Moses doubling down the right-field line.—*Jean Shepherd, writer and actor.*

Cleveland Indians

3280 Forty-one-and-a-half games back! Cleveland's far enough back that they are almost eliminated from next year.—*Ken Singleton, Expos broadcaster, 1985.*

3281 Tomorrow's a new day. If we work hard, we can get back to mediocrity.—*Toby Harrah, Indians third baseman.*

3282 I always liked working Indians games because they were usually out of the pennant race by the end of April, and there was never too much pressure on the umpires.—*Ron Luciano, former umpire. The Tribe went a record 34 years (1960–1993) without consecutive winning seasons.*

3283 It's September and we're 300 games out.—*Doug Jones, Indians reliever, 1991. The Tribe finished 34 games out of first—and 12 games out of sixth—with a 57–108 record.*

3284 I'd rather play big games. We played enough little ones to last us all a lifetime.—*Mike Hargrove, Indians manager, on playing games with playoff implications, 1994. The strike ruined the playoffs in 1994, but the Indians made it to the World Series in 1995 and 1997, losing both times.*

3285 In 25 years, the two most exciting moments have been Tito Francona's TV commercials for Central National Bank and Valmy Thomas' groin injury.—*Bennett Tramer, sportswriter, on the Indians, 1979.*

3286 For some reason the Indians just don't want to get better.—*Catcher Jerry Willard on being released by the Indians after hitting .270 in 1985. In 1986, his replacement, Andy Allanson, hit .225.*

3287 The Indians have only one difficulty. They're the Indians.—*Thomas Boswell, writer, 1986.*

3288 The only thing I know is that a three-time loser is a baseball manager on his way to Cleveland in an Edsel.—*Bobby Bragan, former Indians manager.*

3289 They ought to change our name to the Cleveland Light Company. We don't have anything but utilitymen.—*Lou Camilli, Indians shortstop, 1972.*

3290 The first thing they do in Cleveland, if you've got talent, is try to trade you for three guys who don't.—*Jim Kern, Rangers reliever, 1981. Kern signed with Cleveland in 1967 and was traded to Texas after the 1978 season for Len Barker and Bobby Bonds.*

3291 With the A's (1974–1975) we depended upon pitching and speed to win. With the Giants (1961–1964) we depended upon pitching and power to win. With the Indians (1968–1971) we depended upon an act of God.—*Alvin Dark, former manager, comparing all the teams he managed.*

3292 They say anything can happen in a short series. I just didn't expect it to be that short.—*Al Lopez, Indians manager, on being swept by the New York Giants in the 1954 World Series. Cleveland had won 111 games during the regular season.*

3293 There are now 6 billion people in the world, and the Cleveland Indians still can't find one that can pitch.—*Jay Leno, talk show host, on Cleveland losing the 1999 ALDS to Boston after leading the series 2–0, October 1999. In their three losses, the Indians surrendered 44 runs.*

Colorado Rockies

3294 One man's list of the Rockies' biggest needs: 1. starting pitching, 2. relief pitching, 3. left-handed pitching, 4. right-handed pitching, 5. young pitching, 6. old pitching, 7. any other kind of pitching, 8. a center fielder, 9. a catcher, 10. speed.—*Jim Armstrong, sportswriter, on the last-place Rockies, 1999.*

Detroit Tigers

3295 The Tigers aren't just rebuilding. They've gone back to the primordial ooze to evolve again.—*Michael Knisley, sportswriter, 1996. The Tigers finished with a 53–109 record—39 games out of first place.*

3296 There is hope for the Detroit Tigers if the American League, as expected, brings in the proposed T-ball rule.—*Nick Canepa, sportswriter, 1996.*

3297 The Detroit Tigers are now 0–8. They're having a worse spring than the Republican Guard.—*Jay Leno, talk show host, April 10, 2003.*

3298 Congratulations to Kevin Milwood—he threw a no-hitter. And a pitcher for the Detroit Tigers also threw a no-hitter. Okay, it was during batting practice.—*Jay Leno, talk show host, 2003. Milwood and the Phillies blanked the Giants on April 27.*

3299 How embarrassing is that? Kmart thinks you're a loser.—*Jay Leno, talk show host, on the retail chain ending their sponsorship of the Tigers, 2002. The Tigers began the season 0–11, costing manager Phil Garner his job.*

3300 Over the weekend, I'm watching some war footage, you know? I see a bunch of men in uniform waving white flags and surrendering. And then I realized—Detroit Tigers. Detroit Tigers, that's what it was.—*Jay Leno, talk show host, 2003.*

3301 They've had 100 years to work on this. The Mets had what, 60 days? I think the Detroit organization ought to have a really close look at themselves. The Mets were put together with the tail end of just the National League and picked up strays like me and didn't really have a chance to do any better than we did.—*Ken MacKenzie, former Mets reliever, on the 2003 Tigers challenging the 1962 Mets record for losses in a season (120). Detroit finished with a 43–119 record.*

Florida Marlins

3302 You know how you have to give 100 percent? When you play the Marlins, you gotta give 40 or 50 percent.—*David Letterman, talk show host.*

3303 You know the saying that you learn more from defeats than victories? We're going to become Einsteins.—*John Boles, Marlins manager, 2000.*

Houston Astros

3304 We may lose a lot, but when we win it sure is difficult.—*Tom Griffin, Astros pitcher, 1970.*

3305 We had to go to our passing game much earlier than expected. Of course, a couple of turnovers and we would have been right back in the game.—*Jim Deshaies, Astros pitcher, on falling behind Cincinnati 14–0 after one inning, 1989.*

3306 When I was a batboy for the Astros, the players used to rub my head for good luck. They still haven't won the pennant and I'm going bald.—*Barry Rochkind, radio announcer and former bat boy, 1989.*

3307 Because they play at Enron Field, this might be a good time for the Houston Astros to claim their record in the post-season is the result of accounting errors.—*Michael Ventre, sportswriter, 2002. The Astros finally won their first playoff series when they defeated the Braves in 2004. Their home ballpark name was briefly changed to Astros Field before it was re-launched as Minute Maid Park.*

Kansas City Royals

3308 I've never been on a team where everybody stinks.—*Tony Graffanino, Royals second baseman, July 2004.*

3309 Avoiding 100 losses in a season is sort of like backing your car out of the garage without knocking off a side mirror: It's definitely worth doing, but it isn't something you want to spend a lot of time bragging about.—*Joe Posnanski, sportswriter, on the 2007 Royals who, after three straight years of triple-digit losses, lost only 93 games.*

Los Angeles Dodgers

3310 Here in LA, finding a celebrity to throw out the first ball is not a problem. The hard part is finding a Dodger who can catch it.—*Jay Leno, talk show host, 1993.*

3311 We don't have a guy who can hit a sacrifice fly far enough to score Jesse Owens from third base.—*Fresco Thompson, Dodgers vice president, 1967.*

3312 The Dodgers have not lost to any inferior teams this year. They've lost to everybody.—*Howard Cosell, broadcaster, 1985. Despite their slow start, the Dodgers won the Western Division that season.*

3313 Waiting for the Dodgers and Angels to get back into the pennant race is like leaving the porch light on for Amelia Earhart to return.—*Pat Buttram, radio announcer, 1992.*

3314 Now that the Olympics are over, the only amateur athletes left in town are the Dodgers.—*Johnny Carson, talk show host, 1984.*

3315 The Dodgers are such a .500 team that if there was a way to split a three-game series, they'd find it.—*Vin Scully, Dodgers broadcaster, 1990.*

3316 Good news for the economy. President Bush is off on a 35-day vacation. Who else can take a month off? Besides the Dodgers.—*Jay Leno, talk show host, August 2003.*

3317 In Chicago, a couple who are huge Cubs fans have named their baby Wrigley Field. Here in Los Angeles a couple who are huge Dodgers fans named their new baby Missed The Playoffs Again.—*Jay Leno, talk show host, 2007.*

Milwaukee Brewers

3318 Aren't all contracts with the Milwaukee Brewers minor league contracts?—*Keith Olbermann, broadcaster, on outfielder John Vander Wal signing with the Brewers, 2003.*

Minnesota Twins

3319 The plane hasn't crashed.—*Kent Hrbek, Twins first baseman, when asked if there had been any positive signs after a dismal start to the 1994 season.*

3320 There are a lot of peaks and valleys in this game. We're in a valley—Death Valley.—*Kirby Puckett, Twins outfielder, 1995. Minnesota finished last in the AL Central.*

3321 Through no fault of our own, we find ourselves still in the middle of the race.—*Twins GM Andy MacPhail, July 1993. Minnesota finished 23 games out of first, 71–91.*

Moscow Red Devils

3322 We've got great athletes and now we're learning the game. At first was pretty bad. People slid into first base and ran from home plate to third base. We lost to the Nicaraguan national team 48–0.—*Andrei Tslikovsky, Moscow Red Devils third baseman, 1991.*

New York Mets

3323 From the start, the trouble with the Mets was the fact that they were not too good at playing baseball. They lost an awful lot of games by one run, which is the mark of a bad team. They also lost innumerable games by fourteen runs or so. This is the mark of a terrible team. Actually, all the Mets did was lose. They lost at home and they lost away, they lost at night and they lost in the daytime. And they lost with maneuvers that shake the imagination.—*Jimmy Breslin, columnist.*

3324 From the start, everything was major league with the Mets except the team on the field.—*Richie Ashburn, former Mets outfielder, 1963.*

3325 The Mets is a good thing. They give everybody jobs. Just like the WPA (Works Progress Administration).—*Pitcher Billy Loes on being selected by the Mets in the 1961 expansion draft.*

3326 The only thing worse than a Mets game is a Mets doubleheader.—*Casey Stengel, Mets manager, 1962.*

3327 The Mets have shown me ways to lose I never knew existed.—*Casey Stengel, Mets manager, 1962.*

3328 I don't know what's going on, but I know I've never seen it before.—*Richie Ashburn, Mets outfielder, 1962.*

3329 MVP on the worst team ever. I wonder what exactly they meant by that.—*Richie Ashburn, Mets outfielder, on being named team MVP for the expansion franchise that went 40–120 in 1962. Ashburn hit .306 in what would be his final season.*

3330 I have a son and I make him watch the Mets. I want him to know life. It's a history lesson. He'll understand the depression.—*Toots Shor, restaurateur, 1962.*

3331 Some days they're terrible, others they're bad.—*George Weiss, former Mets GM, 1968.*

3332 It's fall in New York, which means the air is filled with the smell of burning Mets season tickets.—*David Letterman, talk show host, 1993.*

3333 The only difference between the Mets and the *Titanic* is that the Mets have a better organist.—*Jim Murray, sportswriter.*

3334 The only thing wrong with the Mets is that we don't play them enough.—*George Kirksey, Astros vice president, 1965.*

3335 I've covered losing teams before. But for me to be with a non-winner!—*Barney Kremenko, sportswriter, on covering the 1962 Mets.*

3336 A lot of people have written us off, but then, as a former Met, I guess I'm used to it.—*Hubie Brooks, Expos shortstop, 1985.*

3337 Darryl Strawberry was quoted as saying the Mets felt "numb" after Johnson was dropped. Big deal. They've been numb for two months.—*George Vecsey, sportswriter, on the firing of manager Davey Johnson, 1990.*

3338 What do you mean pressure? In New York, I pitched once when we were trying to keep from losing 100 games. That's pressure.—*Nino Espinosa, Phillies pitcher, on his days with the Mets, 1979.*

3339 They will not lose as many games as the Mets.—*Bob Hope, president of the Colorado Silver Bullets (not the entertainer), on the inaugural season of the all-female minor league team, 1993. The Silver Bullets went 6–38 in 1994, 11–33 in 1995, and 18–34 in 1996 before finally having a winning season in 1997 (23–22). The team folded before the 1998 season.*

3340 President Clinton did say that from now on he would try to give more attention to our nation's disasters. In fact, he said in the next few weeks he promises to attend at least one New York Mets game.—*Jay Leno, talk show host, 1993.*

3341 There are a lot of changes coming in baseball. There will be an extra round of playoffs. There will be two new divisions, one in each league. And all the teams have agreed to pitch underhanded to the Mets.—*David Letterman, talk show host, 1994.*

3342 The bad news—there's a strong possibility that there will be a baseball strike this season. The good news—for Met fans—it's impossible to be mathematically eliminated from a strike.—*David Letterman, talk show host, 1994.*

3343 Signs of spring in New York City: Drug arrests soar as Yankees return to town. The Mets are mathematically eliminated from the pennant race.—*David Letterman, talk show host, 1996.*

3344 One thing I've noticed about this franchise is that it's never been mediocre. It's either been a castle or an outhouse.—*Joe Torre, Mets third baseman, 1975.*

3345 If everybody on this team commenced breaking up the furniture every time we did bad, there'd be no place to sit.—*Casey Stengel, Mets manager, on a tirade in which outfielder Ron Swoboda tore up the clubhouse.*

3346 We are a much improved ball club; now we lose in extra innings.—*Casey Stengel, Mets manager.*

3347 The Mets always said I couldn't win the big games. I'd like to know the last time the Mets *had* a big game.—*Pitcher Pete Falcone on leaving the Mets after the 1982 season. Falcone went 26–37 in his four seasons with New York before signing with the Braves.*

3348 People are always saying that one-eighth of an inch is the difference between winning and losing baseball. With the Mets, it's three inches.—*Murray Kempton, journalist, on the 1962 Mets.*

NEW YORK YANKEES

3349 When I covered the Yankees in the '60s, they had players like Horace Clarke, Ross Moschitto, Jake Gibbs and Dooley Womack. It was like the first team missed the bus.—*Joe Garagiola, broadcaster.*

3350 The Yankees are just four players away from contention. And the four players are named Mickey, Babe, Lou and Yogi.—*Bill Robinson, broadcaster, 1990.*

3351 Let's put it this way: It's been a bad year for sleep.—*Wayne Tolleson, Yankees infielder, on the last-place team, 1990.*

3352 George will take away the showers next, so the players will stink when they're on and off the field.—*Graig Nettles, Padres third baseman, on Yankees owner George Steinbrenner eliminating the players' lounge at Yankee Stadium, 1984.*

3353 We're at a point where it feels good to win a game; last year it felt good to win 10 in a row.—*David Cone, Yankees pitcher, on a slow start after winning the World Series, May 1999. New York dropped from 114 wins to 98—yet still won the AL East and swept the Braves to win the second of their three consecutive championships.*

3354 They score about as often as the U.S. World Cup [soccer] team and lose with the same frequency.—*Michael Martinez, sportswriter, on the 1990 Yankees.*

3355 Sympathy is something that shouldn't be bestowed upon the Yankees. Apparently it angers them.—*Bob Feller, Hall of Fame pitcher.*

3356 The stadium will now be imploded. By the way, the team imploded around April.—*David Letterman, talk show host, on the final season of Yankee Stadium, 2008.*

OAKLAND ATHLETICS

3357 We're either in a tough stretch, or we're just not very good.—*Tony LaRussa, Oakland A's manager, on a long losing streak, 1994.*

3358 There are 25 players on the roster. Five of them are happy to be here. The other 20 want like hell to be traded. I'm not exaggerating.—*Dave Revering, Oakland A's first baseman, 1979.*

3359 Losing to the A's or Padres is like drowning in two inches of water.—*Art Spander, sportswriter, 1994.*

3360 We made $40,000 selling our 1997 uniforms. We made an extra $5,000 selling our 1997 players.—*Sandy Alderson, Oakland A's president, 1998.*

PHILADELPHIA PHILLIES

3361 Once I was picked up by a squad car at 4 A.M. on a Philadelphia street. They fined me $75 for being intoxicated and $400 for being with the Phillies.—*Bob Uecker, former Phillies catcher, 1974.*

3362 We called our highlights film from last year *Whatever It Takes,* because last year whatever it took to win, we did. This year the title still works. Whatever it takes to lose a game, we do.—*Bill Giles, Phillies president, 1994.*

3363 Our slogan is "We Can't Possibly Be This Terrible Again."—*Bill Giles, Phillies president, on the worst team in the NL, 1996.*

3364 Show me a Philadelphia team and I'll show you a loser.—*Joe E. Lewis, comedian.*

3365 If we traded him to the Cubs, they'd win by 30 games. If we traded him to the Mets, they'd win by 20 games. If we traded him to the Phillies, they'd have a chance to win.—*Whitey Herzog, Cardinals manager, on All-Star shortstop Ozzie Smith, 1985.*

3366 Any team can have a bad century, but the Phillies have overdone it. Since 1900, they have lost 1,270 more games than they have won, so they need about an eight-season winning streak just to get back to mediocrity.—*George Will, writer, 1998. On July 15, 2007, the Phillies lost their 10,000th game as a franchise—the most of any major professional sports teams.*

3367 There are times when you have to go to the bathroom real bad. You hold off and then finally you get there. And then, amazingly, you have trouble with your zipper. And something happens. Well, here we are on the verge of winning the division and we're peeing on ourselves.—*Tug McGraw, Phillies reliever, September 1976.*

3368 There's no way you can win with the players we have here. I'm sick and tired of keeping my mouth shut. Go get us somebody who can play.—*Mitch Williams, Phillies reliever, 1992. Philadelphia added Kevin Stocker, Pete Incaviglia, Jim Eisenreich, Milt Thompson, Danny Jackson and Larry Andersen in order to win the NL pennant in 1993.*

3369 Over the weekend, Veterans Stadium in Philadelphia was blown up. Fans cried—when they found out that the Phillies weren't in it.—*Craig Kilborn, talk show host, 2004.*

3370 On a clear day they could see seventh place.—*Fresco Thompson, Brooklyn Dodgers executive, on the Phillies.*

Pittsburgh Pirates

3371 They finished last—on merit.—*Branch Rickey, Pittsburgh GM, on the 1952 Pirates (42–112).*

3372 If it's anything like last year, I'll be looking forward to the strike.—*Andy Van Slyke, Pirates outfielder, on the upcoming 1994 season. Pittsburgh was 53–61 when the season was cancelled.*

3373 If we lose this game, I'm walking home.—*Jim Rooker, Pirates announcer, after Pittsburgh took a 10–0 lead on the Phillies in the top of the first inning, June 8, 1989. The Phillies eventually came back and won 15–11. Rooker made good on his promise at the end of the season by making the 300+ mile walk for charity.*

3374 The sequel to the *Pirates of the Caribbean* opens next week. You watch these movies and the pirates always win. You ever notice that? You want to see the Pirates lose? Move to Pittsburgh—*Jay Leno, talk show host, 2007. Pittsburgh set a record with 18 straight losing seasons (1993–2010), and counting...*

St. Louis Browns

3375 The Mets achieved total incompetence in a single year, while the Browns worked industriously for almost a decade to gain equal proficiency.—*Bill Veeck, former St. Louis Browns owner, comparing the Browns to the 1962 Mets.*

St. Louis Cardinals

3376 We've had off days before. We've had off days on days when we played.—*Whitey Herzog, Cardinals manager.*

3377 It's games like this that make you want to see a 10-run rule enforced.—*Whitey Herzog, Cardinals manager, on a 17–2 loss to Houston.*

3378 Dad, they stink! All the kids are going to make fun of me.—*Brian Lamping, 12-year-old son of new Cardinals president Mark Lamping, 1994.*

San Diego Padres

3379 In all my life, I've never been associated with such a born loser.—*Gene Richards, Padres outfielder, 1977.*

3380 I bought the team to have some fun, but it is proving to be as enjoyable as a wake—your own.—*Ray Kroc, Padres owner, 1974.*

3381 You guys are mad about people saying how awful you are. Well, you are awful.—*Jim Riggleman, Padres manager, to his team during a 12-game losing streak, 1994.*

3382 I would never want to be a Padre. I mean, how do you get into the Hall of Fame as a Padre?—*Reggie Jackson, former All-Star outfielder and 1973 AL MVP.*

3383 We know we're better that this, but we can't prove it.—*Tony Gwynn, Padres outfielder, 1989.*

3384 I can't recall. But I've probably seen everything. I played in San Diego.—*Cito Gaston, Blue Jays manager, when asked if he'd seen anything like a play in which Royals catcher Mike Macfarlane made a three-run throwing error with two outs, 1990.*

3385 I bet I'm the only player in the majors who grew up idolizing Ed Spiezio.—*Alan*

Trammell, Tigers shortstop, on growing up a Padres fan, 1984. San Diego finished in last from 1969 to 1971 while Spiezio was the starting third baseman.

3386 We play like King Kong one day and like Fay Wray the next.—*Terry Kennedy, Padres catcher, 1983.*

San Francisco Giants

3387 If we keep this team together, we could finish 30 games out.—*Dave LaPoint, Giants reliever, 1985. With a 62–100 record, San Francisco finished 33 games out.*

3388 We've waited this long and we can wait a couple more years—for a major-league team or the San Francisco Giants, which ever comes first.—*Todd Phipers, sportswriter, on the prospects of getting a team in Denver, 1984. The Giants never relocated, but the expansion Colorado Rockies eventually made it to town in 1993.*

3389 It's a surprise the Better Business Bureau hasn't shut down this franchise.—*Randy Youngman, sportswriter, on the Giants, 1984.*

3390 All anyone here wants is out.—*John D'Acquisto, Giants pitcher, 1976.*

Seattle Mariners

3391 When the end of the world comes, Seattle will still have one more year to go.—*Dick Vertlieb, former Mariners GM.*

3392 Being named manager of the Seattle Mariners is like being named the head chef at McDonald's.—*Charles Bricker, sportswriter, 1981.*

3393 It looked more like Michigan beat Northwestern out there, instead of baseball. It was 36 degrees. We got to freeze our butts and get them kicked at the same time.—*Lou Piniella, Mariners manager, on a 20–3 loss to Detroit at Tigers Stadium, 1993.*

3394 Playing on this team and seeing what is happening around me, I feel that something is beginning to fall apart. But, if I was not in this situation, and I was objectively watching what just happened this week, I would probably be drinking a lot of beers and booing. Usually, I enjoy Japanese beer, but given the situation, if I was objectively watching the game, I wouldn't care if it was Japanese beer, American beer or beer from Papua New Guinea.—*Ichiro Suzuki, Mariners outfielder, on Seattle's atrocious start to the 2008 season.*

Tampa Bay (Devil) Rays

3395 We're not intimidated by anyone because we've been beaten by everyone.—*Hal McRae, Devil Rays manager, 2001.*

3396 It's good for everybody's soul to occasionally win a game because these are the times that try men's souls.—*Hal McRae, Devil Rays manager, on ending a 13-game losing streak, July 21, 2002.*

3397 It's not that the fans don't want to see Tampa Bay. They don't want to see them that often.—*Peter Angelos, Orioles owner, on the poor attendance in Baltimore when the Devil Rays come to town, 2001.*

3398 The only thing that keeps this organization from being recognized as one of the finest in baseball is wins and losses at the major league level.—*Chuck LaMar, Devil Rays GM, 2005.*

Texas Rangers

3399 Who are the Texas Rangers?—*Bo Jackson, Auburn running back, when asked before the Cotton Bowl if he would consider giving up football to play baseball if the Rangers drafted him, 1985.*

3400 He's a 35-year-old rookie. He will make many mistakes through inexperience. Every previous Ranger manager would say he's already made the most elementary error. He took the job.—*Frank Luksa, sportswriter, on new Rangers manager Bobby Valentine, 1985.*

3401 I wanted to know everything my players should forget.—*Bobby Valentine, Rangers manager, on why he read a history of the team, 1986.*

3402 We've really been the Santa Claus, so far, of the American League. We've just given games away.—*Frank Tanana, Rangers pitcher.*

3403 We're better than most people think, though that isn't saying much.—*Buddy Bell, Rangers third baseman.*

Washington Senators/Nationals

3404 For the Washington Senators, the worst time of the year is the baseball season.—*Roger Kahn, sportswriter.*

3405 What we're trying to do here is make chicken salad out of chicken shit.—*Joe Kuhel, Washington Senators manager, 1949.*

3406 Washington, first in war, first in peace, and last in the American League.—*Charles Dryden, sportswriter.*

3407 The Senators this year are so bad they can't even beat themselves.—*Bob Addie, sportswriter, on a split-squad exhibition game that ended in a tie.*

3408 Then why are you covering the Nationals?—*Ralph Nader, presidential candidate, when told the* Washington Post *would no longer cover his campaign because he had no chance of winning, 2008.*

Malapropisms and Fractured Speech

3409 They're coming out in groves.—*Babe Ruth, Yankees outfielder, on attendance at home games*

3410 I have one word for Jim Hendry: Good job.—*Carlos Zambrano, Cubs pitcher, on the Chicago GM pulling off a trade to acquire pitcher Rich Harden, July 8, 2008.*

3411 Man, it was tough. The wind was blowing about 100 degrees.—*Mickey Rivers, Rangers DH, 1983.*

3412 My goals are to hit .300, score 100 runs and stay injury-prone.—*Mickey Rivers, Rangers outfielder/DH, 1984.*

3413 Pitching is 80 percent of the game, and the other half is hitting and fielding, so when you get out to center field the first thing you do is stick up your finger to check the wind-chill factor.—*Mickey Rivers, Rangers outfielder.*

3414 Mark Wagner looked lost out there at shortstop. He looked like the Lost Mohegan.—*Mickey Rivers, Rangers outfielder, on his teammate, 1981.*

3415 I was brought up in Florida, so there isn't much difference between playing there and here. The climax are about the same.—*Mickey Rivers, Rangers outfielder, on playing in Arlington, Texas.*

3416 We'll do all right if we can capitalize on our mistakes.—*Mickey Rivers, Texas Rangers outfielder/DH, 1984.*

3417 I threw about 90 percent fastballs and sliders. Fifty percent fastballs and 50 percent sliders. Hey, wait, I'm starting to sound like Mickey Rivers.—*John Butcher, Rangers pitcher, 1983.*

3418 We've definitely reached the highest level of embarrassivity.—*Jose Rijo, Reds pitcher, on the disappointing 1993 season.*

3419 We're in the doodlums.—*Frank Lucchesi, Rangers manager, on a losing streak.*

3420 Nobody can make me the scrapgoat.—*Frank Lucchesi, Rangers manager.*

3421 I've got a great repertoire with my players.—*Danny Ozark, Phillies manager.*

3422 Even Napoleon had his Watergate.—*Danny Ozark, Phillies manager, 1978.*

3423 That's completely beyond my apprehension.—*Danny Ozark, Phillies manager.*

3424 I will not be co-horsed.—*Danny Ozark, Phillies manager.*

3425 It's got a lot of crooks and nannies.—*Mike Shannon, Cardinals broadcaster, on Florida's Joe Robbie Stadium, 1993.*

3426 The side is out and the runners is left at their respectable bases.—*Dizzy Dean, broadcaster and Hall of Fame pitcher.*

3427 The tying runts are on second and third.—*Dizzy Dean, broadcaster.*

3428 Sin tax? What won't they think of next.—*Dizzy Dean, broadcaster, on complaints about his improper syntax.*

3429 He must think I went to the Massachusetts Constitution of Technology.—*Dizzy Dean, Cardinals pitcher, on manager Branch Rickey.*

3430 I must have had ambrosia.—*Jim Gantner, Brewers second baseman, on why he forgot an appointment.*

3431 I did take a hunting trip to one of those Canadian proverbs.—*Jim Gantner, Brewers second baseman.*

3432 I knew Bud Selig was a moron. I didn't know he was an oxymoron.—*Bill Conlin, sportswriter, on baseball's acting commissioner who set a "tentative deadline" for the cancellation of the 1994 baseball season.*

3433 All I want is for my case to be heard in front of an impractical decision-maker.—*Pete Rose, Reds manager, 1989.*

3434 I will perish this trophy forever.—*Johnny Logan, Milwaukee Braves shortstop.*

3435 I know the name, but I can't replace the face.—*Johnny Logan, Milwaukee Braves shortstop.*

3436 I'm very, very speechless.—*Johnny Logan, former Milwaukee Braves shortstop, on being hired as an announcer, 1973.*

3437 Rome wasn't born in a day.—*Johnny Logan, Milwaukee Braves shortstop.*

3438 I'll probably go into public relationship.—*Johnny Logan, Milwaukee Braves shortstop, on what he would do during the off-season.*

3439 I'll have to go with the immoral Babe Ruth.—*Johnny Logan, Milwaukee Braves shortstop, on who was the greatest ballplayer ever.*

3440 Look at that guy out there in left field. He's in a transom.—*Babe Ruth, Yankees outfielder, on seeing a player lying down in the outfield.*

3441 It's got lots of installation.—*Mike Smith, Reds reliever, on his new coat.*

3442 Make sure you put on a bunch of those neutrons.—*Mike Smith, Reds reliever, when ordering a salad.*

3443 We won a battle of nutrition.—*Tom Kelly, Twins manager, on a 5–4 win over the Angels that lasted almost four hours and featured eight pitching changes, 12 walks, and 343 pitches.*

3444 It would take some of the lust off the All-Star Game.—*Pete Rose, former All-Star, on the prospect of interleague play, 1993.*

3445 They had us with the walls to our back.—*Harvey Kuenn, Brewers manager, on trailing the California Angels 3–1 in the 1982 ALCS before coming back to win the series.*

3446 That's the two-edged sword which Palmer brings to the dance.—*Dick Stockton, Oakland A's broadcaster, on Rangers third baseman Dean Palmer, who hits many homers but also strikes out frequently, 1994.*

3447 I'm not one of those front-office types who hides behind their ivory towers.—*Paul Owens, Phillies GM, who took over the managerial reigns from Pat Corrales midway through the 1983 season and led the "Wheeze Kids" to the World Series, losing to Baltimore in five games.*

3448 Hey, cabbie, could you turn that thing down about a hundred disciples?—*Paul Owens, former GM, to a cab driver with a loud radio.*

3449 We're not really seeing into the bowels of the minds of the parties across the table.—*Bowie Kuhn, former commissioner, on the failure of owner and player representatives to avert a strike, 1994.*

3450 Now, gentlemen, that was a cliff-dweller to end all cliff-dwellers.—*Wes Westrum, Mets manager, after a two-out, ninth-inning rally.*

3451 Jim Fanning lit a torch under our fire.—*Gary Carter, Expos catcher, on his manager, 1981.*

3452 I sat down and I mean I did a lot of soul-searching. I talked to myself like a Dutch oven.—*Calvin Griffith, Twins president, on deciding to give shortstop Roy Smalley and catcher Butch Wynegar long-term contracts.*

3453 They took out the cartridge.—*Calvin Griffith, Twins owner, on his knee surgery, 1983.*

3454 Things started to snowplow.—*Kevin Appier, Royals pitcher.*

3455 I'm going to cancel my prescription.—*Bob Stanley, Red Sox pitcher, after reading a critical newspaper article, 1987.*

3456 I refuse to reveal my identity.—*Boots Poffenberger, Tigers pitcher, in response to an inquiry by manager Mickey Cochrane as to his whereabouts the previous evening, 1938.*

3457 The wind at Candlestick is blowing with great propensity.—*Ron Fairly, Giants broadcaster.*

3458 It got up in the Sandanista winds.—*Andy Van Slyke, Cardinals outfielder, on misjudging a fly ball that was affected by the Santa Ana winds at Dodger Stadium.*

3459 I'm not a meteorologist or a gynecologist or anything like that.—*Earl Weaver, Orioles manager, on his weather expertise, 1985.*

3460 Things happen, injuries. Guys fall down. One of your pitchers can get one of those rotary cuffs.—*Ted Turner, Braves owner, 1997.*

3461 I got a touch of pantomime poisoning.—*Yogi Berra, Yankees catcher.*

3462 Take it with a grin of salt.—*Yogi Berra, Hall of Fame catcher.*

3463 All I know is my players are frosting at the bit.—*Yogi Berra, Yankees manager.*

3464 Well, he'll have to call up a blacksmith. —*Yogi Berra, Yankees catcher, on hearing teammate Billy Martin had locked his keys is his car.*

3465 It ain't the heat, it's the humility.—*Yogi Berra, Hall of Fame catcher.*

3466 We're not exactly hitting the ball off the cover.—*Yogi Berra, Mets manager.*

3467 I'm red as a sheet.—*Yogi Berra, Yankees catcher/outfielder, on the embarrassing flubbing of his lines in the Doris Day–Cary Grant film* That Touch of Mink, *1962.*

3468 Tony Perez is a big clog in their machine.—*Yogi Berra, Mets manager, on facing Perez and the Big Red Machine in the 1973 playoffs.*

3469 Italians are very romantic, a very arduous people.—*Phil Rizzuto, Yankees broadcaster.*

3470 If Don Mattingly isn't the American League MVP, nothing's kosher in China.—*Phil Rizzuto, Yankees broadcaster, 1985. With a .324 average and 145 RBI, Mattingly won the award.*

3471 This is a good story. Usually they just take your biology and rewrite it.—*Harry Coyle, NBC baseball director, on a newspaper column written about him.*

3472 I think Joe Torre is the Mount Rushmore of managers.—*Arn Tellem, agent for pitcher Mike Mussina, after his client signed a free agent contract with the Yankees, 2000.*

3473 To be honest with you, I'll be truthful.—*Sparky Anderson, Tigers manager.*

3474 It's pretty difficult because we've been in heat for a month.—*Ron Romanick, Angels pitcher, when asked how the team would play in cold weather, 1984.*

3475 That picture was taken out of context.—*Jeff Innis, Mets pitcher, on an unflattering photo, 1991.*

3476 Like they say: Don't look back, somebody might be in front of you.—*Barry Bonds, Pirates outfielder, trying unsuccessfully to quote Satchel Paige's expression,* "Don't look back. Something might be gaining on you."

3477 I'm not blind to hearing what everybody else hears.—*Zane Smith, Red Sox pitcher, on rumors he might not make the postseason roster, 1995.*

3478 I've got 20–20 hearing.—*Jimy Williams, Red Sox manager, on listening to complaints from fans, 1998.*

3479 Scott Bullett, as he takes left field, is getting congratulations from everybody. He and his daughter are proud parents of a new baby.—*Harry Caray, Cubs broadcaster, 1995.*

3480 The average attendance at Cubs games this year is 48 degrees.—*Harry Caray, Cubs broadcaster, 1996.*

3481 Jesus Alou is in the on-deck circus.—*Jerry Coleman, Padres broadcaster.*

3482 National League umpires wear inside chest protesters.—*Jerry Coleman, Padres broadcaster.*

3483 If you ask what the Achilles tendon of the team is, it would be pitching.—*Jerry Coleman, Padres manager, 1980.*

3484 I don't look back that far into the future.—*Roger Clemens, Yankees pitcher, on his memories of playing in Boston and losing the 1986 World Series to the Mets, 1999.*

3485 The Brooklyn Dodgers had a no-hitter last night.—*Bob Dole, Republican presidential nominee, in a speech to students at a southern California high school, 1996. Dole was referring Dodgers pitcher Hideo Nomo who no-hit the Rockies in Denver. The Dodgers moved from Brooklyn in 1957.*

3486 Omar Vizquel sympathizes everything that's good about the Cleveland Indians.—*Jim Thome, Indians first baseman, on accepting an award for his teammate, 1997.*

3487 Arguably, we have a great offense, no doubt.—*Terry Bevington, White Sox manager, 1997.*

3488 Our phenoms aren't phenomenating.—*Lefty Phillips, Angels manager, 1971.*

3489 I called the doctor, and he said the contraptions were an hour apart.—*Mackey Sasser, Mets catcher, on his wife going into labor, 1988.*

3490 I want all the kids to do what I do, to look up to me. I want all the kids to copulate me.—*Andre Dawson, Cubs outfielder.*

3491 Okay, now everyone inhale and ... dehale.—*Maury Wills, Dodgers shortstop, leading the team through exercises, 1962.*

3492 Any time I've taken the mound, it's always been the old Samson-and-Goliath story written about me.—*Randy Johnson, 6'10" Diamondbacks pitcher.*

3493 Reggie Smith of the Dodgers and Gary Matthews of the homers hit Braves in that game.—*Jerry Coleman, Padres announcer.*

3494 Me and George and Billy are two of a kind.—*Mickey Rivers, Yankees outfielder, on his relationship with owner George Steinbrenner and manager Billy Martin.*

3495 Edwards missed getting Stearns at third base by an eyeball.—*Jerry Coleman, Padres broadcaster.*

3496 There's two heads to every coin.—*Jerry Coleman, Padres broadcaster.*

3497 I'll tackle that bridge when I get to it.—*Charlie Manuel, Indians manager, 2001.*

3498 I'm going to let the chips fall where they lay.—*Charlie Manuel, Indians manager, 2001.*

3499 I felt a rush of energy.... A miraculous rush of estrogen, or whatever it was—*Baseball fan Charles Murphy on catching the 70th home run ball hit by Giants outfielder Barry Bonds, October 4, 2001.*

3500 I'm going to be MBP this year.—*Outfielder Rickey Henderson on his goals following an off-season trade to the Yankees, 1985.*

3501 We lost a big void.—*Roger Clemens, Red Sox pitcher, on the death of team owner Jean Yawkey, February 26, 1992.*

3502 Nobody wants to be in my pants right now.—*Juan Rincon, Twins reliever, on giving up four runs in just one-third of an inning to the Yankees, 2004.*

3503 I don't believe we ain't going to win.—*Rickey Henderson, Padres outfielder, March 2001. San Diego finished 79–83, fourth place in the NL West.*

3504 We're a team of destination.—*Charlie Kerfeld, Astros reliever, 1986.*

3505 I don't believe in the curse; you make your own destination.—*Manny Ramirez, Red*

Sox outfielder and 2004 World Series MVP, on winning the Series.

3506 If they smell a rat, they have to nip it in the bud.—*Tony Muser, Royals manager, on Kansas City pitcher Chad Durbin receiving a warning from umpires after hitting a batter, 2001.*

3507 You're a liar. There ain't no Hotel Episode in Detroit.—*Rube Waddell, Philadelphia A's pitcher, on receiving a $100 fine for "that disgraceful hotel episode in Detroit."*

3508 Jim Eisenreich is doomed to be an all-star.—*Calvin Griffith, Twins owner, on his rookie outfielder, 1982. Eisenreich played 15 seasons and won a World Series with the 1997 Marlins, but he never made an All-Star team.*

3509 Tomorrow is another day. Unless you're not alive.—*Terry Bevington, White Sox manager.*

Managing to Manage

3510 If you don't win, you're going to be fired. If you do win, you've only put off the day you're going to be fired.—*Leo Durocher on being fired as Cubs manager, 1972. Career managerial record: 2008–1709.*

3511 The secret of managing a club is to keep the five guys who hate you away from the five who are undecided.—*Casey Stengel, Yankees manager. Career record: 1905–1842.*

3512 I became a major league manager in several cities and was discharged. We call it discharged because there was no question I had to leave.—*Casey Stengel, Yankees manager, in his testimony to the U.S. Senate Subcommittee on Antitrust and Monopoly, July 9, 1958. Stengel won 10 pennants and seven World Series titles in 12 seasons as Yankees manager.*

3513 I'm not the manager because I'm always right, but I'm always right because I'm the manager.—*Gene Mauch, Expos manager. Career record: 1902–2037.*

3514 There are only two kinds of managers: winning managers and ex-managers.—*Gil Hodges on being named Mets manager, 1968. The ex–Washington Senators manager (1963–1967) became a winning manager for the 1969 Miracle Mets. Career record: 660–753.*

3515 I can think of three managers who weren't fired. John McGraw of the Giants, who was sick and resigned; Miller Huggins of the Yankees, who died on the job; and Connie Mack of the Athletics, who owned the club.—*Red Smith, sportswriter, to Red Sox manager Don Zimmer, 1979.*

3516 If you don't die on the job or own the ballclub, you're gonna get fired.—*Whitey Herzog, Cardinals manager, 1985. Career record: 1281–1125.*

3517 The only way to make money as a manager is to win one place, get fired and hired somewhere else.—*Whitey Herzog, Cardinals manager, who led St. Louis to the 1982 World Series title.*

3518 Do you know what the average tenure is among big league managers? Two and a half years. Migrant fruit picking is more secure than that.—*Bob Uecker, announcer, 1982.*

3519 There are three secrets to managing. The first is to have patience. The second is be patient. And the third, most important secret is patience.—*Chuck Tanner, manager of the 1979 World Series Champion Pirates.*

3520 Patience is a great thing, but sometimes patience gets you fired.—*Whitey Herzog, Cardinals manager, 1985.*

3521 Managers don't resign. They get fired. —*Walter Alston, Dodgers manager, 1959. Career record: 2040–1613.*

3522 Believe what you like; no manager ever resigns.—*Bucky Harris, Tigers manager. As a 27-year-old player-manager in 1924, Har-*

ris led the Washington Senators to their only World Series championship. Career record: 2157–2218.

3523 Being a winner as a player is getting the most from your ability. Being a winner as a manager is not getting fired.—*Joe Torre, Mets manager, 1978. Torre managed the Yankees to World Series championships in 1996, 1998, 1999, and 2000. Career record: 2326–1997 (as of 2010)*

3524 It's one of the hazards of the job. If a man doesn't want to be fired, he better not manage. He should join the Army.—*Harry Craft, Houston Colt .45s manager, 1964. In seven seasons as a manager, Craft's teams never finished better than seventh. Career record: 360–485.*

3525 If you're looking for job security, drive a mail truck. Managers always get fired.—*Alvin Dark, former manager. In Dark's two seasons in Oakland, the Athletics won the 1974 World Series and lost to the Reds in the 1975 ALCS. Career record: 994–954.*

3526 You never ask why you've been fired because, if you do, they're liable to tell you.—*Jerry Coleman, Padres manager, 1980. Career record: 73–89.*

3527 You never unpack your suitcases in this business.—*Preston Gomez, former manager. In seven seasons with three teams, only his 1974 Astros did not finish in last place. Career record: 346–529.*

3528 They get tired of seeing you. Really, that's all it is.—*Sparky Anderson, Tigers manager, on why even successful managers get fired, 1979. Anderson became the first manager to win 600 games and a World Series in both leagues. Career record: 2194–1834.*

3529 I was in ninth place when I left. Very few managers can remain when they're in ninth place unless they can tell a lot of jokes. And I can't tell a lot of jokes.—*Eddie Stanky on being fired as White Sox manager, 1968. Career record: 467–435. Stanky coached college ball for years before returning to manage Texas in 1977—and quit after just one game.*

3530 Because you can't fire the entire team.—*Dick O'Connell, Red Sox GM, on why he fired manager Darrell Johnson, 1976.*

3531 Architects cover their mistakes with ivy, used car salesmen with paint, young homemakers with mayonnaise, and baseball owners by firing the manager.—*Phil Elderkin, sportswriter, 1986.*

3532 If he had made me a consultant five minutes ago, my first recommendation would have been not to fire the manager.—*John Wathan on being fired as Royals manager and offered a position as a team consultant, 1991. Career record: 326–320.*

3533 When you have a one-year contract, you want to stretch that year as long as possible.—*Chuck Cottier, Mariners manager, on why he arrived for spring training six days early, 1985. Career record: 98–119.*

3534 One-year contract is our policy here. And if it weren't, I'd make it our policy.—*Walter O'Malley, Brooklyn Dodgers owner, to rookie manager Walt Alston, 1954. Alston signed 23 consecutive one-year contracts, winning seven pennants and four World Series titles during his Hall of Fame career.*

3535 It isn't every manager who's offered a multi-hour contract.—*Connie Ryan, Rangers manager, on managing six games in the middle of the 1977 season. Ryan went 2–4 before returning to his coaching duties.*

3536 It's the first time I've had more than a one-year deal since the Army.—*John McNamara, Red Sox manager, on the two-year contract he negotiated with Boston, 1985. Career record: 1150–1215.*

3537 I don't know if I'm a lame duck, but I'm limping a little more and not quacking as much.—*Tom Trebelhorn, Brewers manager, on rumors that he would be fired, 1991. Phil Garner replaced Trebelhorn the next season. Trebelhorn's career record: 471–461.*

3538 I think they recycle more managers than cans.—*Billy North, Oakland A's outfielder.*

3539 You talk about being recycled. Zimmer is the aluminum can of managing.—*Tony Ko-*

rnheiser, sportswriter, on Cubs manager Don Zimmer, 1987. In 13 years of managing, only his 1989 Cubs won a division title. Zimmer's career record: 885–858.

3540 Aren't all managers interim?—*Mike Flanagan, Orioles pitcher.*

3541 All I do is write their names on the lineup card and let them play. It's not a tough job. I haven't misspelled one name yet.—*Harvey Kuenn, Brewers manager, 1982. Taking over after Buck Rodgers was fired, Kuenn led Harvey's Wallbangers to the World Series, losing to St. Louis. Career record: 160–118.*

3542 I just make out the lineup and hide.—*Jack McKeon, Reds manager, 1999. In 15 seasons as a manager, McKeon's teams never won their division, but after he took over the 2003 Marlins, they won the wild card and went on to defeat the Yankees in the World Series. Career record: 1011–940.*

3543 The lineup is set; it's just a matter of who's going to play.—*Pete Rose, Reds manager, during spring training, 1987. Rose's Reds finished second every year from 1985 to 1988. Career record: 412–373.*

3544 I stay in the corner, send them out there and try not to trip anybody on the way by.—*Tom Kelly, Twins manager, on his managerial responsibilities, 1994. Kelly managed Minnesota to World Series victories in 1987 and 1991. Career record: 1140–1244.*

3545 I don't believe it builds character; I believe it builds ulcers.—*Jim Fregosi, Phillies manager, on winning close games, 1993. Career record: 1028–1095.*

3546 A manager gets paid half his salary for winning, half for worrying and nothing for losing.—*Birdie Tebbetts, former manager and All-Star catcher. Career record: 748–705.*

3547 Managing is getting paid for home runs someone else hits.—*Casey Stengel, Hall of Fame manager.*

3548 My only wish in life is that you have a son, that I'm his manager, and I get to tell him, "Sorry, Jim Junior, you're not playing today."—*Junior Ortiz, Pirates backup catcher, to manager Jim Leyland, 1991.*

3549 I could never be a manager. All I have is natural ability.—*Mickey Mantle, Yankees outfielder.*

3550 I learned that I don't want to be a manager. It's a lot easier to hit home runs than to handle 17 guys who think they are home run hitters.—*Jimmie Foxx, three-time MVP, after briefly managing the minor league Portsmouth Cubs in 1944. Foxx later managed the Fort Wayne Daisies of the All-American Girls Professional Baseball League in 1952.*

3551 I'm not sure I'd rather be managing or testing bullet-proof vests.—*Joe Torre, Mets manager, 1981.*

3552 If everyone in this country had to manage a major league team, there would be no need for social security—the job takes 10 to 15 years off your life.—*Rich Donnelly, Pirates coach, 1992.*

3553 Once a man begins managing, his age should be calculated like a dog's—one year equals seven human years.—*Nick Leyva, Phillies manager, 1989. Career record: 148–189.*

3554 If you ask my four-year-old granddaughter what grandpa does, she says, "He kicks dirt on umpires."—*Billy Martin, Yankees manager, 1985. Career record: 1253–1013.*

3555 *TV Producer:* We'll have a camera on you, so don't pick your nose.

Roger Craig (Giants manager, 1987): Whadaya mean? That's one of my signals.

3556 When Leo (Durocher) touched his nose, it meant the hit-and-run was on. But there was a problem. The son-of-a-gun was always picking his nose.—*Herman Franks, former Giants manager. Career record: 605–521.*

3557 Tell a ballplayer something a thousand times, then tell him again because that might be the time he'll understand something.—*Paul Richards, Orioles manager and GM. Career record: 923–901.*

3558 I don't communicate with players. I tell them what to do. I don't understand the meaning of communication.—*Paul Richards, White Sox manager, 1976.*

3559 I had no trouble communicating. The players just didn't like what I had to say.—*Frank Robinson, Orioles coach, on his managerial experiences in Cleveland and San Francisco, 1987. Career record: 1065–1176.*

3560 I want things done right. That is, I want them done my way.—*Frank Robinson, Indians manager.*

3561 There are three ways to do anything: the right way, the wrong way, and my way. If my way turns out to be the wrong way, nobody's ever gonna know because my way is the only way we're ever gonna do it.—*Casey Stengel, Yankees manager, to his players.*

3562 At the end of the tirade, muttering is good. Muttering so they can't quite hear it. That leaves the players not only chagrined and ashamed, but also a little confused.—*Steve Blass, former Pirates pitcher, on managerial speechmaking, 1993.*

3563 This team is going to be unified—even if I have to break necks.—*Russ Nixon, Reds manager, 1982. Career record: 231–347.*

3564 You can beat a dead horse with a two-by-four and you're not going to get much activity.—*Dallas Green, Mets manager, on why he wasn't trying harder to motivate his team, 1993.*

3565 You have to be a psychologist, an accountant and an attorney these days.—*Danny Ozark, Phillies manager, 1978. Career record: 618–542.*

3566 Being a Red Sox manager is like being married to Henry VIII.—*Bob Ryan, sportswriter, on the firing of manager Butch Hobson, 1994. Hobson's career record: 207–232.*

3567 When you're wrong, take the blame. When you're right, the owner will take the credit, so don't worry about it.—*Billy Martin, former Yankees manager, 1984.*

3568 I'm thrilled and sad. It's like watching your mother-in-law drive over the cliff in your new Cadillac.—*Jim Leyland, Pirates manager, on having third base coach Gene Lamont hired as the new manager of the White Sox, 1991. Lamont's career record: 553–562.*

3569 The workout is optional. Whoever doesn't come gets optioned.—*Bobby Valentine, Mets coach.*

3570 Coaches are an integral part of any manager's team. Especially if they're good pinochle players.—*Earl Weaver, Orioles manager, 1972. Career record: 1480–1060.*

3571 A coach sells cars; a manager buys them.—*Jackie Moore, Oakland A's manager. Career record: 163–190.*

3572 My wife doesn't have to buy shoes at a garage sale anymore.—*Doc Edwards, Indians manager, on the difference between being a manager and a coach. Career record: 173–207.*

3573 All coaches religiously carry fungo bats in the spring to ward off suggestions that they are not working.—*Jim Brosnan, Reds reliever, 1960.*

3574 Most coaches remain anonymous until they screw up. If a third base coach goes the entire season without being interviewed after a game, it means he had a perfect season.—*Jay Johnstone, former outfielder.*

3575 I think a coach eats differently after a game. Sometimes a manager does not eat at all.—*Frank Lucchesi, Rangers coach, 1975. Career record: 316–399.*

3576 Being a coach is like being the Queen of England. It's just a title. Coaches mostly hit fungoes.—*Bob Gibson, Hall of Fame pitcher, on being hired as Braves pitching coach, 1981.*

3577 Hotels have maids. Baseball teams have coaches.—*Jose Martinez, Royals coach.*

3578 Frank Robinson can step on your toes and not mess up your shine.—*Joe Morgan, former Giants second baseman, on his manager.*

3579 Would Tim Johnson still be managing the Toronto Blue Jays if he hadn't put "first Man to Walk on the Moon" on his resume?—*Jeff Gordon, sportswriter, on the firing of the Blue Jays manager. Several incidents of lying eventually caught up with Johnson, including exaggerations of his participation in the Vietnam War, 1999.*

3580 I don't fine players. These days if I fine a $4-million player $400, he's liable to tip me $200.—*Jim Leyland, Marlins manager, 1997. Career record: 1493–1518 (as of 2010)*

3581 Most of the managers were lifetime .220 hitters. For years, pitchers have been getting those guys out 75 percent of the time. That's why they don't like us.—*Bill Lee, Expos pitcher, 1979.*

3582 We're about as important as the last player on the bench. That's just the way we get paid, too.—*Larry Dierker, Astros manager. After moving from the broadcast booth to the dugout with no prior managerial experience, Dierker led Houston to four first-place finishes in five years. He was fired, however, largely due to the Astros 2–12 record in the playoffs. Career record: 435–348.*

3583 A baseball manager is a necessary evil. —*Sparky Anderson, Reds manager.*

3584 The players make the manager; it's never the other way.—*Sparky Anderson, Reds manager.*

3585 A manager's job is to select the best players for what he wants done. They're not all great players, but they all do something.—*Earl Weaver, manager of the 1970 World Series Champion Orioles*

3586 The first thing a manager learns is to stay on the bench.—*Pinky Higgins, Red Sox manager. Career record: 560–556.*

3587 Listen, if you start worrying about the people in the stands, before too long you're up in the stands with them.—*Tommy Lasorda, Dodgers manager.*

3588 There are three things the average man thinks he can do better than anybody else: build a fire, run a hotel and manage a baseball team.—*Rocky Bridges, San Jose Bees manager, 1964.*

3589 Every player, in his secret heart, wants to manage someday. Every fan, in the privacy of his mind, already does.—*Leonard Koppett, sportswriter.*

3590 I managed good, but boy did they play bad.—*Rocky Bridges, San Jose Bees manager, 1964.*

3591 Between owners and players, a manager today has become a wishbone.—*John Curtis, pitcher.*

3592 Baseball has been very good to me since I quit trying to play it.—*Whitey Herzog, Cardinals manager.*

3593 They've taken my playing record off and put my managerial record on.—*Sparky Anderson, Reds manager, on why he likes the new baseball cards, 1974.*

3594 Managing is not running, hitting, stealing. Managing is getting your players to put out 100 percent year after year.—*Sparky Anderson, Reds manager.*

3595 A manager really gets paid for how much he suffers.—*Gabe Paul, Indians president, 1963.*

3596 People may think it's easy, but it isn't. Managing is a lonely, difficult job. It's not fun. It's a nightmare. But I enjoy it.—*Maury Wills, Mariners manager, 1980. Wills was fired in 1981 after a 6–18 start. Career record: 26–56.*

3597 Oh, the poor kid. He's going to get an ulcer now.—*Laura Quilici on her son Frank Quilici being named Twins manager, 1972. Career record: 280–287.*

3598 I learned more in one year of managing than I did in the 18 years I played.—*Bob Shaw, former pitcher and Daytona Beach Dodgers manager, 1969.*

3599 It's what you learn after you know it all that counts.—*Earl Weaver, Orioles manager.*

3600 The worst thing about managing is the day you realize you want to win more than the players do.—*Gene Mauch, Twins manager.*

3601 I found out it's much more difficult to get to the majors as a manager than as a player. And it isn't half as much fun.—*Ken Boyer, Cardinals manager, 1978. Career record: 166–190.*

3602 The toughest part about managing is

standing up for nine innings. It's tougher than going shopping with my wife.—*Paul Owens, Phillies manager, 1983. Career record: 161–158.*

3603 They say I have to get to know my players. That arithmetic is bad. Isn't it simpler for 25 of them to get to know me?—*Birdie Tebbetts, Reds manager. In 11 years, none of his teams finished better than third.*

3604 There are only two things a manager needs to know: when to change pitchers and how to get along with your players.—*Bucky Harris, Washington Senators manager.*

3605 Managing isn't difficult. Just score more runs than the other guy.—*Ted Turner, Braves owner and manager for a day, May 11, 1977. Mired in a 16-game losing streak, Turner relieved Dave Bristol as manager and did the job himself. He lost 2–1 to Pittsburgh in his first, last, and only managerial stint.*

3606 Now I'll see if I can control a few knuckleheads.—*Hoyt Wilhelm, ageless knuckleball pitcher, on retiring at age 49 to become a manager for the Class A Greenwood Braves, 1973.*

3607 Me and my owners think exactly alike. Whatever they're thinking, that's what I'm thinking.—*Jim Fregosi, Angels manager, 1980. In 15 seasons, Fregosi only had one World Series appearance with the 1993 Phillies.*

3608 I never pay attention to what ballplayers say. It's just their way of getting newspaper ink.—*Alvin Dark, Indians manager, 1970.*

3609 If I were captain of the *Titanic,* I would tell my passengers we were stopping for ice.—*Chuck Tanner, Pirates manager. Career record: 1352–1381.*

3610 I am the most confident man since General Custer told the troops at Little Big Horn to take no prisoners.—*Frank Lucchesi on being hired as Phillies manager, 1969.*

3611 There is so much talent here that even if these guys had just average seasons, we'd be in the race. Unfortunately, the only one here who's having his average season is me.—*Rene Lachemann, Brewers manager, 1984. Rene's brother Marcel managed three seasons for the Angels. Rene's career record: 428–560.*

3612 Running a ball club is like raising kids who fall out of trees.—*Tom Trebelhorn, Brewers manager, 1989.*

3613 The big secret about managing is to get the players to want to play.—*Ted Williams, Washington Senators manager, 1969. Career record: 273–364.*

3614 I like my players to be married and in debt. That's the way you motivate them.—*Ernie Banks, Cubs assistant coach, 1976. On May 18, 1973, Cubs manager Whitey Lockman was ejected and Banks filled in, thus becoming the first black to serve, albeit for just two innings, as a major league manager.*

3615 Just give me 25 guys on the last year of their contract; I'll win the pennant every year.—*Sparky Anderson, Tigers manager.*

3616 The biggest thing in managing a major league team is to establish some sort of authority without making it smothering discipline.—*Ken Aspromonte, Indians manager. Career record: 220–260.*

3617 With my team I am an absolute czar.—*John McGraw, New York Giants manager. In 33 years as a manager, McGraw won three World Series titles. Career record: 2763–1948.*

3618 Just hold them for a few innings, fellas. I'll think of something.—*John McGraw, New York Giants manager. (Also attributed to Charlie Dressen.)*

3619 I think we can win it—if my brain holds out.—*John McGraw, New York Giants manager, on the 1921 pennant race. The Giants won the NL and defeated the Yankees in the World Series.*

3620 For five innings, it's a pitcher's game. After that, it's mine.—*Fred Hutchinson, Reds manager. Career record: 830–827.*

3621 Run everything out and be in by twelve.—*Red Schoendienst, Cardinals manager, on his two rules, 1968. Career record: 1041–955.*

3622 As long as I can walk out there, managing is what I want to do.—*Leo Durocher, Cubs manager, 1966.*

3623 I love young talent. Give me some scratchers and fighters; give me some guys who make $15,000, who want to make $30,000. You keep the $100,000 players. Give me the ones who want to win.—*Leo Durocher, Astros manager, 1973.*

3624 Yes, and so is everyone else in the league. —*Groucho Marx, comedian, on hearing that Leo Durocher was leading the New York Giants.*

3625 We figured if he can manage, anyone can.—*Bill Rigney, Angels manager, on former manager Leo Durocher, 1966.*

3626 The toughest thing for me as a young manager is that a lot of my players saw me play. They know how bad I was.—*Tony LaRussa, White Sox manager, 1983. Career record: 2638–2293 (as of 2010)*

3627 I pitched and lost 20 games last year. He managed like I pitched.—*Clyde Wright, Brewers pitcher, on manager Del Crandall, 1974.*

3628 I still don't know if I can manage or not. I really haven't had much of a chance so far. When you're behind in the game by three runs all the time, there isn't much to manage. —*Larry Bowa, Padres manager, 1987. Career record: 418–435.*

3629 The only clubhouse meetings I like are the ones dividing up playoff shares.—*Billy Gardner, Royals manager, 1987. Career record: 330–417.*

3630 No matter how good you are, you're going to lose one-third of your games. No matter how bad you are, you're going to win one-third of your games. It's the other third that makes the difference.—*Tommy Lasorda, Dodgers manager. Career record: 1599–1439.*

3631 The doctor said I should do a lot of walking. So I walk to the mound nine or ten times a game.—*Cal Ripken Sr., Orioles manager, 1987. Ripken was fired after losing the first six games of the 1988 season; the Orioles went on to lose their first 21 games. Career record: 68–101.*

3632 It's only the start. So many heads are going to roll it's going to look like a bowling alley around here.—*Jerry Remy, Red Sox second baseman, on the firing of manager Don Zimmer, 1980.*

3633 The weather's cold. My club's bad. My knee hurts. I can't putt no more. I'm off my diet. My wife is nagging me. Other than that, everything's great.—*Don Zimmer, Cubs manager, 1990.*

3634 It couldn't happen to a nicer guy—if you think managing is something nice to happen to you.—*Walter Alston, Dodgers manager, on the hiring of Gil Hodges as Washington Senators manager, 1963.*

3635 Joe Schultz would have been a better manager if he understood more. Of course, if he understood more, he might not have been a manager.—*Jim Bouton, former Seattle Pilots pitcher, on his former manager, 1969.*

3636 He was the greatest hitter I ever saw, but I don't think he was too good a manager. I'd be with him at an All-Star Game and he'd talk to me about hitting. By the time the game started, I didn't have any idea what he was talking about.—*Mickey Mantle, Hall of Fame outfielder, on former Washington Senators manager Ted Williams, 1978.*

3637 My idea of managing is giving the ball to Tom Seaver and sitting down and watching him work.—*Sparky Anderson, Reds manager.*

3638 My best game plan is to sit on the bench and call out specific instructions like, "C'mon Boog," "Get hold of one, Frank" or "Let's go, Brooks."—*Earl Weaver, Orioles manager, 1971.*

3639 Nobody's been more surprised than me that this team has averaged ninety wins the last four years without great overall talent.... So it had to be Earl's doing. The only thing is, I don't know why.—*Jim Palmer, Orioles pitcher, on manager Earl Weaver, 1983.*

3640 The first time Joe said hello to some of the guys, he broke Earl's career record.—*Jim Palmer, Orioles pitcher, on Joe Altobelli, managerial successor to Earl Weaver, 1983.*

3641 I respect anybody who lasts over one year as manager.—*Casey Stengel, former Yankees manager, 1961.*

3642 When I hired you in Atlanta, I said you were a fiery manager. Well, you sure do get fired a lot.—*Eddie Robinson, Braves executive, to manager Dave Bristol, who was fired for the fourth time.*

3643 I think Ray Kroc told 'em to give the job to Gary Coleman and they misunderstood him.—*Jerry Coleman, broadcaster, on being hired as Padres manager, 1980. Coleman lasted one season before returning to the broadcast booth. Gary Coleman, the diminutive child actor, starred in the 1979 TV movie* The Kid from Left Field *in which he becomes manager of the Padres.*

3644 All I know is, I pass people on the street these days, and they don't know whether to say hello or to say goodbye.—*Billy Martin, Yankees manager.*

3645 It's like giving all your love and attention to a woman for 24 years and then finding out she didn't care. It hurt as much as anything.—*Billy Martin on being fired as Twins manager, 1969.*

3646 I'm a one-year manager only if the front office interferes with the ball club. If it leaves me alone, I'm a 20-year manager.—*Billy Martin, Yankees manager, 1976. Martin managed parts of 16 seasons, but never longer than three whole seasons with one team.*

3647 The only real way to know you've been fired is when you arrive at the ballpark and find your name has been scratched from the parking list.—*Billy Martin, Yankees manager.*

3648 When you're a professional, you come back, no matter what happened the day before. —*Billy Martin, Yankees manager, 1979.*

3649 I thought this time it would go nine innings, but I never got out of the first inning.—*Bob Lemon, Yankees manager, on being fired for the second time by owner George Steinbrenner, 1982. Career record: 430–403.*

3650 Playing for Yogi [Berra] is like playing for your father; playing for Billy [Martin] is like playing for your father-in-law.—*Don Baylor, Yankees DH.*

3651 There are close to 11 million unemployed, and half of them are New York Yankee managers.—*Johnny Carson, talk show host.*

3652 Charlie Finley hiring Billy Martin is like Captain Hook hiring the alligator.—*Johnny Carson, talk show host, on the Oakland A's owner and his new manager, 1980.*

3653 "Billy Ball" is a system of play where you fight your own players, the others' players, the umpires, owners, press and strangers in a bar, and then, when you win, and someone wants to know the secret, you say, "Teamwork."—*Nestor Chylak, umpire, on the Oakland A's and manager Billy Martin, 1981.*

3654 When I get through managing, I'm going to open up a kindergarten.—*Manager Billy Martin.*

3655 Anybody who can't get along with a .400 hitter is crazy.—*Joe McCarthy, Yankees manager.*

3656 Sparky [Anderson] came here two years ago promising to build a team in his own image. Now the club is looking for small, white-haired infielders with .212 batting averages.—*Al Ackerman, Detroit broadcaster.*

3657 I don't believe a manager ever won a pennant. Casey Stengel won all those pennants with the Yankees. How many did he win with the Boston Braves and Mets?—*Sparky Anderson, Tigers manager. Stengel's non–Yankee teams never finished better than fifth place.*

3658 No, we don't cheat. And even if we did, I'd never tell you.—*Tommy Lasorda, Dodgers manager.*

3659 The manager of a team is like a stagecoach; he can't move unless he has the horses. —*Pete Rose, Reds manager.*

3660 All managers are losers; they are the most expendable pieces of furniture on the face of the earth.—*Ted Williams, Hall of Fame outfielder and former manager.*

3661 It was like my wedding night. You try to slow it down, but it goes by real fast.—*Carlos Tosca on his first game as Blue Jays manager, after replacing Buck Martinez, 2002. Career record: 191–191.*

3662 I don't know if I'm a leader, but I have the biggest mouth.—*Ozzie Guillen, White Sox manager, 2005. Career record: 600–535 (as of 2010).*

3663 You can't be a micro-manager unless you micro-manage.—*Bob Boone, Reds manager, June 2003. At one point Boone tried both slugger Adam Dunn and slow-footed first baseman Sean Casey batting leadoff. Career record: 371–444*

3664 This squirrel ain't finding no acorns. I can't imagine what he's going through. He has to feel like the guy strapped to the chair with honey and ants on him.—*Sparky Anderson, former Tigers manager, on Detroit manager Alan Trammell, whose team started the 2003 season 1–17. Trammell was fired after the 2005 season with a 186–300 career managerial record.*

3665 These days you have more security if you're an Arthur Anderson auditor than a baseball manager.—*Jon Saraceno, sportswriter, on the early season firings of Joe Kerrigan, Phil Garner, Davey Lopes, Buddy Bell and Tony Muser, 2002. Later that season, Don Baylor and Jerry Manuel were also axed.*

3666 Tony Gwynn says he wants to be the next baseball coach at San Diego State. That pretty much wraps up the interviewing process. —*Bud Geracie, sportswriter, 2001. Gwynn became the manager of his alma mater in 2002.*

3667 When fans come to the ballpark, damn it, every last one of them is a manager.—*Whitey Herzog, Cardinals manager.*

3668 As soon as the season is over, I don't give a shit about my players. They don't give a shit about me, either. I never send anyone a Christmas card, ever, because I don't give a shit about them. Now, during the season, they're my kids. I will kill for them. I guarantee you I will. Now, when the season is over, I got enough with my wife and three kids. But as long as we're here and have the same uniform, I will kill for them. And I hope they kill for me, too.—*Ozzie Guillen, White Sox manager, 2009.*

3669 What I'm trying to convince them is, you're not trying to beat the Yankees or the Red Sox or the Blue Jays; you're trying to beat the game of baseball through execution. When you play the game properly, it really should not matter what name is on the front or back of the shirt. And when you can reduce it to that mentally, I think you have a better chance of repeating the proper things over and over again.—*Joe Maddon, Devil Rays manager.*

3670 Sometimes I would do just the opposite of what George wanted me to do because I won't let anyone tell me how to manage. If I'm going down the tube, I'm going to do it my way.—*Billy Martin, four-time Yankees manager, on his relationship with owner George Steinbrenner.*

3671 The average fan may think a manager has to fight his men off when he's looking for a pinch hitter. Don't kid yourself. You look down the bench and more often than not every eye is averted.—*Manager Leo Durocher.*

3672 The split is amicable. He wants to leave, and we don't want him to stay.—*Woody Paige, sportswriter, on the departure of Rockies manager Jim Leyland after just one season, 1999.*

3673 This is the first time I was ever outmanaged on an off day.—*Jim Leyland, Tigers manager, on an ALDS game that was called on account of weather, 2006. Yankees manager Joe Torre sent his team home, but Leyland—unaware of the cancellation—had his players warming up. The Tigers eventually defeated New York and advanced to the World Series.*

Media Relations

3674 I know what the word "media" means. It's plural for mediocre.—*Rocky Bridges, major league infielder.*

3675 I try to have respect for people in general, whether it's baseball players or low lifes like the media.—*Jim Riggleman, Cubs manager, 1995.*

3676 That's why I don't talk. Because I talk too much.—*Joaquin Andujar, Astros pitcher, on his policy of not talking to the press.*

3677 I got a new word this year: "no comment."—*Joaquin Andujar, Cardinals pitcher, 1984.*

3678 When I have something to say, I won't say anything.—*Luis Polonia, Angels outfielder, when asked about a comment made by former Yankees teammate Pascual Perez, 1991.*

3679 Sometimes they write what I say, not what I mean.—*Pedro Guerrero, Cardinals first baseman, on sportswriters, 1989.*

3680 I know you want great quotes. I just don't have them.—*Paul O'Neill, Yankees outfielder, during the first half of the 1994 season when his batting average was well over .400.*

3681 Writers like to say they've seen a lot of players come and go. I've seen a lot of writers come and go.—*Nolan Ryan, 44-year-old Rangers pitcher, 1991.*

3682 If it isn't, son, you've got one helluva scoop.—*Grantland Rice, sportswriter, when asked by a reporter,* "Isn't that the sun setting in the west?" *(Also attributed to sportswriter Bill Slocum.)*

3683 Do I miss the media there? Sure—like I miss shoulder surgery.—*Sterling Hitchcock, Mariners pitcher, on returning to New York to face the Yankees, 1996.*

3684 I always turn to the sports pages first. That way you've got a 50–50 shot of getting some good news.—*Vice President Gerald Ford, 1974.*

3685 I read every paper I can get my hands on from front to back. And in the business I'm in, that includes the classifieds for unemployment.—*Tommy Lasorda, Dodgers manager.*

3686 I've always said I only read the papers when we're winning. The way we've been playing, I haven't been reading much.—*Jeff Torborg, Mets manager, 1992.*

3687 With the Cardinals, I'd come in and find everyone reading the stock market report. With the Pirates, I come in and find everyone reading the paper to see if Hulk Hogan won.—*Andy Van Slyke, Pirates outfielder.*

3688 I must say I've enjoyed it. I mean, it's bad for readers and reporters, but it's the environmentally correct thing to do.—*Andy Van Slyke, Pirates outfielder, on a Pittsburgh newspaper strike, 1992.*

3689 Ballplayers shouldn't gripe about reporters. A ballplayer should stay on a reporter's good side. Say nice things. Admire his clothes. Compliment him on his T-shirt.—*Andy Van Slyke, Pirates outfielder, 1992.*

3690 The thing is, a lot of the people who make those suggestions would have a hard time filling out the application forms to work at 7-Eleven. People think they know the game because they watch it on TV or they watch it from a distance, like, say, for example, oh, sportswriters.—*Andy Van Slyke, Pirates outfielder, on the multitude of people offering advice on how to cure his season-long slump, 1994.*

3691 You hear players say, "You never played the game." My comeback is, "Hey, pal, you never paid your way in."—*Norm Hitzges, broadcaster, 1990.*

3692 I'd like to thank the writers for ... no, I can't thank them for anything.—*Roger Clemens, Red Sox pitcher, accepting the Boston area writers' award as team MVP, 1991.*

3693 I guess I'll have to gain sixty pounds, start smoking a cigar and wear clothes that don't match.—*Garth Iorg, Blue Jays third baseman, on the possibility of becoming a sportswriter.*

3694 Nah, I just make 'em up like everyone else.—*Dave Kingman, Cubs outfielder and part-time columnist for the* Chicago Tribune, *when asked if he used a tape recorder to get accurate quotations, 1980.*

3695 Yep, I'm joining you baseball writers. I finally hit rock bottom.—*Davey Johnson, former Orioles manager, on agreeing to write an internet column, 1998.*

3696 How can you call yourself a sportswriter? You don't even smoke cigars.—*Dock*

Ellis, Yankees pitcher, to sportswriter Steve Kelley.

3697 *Jason Corrales:* Dad, do all writers dress like slobs?

Pat Corrales (Indians manager, 1986): They're all trying to be Ernest Hemingway. Did you ever see a picture of Hemingway? He was a fat guy with a big beard who dressed terrible.

3698 Rock and roll musicians, they don't step on stage and get booed. Sixteen critics don't come backstage after a concert and say, "You guys screwed up that C-to-the-A change there. Were you aware of that?"—*Jack McDowell, White Sox pitcher, on the difference between playing baseball and being a musician, 1994. Black Jack was also a guitarist for the rock band Stick Figure.*

3699 I like my horses better because they can't talk to sportswriters.—*George Steinbrenner, Yankees owner, on the difference between his race horses and his ballplayers, 1985.*

3700 You can't put much stock in papers. They only cost 50 cents.—*Pete Rose, Reds manager, 1989.*

3701 The papers would screw up a two-car funeral.—*Ted Turner, Braves owner, 1988.*

3702 A ballplayer has two reputations: one with the other players and one with the fans. The first is based on ability. The second the newspapers give him.—*Johnny Evers, Cubs second baseman.*

3703 Hell, if the game was half as complicated as some of these writers make out it is, a lot of us boys from the farm would never have been able to make a living at it.—*Bucky Walters, Reds pitcher and 1939 NL MVP.*

3704 That poll cost me a lot of money. I made about 290 of those calls myself.—*Dave Magadan, Marlins third baseman, on a Florida newspaper survey that asked fans if they favored a proposed trade of Magadan for Expos reliever Mel Rojas, 1994. Three-hundred people phoned in, with 99 percent opposed to the deal.*

3705 I thought there was a rule that you can't write what nobody said, but I found out that around here that's not true.—*Kenny Rogers, Yankees pitcher, on the New York media, 1996.*

3706 I was showing early symptoms of becoming a professional baseball man. I was lying to the press.—*Roger Kahn, sportswriter, on becoming part owner of the Class A Utica Blue Sox, 1985.*

3707 Because you have to lie so much.—*Reggie Jackson, Oakland A's DH, on why he dislikes being interviewed, 1987.*

3708 Them ain't lies, them scoops.—*Dizzy Dean, Cardinals pitcher, on the contradictory stories he frequently told reporters, especially concerning his age and birthplace. Consensus is that Dean was born in Lucas, Arkansas, on January 16, 1911.*

3709 You know what you can do with all those notes you just took? Shred 'em and put 'em around the shrubs at home and watch them grow.—*Don Sutton, Dodgers pitcher, to a reporter who had just finished interviewing manager Tommy Lasorda, 1988.*

3710 My gum company made a $40-million profit last year, and I can't get the financial writers to say a word about it. But I fire a manager and everybody shows up.—*Philip K. Wrigley, Cubs owner.*

3711 Can't you guys cover something more important than this? Aren't there some boat races out there?—*Davey Johnson, Reds manager, to sportswriters still covering his struggling team in September, 1993.*

3712 They ought to be writing for the gossip columns, not the baseball fans.—*Paul Richards, Braves vice president, on reporters, 1969.*

3713 I watched CBS since they lost so much money televising baseball.—*Andy Van Slyke, Pirates outfielder, on what he did during the off-season, 1991.*

3714 Let 'em ask one question, then you keep on talking so they won't ask you another one.—*Casey Stengel, Yankees manager, on how to deal with the media.*

3715 Does everybody get up 365 days a year and feel great, especially when they know they have to talk to the media every day?—*Mark McGwire, Cardinals first baseman, on his sometimes surly attitude toward the media, 1998.*

3716 There are so many papers now that it's going to cost you $12 a day to eat breakfast.—*Rich Donnelly, Pirates bullpen coach, 1989.*

3717 We get paid a lot of money to read nasty stuff about ourselves in the paper.—*Matt Young, Red Sox pitcher, 1993. After two disastrous seasons in Boston, Young was traded to Cleveland.*

3718 Anyone who thinks he can run baseball without a daily paper can't run baseball.—*Walter O'Malley, Los Angeles Dodgers owner.*

3719 I just wanted to see what happens when one mule confronts 300 asses.—*Charles Finley, Oakland A's owner, on taking his mule, Charlie O., to a World Series luncheon for baseball writers.*

3720 Pour hot water over a sportswriter and you'll get instant shit.—*Ted Williams, Hall of Fame outfielder.*

3721 The Lord taught me to love everybody, but the last ones I learned to love were the sportswriters.—*Alvin Dark, Oakland A's manager, 1974.*

3722 I go to the park sick as a dog, and when I see my uniform hanging there, I get well right away. Then I see some of you guys, and I get sick again.—*Pete Rose, Reds third baseman, on the press, 1978.*

3723 I was going to be a sportswriter until I met several.—*Joe Brown, Pirates GM, 1976.*

3724 I never read papers. It isn't healthy for professional athletes.—*R.J. Reynolds, Pirates outfielder.*

3725 The papers aren't going to win a game for me, and I don't need anybody to tell me I lost.—*Harry Walker, Astros manager, 1970.*

3726 The only thing I read in the papers is the comics. When they start mixing in the sports with the comics, I'll stop getting my subscriptions.—*Bo Jackson, Royals outfielder, 1987.*

3727 If you want to survive in New York, you better only read the box scores.—*Billy Martin, Yankees manager, 1979.*

3728 One time I dropped a fly ball in Milwaukee and, after the game, the writers asked me what happened. I told them, "Well, I was looking up and a UFO flew right across. It was weird. I never saw anything like that in my life." Man, I was only joking, and they wrote it up and put it in the paper.—*Jesse Barfield, Blue Jays outfielder, 1986.*

3729 Owner George Argyros, by the way, told a booster club that the reason for the club's poor attendance was the media, which is like blaming the rain in Seattle on the meteorologists.—*Peter Gammons, sportswriter, on the Mariners owner.*

3730 I didn't say the rumors are all bad. I just said they aren't true.—*Derek Jeter, Yankees shortstop, on a report that he was dating supermodel Tyra Banks, 1997.*

3731 Radio created a desire to see something. Television is giving it to them. Once a television set has broken them of the ballpark habit, a great many fans will never acquire it.—*Branch Rickey, Pirates GM.*

3732 No doubt, too big a deal has been made of Clemens vs. Piazza. Just as too big a deal was made of John Rocker's ranting, Al Gore's fibbing and Lady Di's death. All of which were the media's fault.—*David Whitley, sportswriter, on an incident in the 2000 World Series in which Yankees pitcher Roger Clemens threw part of a broken bat at Mets catcher Mike Piazza.*

3733 John Rocker isn't talking to the media. Too bad he didn't think of that earlier.—*Bud Geracie, sportswriter, on the controversial Braves reliever who made racist, homophobic and sexist comments, 2000.*

3734 It's a weird scene. You win a few baseball games and all of a sudden you're surrounded by reporters and TV men with cameras asking you about Vietnam and race relations and stuff about yourself. Man, I'm only a kid. I don't know exactly who I am. I don't have a whole philosophy of life set down.—*Vida Blue, 22-year-old Oakland A's pitcher, August 1971. Blue finished the season 24–8 with 24 complete games, eight shutouts, and a 1.82 ERA, to win both the AL MVP and Cy Young Awards.*

3735 If sportswriters were voting for the Serial Killer Hall of Fame, Charles Manson would have to wait until his third year of eligibility.—*Norman Chad, sportswriter, on the fact that no player has ever been unanimously elected to Cooperstown 2001.*

3736 Nah. Somebody will think of something and designate it to a spokee to be named later.—*Rocky Bridges, Giants coach, when asked if he really said everything that is attributed to him, 1985.*

3737 You want to know the color of my underwear, too? You guys are starting to ask questions like the Japanese writers used to.—*Ichiro Suzuki, Mariners outfielder, on the increased media attention as he pursued the all-time single-season hit record, September 2004. Ichiro set the record with 262 hits, and in his first ten seasons he led the majors in hits seven times.*

3738 I don't give a shit about talk shows; I don't. Those talk shows in Chicago, they're lucky I'm here. Because they would be selling cheeseburgers somewhere or hot dogs somewhere. I don't care what they think about what I do because it's easy when you're behind the mic and criticize people after the thing is done.—*Ozzie Guillen, White Sox manager, April 2010.*

Modesty

3739 If you say you're going to do it, and you go out and do it, it ain't braggin'.—*Dizzy Dean, Hall of Fame pitcher.*

3740 I may not have been the greatest pitcher ever, but I was amongst 'em.—*Dizzy Dean, Hall of Fame pitcher.*

3741 You've got to remember—I'm 73.—*Ty Cobb, Hall of Fame outfielder, on why he thought he would only hit .300 playing in 1960.*

3742 All us Youngs could throw. I used to kill squirrels with a stone when I was a kid, and my granddad once killed a turkey buzzard on the fly with a rock.—*Cy Young, Hall of Fame pitcher.*

3743 My boy, I can't recollect ever having to pitch with the bases full.—*Cy Young, before his Hall of Fame induction, when asked by a reporter what pitch he liked to throw when the bases were loaded, 1939.*

3744 I still don't know why they asked me to do this commercial.—*"Marvelous" Marv Throneberry, former Mets first baseman, in a series of Miller Lite TV commercials.*

3745 *Lady:* I'm shocked! You're a professional athlete and you smoke?

John Kruk (Phillies first baseman, 1993): Lady, I'm not an athlete. I'm a baseball player.

3746 It's amazing that fans want to see me play. What is our society coming to?—*John Kruk, Phillies first baseman, on being voted onto the starting lineup for the 1993 All-Star Game.*

3747 Lou Brock was the symbol of great base stealing. But today I am the greatest of all-time.—*Rickey Henderson, Oakland A's outfielder, after breaking the career stolen base record (938), May 1, 1991. Rickey's modesty was old news later that evening after 44-year-old Rangers pitcher Nolan Ryan threw his seventh career no-hitter.*

3748 Yes, I am a hot dog. Look up all the baseball players who were ever called hot dogs. Every last one of those guys could play. You're not a hot dog unless you can play. Ever hear of a hot dog who couldn't play?—*Rickey Henderson, Oakland A's outfielder, 1992.*

3749 Do I talk to myself? No. I just remind myself of what I'm trying to do. You know, I never answer myself. So how can I be talking to myself?—*Rickey Henderson, all-time stolen base king, who reportedly would stand in front of a mirror and tell himself, "Rickey, you're the greatest."*

3750 Get an intentional walk.—*Nolan Ryan, Rangers pitcher, when asked if there was anything in baseball he hasn't done, 1992.*

3751 They ought to pay me just to walk around here.—*Dave Parker, Pirates outfielder and 1978 NL MVP.*

3752 Because on a scale of one to ten, I'm a 15.—*Dennis Lamp, Cubs pitcher, on why he wears a pendant with the No. 15.*

3753 My problem is I don't have a weakness, but I'm trying to develop one so Adcock can work on it.—*Leon Wagner, Indians outfielder, on manager Joe Adcock, 1967.*

3754 The only way I can't hit .300 is if something is physically wrong with me.—*Pete Rose, Reds third baseman.*

3755 I'm just like everybody else. I have two arms, two legs and 4,000 hits.—*Pete Rose, Reds player-manager, 1984.*

3756 I never said I was the best hitter in the history of baseball, only that I've made the most hits.—*Pete Rose, Reds player-manager, 1986.*

3757 Pitch me outside, I will hit .400. Pitch me inside, and you will not find the ball.—*Roberto Clemente, Pirates outfielder.*

3758 Everybody thinks I've changed, but I'm just a boy from the hills of Indiana. If you don't believe me, ask my butler, Reggie Jackson.—*Don Mattingly, Yankees first baseman, 1987.*

3759 Liberty Bell and I are the only attractions in Philadelphia.—*Ping Bodie, Philadelphia A's outfielder, 1917.*

3760 If they paid you on the basis of personality, I'd make about $2 a year.—*Mike Ivie, Giants first baseman, 1981.*

3761 The night we won the World Series, I was understandably feeling my oats. I asked my wife how many really great managers she thought there were in baseball. Glaring at me, she said, "I think there's one less than you do." —*Danny Murtaugh, Pirates manager, 1961.*

3762 Earl's never wrong. Just ask him.—*Mike Boddicker, Orioles pitcher, on manager Earl Weaver, 1985.*

3763 I don't want to win my 300th game while he's here. He'd take credit for it.—*Jim Palmer, Orioles pitcher, on manager Earl Weaver. Palmer retired with 268 career victories.*

3764 My wife. So I could see how wonderful it is to live with me.—*Andy Van Slyke, Pirates outfielder, when asked with whom he would most like to change places for a day, 1988.*

3765 I don't duck left-handers. I don't duck right-handers. I don't even duck gunshots.—*Kevin Mitchell, Reds outfielder, on missing his first start of the season against a left-handed pitcher, 1994.*

3766 The planes at LaGuardia better not fly too low when I'm at bat.—*George Foster, Mets outfielder, 1982.*

3767 Reggie Jackson wouldn't get in the batter's box until he knew we were back from a commercial. Of course, [Bob] Uecker wanted to hit during the commercial.—*Al Michaels, broadcaster, 1986.*

3768 Anybody with ability can play in the big leagues. But to be able to trick people year in and year out the way I did, I think that was a much greater feat.—*Bob Uecker, former catcher, 1980.*

3769 I didn't get a lot of awards as a player. But they did have a Bob Uecker Day Off for me once in Philly.—*Bob Uecker, former Phillies catcher.*

3770 In 1962, I was named Minor League Player of the Year. It was my second season in the Bigs.—*Bob Uecker, former catcher.*

3771 If a guy hits .300 every year, what does he have to look forward to? I always tried to stay around .190, with three or four RBI. And I tried to get them all in September. That way I always had something to talk about during the winter.—*Bob Uecker, former catcher.*

3772 Baseball hasn't forgotten me. I go to a lot of old-timers' games, and I haven't lost a thing. I sit in the bullpen and let people throw things at me.—*Bob Uecker, former catcher.*

3773 A lot of coaches along the way had a hard time dealing with it. They had the feeling I thought I was better than everyone else. They were right. I do think I'm better than everybody else.—*Charlie Kerfeld, Astros reliever, 1987.*

3774 They finally got around to replacing me. All it took was two quality players and close to $40 million.—*Darryl Strawberry, Dodgers outfielder, on the free agent signings of Eddie Murray and Bobby Bonilla by the Mets, 1991.*

3775 I'm not trying to replace anyone because I can't do what the guys they got rid of did.—*Paul Householder, Reds outfielder, on the departure of outfielders Ken Griffey and George Foster, 1982.*

3776 I only know three or four of the players, but I think they know me.—*Willie Mays, Hall of Fame outfielder, on his first day in spring training camp as a Giants instructor, 1986.*

3777 You sure they got the right Ozzie?—*Ozzie Guillen, White Sox shortstop, on hearing that* Sports Illustrated *was going to write a story about him and not Cardinals shortstop Ozzie Smith, 1989.*

3778 No one knows who I am, so I'd have to kill all the other shortstops. I'd have to take care of Cal Ripken, Alan Trammell, Tony Fernandez and Kurt Stillwell. Then I'd be in jail, and I wouldn't be able to play anyway.—*Ozzie Guillen, White Sox shortstop, on his chances of being selected as an All-Star starter, 1990. Guillen was named as a reserve.*

3779 I came to the Braves on business, and I intended to see that business was good as long as I could.—*Henry Aaron, former Milwaukee/Atlanta Braves outfielder.*

3780 It was a great thrill. Some day he can tell his grandchildren he hit against me.—*Doc Medich, Yankees pitcher, on facing Brewers DH Henry Aaron, 1975.*

3781 If they ever start an Instructional League Hall of Fame, I'll be a charter member.—*David Clyde, former pitching phenom and top draft choice of the Rangers. Rushed to the big leagues at age 18, Clyde developed arm trouble and ended up with a career record of 18–33.*

3782 I don't want to be a star, but I'd like to twinkle a little.—*John Lowenstein, Indians outfielder.*

3783 I don't want to be a star. Stars get blamed too much.—*Enos Cabell, Astros third baseman.*

3784 I don't want to be a hero; I don't want to be a star. It just works out that way.—*Reggie Jackson, Yankees outfielder, 1980.*

3785 I drink beer, I swear and I keep my hair short, so I guess you'd call me an All-American boy.—*Tom Seaver, Mets pitcher, 1969.*

3786 I'll take any way to get into the Hall of Fame. If they want a batboy, I'll go in as a batboy.—*Phil Rizzuto, former Yankees shortstop, 1981. The veterans committee elected Scooter to the Hall in 1994.*

3787 The Yankees, all they needed was someone to catch the ball, make a double play, get hit by a pitch and not get hurt.—*Phil Rizzuto, former Yankees shortstop, at his Hall of Fame induction, 1994.*

3788 Being an opening-day pitcher may just mean you're the best on the team, even if the team stinks.—*Jack McDowell, White Sox pitcher, downplaying his selection to start the first game of 1991.*

3789 I don't know if it's because we've lost a lot of good players or I'm getting better.—*Tim Wallach, Expos third baseman, on being named team MVP for the second straight year, 1990.*

3790 My claim to fame is not leaping. As a matter of fact, I'm not sure what my claim to fame is.—*Chili Davis, Angels outfielder, after making a leaping catch, 1988.*

3791 I don't think I would do as well in American baseball.—*Sadaharu Oh, Yomiyuri Giants first baseman, on surpassing Hank Aaron's world home run record, 1977. Oh finished his illustrious career with 868 homers.*

3792 Not to belittle myself, but there's no telling what the ball was worth before I signed it.—*Gorman Thomas, Mariners DH, on signing a baseball that had been autographed by Hall of Famers Babe Ruth, Joe DiMaggio, Hank Aaron, and Mickey Mantle, 1986.*

3793 This signature might not be worth much now, but five years from now it will be worth even less.—*Tommy Lasorda, Dodgers manager, 1990.*

3794 I've got one fault. I lie.—*Tommy Lasorda, Dodgers manager.*

3795 You know, it used to take 43 Marv Throneberry cards to get one Carl Furillo.—*Marv Throneberry, former Mets first baseman, on the price of baseball cards.*

3796 I'm in the twilight of a mediocre career.—*Ed Kranepool, Mets first baseman, 1975.*

3797 The cream always rises to the top. I'm a good example of that ... not exactly whipped cream. I'm kind of an ugly foam.—*Rex Hudler, Phillies utility player, to a group of minor leaguers, 1997.*

3798 I'm a proven so-so player.—*Jeff Manto, Indians third baseman, 1998.*

3799 It took me twelve seasons to become an overnight sensation.—*Toby Harrah, Indians third baseman, 1982.*

3800 I'm not a Mercedes. I'm a Volkswagen. They get a lot of mileage out of me, but I'm not pretty.—*Dan Quisenberry, Royals reliever.*

3801 Most guys are born to hit. I was born to hit .238.—*Don Zimmer, former infielder, who retired in 1965 with a .235 career average and became a manager in 1972.*

3802 I was a three-way hitter. Right, left and seldom. They kept getting my batting average mixed up with my weight—170. 175.—*Jack McKeon, Royals manager, on his minor league playing career, 1975.*

3803 Comparing me to Sandy Koufax is like comparing Earl Scheib to Michelangelo.—*Don Sutton, Dodgers pitcher, on breaking a record once held by Koufax.*

3804 To be honest, I don't know why teams keep signing me.—*Lance Parrish, 39-year-old catcher, on signing with Pittsburgh, 1996. Parrish never played with the Pirates and retired with three Gold Gloves, six Silver Slugger Awards, and eight All-Star appearances.*

3805 I told him if you keep us within two runs, I'll win it by myself. Four or five, you're on your own.—*Barry Bonds, Giants outfielder, to pitcher Osvaldo Fernandez, 1996.*

3806 Abraham Lincoln, Jesus Christ, John F. Kennedy—if the world can do without them, the Braves can do without me for a year.—*Ted Turner, Braves owner, on being suspended from baseball for one year for tampering, 1977.*

3807 If I only had a little humility, I would be perfect.—*Ted Turner, Braves owner, 1977.*

3808 Fans don't boo nobodies.—*Reggie Jackson, Oakland A's outfielder, 1974.*

3809 Not enough papers here to carry my quotes.—*Reggie Jackson, Orioles outfielder, on Cleveland, 1976.*

3810 This team, it all flows from me. I've got to keep it all going. I'm the straw that stirs the drink.—*Reggie Jackson, Yankees outfielder, 1977.*

3811 Sometimes I underestimate the magnitude of me.—*Reggie Jackson, Yankees outfielder, 1977.*

3812 Love me or hate me, you can't ignore me. —*Reggie Jackson, Yankees outfielder, 1977.*

3813 I represent both the underdogs and the overdog in our society.—*Reggie Jackson, Yankees outfielder.*

3814 The only reason I don't like playing in the World Series is I can't watch myself play.—*Reggie Jackson, Yankees outfielder.*

3815 I was reminded that when we lose and I strike out, a billion people in China don't care.—*Reggie Jackson, Yankees outfielder.*

3816 In the building I live in on Park Avenue, there are ten people who could buy the Yankees, but none of them could hit the ball out of Yankee Stadium.—*Reggie Jackson, Yankees outfielder.*

3817 It boosted my ego, although mine probably doesn't need it.—*Reggie Jackson, Angels DH, on tying Lou Gehrig with his 493rd home run, 1984.*

3818 There's only one thing bigger than me, and that's my ego.—*Dave Parker, Pirates outfielder.*

3819 That's pretty good, considering that Dave's previous idol was himself.—*Willie Stargell, Pirates first baseman, on hearing that teammate Dave Parker called him his idol, 1980.*

3820 Carl Everett is the best player in baseball—just ask Carl Everett.—*Ryan Dempster, Marlins pitcher, on the Red Sox outfielder, 2000.*

3821 The secret to my success was clean living and a fast-moving outfield.—*Lefty Gomez, Hall of Fame pitcher.*

3822 It's right up there with lobster.—*Gary Gaetti, Twins third baseman, on becoming an All-Star, 1988.*

3823 I'm an eclipse player. You don't see me very often.—*Benny Ayala, Orioles utility player, on batting only four times in June, 1984.*

3824 We're the best team in baseball, but not by much.—*Sparky Anderson, Reds manager.*

3825 They throw the ball, I hit it. They hit the ball, I catch it.—*Willie Mays, Giants outfielder.*

3826 It wasn't even close; I was awesome.—*Darryl Strawberry, former All-Star outfielder, on comparisons to Mets outfield prospect Lastings Milledge, 2006. Strawberry was the 1983 NL Rookie of the Year, and he made the All-Star team eight times before turning 30.*

3827 That just shows you how this league has gone to hell.—*Chuck Finley, Angles pitcher, on his selection as AL player of the week.*

3828 When I'm at bat, I'm in scoring position.—*Oscar Gamble, Yankees outfielder.*

3829 Wags could hit more than .300. Wags could hit .350. But I'm a big guy. When I go in to negotiate my contract, the first thing they ask me is, "How many home runs did you hit?"—*First baseman Leon "Daddy Wags" Wagner, on his hitting prowess. Wagner's best average was .294 with the Indians (1965); in 1962 he hit 37 home runs with the Angels.*

3830 By the time they realize I don't have anything, the inning is over.—*Todd Jones, Tigers closer, on how he gets the job done without overpowering stuff, 2006.*

3831 You have to love talent, baby, and I have nothing but talent. Why, I amaze myself.—*Ken Harrelson, Red Sox outfielder.*

Number Problems

3832 I won't play for a penny less than fifteen hundred dollars.—*Honus Wagner, Pirates shortstop, after being offered a contract for $2,000.*

3833 It just as easily could have gone the other way.—*Don Zimmer, Cubs manager, after a 4–4 road trip, 1990.*

3834 Well, the weatherman said fifty percent chance of rain, and he might be right.—*Jerry Doggett, Dodgers broadcaster.*

3835 I don't know which finger, but I'll tell you this—he always gave 60 percent.—*Jack Buck, Hall of Fame broadcaster, on which finger Hall of Fame pitcher Mordecai "Three Finger" Brown was missing, 1996. For the record, Brown had most of his right forefinger amputated due to a farming accident when he was seven years old.*

3836 That's three helmets at two dollars each. Since three and two are five, you owe me five dollars, Buddy.—*Mickey Rivers, Rangers outfielder and kangaroo court judge, to third baseman Buddy Bell, who was fined for breaking batting helmets.*

3837 It's like a 360-degree turnaround. I mean a 180-degree turnaround. I only went to high school.—*Steve Avery, Braves pitcher, on Atlanta's rise from last place in 1990 to first in 1991.*

3838 Better make it six. I can't eat eight.—*Don Osinski, Milwaukee Braves pitcher, on whether he wanted his pizza cut into six or eight pieces, 1965. (Also attributed to Yogi Berra.)*

3839 Dave Dravecky has now thrown 66 pitches through six innings. It doesn't take a smart guy very long to figure out that's 12 an inning.—*Duane Kuiper, Giants broadcaster, 1988.*

3840 Pete Rose has 3,000 hits and 3,014 overall.—*Jerry Coleman, Padres broadcaster.*

3841 So the Padres take a three-game series from the Giants, three games to two.—*Jerry Coleman, Padres broadcaster.*

3842 Rick Miller hit only one home run last year (1978), and that's like hitting none.—*Jerry Coleman, Padres broadcaster, on the Angels outfielder.*

3843 The new Haitian baseball can't weigh more than four ounces or less than five.—*Jerry Coleman, Padres broadcaster.*

3844 Montreal leads Atlanta by three, 5–1. —*Jerry Coleman, Padres announcer.*

3845 Last night's homer was Willie Stargell's 399th career home run, leaving him one shy of 500.—*Jerry Coleman, Padres announcer.*

3846 That's [George] Hendrick's 19th home run. One more and he reaches double figures. —*Jerry Coleman, Padres announcer.*

3847 That was [Andy] Benes' fifth strikeout on the day. He came in with 94, so now he has 104 strikeouts on the year.—*Ralph Kiner, Mets broadcaster, 1993.*

3848 [Bobby] Bonilla has struck out three times in the game—and he's 1-for-2.—*Ralph Kiner, Mets broadcaster, 1994.*

3849 So that would make him 7-foot-10.—*Ralph Kiner, Mets broadcaster, after partner Tim McCarver explained that 6'10" Mets pitcher Eric Hillman was standing on a 10-inch-high mound, 1993.*

3850 And the Mets need at least one run to tie it up.—*Ralph Kiner, Mets broadcaster, during a game in which New York trailed Philadelphia 2–1, 1990.*

3851 Six weeks or maybe longer. Maybe a month and a half.—*Junior Ortiz, Pirates catcher, when asked how long he would be on the disabled list, 1988.*

3852 I felt like I hadn't played in a week.—*Darin Erstad, Angels outfielder, on missing seven days with a concussion, 2002.*

3853 If you're 2-for-2, why isn't your average 2.000, not 1.000?—*Larry Andersen, Astros reliever, 1989.*

3854 If I hit .200 the second half, that's .400, right?—*Julio Cruz, White Sox second baseman, after hitting .201 for the first half of the 1984 season. Cruz finished with a .222 average.*

3855 We're playing the league leaders. If we win three out of four games, we'll pick up three games.—*Mel Hall, Yankees outfielder, on a series against Toronto, 1990.*

3856 Now that we're at .500, there's only two ways to go.—*Dave Winfield, Yankees outfielder.*

3857 That puts me on a pace to hit six.—*Mike Gallego, Oakland A's infielder, on hitting five home runs in one week, 1991.*

3858 Who won the first game?—*Jerry Willard, Indians catcher, on hearing the Twins won a doubleheader.*

3859 Geez, no wonder we lost them all.—*Jim Gantner, Brewers second baseman, after hearing Milwaukee had failed to score any runs in six extra-inning games, 1990.*

3860 Sometimes you have to take two steps backward to take a step up.—*Tom Candiotti, Indians pitcher, on his 7–18 record for the last-place Tribe, 1987.*

3861 Two grand slams in a week—man, that's seven or eight ribbies right there.—*Bill Madlock, Pirates third baseman.*

3862 I talked to him five times. He called me twice, I called him twice.—*Larry Bowa, Padres manager, on conversations with outfielder Stan Jefferson, 1988.*

3863 Don't tell me 2 and 2 is 4. How do you know 2 is 2? That's the real question.—*Steve Carlton, four-time Cy Young Award winner.*

3864 I usually sleep for two hours, from one o'clock to four.—*Yogi Berra, Yankees catcher, on his pregame routine before night games.*

3865 I think we have a better chance of sweeping the series than they do.—*Yogi Berra,*

Yankees manager, after winning the first two games of a three-game series, 1984.

3866 If there's a 50 percent chance we'll have a repeat American League pennant winner, you gotta remember there's also a 75 percent chance we won't.—*Yogi Berra, Yankees manager, 1984.*

3867 In baseball, nine times out of ten you're going to struggle half the time.—*Eddie Williams, Padres first baseman, 1994.*

3868 That's the fourth extra base hit for the Padres—two doubles and a triple.—*Jerry Coleman, Padres broadcaster.*

3869 David Cone is in a class by himself with three or four other players.—*George Steinbrenner, Yankees owner, 1996.*

3870 When you play this game ten years, go to bat 7,000 times and get 2,000 hits, you know what that means? That you've gone 0-for-5,000.—*Reggie Jackson, Oakland A's outfielder, 1974.*

3871 During my 18 years, I came to bat almost 10,000 times. I struck out about 1,700 times and walked maybe 1,800 times. You figure a ballplayer will average about 500 at-bats a season. That means I played seven years without ever hitting the ball.—*Mickey Mantle, former Yankees outfielder, 1970.*

3872 What's the matter with you? Other pitchers win their games 9–3, 10–2. You win yours 2–1, 1–0. Why don't you win your games like the others?—*Jacob Ruppert, Yankees owner, to Waite Hoyt.*

3873 Well, Rickey's not one of them, so that's 49 percent right there.—*Rickey Henderson, Red Sox outfielder, on former MVP Ken Caminiti's assertion that 50 percent of major leaguers use steroids, 2002.*

3874 Fifty percent? That's ridiculous! Fifty percent would mean half our guys.—*Mike Lieberthal, Phillies catcher, on claims of rampant steroid use in the majors, 2002.*

3875 I was only going three-quarters to 75 percent.—*Mike Lieberthal, Phillies catcher, on running again after an injury, 1999.*

3876 You give 100 percent in the first half of the game, and if that isn't enough, in the second half you give what's left.—*Yogi Berra, Yankees coach.*

3877 You can count on the fingers of your right hand the number of times I've hit a homer to the opposite field—about 10.—*Gary Carter, former All-Star catcher.*

3878 His numbers are pretty good.—*Allard Baird, Royals GM, on calling up pitching prospect Jeff Austin, who was 2–7 with a 7.76 ERA for the Omaha Royals, 2001.*

3879 If I hit 30 home runs and Jacque Jones hits 30 home runs and Torii Hunter hits 30 home runs, that's 120 home runs.—*Corey Koskie, Twins third baseman, 2004.*

3880 Everybody knows I should have made that play. I make that play 101 times out of 100. —*Mark McLemore, Mariners third baseman, on booting a grounder that allowed Oakland to tie the game with two outs in the bottom of the ninth, April 18, 2003. McLemore redeemed himself with the game-winning single in the10th inning.*

3881 I think 95 is a good, round number. We had 55 wins at the break, and if we can get another 40 in the 74 we've got left, that's 95 wins. That's a good, round number for winning the West.—*Lou Piniella, Mariners manager, 2001. Sweet Lou's math is fine, but his understanding of roundness leaves something to be desired. The M's won a remarkable 116 games only to lose the ALCS to the Yankees.*

3882 I don't want to go anywhere. I want to be here 150% out of 100.—*Chuck Knoblauch, Yankees outfielder, on trade rumors, 2001.*

3883 Half my stuff was at my mom's, half was at my dad's and half was at my new house.—*John Patterson, second baseman, on why it took him so long to get packed after he was called up by the Giants, 1992.*

3884 Kansas City and Cleveland, a double-header, was postponed because of rain. They'll play four tomorrow.—*Hank Greenwald, Giants announcer.*

3885 He's the best 23-year-old catcher I've seen since Campy—and Campy was 25 years old at the time I saw him—*Hall of Fame manager Casey Stengel comparing Dodgers legend Roy Campanella to Reds catcher Johnny Bench, 1971.*

3886 I know my days are numbered. I just don't know the number.—*Rudy May, Yankees pitcher.*

Uniform Numbers

3887 We're on a first number basis with each other. He calls me 3 and I call him 2.—*Bill "Spaceman" Lee (No. 37) on Mark "The Bird" Fidrych (No. 20), 1977.*

3888 Because if you turn 337 upside down, it spells LEE. And then I could stand on my head and people would know me right away. —*Bill Lee, Expos pitcher, on why he wanted to change his uniform number from 37 to 337.*

3889 There's too many 9s out there. But do you think there's another 09?—*Benito Santiago, Padres catcher, on his new uniform number, 1991.*

3890 It's the closest to 100 that I could get. I'm going out and try to throw every pitch 99 miles an hour.—*Mitch Williams, hard-throwing reliever, on why he changed to uniform No. 99 when he was traded from the Cubs to the Phillies, 1993.*

3891 I was rookie of the year in 1972, my son Carson was born in 1972 and my number in Boston was 27—or 72 backward.—*Carlton Fisk, White Sox catcher, on choosing No. 72 as his new uniform number, 1981. Fisk played 1,421 games with Chicago and 1,078 with Boston.*

3892 I got tired of asking for a number that was already worn by somebody else.—*Willie Crawford, Oakland A's outfielder, on why he chose No. 99, 1977.*

3893 The Tampa Bay Devil Rays are retiring Wade Boggs' No. 12, which is the least they can do for someone who gave the club all those years of service. Both of them, to be specific.—*Tom FitzGerald, sportswriter, 2000. Boggs became the first player to reach 3,000 hits with a home run.*

3894 He can have my wife. But he can't have my number.—*Dwight Gooden, Mets pitcher, after new teammate Frank Viola asked for Gooden's No. 16, 1989.*

3895 Is soon-to-be-44-year-old reliever Jesse Orosco wearing number zero-zero because he's been around so long that his speedometer just turned over?—*Keith Olbermann, broadcaster, on the uniform number change by the Dodgers pitcher, 2001.*

3896 It's only half his number, but if I am half as good as he is, that'll be enough.—*Jeffrey Hammonds, Reds outfielder, on wearing uniform No. 4 in honor of former teammate Eric Davis, who wore No. 24, 1998.*

Statistics

3897 Say you were standing with one foot in the oven and one foot in an ice bucket. According to the percentage people, you should be perfectly comfortable.—*Bobby Bragan, Milwaukee Braves manager, 1963.*

3898 Statistics are used by baseball fans in much the same way that a drunk leans against a street lamp; it's there more for support than enlightenment.—*Vin Scully, Dodgers broadcaster.*

3899 Baseball statistics are like a girl in a fine bikini. They show a lot, but not everything.—*Toby Harrah, Indians third baseman, 1983.*

3900 Statistics are about as interesting as first-base coaches.—*Jim Bouton, former pitcher.*

3901 Statistics can be used to support anything, including statisticians.—*Bill Lyon, sportswriter.*

3902 I don't think baseball could survive without all the statistical appurtenances involved in calculating pitching, hitting and fielding percentages. Some people could do without games as long as they got the box scores.—*John M. Culkin, media scholar, 1976.*

3903 Baseball fans love numbers. They love to swirl them around their mouths like Bordeaux wine.—*Pat Conroy, author.*

3904 Baseball fans are junkies, and their heroin is the statistic.—*Robert S. Wieder, writer.*

3905 Statistics are to baseball what a flaky crust is to mom's apple pie.—*Harry Reasoner, journalist.*

3906 No sport is as obsessed with statistics as baseball is. If you see an armored truck pull up outside the ballpark, it's not bringing cash, it's bringing boxes of decimal points.—*Scott Ostler, sportswriter, 2000.*

Odds and Ends

Football and Other Sports

3907 Soccer proved to be the toughest and motocross racing was second. Pro football came in eighth. It is presumed that baseball players were not tested because doctors did not want to awaken them.—*John Sonderegger, sportswriter, on a scientific study of the most strenuous sports, 1976.*

3908 I wish I could do both. At least I'd like to try it to see if I liked it.—*Bo Jackson, Auburn University senior, on deciding between playing professional baseball or football, 1985. The Tampa Bay Buccaneers selected Jackson with the first overall pick in the 1986 draft, but he declined and signed with the Kansas City Royals.*

3909 You know what baseball is? It's playing cards, sleeping, watching TV. Dress. Batting practice. Fool around with the fans. Joke with teammates. Football is a little different. Before the game, everybody sits on the floor, quietly, thinking of whose head they're going to take off.—*Bo Jackson, Kansas City Royals All-Star outfielder and Los Angeles Raiders All-Pro running back, 1990.*

3910 Baseball and football are very different games. In a way, both of them are easy. Football is easy if you're crazy as hell. Baseball is easy if you've got patience. They'd both be easier for me if I were a little more crazy—and a little more patient.—*Bo Jackson, Royals outfielder and Raiders running back.*

3911 Football is to baseball as blackjack is to bridge. One is the quick jolt; the other the deliberate, slow-paced game of skill.—*Vin Scully, Dodgers broadcaster.*

3912 It ain't like football. You can't make up no trick plays.—*Hall of Famer Yogi Berra comparing baseball and football.*

3913 What do you want, a bonus or a limp? —*Fresco Thompson, Dodgers executive, on whether a player should choose baseball or football.*

3914 The year you coached [1955], Northwestern was 0–8–1. You guys must have prepared so much for that tie, the other eight games got away.—*Lou Piniella, Cincinnati Reds manager, to Yankees owner George Steinbrenner, a former Northwestern assistant football coach, 1992.*

3915 If I dance after a home run, I don't think the pitchers would appreciate it. Baseball is a different game. In football, you're free to make a fool of yourself.—*Deion Sanders, two-sport star.*

3916 The thing to remember is, no matter what happens, three days after the World Series, everyone will be talking about football.—*David Justice, Oakland A's outfielder, on postseason pressure, October 2002. After the A's lost to the Twins in the ALDS—his 21st postseason series—Justice retired.*

3917 No, the ball's too big, and there's no chance of a rainout.—*Eric Hillman, 6'10" Mets pitcher, when asked if he liked basketball, 1993.*

3918 Basketball is really my game. Problem was the other kids got bigger and quicker and I stayed short and slow.—*Don Mattingly, Yankees first baseman, 1989.*

3919 If you see me watching a soccer game, you can beat me over the head with a shovel.—*Mike Macfarlane, Royals catcher, on the likelihood he would watch any of the 1994 World Cup.*

3920 I think I'll stick to this profession. I want to be talking when I'm 40.—*Stan Belinda, Pirates reliever, on whether he would consider becoming a professional boxer, 1991.*

3921 If you picked up a tennis racket in the neighborhood where I grew up, you'd get your butt kicked. Besides, where would you get money for a racket?—*Billy Martin, Yankees manager, 1985.*

3922 We were talking tennis. We asked each other how come our girlfriends can't beat Venus Williams.—*Brady Anderson, Orioles outfielder, on a pregame conversation with Indians second baseman Roberto Alomar about their tennis-playing girlfriends, 1999. Anderson was dating Amanda Coetzer and Alomar was engaged to Mary Pierce.*

3923 The first time I heard about spelunking, I thought it had something to do with pornography.—*Trevor Hoffman, Padres closer, on the activity otherwise know as cave exploration, 1999.*

3924 Croquet was really my kind of sport. That big wooden ball is just laid there, begging to be hit. And there are no curve balls in croquet.—*Catcher Marc Hill, a career .223 hitter.*

3925 When he captures your pieces, he puts them in his nose.—*Joe Ausanio, former Yankees reliever and member of the United States Chess Federation, on playing chess against Reds pitcher Pete Harnisch, 2001.*

3926 We love it when everyone gets into the game, as long as it's *our* game.—*Shawn Green, Blue Jays outfielder, on fans who cheer during scoreboard updates for Toronto Maple Leaf hockey games, 1999.*

3927 Now we know how many people hate hockey and the Maple Leafs in Toronto.—*Mike Rutsey, sportswriter, on a Blue Jays crowd of 12,751 at SkyDome—the smallest crowd in the history of the stadium—on the same night as Game 7 of the Maple Leafs playoff series against the New York Islanders, April 30, 2002.*

3928 It's real, because you have to put a lot of time into learning not how to kill someone by accident.—*Phil Coke, Yankees reliever, on professional wrestling, 2009.*

3929 Getting into baseball was refreshing. So many players have paid their dues and are appreciative of what they have. Baseball is a breath of fresh air. It's a different culture.—*Jerry Colangelo, Arizona Diamondbacks and Phoenix Suns owner, on the difference between owning a baseball and basketball team, 2002.*

NBA All-Stars

3930 If I hear Mike Scioscia right, he's always talking about "staying focused." I thought they were really able to maintain that focus that is so easy to lose in baseball because it's such a boring game.—*Phil Jackson, Los Angeles Lakers head coach, on the 2002 World Series Champion Anaheim Angels.*

3931 Baseball has as good a chance of having a salary cap as Michael Jordan has of wearing a White Sox cap; neither is going to happen.—*Andy Van Slyke, Pirates outfielder, on Jordan's attempt to become an outfielder for the White Sox after leaving the Chicago Bulls, 1994.*

3932 I can just see the American League catchers now. "Sorry about that third strike, Michael. Can I have your autograph?"—*Andy Van Slyke, Pirates outfielder, on what would happen if Michael Jordan played for the White Sox, 1994.*

3933 Michael told me how great retirement was, playing golf all the time. That didn't last long. In a week or two I might go to the [Milwaukee] Bucks and ask for a tryout.—*Robin Yount, former Brewers outfielder, on his retirement, 1994.*

3934 I think it's the greatest shot in the arm baseball could get. Once upon a time, all kids wanted to be baseball players, but nowadays a young kid dreams about playing basketball or football and making millions. I think it's great to see a man who has reached the pinnacle of his career, and now he wants to go back and do what he wanted to do as a kid—play baseball.—*Harry Caray, Cubs announcer, on Michael Jordan's decision to play baseball, 1994. Jordan hit .202 with three homers in his only minor league season.*

3935 The first person who asks me about Michael Jordan, I'm kicking their butt.—*Bo Jackson, Angels outfielder and former two-sport superstar, during spring training, 1994.*

3936 He's not a natural hitter. He couldn't hit a curveball with an ironing board.—*Bob Feller, Hall of Fame pitcher, on Birmingham Barons outfielder Michael Jordan, 1994.*

3937 This is definitely not the way I wanted my first ESPN highlight to go.—*Joe Ganote, Knoxville Smokies pitcher, on surrendering the first hit of Michael Jordan's baseball career. Jordan played right field for the Birmingham Barons, 1994.*

3938 There's something odd about going up to Michael Jordan and slipping him $16 a day.—*Terry Francona, Birmingham Barons manager, on giving his outfielder meal money, 1994.*

3939 Bad news for Michael Jordan: Today, Nike cut him from the company softball team. —*Jay Leno, talk show host, 1994.*

3940 Strikes.—*Tippy Martinez, Orioles pitcher, when asked what kind of pitches he would throw to Blue Jays shortstop Danny Ainge, who struck out 128 times in 665 career at-bats before switching to basketball with the Boston Celtics.*

3941 No matter how long he played, he could never have hit a fastball to the left of the first base coach.—*Jim Palmer, Hall of Fame pitcher, on former Blue Jays infielder Danny Ainge, 1994. Ainge hit .220 in the majors, but he won two NBA titles with Boston in 1984 and 1986.*

3942 I'm not really understanding a baseball game. I know a couple rules, but not all the rules. I like to see those fans. I can feel the heat.—*Yao Ming, Houston Rockets center, 2006.*

The Name Game

3943 Sixto Lezcano is the only major league baseball player who will get you 80 points in a Scrabble game.—*Roy Firestone, broadcaster, 1984.*

3944 We'll see if he can spell Mientkiewicz.—*Patrick Klinger, Twins executive, on the team's plans to honor 13-year-old Sean Conley, who won the National Spelling Bee, 2001.*

3945 Proving there are two sides to everything, Doug Mientkiewicz is leading the Twins with a .389 batting average but is having to sign that name on a lot more baseballs.—*Bud Geracie, sportswriter, May 2001.*

3946 Every time I sign a ball, and there have been thousands, I thank my luck that I wasn't born Coveleski or Wambsganss or Peckinpaugh.—*Mel Ott, Hall of Fame outfielder.*

3947 In the hills where I come from, we would take a name like that, get two girls' names out of it, and have enough left over for three boys.—*Arkansas Governor Orval Faubus on catcher Joe Garagiola.*

3948 That Bobby guy was always hurt.—*Roberto Kelly, Reds outfielder, on why he changed his name to Bobby during the 1993 season and then back to Roberto before the 1994 season. When he switched the first time, Kelly said of the name change,* "It's permanent for now."

3949 Jose truly was the player to be named later.—*Rocky Bridges, Giants coach, on shortstop José González, who changed his name to Uribe Gonzalez and then Jose Uribe, 1985.*

3950 The thing I got most excited about was forming the world's only Q-initialed battery with Jamie Quirk.—*Dan Quisenberry, Royals reliever, 1981.*

3951 It was a conspiracy. They thought the Zs had become too powerful and they had to break it up.—*Jeff Zimmerman, Rangers reliever, on the off-season trade of Gregg Zaun, the departure of Todd Zeile as a free agent, and the demotion of outfielder Mike Zywica, 2000.*

3952 Wow!—*Robb Nen, Marlins reliever, on learning that in a game against Chicago, he and Cubs reliever Dave Otto became the first two players whose last names are palindromes to appear in the same game, 1994. The only other palindrome players to appear in the majors were Truck Hannah, Toby Harrah, Eddie Kazak, Johnny Reder, Mark Salas, and Robb's father, Dick Nen.*

3953 I'd like you all to meet Mookie Wilson.—*Harry Weltman, GM of the NBA's New Jersey Nets, introducing the team's No. 1 draft pick, Mookie Blaylock, 1989.*

3954 It is a pleasure to be up here with Joe Torrez, a fellow New Yorker.—*New York Mayor Michael Bloomberg on sharing the dais at the NYU commencement ceremony with Yankees manager Joe Torre, May 2003.*

3955 I don't know how to pronounce his last name. He's the fighter. Ali Muhammad, that's it.—*Calvin Griffith, Twins president, looking at a baseball signed by former heavyweight champion Muhammad Ali, 1983.*

3956 I knew someday I'd be Schott at sunrise.—*Lou Piniella, Reds manager, after getting a kiss from team owner Marge Schott on an early morning television show.*

3957 I got a letter from a woman suggesting that Hall be traded to Kansas City, so he could be Royal Albert Hall.—*Skip Caray, Braves broadcaster, on outfielder Albert Hall, 1986.*

3958 I can't understand why he hasn't been nicknamed Chicken. Don't you get it? Chicken Catcher Torre.—*Bobby Bragan, Milwaukee Braves manager, on Joe Torre, 1963.*

3959 I asked him if he meant, "You're not ready yet" or "You're not ready, Yett."—*Rich Yett, Indians pitcher, on being sent to the minors by manager Pat Corrales, 1986.*

3960 I'm thinking of bottling it and going into business. We can call it Leiter Fluid.—*Al Leiter, Blue Jays pitcher, on a substance that helped to cure his finger blisters, 1991. In an unrelated note, Leiter optimistically negotiated a clause in his contract for a $50,000 bonus if he won the Associated Press Comeback Player of the Year Award. The award was given by UPI.*

3961 I'm a household name, but not a household word.—*Paul Householder, Reds outfielder, 1982.*

3962 Does that make me a Hart specialist? Or the designated Hart transplant.—*Ron Swoboda, Yankees outfielder, on pinch-running for designated hitter Jim Ray Hart in consecutive games, 1973.*

3963 At some point, they ought to call you Senior Junior—*Ralph Kiner, Mets announcer, to Expos utility player Junior Noboa, 1990.*

3964 Think of the promotional possibilities. On Reynolds-Rapp night, the first 25,000 fans get free tin foil.—*Jeff Conine, Marlins first baseman, on a pitching matchup between Houston's Shane Reynolds and Florida's Pat Rapp, 1997.*

3965 Hopefully, the next time I get an Opening Day start, there won't be any other instruments in the lineup.—*Bret Saberhagen, Royals pitcher, on giving up home runs to George Bell, Sam Horn and Albert Belle on consecutive opening days.*

3966 Get the presidents out of the game. If I come up and Joe Carter's out there, I'll give up.—*Andy Van Slyke, Pirates outfielder, after outfielders Claudell Washington and Otis Nixon robbed him of home runs, 1992.*

3967 We needed to buy a vowel.—*Steve Phillips, Mets GM, on signing Dutch-born infielder Robert Eenhoorn, 1998.*

3968 The Expos latest-and-greatest prospect is outfielder Milton Bradley. I don't know what the future holds for the kid, but with a name like that, he's gotta have game.—*Jim Armstrong, sportswriter, 1999. After making his debut in 2000, the highly volatile Bradley played for eight teams in his first eleven seasons.*

3969 Seems like a good time for the Baltimore Orioles to see what little-used catcher Fernando Lunar can do in a night game.—*Dwight Perry, sportswriter, 2002. Lunar went 0 for 2 that season, his last in the majors.*

3970 His control isn't much to talk about, but they say the kid's got a gun for an arm.—*Jim Armstrong, sportswriter, on Carolina Mudcats pitcher John Dillinger, 1997. In twelve minor league seasons, Dillinger went 68–70, but he never made it to the Show.*

3971 No one will have a harder time living up to his name than Met outfielder Wonderful Terrific Monds III, who signed a one-year deal last week.—*Gene Wojciechowski, sportswriter, 1996. The name goes back to his great-grandfather who, after 11 daughters, was so thrilled* *to have a son that all he could say was "Wonderful! Terrific!"*

3972 He'll be okay if he keeps his hand out of his shirt.—*Casey Stengel, Mets manager, on outfielder Danny Napoleon, 1965.*

3973 It might not amount to a hill of beans in this crazy baseball season. But even if the fog never lifts, the Phillies will always have Parris.—*Frank Fitzpatrick, sportswriter, on Philadelphia breaking out of a hitting slump by shelling Pirates pitcher Steve Parris, 1997.*

3974 My ultimate dream is to have my own bank, maybe in Paris. I'd call it Banks' Bank on the Left Bank.—*Ernie Banks, Hall of Fame infielder.*

3975 If the Dodgers go to the expense of putting my name on the back of a uniform, I know darn well they aren't going to trade me.—*Bill Grabarkewitz, Dodgers infielder, 1972. Grabarkewitz was traded after the season to the Angels.*

3976 I told Roland Hemond to go out and get me a big name pitcher. He said, "Dave Wehrmeister's got 11 letters. Is that a big enough name for you?"—*Eddie Einhorn, White Sox owner, 1985.*

3977 Who wants to be a Cardinal beat writer? I mean, not even spell check will help when Jason Simontacchi starts, Gene Stechschulte relieves, and Jason Isringhausen closes. —*Dave van Dyck, sportswriter, 2002.*

3978 When I'm commissioner of baseball, Mark Grudzielanek changes his name to Mark Grud.—*Jerry Greene, sportswriter, on the Dodgers second baseman, 2001.*

3979 The L.A. Dodgers signed shortstop Mark Grudzielanek to a four-year contract. The contract was six pages long. One page for the terms of the agreement, five pages for Grudzielanek's signature.—*Jerry Perisho, comedy writer, 2000.*

3980 You know when you got it made? When you get your name in the crossword puzzles.—*Rocky Bridges, San Jose Bees manager, 1964.*

3981 Your first name's white, your second is Hispanic and your third belongs to a black. No wonder you don't know who you are.—*Mickey Rivers, Yankees outfielder, to Reginald Martinez Jackson, better known as Reggie, 1977.*

3982 I thought I had to show all my stuff. I threw the ball so hard I tore a couple of boards off the grandstand. One of the fellows said that the stand looked like a cyclone struck it. That's how I got the name that was shortened to Cy.—*Denton True "Cy" Young, Hall of Fame pitcher.*

3983 I refuse to call a 47-year-old, white-haired man Sparky.—*Al Clark, umpire, on Tigers manager George "Sparky" Anderson, 1981.*

3984 In Japan, Godzilla is actually very humble, very kind, gentle. He goes around breaking things and stepping on people, but the heart of Godzilla is very pure, very gentle.—*Hideki Matsui, Yankees rookie outfielder, on his nickname, which he picked up in high school, 2003.*

3985 I couldn't pronounce it myself.—*Bob Miller, Mets pitcher, on why he changed his last name from Gmeinweiser, 1974.*

3986 I like to have broken my jaw trying to pronounce that one, but I said his name just by holding my nose and sneezing.—*Dizzy Dean, announcer, on Cubs pitcher Ed Hanyzewski.*

3987 They got their pitching staff when a U-Boat surfaced off San Diego.—*Jack Buck, broadcaster, on the Padres pitching staff that included Butch Metzger, Dave Freisleben and Dave Wehrmeister, 1976.*

3988 I'm sure the Yankee Clipper would be proud to have his name on that potholed, garbage-covered stretch of hell. Thanks for the memories, Joe.—*Comedian Dennis Miller on renaming New York's West Side Highway after the late Joe DiMaggio, 1999.*

3989 He came over to me and said he didn't have a problem getting a reservation in New York anymore. I asked him when my name is going to be on the money. He said real soon.—*Paul O'Neill, Yankees outfielder, on meeting the recently appointed Secretary of the Treasury Paul O'Neill, 2001.*

3990 I should have named my kid Tidewater.—*Ron Gardenhire, Twins manager, on learning that Chipper Jones named his son Shea because he hits so well in New York, 2004.*

3991 Chris Assenheimer is the guy who didn't vote Ichiro rookie of the year, and boy does he look like one.—*Bud Geracie, sportswriter, 2001. Ichiro hit .350 as a 27-year-old rookie. Assenheimer's first-place vote went to Indians pitcher C.C. Sabathia (17–5, 4.39 ERA).*

3992 Everybody has a nickname. It beats being called "bum."—*Mitch Williams, Astros reliever, on being called Wild Thing, 1994.*

3993 I owe it all to my parents.—*David Aardsma, Giants reliever, on replacing Hank Aaron as the first player listed alphabetically in the Baseball Encyclopedia, 2004.*

Politics

3994 I'm a Dominican.—*José Rijo, Reds pitcher, when asked if he was a Democrat or a Republican.*

3995 If the World Series runs until Election Day, the networks will run the first one-half inning and project the winner.—*Lindsey Nelson, announcer, during the 1980 World Series.*

3996 He wanted to see poverty, so he came to see my team.—*Casey Stengel, Mets manager, on President Lyndon B. Johnson visiting Shea Stadium to see the Mets who finished 53–109 in 1964.*

3997 I don't know a lot about politics, but I know a lot about baseball.—*Richard M. Nixon, former President of the United States, 1981.*

3998 All you have to do is sit Molotov down between Branch Rickey and Casey Stengel, and in four years Russia will have nothing left but Siberia and a couple of left-handed pitchers.—*Frank Lane, White Sox GM, on how to deal with the Soviet Union, 1955.*

3999 We need a lefty in the bullpen!—*Mike Sweeney, Royals first baseman, to members of the Russian national baseball team that were in attendance, May 2000.*

4000 The President took all the news very calmly. I'd seen Enos Slaughter get more upset about an umpire say "strike two" than Gerald Ford did when he realized he wasn't going to win a presidential election.—*Joe Garagiola, broadcaster, on Jimmy Carter's defeat of Ford in 1976.*

4001 I heard Jimmy Carter say he has lost control of the U.S. Government. That shows you how dumb he is. He thought he had control to begin with.—*Bill Lee, Red Sox pitcher, 1978.*

4002 He's sitting over there and says, "Hey, Grover Cleveland. I played him in the movies." I said no, you played Grover Cleveland Alexander, the baseball player. And then I knew the nation was in tough shape from that moment on.—*Tip O'Neill, Speaker of the House, on a discussion with Ronald Reagan, who portrayed Pete Alexander in* The Winning Team (1952). *Alexander is the only ballplayer named after one president and portrayed by another on film.*

4003 Mr. President, you go tell the Russians we're having an awful good time over here playing baseball.—*Rick Dempsey, Orioles catcher, to President Ronald Reagan, who had called the Baltimore locker room to congratulate the Orioles on winning the 1983 World Series.*

4004 Mr. President! How the hell are you?—*Bret Saberhagen, Royals pitcher, to President Ronald Reagan, who had called the Kansas City locker room to congratulate the Royals on winning the 1985 World Series.*

4005 I'll live in Washington and I'll pitch for the Washington Senators. I'll bring baseball back to the city. It'll be the law.—*Bill Lee, former All-Star pitcher, announcing his candidacy for President with the Rhinoceros Party, 1987. One of Lee's former teams, the Montreal Expos, became the Washington Nationals in 2005.*

4006 Nobody knows more about vice than he does.—*Bill "Spaceman" Lee, presidential candidate of the Rhinoceros Party, on why he would name gonzo journalist Hunter S. Thompson as his vice presidential running mate, 1988.*

4007 The season was off to a great start until Defense Secretary Richard Cheney showed up at Yankee Stadium and closed two bases.—*Jay Leno, talk show host, 1991.*

4008 The Yankees and the Clinton administration have led different lives. One group has a history of drug problems. The other plays baseball.—*Alan Ray, comedy writer, on a visit to the White House to commemorate New York winning the 1996 World Series.*

4009 The New York Yankees are in the Fall Classic again. And Hillary Clinton says she's elated. She's never been to a Super Bowl.—*Alan Ray, comedy writer, October 1999. Clinton switched her loyalty from the Cubs to the Yankees as she campaigned during her successful New York Senate race.*

4010 If he's out of a job, spring training begins in Florida, but I hear he's looking for a four-year deal with a four-year extension.—*Steve Lubratich, Tigers assistant GM, on Vice President Al Gore, who took a break from his presidential campaign to throw batting practice at Comerica Park, 2000. None of the Tigers managed to take Gore deep.*

4011 I tried to turn on the game, and they had these two dudes talking. I don't know who they were. They didn't have their names on the screen.—*Eric Davis, Cardinals outfielder, on a blackout of Game 1 of the 2000 ALDS between the A's and Yankees. Instead, the NBC affiliate in St. Louis was broadcasting the presidential debate between Al Gore and George W. Bush.*

4012 I finally won an election on my own. It's the first time the Bush family ever won an election by unanimous vote.—*George W. Bush on being approved as the managing partner of the Rangers, 1989. Bush was elected governor of Texas in 1994 and President of the United States in 2000.*

4013 Back in 1973, we rolled a couple of doobies and smoked them together. And I can tell you—he definitely inhaled.—*Bill "Spaceman" Lee, on Texas Governor George W. Bush, 2000.*

4014 I'm always suspicious of guys who've got a famous father.—*George W. Bush, President of the United States, on meeting Diamondbacks GM Joe Garagiola Jr., January 2002.*

4015 I guess the president's groupies are a bit different.—*Denny Neagle, Rockies pitcher, on staying at the same hotel in Los Angeles as President George W. Bush, where there were numerous protesters, 2001.*

4016 Major League Baseball is sending All-Star ballots to Japan, Dominican Republic, Mexico, Puerto Rico and Venezuela. That's great. Just don't send any to Florida.—*Scott Ostler, sportswriter, on the contested 2000 presidential election, 2001.*

4017 The 2001 Hall of Fame ballot leaves little margin for error. There are no butterflies, no chads (certainly not Chad Curtis). It's arranged in the shape of a batter's box and even the writers from Florida papers should be able to handle it.—*Dan Shaughnessy, sportswriter, 2000.*

4018 Congratulations to George W. Bush. Last night the Supreme Court declared him the winner of last night's All-Star Game.—*David Letterman, talk show host, on the 2002 midsummer classic that ended after 11 innings in a 7–7 tie.*

4019 It's never OK, OK? Not now. Not ever. To love the Yankees would mean, among other things, that you've cuddled up with owner George Steinbrenner [...]. And another thing. During these troubled times, our leader, George W. himself, has asked for a return to normalcy. Is there anything more abnormal in America than loving the Yankees? —*Randy Galloway, sportswriter, on the changing public sentiment towards New York after 9/11, 2001.*

4020 The president threw one more strike than I did.—*Ray King, Cardinals reliever, on going 3–0 on the first two batters he faced on Opening Day, 2004. President Bush began the day by throwing a strike during the ceremonial first pitch.*

4021 I ask, what does it say about this country when Jesse Ventura can get elected but Bill Mazeroski can't?—*Gary Shelton, sportswriter, 2000. The former wrestler was elected governor of Minnesota and Maz was eventually voted into the Hall of Fame in 2001.*

4022 Now I not only have to answer to [owner] Jerry Reinsdorf about pitching, I have to answer to the President.—*Kenny Williams, White Sox GM, on President Barack Obama being a Chicago fan, 2008.*

4023 He would be good at filibustering.—*Theo Epstein, Red Sox GM, on the strengths that former Boston pitcher Curt Schilling would possess if he ran for the late Ted Kennedy's Senate seat, 2009. Schilling chose not to run.*

Small Towns

4024 There's not as much night life at home as there is here. And there's not as much day life, either.—*Ron Guidry, Yankees pitcher, comparing his home town of Lafayette, Louisiana, to New York City, 1978.*

4025 It's so small we don't even have a town drunk. Everybody has to take a turn.—*Stan Hack, Cubs third baseman, on his hometown of Sacramento, California, 1909 (population 29,282 in 1900).*

4026 I live so far out in the sticks that when I want to go hunting I walk toward town.—*Rocky Bridges, Phoenix Giants manager, on his hometown of Couer d'Alene, Idaho, 1979 (population 24,563 in 1990).*

4027 How cold is it? It's so cold the ice feels warm compared to the air.—*Bill Lee, former All-Star pitcher, on living in northern Vermont, 1987.*

4028 I live on Rural Route 1 in Vermont. The state came to me and told me they were naming the roads, and I could name mine. I told 'em I didn't want to name mine because I didn't want anyone to know where I live. They said, "You name it, or we'll name it for you." I told them to call it the Ted Kaczynski Memorial Highway.—*Bill Lee, former pitcher, 2002. Kaczynski was better known as the Unabomber.*

4029 The telephone directory has only one yellow page.—*Toby Harrah, Rangers shortstop, on his hometown of Sissonville, West Virginia, 1974 (population 4,399 in 2000).*

4030 The average age in Sun City, Arizona, is deceased.—*Bob Uecker, Brewers broadcaster, 1982.*

4031 The only thing easier than finishing in the top ten was getting a date for the senior prom.—*Travis Hafner, Indians first baseman, on his high school in Jamestown, North Dakota (population 15,527 in 2000, which ranks as the seventh largest city in the state). Hafner was the valedictorian in a class of eight—four boys and four girls.*

4032 It was the first time I met anyone I hadn't met before.—*John Kruk, Phillies first baseman, on playing in the minor leagues in 1981—the first time he had ever left his small hometown of Keyser, West Virginia (population 5,303 in 2000).*

Little League

4033 It's just like the major league World Series, except the players are smaller and more mature.—*Conan O'Brien, talk show host, on the Little League World Series, 1994.*

4034 It was long past midnight by the time the 13 little delinquents on our bus finally fell asleep. The relief was tremendous. I felt the way America feels when the State of the Union address ends or when sportscaster Dick Vitale signs off.—*Jeff Burroughs, 1974 AL MVP and coach of the 1993 Little League Champions from Long Beach.*

4035 The last time I saw anything like this, I was playing for Tasty Freeze in the Little League.—*Dave Smith, Astros reliever, on falling behind 14–0 to Cincinnati after just one inning, 1989.*

4036 My wife is probably going to organize a Little League team for me just to get me out of the house.—*Terry Collins, Astros manager, on the 1994 baseball strike.*

4037 The biggest thrill a ballplayer can have is when your son takes after you. That happened when my Bobby was in the championship Little League game. He really showed me something. Struck out three times. Made an error that lost the game. Parents were throwing things at our car and swearing at us as we drove off. Gosh, was I proud.—*Bob Uecker, former catcher.*

4038 Nothing matters after Little League.—*Kenneth Herz, sportswriter, 1985.*

4039 I think Little League is wonderful. It keeps the kids out of the house.—*Yogi Berra, Hall of Fame catcher.*

4040 Little League is a disaster. It exists for parents who are trying vicariously to recover an ability of their own that never really existed.—*Bill Veeck, White Sox owner, 1973.*

4041 He's hitting .450. Of course, everybody is hitting .450.—*Marquis Grissolm, Braves outfielder, on the batting skills of his four-year-old son D'Monte, who was playing t-ball.*

4042 A reason you may suspect a Little Leaguer is too old: Teammates put their teeth under their pillows. He puts his in a glass of water.—*David Letterman, talk show host, on 14-year-old Danny Almonte, who played for the Bronx in the 2001 Little League World Series.*

4043 Nice to hear Danny Almonte has enrolled in school. I'm told he's attending Jack Benny Middle School.—*Scott Ostler, sportswriter, 2001. For those too young to know, comedian Jack Benny claimed for decades that he was 39 years old.*

4044 Danny Almonte has been voted into the Little League Hall of Fame by the veterans committee.—*Scott Ostler, sportswriter, 2001.*

4045 When investigating suspicious Little Leaguers, check players' equipment bags for wedding rings, car keys and shaving kits.—*Dan Shaughnessy, sportswriter, 2001.*

Show Business

4046 Models are like baseball players. We make a lot of money quickly, but all of a sudden we're 30 years old, we don't have a college education, we're qualified for nothing, and we're used to a very nice lifestyle. The best thing is to marry a movie star.—*Supermodel Cindy Crawford, who was married to movie star Richard Gere from 1991 to 1995.*

4047 He must have done that one before he died.—*Yogi Berra, Hall of Fame catcher, on the Steve McQueen movie* The Magnificent Seven, *1982.*

4048 This is not ballet dancing, okay? Let's get that straight. This isn't ballet. We're soldiers marching around.—*Mark McGwire, Oakland A's first baseman, on performing with manager Tony LaRussa and teammates Steve Howard and Dave Stewart in the Oakland Ballet's production of* The Nutcracker, *1990.*

4049 I've never been able to figure out what that song means.—*Joe DiMaggio, Hall of Fame outfielder, on Simon and Garfunkel's classic "Mrs. Robinson," which features the line,* "Where have you gone, Joe DiMaggio?" *1984.*

4050 I don't know why they ever picked Anthony Perkins to play me. He threw a baseball like a girl. I hated the movie.—*Jimmy Piersall, former All-Star shortstop, on the star of his biopic* Fear Strikes Out *(1957).*

4051 What a lousy picture that was. They had Babe Ruth drinking milk. I don't think he drank a glass of milk in his life.—*Mark Koenig, former Yankees shortstop, on* The Babe Ruth Story (1948), *which is often cited as the worst baseball film ever made.*

4052 John Goodman can act. Utterly persuasive as the man-child Ruth. But Goodman at bat as Babe Ruth is the visual equivalent of Roseanne Arnold in a bikini as Marilyn Monroe.—*Dave Kindred, sportswriter, in a review of* The Babe, *1992.*

4053 My big lines were, "Ubba, gooba."—*Jim Lefebver, Mariners manager, on his 1966 appearance as a cannibal on* Gilligan's Island, *1989.*

4054 I had to join the Screen Actors Guild to be in the show. Between that and taxes, I lose $17 every time it airs.—*Buck Showalter, Yankees manager, on making a cameo appearance on* Seinfeld, *2003.*

4055 If the series doesn't work out, I think I'll go to Japan and try to get a job as a catcher. They don't know about me over there.—*Bob Uecker, career .200 hitter, on starring in the TV sitcom* Mr. Belvedere, *1985.*

4056 If the World Series goes seven games, it will be NBC's longest-running show this fall.—*Johnny Carson, talk show host, 1978.*

4057 Well, she's already had so much experience grabbing herself, she should be great.—*Jay Leno, talk show host, on the casting of Madonna as a ballplayer in* A League of Their Own, *1992. The decision to cast Madonna caused Debra Winger to leave the film; she was replaced by Geena Davis.*

4058 Three hours and seventeen minutes. Just like an American League game.—*Ed Lynch, Cubs GM, on what he thought of the movie* Titanic, *1998.*

4059 We have all the equipment, we have all the songs. Right now we have everything but the talent.—*Scott Spiezio, Oakland A's second baseman, on his heavy metal band Spastic Dysphonia, 1998.*

4060 He asked me one day, "What do you guys do at half time?" That's when I knew it was going to be one long damn movie.—*John Kruk, former first baseman, on a conversation with movie director Tony Scott, who was directing* The Fan *in which Kruk had a small part, 1996.*

4061 I heard that actors start work at six o'clock in the morning. That sort of soured me on the whole thing.—*Bo Belinsky, Angels pitcher, on considering a future in show business.*

4062 Back then, my idol was Bugs Bunny because I saw a cartoon of him playing ball —you know, the one where he plays every position himself with nobody else on the field but him? Now that I think of it, Bugs is still my idol. You have to love a ballplayer like that.—*Nomar Garciaparra, Red Sox shortstop, 1999.*

4063 Next time they try, I'll be like Tanner in the Astrodome in *Bad News Bears,* running around the outfield making them try to catch me.—*Ken Griffey Jr., Reds outfielder, on being removed from a game in the middle of an inning as part of a double-switch, 2007. Actually, the movie was* The Bad News Bears in Breaking Training (1977) *that featured a road trip to the Astrodome for the Bears.*

4064 I don't know how you can screw up playing yourself, but I'm afraid I will.—*Scott Hatteberg, former A's first baseman, on being cast to play himself in the proposed film version of* Moneyball, *2009.*

4065 You are far from supporting our troops, defying the noblest of the American spirit. You are choking freedom of dissent. How ironic.—*Roger Kahn, renowned baseball writer, on why he was cancelling an appearance at the Hall of Fame, April 2003, as written in a letter to Hall of Fame president Dale Petroskey, who had himself cancelled a planned celebration of the 15th anniversary of* Bull Durham *because he did not want the politically active couple of Tim Robbins and Susan Sarandon to appear.*

4066 You belong with the cowards and ideologues in a hall of infamy and shame.—*Actor Tim Robbins on the cancellation of the* Bull Durham *celebration at the Hall of Fame by President Dale Petroskey, April 2003. Petroskey objected to Robbins' outspoken opposition to the war in Iraq, claiming that he and Susan Sarandon "could ultimately put our troops in even more danger."*

4067 It's an outrage. I don't want to shoot them or anything. I just want them to move to Oklahoma.—*Lance Berkman, Astros outfielder, on the disparagement of President George W. Bush by Natalie Maines of the Dixie Chicks, March 2003.*

4068 Now instead of being demoted to the minors, players will be forced to appear on an episode of *Melrose Place.*—*Alex Kaseberg, comedy writer, on the purchase of the Dodgers by Rupert Murdoch, whose News Corporation also owned Fox Television, 1995.*

4069 I thought it was from a funeral home. —*Roger Craig, San Francisco Giants manager, on a congratulatory telegram from the Grateful Dead.*

4070 Yesterday there were rallies for me in cities across the country, including Chicago. You can tell things are bad when even Cubs fans feel sorry for you.—*Comedian Conan O'Brien on the controversy surrounding his demotion as host of* The Tonight Show, *January 19, 2010.*

4071 Baseball has been the most exciting and frustrating experience of my life. In movies, I never lost a fight. In baseball, I hardly ever won one.—*Gene Autry, Angels owner and movie legend. Autry died in 1998—four years before his beloved team won the World Series.*

Owners and Executives

4072 Baseball must be a great game to survive the fools who run it.—*Bill Terry, Hall of Fame first baseman.*

4073 Baseball has always chosen the longest way around and never been administered with real intelligence.—*Paul Gallico, sportswriter.*

4074 The owners aren't bad. They're dumb. —*Paul Richards, former player, manager, and executive, 1973.*

4075 Most of the owners in baseball today couldn't care less about the future of the game. They have no interest in, nor any consideration for, the American people, who pay the bills.—*Happy Chandler, former commissioner, 1964.*

4076 When you come right down to it, the baseball owners are really little boys with big wallets.—*Harold Parrott, writer.*

4077 Baseball owners have moral scruples against taking any man's dollar when there is a chance to take a dollar and a quarter.—*Red Smith, sportswriter.*

4078 I'll try to sell, but sooner or later there aren't going to be any suckers left out there.—*Eddie Chiles, Rangers owner.*

4079 The dumbest NFL owner is equal to the smartest baseball owner.—*Edward Bennett Williams, owner of the Baltimore Orioles and Washington Redskins. Both teams won a championship in 1983.*

4080 National League owners are one hundred percent for progress and one hundred percent against change.—*Edward Bennett Williams, Orioles owner.*

4081 Somebody said we couldn't even get 21 votes to go home.—*Jerry Reinsdorf, White Sox owner, on the inability of the owners to agree on anything during the winter meetings, 1994.*

4082 I've been to the last two owners' meetings, and these guys couldn't decide where to go to lunch together.—*Chuck Armstrong, Mariners president, 1986.*

4083 The owners claim they're going to put their foot down. Then they turn around and wrap their mouths around it.—*Keith Moreland, Cubs outfielder.*

4084 Do you ever get the impression that if it was raining soup, the lords of baseball would stand outside with forks?—*Bill Conlin, sportswriter, 1993.*

4085 Let's put the baseball owners in the next Biosphere experiment and, you know, see what happens.—*John Eisenberg, sportswriter, 1993.*

4086 Honestly, these owners aren't smart enough to juice a ball. They can't even operate a juice machine. And they couldn't keep quiet about it if they did. They don't leak private information; it floods from their mouth.—*Woody Paige, sportswriter, on the possibility of a juiced baseball, 1998.*

4087 As men get older, the toys get more expensive.—*Marvin Davis, Denver Broncos owner, on his $12-million bid to buy the Oakland A's, which was rejected.*

4088 Circumstances alter cases.—*Bill Veeck, St. Louis Browns owner, on why he was in favor of a petition to equally distribute radio and TV revenue to all ballclubs, 1951. Years earlier, Veeck had opposed a similar revenue-sharing plan while he was running the more profitable Cleveland Indians.*

4089 I found out a long time ago there is no charity in baseball. Every club owner must make his own fight for existence. I went into baseball purely for the fun of it. I had no idea I would spend so much money.—*Jacob Ruppert, Yankees owner, who bought the team (with Tillinghast Huston) in 1915 for $450,000. He bought out Huston in 1922 for $1.2 million and opened Yankee Stadium in 1923 at a cost of $2.5 million.*

4090 Werner was to baseball what pigeons are to the Statue of Liberty.—*Mark Whicker, sportswriter, on Padres owner Tom Werner, 1994.*

4091 We're operating now under seagull management. You know, George flies in, he eats a little bit, then he shits all over everybody and flies out.—*Chuck Armstrong, Mariners president, on team owner George Argyros.*

4092 I understand it's business, but the bad part of it is I haven't gotten a pair of Levis out of the deal yet.—*Troy Neel, Oakland A's DH, on the 1994 sale of the team by the Haas family, owners of Levi Strauss.*

4093 There's nothing in the world I wouldn't do for Walter O'Malley. There's nothing he wouldn't do for me. That's the way it is. We go through life doing nothing for each other.—*Gene Autry, Angels owner, on the Dodgers owner, 1965.*

4094 When [Tom] Monaghan's lawyers had their meeting with [Michael] Ilitch's lawyers, presumably they met at a neutral site—Pizza Hut.—*Bob Elliott, sportswriter, on the sale of the Tigers from Monaghan, owner of Domino's, to Ilitch, owner of Little Caesar's, 1992.*

4095 He sold the whole team down the river to keep his dirty head above water.—*Harry Hooper, Red Sox outfielder, on owner Harry Frazee. Besides selling Babe Ruth, Frazee also sold off Carl Mays, Everett Scott, Joe Dugan, Waite Hoyt, and Herb Pennock to the Yankees. Frazee bought the Red Sox in 1916 for $400,000, they won the 1917 World Series, and he sold the last-place team on July 11, 1923, for $1.5 million.*

4096 He'd go into the vault to get a nickel change.—*Enos Slaughter, Cardinals outfielder, on GM Branch Rickey, 1934.*

4097 He had a Puritan distaste for money in someone else's hands.—*Roger Kahn, sportswriter, on Brooklyn Dodgers GM Branch Rickey.*

4098 Rickey had both money and players. He just didn't like to see the two of them mix.—*Chuck Connors, actor and former Brooklyn Dodgers prospect, on Branch Rickey.*

4099 There is nothing in baseball I dislike. I'll stay in the game as long as my mind is clear. When I reach the stage when I don't know my business, or trade a .300 hitter for a .200 hitter, then you'll know I'm unfit.—*Connie Mack, Philadelphia A's owner-manager.*

4100 I get tired of hearing my ballplayers bellyache all the time. They should sit in the press box sometimes and watch themselves play.—*Buzzie Bavasi, Padres president, 1973.*

4101 Every time baseball's owners meet, an angel loses its faith.—*Steve Hummer, sportswriter, 2001.*

4102 If you put these guys in a room with flooding and a leaking roof, they would vote unanimously to paint the walls.—*Dan LeBatard, sportswriter, on baseball owners, 2001.*

4103 Horace Stoneham has only two occupations in life. He owns the Giants and he drinks.—*Bill Veeck, former baseball owner, 1965.*

4104 Bob Short should be named Minor League Executive of the Year—*Russ White, writer, on the Texas Rangers owner who relocated the Washington Senators to Arlington for the 1972 season and finished 54–100, worst in the majors.*

4105 The worst decision was hiring Harrelson as general manager, and the second worst was letting him fire the manager.—*Jerry Reinsdorf, White Sox owner, on the 1982 hiring of Ken "Hawk" Harrelson and the 1986 firing of manager*

Tony LaRussa, who went on to become the third-winningest manager of all-time while Harrelson returned to the broadcast booth, 2006.

The Front Office

4106 I have a darn good job, but please don't ask me what I do.—*Stan Musial, Hall of Fame outfielder, on his job as senior vice president of the Cardinals, 1988.*

4107 I'm a vice president in charge of special marketing. That means I play golf and go to cocktail parties. I'm pretty good at my job.—*Mickey Mantle, Hall of Fame outfielder and Yankees executive.*

4108 I'm not here all the time, so you can use mine. Here, this drawer is yours.—*Charlie Finley, Oakland A's owner, to vice president Joe DiMaggio, who asked Finley for an office desk, 1968.*

4109 I think that means I'm the general manager.—*Jim Frey on his title of Cubs vice president of baseball operations, 1988.*

4110 We in management are united by our problems and divided by our solutions.—*Frank Cashen, Mets GM.*

4111 Oh, until about five minutes after I'm dead.—*Bill Shea, Mets executive, when asked how long Shea Stadium would bear his name. Shea was an attorney who led the effort to bring an expansion team to New York in 1962. Shea died in 1991, but the stadium retained his name until the Mets moved to Citi Field in 2009.*

4112 That's perfect for a GM, a baby to be named later.—*Steve Lubratich, Tigers assistant GM, on team GM Randy Smith, who was late in returning from a scouting directors meeting to be with his wife in time for the birth of their second child. They waited until the next day to name the baby Shane, 2000.*

4113 You have to bear in mind that Mr. Autry's favorite horse was named Champion. He ain't ever had one called Runner Up.—*Gene Mauch, Angels manager, on team owner Gene Autry.*

4114 Disney's venture into baseball comes as very good news, and I am particularly looking forward to their Pittsburgh Pirates of the Caribbean ride.—*Mike Downey, sportswriter, on Angels owner Gene Autry selling 25 percent of his team to the Walt Disney Company, 1995.*

4115 There are more lies told in the lobby of winter meetings than anywhere on the face of the earth at any one time.—*John Schuerholz, Braves GM, 1999.*

4116 He's made some shrewd deals. In fact, I think he's craftier than my father, who was a Texas horse trader. As far as I'm concerned, he holds a position unique in baseball: general manager for life, if he wants it that long. —*Gene Autry, Angels owner, on GM Fred Haney, 1961. Haney took the expansion team through the 1968 season before becoming a team consultant.*

Charles O. Finley Oakland A's Owner

4117 My middle initial stands for Owner.

4118 I wanted to get into baseball in the worst way, and that's exactly what I did.

4119 I always wanted to be a player, but I never had the talent to make the big leagues. So I did the next best thing: I bought a team.

4120 Anyone can manage a baseball team. The owner runs the team anyway.

4121 Pigs get fat, hogs go to market. Modern professional athletes are like hogs. They're gluttons.—*1974.*

4122 If a general manager of mine ever said someone was indispensable, I'd fire him.—*As Kansas City A's president, 1963.*

4123 We run our club like a pawn shop—we buy, we trade, we sell.—*1977.*

4124 It is my ball club, my money and I don't appreciate anyone telling me how to spend my money to run my business. As long as I own this ball club, I will operate my way.—*1973.*

4125 Dick Williams is the best manager I've

ever had. I ought to know, I've fired enough of them.—*1972.*

4126 We had a common bond on the A's: everybody hated Charlie Finley.—*Reggie Jackson, former Oakland A's outfielder.*

4127 I hope to do a good enough job managing that maybe Charlie can trade me for $200,000 and a couple of ballplayers.—*Jack McKeon, Oakland A's manager, on replacing manager Chuck Tanner, who was traded to Pittsburgh for catcher Manny Sanguillen, 1977.*

4128 Finley is a self-made man who worships his creator.—*Jim Murray, sportswriter.*

4129 Charlie Finley is a menace to baseball.—*Ken "Hawk" Harrelson, Kansas City A's first baseman, on the team owner, 1967. Harrelson was released by the A's shortly after making this remark.*

4130 I'm not upset at all. Mr. Finley owns the team and if he assumes he can win without me, that's okay. I'm sure they can find somebody who can hit 30 homers, knock in 100 runs and steal 25 bases. You can find that anyplace, can't you?—*Reggie Jackson, Oakland A's outfielder, on trade rumors, 1974.*

4131 Finley's so cold-blooded, he ought to make antifreeze commercials.—*Reggie Jackson, Oakland A's outfielder, on owner Charlie Finley.*

4132 When Charlie Finley had his heart operation, it took eight hours—seven just to find his heart.—*Steve McCatty, Oakland A's pitcher, 1981.*

4133 He never interfered with me. That's because I never worked for him.—*Casey Stengel, Hall of Fame manager, on Charlie Finley.*

4134 *Charlie Finley (A's owner, 1969):* I noticed when you went out to the mound, you had grass stains on the seat of your pants. That's not a good example to set for your players.

Hank Bauer (A's manager): Those weren't grass stains, Charlie. That was mistletoe.

4135 Charlie Finley wouldn't think God would make a good commissioner.—*Warren Giles, NL president.*

4136 One day we woke up and the Wicked Witch of the North was dead and we were all the children of Oz.—*Matt Keough, Oakland A's pitcher, on the sale of the team by Charlie Finley, 1981.*

4137 Catfish Hunter had the distinction of playing for both Charlie Finley and George Steinbrenner, which is enough in itself to put a player in the Hall of Fame.—*Peter Ueberroth, baseball commissioner. Hunter was elected to the Hall of Fame in 1987.*

Calvin Griffith
Minnesota Twins Owner

4138 This is a very close-knit family. I imagine you talked to my son Clark yesterday, and I imagine he told you we don't talk.

4139 Money does nothin' but ruin ball players.

4140 People who call me cheap never had to make a payroll. I'll pay them what they deserve and not what their agents think they deserve.

4141 You don't see anyone with 50 years of age or responsibilities hollering about me. It's the young ones that never had to make a bigger decision than what subject to take. I don't mind being called a dinosaur. A dinosaur, from what I've seen on TV, is a pretty powerful person. A dinosaur usually pushes himself around to where he doesn't get hurt.—*1983.*

4142 If I have the smallest payroll in the majors, I'm proud of it. Those other owners, they're all egotists. They've got so much money, but nobody knew who they were before baseball. Who the hell ever heard of Ted Turner or Ray Kroc or George Steinbrenner?

4143 I can't tell you what I intend to do. But I can tell you one thing; it won't be anything rational.—*On firing manager Billy Martin, 1969.*

4144 He's the perfect businessman. He likes to get the most for the least. And he likes the least part best.—*Dave Goltz, Twins pitcher, on owner Calvin Griffith, 1979.*

4145 He's got money stashed in the cobwebs of his vault.—*Yankees catcher Butch Wynegar on his previous employer, Twins owner Calvin Griffith, 1983.*

4146 Everyone who plays for Griffith hustles like crazy so that some other club will make a trade and get the player away from Griffith.—*Bill Lee, former Red Sox pitcher, on Twins owner Calvin Griffith.*

4147 I know winning isn't everything, but with Calvin Griffith winning isn't anything.—*Ron Davis, Twins reliever, 1982.*

4148 He returned from the fishing season opener with his limit of walleyes. Calvin immediately took them to a grocery store and traded them for a package of Mrs. Paul's frozen fish sticks and 10 dollars in cash.—*Charley Walters, sportswriter, on parsimonious Twins owner Calvin Griffith, 1982.*

4149 It's not just that he marches to his own drum; I don't even think he *hears* anyone else's. He doesn't identify with the fans—never has. He doesn't do things because they're good [public relations] or politically smart. It's a strange thing to say, with that big fat belly of his, but in a perverse way I find him gallant.—*Bill Veeck, former owner, on Calvin Griffith, 1983.*

Marge Schott Cincinnati Reds Owner

4150 Is Marge Schott feeling all right? She's been back in her office at least two or three weeks now and as far as I can tell she hasn't insulted a single person on the basis of race, color or creed.—*Ron Rapoport, sportswriter, 1993.*

4151 Owner Marge Schott says the Reds have embarrassed her this year. Does that mean they're even?—*Jim Henneman, sportswriter, 1993.*

4152 Trying to teach sensitivity to Marge Schott is like trying to teach typing to Schottzie 02.—*Scott Ostler, sportswriter, on the Reds owner and her St. Bernard, 1993. Both were suspended from baseball that season after Schott made racially insensitive remarks.*

4153 I don't think the ball is juiced. I think Marge is.—*Mike Downey, sportswriter, on Marge Schott, 1994.*

4154 He was happier to get away from Marge Schott than people were to chopper out of Saigon at the end of Vietnam.—*Mike Lupica, sportswriter, on former Reds manager Davey Johnson becoming manager in Baltimore, 1996.*

4155 Marge Schott, recovering from pneumonia, is in stable condition. For the first time in her life.—*Nick Canepa, sportswriter, 1996,*

4156 Doctors are tentative about Cincinnati Reds owner Marge Schott's hip replacement operation, saying she'll have 80 percent recovery in six weeks. But it may be as much as three months before she can get her foot in her mouth.—*Craig Kilborn, talk show host, 1998.*

4157 You know, I love baseball, okay? But if we finally got Marge Schott and George Steinbrenner to shut up, maybe we should think twice about resolving this thing, don't you think?—*Jay Leno, talk show host, on the gag order imposed on owners during the 1994 baseball strike.*

4158 I wish they'd give me a scorecard with pictures because I still get everybody mixed up.—*Marge Schott, Reds owner.*

George Steinbrenner New York Yankees Owner

4159 Some guys can lead through genuine respect. I'm not that kind of leader.

4160 What happens is that all your life you operated businesses in such a way that you could afford to buy a baseball team. And then you buy the team and forget all the business practices that enabled you to buy it.

4161 I used to be very hands-on, but lately I've been more hands-off, and I plan to become more hands-on and less hands-off and hope that hands-on will become better than hands-off, the way hands-on used to be.—*1990.*

4162 I just can't understand all these teams changing managers the way they do. The lack of stability is alarming.—*Announcing that Yogi Berra would remain manager, 1984. Berra was fired the next season after 16 games.*

4163 He's the manager—until he screws up.—*On Billy Martin.*

4164 Owning the Yankees is like owning the Mona Lisa. That's something you never sell.

4165 There are two things George Steinbrenner doesn't know about: baseball and weight control.—*Graig Nettles, Yankees third baseman.*

4166 It's a good thing Babe Ruth still isn't here. If he was, George would have him bat seventh and say he's overweight.—*Graig Nettles, Yankees third baseman.*

4167 Above all else stands Steinbrenner's greatest talent—nay, genius; his uncanny knack of never being responsible for anything that goes wrong.—*Scott Ostler, sportswriter.*

4168 I know how to tell when George Steinbrenner is lying—his lips move.—*Jerry Reinsdorf, White Sox owner.*

4169 Nothing is more limited than being a limited partner of George's.—*John McMullen, Astros owner, on his prior business dealings with George Steinbrenner, 1980.*

4170 George Steinbrenner has one simple ambition in life. He wants to own all the land next to his.—*Dan Quisenberry, Royals reliever.*

4171 Instead of identifying somebody as their manager, the Yankees should appoint him "vice president, dugout decisions."—*Dave Anderson, sportswriter, 1982.*

4172 George Steinbrenner is the salt of the earth, and the Yankees players are open wounds.—*Scott Ostler, sportswriter.*

4173 I'm gonna buy the Suez Canal. When one of his ships comes through there, I'm gonna blow it up.—*Dock Ellis, Yankees pitcher, on owner and shipping magnate George Steinbrenner.*

4174 If a guy hit a home run, George would say it wasn't long enough.—*Lou Piniella, Reds manager, on former boss George Steinbrenner, 1992.*

4175 George is always trying to patch the tire when the car needs new wheels.—*Lou Piniella, Mariners manager, on George Steinbrenner, 1993.*

4176 Getting fired by George doesn't mean too much. It's not a true measure of your qualifications.—*Lou Piniella, Reds manager, on being fired twice as Yankees manager by George Steinbrenner, 1990.*

4177 The two biggest expenses for Yankee employees are housing and going-away parties.—*Bob Quinn, Reds GM, 1990.*

4178 The only thing that surprises me is that people are still surprised when something happens.—*Gene Michael, former Yankees manager, on the revolving door of managers, general managers, and players under George Steinbrenner, 1989.*

4179 Changing the manager is a step in the right direction. Now if they'd change the owners, maybe I'd stay.—*Don Baylor, Yankees DH, on the firing of manager Billy Martin after the 1985 season. Upon leaving New York, Baylor set a record by playing in three consecutive World Series with three different teams: Boston (1986), Minnesota (1987) and Oakland (1988).*

4180 Every year is like being traded—a new manager and a whole new team.—*Graig Nettles, Yankees third baseman, on playing for George Steinbrenner. The Boss made 17 managerial changes in his first 17 years as owner.*

4181 They deserve each other.—*Cleveland Amory, sportswriter, on Yankees owner George Steinbrenner and manager Billy Martin, 1983.*

4182 The more we lose, the more he'll fly in. And the more he flies in, the better chance there'll be a plane crash.—*Graig Nettles, Yankees third baseman, on George Steinbrenner, 1977.*

4183 Everything you read about George Steinbrenner is true. That's the problem.—*Dave Winfield, Yankees outfielder, 1985.*

4184 It's a beautiful thing to behold, with all 36 oars working in unison.—*Jack Buck, broadcaster, on the yacht belonging to Yankees owner George Steinbrenner, 1981.*

4185 Turner has gone to great financial lengths to save the world, and Steinbrenner has gone to great lengths to control it.—*I. J. Rosenberg, sportswriter, on Braves owner Ted Turner, who donated $1 billion to the United Nations, and Yankees owner George Steinbrenner, 1998.*

4186 Just six months ago, Orlando Hernandez escaped the island of Cuba, and recently he pitched his first winning game in Yankee Stadium. He's a very lucky man. He escapes the dictatorial reign of a ruthless tyrant and ends up working for George Steinbrenner.—*David Letterman, talk show host, 1998.*

4187 Steinbrenner was born on third base and thinks he hit a triple.—*Jim Bouton, former Yankees pitcher, on owner George Steinbrenner.*

4188 He has a knowledge of the game. The only thing he doesn't have is patience.—*Joe Torre, Yankees manager, on owner George Steinbrenner, 1998.*

4189 George Steinbrenner buys up every high-ticket free agent in baseball, and he's got enough left over to kick in $400 million to build a new stadium. Why isn't this guy secretary of the treasury?—*Scott Ostler, sportswriter, 2002.*

Ted Turner Atlanta Braves Owner

4190 I bought the Braves for two reasons—to get an autographed ball without pleading for it and to get good seats.—*On buying the Braves in 1976.*

4191 If you can't do anything else, make a lot of noise.

4192 I'm not interested in selling the Braves ... but I don't know why not.—*1978.*

4193 One of my goals in life was to be surrounded by unpretentious, rich young men. Then I bought the Braves, and I was surrounded by 25 of them.—*1976.*

4194 Baseball is a game, a big game, but only a game. Collecting garbage is more important. What would you rather have, a yard filled with garbage or a ticket to a ball game?—*1978.*

4195 There's a fine line between being colorful and being an asshole, and I hope I'm still just colorful.—*1978. Turner took his colorful ideas one step too far in the 1980's by colorizing film classics such as* Casablanca *and* Yankee Doodle Dandy *for his cable TV channels.*

The Commish

4196 We've got to keep baseball on a high standard for the sake of the youngsters—that's why I took the job, because I want to help.—*Kenesaw Mountain Landis, baseball's first commissioner, 1920.*

4197 His career typifies the heights to which dramatic talent can carry a man in America, if only he has the foresight not to go on the stage.—*Heywood Broun, sportswriter, on commissioner Kenesaw Mountain Landis.*

4198 I thought baseball was a sport when I became commissioner. I was mistaken. The semi-bandits own it.—*Happy Chandler, former baseball commissioner, 1962. Chandler, baseball's second commissioner, was voted out of office by the owners after one term (1945–1951).*

4199 I decided to withdraw my name when I didn't get a single vote on the first 19 ballots. —*Bill Veeck, former owner, on running for commissioner, 1969. Bowie Kuhn was selected as the fifth commissioner, serving from 1969 to 1984.*

4200 Resign.—*Bill Veeck, former White Sox owner, on the first thing he would do if elected baseball commissioner.*

4201 There was a vacancy when I left, and the owners decided to continue with it.—*Happy Chandler, former baseball commissioner, on his successor, Ford Frick, 1978.*

4202 Bowie Kuhn is the best commissioner in baseball today.—*Jim Bouton, Braves pitcher, 1978.*

4203 If I hear him say just once more he's doing something for the betterment of baseball, I'm going to throw up.—*Sparky Anderson, Reds manager, on commissioner Bowie Kuhn, 1978.*

4204 I'd like to hire Bowie Kuhn so I could have the pleasure of firing the clown the very next day.—*Charlie Finley, Oakland A's owner, 1981.*

4205 A woman asked me the other day if there was any truth to the rumor that Charlie Finley was out to get me. I said, "Honey, that ain't no rumor."—*Bowie Kuhn, baseball commissioner, 1978.*

4206 I have often called Bowie Kuhn the village idiot. I apologize to the village idiots of America. He's the nation's idiot.—*Charlie Finley, Oakland A's owner, 1980.*

4207 I put Kuhn in the same category as Jimmy Carter. Neither one is qualified to hold the position he has.—*Gene Autry, Angles owner, on Commissioner Bowie Kuhn, 1978.*

4208 We've got a commissioner who doesn't represent both sides. He doesn't even know who's playing the game. I've been introduced to him eight or nine times over the years and every time he says, "Nice to meet you."—*Buddy Bell, Rangers third baseman, on Commissioner Bowie Kuhn, 1981.*

4209 I'm not very smart. I think I can prove that. Who would accept a job with Marge Schott's dog, Ted Turner and George Steinbrenner as your boss?—*Peter Ueberroth, baseball commissioner.*

4210 If Bud had been the captain of the *Titanic*, he'd have survived, blamed the iceberg and been given a bigger ship.—*Tom Boswell, sportswriter, on Brewers owner Bud Selig being named baseball commissioner after holding the title of "acting commissioner" for several years, 1998.*

4211 Sitting side by side at the game in Havana were Fidel Castro, who hijacked a nation in 1959, and baseball commissioner Bud Selig, the used car salesman who hijacked the Seattle Pilots in 1970. Have there ever been two men who have ascended so dubiously, accomplished so little and stayed in power so long?—*Art Thiel, sportswriter, during an exhibition game between the Baltimore Orioles and Cuban All-Star team, 1999.*

4212 He is a decent and honorable man, but he has as much business being commissioner as I have playing power forward for the Lakers.—*Bob Costas, broadcaster, on acting commissioner Bud Selig, 1997.*

4213 I've watched the [Los Angeles] Clippers do one silly thing after another. Do you see [NBA Commissioner] David Stern doing anything about it?—*Bud Selig, acting baseball commissioner, on why he doesn't void seemingly lopsided trades, 1998.*

4214 The primary qualification for the Supreme Court these days seems to be a complete absence of opinion and knowledge about anything. This is pretty much top of the résumé for baseball also.—*Bernie Lincicome, sportswriter, on U.S. Senator George Mitchell, who refused to be considered for a Supreme Court nomination, possibly becoming baseball commissioner, 1994.*

4215 If you want a commissioner who would please the owners, we should hire Madonna.—*Marge Schott, Reds owner, 1992.*

4216 Baseball will hire Billy Crystal as next commissioner, on the premise that if you're going to laugh at the guy in charge, there might as well be a legitimate reason.—*Art Spander, sportswriter, 1992.*

4217 I love the game, but I don't need that kind of turmoil.—*George Bush, former President of the United States, on the possibility of becoming baseball commissioner, 1993.*

4218 Baseball commissioner Bud Selig is now five points behind Osama bin Laden in the popularity polls.—*Jay Leno, talk show host, on the decision to have the 2002 All-Star Game end in a 7–7 tie after 11 innings.*

4219 The guy who ought to be commissioner of baseball is Fidel Castro because he speaks Spanish, he's had a lot of dealings with Washington, and he played the game.—*Dick Schaap, sportswriter.*

Physical Fitness

4220 They examined all my organs. Some of them are quite remarkable, and others are not so good. Several museums are bidding on them.—*Casey Stengel, Mets manager, after receiving a physical examination.*

4221 When you get guys out, you're big. When you don't get guys out, you're fat.—*Ozzie Guillen, White Sox manager, on 270-pound closer Bobby Jenks, 2006.*

4222 I got a jackass back in Oklahoma, and you can work him from sunup till sundown and he ain't never going to win the Kentucky Derby.—*Pepper Martin, Cardinals outfielder, on explaining to manager Ray Blades that St. Louis didn't need to work out twice a day during spring training.*

4223 Watching Fernando Valenzuela force himself into a Los Angeles Dodgers uniform is something like seeing Kate Smith struggling to fit into a pair of Brooke Sheilds' designer jeans.—*H.G. Reza, sportswriter, 1981.*

4224 His uniform fits him like a banana peel over a watermelon.—*Mike Krukow, Giants broadcaster, on portly Phillies pitcher Fernando Valenzuela, 1994.*

4225 I don't know, I'm not in shape yet.—*Yogi Berra, Yankees catcher, when asked what his cap size was in spring training.*

4226 The best knee I saw belonged to a 77-year-old woman.—*Dr. Phillip Marone, Phillies orthopedic surgeon, after completing four arthroscopic knee surgeries in one morning, including operations on first baseman John Kruk and coach Mike Ryan, 1993.*

4227 At least now I know I have a muscle in my stomach. A lot of people didn't think I did.—*John Kruk, Phillies first baseman, after doctors discovered abdominal lumps caused by a muscle strain, 1994.*

4228 I wasn't in shape during the season, so why should I stay in shape during the strike?—*Rod Beck, Giants reliever, 1994.*

4229 I've never seen anyone on the disabled list with pulled fat.—*Rod Beck, Cubs closer, on why he doesn't worry about his physique, 1998.*

4230 All that running and exercise can do for you is make you healthy.—*Denny McLain, Washington Senators pitcher, 1971. (Also attributed to Tigers pitcher Mickey Lolich.)*

4231 I watched aerobics on TV.—*Rickey Henderson, Oakland A's outfielder, on how he stayed in shape during the 1990 spring training lockout.*

4232 He told me he couldn't wait for the basketball season to end, so he could go back to baseball and get out of shape.—*Bill Russell, Hall of Fame basketball player, on former Boston Celtics teammate Gene Conley, who also pitched for the Milwaukee Braves.*

4233 If baseball players had to jump around for one season of a basketball schedule in our league, they'd never gripe about anything again.—*Ben Kerner, St. Louis Hawks owner, 1958.*

4234 Physically, I feel fine. It's my ERA that's not in too good shape.—*Nolan Ryan, Rangers pitcher, 1992.*

4235 My hope for Nolan Ryan after he hangs up his spikes next year: Go to Harvard med school. Not to study, but to be studied.—*Blackie Sherrod, sportswriter, on the 46-year-old Rangers pitcher, 1993.*

4236 My arm has felt so bad since I retired that I can't even throw a tantrum.—*Steve Stone, Cubs broadcaster, on why he wouldn't consider making a comeback, 1991.*

4237 Jesse Owens never won a baseball game in his life.—*Jim Kaat, former All-Star pitcher, on why he doesn't believe in pitchers running wind sprints, 1984.*

4238 I don't generally like running. I believe in training by rising gently up and down from the bench.—*Satchel Paige, Hall of Fame pitcher.*

4239 If you can't get in shape in three weeks, you should be a plumber.—*Bob Feller, Hall of Fame pitcher, on an abbreviated spring training after an owners' lockout, 1990.*

4240 I don't lift weights or anything, I just dance the polka.—*Phil Niekro, 46-year-old Yankees pitcher, on staying in shape, 1985.*

4241 You don't run the damn ball across the plate.—*Johnny Sain, Boston Braves pitcher, on why running is unimportant for pitchers.*

4242 I had my two-year-old counting sit-ups for me. He can count to ten, and he skips some of the numbers.—*Lee Smith, Cardinals reliever, on why he reported overweight to spring training, 1991.*

4243 I'm not even going to lift a baseball bat unless it's to swing at any owner I see.—*Barry Larkin, Reds shortstop, on his plans for staying in shape during the 1994 baseball strike.*

4244 Let's not overdo this. I only have to call the bases, not steal them.—*Eric Gregg, 325-pound NL umpire, to his new trainer.*

4245 Medical people tell me I have the body of a 30-year-old. I know I've got the brain of a 15-year-old. You got both, you can play baseball.—*Pete Rose, 44-year-old Reds player-manager, 1985.*

4246 You don't have to be in shape to play baseball. There are guys who have played well overweight. I have the highest fat level of anybody on the team, but I know guys in shape who hit .180.—*Bill Madlock, Pirates third baseman, 1984.*

4247 I'm tired of hearing people ask me, for 13 years, how much I weigh. What's the difference? I never ride that pine. I play 158 games a year. The guys with the beautiful bodies are always hurt.—*George Scott, Red Sox first baseman, 1978.*

4248 When the season is over, I feel like a used car.—*Bob Brenly, Giants catcher.*

4249 I always loved the game, but when my legs weren't hurting, it was a lot easier to love.—*Mickey Mantle, Hall of Fame outfielder.*

4250 The doctor wanted me to have a pacemaker put in, but I refused because my brother had one installed and every time he sneezes the garage door flies open.—*Ellis Clary, Twins scout, 1985.*

4251 I believe there are a bunch of orthopedic surgeons behind this league, if you want to know the truth.—*Brooks Robinson, Hall of Fame third baseman, on the Senior Professional Baseball Association, 1989.*

4252 You don't need a trainer down here. You need a paramedic.—*Clete Boyer, manager of the Senior League Bradenton Explorers, 1990.*

4253 I said I could pitch as good as most of these fellows, and I can. But I'll be dog-goned if I'm ever going to try this stunt again. Talking's my game now, and I'm just glad that the muscle I pulled wasn't in my throat. —*Dizzy Dean, St. Louis Browns broadcaster, on coming out of retirement to pitch one game against the White Sox, September 28, 1947. Dean pitched four shutout innings but left the game with a pulled leg muscle. Dean had retired back in 1941.*

4254 My off-season conditioning is probably the worst in the world. When baseball's over, I don't do anything except go out and drink beer with the boys.—*David Wells, Orioles pitcher, 1996.*

4255 Ballplayers usually announce personal goals when they report to camp. Wells' goal is not to get stuck in the team Jacuzzi. Mitchell's goal is not to require a fan belt from a Greyhound bus to hold up his pants.—*Scott Ostler, sportswriter, on the girth of Yankees pitcher David Wells and Indians outfielder Kevin Mitchell, 1997.*

4256 I'm running on retreads. There are no fresh tires on my body. I'm that foam plug that you buy at the local auto store just to get to the next station.—*Andy Van Slyke, 36-year-old former outfielder, on trying to make the Cardinals in spring training, 1997. Van Slyke came close, but injuries kept him from completing the comeback.*

4257 This isn't a body. It's a cruel family joke.

—Curt Schilling, Phillies pitcher, on his physique, 1997.

4258 I kind of like having them in here. It makes me feel a lot better about my body.—*Curtis Leskanic, Brewers pitcher, on coaches moving their lockers into the same room with the players, April 2003.*

4259 You know what jogging has done for America? Now, when a jogger drops dead on the road, he's in shape. And when the guy at the wake says, "He sure looks good," his widow says, "He oughta. He ran three miles every morning."—*Tommy Lasorda, Dodgers manager, 1986.*

4260 I ran 2 ½ miles every day, and I gained two pounds. My stomach got smaller, but my butt got bigger.—*Mickey Rivers, Rangers outfielder, 1981.*

4261 I don't need a chest protector, I need a bra.—*Gus Triandos, former Orioles catcher, at an old-timers' game, 1979.*

4262 I definitely know one thing about Ernie Banks and his "Let's play two" thing—Ernie Banks ain't never strapped on catcher's gear.—*Gregg Zaun, Blue Jays catcher, on catching all 18 innings of a game against the Angels, August 8, 2005.*

4263 I could feel my love handles jiggling as I ran in from the bullpen.—*Kent Mercker, 40-year-old Reds reliever, on how it felt to return to action for the first time in two seasons, 2008.*

4264 I need cortisone for both knees. I take butazolidin, endizine and muscle relaxer. If I were a race horse, I would be disqualified.—*Johnny Bench, Reds catcher, 1981.*

4265 I was thinking about making a comeback—until I pulled a muscle vacuuming.—*Johnny Bench, Hall of Fame catcher, 1990.*

4266 My workout was running down fly balls, stealing a base, or running for my life on the football field.—*Bo Jackson, two-sport star.*

4267 Back before I injured my hip, I thought going to the gym was for wimps.—*Bo Jackson, White Sox DH.*

4268 Because I want to have my arm in good shape, I need to have my legs in good shape. Without a leg, there is no arm.—*Pedro Martinez, New York Mets pitcher, 2006.*

4269 If the human body recognized agony and frustration, people would never run marathons, have babies or play baseball.—*Carlton Fisk, White Sox catcher, 1990.*

4270 I've buried people in better shape than I'm in.—*Richie Hebner, Detroit Tigers third baseman, after a two-mile run during spring training, March 1980. Hebner worked in the off-season as a gravedigger at his father's cemetery.*

4271 Every spring is like an instant replay. I'm sore in the same places I was eight years ago.—*Lee May, Orioles DH, 1979.*

4272 The way to make coaches think you're in shape in the spring is to get a tan.—*Whitey Ford, Yankees pitcher.*

4273 I used to pitch, golf, have fun, rest and pitch again. Now, I pitch, recover, recover, recover, rest and pitch again.—*Don Sutton, Angels pitcher, 1986.*

4274 If it blows out, it blows out. Somebody will be there to fix it. They put Humpty Dumpty back together again, didn't they?—*David Segui, Orioles first baseman, on returning to the lineup after recovering from an injured left wrist, May 2002.*

4275 I think I'd look great in a Speedo right now.—*Reliever Mitch Williams on an attempted comeback with the Phillies, 1996. Wild Thing pitched in Philadelphia's minor league system but was released after compiling a 10.20 ERA in 10 appearances with the Scranton/Wilkes-Barre Red Barons.*

4276 Your body is just like a bar of soap. It gradually wears down from repeated use.—*Dick Allen, White Sox first baseman, 1972.*

Pitching In

4277 Let's face it, pitchers are some kind of freaks.—*Frank Lane, Brewers GM, 1972.*

4278 Pitchers, like poets, are born not made. —*Cy Young, Hall of Fame pitcher.*

4279 I always thought the pitcher was a higher level of primate. Hitting is a reactive process, whereas pitching is an initiative process. We have to do a lot more planning.—*Jim Bouton, former pitcher, 2003.*

4280 It's a hitter's game. They have pitchers because somebody has to go out there and throw the ball to the plate.—*Clay Carroll, Reds pitcher.*

4281 All pitchers are liars and crybabies.—*Yogi Berra, Hall of Fame catcher.*

4282 The only thing dumber than a pitcher is two pitchers.—*Ted Williams, Hall of Fame outfielder.*

4283 I don't think enough of them are good athletes. They can't hit, can't field, can't bunt, can't run. I wouldn't want a job where I played only once every fifth game.—*Pete Rose, Reds third baseman, 1975.*

4284 They're like a tick on a dog; they're worthless for four days, but then they have to suck the blood on that fifth day.—*John Kruk, Phillies first baseman, on starting pitchers, 1994.*

4285 Pitching is not a position. Pitchers are flakes. Every pitcher I've ever met in my life is short upstairs. I think it's a requirement.—*Jay Schroeder, Washington Redskins quarterback and former Blue Jays minor league catcher-outfielder, 1985.*

4286 Pitchers, as a group, are pampered little swine with too much money and no real effect on the game except to drag it out and interrupt the action.—*Hunter S. Thompson, gonzo journalist, on his proposal to replace pitchers with machines, 2000.*

4287 I remember one time going out on the mound to talk with Bob Gibson. He told me to get back behind the batter, that the only thing I knew about pitching was it was hard to hit.—*Tim McCarver, former Cardinals catcher.*

4288 I think pitchers are a better judge of what to throw than catchers. The pitcher's throwing it, ain't he?—*Dizzy Dean, Hall of Fame pitcher.*

4289 When I started to throw the ball back to the pitcher harder than he was throwing to me, we changed positions.—*Bert Blyleven, Twins pitcher, on why he switched from playing catcher.*

4290 To a pitcher, a base hit is the perfect example of negative feedback.—*Steve Hovley, Seattle Pilots outfielder, 1969.*

4291 It helps a pitcher to be exposed to the enemy camp.—*Al Dowling, Dodgers pitcher, on why he preferred to room with position players while traveling on the road.*

4292 The pitcher is happiest with his arm idle. He prefers to dawdle in the present, knowing that as soon as he gets on the mound and starts his windup, he delivers himself to the uncertainty of the future.—*George Plimpton, writer.*

4293 If the double play is a pitcher's best friend, what is a fielder's choice? An acquaintance?—*Tim McCarver, announcer, 2004.*

Pitching Fundamentals

4294 I became a good pitcher when I stopped trying to make them miss the ball and started trying to make them hit it.—*Sandy Koufax, Hall of Fame pitcher.*

4295 Show me a guy who can't pitch inside and I'll show you a loser.—*Sandy Koufax, Hall of Fame pitcher.*

4296 Pitching is the art of instilling fear by making a man flinch.—*Sandy Koufax, Hall of Fame pitcher.*

4297 You're supposed to win when you have all your pitches going for you. You haven't become a good pitcher until you can win when you don't have anything.—*Sandy Koufax, Hall of Fame pitcher.*

4298 You've got to be lucky, but if you have good stuff, it's easier to be lucky.—*Sandy Koufax, Dodgers pitcher, on what it takes to pitch four no-hitters.*

4299 There never is any set way to pitch to a great hitter. If there were, he'd be hitting .220.—*Don Drysdale, Dodgers pitcher.*

4300 A pitcher pitches low instead of high because how often have you seen a 420-foot ground ball?—*Pitcher Jim Bunning.*

4301 Pitch inside more and spread a few rumors about your sanity—or lack of it.—*Al Hrabosky, former Cardinals reliever, on his advice to St. Louis closer Todd Worrell, 1987.*

4302 It helps if the hitter thinks you're a little crazy.—*Nolan Ryan, Hall of Fame pitcher.*

4303 Roy Oswalt is a drop and drive pitcher. What is a drop and drive pitcher? He is a guy who drops and drives. Very simple.—*Tim McCarver, announcer, 2005.*

4304 Carlton does not pitch to the hitter, he pitches through him. The batter hardly exists for Steve. He's playing an elevated game of catch.—*Tim McCarver, Phillies catcher, 1980.*

4305 Randy's pitches are too good to take—and not good enough to hit.—*Bob Skinner, Pirates batting coach, on Padres pitcher Randy Jones, 1976. Jones finished his Cy Young Award season 22–14.*

4306 If you make a mistake on a patient, you don't get another start.—*Doc Medich, Pirates pitcher, on the difference between being a medical intern and a pitcher, 1976.*

4307 That space between the white lines—that's my office. That's where I conduct my business.—*Early Wynn, Hall of Fame pitcher.*

4308 I figured the old arm just had so many throws in it, and there wasn't any use wasting them.—*Cy Young, Hall of Fame pitcher, on why he hardly warmed up before entering a game. (Also attributed to Grover Cleveland Alexander.)*

4309 What do you want me to do? Let those sons of bitches stand up there and think on my time.—*Grover Cleveland Alexander, Phillies pitcher, on why he pitches so fast.*

4310 Gibson pitches as though he's double parked.—*Vin Scully, Dodgers broadcaster, on Cardinals pitcher Bob Gibson, 1972.*

4311 If the game lasts more than two hours, my pitches turn into pumpkins.—*Jim Kaat, Phillies pitcher, on why he pitches quickly, 1976.*

4312 I can remember catcher Jim Hegan reaching over and grabbing a towel to wipe off the plate. I told him there weren't no need of doing anything like that. I gave him this gum wrapper and told him to lay it the long way of home plate. After I split that wrapper a few times with my fast ball, they sort of decided I still had my control.—*Satchel Paige, Hall of Fame pitcher, on his 1948 debut with the Indians at age 42, 1973.*

4313 I wasn't afraid of anybody I'd seen in that batter's box. I'd been around too long for that. I wasn't as fast as I used to be, but I was a better pitcher. If I couldn't overpower them, I'd outcute them.—*Satchel Paige, Indians pitcher, on his major league debut at age 42, July 9, 1948.*

4314 Just take the ball and throw it where you want to. Throw strikes. Home plate don't move.—*Satchel Paige, former pitcher, 1965.*

4315 I throw the ball right down the middle. The high ball hitters swing over it and the low ball hitters swing under it.—*Saul Rogovin, Phillies pitcher, 1956.*

4316 You would be amazed how many important outs you can get by working the count down to where the hitter is sure you're going to throw to his weakness and then throw to his power instead.—*Whitey Ford, Yankees pitcher.*

4317 It's no fun throwing fastballs to guys who can't hit them. The real challenge is getting them out on stuff they can hit.—*Sam McDowell, Indians pitcher.*

4318 If it was, more pitchers would be soaking their heads instead of their arms.—*Jim Lonborg, 1967 Cy Young winner, when asked if pitching was more mental than physical.*

4319 A pitcher needs two pitches—one they're looking for and one to cross 'em up. —*Warren Spahn, Boston Braves pitcher. Spahn won 363 games—sixth all-time and first among left-handers.*

4320 Mike always thinks two pitches ahead. When they make an out on one of his "set-up" pitches, he looks like they've spoiled his fun.—*Elrod Hendricks, Orioles catcher, on pitcher Mike Cuellar. Following a trade from Houston after the 1968 season, Cuellar won 20 or more games in his first three seasons in Baltimore.*

4321 Hitting is timing. Pitching is upsetting timing.—*Warren Spahn, Boston Braves pitcher.*

4322 A pitcher's speed is worth nothing if he cannot put the ball where he wants to. To me, control is the first requirement of good pitching.—*Christy Mathewson, New York Giants pitcher.*

4323 I exploit the greed of all hitters.—*Lew Burdette, Milwaukee Braves pitcher.*

4324 Pitching is simple—cheese for the kitchen and a yakker for the kudo.—*Dennis Eckersley, Red Sox pitcher, 1978.*

4325 I always thought the pitcher had the advantage. It's like serving in tennis.—*Allie Reynolds, Yankees pitcher.*

4326 The first commandment is observation. Look around, notice the little quirks in the batter, and notice your own quirks. Your doctor never stops learning. The great pitcher imitates him.—*Herb Pennock, Yankees pitcher.*

4327 Pitching is really just an internal struggle between the pitcher and his stuff. If my curve ball is breaking and I'm throwing it where I want, then the batter is irrevelant.—*Steve Stone, Orioles pitcher, 1980.*

4328 If you can get the ball over with something on it, there's no call to be smart and try to get it to certain parts of the plate. That plate's only a few inches wide, and the ball park is as big as all get out.—*Dizzy Dean, Hall of Fame pitcher.*

4329 A pitcher has to look at the hitter as his mortal enemy.—*Early Wynn, White Sox pitcher.*

4330 I was never nervous when I had the ball, but when I let it go I was scared to death. —*Lefty Gomez, former Yankees pitcher, 1961.*

4331 I'm still excited to pitch, but I'm able to get those butterflies flying in formation.—*Chad Durbin, Royals pitcher, on his second year in the majors, 2001.*

4332 The best pitchers have the worst moves to first base, probably because they let so few runners get there.—*Tommy Harper, Red Sox outfielder, 1973.*

4333 You can't hit what you can't see.—*Walter Johnson, Hall of Fame pitcher.*

4334 Go on up there and hit what you see. If you can't see it, come on back.—*Bucky Harris, Washington Senators manager, to his players whenever they faced Indians pitcher Bob Feller.*

4335 Strikeouts are boring. Besides that, they're fascist. Throw some ground balls, it's more democratic.—*Kevin Costner (as Crash Davis) to pitcher Nuke LaLoosh (played by Tim Robbins) in Ron Shelton's* Bull Durham, *1988.*

4336 My only day off is the day I pitch.—*Roger Clemens, seven-time Cy Young winner.*

4337 Nothing makes a pitcher feel more secure than the sight of his teammates circling the bases during a ball game.—*Jim Brosnan, Reds pitcher.*

The Pitching Repertoire

4338 I never threw an illegal pitch. The trouble is, once in a while I toss in one that ain't been seen by this generation.—*Satchel Paige, Hall of Fame pitcher, 1982. Paige gave names to his distinctive pitches including the "two-hump blooper," a moving changeup; "Long Tom," a hard fastball; and his renowned "hesitation pitch" in which he stopped in mid-delivery.*

4339 It's called a nudist ball; it's got nothing on it.—*Phil Hennigan, Indians pitcher, on his new pitch, 1973.*

4340 He throws a "radio ball," a pitch you hear, but you don't see.—*Gene Mauch, Phillies manager, on Dodgers pitcher Sandy Koufax.*

4341 I used to throw a loan pitch. I kept loaning it to the hitters, and they never returned it.—*Bert Blyleven, Angels pitcher, 1990.*

4342 It was either going to be Nanu Nanu or the Vulcan. Spock just seemed like a cooler character than Mork.—*Joe Nelson, Rays reliever, on why he calls his split-finger pitch the Vulcan Changeup, May 2009.*

4343 I have a curveball that sometimes acts like a slider, sometimes acts like a curve, and sometimes acts like a batting-practice fastball.—*Brett Tomko, Reds pitcher, 1997.*

4344 I think I'll call it the "flu ball." You see, I mask its delivery. And if a batter ever gets hit with it, he'll go to the hospital.—*Spider Baum, San Francisco Seals pitcher, on his latest creation, 1919. Baum shares the record with nine 20-win seasons in the minor leagues.*

4345 I was throwing between starts in Baltimore, and I found my curveball. I looked under the bench, and it was just sitting there ... I once found my fastball in Cleveland. It was in the lost-and-found. Last year, I lost my mechanics in Toronto. There are parts of me all over the league.—*Bert Blyleven, Twins pitcher, 1986.*

4346 I can't throw one, so I bought one.—*Curt Schilling, Phillies pitcher, on getting a dog named Slider, 1992.*

4347 With that dinky slider, he's so bad he's the only batting practice pitcher who can get people into slumps.—*Charlie Smith, Mets third baseman, on coach Yogi Berra throwing batting practice, July 1965.*

4348 When you have a good screwball, hitters don't like it. As soon as you throw enough of them, hitters start looking at ads for broadcasting school.—*Joe Garagiola, broadcaster.*

4349 It was a cross between a screwball and a changeup—a screwup.—*Bob Patterson, Cubs reliever, on a home run pitch, 1996.*

4350 They called it a Cuban fastball back then until they stopped getting guys from Cuba who threw it. Then they just called it a forkball.—*Gaylord Perry, Hall of Fame pitcher.*

4351 I'll tell you why I started throwing a forkball. The idea came from watching so many of my balls going out of the park.—*Steve Stone, White Sox pitcher, 1978.*

4352 You put that idiot behind a tree that's 60-feet, 6-inches away and I'll womp him with that optical illusion.—*Dizzy Dean, Cardinals pitcher, when told that a scientist considered the curve ball an optical illusion.*

4353 I've been trying to see if it's Brown's grip, due to his loss of two fingers, that gives him that sharp break on his curve. I've decided it isn't. And it's lucky for some of you pitchers that I haven't, because if I thought it was his loss of two fingers that made Brown the pitcher he is, I'd get a hatchet and start working on you guys.—*John McGraw, New York Giants manager, on Cardinals rookie pitcher Mordecai "Three-Finger" Brown, 1903. Brown lost his forefinger and part of his middle finger in a farm accident when he was seven years old.*

4354 If it breaks over the plate, it ain't a curve ball.—*Casey Stengel, Hall of Fame manager.*

4355 That wasn't Uncle Charlie. That was Lord Charles.—*Chipper Jones, Braves outfielder, on teammate Kevin Milwood's curveball, 2002.*

4356 Natural grass is a wonderful thing for little bugs and sinkerball pitchers.—*Dan Quisenberry, Royals reliever.*

4357 The batter still hits a grounder. But in this case the first bounce is 360 feet away.—*Dan Quisenberry, Royals reliever, on what happens when his sinker isn't sinking, 1980.*

4358 If a guy is a good fastball hitter, does that mean I should throw him a bad fastball?—*Larry Andersen, Phillies reliever, 1993.*

4359 My father once told me the harder you throw it, the less time you have to duck.—*Doug Jones, soft-tossing Indians reliever, 1988.*

4360 Ross Grimsley has three speeds—slow, slower and hurry up, already.—*Dale Singer, sportswriter.*

4361 Cleveland left-hander Ross Grimsley beat his own record and had a pitch timed at forty-two miles per hour. His old record was forty-four mph.—*Peter Gammons, sportswriter, 1980.*

4362 I throw steak. He throws salad.—*Dennis Eckersley, Red Sox pitcher, comparing his pitching style with teammate Bill Lee.*

4363 Some night Zahn's going to deliver the ball, and by the time it gets there, he's going to find out the batter has been waived out of the league or traded.—*Bob Lemon, Yankees manager, on Twins pitcher Geoff Zahn.*

4364 Teams can't prepare for me in batting practice. They can't find anyone who throws as slow as I do.—*Dave LaPoint, White Sox pitcher, 1988.*

4365 You could catch him with a pair of pliers.—*Ed Bailey, San Francisco Giants catcher, on soft-tossing reliever Stu Miller.*

4366 Nobody knows how fast I am. The ball doesn't get to the mitt that often.—*Lefty Gomez, Yankees pitcher.*

4367 One day I was pitching against Washington, and the catcher called for a fastball. When it got to the plate, it was so slow that two pigeons were roosting on it. I decided to quit.—*Dizzy Trout, former All-Star pitcher.*

4368 We had him clocked at 92—45 going to Rick Dempsey and 47 coming back.—*Tommy Lasorda, Dodgers manager, on 43-year-old pitcher Don Sutton, 1988. After going 3–6, Sutton suffered an elbow injury and retired with 324 career wins—14th on the career list (tied with Nolan Ryan).*

4369 I think some of the guys over there thought, "Geez, he's throwing a lot of changeups." Those were fastballs.—*Bret Saberhagen, Red Sox pitcher, on his 80-mph fastball, 1998.*

4370 I'm getting by on three pitches now: a curve, a changeup and whatever you want to call that thing that used to be my fastball.—*Frank Tanana, Angels pitcher, 1978.*

4371 I got three pitches: my change, my change off my change, and my change off my change off my change.—*Preacher Roe, Brooklyn Dodgers pitcher.*

4372 When you start to lose it, your fastball and your change-up keep getting closer to one another.—*Scott McGregor, Orioles pitcher.*

4373 Most pitchers fear losing their fastball and, since I don't have one, the only thing I have to fear is fear itself.—*Dan Quisenberry, Royals pitcher, 1985.*

4374 I knew I was in trouble when the guy was clocking me with a sundial.—*Joe Magrane, Cardinals pitcher, 1987.*

4375 There are two theories on hitting the knuckleball. Unfortunately, neither of them work.—*Charlie Lau, White Sox coach, 1982.*

4376 It's like watching Mario Andretti park a car.—*Ralph Kiner, Mets broadcaster, on watching knuckleball pitchers, 1973.*

4377 I'd have a better chance of catching flies with Chinese chopsticks.—*Andy Van Slyke, Pirates outfielder, on hitting the knuckleball, 1992.*

4378 It's not something you can practice. It's like practicing javelin catching.—*Andy Van Slyke, Pirates outfielder, on hitting the knuckleball, 1993.*

4379 The best way to catch a knuckleball is to wait until the ball stops rolling and then pick it up.—*Bob Uecker, broadcaster and former catcher.*

4380 It was great. I got to meet a lot of important people. They all sit behind home plate.—*Bob Uecker, Braves catcher, on handling Phil Niekro's knuckleball in 1967.*

4381 My teammates have nicknamed me "Retriever." All I ever seem to be doing is going back to the screen.—*Bruce Benedict, Braves catcher, on trying to handle Phil Niekro's knuckler, 1981.*

4382 It was like talking to Thomas Edison about light bulbs.—*Tom Candiotti, Indians pitcher, on discussing the knuckleball with teammate Phil Niekro, 1986.*

4383 It actually giggles at you as it goes by.—*Rick Monday, Dodgers outfielder, on the knuckleball of Braves pitcher Phil Niekro, 1983.*

4384 As you recall, the Marlins won, largely because a number of Dodger hitters dozed off while waiting for Charlie Hough's knuckleball to reach home plate.—*Dave Barry, humorist, on the first win for the Florida Marlins franchise, April 5, 1993.*

4385 He can embarrass a hitter on one pitch and embarrass a catcher on the next.—*Ron Tingley, Marlins catcher, on knuckleball pitcher Charlie Hough, 1994. Tingley, who was Hough's personal catcher, got embarrassed once too often and was released in June.*

4386 I hate to see my guys bat against him. They swing three times before the knuckler is halfway to the plate.—*Billy Rigney, Twins manager, on knuckleball pitcher Hoyt Wilhelm, who became the first reliever elected to the Hall of Fame in 1985.*

4387 If you want to know how it feels to catch the knuckleball, ask the backstop, not me.—*Sandy Alomar Jr., Indians catcher, after handling pitcher Tom Candiotti, 1990.*

4388 You feel great about him being out there until he throws the ball.—*Rich Donnelly, Pirates coach, on knuckleball pitcher Tim Wakefield, 1993. As a mid-season call-up, Wakefield went 8–1 for the division-winning Pirates. Despite tossing two complete game victories in the NLCS, Atlanta defeated Pittsburgh in seven games.*

4389 Like some cult religion that barely survives, there has always been at least one but rarely more than five or six devotees throwing the knuckleball in the big leagues.... Not only can't pitchers control it, hitters can't hit it, catchers can't catch it, coaches can't coach it, and most pitchers can't learn it. The perfect pitch.—*Ron Luciano, former AL umpire.*

4390 You don't catch the knuckleball, you defend against it.—*Joe Torre, manager and former catcher.*

4391 I'd rather have my leg cut off than do that all day. You just hope it hits your bat in a good spot.—*John Kruk, lifetime .300 hitter, on facing the knuckleball.*

4392 Throwing a knuckleball for a strike is like throwing a butterfly with hiccups across the street into your neighbor's mailbox.—*Willie Stargell, Hall of Fame first baseman.*

4393 Hitting that thing is like trying to catch a butterfly with a pair of tweezers.—*Catcher Tim McCarver on the knuckleball.*

4394 I never worry about it. I just take my three swings and go sit on the bench. I'm afraid if I ever think about hitting it, I'll mess up my swing for life.—*Dick Allen on facing the knuckleball.*

4395 [A knuckleball is] a curve ball that doesn't give a damn.—*Jimmy Cannon, sportswriter.*

4396 I work for three weeks to get my swing down pat and Phil [Niekro] messes it up in one night.—*Pete Rose, Reds third baseman.*

4397 I'd rather try hitting a hummingbird than a knuckleball.—*Pete Rose, Reds third baseman.*

4398 You don't want a knuckleballer pitching for you. Of course, you don't want one pitching against you either.—*Paul Richards, White Sox manager.*

4399 When he changes balls to the umpire, he throws as hard as I do.—*Steve Sparks, Tigers knuckleball pitcher, on reliever Matt Anderson, whose pitches were clocked at 100 mph, 2001.*

4400 You know, catching the knuckleball, it's like trying to catch a fly with a chopstick.—*Jason Varitek, Red Sox pitcher, on catching Tim Wakefield's knuckler.*

4401 You need the fingers of a safecracker and the mind of a Zen Buddhist to throw it.—*Pitcher Jim Bouton on the knuckleball, 1970.*

4402 I don't put any foreign substances on the baseball. Everything I use comes from the good old U.S.A.—*George Frazier, Yankees reliever. Pitching in middle relief, Frazier tied a World Series record with three losses against Los Angeles, 1981. The only other three-time loser was "Black Sox" pitcher Lefty Williams, who was paid to lose games during the 1919 World Series.*

4403 You're getting warm, but it's not here.—*Note inside the glove of Dodgers pitcher Don Sutton. Umpires frequently checked Sutton for suspected illegal substances.*

4404 Sutton has set such a fine example of defiance that someday I expect to see a pitcher walk out to the mound with a utility belt on—you know, file, chisel, screwdriver, glue. Sutton will throw a ball to the plate with bolts attached to it.—*Ray Miller, Orioles pitching coach, on pitcher Don Sutton.*

4405 He handed me a tube of Vaseline. I thanked him and gave him a sheet of sandpaper.—*Don Sutton, Dodgers pitcher, on an encounter with Padres pitcher Gaylord Perry, 1979.*

4406 Gaylord is a very honorable man. He only calls for the spitter when he needs it.—*Gabe Paul, Indians president, on pitcher Gaylord Perry.*

4407 I once called the president of Vaseline and told him he should use me in a commercial since I used his product all the time. He got a little upset when he found out what I used it for. He said Vaseline is only for babies and fannies.—*Gaylord Perry, Rangers pitcher, 1980.*

4408 He has been approached by every investment firm in San Francisco. After all, he's the man who took a 39-cent jar of Vaseline and made himself a $100,000 pitcher.—*Bob Bolin, former Giants pitcher, on Gaylord Perry.*

4409 It's a hard slider.—*Allison Perry, five-year-old daughter of Giants pitcher Gaylord Perry, when asked if her father threw a grease ball, October 1971.*

4410 I reckon I tried everything on the old apple but salt and pepper and chocolate sauce topping.—*Gaylord Perry, Cleveland Indians pitcher, 1974.*

4411 I'd like to see the spitball legalized. I never threw one, but I used to sweat very easily.—*Lefty Gomez, former Yankees pitcher, 1969.*

4412 Why, Mr. Summers, don't you know that the spitter has been outlawed for years? How would I ever learn to throw one?—*Tommy Bridges, Tigers pitcher, to plate umpire Bill Summers, who accused him of throwing a spitball.*

4413 I don't cheat out there—at least I don't get caught.—*Milt Wilcox, Tigers pitcher.*

4414 My best pitch is the one I do not throw. —*Lew Burdette, Milwaukee Braves pitcher, on his spitball.*

Getting Shelled

4415 You know you're having a bad day when the fifth inning rolls around and they drag the warning track.—*Mike Flanagan, Orioles pitcher, 1992.*

4416 I once scouted a pitcher who was so bad that when he came into a game the ground crew dragged the warning track.—*Ellis Clary, White Sox scout.*

4417 It couldn't have been a perfect pitch. Perfect pitches don't travel that far.—*Casey Stengel, Mets manager, after pitcher Ray Daviault surrendered one of his 14 homers in just 81 innings pitched, 1962.*

4418 Where in the world have you been? I thought you'd never get here.—*Fred Talbot, Seattle Pilots pitcher, as manager Joe Schultz finally came to remove him from a game, 1969.*

4419 So much for a clean slate.—*Walt Terrell, Tigers pitcher, after giving up 10 runs in his first 11 innings with Detroit, 1990.*

4420 Right now I would have to say one through nine.—*Joe Magrane, California pitcher, on which AL hitters he was having the most difficulty with, 1994.*

4421 I'm not a home run pitcher. I'm a singles pitcher.—*Mike Smith, Reds pitcher.*

4422 Say one thing for Phils manager Jim Fregosi, he's got more faith than the Pope.

The current population of the United States is 252,686,000. Only Fregosi would have brought in Wild Thing to protect a one-run lead in the ninth.—*Thomas Boswell, writer, on reliever Mitch Williams giving up a walk-off home run to Joe Carter in Game 6 of the 1993 World Series.*

4423 If I hear anybody try to put the blame on Mitch, I'm going to slap them in the face—unless they're bigger or stronger.—*Larry Andersen, Phillies reliever, on teammate Mitch Williams who concluded a disastrous World Series by surrendering a game-winning home run to Blue Jays outfielder Joe Carter that ended the 1993 Series.*

4424 He wasn't locating the ball at all. He was missing. But he wasn't missing their bats. —*Lou Piniella, Mariners manager, on pitcher Ken Cloude giving up four home runs in three innings, 1998.*

4425 My three brothers taught me how to throw strikes, and thanks to them I gave up 379 home runs in the big leagues.—*Catfish Hunter on being inducted into the Hall of Fame, 1987.*

4426 I always wanted to throw a no-hitter. Then, after the first batter, I worked on the one-hitter. After I faced the second hitter, I wanted to keep it down to a nice two-hit shutout. After the third batter, I wanted to pitch a three-hit, one-run game.—*Red Adams, Dodgers pitching coach. In 1946, his only major league season with the Cubs, Adams was 0–1 with an 8.25 ERA in eight games.*

4427 I've seen guys pitch bad, and I've seen guys pitch in bad luck, but you've done an outstanding job putting it all together.—*Sparky Lyle, Rangers reliever, to Jim Kern on his 3–11 record, 1980.*

4428 I always wanted to be a pilot when I was growing up. I always was fascinated with airplanes. Of course, later, I saw a lot of flights leaving Busch Stadium when I was on the pitching mound.—*Danny Cox, Blue Jays reliever, on his days with St. Louis, 1997.*

4429 When I came in there, I figured, well, the good thing is, at least I'll bring my ERA down. It started at 45.00, so it would be tough to go up—but I found a way.—*Paul Janish, Reds shortstop, on giving up six runs in his second pitching appearance of the 2009 season.*

4430 I see he gives up runs every time he pitches.—*Lou Piniella, Cubs manager, when asked what he sees in reliever Neal Cotts, who had a 7.20 ERA early in 2007.*

4431 They should have had the bases loaded because every time I pitched for them, that's what happened.—*Roger Craig, Giants manager and former Mets pitcher, on throwing out a ceremonial first pitch to commemorate the 25th anniversary of the Mets, 1987.*

4432 Balls I didn't even throw were getting hit.—*Ben Sheets, Brewers pitcher, on a spring training outing in which he gave up 10 runs and 13 hits in just 2 ⅓ innings, 2002. And in a 2010 spring training start with Oakland, Sheets gave up 10 runs without recording an out.*

4433 I tried to throw a sinker, and it was as straight as uncooked pasta.—*David Weathers, Reds reliever, on surrendering a colossal home run to Mets outfielder Xavier Nady, June 2006.*

4434 Go out there and pitch three innings or four hours, whichever comes first.—*Danny Murtaugh, Pirates manager, to Steve Blass, 1967. After finishing second in the Cy Young voting in 1972, Blass came unglued in 1973—he went 3–9 with a 9.85 ERA—and was out of baseball following one start the next season.*

4435 My fastball, my slider, my ERA and my blood pressure.—*Pitcher Rich Gale when asked, "What's up?"*

Control Problems

4436 They want me to throw it over the plate, and I can't pitch that way.—*Rick Ownbey, Mets pitcher, 1982.*

4437 I'm working on a new pitch. It's called a strike.—*Jim Kern, Indians pitcher, 1986.*

4438 Actually, my control wasn't that bad. I was just missing with pitches.—*Harry Parker,*

Mets pitcher, on walking nine batters in one game, 1974.

4439 I think the surgery might have screwed me up. I've never had control like this.—*Turk Wendell, Phillies reliever, on coming back with better control after elbow surgery, 2003.*

4440 A pitcher who walks Babe Ruth throws a party. A pitcher who walks Freddie Patek wants to go home and kick the dog.—*Whitey Herzog, Royals manager, on his light-hitting shortstop.*

4441 After a while I asked if I could pitch from closer in.—*Charlie Hough, White Sox pitcher, on walking five batters in a row, 1992.*

4442 The middle of the plate is where offensive history is written.—*Dan Quisenberry, Royals reliever, 1984.*

4443 Home plate is 17 inches wide. But to Don Drysdale it is divided into three parts—the inside four inches, the middle nine inches and the outside four inches. To him only the middle part belongs to the hitter; the inside and outside part belong to the pitcher.—*Dave Anderson, sportswriter.*

4444 When I got to the mound, catcher Johnny Oates reminded me that the lower mask was his and the upper one was the umpire's.—*Doyle Alexander, Orioles pitcher.*

4445 He's so nearsighted he hardly can see a sign, and even if he does, he's likely to forget it.—*Bill Dickey, Yankees catcher, on why he and pitcher Lefty Gomez never used signs.*

4446 Well, that's one way to pitch out of a bases-loaded jam.—*Tom Trebelhorn, Brewers manager, on pitcher Mark Knudson allowing three runs to score on two wild pitches, 1990.*

4447 If the arms were on the knees instead of the shoulders, you would pitch everybody high. Where the arms are is where the action is.—*Curt Simmons, Phillies pitcher.*

4448 I used more effort winding up than he did in pitching nine innings.—*Burleigh Grimes, Hall of Fame pitcher, on fellow Hall of Famer Grover Cleveland Alexander.*

4449 Fay Vincent was the guest. He threw out the first ball and sat in the third row. My pitches were landing in his beer.—*Pete Harnisch, Astros pitcher, on a shaky opening day start, 1991.*

4450 Rex Barney would be the league's best pitcher if the plate were high and outside.—*Bob Cooke, sportswriter, 1940s. In his six-year career, only once (1948) did Barney strike out more batters than he walked.*

4451 He has the power to throw the ball through a wall, but you couldn't be quite sure which building.—*Casey Stengel, Yankees manager, on Brooklyn Dodgers pitcher Rex Barney.*

4452 Some people throw to spots, some people throw to zones. Renie throws to continents.—*Dan Quisenberry, Royals reliever, on pitcher Renie Martin, 1981.*

4453 Maybe now he'll get a complete game.—*Rich Donnelly, Pirates third base coach, on former pitcher Bob Walk, who joined the Pirates broadcast crew, 1994. In 250 career starts, Walk pitched just 16 complete games.*

4454 He can pitch when he's relaxed, and he'll be happy and relaxed here. If he isn't, we'll kill him.—*John Kruk, Phillies first baseman, on reliever Mark Davis, 1993. The 1989 NL Cy Young winner was released on July 2 after posting a 5.17 ERA.*

4455 I wouldn't admire hitting against Duren because if he ever hit you in the head, you might be in the past tense.—*Casey Stengel, Yankees manager, on reliever Ryne Duren, 1959. Duren combined a blazing fastball with a frightening lack of control.*

4456 Whenever he came into a game, people would stop eating their popcorn.—*Casey Stengel, Yankees manager, on reliever Ryne Duren, who squinted through bottle-thick glasses and once hit the on-deck batter.*

4457 Ryne Duren was a one-pitch pitcher. His one pitch was a wild warm-up.—*Jim Bouton, Yankees pitcher.*

4458 I've never taken batting practice against him, and I never will. I have a family to think of.—*Bob Watson, Astros first baseman, on pitcher*

J.R. Richard, 1979. Richard posted back-to-back 300-strikeout seasons in 1978 and 1979, but a stroke midway through the 1980 season effectively ended his career.

4459 You've got to get him out of there before he kills someone. He's more dangerous than cigarettes.—*Earl Weaver, Orioles manager, on Rangers rookie pitcher Williams hitting three batters in a row, 1986.*

4460 I pitch like my hair's on fire.—*Mitch Williams, Cubs reliever, 1989.*

4461 *Peter Gammons (sportswriter):* What was it like when you two played catch?

Mitch Williams (Phillies reliever): It wasn't catch. It was fetch.—*Wild Thing's brother Bruce was a minor league pitcher with control problems, 1993*

4462 He asked if any of us had a trick pitch and I said, "Yeah, I'll throw a strike once in a while."—*Mitch Williams, Cubs reliever, on being a member of the 1989 NL All-Star Team headed by Dodgers manager Tommy Lasorda.*

4463 Don't worry, Skip. What little hair you got you won't have when I get through with you.—*Reliever Mitch Williams to Cubs manager Don Zimmer after coming to Chicago in a trade for first baseman Rafael Palmeiro, 1989.*

4464 If everyone were like him, I wouldn't play. I'd find a safer way to make a living.—*Andy Van Slyke, Pirates outfielder, on Cubs reliever Mitch Williams, 1989.*

4465 Our concessionaires will love him. No one will leave the park early. But Terry Collins and myself will have to invest in some Maalox and Grecian Formula.—*Bob Watson, Astros GM, on trading pitchers Doug Jones and Jeff Juden to Philadelphia for Mitch Williams, 1993.*

4466 He doesn't have ulcers, but he's one of the biggest carriers there is.—*Jim Fregosi, Phillies manager, on reliever Mitch Williams, 1993.*

4467 But at least I know when he comes in, someone's going to come down to first and I can talk to someone. I just hope the guy who leads off the inning is a nice guy and likes to talk.—*John Kruk, Phillies first baseman, on reliever Mitch Williams, 1993.*

4468 Mitch Williams has walked more people than a seeing-eye dog.—*Frank Luksa, sportswriter.*

4469 *Mitch Williams (Astros reliever, 1994):* You'll go through a lot of cigarettes when I pitch.

Terry Collins (Astros manager): But I don't smoke.

Williams: Well, you'd better start.

4470 If I'm not gonna tame the Wild Thing, I might as well make as many glove saves as I can.—*Eddie Taubensee, Astros catcher, on the possibility of catching Williams with a hockey goalie's glove, 1994.*

4471 If they're thinking about living through the at-bat, it takes their minds off hitting a little bit.—*Mitch Williams, Phillies reliever, 1993.*

4472 The latest manager of the Atlantic City Surf of the independent Atlantic Coast League is—Mitch Williams. [...] Wild Thing took over for Tommy Helms this week, and the last-place Surf lost his debut on, ahem, a wild pitch in the 10th inning.—*Ron Rapoport, sportswriter, July 2002. Wild Thing had been pitching for the Surf before being named manager. Previously, Williams had been managing a bowling alley before returning to baseball. In 2007, Williams began working as a broadcaster.*

4473 He had Whitey Ford's pitches and Edsel Ford's luck.—*Richie Ashburn, former Mets outfielder, on pitcher Ken MacKenzie. Despite a less-than-stellar career, MacKenzie was the only pitcher on the 1962 expansion Mets to post a winning record (5–4).*

4474 I'm the greatest 60-foot pitcher in baseball. If I can conquer those last six inches, I'll be on my way.—*Barry Latman, Angels pitcher, 1964.*

4475 It doesn't matter how many you walk, just so long as they don't score.—*Nolan Ryan, Angels pitcher, 1977.*

4476 Don't get used to it.—*Mitch Williams, Phillies reliever, after tossing a 1–2–3 inning, 1992.*

4477 What's the matter? Didn't the bullpen have any home plates.—*Graig Nettles, Yankees third baseman, to reliever Goose Gossage who entered a game by throwing eight straight balls.*

4478 Actually, my control wasn't that bad. I was just missing with my pitches.—*Harry Parker, Mets pitcher, on walking nine Padres in one game, 1974. Parker finished the season 4–12.*

4479 I've got to keep 'em guessing.... Actually, I keep myself guessing—I don't know where the ball is going.—*Bob Walk, Pirates pitcher, 1991. Walk was a misnomer—he only surrendered 606 bases on balls in 1,666 innings pitched.*

4480 As pitches go, this one was the wildest of the wild. Nomo uncorked one Saturday against the Padres that a catcher could have tracked only on a Global Positioning System.—*Tom FitzGerald, sportswriter, on a wild pitch by Dodgers starter Hideo Nomo that landed halfway up the screen behind home plate, April 2003.*

4481 I'd never been asked to throw an intentional walk in my life. I didn't know how to do it [...]. It's not like something you work on in the bullpen between starts.—*Bobby Bradley, Pirates pitching prospect, on surrendering the game-winning run in an exhibition game on a wild pitch—during an intentional walk, March 2001. Bradley played six minor league seasons but never made it to the majors.*

4482 If this was a walkathon, how much money could we have raised?—*Jim Deshaies, Astros broadcaster, on Houston and Milwaukee combining for 23 walks, May 2000.*

4483 He had good command, though. He didn't hit any cars or anything.—*Ned Colletti, Dodgers GM, on seeing pitcher Chein-Ming Wang throw in a parking lot before signing with the Nationals, 2010.*

4484 Oh, those bases on balls!—*George Stallings, Boston Braves manager, suggesting his epitaph, 1914.*

Beanballs

4485 You know my favorite play in baseball? The bean ball. It's great, isn't it? It's dramatic. Especially if the guy is really hurt. Sometimes the ball hits the helmet, and you feel kind of disappointed even though it makes a good loud noise.—*George Carlin, comedian, 2001.*

4486 Any pitcher who throws at a batter and deliberately tries to hit him is a Communist.—*Alvin Dark, Giants manager.*

4487 None of Martinez's "purpose" pitches target the hitter's legs or hips. He doesn't throw at your ribs or even your shoulder. When Pedro J. sends you a message, it goes right to your head.—*Bruce Keidan, sportswriter, on Expos pitcher Pedro J. Martinez, 1994. Martinez hit 141 batters in his career.*

4488 I hated to play against Drysdale. After he hit you, he'd come around, look at the bruises on your arm and say, "Do you want me to sign it?"—*Mickey Mantle, Hall of Fame outfielder, on Hall of Fame pitcher Don Drysdale.*

4489 The pitcher has to find out if the hitter is timid. And if the hitter is timid, he has to remind the hitter he's timid.—*Don Drysdale, former Dodgers pitcher, on why he threw at batters, 1979.*

4490 If one of our guys went down, I just doubled it. No confusion there. It didn't require a Rhodes Scholar. If two of my teammates went down, four of yours would. I had to protect my guys.—*Don Drysdale, former Dodgers pitcher, on hitting 154 batters in his career.*

4491 The second one makes the hitter know you meant the first one.—*Don Drysdale, Dodgers pitcher, on why he would throw two brushback pitches in a row.*

4492 The easiest pitch to get out of the way of is the one coming right at your head. You see it all the way.—*Don Drysdale, Hall of Fame pitcher.*

4493 The trick against Drysdale is to hit him before he hits you.—*Orlando Cepeda, Giants first baseman, on Dodgers pitcher Don Drysdale.*

4494 Don Drysdale would consider an intentional walk a waste of three pitches. If he wants to put you on base, he can hit you with one pitch.—*Mike Shannon, Cardinals outfielder.*

4495 If you go 3-and-0 on a guy, go ahead and flatten his ass. You're going to walk him anyway. If you're going to do it, do it real good.—*Sal "The Barber" Maglie, former pitcher.*

4496 Freddie Fitzsimmons is my man. He once hit me in the on-deck circle.—*Billy Herman, Red Sox manager, on his choice for the best brush-back pitcher in baseball, 1966.*

4497 Who's going to waste their time hitting me?—*Ozzie Guillen, light-hitting Braves shortstop, on getting hit by a pitch for the first time in eight years, July 1998.*

4498 I never hit anybody on the head intentionally. If a guy got hit on the head it was his own fault. The head is the easiest part of the body to get out of the way. I hit guys in the ribs. The ribs don't move.—*Bob Gibson, Hall of Fame pitcher, 1981.*

4499 After a while you realize he doesn't hit every batter.—*Terry Pendleton, Braves third baseman, on Phillies reliever Mitch Williams, 1993.*

The Pitching Staff

4500 Our pitching staff is a conspiracy of ifs.—*Branch Rickey, Cardinals GM, 1963.*

4501 We can't agree on revenue sharing, interleague play or the DH, but the one thing we finally agree on is that there isn't any pitching.—*Jim Bowden, Reds GM, 1999.*

4502 The Cubs do not have pitchers, they have donors.—*Bernie Lincicome, sportswriter, on Chicago's lowly pitching staff, 1994.*

4503 The secret of success as a pitcher lies in getting a job with the Yankees.—*Waite Hoyt, Yankees pitcher, 1927.*

4504 *Carl Blando (Royals scout):* There are truck drivers who throw 90 miles an hour who can't pitch.

Russ Sehon (Yankees scout): You got the names of those truck drivers?

4505 *Cubs scout:* Charlie, I've landed the greatest young pitcher in the land. He struck out every man who came to bat—27 in a row. Nobody even got a foul until two out in the 9th. The pitcher is right here with me. What shall I do?

Charlie Grimm (Cubs manager): Sign up the guy who got the foul. We're looking for hitters.

4506 He's left-handed and he's breathing.—*Tom Kelly, Twins manager, relating everything he knew about pitcher Keith Garagozzo, whom Minnesota claimed from the Yankees farm system, 1993.*

4507 Curt [Schilling's] gone. Can't bring him back. Move on. Wish him well. He wished us well. What else can you say? I like Brandon Webb. I like Shane Reynolds. I like Elmer Dessens. And whoever we get for that fifth spot, I like him.—*Randy Johnson, Diamondbacks pitcher, 2004. While Schilling and the Red Sox won the World Series, Arizona went 51–111. Johnson had a 16–14 record, but Webb (7–16), Reynolds (0–1), and Dessens (1–6) didn't fare so well. Oh, and that fifth starter? There wasn't much to like from Casey Fossum (4–15), Steve Sparks (3–7) and Edgar Gonzalez (0–9).*

4508 It's like having twin daughters and they're both up for homecoming queen.—*Bob Brenly, Diamondbacks manager, on which of his pitchers he would support for the Cy Young Award—Randy Johnson or Curt Schilling, September 2002. The Big Unit was the unanimous winner while Schilling finished second.*

4509 Give Rick Reed 23 runs, and he's tough to beat.—*Mike Krukow, Giants announcer, on hearing Reed and the Twins defeated Cleveland 23–2, June 4, 2002.*

4510 That poor kid is going to get his first home run ball and it's off Mark Grace. I feel sorry for him.... I didn't have a scouting report on him. Obviously he can hit 65-mph fastballs.—*Mark Grace, Diamondbacks first baseman, on being pressed into service as a pitcher in a blowout loss to the Dodgers and surrendering the first career home run to catcher David Ross, September 2002.*

4511 I don't know, but we're leading the league in third-down conversions.—*Charlie*

Hough, Rangers pitcher, on whether the pitching staff was benefiting from throwing footballs in workouts.

4512 We cannot permit that to ever happen again. I'm going to have all of our present bat boys throw a bullpen session tomorrow, just to see what we have going on here.—*Joe Maddon, Devil Rays manager, on losing to Blue Jays pitcher—and former Rays batboy—Jesse Litsch, 2007.*

4513 The ERA of Twins' starters has surpassed the average interest rate on a 30-year mortgage, a bit of information that doesn't figure to be of much use to Twins pitchers. Commitments for long-term housing are not recommended.—*Dennis Brackin, sportswriter, May 1995. The last-place Twins finished the season with a 5.77 ERA—worst in the AL.*

4514 He should have been better, pitching on 3,195 days rest.—*Steve Blass, Pirates announcer, on Pittsburgh replacement pitcher Jimmy Boudreau, who had last pitched in the minors in 1986, during spring training, 1995.*

4515 Everybody wants pitching. Even our pitching.—*Jim Frey, Cubs GM, 1991. Chicago finished the season 11th (out of 12 teams) in NL ERA.*

4516 We have a lot of pitchers capable of stopping a winning streak.—*Bruce Hurst, Red Sox pitcher, March 1986.*

Predictions

4517 It's tough to make predictions, especially about the future.—*Yankees legend Yogi Berra (also attributed to Danish physicist Niels Bohr).*

4518 Ruth had become simply impossible, and the Boston club could no longer put up with his eccentricities. I think the Yankees are taking a gamble. While Ruth is undoubtedly the greatest hitter the game has ever seen, he is likewise the most selfish and inconsiderate man ever to put on a baseball uniform.—*Harry Frazee, Red Sox owner, on selling Babe Ruth to the Yankees for $100,000 and a $300,000 loan, 1920.*

4519 Ruth made a grave mistake when he gave up pitching. Working once a week, he might have lasted a long time and become a great star.—*Tris Speaker, Indians player-manager, 1921. Ruth went 94–46 with a 2.28 ERA as a pitcher, and then he re-wrote the entire offensive record book as a Yankees outfielder.*

4520 No man who smokes will ever be a big league player.—*Barney Dreyfuss, Pirates owner, on Houston Buffs outfielder Tris Speaker, 1907. Speaker's Texas League contract was purchased for $750 by the Red Sox later that season. After a 22-year career, Speaker was elected to the Hall of Fame in 1937.*

4521 There's no chance of night baseball ever becoming popular in the bigger cities because high-class baseball cannot be played under artificial lights.—*Clark Griffith, Washington Senators owner, 1935. Starting that season, the Reds played seven night games—one against each of the other NL teams.*

4522 I am more convinced than ever that there is no future in electric-lighted play.—*Ed Barrow, Yankees president, 1944. The Cubs were the last team to institute night games in 1988.*

4523 You've bought yourself a cripple.—*Bill Terry, New York Giants manager, to Yankees farm system director George Weiss, who purchased the contract of outfielder Joe DiMaggio from the San Francisco Seals for $25,000, 1935. The previous year, DiMaggio had injured his knee in a non-baseball incident. DiMaggio was named an All-Star every year in his 13 seasons, won three MVP Awards (finishing second twice), and was inducted into the Hall of Fame in 1955.*

4524 This series is already won, but I don't know by which team.—*Dizzy Dean, Cardinals pitcher, before the 1934 St. Louis–Detroit World*

Series. Ol' Diz was right—the Cardinals won in seven games.

4525 If them guys are thinking, they're as good as licked right now.—*Dizzy Dean, Cardinals pitcher, on the Detroit Tigers, 1934.*

4526 Tell them I'll be back, and tell them I'm going to wind up making more money in this game than the three of them put together.—*Ted Williams, 19-year-old outfielder, on being razzed about his assignment to the minor leagues by Red Sox outfielders Doc Cramer, Joe Vosmik and Ben Chapman, 1938. Williams hit .366 with 43 homers in the minors and then came up the big leagues to stay in 1939.*

4527 Who needs New York?—*Warren Giles, NL president, when asked if the relocation of the Giants and Dodgers to California would have any effect on baseball, 1958.*

4528 In the most momentous accident since Columbus set out for India, the Amazin' Mets last night clinched the National League East. The rest will be easy.—*Dick Young, sportswriter, 1969. Young was right—the Mets swept the Braves in the NLCS and upset the Orioles to win their first World Series. Seven years earlier, the expansion Mets recorded the worst single season in the modern era (40–120).*

4529 If everyone contributes what their agents say they'll contribute, we'll have 172 wins and no losses in 162 games.—*Dave Garcia, Indians manager, 1981.*

4530 In 10 years, Ed Kranepool has a chance to be a star. In 10 years, Greg Goossen has a chance to be 30.—*Casey Stengel, Mets manager, on a pair of 20-year-old prospects, 1965. While never a superstar, Kranepool was an All-Star in 1965 and retired in 1979 as the team leader in eight batting categories. Goossen was a backup catcher who retired after the 1970 season.*

4531 I'm 0-for-5 predicting a world championship for this club since I became manager, and that's about the way I used to hit, so I'm through making predictions.—*Sparky Anderson, Reds manager, 1975. Cincinnati won the World Series that year, defeating Boston in seven games.*

4532 Is Brooklyn still in the league?—*Bill Terry, New York Giants first baseman-manager, when asked what he though of Brooklyn's chances to win the pennant, 1934. Although the Dodgers didn't win the pennant, they defeated the Giants in the final two games of the season to allow the Cardinals to overtake the Giants and win the pennant.*

4533 The Giants is dead.—*Charlie Dressen, Brooklyn Dodgers manager, when asked about New York's chances of winning the pennant, August, 1951. The Giants proceeded to erase a 13 ½-game deficit and tie the Dodgers on the last day of the season. The Giants won the three-game playoff, capped by Bobby Thomson's "Shot Heard Round the World."*

4534 I was misquoted, Skip. I picked 'em in six.—*Billy Loes, Brooklyn Dodgers pitcher, explaining to manager Charlie Dressen his quotation in the newspaper predicting that the Yankees would beat the Dodgers in seven games in the 1952 World Series, which they did.*

4535 If I played there they'd name a candy bar after me.—*Reggie Jackson, Oakland A's outfielder, on the prospect of playing in New York, 1973. Four years later he would join the Yankees and fulfill his destiny by winning the World Series his first two years in the Bronx and seeing the creation of the Reggie Bar.*

4536 Anyone who tells himself he can win a pennant with an expansion team is just spitting into a gale.—*Roy Hartsfield, Blue Jays manager, 1978. Toronto finished in last place with a 59–102 record—40 games out of first place.*

4537 The only guys not picking us last are our writers because they know they have to deal with us. They're picking us fifth.—*Tom Pagnozzi, Cardinals catcher, 1991. St. Louis placed second but finished a distant 14 games behind Pittsburgh.*

4538 Boston is going to be tough. If they get out by six or eight games, they will be hard to catch. Our guys have a lot of work to do.—*George Steinbrenner, Yankees owner, on the 1978 season. The Red Sox held a 14-game lead over New York on July 17 before finishing in a first-place tie. The Yankees won the one-game playoff on the strength of a home run by shortstop Bucky Dent.*

4539 If anyone offers you 100-to-1 odds on the Cubs winning the National League East in 1984, take them up on it. If I've ever seen a dead giveaway setup for a miracle, this is it.—*Bill James, baseball analyst, 1984. The Cubs won the division by 6 ½ games over the Mets.*

4540 Every season it's predicted that the Padres are about to go somewhere. And every year it turns out to be the beach.—*Thomas Boswell, writer, 1981.*

4541 There's no tomorrow if we don't win tomorrow.—*Tony Gwynn, Padres outfielder, on losing the first two games of the 1984 NLCS. San Diego rallied to win three straight to defeat the Cubs.*

4542 Right now I'm expecting him to do what he did for the Mets last year, which was very little. If he does that, I won't be disappointed.—*Buzzie Bavasi, Angels GM, on outfielder Ellis Valentine, 1983.*

4543 Everyone was screaming about Denny McLain and Mark Fidrych after a season or two, but they didn't hold up for long. Give Gooden time, a chance to louse up his life. If he shows discipline and doesn't do it, I'll offer him my congratulations.—*Bob Feller, Hall of Fame pitcher, on Mets pitcher Dwight Gooden, 1985. After winning Rookie of the Year in 1984 and the Cy Young in 1985, Gooden underwent drug rehabilitation in 1987. He was suspended for 60 days in 1994 for cocaine use and was banned for the entire 1995 season for another substance abuse infraction. He retired in 2000 with a 194–112 record.*

4544 It might turn from a hobby to a hobble.—*Gene Mauch, Angels manager, on the decision by Royals outfielder Bo Jackson to continue playing pro football as a "hobby," 1987. A football injury in 1991 led to hip-replacement surgery and a baseball-only career. Jackson completed rehabilitation and ultimately won the Comeback Player of the Year Award with the White Sox in 1993.*

4545 Don't ever bet against the Dodgers pitching and Kirk Gibson.—*Roger Craig, Giants manager, before the 1988 postseason. The underdog Dodgers defeated the Mets in the NLCS and then beat the heavily favored Oakland A's in the World Series.*

4546 The man who is the spearhead of the Dodger offense throughout the year, who saved them in the League Championship, will not see any action tonight, for sure.—*Vin Scully, broadcaster, on Dodgers outfielder Kirk Gibson in the eighth inning of Game 1 of the 1988 World Series. Gibson won the game with a walk-off, pinch-hit home run in the ninth off Oakland closer Dennis Eckersley. It was his only at-bat of the Series in the defeat of the heavily favored A's.*

4547 Hey, this isn't over until they beat us tomorrow.—*Cito Gaston, Blue Jays manager, after a loss to the Twins in the 1991 ALCS. As Gaston inadvertently predicted, Minnesota won the next game and went on to defeat the Braves in the World Series.*

4548 We finished last with you, we can finish last without you.—*Branch Rickey, Pirates GM, explaining to outfielder Ralph Kiner why the team was willing to trade him despite Kiner leading the majors in home runs for six straight seasons, 1953. After Kiner was dealt to the Cubs, Pittsburgh went on to finish last again in 1954, 1955 and 1957.*

4549 If I'd done everything I was supposed to, I would be leading the league in home runs, have the highest batting average, have given $1,000 to the cancer fund and have married Marie Osmond.—*Clint Hurdle, Royals utility player, 1978.*

4550 It could be today. It could be tomorrow. Or it could be next Saturday in a softball league.—*Walt Terrell, Tigers pitcher, on when he would make his next start, 1991.*

4551 Do I believe it can happen? Of course. But I also believe in the Easter Bunny, the Tooth Fairy and the presidential prospects of George McGovern.—*Ray Sons, sportswriter, on the odds of an all-Chicago World Series, 1991. That year the White Sox placed second and the Cubs fourth.*

4552 I hate to brag, but at the beginning of the season I predicted the Dodgers would have good luck getting to the World Series. And sure enough, it's a short drive to San Diego. They can be there in two hours.—*Jay Leno, talk show host, on LA's disappointing season, 1998. The Yankees swept the Padres in the World Series.*

4553 One of three things is going to happen to you. You're either going to kill somebody, somebody is going to kill you, or you're going to kill yourself.—*Bob Short, former Rangers owner, to manager Billy Martin. On December 25, 1989, Martin died in a one-car accident when his truck, which was driven by a friend, crashed after both men had been drinking heavily.*

4554 I won't be active in the day-to-day operations of the club at all.—*George Steinbrenner, businessman, on buying the Yankees from CBS, 1973.*

4555 Bob Lemon is going to be our manager all year. You can bet on it. I don't care if we come in last. I swear on my heart he'll be the manager all season.—*George Steinbrenner, Yankees owner, before the 1982 season. Lemon was fired after a 6–8 start. His replacement, Gene Michael, was fired later that season after going 44–42. Clyde King ended the season as manager (29–33), but he was replaced by Billy Martin before the 1983 season.*

4556 Yogi will be the manager the entire season, win or lose.—*George Steinbrenner, Yankees owner, on manager Yogi Berra, February 20, 1985. Berra was fired April 28—after a 6–10 start.*

4557 I knew I was in for a long year when we lined up for the national anthem on opening day and one of my players said, "Every time I hear that song I have a bad game."—*Jim Leyland, Pirates manager, 1986. Pittsburgh finished 44 games out of first place.*

4558 By the end of the century the white baseball will be obsolete.—*Charlie Finley, Oakland A's owner, on his proposed orange baseball, which never gained acceptance.*

4559 Some day all stadiums will have domes, and they'll seat around 2,500. They'll sell the television rights for about $3 million, and seeing the game live will be on a very exclusive basis, like *Queen for a Day*. When will that be? In about 40 years. That's how long it takes for baseball to make a change.—*Bobby Bragan, Houston Colt .45s coach, 1962. By 2002, there were nine domed stadiums and Fox had signed a six-year, $2.5 billion television contract.*

4560 Relax. We've been playing these guys for 80 years. They're never gonna beat us.—*Yankees legend Yogi Berra to outfielder Bernie Williams before the 1999 ALCS against the Red Sox. In 2004 Boston would eventually break the curse.*

4561 The only way we're going to improve is if we actually go out and get better.—*Jason Bay, Pirates outfielder, 2006. Pittsburgh had not finished with a winning record since 1992, a record losing streak that's still going as of 2010.*

4562 There'll be a man on the moon before Gaylord Perry hits a home run.—*Alvin Dark, Giants manager, on his rookie pitcher, 1962. On July 20, 1969—less than one hour after Neil Armstrong walked on the moon—Perry hit his first career homer.*

4563 I'm sorry, but I don't see the Diamondbacks repeating this year. After [Randy] Johnson and Curt Schilling, their pitching is thinner than Gwyneth Paltrow's Oscars dress.—*Jim Armstrong, sportswriter, 2002. Arizona went 98–64 to repeat as Western Division champions (they lost to St. Louis in the NLDS). The Big Unit won his fourth straight Cy Young Award and Schilling finished second.*

4564 When Ken Griffey, Jr., breaks Roger Maris' single-season home run record, he should get three asterisks: one for batting indoors, one for hitting a juiced baseball and one for inheriting superior genes.—*Bernie Lincicome, sportswriter, 1994. Griffey hit 56 homers in 1997 and 1998, but Mark McGwire (70) and Sammy Sosa (66) beat him to Maris' record in 1998.*

4565 I promise you from the bottom of my heart. I won't be in the game that long. I guarantee you that I'm going to be on vacation.—*Barry Bonds, Giants outfielder, 2001. Barry reneged on that promise in 2007, breaking Aaron's career mark of 755 and finishing with 762 home runs.*

4566 There are many things I'm troubled and concerned about, but Belle's Hall of Fame status isn't one of them. In fact, here's a partial list of things that concern me more than Belle getting into the Hall: 1. The Major League Soccer draft. 2. The results of the U.S. Alpine Nationals. 3. Static cling.—*Mike Bianchi, sportswriter, on the retirement of surly slugger Albert Belle, 2001. In his 12-year career, Belle hit .295 with 381 home runs and finished in the top ten of the MVP voting five times. In 2006, he got just 7.7% of the vote, and after just 3.5% the next year, he was removed from the ballot.*

4567 Word out of the Padres' camp is that Tony Gwynn can bend over and tie his shoes. In other words, pencil him for .340.—*Jim Armstrong, sportswriter, March 2001. In what would be his final season, Gwynn hit .324 and finished his career with a .338 average.*

4568 You only need 2,999 more, kid.—*Jerry Remy, Red Sox second baseman, to rookie third baseman Wade Boggs, on getting his first hit, 1982. Boggs picked up No. 3000—a homer—on August 7, 1999.*

4569 When the leaves turn brown, I'll wear the batting crown.—*Dave Parker, Pirates outfielder, July 1978. Parker completed his back-to-back batting titles by hitting .334 en route to winning NL MVP.*

4570 The world will end before there's another .400 hitter. I think that was mentioned in the Bible.—*Lenny Dykstra, Phillies outfielder, 1990.*

Religion

4571 Next to religion, baseball has furnished a greater impact on American life than any other institution.—*President Herbert Hoover.*

4572 Baseball is like church. Many attend, but few understand.—*Wes Westrum, Giants coach, 1962.*

4573 Well, that kind of puts the damper on even a Yankee win.—*Phil Rizzuto, Yankees broadcaster, on hearing that Pope Paul VI had died, August 6, 1978.*

4574 I began to wake up in the morning and say, "Good morning, Lord," instead of "Good Lord, morning."—*Clint Hurdle, Mets catcher-outfielder, on becoming a born-again Christian, 1985.*

4575 Maybe he doesn't want to hurt the ball. —*Mike Littwin, sportswriter, on whether the play of Dodgers outfielder Darryl Strawberry had been affected by becoming a born-again Christian, 1991.*

4576 A religious fanatic is somebody who knows Jesus Christ better than you do.—*Jim Kaat, White Sox pitcher, 1975.*

4577 I don't think God cares that we're not hitting. If he did, then Billy Graham would be hitting .400.—*Chris Sabo, Reds third baseman, when asked if prayer might help the team, 1989.*

4578 Billy Graham is a cracker.—*Outfielder Steve Hovley.*

4579 A man once told me to walk with the Lord. I'd rather walk with the bases loaded.—*Ken Singleton, Orioles DH, 1983.*

4580 *Pat Kelly (Orioles outfielder):* When was the last time you were on your knees?

Earl Weaver (Orioles manager): The last time I sent you up to pinch-hit.

4581 Turn the other cheek? Do you know what I think? I think they must have said that before there were sports.—*Manager Billy Martin.*

4582 When I tell a player to hustle and he says to me that God will take care of his slump, I tell him God may do a lot of things, but he don't know nothing about hitting.—*Whitey Herzog, Cardinals manager.*

4583 It doesn't surprise me that the Mariners want to get God out of their locker room. They've gotten rid of all their other good players, too.—*Steve Largent, Seattle Seahawks wide receiver, on claims by the Mariners front office that players put too much faith in religion.*

4584 God is still my amigo, but he must be someplace else. Maybe he's watching the American League.—*Joaquin Andujar, Cardinals pitcher, on leading the league with 13 losses in July, 1983.*

4585 God is back in the National League. Matter of fact, he is staying at my house. I'll have to have a barbecue for him.—*Joaquin Andujar, Cardinals pitcher, on ending a long losing streak, 1983. He finished the year 6–16.*

4586 We pray this year that from your great Heaven we receive the world championship.—*The Rev. William Kalaidjian in an opening day prayer at Yankee Stadium, 1977. New York won the World Series that season, defeating Los Angeles in six games.*

4587 I feel sorry for Tommy Lasorda. He keeps talking about the Lord and Dodger Blue, but one of these days Tommy's going to meet the Lord and Tommy's mouth will drop open because the Lord will be wearing pinstripes.—*Billy Martin, Yankees manager, 1988.*

4588 I studied to be a priest. I didn't think I'd be a Padre.—*Joe McIlvaine, Padres GM and executive vice president, 1990.*

4589 Aw, I can't make no goddamn speech. —*Charles Barrett, St. Louis Browns scout, at a sports dinner sponsored by the Holy Name Society, an organization created to combat taking of the Lord's name in vain.*

4590 If Jesus were on the field, he'd be pitching inside and breaking up double plays.—*Tim Burke, Expos pitcher.*

4591 If Jesus Christ were to show up with his old baseball glove, some guys wouldn't vote for him. He dropped the cross three times didn't he?—*Dick Young, sportswriter, on why no player will ever gain unanimous election into the Baseball Hall of Fame, 1979.*

4592 If God let you hit a home run your last time up, who struck you out the time before that?—*Sparky Anderson, Tigers manager.*

4593 The Lord helps in many ways, but you have to help yourself on the field. After all, the pitcher may be praying, too.—*Mike Easler, Red Sox DH and ordained Baptist minister, 1986.*

4594 People say it seems like the Lord wants the Cubs to win. Well, I think the Lord has more important things on his mind. But I hope he likes us a little.—*Jim Frey, Cubs manager, 1984. The Cubbies won the Eastern Division and led the NLCS 2–0 before San Diego swept the final three games.*

4595 There are three things in my life which I really love: God, my family and baseball. The only problem—once baseball season starts, I change the order around a bit.—*Al Gallagher, Giants third baseman, 1971.*

4596 If God wanted football to be played in the spring, he would not have invented baseball.—*Sam Rutigliano, former Cleveland Browns football coach, on the creation of the United States Football League.*

4597 He thinks I'm Jewish.—*Gene Oliver, Braves catcher, explaining why he was hitting .415 against Dodgers pitcher Sandy Koufax.*

4598 Why couldn't you be Jewish, too?—*Walter Alston, Dodgers manager, to pitcher Don Drysdale, after taking him out in the third inning of Game 1 of the 1965 World Series. Drysdale allowed seven runs (3 earned) starting in place of Sandy Koufax, who was observing Yom Kippur. Koufax surrendered one run and took the loss in Game 2, then pitched shutouts in Games 4 and 6 with just two days of rest in between.*

4599 I've been a DH all my life: Designated Hebrew.—*Ron Blomberg, Yankees designated hitter, 1973. Blomberg holds the distinction of being the first DH in major league history.*

4600 I'm a David and I'm a star.—*Dave Parker, Pirates outfielder, on why he wears a Star of David pendant, 1977.*

4601 I've been tempted sometimes to say into a microphone that I feel I won tonight because I don't believe in God.—*Jim Bouton, major league pitcher.*

4602 We have very good ratings. Of course, we have a pretty good lead-in audience. Our show is at 12:30. On the same station at noon is the Pope's weekly half-hour program.—*Salvatore Varriale, host of the Italian version of* This Week in Baseball, *1994.*

4603 After the kind of year we had, I've got to touch all the bases.—*Bud Selig, Brewers owner, on an off-season vacation during which he met the Pope in Rome and the Rabbi of Jerusalem in Israel, 1984.*

4604 We're 24 morons and a Mormon.—*John Kruk, Phillies first baseman, on the Phillies and outfielder Dale Murphy.*

4605 You don't have to be a wimp to be a Christian.—*Orel Hershiser, Dodgers pitcher and 1988 NL Cy Young winner.*

4606 Fingers has 35 saves. Rollie has a better record than John the Baptist.—*Lon Simmons, Oakland A's broadcaster.*

4607 A fellow has to have faith in God above and Rollie Fingers in the bullpen.—*Alvin Dark, Oakland A's manager.*

4608 I believe everyone should carry some type of religious artifact on his or her person at all times.—*Bob Costas, broadcaster, on why he carries two Mickey Mantle baseball cards in his wallet, 1984.*

4609 Your Holiness, I'm Joseph Medwick, and I used to be a Cardinal.—*Joe Medwick, former Cardinals outfielder, during a visit to the Vatican to see the Pope.*

4610 You know, the Pope will be coming to New York soon for three days. The first day, he'll say Mass at Shea Stadium. The next two days, he'll be hearing confessions from Darryl Strawberry and Dwight Gooden.—*David Letterman, talk show host, May 1995.*

4611 People are saying it was a great mass. As a matter of fact, afterward the Yankees retired Roman numeral XVI.—*David Letterman, talk show host, on Pope Benedict's appearance at Yankee Stadium, April 20, 2008.*

4612 Don't pray when it rains if you don't pray when the sun shines.—*Satchel Paige, Hall of Fame pitcher, 1974.*

4613 He cussed so awful last year, I finally told him I wasn't going to sit beside him anymore because the Lord was going to strike him dead if he kept talking like that, and I didn't want to be there when it happened.—*Scott McGreggor, Orioles pitcher, on manager Earl Weaver, 1983.*

4614 The Lord knows I have a bad knee and can't run the bases too good, so he blessed my bat and let me hit all those home runs to save my knees. The Lord knows his baseball.—*Jack Clark, Giants outfielder, 1978.*

4615 I knew Alvin Dark was a religious man, but he's worshipping the wrong god—Charles Finley.—*Vida Blue, Oakland A's pitcher, on his manager and owner, 1974.*

4616 Please God, let me hit one. I'll tell everybody you did it.—*Slugger Reggie Jackson.*

4617 For all I know, God may not even like baseball. He may be a football fan.—*Don Sutton, Dodgers pitcher.*

4618 After all, I don't think God really cares about baseball. He's got more important things on his mind.—*Dan Quisenberry, Royals reliever.*

4619 I believe in God, but I'm not too clear on the other details.—*Bill Veeck, White Sox owner.*

4620 I believe in the Church of Baseball. I've tried all the major religions, and most of the minor ones. I've worshiped Buddha, Allah, Brahma, Vishnu, Siva, trees, mushrooms, and Isadora Duncan. I know things. For instance, there are 108 beads in a Catholic rosary and there are 108 stitches in a baseball. When I heard that, I gave Jesus a chance. But it just didn't work out between us. The Lord laid too much guilt on me. I prefer metaphysics to theology.—*Susan Sarandon (as Annie Savoy) in Ron Shelton's* Bull Durham, *1988.*

4621 I don't do miracles. They're flashy and they upset the natural balance. Oh, maybe I'll do a miracle now and then, just for fun—if it's not too important. The last miracle I did was the 1969 Mets. Before that, I think you have to go back to the Red Sea.—*George Burns (as God) in* Oh God! *(1977).*

4622 God is living in New York, and he's a Mets fan.—*Tom Seaver, Yankees pitcher, 1969. Seaver might have been right, the "Miracle Mets" beat Baltimore in the World Series in five games.*

4623 I guess this is like Holy Week, isn't it.... We had Palm Sunday. It's also Passover. This week is also Easter. You know, between the rescue of our POWs and the Tigers winning a game, this is truly a week of miracles, isn't it.—*Jay Leno, talk show host, 2003. Detroit finished 43–119, an ungodly 47 games behind the Twins.*

4624 There are differences between baseball and religion, no way around it. Religions have at least one god. Baseball only has demigods. Religions know the Truth. Baseball only has statistics. Still, nit-picking aside ... they're about the same. Baseball is religion without the mischief.—*Thomas Boswell, writer, 1982.*

4625 God watches over drunks and third basemen.—*Leo Durocher, manager.*

4626 I believe him because he's a real religious guy. Someone else tells me they have a migraine, I know they are hung over.—*Ozzie Guillen, White Sox manager, on reliever Scott Linebrink, 2008.*

4627 We're dirtbags like 99 percent of the world. Maybe worse, because we are all baseball players.—*Todd Helton, Rockies first baseman, on a news story that said the team was built around a "Christian-based code of conduct," 2006.*

4628 Jesus is the answer.
What is the question?
Who is Matty and Felipe's brother?
—*Bathroom graffiti circa 1960s San Francisco, on the Alou brothers.*

4629 If the Lord were a pitcher, he would pitch like Pedro [Martinez].—*David Segui, Mariners first baseman, 1999.*

4630 *Jewish Red Sox fan:* I know it's Rosh Hashanah, but it's the Yankees and Red Sox, and Pedro Martinez is pitching.

Rabbi: It's not such a problem. That's why God invented VCRs.

Jewish Red Sox fan: You mean, I can tape the Rosh Hashanah services?—*As told by sportswriter John Feinstein, 1999.*

4631 The Red Sox are a religion. Every year we re-enact the agony and the temptation in the Garden. Baseball child's play? Hell, up here in Boston it's a passion play.—*George V. Higgins, writer, 1980.*

4632 Can't you see we're having a fucking chapel in here!—*Dwight Evans, Red Sox outfielder, to a reporter who accidentally interrupted a Sunday morning service in the Boston clubhouse.*

4633 I feel like Job. I can't get mad at anybody except the Lord, and if I do that I'm afraid things will get worse.—*Sandy Koufax, Dodgers pitcher, on getting injured in the middle of the season, August 1962. Koufax recovered to win three of the next four Cy Young Awards and the 1963 MVP.*

4634 The wasting of good pitching is a mortal sin, according to the Catholic Church. [...] It's actually the 11th commandment.—*Joe Maddon, Devil Rays manager, May 2006.*

4635 There are days when you know that God invented baseball to give us all a sense of eternity—*Michael Olesker, columnist, 1983.*

Road Trips

4636 On the road when you go downstairs for coffee in your underwear, they throw you out of the kitchen.—*Andy Van Slyke, Pirates outfielder, on the difference between playing at home and on the road.*

4637 Actually, the best thing about playing at home is that you are not on the road.—*Darrell Porter, Cardinals catcher.*

Anaheim

4638 It was like playing a midnight game in the losers bracket of one of those softball tournaments. It's too laid-back for me there.—*Bill Wegman, Brewers pitcher, on a game played before a silent crowd of 20,000 at Anaheim Stadium, 1992.*

4639 It's just too dusty, and it smells. It smells like ... tractor pulls.—*Gary Allenson, Red Sox bullpen coach, on Anaheim Stadium, 1993.*

4640 I got to go to Chicago, Oakland and California ... and California is one of the best cities in the United States.—*Ivan Rodriguez, Rangers rookie catcher, on his first big league road trip, 1991.*

4641 The way they dress here, your head is always in the stands. All those bikinis, your eyes get tired.—*Rod Carew, Angles first baseman, on the difference between playing in California and Minnesota.*

4642 It looks like a miniature golf course on steroids.—*Robin Williams, comedic actor, on the outfield rock formation at Edison Field, 2002.*

Arizona

4643 The primary diversionary feature of Yankee Stadium is Monument Park, a celebration of the team's unmatched baseball history and accomplishments. The primary diversionary feature of Bank One Ballpark is a swimming pool behind the right-center-field fence.—*Bob Ryan, sportswriter, before the Diamondbacks played the Yankees in the 2001 World Series.*

4644 That's our advantage. Teams come here and can't take their eyes off all the breasts.—*Mark Grace, Diamondbacks first baseman, on the distractions at the Bank One Ballpark, 2001.*

4645 A thought about the swimming pool at Bank One Ballpark: Could this be the first time in baseball history that a World Series share goes to a lifeguard?—*Tom FitzGerald, sportswriter, 2001.*

4646 You can drive down the street and, if you didn't know what it was, you'd never guess it was a ballpark. From the air, it looks like a hangar that might have housed the Hindenberg.—*Nick Canepa, sportswriter, on the opening of the Bank One Ballpark in Phoenix, 1998.*

4647 I told them spring training curfew is 1 A.M. I also told them if they could find anything to do in Tucson that would keep them out to 1 in the morning, please let the staff know. —*Bob Brenly, Diamondbacks manager, on his relaxed spring training rules, March 2001. Perhaps this explains how Arizona was able to win the 2001 World Series.*

Arlington

4648 There are Cubs fans.—*Mitch Williams, Cubs reliever, when asked the difference between Chicago fans and Texas Rangers fans, 1989.*

4649 The real legacy of [Arlington Stadium], which gives way to the new Ball Park in Arlington this season: Warm beer, cold nachos and bad baseball. Bring on the bulldozers.—*Bill Sullivan, sportswriter, 1994.*

4650 A guy's got a chance to settle down virtually anywhere on the map, and he picks a place where the 110-degree summer days are used to count down the opening of football training camp.—*John McGrath, sportswriter, on shortstop Alex Rodriguez signing a 10-year, $252-million contract to play for the Texas Rangers, December 2000.*

Atlanta

4651 It's so hot here they give their chickens ice cubes so that they don't lay hard-boiled eggs. —*Tommy Lasorda, Dodgers manager, on Atlanta, 1978.*

4652 It's pitiful, strictly a launching pad.—*Sparky Anderson, Reds manager, on Atlanta–Fulton County Stadium, 1977.*

4653 It's like breathing through mud.—*Chipper Jones, Braves third baseman, on the humid weather in Atlanta, 1996.*

4654 For the fifth time in this decade, we're going to be subjected to Ted and Jane, the moronic Tomahawk Chop, protests from American Indian groups, and the virtues of Tom Glavine and John Smoltz.—*Dan Shaughnessy, sportswriter, on the World Series returning to Atlanta, October 1999. Despite winning their* *division 14 consecutive years (1991–2005, minus the 1994 strike-cancelled season) and claiming the pennant five times, Atlanta won the World Series just once in 1995.*

Baltimore

4655 The trouble with Baltimore is it's in Baltimore.—*Reggie Jackson, Angels outfielder, who played the 1976 season with the Orioles.*

4656 Baltimore is a very exciting town—for excitement just before the game I went down the street and watched a hubcap rust.—*Norm Cash, broadcaster and former Tigers first baseman, 1976.*

4657 The weather is like the team. Gray. Colorless. Drab. The climate would have to improve to be classified as merely lousy. It would be a great place to stage "Hamlet" but not baseball games. It doesn't really rain, it just kind of leaks. You get a picture of Baltimore as a guy just standing on a corner with no place to go and rain dropping off his hat. Baltimore's a great place if you're a crab.—*Jim Murray, Los Angeles sportswriter.*

4658 Baltimore's such a lousy town, Francis Scott Key went out on a boat to write "The Star Spangled Banner."—*Billy Martin, Yankees manager.*

4659 If you find a girl with a full set of teeth, you have to marry her.—*Mark Smith, Hagerstown Suns (Orioles Class AA affiliate) outfielder, 1992.*

4660 I tried to call one of my coaches, and they told me I had to dial a "1" first.—*Johnny Oates, Orioles manager, on the expansive new Oriole Park at Camden Yards, 1992.*

4661 I liked our old ballpark better. People would ask if the beer was cold. Today, they say, "Is the Chardonnay chilled yet?"—*Wild Bill Hagy, Orioles fan, on Oriole Park at Camden Yards, 1994. The new park replaced Memorial Stadium in 1992.*

4662 This is like pitching inside a Volkswagen.—*Chuck Finley, Angles pitcher, on Camden Yards, 2002.*

Boston

4663 Fenway Park, in Boston, is a lyric little bandbox of a ball park. Everything is painted green and seems in curiously sharp focus, like the inside of an old-fashioned peeping-type Easter egg.—*John Updike, writer.*

4664 I love it here. Everywhere you look you can feel the walls pulsating like Edgar Allan Poe's Telltale Heart.—*Dan Quisenberry, Royals reliever, on Fenway Park, 1984.*

4665 When I saw the left-field fence, I thought we were going to play softball.—*Joaquin Andujar, Oakland A's pitcher, on Fenway Park, 1986.*

4666 Do they leave it there during games?—*Bill Lee, Red Sox rookie pitcher, on Fenway Park's Green Monster, 1969. The 37-foot-high wall is only 315 feet down the left field line.*

4667 I was always afraid that it would fall down and kill Rico Petrocelli at short.—*Bill Lee, former Red Sox pitcher, on the Green Monster.*

4668 I've never played in a phone booth before.—*Gene Conley, Red Sox pitcher, before his first game at Fenway Park, 1961.*

4669 Pitching in Fenway is like playing baseball in this room. You can't throw sidearm without bruising your knuckles.—*Lefty Gomez, Yankees pitcher, 1938.*

4670 I've hit balls off the end of the bat that go over the light towers in that park. It's ridiculous.—*Jose Canseco, Oakland A's outfielder, on Fenway Park. Canseco signed with Boston as a free agent and hit 52 homers in his two seasons with the Red Sox (1995–1996).*

4671 For a year and a half, I never heard my last name at Fenway Park. I heard, "Now pitching for Boston, Tom Boooooo."—*Tom House, former Red Sox reliever.*

4672 First you have to flunk an IQ test. Second, you have to be able to drink a gallon of beer. If you can drink more than a gallon, they give you a seat in the front row behind the Boston bullpen.—*Joe Sambito, Red Sox reliever, on fans in the Fenway Park bleachers, 1987.*

4673 Boston has two seasons: August and winter.—*Billy Herman, Red Sox manager, 1965.*

4674 When I took this job, everyone in California warned me that it would snow. What they didn't tell me was the snow would stay.—*Mike Port, Red Sox assistant GM, on the weather in New England, 1996.*

4675 It now takes a 36-month payment booklet to get a hot dog and beer at Fenway Park.—*Andy Moss, broadcaster.*

4676 The one thing I wanted most to accomplish in my athletic career was to get a standing ovation at Fenway Park. I got one for being thrown out of the game.—*Brad Ausmus, Tigers catcher, 1999. Ausmus did make the All-Star team that season, which was played at Fenway.*

4677 I could care less if they bomb the town. The people have no manners. They have no respect for anything. They raise their kids to get on people.—*Jeff Russell, Indians reliever, after being traded from Boston, 1994.*

4678 There's no mystique there. They should burn it down.—*Sparky Anderson, Tigers manager, on Fenway Park, 1991.*

Brooklyn

4679 Brooklyn, that borough of churches and bad ballclubs, many of which I had.—*Casey Stengel, former Brooklyn Dodgers outfielder and manager.*

4680 It has always been my ambition to play in New York City. Brooklyn is all right, but if you're not with the Giants, you might as well be in Albany.—*Bill Dahlen, New York Giants shortstop, 1904.*

Canada

4681 Canada is a country whose main exports are hockey players and cold fronts. Our main imports are baseball players and acid rain.—*Pierre Trudeau, Canadian Prime Minister, 1982.*

4682 Well, you see they have polar bears up there and lots of fellows trip over them trying to run the bases, and they're never much good anymore except for hockey and hunting deer.—*Casey Stengel, Hall of Fame manager.*

4683 Sure, I'm proud to be an American.—*Steve Foster, Reds reliever, when asked by a Canadian customs agent if he had anything to declare, 1991.*

4684 They use Monopoly money. Milk comes in a bag. It's a very bizarre place.—*Bob Brenly, Blue Jays catcher, on Canada, 1989.*

4685 I think what keeps them coming back to the ballparks is their mutual affection for ale and for drinking it in the company of tens of thousands of their fellow countrymen.—*Phil Niekro, Yankees pitcher, on Canadian fans, 1985.*

4686 It'll be great not to have to listen to two different national anthems.—*Mitch Webster, outfielder, on being traded to the Cubs after playing six seasons for Toronto and Montreal, 1988.*

Chicago

4687 Noise pollution at Wrigley Field can't be that much of a problem. There's nothing there to cheer about.—*Illinois congressman John F. Dunn, arguing for the installation of lights at Wrigley, which became the last major league ballpark to play only day games until 1988.*

4688 I'd play for half my salary if I could hit in this dump all the time.—*Babe Ruth, Yankees outfielder, on Wrigley Field, which was the scene of Ruth's alleged "called shot" home run in Game 3 of the 1932 World Series. It was Ruth's final World Series homer.*

4689 It looks like they mowed it with a helicopter.—*Dave LaPoint, Giants pitcher, on the high infield grass at Wrigley Field, 1985.*

4690 It's almost like people go there because Wrigley is like an amusement park.—*Tim Raines, White Sox outfielder, on why more people attend Cubs games than White Sox games even though the Sox won more games, 1993.*

4691 They show up wearing ties, their Rolexes and some even bring their cellular phones. —*Jerry Pritkin, Cubs fan, on the yuppie invasion of the Wrigley Field bleachers, 1991.*

4692 It's hard to see the ball in the daytime here.—*Joaquin Andujar, Cardinals pitcher, on playing in Wrigley Field, 1984. Lights were not installed until 1988.*

4693 Putting lights in Wrigley Field is like putting aluminum siding on the Sistine Chapel. —*Roger Simon, sportswriter, 1988.*

4694 The first time I tried it with the lights on, it was pretty much a washout, too.—*David Letterman, talk show host, on the first night game ever played at Wrigley Field, which was called on account of rain, August 8, 1988.*

4695 Wrigley Field—it sort of reminds you of some of the old ballparks.—*Jeff Torborg, broadcaster and former manager, 1995.*

4696 At Wrigley I feel like King Kong. Here, I feel like Donkey Kong.—*Gary Gaetti, Cardinals third baseman, on hitting .421 at Wrigley Field and .215 at Comiskey Park, 1998. Later that season, Gaetti was released by St. Louis and signed by the Cubs.*

4697 The Chicago Cubs are like Rush Street —a lot of singles, but no action.—*Joe Garagiola, broadcaster and former Cubs catcher.*

4698 If I ever die, I want to die in Chicago. —*Minnie Minoso, former White Sox outfielder, 1976.*

4699 Chicago Cub fans are the greatest fans in baseball. They've got to be.—*Herman Franks, Cubs manager, 1978.*

4700 Cubs fans are 90 percent scar tissue.— *George Will, writer.*

4701 I was in Chicago last weekend.... It was so cold it froze your thoughts.—*Rick Monday, Dodgers outfielder, 1977.*

4702 Wrigley Field is a Peter Pan of a ball park. It has never grown up and it has never grown old. Let the world race on—they'll still be playing day baseball in the friendly confines of Wrigley Field, outfielders will still leap up against the vines, and the Cubs ... well, it's the season of hope. This could be the Cubbies' year.—*E.M. Swift, sportswriter.*

4703 There is no off-season in Chicago. It is only when the teams start playing that the fans lose interest.—*Steve Daley, sportswriter.*

4704 I certainly won't miss the booing in Chicago. They even booed my kids at the father-son game last season. Now that was the last straw.—*Bill Melton, Angels third baseman, on being traded from the White Sox, 1975.*

4705 This place was built on a dump. One day, I dug up an old blue-and-white coffee cup out at shortstop. They had to stop the game and come out with a couple of shovels of dirt.—*Luke Appling, former White Sox shortstop, on playing at Comiskey Park, 1988.*

4706 At Yankee Stadium, the fans throw bottles from the outfield. At Comiskey Park, they throw them from the box seats.—*Eddie Einhorn, White Sox owner, 1982.*

4707 Chicago is the best place to play if an athlete doesn't care about winning or losing. You don't have to win to be revered in Chicago, especially if you're a Cub. In New York, you've got the garbage man yelling at you if you didn't get a hit last night.—*Brian McRae, former Cubs outfielder, 2002.*

4708 You are going to take batting practice, and the rats look bigger than a pig out there. You want to take a look? I think the rats out there are lifting weights.—*Ozzie Guillen, White Sox manager, on Wrigley Field, 2008.*

4709 I just hate Wrigley Field. I wish I could do something about it. The Governor of Chicago, please build another one. I don't know why people make such a big deal that I don't like Wrigley Field.—*Ozzie Guillen, White Sox manager, 2009.*

4710 A girls' soccer league in Cleveland has banned cheering. It's being hailed as precedent-setting. Like they haven't done that for years at Comiskey.—*Steve Rosenbloom, sportswriter, 1999.*

4711 The motherfuckers don't even work. That's why they're out at the fuckin' game.

They oughta go out and get a fuckin' job and find out what it's like to go out and earn a fuckin' living. Eighty-five percent of the fuckin' world is working. The other fifteen percent come out here.—*Lee Elia, Cubs manager, during an epic rant about Chicago fans, April 29, 1983.*

Cincinnati

4712 In Cincinnati after two o'clock (A.M.), the only people you see are bartenders, ballplayers and cab drivers.—*Jim Brosnan, Reds reliever, 1962.*

4713 They still haven't finished the freeway outside the stadium ballpark ... it's Kentucky's turn to use the cement mixer.—*Jim Murray, Los Angeles sportswriter, on Riverfront Stadium.*

4714 Cincinnati should be evacuated and marked, "Closed for Repairs."—*Jim Murray, Los Angeles sportswriter.*

4715 The principle sport in Cincinnati is for people to sit on the front porch and watch tar bubble in the street.—*Jim Murray, Los Angeles sportswriter.*

4716 If Cincinnati were human, they'd bury it. It's the only municipal rubble heap this side of occupied Germany. If war came, the Russians would bypass it because they'd think it had already been bombed.—*Jim Murray, Los Angeles sportswriter.*

4717 It's a good thing I stayed in Cincinnati for four years (1953–1957)—it took me that long to learn how to spell it.—*Rocky Bridges, San Jose Bees manager, 1964.*

4718 I'm looking forward to that place coming down. Nothing against Cincinnati—Cincinnati is a great town. But that stadium ... it's just like a big ashtray.—*Jon Lieber, Cubs pitcher, on Cinergy Park (aka Riverfront Stadium), 2003. It was replaced by the Great American Ball Park.*

4719 Maybe we could rename it Pretty Good American Ball Park.—*Paul Daugherty, sportswriter, on the debut of the Great American Ball Park, 2003.*

Cleveland

4720 We are now arriving in Cleveland. Set back your watches forty-two minutes.—*Tim McCarver, Red Sox catcher, 1975.*

4721 The only good thing about playing in Cleveland is you don't have to make road trips there.—*Richie Scheinblum, Angels outfielder, 1973.*

4722 Flying into Cleveland last night, I thought of life in this great American city and decided if you were going to crash on a Cleveland flight, it would be better if it was an inbound flight.—*Jim Bouton, Seattle Pilots pitcher, 1969.*

4723 I'm not sure how much I'll play, but if I have to sit, I'd rather sit in Chicago than Cleveland.—*Jack Brohamer, White Sox second baseman, on being traded from Cleveland, 1976.*

4724 The only difference between Cleveland and the *Titanic* is that the *Titanic* had better restaurants.—*Barney Nagler, sportswriter, 1986.*

4725 Where else is the lake brown and the river a fire hazard?—*Ken Harrelson, announcer, on Cleveland, 1981.*

4726 I went through Cleveland one day, and it was closed.—*Jay Johnstone, Yankees outfielder, 1978.*

4727 I got in a cab and asked the driver to take me to some places of interest. He took me around the block and dropped me off back at the hotel.—*Jim Palmer, Orioles pitcher, on Cleveland, 1984.*

4728 If they had 75,000 fans in Cleveland for the opener, they must have passed out 300,000 free tickets.—*Graig Nettles, Yankees third baseman, 1973.*

4729 In Cleveland, pennant fever usually winds up being just a 48-hour virus.—*Frank Robinson, Indians manager.*

4730 I'm not used to being funny and cracking jokes like everyone else is doing. In Cleveland we took our banquets seriously and saved the jokes for our games.—*Von Hayes, Phillies outfielder, at a sports banquet, 1983.*

4731 There's nothing wrong with the stadium that a case of dynamite wouldn't cure.—*Mike Hargrove, Indians first baseman, on Municipal Stadium.*

4732 Don't tear the spider webs down. That's what's holding the stadium up.—*George Vukovich, Indians outfielder, on Municipal Stadium, 1985.*

4733 It's the worst field in the country. Russia probably has better fields. A mine field would be better.—*Joe Carter, Indians outfielder, on Municipal Stadium.*

4734 How could it have been a perfect game? It was in Cleveland.—*Randy Galloway, sportswriter, on a perfect game by Indians pitcher Len Barker against Toronto, May 15, 1981.*

4735 Cleveland's not the end of the world, but you can see it from there.—*John Lowenstein, former Indians utility player.*

4736 The A's leave after this game for Cleveland. It was by a 13–12 vote they decided to go. —*Lon Simmons, Oakland A's broadcaster.*

4737 This is the best seat in the house. It's the farthest from home plate.—*John Adams, Indians fan, on his seat in the last row of Section 54 in the right field bleachers, 1985.*

4738 I miss innings one through nine, but not Cleveland or Detroit.—*Gene Mauch, former manager, on what he missed most about life in the big leagues.*

4739 I remember the wet, the cold and the stench when the sewers backed up.—*Lary Sorensen, former Indians pitcher, on Cleveland, 1993.*

4740 Cleveland Stadium is not a baseball park. It's a museum. A museum of unnatural history.—*Doug Jones, Indians reliever, 1989.*

4741 I don't know what the fence looks like. I haven't seen it yet, but I heard it's right over the horizon.—*Mike Hargrove, Indians manager, on the renovated center field fence at Cleveland Stadium, which was moved back to 415 feet from home plate and raised to 16 feet high, 1991.*

4742 What's worse than one day off in Cleveland? Two.—*Randy Youngman, sportswriter.*

4743 I'd rather be the number ten pitcher on the Yankees than a starter in Cleveland.—*Ron Davis, Yankees reliever, 1982.*

4744 If I could get a king-sized bed down here, I wouldn't have to pay rent on my apartment.—*Alvaro Espinosa, Indians infielder, on their expansive new home park, Jacobs Field, 1994.*

4745 I think there's a nice symmetry to the relationship between the town and the fans because the team has driven people to drink for 40 years now, and the liquor tax was used to build the new stadium.—*Bud Shaw, sportswriter, on Jacobs Field, 1994.*

4746 It's hard to believe we're in Cleveland. —*Paul Sorrento, Indians first baseman, on the beauty of Jacobs Field, 1994.*

4747 David Wells was warming up for a start here in the postseason, and he heard some things that he hadn't heard before, which is saying something.—*Joe Torre, Yankees manager, on profane fans in Cleveland, 2007.*

4748 I'm not excited to go to Cleveland, but we have to. If I ever saw myself saying I'm excited going to Cleveland, I'd punch myself in the face because I'm lying.—*Ichiro Suzuki, Mariners outfielder, on having to make three trips to Cleveland due to a four-game snowout to start the season, April 2007.*

Colorado

4749 You can play for the three-run homer there a lot. Like every inning.—*Joe Girardi, Yankees catcher and former Rockies backstop, on the thin air at Coors Field, 1996.*

4750 Thanks to interleague play, McGwire, Canseco, Griffey, Buhner and Juan Gonzalez will visit Coors Field this year. NASA officials have been alerted.—*Jayson Stark, sportswriter, 1997.*

4751 They couldn't pay me enough money to play here. It ruins the back of your baseball card.—*Steve Trachsel, Cubs pitcher, on Coors Field, 1999.*

4752 Man, this place is so tough you should get a save with a four-run lead here.—*Jeff Brantley, Reds reliever, on Coors Field, 1996.*

4753 Playing here is like hitting with no gravity. Even I've got power here.—*Mark Grace, Cubs first baseman, on Coors Field, 1999.*

4754 The Rockies may be the first team in history to draw 4 million fans and give up 4 million runs.—*Woody Paige, sportswriter, 1993.*

4755 I don't know how anybody lasts here mentally for 80 days, especially the manager. If you don't have gray hair when you get here, you will when you leave.—*Mike Williams, Pirates reliever, on Coors Field, 1999.*

4756 You don't need an official scorer at Coors Field. You need a certified public accountant.—*Vin Scully, Dodgers announcer.*

Cuba

4757 They'll be observing slightly different rules. In Cuba, no one is ever safe at home.—*Alan Ray, comedy writer, on the Orioles playing a preseason exhibition in Havana against the Cuban national team, 1999. The Orioles won the game in Cuba but later lost an exhibition in Baltimore.*

4758 I think we're tapping into a powerful karmic dynamic—literature, baseball, communism—plus I hear the island distillers make excellent rum.—*Bill "Spaceman" Lee, former pitcher, on a visit to Cuba to help fund a team founded by Ernest Hemingway in the 1950's, September 2000.*

Detroit

4759 It's like a submarine, you can't wait to get out of it.—*Gary Allenson, Red Sox bullpen coach, on Tiger Stadium, 1993.*

4760 Detroit fans don't know anything about baseball. They couldn't tell the difference between baseball players and Japanese aviators.—*Mayo Smith, Tigers manager, 1970.*

4761 If you look in the stands in Arlington, you see some pretty nice scenery. In Detroit all you're likely to see is a fight.—*Jimmy Piersall, announcer, 1979.*

4762 They don't have a father-son game here because the kids would get lost.—*Graig Nettles, Yankees third baseman, on the high infield grass at Tiger Stadium, 1980.*

4763 If your lawn looked like Detroit's infield, you'd be saying, "Honey, I'll get to it tomorrow, I promise."—*Bobby Valentine, Rangers manager, 1990.*

4764 I grew up going to Briggs Stadium in Detroit. It, too, is a nice place to watch a ballgame when you can see it. There are 52,000 seats in Briggs Stadium and 51,000 of them are behind posts. I know; I've sat in all of them. —*Donald Kaul, sportswriter, 1992. Tiger Stadium was originally named Navin Field, after team president Frank Navin, then changed to Briggs Stadium in 1938 by new owner Walter Briggs Sr. It became Tiger Stadium in 1961.*

Florida

4765 Florida is for old people and their parents.—*Harry Dalton, Brewers GM, on why he prefers Arizona as a spring training site.*

4766 A word about Florida. It's as flat as a barber shop quartet after midnight. It's surrounded by salt water and covered by fresh air. It's a great place if you're a mosquito. An old mosquito.—*Jim Murray, Los Angeles sportswriter, 1965.*

4767 People don't visit South Florida in the summer; they evacuate it. Three things stand out about South Florida summers. In no particular order they are the heat, the humidity and the thundershowers.—*Bob Smizik, sportswriter, lamenting the selection of Miami as an expansion city, 1991.*

4768 Miami is a wonderful town, but you can't look around and say these are baseball fans. You even have jai alai fans. Jai alai fans and baseball fans don't even drink in the same places.—*Mario Cuomo, New York Governor, on a bid by Miami for an NL expansion team, 1990. Cuomo lobbied unsuccessfully for Buffalo to receive a franchise.*

4769 There were more bees in this stadium than fans—first buzz this ballpark had in weeks. —*Dave Joseph, sportswriter, after the Marlins had to rope off a section of the stadium due to a swarm of roughly 20,000 bees.*

Houston

4770 Houston is the only city in the country where women wear insect repellent instead of perfume—*Richie Ashburn, Mets outfielder, 1962.*

4771 Some of the bugs there are twin-engine jobs.—*Sandy Koufax, Dodgers pitcher, on Houston, 1961.*

4772 People around America do not consider this a major league town. But if we get the Dome and get a team, then every day in every newspaper the sports section will show us in the major league standings and the same papers will show Dallas still in the Texas League.—*George Kirksey, Houston Colt .45s executive, encouraging Houston to build the world's first domed stadium, the Astrodome, which opened April 9, 1965.*

4773 This is one heck of a place just to be in and watch whatever is going on. If they had a maternity ward and a cemetery, you'd never have to leave!—*Bob Hope, entertainer, on the opening of the Astrodome, 1965.*

4774 Well, you have to expect a few bugs in any new park.—*Warren Giles, NL president, on the blinding sunlight that made catching fly balls in the Astrodome impossible, 1965. When the glass-tiled ceiling was painted, the grass died. AstroTurf was the solution.*

4775 Personally, I like to get rained out once in a while.—*Jim Beauchamp, former Astros outfielder, on the Astrodome, 1966.*

4776 This is a tough yard for a hitter when the air conditioning is blowing in.—*Bob Boone, Phillies catcher, on the Astrodome, 1976.*

4777 How can you hit inside a dome when you grew up listening to your mother tell you not to play ball inside the house.—*Kurt Bevacqua, Padres utility player, on the Astrodome.*

4778 The Houston Astros play in a vast indoor stadium known as the Astrodome, but the problem is they field a half-vast team.—*Kurt Bevacqua, Padres utility player, 1984.*

4779 No one booed an Astro player. No one got into a fight; a fight at the Astrodome would be as shocking as fisticuffs in the College of Cardinals.—*Roger Angell, sportswriter, 1966.*

4780 If Houston and Montreal stay on top, it will be the first time the National League playoffs will take place entirely outside the United States.—*Hank Greenwald, Giants announcer, 1979.*

4781 It reminds me of what I imagine my first ride would be like in a flying saucer.—*Mickey Mantle, Yankees outfielder, on the Astrodome, 1965. Mantle is credited with hitting the first home run in the Dome during an exhibition game on April 9, 1965.*

4782 When Bush and Gorbachev have their summit meeting, they should agree on a missile test—one missile each. We get to test ours wherever in Russia we want. They have to test theirs at the Astrodome.—*Andy Van Slyke, Pirates outfielder, 1990.*

4783 The Houston Astrodome is the biggest hairdryer in the world.—*Joe Pepitone, Astros first baseman, 1970.*

4784 *Astrodome Host:* How would you like to have the Astrodome in Monaco?

Prince Ranier of Monaco: Marvelous. Then we could be the world's only indoor country.

4785 Don't get in a slump here because they don't force you to take extra batting practice—they make you wash the windows.—*Al Spangler, Houston outfielder, on the Astrodome, 1965. One of the original Colt .45's, Spangler was released that year following a prolonged slump.*

4786 Everything you do is under the microscope in New York. Here, it takes a month for half the country to know what's going on.—

Gerry Hunsicker, Astros GM, on the difference between working for the Mets and Astros, 1998.

4787 The Astros' pitchers have come up with a nickname for the place: Ten Run Field.—*Jim Armstrong, sportswriter, on the opening of Enron Field, 2000.*

4788 It's certainly a new twist. What's next—an alligator pit?—*Doug Glanville, Phillies outfielder, on a hill and flag pole in center field at Houston's new home park, Enron Field, 2000.*

4789 They ought to put on the tickets that you have to wear a helmet and bring your glove if you're going to sit there.—*Tim Bogar, Astros shortstop, on Section 106 at Enron Field, which juts out down the left-field line and is just 220 feet from home plate, 2000.*

4790 When the game starts, do the walls move back?—*Andy Ashby, Phillies Pitcher, on Enron Field, 2000.*

4791 This city always smells like meat.—*Jimmy Kimmel, comedian, on Houston, 2004.*

Japan

4792 They're really rude and follow you around everywhere. And some of the questions are bizarre. They ask what kind of teeth you have, as if that has something to do with being a good hitter. And if your ears are a certain size, they think you can run fast.—*Dan Gladden, Yomiuri Giants outfielder, on his first season in Japan, 1994.*

4793 This is the first time I've ever played in the United States. I've played in Montreal, Venezuela, Japan and Alaska.—*Warren Cromartie, Royals first baseman, on returning to the majors after spending eight seasons playing for the Yomiuri Giants in Japan, 1991.*

4794 No good. Everything made in Japan.—*Masanori Murakami, Giants reliever, on why he won't buy any souvenirs in the United States, 1965.*

4795 I went to a steak house one night and the price for a filet—just the filet—was $150. You learn to eat rice over there in a hurry.—*David Cone, Mets pitcher, after playing an exhibition tournament in Japan, 1988.*

4796 It was strange. The only English words I saw were Sony and Mitsubishi.—*Pitcher Bill Gullickson on playing with the Yomiuri Giants, 1988. After a two-year stint in Japan, Gullickson returned to the U.S. in 1990 and led the majors with 20 wins in 1991.*

4797 Guys who play there say it gets awfully lonely. Hell, for the money they're talking, I can buy some friends and take them with me.—*Reggie Jackson, Angels outfielder, on the possibility of playing in Japan, 1989.*

4798 When we went on the road, we ate as a team, so we had to eat the Japanese stuff. All kinds of stuff, moving stuff, live stuff, stinky stuff, ugly stuff. We talked to the interpreter to make sure they had some baked or fried chicken, or else we would have starved.—*Brian Williams, Cubs pitcher, on playing in 1998 for the Fukouka Daiei Hawks, 2000.*

4799 It is our game, our pastime, our opener, our holiday. So why are we exporting it like a crate of oranges? Why must something as sacred as the beginning of baseball season be merrily donated to the world, forcing the inconvenience of a 4 A.M. first pitch—jeez, Cub fans are just getting in then—to enjoy an American birthright?—*Jay Mariotti, sportswriter, on the Mets and Cubs starting the 2000 season in Japan.*

Kansas City

4800 What could be better than a Fourth of July doubleheader in Kansas City? Anything up to and including a kick in the ass.—*Jim Bouton, Yankees pitcher.*

4801 Kansas City has great, enthusiastic fans, except those who call you up and threaten to kill you.—*Buddy Bell, Rangers third baseman, 1979.*

Los Angeles

4802 When you say you're a Padre, people ask when did you become a parent. When you say you're a Cardinal, they tell you to work hard because the next step is Pope. But when you say you're a Dodger, everybody knows you're in the major leagues.—*Tommy Lasorda, Dodgers manager.*

4803 In Los Angeles, 20,000 people would show up at the park accidentally, just to see what the lights were about.—*Buzzie Bavasi, Padres president, 1970.*

4804 I can't think of a worse place to have a birthday.—*Pete Rose, Reds third baseman, on being in Los Angeles, April 14, 1975.*

4805 It's 400 miles of slide area. One minute you're spreading a picnic lunch on a table at the Palisades and the next minute you're treading water in the Pacific. It's a place that has a dry river but 100,000 swimming pools. It's a place where you get 100 days for murder but six months for whipping your dog.—*Jim Murray, Los Angeles sportswriter, showing that he can make fun of his home town too.*

4806 People recognize me wherever I go, where it used to be just New York. I guess people who aren't even baseball fans watch the World Series. I was driving down the freeway in Los Angeles this winter, and a guy pulled up next to me and gave me the finger.—*Graig Nettles, Yankees third baseman.*

4807 They had room at the LA Coliseum for 93,000 people and two outfielders.—*Lindsey Nelson, sportscaster, on the first home stadium of the Dodgers (1958–1961), which featured a 250-foot left field foul line. In 1958, there were 182 home runs hit to left field, three to center, and eight to right.*

4808 I was hoping they would move 200 miles further west.—*Tallulah Bankhead, actress and die-hard New York Giants fan, on the move of the Dodgers from Brooklyn to Los Angeles, 1958. Her beloved Giants also made the move west that year.*

4809 Los Angeles is where people carry radios to ball games so that they can be told what's happening before their eyes.—*Joel Oppenheimer, sportswriter, 1985.*

4810 It's the most laid-back town I've ever played in, and that kind of drags you down.—*Catcher Todd Hundley, on Los Angeles, 2003.*

Mexico

4811 He is only 21, but he played several years in the Mexican League, where you have to be good or they throw tequila bottles, lemons and batteries at you. If they left their guns at home.—*Dimitri Young, Reds outfielder, on pitcher Dennis Reyes, 1998.*

4812 Not a bit; we lose at any altitude.—*Casey Stengel, Mets manager, when asked if playing in the high altitude of Mexico City affected his team in a 6–4 exhibition loss to the Mexico City Red Devils, March 1964.*

Milwaukee

4813 They know when to cheer and they know when to boo. And they know when to drink beer. They do it all the time.—*Gorman Thomas, Brewers outfielder, on the hometown fans, 1980.*

4814 I didn't like playing in Milwaukee. I didn't go out there for a year. I hated to walk the streets or eat the food there. The people don't look right, like they're from London, Jamaica, or another planet. I don't like the town. The only place worse is Cleveland.—*George Scott, first baseman, on his experience in Milwaukee (1972–1976).*

4815 The blankets in July.—*Dave Parker, Angels DH, on what he will miss most about playing in Milwaukee, 1991.*

4816 By the time this series is over, these players will have qualified for the Iditarod.—*Lon Simmons, Oakland A's broadcaster, on playing the opening series of the 1994 season in freezing Wisconsin temperatures.*

Minnesota

4817 I don't think there are good uses for nuclear weapons, but this place might be one.—*Dan Quisenberry, Royals reliever, on the Hubert H. Humphrey Metrodome.*

4818 There's no lead safe in this yard. There's no fail-safe zone. It's condition red all the time.—*Dan Quisenberry, Royals reliever, on the Metrodome, 1982.*

4819 I think this is great. The ball really shoots out of here. Now if we can only learn to hit.—*Calvin Griffith, Twins owner, on the opening of the Metrodome, 1982.*

4820 It's a mockery of baseball. This place should go down as the biggest joke in baseball history.—*Billy Martin, Yankees manager, on the Metrodome, 1982.*

4821 If this is a ballpark, I'm a Chinese aviator.—*Billy Martin, Yankees manager, on the Metrodome.*

4822 This place stinks. It's a shame a great guy like Hubert H. Humphrey had to be named after it.—*Billy Martin, Yankees manager, on the Metrodome, 1985.*

4823 It's a travesty. Hit the ball on the ground and it bounces over your head. Hit it in the air and you can't see it.—*Bobby Cox, Blue Jays manager, on the Metrodome, 1985.*

4824 This is the weirdest place I've ever seen. It's like being inside the Goodyear blimp.—*DeWayne Buice, Angels reliever, on the Metrodome, 1987.*

4825 Ninety-nine percent of the guys in the league with no-trade contracts had it in their contracts they wouldn't play for us. The other one percent were already here.—*Tom Brunansky, Twins outfielder, 1987.*

4826 It was so quiet I heard a guy in the upper deck burp, and then I heard a woman in the left-field stands yell, "Pardon you!"—*Bill Caudill, Mariners pitcher, on the small crowds at the Metrodome, 1982.*

4827 I could hit three or four home runs there. If I hit five or six they ought to condemn the place. If I don't hit any, they ought to condemn me.—*Wally Backman, Twins second baseman, on the Metrodome, 1988. Backman hit just one homer in 1989, his only season in the AL.*

4828 I said Minneapolis and St. Paul didn't like each other, and from what I could see, I didn't blame either of them.—*Jim Murray, Los Angeles sportswriter, on the Twin Cities.*

4829 In '99 we could hear a guy buying a hot dog in the upper deck.—*Doug Mientkiewicz, Twins first baseman, on the increased attendance at the Metrodome, 2002.*

4830 It will be great to see somebody riding a mower instead of a vacuum cleaner.—*Dave St. Peter, Twins president, on having real grass instead of artificial turf in the new Minnesota ballpark, September 2007. After playing in the Metrodome for28 seasons, the Twins moved to Target Field in 2010.*

Montreal

4831 Most people up here speak French. However, they are nice people.—*Byrum Saam, Phillies broadcaster, 1969.*

4832 The place was always cold, and I got the feeling that the fans would have enjoyed baseball more if it had been played with a hockey puck.—*Andre Dawson, former Expos outfielder and 2009 Hall of Fame inductee.*

4833 Montreal was always good to me. I could fall in a gutter at 4 A.M. with a fistful of $50 bills, and I'd wake up with a fistful of $50 bills.—*Bill Lee, former Expos pitcher.*

4834 It looks like the same thing George Scott wore around his waist when he was trying to lose weight.—*Bill Lee, former Expos pitcher, on the retractable orange roof of Olympic Stadium, 1987.*

4835 I didn't have any trouble ordering at restaurants. French toast for breakfast. French onion soup for lunch. French dip for dinner.—*Mickey Cobb, Royals trainer, on visiting Montreal, 1982.*

4836 You know how you usually say, "You can feel the electricity in the air"? Here, they say, "Can you hear the electricity?" This place is brutal.—*Dann Bilardello, Padres catcher, on Olympic Stadium, 1992.*

4837 They discovered *boo* is pronounced the same in French as it is in English.—*Harry Caray, Cubs announcer, on fans in Montreal.*

4838 A total of 5,548 bottled water-sipping, environment-loving, baseball-loathing Quebecois came to the stadium to prove to the world that their beloved club should not move to the Washington area. [...] When will baseball finally get the message? Montreal hates baseball, hates the Expos, couldn't care less if the team leaves and doesn't deserve to have a major league team. Half the time, Montreal even hates being in Canada.—*Thomas Boswell, writer, on the miniscule crowds at Olympic Stadium, September 1999. The Expos were relocated to Washington DC and renamed the Nationals after the 2004 season.*

4839 I want to apologize to the people of Montreal. A lot of people thought we were going to actually blow up Olympic Stadium and were very disappointed when they learned we weren't.—*Phil Alden Robinson, movie director, on a scene in his film* The Sum of All Fears, *2002. Shot in Montreal, Olympic Stadium was a stand-in for a stadium in Baltimore where the Super Bowl takes place. Robinson also directed the baseball classic* Field of Dreams.

4840 The Montreal Expos have announced practices will be closed to the public. They want to simulate a real game atmosphere.—*Alan Ray, comedy writer, before spring training, 2002.*

New York

4841 The first big league game I ever saw was at the Polo Grounds. My father took me. I remember it so well—the green grass and the green stands. It was like seeing Oz.—*Pitcher John Curtis.*

4842 The only thing I found difficult about New York was enjoying a $20 omelette.—*Ron Kittle, White Sox outfielder, 1983. Kittle was traded to the Yankees in 1986.*

4843 I'm from The Bronx, and I have an aversion to New York.—*Alan Meersand, agent, on why so few ballplayers want to play for New York teams, 1991.*

4844 People in New York have black teeth, and their breath smells of beer. And the men are even worse.—*Charlie Kerfeld, Astros reliever, 1986.*

4845 Seeing Yankee fans up close for the first time is like waking up in a Brazilian jail.—*Art Hill, writer, 1988.*

4846 I've been in jail before, and it's more comfortable than being in this place.—*Steve Howe, Yankees reliever, on Yankee Stadium, 1996.*

4847 Hate the city, hate the ball park, hate the Mets. Other than that, it's great.—*Tom Pagnozzi, Cardinals catcher, 1991.*

4848 The Indians who sold that island for 24 bucks made a helluva deal.—*Allie Reynolds, former Yankees pitcher, 1983. Reynolds was one-quarter Creek Indian.*

4849 The only way I like New York is when I'm flying over it.—*George Foster, Reds outfielder. Foster was traded to the Mets in 1982 and released in August of 1986, the year the Mets won the World Series.*

4850 No other city is so confident in its own preeminence that it could afford to take such open delight in its own bad taste.—*Bill Veeck, White Sox owner, on New York City.*

4851 One bedroom in the Bronx. Eleven hundred a month! It's a good thing they've got a good spread in the clubhouse or I wouldn't survive.—*Fernando Vina, Mets rookie infielder, 1994.*

4852 In Cincinnati, I owned a house. Here, I can't find an apartment I can afford.—*Doug Flynn, Mets infielder, 1977.*

4853 Hating the Yankees is as American as pizza pie, unwed mothers and cheating on your income tax.—*Mike Royko, Chicago columnist, 1981.*

4854 The first thing I do is go to my room, bolt the door and then put a chair against it.—*Phil Niekro, Braves pitcher, on visiting New York.*

4855 Yesterday, Mayor Giuliani urged New Yorkers to go to Yankees games at the Stadium. Easy for him to say—he's got body guards.—*David Letterman, talk show host, 1994.*

4856 Whitey [Ford] and I figured out once that each year I hit about fifteen long outs at

Yankee Stadium that would have been home runs in Ebbets Field. In my eighteen years, I would have gotten 270 additional home runs if I'd been a Dodger.—*Mickey Mantle, Yankees outfielder.*

4857 Usually a perfect game at Yankee Stadium is when nobody gets hit by a chunk of concrete.—*David Letterman, talk show host, on two memorable events at Yankee Stadium, 1998. Earlier in the year, a 500-pound concrete beam collapsed. Weeks later, pitcher David Wells threw a perfect game.*

4858 There's no way they could bury 12 people out there.—*Bob Kearney, Seattle catcher, on the 12 monuments behind center field of Yankee Stadium.*

4859 Anyone who insists on being in New York obviously never has been there.—*Steve Rosenbloom, sportswriter, on Japanese pitcher Hideki Irabu, who refused to play for any major league team except the Yankees, 1997.*

4860 When I was a little boy, I wanted to be a baseball player and join the circus. With the Yankees, I've accomplished both.—*Graig Nettles, Yankees third baseman.*

4861 I fit right in with the zoo. The animals here have their own keys to the cages. Everybody here is a story in himself. It really is a zoo with all kinds of different animals.—*John "The Count" Montefusco, Yankees pitcher, 1984.*

4862 I would retire first. It's the most hectic, nerve-racking city. Imagine having to take the 7 Train to the ballpark looking like you're riding through Beirut next to some kid with purple hair, next to some queer with AIDS, right next to some dude who just got out of jail for the fourth time, right next to some 20-year-old mom with four kids. It's depressing.... The biggest thing I don't like about New York are the foreigners. I'm not a very big fan of foreigners. You can walk an entire block in Times Square and not hear anybody speaking English. Asians and Koreans and Vietnamese and Indians and Russians and Spanish people and everything up there. How the hell did they get in this country?—*John Rocker, Braves closer, on if he would ever play for a New York team, 1999. Rocker raised the ire of New Yorkers with some inflammatory statements during the 1999 NLCS, but nothing compared with this statement he made after the season.*

4863 I would never pitch for the Yankees because they represent everything wrong with America.—*Bill Lee, Red Sox pitcher, 1978.*

4864 I could never play in New York. The first time I came into a game there, I got into the bullpen car and they told me to lock the doors.—*Mike Flanagan, Orioles pitcher, 1979.*

4865 The first time I was there was in 1965, and I was scared to go out of my hotel room. Now I'm scared to stay in the room.—*Catfish Hunter, Yankees pitcher, on New York City, 1975.*

4866 It's always a pleasure to be in New York in the winter because that means you're either doing a commercial or winning an award.—*Pete Rose, Reds third baseman, 1975.*

4867 The fans are the worst. The city is the worst. Of course, if you live here long enough I guess it's only natural that you become an asshole.—*Bill Russell, Dodgers shortstop, on New York, 1978.*

4868 This is a town where fans know your mother's name, and they do not like her.—*Steve Lyons, announcer and former utility player, 2000.*

4869 One night earlier this month, the Florida Marlins had a home attendance of only 4,500. At any one time in Yankee Stadium, there are more than that just throwing used flashlight batteries at opposing outfielders.—*Jerry Perisho, comedy writer, April 2002.*

4870 The best solution for the overcrowding in New York would be to combine Nickel Beer Night with a baseball bat promotion at Yankee Stadium.—*Neil J. Liss, announcer, 1985.*

4871 I hate the Mets more than the Communists. At least the Communists don't have off-season problems.—*Bill Murray, comedic actor, 1987.*

4872 All the foreigners are already there, and the Mets are helping out with drug testing.—*Billy Crystal, comedian, on why New York would be an ideal choice to host the 2012 Summer Olympics, 2002. The Games were awarded to London.*

4873 The team itself won't start collapsing until September.—*David Letterman, talk show host, on the crumbling Yankee Stadium, April 20, 1998.*

4874 The stadium will now be imploded. By the way, the team imploded around April.—*David Letterman, talk show host, on Yankee Stadium, 2008.*

4875 Paul McCartney is here tonight. [...] Paul's going to be in town this week doing two shows this weekend out at Citi Field, home of the Mets. The reason he's doing the two shows [...] is that he hopes from those concerts to raise enough money to buy a couple of tickets to go see the Yankees.—*David Letterman, talk show host, 2009.*

4876 They're talking about a bumper sticker in New York that says "Honk if you *haven't* hit a home run at Yankee Stadium."—*Diane Sawyer, talk show host, on the launch pad that is the new Yankee Stadium, 2009.*

4877 The NYU graduation speaker is Secretary of State Hillary Clinton. [...] She told the grads, "Work hard. Save your money. And one day you might be able to afford to attend a Yankees game."—*David Letterman, talk show host, 2009.*

4878 When you're going good, it doesn't get any better than being in New York. But when you're going bad, it doesn't get any worse.—*Davey Johnson, Mets manager. Johnson led New York to a first or second place finish every year from 1984 to 1989, including a World Series victory in 1986. He was fired in 1990 after starting the season 20–22.*

4879 A Subway Series will not save baseball, but it might destroy New York, not a bad consolation prize.—*Jay Mariotti, sportswriter, on the 2000 World Series.*

Oakland

4880 At night that place is a graveyard with lights.—*Whitey Herzog, Cardinals manager, on the Oakland–Alameda County Coliseum.*

4881 You have to pay 50 cents to go from Oakland to San Francisco. Coming to Oakland from San Francisco is free.—*Jim Murray, Los Angeles sportswriter, on the Bay Area toll roads.*

4882 I've always been partial to getting a dead whale and rolling it over the dirt. Really works. Of course, it's smelly, and a lot of people don't like it.—*Dan Quisenberry, Royals reliever, on how to smooth out the infield in Oakland.*

4883 It's nice pitching in an airport.—*Vida Blue, Oakland A's pitcher, on the spacious Oakland–Alameda County Coliseum, 1971.*

4884 You could graze 300 sheep in foul territory of this ballpark, and they would never go hungry.—*Norm Hitzges, broadcaster, on the Oakland–Alameda County Coliseum, 1990.*

4885 Oakland's the luckiest city since Hiroshima.—*Missouri Senator Stuart Symington, on the move of the A's from Kansas City to Oakland, 1967.*

4886 If he wants to move, I'll get him a bus ticket and help him.—*Bob Lurie, Giants owner, on Charlie Finley's proposed move of the A's from Oakland to Washington, D.C., 1977.*

4887 Look how drab this place is. All gray cement. Players call it the Oakland Mausoleum.—*Sal Bando, Oakland A's third baseman, 1973.*

4888 I'll tell you, if Cleveland had our club, we'd draw two million people here. But in Oakland, we get nobody, even though we've won the World Series twice.—*Sal Bando, Oakland A's third baseman, 1974. The A's won a third straight World Series that season.*

Philadelphia

4889 I saw a fan fall out of the upper deck in Philadelphia's Connie Mack Stadium. When he got up and walked away, the crowd booed.—*Bob Uecker, Brewers broadcaster and former Phillies catcher (1966–1967).*

4890 Even if you win a rowing race in Philly, they boo you unless you go over the rapids.—*Bob Uecker, Brewers broadcaster.*

4891 Philly fans are so mean that one Easter Sunday, when the players staged an Easter-egg hunt for their kids, the fans booed the kids who didn't find any eggs.—*Bob Uecker, former Phillies catcher.*

4892 If Ben Franklin played shortstop here and made an error, they'd probably boo him for a week, too.—*Russ Hodges, broadcaster, on Philly fans.*

4893 They had the worst fans in the world. They'd boo a wake.—*Joe Dugan, former Philadelphia A's infielder.*

4894 In Philadelphia, fans even boo Santa Claus.—*Frank Sullivan, Phillies promotional director, 1980.*

4895 Some of those people would boo the crack in the Liberty Bell.—*Pete Rose, Reds third baseman, 1976.*

4896 We do so well on the road because the fans don't boo us so much.—*Sixto Lezcano, Phillies outfielder, 1984.*

4897 You know what they do when the game's rained out? They go to the airport and boo bad landings.—*Bob Uecker, broadcaster, 1975.*

4898 The only thing I know about it is that it's in New Jersey.—*Michael Crouhel, catcher for the Dutch national team, when asked what he knew about Philadelphia, 1992. Crouhel had just signed a minor league contract with the Phillies.*

4899 Philadelphia is the only city in the world where you can experience the thrill of victory and the agony of reading about it the next day.—*Mike Schmidt, Phillies third baseman, 1981.*

4900 They read their sports pages, know their statistics and either root like hell or boo our butts off. I love it. Give me vocal fans—pro and con—over the tourist types who show up in Houston or Montreal and just sit there.—*Mike Schmidt, Phillies third baseman, 1975.*

4901 Kansas City fans don't know how to be mean. They know how to be mean in Philadelphia.—*Larry Bowa, Phillies shortstop, 1980.*

4902 I'll play first, third, left. I'll play anywhere—except Philadelphia.—*Dick Allen, former Phillies All-Star, on being traded to St. Louis, 1970. In 1975, Allen returned to play in Philadelphia.*

4903 Over the weekend, Veterans Stadium in Philadelphia was blown up. Fans cried—when they found out that the Phillies weren't in it.—*Craig Kilborn, talk show host, 2004.*

4904 I did get a standing O in Philly. And not many visiting players can say *that.*—*Paul Janish, Reds shortstop, on coming in to pitch late in a game and surrendering six runs in one inning, including a grand slam to outfielder Jayson Werth, 2009.*

4905 You realized the healing had started when they booed Chipper.—*Larry Bowa, Phillies manager, on Philadelphia fans booing Braves third baseman Chipper Jones for hitting a home run in the first inning of the first game in Veterans Stadium following 9/11, 2001.*

Pittsburgh

4906 [The fans] think they pay our salaries, but what about Pittsburgh? No one goes to the stadium there, and the players still get paid.—*Joaquin Andujar, Oakland A's pitcher, 1987. Even during their three consecutive NLCS appearances (1990–1992), the Pirates had trouble selling out Three Rivers Stadium.*

4907 If they had told me four years ago I was going to Pittsburgh, I'd have said, "Oh, no, c'mon, not there, not Pittsburgh."—*Ken Oberkfel, Pirates infielder, 1989.*

4908 Pittsburgh is such a tough town that even the canaries sing bass there.—*Arthur "Bugs" Baer, columnist.*

4909 He's spent several years in the majors plus several more with the Pirates.—*Don Mattingly, Yankees first baseman, on pitcher Rick Rhoden, 1987.*

4910 Some parks have those games where you guess the number of people in the park. Here, you have to identify them, too.—*Lee Mazzilli, Pirates outfielder, on the small crowds at Three Rivers Stadium, 1984.*

4911 My father's cemetery has more life than this ballpark.—*Richie Hebner, Mets third baseman, on Three Rivers Stadium, 1979.*

4912 The Pirates offered free coffee and hot chocolate after the third inning. You should have seen the fans—hundreds of them—running to the concession stands [...]. Although it's a proven fact people will accept a bag of garbage if it's free, this was about survival. Who wants frostbite at a baseball game?—*Ron Cook, sportswriter, on opening day in Pittsburgh, 2000.*

4913 The place has too many views. Nobody's watching us play. They're all looking at the buildings, looking at the bridge, looking at the river, looking at other parts of the stadium. I don't think anybody here even knows who's on our team.—*Terry Mulholland, Pirates pitcher, on playing in the new PNC Park, 2001.*

4914 Have you ever noticed that sporting events in Pittsburgh are the only time the word *confluence* is ever used?—*Jim Deshaies, Astros announcer, on the location of Three Rivers Stadium at the confluence of the Allegheny, Monongahela and Ohio rivers, 2002.*

St. Louis

4915 Sure holds the heat well.—*Casey Stengel, Hall of Fame manager, on Busch Stadium, 1966.*

4916 It had a bond issue recently and the local papers campaigned for it on a slogan "Progress or Decay," and decay won in a landslide. —*Jim Murray, Los Angeles sportswriter, on St. Louis.*

4917 What? The St. Louis Cards are threatening to move to East St. Louis? [...] The only way anybody goes to East St. Louis is in the trunk of their own car.—*Jerry Greene, sportswriter, on a rumored move, 2002.*

San Diego

4918 The good news is that we may stay in San Diego. The bad news, I guess, is the same thing.—*Buzzi Bavasi, Padres president, on the possibility of moving the club to Washington D.C., 1973.*

4919 Tradition in St. Louis is Stan Musial coming into the clubhouse and making the rounds. Tradition in San Diego is Nate Colbert coming into the clubhouse and trying to sell a used car.—*Bob Shirley, Cardinals pitcher, on being traded to San Diego, 1980.*

4920 Yankees tradition is Robert Merrill belting out the national anthem in full operatic voice. Padres tradition is Roseanne grabbing her crotch after singing the national anthem.—*Steve Campbell, sportswriter, on the two teams competing in the 1998 World Series, which the Yankees swept.*

4921 You've got a lot of beaches in San Diego. Some of them are nude beaches. Why would someone want to watch someone in uniform when they could watch somebody nude?—*Pete Rose, Reds manager, 1988.*

4922 Being booed in New York or St. Louis is not like it is down here. The fans here just go, "Boo, dude!"—*Jack Clark, Padres first baseman, 1990.*

4923 Some of the beach people in San Diego still cheer pop flies.—*Jay Johnstone, Padres outfielder, 1979.*

4924 They use more beach balls during a game in San Diego than baseballs.—*Larry Andersen, Phillies reliever, 1993.*

4925 At least [New York fans] know what a double-switch means. In San Diego, they think it's something you spank twins with.—*Mike Krukow, Giants broadcaster, 1994.*

4926 In this park without charm you'll find a team without talent and management without a conscience. It's a rare trifecta.—*Jon Heyman, sportswriter, on San Diego, 1993.*

4927 I come from San Diego, where if they had a baseball writers' dinner in the middle of winter, it would be in a drive-thru restaurant with 4 ½ people.—*Larry Lucchino, part owner of the Red Sox, 2002.*

4928 It's so ironic to have this happen in San Diego because they're never going to have a rain delay. I don't even know if they have a tarp. But they have a beekeeper on speed dial.—*Jim Deshaies, Astros broadcaster, on a 52-minute delay caused by a swarm of bees, July 2, 2009.*

San Francisco

4929 The coldest winter I ever spent was a summer in San Francisco.—*Mark Twain, humorist.*

4930 It's like playing a game on an aircraft carrier in the North Atlantic.—*Rich Donnelly, Pirates third base coach, on the cold and windy conditions at Candlestick Park, 1992.*

4931 You know it's summertime at Candlestick when the fog rolls in, the wind kicks up and you see the center fielder slicing open a caribou to survive the ninth inning.—*Bob Sarlatte, comedian, 1993.*

4932 Never mind the coffee. Get a priest.—*Joe Garagiola, announcer, during a cold night game at Candlestick Park after being offered a cup of coffee.*

4933 I guess they can make Candlestick Park a dump sight now.—*Brett Butler, Dodgers outfielder, before the Giants abandoned a plan to relocate to St. Petersburg, Florida, 1992.*

4934 The Candlestick wind is not fun. It is evil and cold and turns baseball into slapstick with goose bumps.—*Scott Ostler, sportswriter, 1992.*

4935 Candlestick Park is cold, miserable, uncomfortable and hard to access from the freeway. And that's not even bringing up the bad points.—*Art Spander, sportswriter, 1992.*

4936 Any city that would call an earthquake a fire would call Candlestick a ballpark.—*Jim Murray, Los Angeles sportswriter.*

4937 It has a nice, even climate. It's always winter.—*Jim Murray, Los Angeles sportswriter, on San Francisco.*

4938 San Francisco is not so much a city as a myth. It is in the United States but not of it. It is so civilized, it would starve to death if it didn't get a salad or the right wine. It fancies itself Camelot, but it comes off more like Cleveland. Its legacy to the world is quiche.—*Jim Murray, Los Angeles sportswriter.*

4939 You should get caught doing something bad, like throwing bombs at archdukes, for them to put you there.—*Bob Knepper, former Giants pitcher, on Candlestick Park.*

4940 How come "the greenhouse effect" has warmed the earth everywhere but Candlestick Park?—*Bob Hertzel, sportswriter, 1991.*

4941 There's a good crowd tonight. I was going to say people were strung out all over the place, but people might take that literally.—*Hank Greenwald, Giants broadcaster, 1981.*

4942 I'll be prepared. Our seventh grade trip was to Antarctica. I'll take a Bunsen burner over there. And maybe some powdered food. For lack of a better word, by the end of the game, I'd like to say I breezed through nine innings.—*Joe Magrane, Cardinals pitcher, on his first visit to Candlestick Park.*

4943 The wind, the fog rolling in.... If that's not excitement enough, they ought to just plant land mines arbitrarily in the outfield.—*Joe Magrane, Cardinals pitcher, on Candlestick Park, 1988.*

4944 I'd rather have started at Alcatraz than Candlestick.—*Steve Blass, broadcaster and former Pirates pitcher, 1996.*

4945 Show me somebody who likes to play here, except the Giants, and I'll show you either a moron or a liar. Whoever built this place is an idiot.—*Rob Dibble, Reds reliever, on Candlestick Park, 1990.*

4946 Sitting in the dugout is like sitting in the bottom of a toilet. All that tissue blows in, and no one flushes it.—*Whitey Herzog, Cardinals manager, on the playing conditions at Candlestick Park.*

4947 This wouldn't be such a bad place to play if it wasn't for that wind. I guess that's like saying hell wouldn't be such a bad place if it wasn't so hot.—*Jerry Reuss, Dodgers pitcher, on Candlestick Park.*

4948 I have to think the wind got hold of it. Otherwise, my mind tells me my fielders would have been running towards it instead of away from it.—*Casey Stengel, Mets manager, on a pop fly at Candlestick Park, 1962.*

4949 Every time I leave this place I need therapy.—*Reggie Sanders, Reds outfielder, on the difficulty of playing defense in San Francisco, 1997.*

4950 I knew about the wind. After all, it was my home park. But I wasn't ready for that one gust.—*Stu Miller, Giants pitcher, on being blown off the mound during the 1961 All-Star Game. Miller was called for a balk but eventually won the game for the NL.*

4951 Candlestick was built on the water. It should have been built under it.—*Outfielder Roger Maris.*

4952 The only difference between Candlestick and San Quentin is that at Candlestick they let you go home at night.—*Jim Wohlford, Giants outfielder.*

4953 They've played on grass, and they've played on AstroTurf. They should put down a layer of paper in Candlestick Park, because the Giants always look good on paper.—*Don Rose, broadcaster, 1984.*

4954 This is the worst place I've ever seen. It's summertime everywhere around the United States but here. I wouldn't come to a game here if they were playing a World Series. I'm just glad I don't have to pay to get in.—*Bobby Murcer, Giants outfielder, 1975.*

4955 The Bay Area is the center of devil worship, radical groups and homosexuality in this country. It is a satanic region.—*Gary Lavelle, Giants pitcher, 1979.*

4956 This is the only stadium in the country where home runs land in the water [McCovey Cove] if you don't count Phoenix's swimming pool, Kansas City's waterfall, Detroit's synchronized water fountains or New York's open sewer.—*Alex Kaseberg, comedy writer, on San Francisco's Pac Bell Park, 2000.*

Seattle

4957 In this ball park, I feel that when you walk to the plate you're in scoring position.—*Don Baylor, Yankees DH, on the Seattle Kingdome, 1984.*

4958 This place is so dim it looks like a Gothic cathedral. I guess Gothic cathedrals are good for hitting.—*Dan Quisenberry, Royals reliever, on the Kingdome, 1981.*

4959 It's a comment on the attendance in Seattle that fewer than twenty-eight thousand fans showed up to see Gaylord Perry's three hundredth win, but thirty-six thousand showed up a few days later to get free "funny nose glasses."—*Raymond Mungo, sportswriter.*

4960 I like it better than the Metrodome. Of course, that isn't saying much. It's kind of like saying you like influenza better than beriberi.—*Roger Angell, sportswriter, on the Kingdome, 1988.*

4961 If they'd stop blowing off those fireworks up there in that Kingdome every time [Ken] Griffey hits a home run, maybe the ceiling tiles would stay up.—*Steve August, Red Sox traveling secretary, 1994. Falling ceiling tiles led Kingdome officials to approve a mid-season replacement of all 40,000 tiles, forcing the Mariners on an unexpected month-long road trip.*

4962 Seattle is not a baseball city; it is a coffee stand with computer geeks chattering over scones.—*Rick Telander, sportswriter, 2000.*

Tampa Bay

4963 In July, you can see a dog chasing a cat, and they'll both be walking.—*Chuck LaMar, Devil Rays GM, on the Florida heat and why the team will play its inaugural season at air-conditioned Tropicana Field, 1998.*

4964 Petco also has Picnic Hill, a place for ticket holders to enjoy both a picnic and, should they desire it, a "limited view" of the Padres game. (Tampa's Tropicana Field has a similar location, where fans can, for an additional fee, have no view of the Devil Rays at all.)—*Steve Rushin, sportswriter, June 2004.*

4965 I enjoy coming back here, especially when it's only for three days.—*Joe Kennedy, A's pitcher and former Devil Ray, on returning to Tropicana Field, 2007.*

Toronto

4966 They speak American up there, don't they? It's not like Montreal, is it?—*Tom Underwood, Cardinals pitcher, on being traded to Toronto, 1977.*

4967 This place is great. It's like something out of *2001.*—*Bret Saberhagen, Royals pitcher, on the futuristic Toronto SkyDome, 1989.*

4968 There's just so much inside here. It's like a shopping center.—*Wayne Terwilliger, Twins coach, on SkyDome, 1989.*

4969 You can ask your kid, "Do you want to go to the SkyDome or Europe?"—*Pat Sheridan, Tigers outfielder, on the high prices at Toronto's new ballpark, 1989.*

4970 What do the people in the SkyDome hotel look at during the winter?—*Joe Falls, sportswriter, 1993. The SkyDome complex features 75 rooms overlooking the field.*

4971 I remember walking into Wrigley Field and bursting into tears, it was so lovely. I walk into SkyDome, and what I burst into is laughter.—*Christie Blatchford, columnist, 1991.*

4972 I'm not saying the SkyDome is sterile and plastic, but when you come through the turnstiles, Barbie and Ken tear your ticket.—*Scott Ostler, sportswriter, 1992.*

4973 It's big enough for deer hunting.—*Ellis Clary, Blue Jays scout, on SkyDome, 1989.*

4974 Most of them would heckle the Special Olympics.—*Dennis Lamp, former Blue Jays reliever, on Toronto fans.*

4975 Toronto's just like Detroit or Cleveland or Chicago or all the other American cities. The only difference is that it's cleaner and maybe smells a little better.—*Sparky Anderson, Tigers manager, 1992.*

4976 Yeah, that Toronto is the fajitas capital of the world, all right.—*Jayson Stark, sportswriter, on a comment by Blue Jays pitcher Roger Clemens that he liked Toronto because it was so much like Houston, 1996.*

Washington, D.C.

4977 The only way they'd get me back to Washington is to subpoena me.—*Calvin Griffith, Twins owner, on the move of the Senators to Minnesota, 1971.*

4978 Washington is where you cannot swing a fungo bat without hitting a lawyer, which is a good reason for swinging fungo bats.—*George Will, writer.*

4979 They put a lot of makeup on her, a lot of lipstick on her. She's still an old girl, but an old girl is still a pretty girl if you ask me.—*Mark Grace, Diamondbacks broadcaster, on RFK Stadium.*

Sex: The Other National Pastime

4980 One percent of ballplayers are leaders of men, the other 99 percent are followers of women.—*John McGraw, New York Giants manager.*

4981 *Reporter:* What's the most difficult thing about playing major league baseball?

Mike Hegan (Seattle Pilots catcher, 1969): Explaining to your wife why she needs a penicillin shot for your kidney infection.

4982 All right, you guys, look horny.—*Jim Bouton, Seattle Pilots pitcher, to his teammates upon returning from a long road trip, 1969.*

4983 In general, I find boxers possess more wisdom than baseball players. In baseball, the principle level of conversation is about last night's sexual conquest.—*Howard Cosell, broadcaster.*

4984 I've seldom seen a horny player walk into a bar and not let out exactly what he did for a living.—*Johnny Bench, Reds catcher, 1979.*

4985 If they can produce on the field as well as off, we'll win the pennant.—*Casey Stengel, Mets manager, on outfielders Frank Thomas, Gus Bell and Richie Ashburn, who had combined to father 20 children, 1962.*

4986 Who says this hasn't been a productive season?—*Phil Garner, Brewers manager, on five of his players who became parents during the 1994 season and three others who were expecting in the off-season.*

4987 Back then in the Dominican, nobody had a TV. They had to go to bed at 6 o'clock.—*Josias Manzanillo, Mets pitcher, on how he became one of 18 children, 1993. One brother, Ravello, became a reliever for the Pirates in 1994.*

4988 You know why I get all the women? Because I go in head first.—*Pete Rose, major league All-Star.*

4989 Boys, I had all the ingredients for a great piece of ass last night—plenty of time and a hard-on. All I lacked was a broad.—*Ray Oyler, Seattle Pilots shortstop, 1969.*

4990 Mitch found God in spring training, then every night he tried to find a goddess.—*Lenny Dykstra, Mets outfielder, on former teammate Kevin Mitchell, who was a born-again Christian, 1987.*

4991 The only girl I ever saw him around was his sister.—*Mark Lemke, Braves second baseman, on Pirates outfielder Andy Van Slyke, 1991. Both players grew up in Utica, New York.*

4992 *Wes Westrum (Mets manager, 1965):* Okay, from now on, no more broads in the hotel rooms.

Jack Hamilton (Mets pitcher): You mean it was okay before this? Nobody told me.

4993 The last time I was surrounded by this many beautiful women was when I spent Father's Day at Steve Garvey's house.—*Bob Hope, entertainer and former Indians board member. Garvey admitted to fathering children with several different women.*

4994 I'm much more sexual than my husband. I need a man more than he needs a woman.—*Cyndy Garvey, ex-wife of Dodgers first baseman Steve Garvey, 1980.*

4995 Steve Garvey a womanizer?! St. Steve?! When we called him "Father Garvey," we meant the Roman-collar type, not the paternity-suit type.—*Jim Murray, sportswriter, 1989.*

4996 According to *The Sporting News*, over the last four years, Wade Boggs hit .800 with women in scoring position.—*David Letterman, talk show host, on the Red Sox third baseman who reportedly had a long-term affair with Margo Adams, 1989.*

4997 If I led any cleaner of a life than I do now, I'd be a monk.—*Wade Boggs, Red Sox third baseman, on his life following the discontinuation of his affair with Margo Adams, 1990.*

4998 Why didn't they just do what every other professional athlete who visits New York does —call Madonna?—*David Letterman, talk show host, on Padres outfielder Derek Bell and pitcher Scott Sanders being arrested for solicitation while in town for a series against the Mets, 1994. Even at age 50, Madonna was romantically linked to Yankees third baseman Alex Rodriguez in 2009—although both were married to other people.*

4999 I blame it on expansion, which has thinned the baseball groupie talent pool.—*Scott Ostler, sportswriter, on the Derek Bell–Scott Sanders solicitation arrests, 1994.*

5000 If you were me, would you go around denying rumors like that?—*Harry Caray, Cubs broadcaster, on a rumor that he was fired by the Cardinals in 1969 because of an affair with the young wife of an Anheuser-Busch executive, 1989.*

5001 Say you pick her up at seven o'clock. Well, then grab her where it tickles at 7:05. No go? Tough, but hell it's early yet. There's still time to call another broad. You'd be surprised. Some damned famous broads say okay quick.—*Leo Durocher, Astros manager, 1972.*

5002 A poll revealed that because of the baseball strike, men are having more sex. But the sex doesn't last very long because there's no baseball to think about.—*Conan O'Brien, talk show host, 1994.*

5003 I spent 15 years honing my baseball skills, $110 at the tanning salon and $35 having my hair styled. Then I get benched on National Secretaries Day. There is no justice.—*Bobby Grich, Angels second baseman, 1985.*

5004 Murphy doesn't even wear short sleeve shirts.—*Wayne Minshaw, Braves publicist, on outfielder Dale Murphy, who turned down a request to pose nude for* Playgirl, *1984.*

5005 *Harry Kalas (Phillies broadcaster):* Rich, the game bat must be very important to you.

Richie Ashburn (Phillies broadcaster): Harry, it really is. In fact, when I was playing and going well with a certain bat, I wouldn't trust leaving it around the dugout. I used to take it back to the room and go to bed with it. In fact, I've been to bed with a lot of old bats in my day.

5006 I'd rather hit than have sex.—*Reggie Jackson, Oakland A's outfielder, 1974. Reggie holds the record for striking out 2,597 times ... on the field.*

5007 The mare I bought kept coming up barren, and my wife kept coming up pregnant, so finally I decided I was in the wrong line of work.—*Frank Cashen, Mets GM, on why he gave up horse breeding for baseball.*

5008 Being with a woman all night never hurt no professional ball player. It's staying up all night looking for a woman that does him in.—*Casey Stengel, Yankees manager.*

5009 If I can't get it between seven P.M. and midnight, the hell with it.—*Rogers Hornsby, Cardinals second baseman, on ballplayers seeking female companionship.*

5010 You gotta learn that if you don't get it by midnight, chances are you ain't gonna get it, and if you do, it ain't worth it.—*Casey Stengel, Yankees manager, on looking for love.*

5011 His phallus and his home-run bat were his prize possessions, in that order.—*Fred Lieb, sportswriter, on Yankees slugger Babe Ruth.*

5012 Anybody who doesn't want to fuck can leave now.—*Babe Ruth, Yankees outfielder.*

5013 With women it's like this: I'm not married, but I'm in great demand.—*Satchel Paige, Indians pitcher.*

5014 Baseball makes broads aggressive.—*Jim Brosnan, Reds reliever.*

5015 I remember the first time I touched my first girlfriend. She threw me through the backyard fence and dislocated my shoulder.—*Bill Lee, Expos pitcher, 1980.*

5016 We may have to call off Family Day.—*Lee MacPhail, Yankees GM, on a wife swap between Yankees pitchers Fritz Peterson and Mike Kekich, 1972.*

5017 If this had happened eleven years ago, Mama never would have let me play ball.—*Reggie Smith, Red Sox outfielder, on the Fritz Peterson–Mike Kekich wife swap, 1973.*

5018 It's the commissioner's role to try to protect the image and honesty of the game. This does not help the image of the game.—*Bowie Kuhn, baseball commissioner, on the Fritz Peterson –Mike Kekich wife swap, 1973. Peterson remained married to Susanne Kekick while Kekich and Marilyn Peterson separated shortly after the swap.*

5019 I thought the only thing you ever did in the minors was chase broads. When did you have time to learn how to pitch?—*Steve Barber, Orioles pitcher, to Angels pitcher Bo Belinski, 1962.*

5020 I don't swear or smoke, don't drink much and don't chase girls.... But it's all right if they chase me.—*Butch Wynegar, Twins catcher, 1976.*

5021 He was playing hands with his wife during spring training, and instead of running around the outfield, he did his running in the bedroom. Now, love is love. But it comes pretty cheap for these young ballplayers these days, and I think they should take advantage of that and wait to get married.—*Calvin Griffith, Twins owner, on catcher Butch Wynegar, 1978.*

5022 We had to get married. That's the only way she could get on the team plane to Montreal. They don't fly girlfriends, only wives.—*Pete Rose, Expos first baseman, on his wedding, 1984.*

5023 We've got 25 guys that all have their catcher's mitts on.—*Bruce Bochy, Padres manager, on the willingness of his players to catch the ceremonial first pitch thrown by tennis star Anna Kournikova, 2005.*

5024 It was exciting and actually a turning point in our relationship. It was exciting because it was Fenway Park.—*Jessica Canseco, ex-wife of former Red Sox slugger Jose Canseco, on making whoopee in a Fenway Park office, 2006. Canseco played in Boston in 1996 and 1997.*

5025 We want to christen every city that Kris has played in during his professional career.—*Anna Benson, wife of Pirates pitcher Kris Benson, 2004.*

5026 I told him, cheat on me all you want. If you get caught, I'm going to screw everybody on your entire team—coaches, trainers, players. I would do everybody on his whole team.—*Anna Benson, wife of Mets pitcher Kris Benson, 2005.*

5027 Phillies outfielder Pat Burrell and Pittsburgh pitcher Kris Benson, both of whom confessed to assorted shenanigans in *Penthouse*, will confer and agree that both thought they were talking to *Popular Mechanics*.—*Bernie Lincicome, sportswriter, March 2001.*

5028 This is a tease, man. It's like when you have a girlfriend and you are kissing her all over the place and you get to the Mambo, and she say no. That's where we are right now.—*Ozzie Guillen, White Sox manager, on falling out of the pennant race, September 2009.*

5029 I roomed with this goddamn Rudy York. He was the silliest bastard I ever met in my life. He was a third-string catcher at the time, and I was a regular, and all night long that goddamn phone was ringing. He knew every whore in New York.—*Billy Rogell, Tigers shortstop and teammate from 1939–1941, 1991.*

5030 If you believe [Roger Kahn's] *The Boys of Summer*, you believe that in one week in 1952, I slept with five women of different nationalities. [...] That's wrong. Took me at least two weeks.—*Dick Williams, Hall of Fame manager and former Brooklyn outfielder, 1990.*

5031 Billy Martin took advantage of one perk fame gave him. There are women, young and old, who love to love famous sports personalities, if only for a night. One of Billy Martin's missions in life, it seemed, was to reciprocate.—*Peter Golenbock, sportswriter.*

5032 Top Ten Baseball Euphemisms For Sex

10. Working the rosin bag
9. Comebacker
8. Charging the mound
7. Riding the pine
6. Jerking one into the seats
5. Coming from behind
4. Doubleheader
3. Going deep in the hole
2. The big unit
1. Visiting Busch Stadium—*David Letterman, talk show host, September 20, 2001.*

Slump-Busting

5033 Most slumps are like the common cold. They last two weeks no matter what you do.—*Terry Kennedy, Padres catcher.*

5034 A slump starts in your head and winds up in your stomach. You know that eventually it will happen, and you begin to worry about it. Then you know you're in one. And it makes you sick.—*Billy Williams, Cubs outfielder.*

5035 Slumps are like a soft bed—they're easy to get into and hard to get out of.—*Johnny Bench, former Reds catcher, 1987.*

5036 If you have a batting slump or a cold,

you will get plenty of advice.—*Hank Greenwald, announcer.*

5037 When you get in a slump on the road the best thing to do is get home. When you get in a slump at home the best thing is to get on the road.—*Ralph Houk, Tigers manager, 1974.*

5038 So many ideas come to you and you want to try them all, but you can't. You're like a mosquito in a nudist camp. You don't know where to start.—*Reggie Jackson, Oakland A's outfielder, on hitting slumps, 1970. Reggie went through an 0-for-35 slump with the Angels in 1985.*

5039 You know you're going bad when your wife takes you aside and tries to change your batting stance. And you take her advice.—*Thomas Boswell, writer, 1982.*

5040 Not many people talk to you when you're hitting .195.—*Dwight Evans, Red Sox outfielder, when asked if he was receiving hitting advice during an early-season slump, 1981. Dewey recovered to hit .296 and lead the AL in homers.*

5041 When you're in a slump, it's almost as if you look up at the field and it's one big glove.—*Vance Law, infielder and son of 1960 NL Cy Young winner Vern Law.*

5042 When you're going like this, it looks like even the umpires have gloves.—*Pete Rose, Reds All-Star.*

5043 When you are in a slump and you have all that stuff in your mind, medically speaking, you need a mental enema.—*Fran Healy, broadcaster and former catcher.*

5044 When the pressure builds up, it's like being on a bus in a mudhole. The harder you press on the pedal, the further you sink in the mud.—*Bob Watson, Yankees first baseman, 1980.*

5045 Slump? I ain't in no slump. I just ain't hitting.—*Yogi Berra, Yankees catcher.*

5046 I broke my slump when I found a delivery in my flaw.—*Dan Quisenberry, Royals reliever, 1981.*

5047 I had slumps that lasted into the winter.—*Bob Uecker, announcer and former catcher.*

5048 I hadn't hit the ball since Moby Dick was a minnow.—*Jerry Martin, Phillies outfielder, 1978.*

5049 I'm hitting so bad I could go into a slump and raise my average.—*Bill Grabarkewitz, Angels infielder, 1973. After hitting .163 for Anaheim, he was traded to Philadelphia in August.*

5050 The way things are going for me, if I'd buy a pumpkin farm, they'd cancel Halloween.—*Billy Gardner, Twins manager, 1983.*

5051 In baseball there are only two things I'm an expert in—trades and slumps.—*Joe Garagiola, broadcaster and former catcher, 1974.*

5052 What we could use is a couple of shutouts, but I don't know if that would be good enough to win.—*Whitey Herzog, Cardinals manager.*

5053 All I know is that the way we're hitting, sick people are getting out of bed and wanting to pitch against us.—*Bob Lemon, Yankees manager.*

5054 Baseball is supposed to be a non-contact sport, but our hitters seem to be taking that literally.—*Larry Doughty, Pirates GM, 1989.*

5055 Maybe Jesse Jackson can get some guys home for us. I should give him a call.—*Jerry Manuel, White Sox manager, on his team scoring just three runs in a 26-inning stretch, 1999. Jackson had recently negotiated the release of three captured American soldiers from Yugoslavia.*

5056 I managed a team that was so bad we considered a 2-and-0 count on the batter a rally.—*Rich Donnelly, Pirates coach, 1989.*

5057 I would have jumped off a tall building. But the way I'm hitting, I wouldn't have hit the ground.—*Phil Garner, Dodgers infielder, 1987. After a trade from Houston, Scrap Iron hit .190 in 70 games with Los Angeles.*

5058 I've heard of guys going 0-for-15, or 0-for-25, but I was 0-for-July.—*Bob Aspromonte, Astros third baseman, 1965. Aspromonte finished the season with a .263 average.*

5059 You hate to come out of a game when you're hot.—*Mark Smith, Pirates outfielder, on breaking an 0-for-31 slump to start the season before being taken out of a game for defensive purposes, 1998. Smith finished the season hitting .195.*

5060 I've forgotten where first base is. They tell me it's not in the dugout, but I don't believe them.—*Bob Kearney, Mariners catcher, on an 0-for-31 slump, 1985. Despite the bad stretch, Kearney finished the year with a .243 average.*

5061 I was 0 for 32 and hit a homer on the first pitch. That's the only time I've ever worn it.—*Derek Jeter, Yankees shortstop, on wearing a gold lamé thong in a game, 2008. The slumpbusting undergarment was owned by first baseman Jason Giambi.*

5062 I'm getting close to hitting my age.—*Bob Kearney, 28-year-old Mariners catcher, on his .029 average at the end of April, 1985.*

5063 I've been 0 for 40 before.... Just not consecutively.—*Brad Ausmus, Astros catcher, on snapping a long hitless skid, 2007.*

5064 We lost 14 straight. Then we had a game rained out, and it felt so good we had a victory dinner.—*Lefty Gomez, Hall of Fame pitcher, on his short stint (1946–1947) as manager of the Binghamton Triplets of the Eastern League, 1962.*

5065 I was due for a bad outing.—*Bill Bonham, Cubs pitcher, on failing to retire any of the four batters he faced in his major league debut, 1971.*

5066 My earned run average is so high it looks like an AM radio station.—*Jim Gott, Pirates pitcher, 1989.*

5067 Our earned run average looks like the national debt.—*Charlie Fox, Giants manager, 1973.*

5068 It's not big if you look at it from the standpoint of the national debt.—*Bill Rigney, Twins manager, on his team's earned run average.*

5069 There were times last year when people looked at the scoreboard and thought my batting average was the temperature.—*Buck Martinez, Blue Jays catcher, 1985.*

5070 I was going so bad that last week I skipped dinner two days because I was down to .198 and I didn't want anyone saying I wasn't hitting my weight.—*Jesse Barfield, Blue Jays outfielder, 1986. Barfield recovered to have the best year of his career, making the All-Star team and leading the majors with 40 homers.*

5071 It's not easy to hit .215. You have to be going terrible and have bad luck, too.—*Steve Kemp, Pirates outfielder, 1985.*

5072 The only people in the U.S. who had a worse night than me died.—*Steve Kemp, Pirates outfielder, 1985.*

5073 We were as flat tonight as people used to think the earth was.—*Danny Ozark, Phillies manager, 1979.*

5074 I couldn't drive home Miss Daisy.—*Lee Tinsley, Red Sox outfielder, on his inability to hit with runners in scoring position, 1996.*

5075 I don't care what the writers say. I still say I got a chance to win five games this season.—*Denny McLain, Washington Senators pitcher, 1971. McLain won 10 games, but lost a league-high 22.*

5076 I had nothing to lose, everything to gain. I gained a lot of losses.—*Mike Morgan, Dodgers pitcher, on signing at age 18 with Oakland, 1989. In 1979, his first full season, Morgan went 2–10.*

5077 I hope not.—*Brad Komminsk, Braves outfielder, when asked if he thought there was such a thing as the sophomore jinx, 1985. After hitting .203 as a rookie in 1984, Komminsk improved to .227 the next season.*

5078 With the kind of year I had, I'm ready to try anything.—*Paul Householder, Reds outfielder, on getting engaged in the off-season after batting .211, 1982.*

5079 When I struggle at the plate I ask the trainer for eye drops and put them right on my bat so my bat can see the ball good.—*Ozzie Guillen, White Sox shortstop, 1987.*

5080 I got an out! I almost moonwalked off the field.—*Mitch Williams, Angles reliever, on surrendering a sacrifice fly—his first out recorded* *during a span of three appearances and seven batters, May 1995. In 20 appearances, Williams had a 6.75 ERA for Anaheim.*

5081 You decide you'll wait for your pitch. Then, as the ball starts toward the plate you think about your stance; and then you think about your swing; and then you realize the ball that went past you for a strike was your pitch. —*Bobby Murcer, Yankees outfielder, on batting slumps.*

5082 It's easy to enjoy your job and enjoy other people when things are going good. When you're faced with adversity is when the character of men is measured. There's a Mennonite proverb, "Man, like a tree, is measured best when cut down."—*Dan Quisenberry, Royals reliever.*

5083 Every season has its peaks and valleys. What you have to try to eliminate is the Grand Canyon.—*Andy Van Slyke, Cardinals outfielder.*

5084 I'm surprised I didn't break out in a rash, the way I've been handling the bat this year.—*Andy Van Slyke, Pirates outfielder, on picking up a live bat that landed on the field, 1994. After several All-Star appearances and hitting over .300 the previous two seasons, Van Slyke dropped to .246 in 1994.*

5085 In batting practice, I've been like Reggie Jackson. In the games, I've been like Michael Jackson.—*Torii Hunter, Twins outfielder, on a hitting slump, June 2006.*

5086 I'm Ichiro without speed and without batting average.—*Jeff Bagwell, Astros first baseman, on going 35 games without a home run, June 2003.*

5087 He just took a bag of our bats and put them in the window. He knew nothing would hit it.—*Ron Gardenhire, Twins manager, on the quick thinking of coach Steve Liddle during a tornado warning in Kansas City, 2004.*

5088 The Houston Astros will be doing one of those bobble-head doll giveaways soon. It's a natural because Jose Lima already has that motion as he watches his pitches leave the park.—*Jerry Greene, sportswriter, 2001. After making the All-Star team and winning 21 games in 1999, Lima Time imploded when Houston moved to Enron Field, going 7–16 with a 6.65 ERA and surrendering a league-high 48 homers. He was soon traded to Detroit.*

5089 If I were a horse, I'd shoot myself.—*Trever Miller, Astros reliever, on giving up 14 runs over five outings, July 1999.*

Strategy

5090 Percentage baseball must be good. If it weren't, it wouldn't work so often.—*Pinky Higgins, Red Sox manager, 1961.*

5091 You can't sit on a lead and run a few plays into the line and just kill the clock. You've got to throw the ball over the goddamn plate and give the other man his chance. That's why baseball is the greatest game of them all.—*Earl Weaver, Orioles manager.*

5092 The key to winning is pitching, fundamentals and three-run homers.—*Earl Weaver, Orioles manager, 1980.*

5093 Actually, I prefer four-run homers.—*Earl Weaver, Orioles manager, when asked about his philosophy of playing for three-run homers, 1985.*

5094 Please tell me you were trying to stop the clock because we were out of timeouts.—*Jim Leyland, Pirates manager, to shortstop Jay Bell, who threw a ground ball into the stands, 1992.*

5095 The clock doesn't matter in baseball. Time stands still or moves backward. Theoretically, one game could go on forever. Some seem to.—*Herb Caen, sportswriter, 1979.*

5096 I don't like them fellas who drive in two runs and let in three.—*Casey Stengel, Hall of Fame manager.*

5097 *Deion Sanders (Braves outfielder, 1994):* I'll do anything possible to help the team. Steal, walk, bunt. Anything.

Steve Marantz (sportswriter): Get hit by a pitch?

Sanders: No.

5098 I got into computers four or five years ago. I fed all the information in and pushed the button. It said, "Fire the manager."—*Buck Rodgers, Expos manager, 1984.*

5099 I used to send myself up to pinch hit whenever the wind was blowing out from home plate.—*Joe Cronin, Hall of Fame shortstop, on his days as Red Sox player-manager.*

5100 When I can't make up my mind about changing a pitcher or putting in a pinch hitter, I listen for ideas the announcer has, then do the opposite.—*Ben Chapman, Phillies manager, on keeping a radio in the dugout in order to listen to the broadcast.*

5101 I'd yank my own son if it was the right move.—*Eddie Stanky, White Sox manager.*

5102 I was afraid I might strangle him if I had him in the dugout.—*Gene Mauch, Twins manager, on why he let pitcher Pete Redfern struggle through four bad innings, June 1980.*

5103 He got hit so hard, I had to get all of the married men off the field.—*Whitey Herzog, Cardinals manager, on a bad outing by reliever Ken Dayley.*

5104 I laid it in there hoping he'd hit it hard at someone. He did, but the someone he hit it at was sitting in the seats.—*Bob Walk, Pirates pitcher, after serving up a home run to Reds second baseman Bill Doran, 1991.*

5105 I would love for one of our starters other than Randy Johnson to get past the sixth inning, but that is starting to seem like hurdling the Great Wall of China.—*Lou Piniella, Mariners manager, 1994.*

5106 Suffering a toothache, eh? Well, why doesn't he go and have them pulled? He pulls his pitchers when they're going bad, doesn't he?—*Joe McCarthy, Yankees manager, on Indians manager Ossie Vitt, 1938.*

5107 Let's try this against the Dodgers. On any ball hit to center field, let's just let it roll to see if it might go foul.—*Catfish Metkovich, Pirates first baseman, on the team's horrific defense, 1952.*

5108 If the season started tomorrow, Nick Esasky would be the first baseman, but it's too damn cold to start the season tomorrow, so we don't know.—*Pete Rose, Reds manager, January, 1987.*

5109 The big focus, right now, is on center field, left field, third base, the starting rotation, the bullpen, the catchers, the bench and the new manager.—*Jim Bowden, Reds GM, on his preseason concerns, 1996.*

5110 The DH serves one useful purpose. It relieves the manager of all responsibility except to post the lineup card on the dugout wall and make sure everybody gets to the airport on time.—*Bill Lee, former pitcher, 1984.*

5111 The only decision a manager has to make after filling out the lineup is where he's going to eat dinner that night.—*Bob Feller, Hall of Fame pitcher, on the designated hitter rule.*

5112 The only pitcher I had left was Mike Armstrong, and the reason I didn't use him was that I wanted to win the game.—*Billy Martin, Yankees manager, 1985.*

5113 *Earl Weaver (Orioles manager):* When I put you in the game I want you to stand right here and don't move. If the ball is hit to you, all I want you to do is throw it to second base.

Pat Kelly (Orioles outfielder): What if we're up a run in the ninth inning and a man is trying to score from second base?

Earl Weaver: Don't worry about that—if we're up by a run in the ninth inning, you aren't out there anyway.

5114 I want them close together so I can coach them in Little League and I can use them in double switches. Then they'll know what their Daddy's career was like.—*Eddie Taubensee, Reds catcher, on his two sons, 1997.*

5115 *Darryl Strawberry:* What, you're pinch-hitting for me?

Montgomery Burns (manager): Yes, you see,

you're a left-hander and so is the pitcher. If I send up a right-handed batter, it's called playing the percentages. It's what smart managers do to win ballgames.

Strawberry: But I've got nine home runs today.

Burns: You should be very proud of yourself. Sit down. Simpson, you're batting for Strawberry.—*With two outs in the ninth, bases loaded, and the score tied, Homer J. Simpson gets hit in the head by a pitch to drive in the winning run. (From* The Simpsons, *"Homer at the Bat," 1992.)*

5116 Did they tell me how to pitch to Williams? Sure they did. It was great advice, very encouraging. They said he had no weakness, won't swing at a bad ball, has the best eyes in the business, and can kill you with one swing; he won't hit at anything bad, but don't give him anything good.—*Bobby Shantz, Philadelphia A's pitcher, on facing Red Sox outfielder Ted Williams.*

5117 Yeah, you can pitch him low, but as soon as you throw the ball, run and hide behind second base.—*Lou Boudreau, Indians shortstop, on pitching to Ted Williams.*

5118 No use throwing at him. First of all, you're not going to hit him. And second of all, you're not going to bother him. Let him do what he was going to do anyway and then concentrate on getting the next man out.—*Paul Richards, Orioles manager and GM, on Red Sox outfielder Ted Williams.*

5119 Throw it ten feet in front of the plate and hope he doesn't hit it on the first hop.—*Mike Hargrove, Indians manager, on how to pitch to White Sox first baseman Frank Thomas, 1994.*

5120 Pitch him low and behind.—*Buck Rodgers, Angels manager, on how to pitch to Blue Jays rookie outfielder Carlos Delgado, who hit eight home runs in his first fifteen games 1994.*

5121 The way to fool Manny Sanguillen is to throw him right down the middle. He'll hit anything but a perfect pitch.—*Billy DeMars, Phillies batting coach, on the free-swinging Pirates catcher 1978.*

5122 *Bill Dickey (Yankees catcher):* What do you want to throw him?

Lefty Gomez (Yankees pitcher): I don't want to throw him nothin'. Maybe he'll just get tired of waitin' and leave.—*On facing Philadelphia A's first baseman Jimmie Foxx.*

5123 Throw him four wide ones and then I try to pick him off first base.—*Preacher Roe, Brooklyn Dodgers pitcher, when asked how to pitch to Cardinals outfielder Stan Musial.*

5124 I had pretty good success with Stan—by throwing him my best pitch and backing up third.—*Carl Erskine, former Brooklyn Dodgers pitcher, on Stan Musial.*

5125 It's very simple. Keep it low and outside and high and inside, and make damn sure it's low and inside and high and outside.—*Loren Babe, White Sox scout, on how to pitch to the powerful Brewers lineup, 1982.*

5126 I don't know what he would do overall, but I know what he would do when I'm pitching—four walks.—*Dwight Gooden, Mets pitcher, on how he would pitch to Dodgers outfielder (and former teammate) Darryl Strawberry, 1990.*

5127 Roll it up there and hope it doesn't bounce.—*Jim Leyland, Marlins manager, on how to pitch to Cardinals first baseman Mark McGwire, 1997.*

5128 The strategy is: Throw it over the plate and hide my eyes. From now on, I'm going to the bathroom while he bats.—*Bob Boone, Royals manager, on Mariners outfielder Ken Griffey Jr., 1997.*

5129 If a man can beat you, walk him.—*Satchel Paige, Hall of Fame pitcher.*

5130 It's smarter to give the big man four balls for one base than one ball of four bases.—*Roger Maris, Yankees outfielder, on teammate Mickey Mantle.*

5131 Keep those nits and gnats off the base, 'cause those lions and tigers will get ya.—*Sam Narron, Cardinals catcher.*

5132 You don't let Superman beat you when you have Wonder Woman on deck.—*Troy Percival, Rays reliever, on the decision by manager Joe Maddon to walk Rangers slugger Josh Hamilton with two outs, bases loaded, and a four-run lead in the ninth inning, August 17, 2008. After* *issuing the free pass, reliever Grant Balfour got the next batter, outfielder Marlon Byrd, to strike out to end the game.*

5133 We tried to set up the double play. But the shortstop doesn't play in the bullpen.—*Lou Piniella, Cubs manager, on intentionally walking the bases full in order to face Nationals first baseman Dimitri Young who promptly hit a grand slam, July 4, 2007.*

5134 I'd throw me a fastball right down the middle. What do you think, I'm going to try and get myself out?—*Joaquin Andujar, Oakland A's pitcher, when asked how he would pitch to himself, 1987.*

5135 What we need now is a second-base coach.—*Graig Nettles, Yankees third baseman, after Minnesota turned an unorthodox triple play against the Yankees on a strikeout and an attempted double steal, May 29, 1982.*

5136 He told us we had to stay out of double plays, and we did.—*Dennis Lamp, Red Sox pitcher, on Boston hitting into two triple plays in one game against Minnesota, July 17, 1990.*

5137 You're thinking he's a good guy to stay out of the double play. Well, we did that.—*Bruce Bochy, Padres manager, on sending outfielder Kerry Robinson in to pinch hit—and hit into a triple play, May 6, 2004.*

5138 No, let us score our runs in an honorable way.—*Judge Fuchs, Boston Braves manager, on a suggestion to try a squeeze play, 1929. The Braves finished the year in last place, an honorable 43 games behind the Cubs.*

5139 Craig likes to squeeze more than Mr. Whipple.—*Tim McCarver, broadcaster, on Giants manager Roger Craig, 1989.*

5140 The squeeze bunt works less often than it succeeds.—*Jerry Coleman, Padres broadcaster.*

5141 I've got nothing against the bunt—in its place. But most of the time, that place is at the bottom of a long-forgotten closet.—*Earl Weaver, Hall of Fame manager, 2002.*

5142 People from Sandusky don't drive here to see Jim Thome bunt.—*Grady Little, Indians coach, on why his first baseman shouldn't bunt against an infield shift, 2001.*

5143 It's easy to beat the shift. All you got to do is hit it in the stands.—*Clarence Jones, Indians hitting coach, 2001.*

5144 Man may penetrate the outer reaches of the universe, he may solve the very secret to eternity itself, but for me, the ultimate human experience is to witness the perfect execution of the hit-and-run.—*Branch Rickey, Brooklyn Dodgers GM.*

5145 If Joe Torre orders a hit-and-run and it works, I pat him on the back and say, "Smart move." If it doesn't work, I go down and hang around the water cooler.—*Don Zimmer, Yankees bench coach, on his job description, 2002.*

5146 There's not much to it. You put a right-handed hitter against a left-handed pitcher and a left-handed hitter against a right-handed pitcher, and on cloudy days, you use a fastball pitcher.—*Manager Casey Stengel.*

5147 You never save a pitcher for tomorrow. Tomorrow it may rain.—*Manager Leo Durocher.*

5148 I'll never forget September 6, 1950. I got a letter threatening me, Hank Bauer, Yogi Berra and Johnny Mize. It said if I showed up in uniform against the Red Sox, I'd be shot. I turned the letter over to the FBI and told my manager Casey Stengel about it. You know what Casey did? He gave me a different uniform and gave mine to Billy Martin. Can you imagine that! Guess Casey thought it'd be better if Billy got shot.—*Phil Rizzuto, announcer and former Yankees shortstop.*

5149 He was the type of fellow who would call all the pitches until you got in a spot, then he'd leave you on your own.—*Bill Terry, New York Giants first baseman, on Giants manager John McGraw.*

5150 Whatever you just told Lowe, don't ever tell him again.—*Dodgers manager Grady Little to pitching coach Rick Honeycutt after pitcher Derek Lowe surrendered a three-run homer on the first pitch following a mound visit from Honeycutt, April 2006.*

5151 I told myself that at least that way, even if I didn't hit *any* home runs, at least I'd be on TV for 15 minutes.—*Lance Berkman, Astros outfielder, on his strategy of taking a lot of pitches during the 2004 Home Run Derby. Berkman reached the finals but lost to Orioles shortstop Miguel Tejada.*

5152 The Reds plan to use 6-foot-6 Adam Dunn, who struck out 170 times last year, as their leadoff hitter. If he's your table setter, it must be a table for one.—*Tom FitzGerald, sportswriter, 2003.*

5153 Baseball isn't keeping up with science. Satellites are sending accurate signals from outer space to earth, but coaches still have trouble transmitting signals from third base to home.—*Ellis Clary, Senators third base coach.*

5154 I get a kick out of watching a team defense me. A player moves two steps in one direction, and I hit it two steps the other way. It goes right by his glove and I laugh.—*Rod Carew, Angels first baseman, 1979.*

5155 It's better to lose a game by making a move than lose it sitting on my ass.—*Earl Weaver, Orioles manager, 1972.*

5156 Our goal is to get as many games rained out as we can.—*Dan Quisenberry, Royals reliever, on the team philosophy in dealing with an injury to third baseman George Brett.*

5157 The short-term goal right now would be to take the field without embarrassing ourselves.—*Todd Zeile, Cardinals third baseman, 1993.*

5158 There'll be two buses leaving the hotel for the park tomorrow. The two o'clock bus will be for those of you who need a little extra work. The empty bus will leave at five o'clock.—*Dave Bristol, Giants manager, 1980.*

Today and Yesterday

5159 The strongest thing baseball has going for it today is its yesterdays.—*Lawrence Ritter, baseball historian.*

5160 I believe in the Rip Van Winkle theory—that a man from 1910 must be able to wake up after being asleep for seventy years, walk into a ballpark, and understand baseball perfectly.—*Bowie Kuhn, baseball commissioner, 1980.*

5161 People who live in the past generally are afraid to compete in the present. I've got my faults, but living in the past is not one of them. There's no future in it.—*Sparky Anderson, former manager.*

5162 When I played the players were dumb. Now the owners are.—*Mickey Mantle, Hall of Fame outfielder, 1991.*

5163 When I began playing the game, baseball was about as gentlemanly as a kick in the crotch.—*Ty Cobb, Hall of Fame outfielder.*

5164 Well, this year I'm told the team did well because one pitcher had a fine curve ball. I understand that a curve ball is thrown with a deliberate attempt to deceive. Surely that is not an ability we should want to foster at Harvard.—*Charles William Eliot, President of Harvard University (1869–1909), on why he wished to drop baseball as a collegiate sport.*

5165 Something must be done to speed up play, as the public does not like to see unnecessary wrangling on the field and a slow, dragging game.—*James A. Gilmore, Federal League president, during a time when baseball games typically lasted less than two hours, 1915.*

5166 Two hours is about as long as an American can wait for the close of a baseball game—or anything else, for that matter.—*Albert Spalding, Boston Red Stockings pitcher, 1881. Spalding was baseball's first 200-game winner, pitching in all of Boston's games in 1874 and recording a 57–5 record in 1875.*

5167 I don't believe there is one real fan in a big-league town who wouldn't be willing to fork up the extra $10 it would cost him for attending practically every game of the season if he was told it was either pay more or lose the club.—*Clark Griffith, Washington Senators owner, March 9, 1920. Griffith placed himself in ever-increasing debt by continuously purchasing control of the team during his tenure as manager, which began in 1912. The Senators left Washington, sort of, in 1960. The "old" Senators, led by Griffith's nephew Calvin, became the Minnesota Twins, while the AL expanded by creating a "new" Senators club, which eventually left town in 1972 to become the Texas Rangers.*

5168 Disregard any reports you hear that involve moving the franchise, because baseball franchises do not move.—*Commissioner Ford Frick on rumors that the Phillies might move. The team did stay in Philadelphia, but within ten years the Milwaukee Braves, Kansas City Athletics, St. Louis Browns, Brooklyn Dodgers and New York Giants had all relocated.*

5169 I was a bonus baby. I got two autographed baseballs and a scorecard from the 1935 All-Star Game.—*Bob Feller, Hall of Fame pitcher, on signing in 1936 with the Indians, 1972.*

5170 Mickey Mantle's 1952 salary was $5,000. His baseball card from that season is now selling for $8,000.—*Alan Robinson, sportswriter, 1990.*

5171 Gosh, all a kid has to do these days is spit straight and he gets $40,000 to sign.—*Cy Young, Hall of Fame pitcher.*

5172 When I first signed with the Yankees, the regulars wouldn't talk to you until you were with the team three or four years. Nowadays the rookies get $100,000 to sign and they don't talk to the regulars.—*Lefty Gomez, former Yankees pitcher, 1970.*

5173 It could be one of the biggest mistakes baseball ever made. Who voted for the rule? The National League voted unanimously to let the American League use it.—*Billy Martin, Tigers manager, on the designated hitter rule, 1973.*

5174 I hated the DH and all the other new wrinkles that had been introduced in an attempt to corrupt the game. I wanted to go back to natural grass, pitchers who hit, Sunday doubleheaders, day games, and the nickel beer.—*Bill Lee, former pitcher, 1984.*

5175 I've changed my mind about it—instead of being bad, it stinks.—*Sparky Anderson, Tigers manager, on the designated hitter rule.*

5176 I flush the john between innings to keep my wrists strong.—*John Lowenstein, Orioles DH, 1982.*

5177 It seems like Satan has thrown the DH into our game.—*Andy Van Slyke, Pirates outfielder, 1988.*

5178 The designated hitter rule is like letting someone else take Wilt Chamberlain's free throws.—*Rick Wise, Red Sox pitcher, 1974. Chamberlain was a career 51 percent free throw shooter.*

5179 The DH is a tenth player. Softball has ten guys. Baseball is nine.—*Joaquin Andujar, Oakland A's pitcher, 1986. (Also attributed to Mets pitcher Dwight Gooden.)*

5180 If I strike out with the bases loaded and two out, I want to be able to pick up my glove and try to redeem myself with a big play in the field.—*Henry Aaron, Braves outfielder, on the DH rule, 1973.*

5181 I wish I were still active in baseball. The designated hitter rule was made for me.—*Dean Chance, former All-Star pitcher and lifetime .066 hitter. Chance retired after the 1971 season, two years before the DH rule was approved by the AL.*

5182 It will revolutionize baseball. It will open a new area of alibis for the players.—*Gabe Paul, Indians president, on the first indoor stadium, the Astrodome, 1964.*

5183 If a horse can't eat it, I don't want to play on it.—*Dick Allen, Cardinals first baseman, on artificial turf, 1970.*

5184 It's like playing with marbles in a bathtub.—*Dave Lemonds, White Sox pitcher, on artificial turf, 1973.*

5185 We should redesign the parks so they're clean and organic. Use natural grass—it's nice and soft, and it grows, and you don't get hurt.

Artificial turf is reincarnated dinosaurs. It's petroleum. We're wasting a non-renewable resource by making artificial turf. Cut a hole in it and let the sun shine through.—*Bill Lee, Expos pitcher, 1979.*

5186 Every ballpark used to be unique. Now it's like women's breasts—if you've seen one, you've seen 'em both.—*Jim Kaat, former Cardinals pitcher.*

5187 The new ballparks are great and they hold a lot more people and the facilities are better. But the old parks had to have a charm we can't match today.—*Ted Simmons, Cardinals catcher, 1976.*

5188 Looking back over the last two decades, I feel that right now I'm playing in the best era of baseball. I saw the change from a pitcher's game to a hitter's game. I saw the introduction of the livelier ball, and I saw the breakdown of the color line. All these changes were for the better.—*Stan Musial, Cardinals first baseman, 1962.*

5189 When I started, baseball was played by nine tough competitors on grass in graceful ballparks. By the time I finished, there were ten men on a side, the game was played indoors on plastic, and I spent half my time watching out for a man dressed in a chicken suit who kept trying to kiss me.—*Ron Luciano, former umpire, 1991.*

5190 When I broke into baseball, each club had two scouts—one west of the Mississippi and the other east of the Mississippi. Now the Dodgers have a scout who works the west side of Wilshire Boulevard and another who works the east side.—*Fresco Thompson, Dodgers vice president, 1965.*

5191 I'm glad I don't play anymore. I could never learn all those handshakes.—*Phil Rizzuto, Yankees broadcaster and 1950 AL MVP.*

5192 You can't drive players anymore, the way they were driving in John McGraw's day. We have college boys, young men who have been pampered. Baseball is handed to them on a silver platter.—*Billy Southworth, Cardinals manager, 1942.*

5193 They give them everything. They've shortened the fences, lowered the mound, reduced the strike zone and put in AstroTurf.—*Juan Marichal, Giants pitcher, on the advantages given to hitters, 1970.*

5194 If the game becomes any more namby-pamby, they may have to put the ball on a batting tee.—*Don Drysdale, Hall of Fame pitcher, 1988.*

5195 When I broke in, we didn't have bats. We just grabbed a branch off a tree.—*Charlie Hough, 46-year-old Marlins pitcher, 1994.*

5196 Whatever happened to the on-deck hitter limbering up while swinging two bats? Now players swing a bat with a weighted doughnut on it, or they swing a metal stick, or a sledgehammer. Do these guys have endorsement deals with Ace hardware?—*Scott Ostler, sportswriter, 2001.*

5197 My father taught me and my brother how to play in the front yard. One day my mother came out and told him we were ruining the lawn. My father told her, "We're raising kids, not raising grass."—*Harmon Killebrew at his Hall of Fame induction, 1984.*

5198 I quit driving in '36 'cause I thought there were too many people on the road.—*Albert "Happy" Chandler, 86-year-old former baseball commissioner, on why he used a chauffeur, 1986.*

5199 In 1971, I had 17 saves and got a raise. In 1985, I had 17 saves and got released.—*Rollie Fingers, former All-Star reliever, 1991.*

5200 One year I hit .291 and had to take a salary cut. If you hit .291 today, you'd own the franchise.—*Enos Slaughter, former All-Star outfielder, 1973.*

5201 Back then, if you had a sore arm, the only people concerned about you were you and your wife. Now it's you, your wife, your agent, your investment counselor, your stockbroker and your publisher.—*Jim Bouton, former All-Star pitcher, 1991.*

5202 They've got stretching instructors, eating instructors, body-building instructors, instructors on how to get out of bed in the morning. But they keep breaking down. Stan Musial, you think he ever lifted weights?—*Don Zimmer, Rockies third base coach, on injuries, 1994.*

5203 Baseball teams go south every spring to cripple their players. In the old days they only stayed a couple of weeks, and they couldn't get many of them hurt in that time, but, nowadays, they stay till they get them all hurt.—*Will Rogers, humorist.*

5204 *Ron Santo (Cubs radio announcer, 1990):* In my day we didn't have all these fancy training aids, like magnetic resonance imaging.

Bob Brenly (Cubs announcer): In your day, they were still using leeches.

5205 When I was in baseball and you went into the clubhouse, you didn't see ballplayers with curling irons.—*Red Barber, former Brooklyn Dodgers announcer, 1988.*

5206 Your butt was market meat back then if you didn't keep your mouth shut. I even saw pitchers throw at guys in the on-deck circle.—*Sparky Anderson, Tigers manager, 1994.*

5207 When I was a young fellow, you knew damned well the pitchers were throwing at you. The first month I was in the league I spent two weeks on my back at the plate.—*Casey Stengel, Hall of Fame manager.*

5208 In the olden days, the umpire didn't have to take any courses in mind reading. The pitcher told you he was going to throw at you.—*Leo Durocher, manager.*

5209 The strike zone used to be anywhere between the knees and the chest. It is now anywhere between the top and bottom of the belt buckle.—*Mitch Albom, sportswriter, 1994.*

5210 It used to be you could kick a player's butt; now you have to kiss it.—*Herman Franks, former manager.*

5211 I remember one game I got five hits and stole five bases, but none of it was written down because they didn't bring the scorebook to the game that day.—*James "Cool Papa" Bell, Hall of Fame outfielder, on a game in the Negro Leagues.*

5212 The game has changed a lot since I played.—*John Wathan, former Royals catcher, on being released by the team and then hired back as a coach the same day, 1986.*

5213 Once upon a time it was an institution. Now it belongs in one.—*Dave Kindred, sportswriter, on baseball, 1992.*

5214 The only problem would be finding enough jaundiced horses to keep up the supply.—*Bob Uecker, broadcaster, on the possibility of using yellow baseballs, 1979.*

5215 Baseball has prostituted itself. Pretty soon we'll be starting games at midnight so the people in outer space can watch on prime-time television. We're making a mistake by always going for more money.—*Ray Kroc, Padres owner, 1977.*

5216 I think they should put a banner on my tombstone. It should read, "Here lies Ted Turner, sponsored by Coca-Cola."—*Ted Turner, Braves owner, on reports that he would sell the naming rights to Turner Field, 2001.*

5217 There's going to come a day when we're going to price ourselves so high that the ordinary fan can't afford the ticket prices the clubs have to charge to pay the players' salaries. And then where are we going to be?—*Darrel Chaney, Reds infielder, 1975.*

5218 If they legalized the aluminum bat, I wouldn't play third any more. Or catch. You'd go deaf. You'd be sleeping in the middle of the night, all of a sudden your ears would be going, "Ding, ding, ding."—*George Brett, Royals third baseman, 1979.*

5219 The difference between the old ballplayer and the new ballplayer is the jersey. The old ballplayer cared about the name on the front. The new ballplayer cares about the name on the back.—*Steve Garvey, Dodgers first baseman.*

5220 I don't know anything about Mantle or DiMaggio. Were they as good as Ken Griffey Jr.?—*Ruben Rivera, Yankees outfield prospect, on being labeled the "next Mantle or DiMaggio."*

5221 I'm playing against guys I've only seen on video games.—*Warren Morris, Pirates rookie second baseman, 1999.*

5222 When I first came to big league camp, you'd go bum a chew or smoke. Now you bum carrot sticks and metric shakes.—*Mark Grace, Cubs first baseman, 1999.*

5223 It used to be that when somebody ran out onto the field it was a pretty woman. Now, if somebody runs out, he jumps you.—*Jeff Datz, Indians first base coach, 2003.*

5224 Who says baseball can go 100 years between good ideas? What a radical concept. Even Marge Schott, who has her doubts about the telephone and the automobile, voted for it.—*Thomas Boswell, sportswriter, on the ratification of interleague play, 1996.*

5225 Interleague play is a novelty hatched from desperation, an old idea that was stashed in there with Charles Finley's Day-Glo baseballs and Bill Veeck's circus freaks. That is where it should have stayed.—*Bernie Lincicome, sportswriter, 1996.*

5226 When I broke in, we had one trainer who carried a bottle of rubbing alcohol—and by the seventh inning he had drunk it all.—*Tommy Lasorda, Dodgers manager.*

5227 When I signed my first contract, I got $140 a month. When we left on our last road trip, I got meal money for 13 days—$540. You think this game hasn't gone crazy?—*Don Zimmer, Cubs coach, 1984.*

5228 It used to be you got paid after you did it. Now you get paid before.—*Rick Waits, Indians pitcher, on contracts with bonus clauses.*

5229 Back home in Puerto Rico, it used to be that mothers would tell their sons to put down their bats and gloves and come in and read their books and homework. After all the money that's floating around, the mothers say, "Put down those books and get out there with that ball and bat."—*Jose Morales, Dodgers pinch-hitter.*

5230 I don't think there's anybody left in the Dominican. Everybody that was born there is playing major league baseball.—*Steve Blass, broadcaster and former pitcher, 1998.*

5231 When we played, World Series checks meant something. Now all they do is screw up your taxes.—*Don Drysdale, former Dodgers pitcher, 1978.*

5232 The players are too serious. They don't have any fun any more. They come to camp with a financial adviser and they read the stock market page before the sports pages. They concern themselves with statistics rather than simply playing the game and enjoying it for what it is.—*Rocky Bridges, Angels coach, 1970.*

5233 We used to go to the racetrack after spring training practice in my day. Four of us would chip in fifty cents each to go to the two-dollar window. Yesterday I asked a player how he did at the track. He said "my horse won." I said, "How much did it pay?" The player said, "No, coach, I didn't bet on the horse, I own it."—*Mickey Vernon, Yankees coach, 1985.*

5234 Problems are the price you pay for progress.—*Branch Rickey, Brooklyn Dodgers GM.*

5235 If I was playing today, I'd be a million-dollar player. Is that scary or what?—*Bob Uecker, Brewers broadcaster and former catcher, 1992.*

5236 Guys like Willie Mays, Catfish Hunter and Juan Marichel, all Hall of Famers, must look at today's salaries like Frank Sinatra looks at rap music.—*Jack Clark, Red Sox DH, 1992.*

5237 The great trouble with baseball today is that most of the players are in the game for the money that's in it—not for the love of it, the excitement of it, the thrill of it.—*Ty Cobb, Tigers outfielder—in 1925!*

5238 I measure it by Cadillacs. I used to pay $5,000 for mine. They pay $20,000 now. So, if they make three times as much as I did, what's the difference?—*Mickey Mantle, Hall of Fame outfielder, on spiraling player salaries, 1979.*

5239 Twenty years and 1,000 miles later, every man becomes a second team All-American.—*Irwin Herz, sportswriter, 1961.*

5240 The older they get, the better they were when they were younger—*Jim Bouton, on old timers' days. For almost 30 years, Bouton was not invited back to Yankee Stadium for their Old Timers' Day due to the fallout over revelations he made in* Ball Four (1970). *After a letter from his son Michael was published in the New York Times asking George Steinbrenner and the Yankees to forgive and forget, Bouton was finally invited back in 1998.*

5241 Today's batter gets mad at the first pitch that comes near him. He's ready to fight. When I was playing, they threw at you to see what kind of man you were.—*Lou Boudreau, Hall of Fame shortstop, 1978.*

5242 You go through the *Sporting News* for the last 100 years and you will find two things are always true: you never have enough pitching and nobody ever made money.—*Donald Fehr, head of the baseball players' union, 1995.*

5243 Baseball is too much a business to them now. I loved baseball. I ate and slept it. But now the players, instead of picking up the sports page, pick up the *Wall Street Journal.*—*Satchel Paige, Hall of Fame pitcher.*

5244 Today's players are more concerned about what the press says [...]. Those guys long ago didn't really care that much about it—a lot of them couldn't read.—*Elrod Hendricks, Orioles coach.*

5245 Baseball hasn't been the national pastime for many years now—no sport is. The national pastime, like it or not, is watching television.—*Bob Greene, writer.*

5246 I don't think we had the pressures then that ballplayers have now because there was no television.—*Ralph Kiner, Mets broadcaster.*

5247 Now you get the manager outraging traditionalists like myself when he signs a pitcher and says, "I hope you can give me five good innings." If you pitched only five good innings in the old days you were a bum.—*Shirley Povich, sportswriter.*

5248 Gas prices are headed through the roof, everyone in the Middle East hates us, Toronto and Seattle are in last place—Happy 1978, everybody!—*Bill Scheft, comedy writer, 2004.*

5249 Ballplayers used to sit in the dining car and discuss baseball when they traveled by train. Now they get on a jet plane and 80 percent have attaché cases and some kind of musical box with earphones on. The money is so easy they don't have to struggle or become students of the game. The talent has become watered down. The players today wear gloves that are like nets—they just look at the ball and it's caught. They were better hitters back in the olden days, too, because they would stay after a game and take batting practice. A player today wouldn't *think* of staying after.—*Calvin Griffith, Twins owner, 1983.*

5250 I believe if "Shoeless" Joe Jackson were playing today, he'd have a shoe contract.—*Don Mattingly, Yankees first baseman.*

5251 I'm throwing just as hard as I ever did. The ball's just not getting there as fast.—*Lefty Grove, Red Sox pitcher.*

5252 I'm throwing the ball twice as hard, but the ball is getting there half as fast.—*Lefty Gomez, Yankees pitcher.*

5253 I throw as hard as ever. It just takes longer to get to the plate.—*Don Newcombe, Cincinnati Reds pitcher, 1960.*

5254 I throw the ball harder than Nolan Ryan. It just doesn't get there as fast.—*Steve Busby, Royals pitcher, 1975.*

5255 I'm throwing the ball as hard as I ever did. It just takes a detour before it gets there.—*Gaylord Perry, Mariners pitcher, 1982.*

5256 I think I throw the ball as hard as anyone. The ball just doesn't get there as fast.—*Eddie Bane, Twins pitcher, 1976.*

Transactions

Trades

5257 It's a lot more fun trading a player than signing him.—*Roland Hemond, White Sox GM, 1980.*

5258 Trade a player a year too early rather than a year too late.—*Branch Rickey, Brooklyn Dodgers GM.*

5259 Being traded is like celebrating your 100th birthday. It might not be the happiest occasion in the world, but consider the alternatives.—*Joe Garagiola, broadcaster and former catcher.*

5260 Sometimes the best deals are the ones you don't make.—*Bill Veeck, White Sox owner.*

5261 I always felt the more Browns I could place on the other teams, the better off I'd be.—*Bill Veeck, St. Louis Browns owner.*

5262 Great trade! Who'd we get?—*Lenny Dykstra, Phillies outfielder, after hearing the team had traded first baseman Von Hayes to the Angels, 1991. For the record, Philadelphia got outfielder Ruben Amaro (.219 in 373 AB) and pitcher Kyle Abbott (1–14, 5.13 ERA). Hayes hit .225 with California in 1992, his final season.*

5263 Every time the Giants trade a starter like a Dan Gladden, they get three minor-league pitchers named Juan.—*Dave Newhouse, sportswriter, 1991.*

5264 You mean I got traded for Dooley Womack? *The* Dooley Womack?—*Jim Bouton, pitcher, on being traded from the Seattle Pilots to the Houston Astros, 1969. Bouton and Womack had been teammates with the Yankees the previous season.*

5265 What's the problem? All I did was trade a hamburger for steak.—*Frank Lane, Indians GM, on trading outfielder Rocky Colavito to Detroit for outfielder Harvey Kuenn following the 1959 season. The trade proved one of the most unpopular in Cleveland history and began a string of 33 seasons in which the Indians were out of contention. From 1960 to 1993, the Tribe's best finish was third place in 1968.*

5266 Hells bells! I traded [Red] Schoendienst, I didn't kill him.—*Frank Lane, Cardinals GM, on the negative fan reaction surrounding a nine-player trade with the New York Giants that included the popular second baseman, 1956.*

5267 This trade could hurt both teams.—*Branch Rickey, Pirates GM, on a multi-player deal that sent Ralph Kiner, Joe Garagiola, Catfish Metkovich, Bill Howerton and Howie Pollet to the Cubs for Gene Hermanski, Toby Atwell, Preston Ward, Bob Addis and Bob Schultz, June 3, 1953. Kiner requested the trade because Rickey refused to give him a raise even though he won seven consecutive home run titles.*

5268 That's too bad; they're the only team I can beat.—*Dave Cole, Cubs pitcher, on being traded to the Phillies, 1955. True to his word, Cole went 0–3 with Philadelphia and was out of baseball the following year.*

5269 We played him and now we can't trade him—*Buzzie Bavasi, Brooklyn Dodgers GM, after infielder Don Zimmer issued a play-me-or-trade-me ultimatum.*

5270 What did we get for him? We got someone who'll pay his salary.—*Ted Turner, Braves owner, on selling pitcher Andy Messersmith and his $330,000 salary to the Yankees, 1978. Messersmith appeared in just six games for the Yankees that season, going 0–3 with a 5.64 ERA.*

5271 I tried growing a beard. That didn't work. I became the player rep. That didn't work. Then I bought a house. That worked.—*Dave Heaverlo, Mariners pitcher, explaining what it took for the Oakland A's to trade him, 1979. After one season with Seattle, he returned to Oakland in 1981.*

5272 If you want to get off this team you have to take a number.—*Dave Revering, Oakland A's first baseman, 1981. Revering was traded to the Yankees the next season.*

5273 You think Ron Davis isn't trying to get traded? He's done everything but light himself on fire in Minnesota.—*Al Michaels, Oakland A's broadcaster, on the Twins reliever, 1982. Davis remained in Minnesota until a 1986 trade sent him to the Cubs.*

5274 No more Hank Aaron, Billy Williams or Bobby Bonds. I like that.—*Steve Carlton, Phillies pitcher, on trades that sent the three sluggers to the AL, 1974.*

5275 With the Dodgers, it's time to move on when you reach a certain salary figure. That's just the way they operate.—*Ron Cey, former Dodgers third baseman, on being traded to the Cubs, 1983.*

5276 You have two alternatives. You can play in Philadelphia or you can quit.—*Marvin Miller, executive director of the Players Association, to pitcher Steve Carlton, who was traded by St. Louis to Philadelphia, 1972. Carlton chose to play with the Phillies and won the Cy Young Award with a 27–10 record for a team that won only 59 games.*

5277 It makes no difference where I go or what happens, so long as I can play the full nine.—*Rogers Hornsby, two-time MVP, on being traded late in his career.*

5278 Budweiser traded me. They're more worried about beer than Joaquin Andujar.—*Pitcher Joaquin Andujar on being traded by St. Louis to Oakland, 1986.*

5279 Baseball is just like the Army. Sometimes you're in Arizona and then you have to go to Libya and fight. You never know when you're going to be traded.—*Joaquin Andujar, Oakland A's pitcher, 1986.*

5280 Both teams got nothing, but our nothing was louder than theirs.—*Sandy Alderson, Oakland A's GM, on the 1986 trade of catcher Mike Heath to St. Louis for outspoken pitcher Joaquin Andujar, 1988.*

5281 I've got my nine-year-old on one extension and my eleven-year-old on the other, and I'm trying to explain to them that I've just been traded from Chicago to Chicago.—*Outfielder George Bell on being traded from the Cubs to the White Sox, 1992. Bell played two seasons and hit 38 homers for the Chisox before retiring. The other player in the trade, Sammy Sosa, played 13 seasons with the Cubs and hit 545 home runs for them.*

5282 It makes sense. Considering the trades Jim Frey has made, they're already operating in the dark.—*Bryant Gumble, talk show host and Cubs fan, on the installation of lights at Wrigley Field, 1988.*

5283 McReynolds acted as if he were serving a career sentence in Babel.—*George Vecsey, sportswriter, on outfielder Kevin McReynolds being traded from the Mets to Kansas City, 1991.*

5284 Vince Coleman for Kevin McReynolds raises the question: "Is there déjà vu in hell?"—*Ray Ratto, sportswriter, on the Royals-Mets swap that returned McReynolds to the Mets and Coleman to Missouri (Coleman came up with the St. Louis Cardinals), 1994.*

5285 I've found that every five years a man has to change his Sox.—*Steve Lyons, utility player, on being traded from the Red Sox to the White Sox in 1986 and back to the Red Sox in 1991.*

5286 I was a Yankee for 22 minutes, and that was 22 minutes too long.—*Bill Caudill, Mariners pitcher, who was traded by the Cubs to New York on August 19, 1981, but never played for the Yankees. He was dealt to Seattle just before the season, on April 1, 1982.*

5287 They told me they want me to be in their future. I told them I don't want to be in their future. It's frustrating enough to be in their present.—*Roger Erickson, Yankees pitcher, 1983.*

5288 I'd rather play in hell than for the Angels.—*Alex Johnson, Reds outfielder, on being traded to California, 1969. Johnson won the AL batting title in 1970 with the Angels.*

5289 I felt like the hostages when they were let out of Iran.—*Pitcher Dave LaPoint after being traded from San Francisco to Detroit, 1986.*

5290 I picked up 22 games in one day.—*Pitcher Rick Sutcliffe after being traded from the Indians to the Cubs, 1984. Sutcliffe was 4–5 before the trade but went 16–1 for the Cubs, leading them to a division title and winning the Cy Young Award by a unanimous vote, becoming the first recipient to split time between both leagues during the season.*

5291 I felt like a stolen car. I was waiting for them to strip me for parts.—*Tommy Lasorda, Dodgers manager and former pitcher, on being sold three times during the 1956 season, 1988.*

5292 There are three signs that you're about to be traded: One, Al Campanis says there's no trade in the making. Two, Tom Lasorda says he loves you like a son. Three, you get your meal money one day at a time.—*Pitcher Jerry Reuss on being released by the Dodgers, April 10, 1987.*

5293 There have been a lot of talks in which Dave Henderson's name has come up. Unfortunately, I'm the only one who ever brought it up.—*Lou Gorman, Red Sox GM, 1987. Henderson was finally traded to San Francisco on September 1, 1987.*

5294 They've changed my title. I'm no longer captain; I'm platoon leader.—*Graig Nettles, Padres third baseman, on being traded from the Yankees, where he was team captain, to San Diego, where he was platooned at third base, 1984.*

5295 John Smiley is going to change his name to John Frowney.—*Tony Perez, Reds coach, on hearing that Smiley was unhappy about being traded from Pittsburgh to Minnesota, 1992. After signing as a free agent with Cincinnati the next season, the frowns continued when Smiley went 3–9 with a 5.62 ERA. New manager Perez was fired after 44 games.*

5296 The A's didn't trade Canseco, they banished him to baseball oblivion with a little note reading, "Thanks for all the headaches."—*Bruce Jenkins, sportswriter, on the trade of outfielder Jose Canseco to the Rangers for DH Ruben Sierra and pitchers Jeff Russell and Bobby Witt, August 31, 1992.*

5297 My wife had to write to me in care of [commissioner] Ford Frick.—*Rocky Bridges, San Jose Bees manager, on playing for seven teams in eleven seasons, 1964.*

5298 I've had more numbers on my back than a bingo board.—*Rocky Bridges, San Jose Bees manager, 1964.*

5299 The way I look at it, either I'm a bum or everybody wants me.—*Pitcher Dave Roberts on playing for seven teams in his 13-year career.*

5300 When I retire, I can make a living playing in Old-Timers' games. I'll be able to go to nine of them, and they pay $2,000 a game.—*Dave LaPoint, Phillies reliever, on playing for nine teams in twelve seasons, 1991.*

5301 I presume the names were withheld pending notification of their next of kin.—*Duane Kuiper, Giants infielder, on the trade of Indians pitcher Len Barker to the Braves in exchange for $150,000 and three players to be named later (Brett Butler, Brook Jacoby and Rick Behenna), August 28, 1983.*

5302 They kept saying we're all supposed to be a family here. If you're a family, you don't send your kids to Cleveland.—*Bill Lee, Red Sox pitcher, on the sale of DH Bernie Carbo to the Indians, June 15, 1978.*

5303 I've experienced a lot of things in baseball, but I've never been traded during a strike. At least I know I'll be in a new uniform the next time I put one on.—*Designated hitter Dave Winfield on being traded from Minnesota to Cleveland during the 1994 strike.*

5304 How could I be surprised? That's the team that traded Babe Ruth.—*George Scott, Brewers first baseman, on why he wasn't shocked that the Red Sox had traded him, 1972. Milwaukee traded Scott back to Boston on December 6, 1976.*

5305 Chance traded Chase for a bunion and an onion.—*Mark Roth, sportswriter, on Yankees manager Frank Chance trading first baseman Hal Chase to the White Sox for first baseman Babe Borton and infielder Rollie Zeider, who was playing with a painful bunion, 1913. Chase was a talented fielder but was frequently traded due to his habit of throwing games for money. Chase was eventually banned for life due to his involvement in the 1919 Chicago Black Sox scandal.*

5306 It's an even trade, and it will strengthen our ball club.—*Clark Griffith, Washington Senators owner, to pitcher Joe Engel whom he had just* *traded to the Minneapolis Millers of the American Association in exchange for nothing in return, 1915.*

5307 The manager told me I was traded. I asked him how many players did you get for me? And if it helped the ball club. He said, "We didn't get any players for you. And, yes, it helped the club."—*Jim Frey, former manager and GM, on his days as a minor league outfielder in the Cardinals organization, 1998.*

5308 Cleveland got the better of the deal. They didn't get anybody.—*Davey Johnson, Reds manager, on getting five replacement players from the Indians in exchange for "future considerations," 1995.*

5309 The Cubs traded a horse and they came away with two ponies.—*Frank Robinson, Orioles manager, on the Cubs trading reliever Lee Smith to the Red Sox for pitchers Calvin Schiraldi and Al Nipper, December 8, 1987.*

5310 He doesn't look like much, but I guess he'll help.—*Hal Lanier, Astros manager, on acquiring shortstop Buddy Biancalana from Kansas City, July 30, 1987. Lanier was wrong—Biancalana went 1 for 24 as an Astro, including 12 strikeouts, and was released after the season.*

5311 There are so many new faces around here, I thought I'd been traded.—*Ken Oberkfell, Cardinals second baseman, during spring training, 1981.*

5312 Every time I see Texas, I see different names on the uniforms.—*Ichiro Suzuki, Mariners outfielder, on the ever-changing cast of characters playing for the Rangers, 2003.*

5313 So many guys come and go here that if we won the pennant, our shares would be $50 apiece.—*Danny Cater, Cardinals first baseman, 1975.*

5314 If it'll help us win, we'll trade Marge Schott for Joan Kroc.—*Pete Rose, Reds player-manager, on the controversial female owners of the Reds and Padres, 1987.*

5315 We didn't want to weaken the rest of the league.—*Frank Lane, Brewers GM, on why he made no off-season trades, 1972.*

5316 I'm not sure which is more insulting, being offered in a trade or having it turned down.—*Claude Osteen, Dodgers pitcher, 1972.*

5317 Sometimes a trade is the best thing for a ballplayer because it makes him take stock of himself.—*Nelson Briles, Pirates pitcher, on being traded by St. Louis, January 29, 1971. Briles was traded three more times in his career.*

5318 I'm the only player on the team with a perforated page in the media guide. That way, it's easier to take out when I'm traded.—*Brian Kingman, Oakland A's pitcher, who was eventually purchased (and released) by Boston, 1983. Kingman was the last pitcher to record 20 losses in one season (1980), going 8–20 with a respectable 3.84 ERA until Mike Maroth went 9–21 in 2003.*

5319 I'm not going to second-guess Dallas Green. All I'm going to say is that Dallas Green traded his best pitcher for a sack of garbage.—*Whitey Herzog, Cardinals manager, after the Cubs GM traded Mike Krukow for Dan Larson, Keith Moreland and Dickie Noles, December 8, 1981.*

5320 I'm mad at the Cub management for trading Jose Cardenal, the only player I saw who could sleep between innings. In fact, Jose could sleep between pitches. With his potential, I had hoped he would remain in Chicago and someday become a distinguished alderman.—*Mike Royko, columnist, 1977*

5321 I feel better since I left. I don't have a grey hair anymore.—*Outfielder Dave Winfield on being traded by the Yankees to the Angels, May 11, 1990.*

5322 Was it difficult leaving the *Titanic*?—*Sal Bando, third baseman, on signing with the Brewers after spending 11 seasons with the Oakland A's, 1976.*

5323 It's like going to the dentist to get a tooth pulled. It's a great pain to lose a bat like that, but eventually the pain goes away, and you feel a whole lot better.—*Bill Caudill, Cubs pitcher, on the trade of outfielder Dave Kingman to the Mets, February 28, 1981.*

5324 All I said was that the trades were stupid and dumb, and they took that and blew it all out of proportion.—*Ron Davis, Twins reliever, 1982.*

5325 He went from Cy Young to sayonara in a year.—*Graig Nettles, Yankees third baseman, on reliever Sparky Lyle being traded to the Rangers following the 1978 season after winning the Cy Young Award in 1977.*

5326 I would like to find a home in baseball. The only thing I've been a part of the last six years is American Airlines.—*Bobby Bonds, All-Star outfielder, on being traded seven times in his career, 1981.*

5327 I've played in more towns than *Gone with the Wind.*—*Frank Lucchesi, Rangers manager, 1975.*

5328 I once loved this game. But after being traded four times, I realize that it's nothing but a business. I treat my horses better than the owners treat us. It's a shame they've destroyed my love for the game.—*Dick Allen, White Sox first baseman.*

5329 My shoulder's okay, but I've still got a scar where the Mets stuck the knife in my back.—*Tug McGraw, Phillies reliever, on being traded by New York, 1976.*

5330 No truth to the rumor the White House also invited the '27 Yankees because it thought more of them might show up.—*Jayson Stark, sportswriter, on the visit by 1997 World Series champion Florida Marlins to the White House, February 1998. After winning the Series, the Marlins traded away or released over half of the players from their championship team by the middle of the 1998 season.*

5331 The movie *Six Days, Seven Nights* opened recently. It's the story of Mike Piazza's career with the Florida Marlins.—*Jerry Perisho, comedy writer, on a series of trades that sent the All-Star catcher from the Dodgers to the Marlins to the Mets, 1998. Piazza played just five games for Florida.*

5332 You know how baseball lingo refers to a short stay as a "cup of coffee"? This fella wasn't here long enough for the water to boil.—*Greg Cote, sportswriter, on catcher Mike Piazza's five-game stint with the Marlins, 1998.*

5333 Thanks to a certain airline that specializes in losing luggage, I've had golf clubs spend more time in Florida than Mike Piazza did.—*Bob Verdi, sportswriter, 1998.*

5334 It's a good thing he left. Our players were about to elect him player rep.—*Rich Donnelly, Marlins coach, on catcher Mike Piazza, 1998.*

5335 The Florida Marlins are offering 3.9 percent APR financing on Todd Zeile, or any other veteran on the lot.—*Dan O'Neill, sportswriter, on the wholesale dismantling of the 1997 World Series Champions, 1998.*

5336 When you play on a team like Cleveland, what you are trying to do is impress other general managers. What you are trying to say is, "Look at me. I'm a good player. Make a deal for me."—*Graig Nettles, Yankees third baseman, who was traded after the 1972 season by Cleveland to New York.*

5337 New York needs Clemens like it needs another pothole. This is like Bill Gates making another billion, Tiger Woods getting another car, Jay Leno growing a double chin. This is excess like we've never seen before.—*Nick Canepa, sportswriter, on the Blue Jays trade of five-time Cy Young Award winner Roger Clemens to the World Champion Yankees in exchange for pitcher David Wells and second baseman Homer Bush, 1999.*

5338 Roger in pinstripes? What's next, Ted Kennedy delivering the keynote speech at the Republican National Convention?—*Dan Shaughnessy, sportswriter, on the trade of pitcher Roger Clemens from the Blue Jays to the Yankees, 1999.*

5339 I found out a long time ago that everybody's dispensable. If any of those other guys thinks differently, let him quit and go look for a job.—*Bobby Murcer, Cubs outfielder, 1977.*

5340 After twelve years of being in the major leagues, I do not feel I am a piece of property to be bought and sold irrespective of my wishes.—*Outfielder Curt Flood on being traded from St. Louis to Philadelphia, 1969. Flood refused his assignment to the Phillies, sat out the 1970 season, and lost a landmark Supreme Court case challenging baseball's reserve clause.*

5341 Once you sign a contract, you're little more than cattle. If they don't want you, they sell you or trade you, and you just moo and move along.—*Danny Darwin, Rangers pitcher, who was traded four times in his 21-year career.*

5342 We would only hope that future poster promotions don't scare away our players when we go to them with the idea early in the season.—*Laurel Prieb, Brewers vice president, on the fiasco that was Bob Wickman Poster Night, which took place the day after Wickman was traded to Cleveland, July 28, 2000.*

5343 Over the last three years, the Mariners have lost Randy Johnson (trade to Houston), Ken Griffey Jr. (trade to Cincinnati) and Alex Rodriguez (free agent)—and today have the best record in baseball. This would be like the Beatles losing Paul, John and George and then recording "Can't Buy Me Love."—*Norman Chad, sportswriter, 2001.*

5344 If Cleveland can survive George Steinbrenner and Don King, it can survive John Rocker.—*Dick Schaap, sportswriter, on the trade of Rocker from Atlanta to Cleveland, 2001.*

5345 Geez, what are you guys all doing here? I thought I traded all of you guys.—*Allard Baird, Royals GM, on walking through the clubhouse after the trading deadline, 2002.*

5346 Say this about the Vaughn trade: It spread happiness from coast to coast. One side couldn't wait to reel him in and the other couldn't wait to shove him out.—*Shaun Powell, sportswriter, on the trade of first baseman Mo Vaughn from the Angels to Mets for pitcher Kevin Appier, December 27, 2001.*

5347 It's quite a compliment. To not be traded for someone the caliber of Kevin Brown is something.—*Matt Clement, San Diego minor league pitcher, on hearing that the Padres refused to include him in a trade to Florida for Kevin Brown, December 1997. Clement was eventually traded to Florida in 2001, this time for Cesar Crespo and Mark Kotsay.*

5348 If I knew then what I know now, I wouldn't have made the trade. But if I knew what I know now, I wouldn't have voted for Richard Nixon.—*Hank Peterson, Orioles GM, on the April 2, 1976, trade for slugger Reggie Jackson, only to lose him to free agency following the season.*

5349 When the year was over, they wanted to give me back as the player to be named later.—*Richie Scheinblum, Reds outfielder, on his 1971 trade from Cleveland to Washington for cash and a player to be named later, 1973. Scheinblum hit .143 in his lone season with the Senators.*

5350 Wonder whether he knew that trade winds were blowing?—*James Jahnke, sportswriter, after Tigers pitcher Mike Maroth was traded to the Cardinals just hours after doing a guest forecast for The Weather Channel, June 22, 2007. In Detroit, Maroth had the dubious distinction of being the first pitcher since 1980 to lose 20 or more games in a season (21 in 2003).*

Free Agent Signings

5351 The fan is the one who suffers. He cheers a guy to a .350 season, then watches that player sign with another team. When you destroy fan loyalties, you destroy everything.—*Frank Robinson, Rochester Red Wings manager, on free agency, 1978.*

5352 I am not an Abraham Lincoln signing the Emancipation Proclamation. Involuntary servitude has nothing to do with this case. This decision does not destroy baseball.—*Peter Seitz, arbitrator, ruling that pitchers Andy Messersmith and Dave McNally were not bound by their contracts and were thus declared free agents, 1975.*

5353 I told Bobby's representatives that if he were interested in coming to Philadelphia, we were interested in having him. I also told him we'd name the city after him.—*Lee Thomas, Phillies GM, on free agent outfielder Bobby Bonilla, who ultimately signed with the Mets, 1991.*

5354 Most of the San Diego fans didn't even know my name. They just called me 2.85. It was a long, long year.—*Outfielder Oscar Gamble on being traded to the Rangers after playing one year of a six-year, $2.85-million contract with the Padres, April 1979.*

5355 I signed Oscar Gamble on the advice of my attorney. I no longer have Gamble, and I no longer have my attorney.—*Ray Kroc, Padres owner, 1978.*

5356 Not really. They lean toward cash.—*Bill Veeck, White Sox owner, when asked if free agent players lean toward playing in big cities.*

5357 You have pets for loyalty.—*Third baseman Wade Boggs on signing a free agent contract with the Yankees rather than return to the Red Sox, 1993.*

5358 First time I put those things on, I felt like clicking my heels and yelling, "We're going back to Kansas."—*Will Clark, Rangers first baseman, on wearing red uniform shoes, 1994. Clark signed with Texas as a free agent after eight seasons with San Francisco.*

5359 Every 40 years I change jobs.—*Ellis Clary, White Sox scout, on why he left the Twins, 1987.*

5360 In this era, Benedict Arnold would be considered a free agent, not a traitor.—*Bill Conlin, sportswriter, 1994.*

5361 Maybe they'll be some good after-Christmas sales.—*John Schuerholz, Braves GM, rationalizing his failure to pursue a closer during the off-season, 1993.*

5362 In awarding Dean Palmer a five-year, $36-million deal, the Tigers have assured themselves of a solid 30–30 third baseman for years—that's 30 homers and 30 errors.—*Garth Woolsey, sportswriter, 1998. Palmer hit 38 homers with 19 errors in 1999 and 29 homers with 25 errors in 2000 before injuries reduced his playing time for the remainder of the contract.*

5363 I liked George's style. He hustled me like a broad.—*Reggie Jackson, Yankees outfielder, on why he chose to sign with George Steinbrenner and New York in 1977.*

5364 I let Mr. October get away and I got Mr. May.—*George Steinbrenner, Yankees owner, on allowing outfielder Reggie Jackson to sign as a free agent with the Angels and inking Dave Winfield to take his place, 1991.*

5365 Matt Young is to Lou Gorman what Al Capone's vault is to Geraldo Rivera.—*Dan Shaughnessy, sportswriter, on the release of pitcher Matt Young by the Red Sox, 1993. Young was signed as a free agent by Gorman for $6.35 million but won only three games over three years.*

5366 You could probably buy half the province of Manitoba for what the Toronto Blue Jays paid for Roger Clemens.—*Jayson Stark, sportswriter, on the free agent acquisition, 1996. Signed for $17 million, Clemens won the Cy Young Award both years he played for Toronto.*

5367 We've got a whole bunch of new players. But I don't think they're the right ones.—*Ozzie Smith, Padres shortstop, 1981. By the time the season was over, San Diego traded Smith to St. Louis for Garry Templeton, who wasn't the right one either.*

5368 It was like Bush coming back to the Clinton inauguration.—*Andy Van Slyke, Pirates outfielder, on former teammate Barry Bonds returning to Pittsburgh for the first time since signing with the Giants, 1993.*

5369 Hello, my name is Orel Hershiser and I'm a reformed Dodger. I spent three years in Cleveland in detox, and I'm much better now. —*Pitcher Orel Hershiser at a San Francisco charity dinner after he signed with the Giants, 1998.*

5370 No. Every team I throw against is my ex-team.—*Mike Morgan, Rangers pitcher, when asked if he was inspired to beat the Twins, one of his former teams, 1999. Morgan set a record by recording a win for 10 different pro teams. He added to his record by getting a win for Arizona in 2000 (he went 0–3 with a 12th team, Toronto, in 1983).*

5371 Work hard, eat right, and thank God there are 30 teams.—*Mike Morgan, Rangers pitcher, on his longevity, 1999. Morgan finished his 22-year career in 2002 after playing for 12 teams.*

5372 You know what the bounty is on [Osama] bin Laden? $25 million. It sounds like a lot—until you realize the Texas Rangers paid $250 million to get Alex Rodriguez.—*Jay Leno, talk show host, on the most expensive free agent signing in the history of baseball, 2001.*

5373 The Yankees treat the winter meetings like a trip to Nieman Marcus. They knew what they wanted. They just didn't worry about the price—and then, on the way out of the store, they said, "As long as we're here, we'll take one more thing."—*Lou Piniella, Mariners manager, on New York acquiring first baseman Jason Giambi, outfielder Rondell White, pitcher Steve Karsay, and outfielder John Vander Wal, 2001.*

5374 I think I look good in purple. It matches my underwear.—*Mark Grace, Diamondbacks first baseman, on leaving the Chicago Cubs, 2001.*

5375 I tell you what, I'm getting good at packing.—*Pitcher Bruce Chen on playing for five teams in 14 months, 2003. As of 2010, Chen played for 10 major league teams: traded five times, signed as a free agent four times, and claimed off waivers once.*

5376 I'm amazed at how quick they've made me feel welcome. I mean, there's a lot of guys on the ball club I've probably hit.—*Pitcher Todd Stottlemyre on signing with Oakland, 1995. In seven seasons with Toronto, Stottlemyre plunked 49 batters.*

5377 He has changed teams so many times and lived in so many hotels that he dials nine to get an outside line even when he's home.—*Jim Caple, sportswriter, on the well-travelled Rickey Henderson, 2000. Rickey played for nine teams (and sixteen managers) in his 25 big league seasons, including four separate stints in Oakland and two in San Diego. Later in his career, Henderson also spent time playing for several independent minor league teams: Portland Beavers, Newark Bears, and San Diego Surf Dawgs.*

5378 He must've got Obama stimulus money. Wake me when he wins his first 100 games.—*Bob Feller, 91-year-old Hall of Fame pitcher, on rookie pitcher Aroldis Chapman, who signed with the Reds for $30.25 million after defecting from Cuba, 2010.*

Demotions and the Minor Leagues

5379 I was downgraded from a hurricane to a tropical depression.—*Rex "Hurricane" Hudler, utility player, after being released by the Giants in spring training, 1994. The Hud-Man quickly found a job with the Angels.*

5380 You just get caught in a position where you have no position.—*Sparky Anderson, Tigers manager, on demoting utility player Skeeter Barnes, 1994.*

5381 Kid, you've got lots of stuff, but wild men belong out west. I'm going to send you as far west as I can. Here's a ticket to Portland, Oregon.—*Nap Lajoie, Indians manager, to pitching prospect Jack Graney, 1908. Graney was converted to an outfielder and played 14 seasons in Cleveland. He later became the first former ballplayer to work as a play-by-play radio announcer.*

5382 I'd feel sorry for him if he were a player. —*Sal Bando, Oakland A's third baseman, on the release of A's pinch runner Herb Washington, 1975.*

5383 I expected it. Let's face it: Would you want me on your pitching staff?—*Kurt Knudsen, Tigers pitcher, on being sent to Triple A Toledo after posting a 13.50 ERA, 1994.*

5384 I've heard of the guillotine falling, but they took a chainsaw through here today.—*Ozzie Virgil, Braves catcher, on the release of pitchers Len Barker, Rick Camp, Terry Forster, and Pascual Perez on April 1, 1986. The previous season the quartet compiled a 9–31 record.*

5385 I never cut a guy hitting that high before. But he was making the rest of us look bad with that average.—*Earl Weaver, Orioles manager, on sending outfielder Drungo Hazewood to the minors after he hit .583 in spring training, 1980.*

5386 I hit a grand slam off Ron Herbel, and when his manager Herman Franks came out to get him, he was bringing Herbel's suitcase.—*Bob Uecker, former catcher, on the Giants pitcher.*

5387 I'd rather go out with my ex-wife's attorney than play in the minor leagues.—*Dave Collins, Reds outfielder, 1987.*

5388 I'd like to stay in baseball long enough to buy a bus—then set fire to it.—*Joe Grzenda,*

Washington Senators pitcher, on spending 11 years in the minor leagues, 1971.

5389 I'd rather be the shortest player in the majors than the tallest player in the minors.—*Freddy Patek, 5'4" Royals infielder, 1974.*

5390 Every player who has played in three straight years in the majors I'd send back to Triple A for a month, just to let them see what it was like so they won't forget how good they have it.—*Mickey Mahler, Rangers pitcher, who was sent down to Triple A Oklahoma City the next day, 1986.*

5391 In Kansas City, I had a phone in my bathroom. In the minors, I stayed in hotels where the fire escape was a rope.—*Tony Torchia, Red Sox bullpen coach, 1985.*

5392 In the minor leagues, when you get off a bus at the hotel after the game, there's always a convenience store you can walk to to buy beer. In the major leagues, it takes some searching.—*Gary Varsho, Wisconsin Timber Rattlers manager, 1998.*

5393 Last year, I could barely fit into the hotel bathroom. This year, there's a television in my bathroom.—*Sean Runyan, Tigers rookie pitcher, on the move from Double-A to the majors, 1998. Runyan set a rookie record in 1998 by appearing in 88 games.*

5394 The lighting is better at some of the night games up here than at some of the day games in the minors.—*Kerry Dineen, Yankees rookie outfielder, on the difference between playing in the Show and the minors, 1975.*

5395 The grass is greener, the sun's not as hot and the dirt is not as dirty.—*Bobby Dues, Braves coach, on the difference between the majors and minors, 1979.*

5396 You know when you realize you're not in the major leagues any more? When you have to get up at 3 o'clock in the morning to take a bus three hours from Vancouver to catch a plane in Seattle for Phoenix.—*J.T. Snow, Vancouver Canadians first baseman, after being demoted by the Angels, 1994. Snow was recalled before the All-Star break.*

5397 I've been to every baseball park in America except those in the American League and National League.—*Rich Amaral, Mariners shortstop, on spending nine seasons in the minors before becoming a 30-year-old rookie, 1992.*

5398 My wife and I figured out the other day that our 12-year-old daughter has lived in 72 different homes. We sometimes forget her age, but we know she's got about 89,000 miles on her already.—*Frank Quilici, Twins manager, on spending 12 years in the minors, 1972.*

5399 I'd rather ride the buses, managing in Triple A, than be a lawyer.—*Tony LaRussa, Oakland A's manager and graduate of Florida State Law School, 1986.*

5400 Say, I've got a tip on the market for you fellows—buy Pennsylvania Railroad because by tomorrow night about a dozen of you bums will be riding on it.—*Casey Stengel, Toledo Mudhens manager, 1929.*

5401 Think of him as a recording star who used to pack stadiums and who now works Holiday Inn lounges.—*Tom Keegan, sportswriter, on 36-year-old Bridgeport Bluefish DH Jose Canseco, who was attempting to make it back to the majors, 2001.*

5402 I've got tar lag.—*Johnny Ruffin, Reds reliever, on being optioned four times from Cincinnati to Indianapolis, a 90-mile drive that crosses time zones, 1995.*

5403 I think you're going to hit .290 this year—but you're going to be doing it in Montgomery, Alabama.—*Mayo Smith, Tigers manager, on sending down outfielder Wayne Comer, 1967. Comer did hit .290, but for the Toledo Mud Hens.*

5404 One day everything is fine and the next they treat you like you murdered someone.—*Mark McLemore, Orioles second baseman, on playing for 10 teams (six minors, four majors) in two years, 1992.*

Umpires

5405 I never questioned the integrity of an umpire. Their eyesight, yes.—*Leo Durocher, former manager and All-Star shortstop.*

5406 Argyin' with an umpire is like argyin' with a stump. Maybe you city folks don't know what a stump is. Well, it's somethin' a tree has been cut off of.—*Dizzy Dean, broadcaster and Hall of Fame pitcher.*

5407 Umpiring is best described as the profession of standing between two seven-year-olds with one ice cream cone.—*Ron Luciano, former umpire, 1982.*

5408 If the Pope was an umpire he'd still have trouble with Catholics.—*John "Beans" Reardon, former NL umpire, 1980.*

5409 I have never missed one in my life and it's too late to start now. The Pope for religion, O'Loughlin for baseball. Both infallible.—*Silk O'Loughlin, AL umpire, when a player questioned his calls.*

5410 Boys, I'm one of those umpires that can make a mistake on the close ones. So, if it's close, you'd better hit it.—*Umpire Cal Hubbard.*

5411 That ball was low. You missed it. If it had been a hamburger, you wouldn't have missed it.—*Pete Rose, Reds first baseman, to 300-pound umpire John McSherry, 1985. On opening day in Cincinnati the next season, McSherry suffered a fatal heart attack.*

5412 While baseball's new strike zone may not be popular with players, it has proven to be a real boon for overweight umpires. Now they don't have to bend over so much when calling high strikes.—*Earl Hochman, comedy writer, 2001.*

5413 Have you looked at some of the umpires lately? Judging from their waistlines, throwing Earl Weaver out of games is the only exercise they get.—*Scott Ostler, sportswriter.*

5414 Throwing people out of a game is like learning to ride a bicycle—once you get the hang of it, it can be a lot of fun.—*Ron Luciano, AL umpire. Earl Weaver was Luciano's favorite manager to ride out of a game. Luciano tossed the Baltimore skipper eight times. In order to prevent further altercations, the AL stopped scheduling Luciano's crew for any Orioles games.*

5415 In the thirteen years I managed in the big leagues, they must have made a million calls—and they were wrong just 91 times.—*Earl Weaver, at his Hall of Fame induction, on the 91 times umpires ejected him in his career, August 1996.*

5416 If you do the screaming, the players won't. If you get thrown out, they won't. You've got to keep the players in the lineup.—*Earl Weaver, Orioles manager, on getting ejected, 1979.*

5417 Unfortunately, a player can't throw an umpire out of a game—even though Earl Weaver has tried it a couple of times.—*Lon Simmons, announcer.*

5418 If an umpire can't handle the glare of the sun, he should get a job in a bank.—*Marty Springstead, AL umpire, when asked if umpires should be allowed to wear sunglasses, 1994.*

5419 *Jimmy Dykes (Philadelphia A's infielder):* How do you spell your name?

George Moriarty (AL umpire): M-o-r-i-a-r-t-y.

Jimmy Dykes: That's what I thought. Only one i.

5420 Despite all the nasty things I have said about umpires, I think they're 100 percent honest. But I can't for the life of me figure out how they arrive at some of their decisions.—*Jimmy Dykes, Philadelphia A's manager. The A's hired Dykes in 1951 after being led by Connie Mack for 50 years.*

5421 Umpires sleep with their eyes open.—*Lon Simmons, Oakland A's broadcaster.*

5422 I know there's a fan here attending his first game, and he wants to know where to sign up for the fantasy umpire contest.—*Jeff Blauser,*

Braves shortstop, on a game in which the umpires had to officiate while dressed in shorts and T-shirts because an airline lost their luggage, 1994.

5423 Those amateur umpires are certainly flexing their fangs tonight.—*Jerry Coleman, Padres broadcaster, on replacement umpires working the 1984 NLCS due to a strike that was ultimately resolved before the World Series.*

5424 Son, if that bat comes down, you're out of the game.—*Bill Guthrie, AL umpire, to a player who had just tossed his bat into the air after striking out.*

5425 Frisch, dead or alive, you're out of the game.—*Bill Klem, NL umpire, to Cardinals player-manager Frankie Frisch, who had feigned a heart attack to protest a call on a close play.*

5426 Son, you just keep on swinging and nobody but me, you, and the catcher will ever know you're losing your eyesight.—*Bill Guthrie, AL umpire, to Philadelphia Athletics third baseman Jimmy Dykes, who had just taken two called strikes.*

5427 When I have fingers run through my hair, I usually get kissed.—*Don Drysdale, Dodgers pitcher, on umpires checking to see if he was hiding illegal foreign substances in his hair for use on baseballs.*

5428 Mr. Manager, if it's possible for you to take my job away from me, I don't want it.—*Bill Klem, NL umpire, to New York Giants manager John McGraw, who had threatened to have Klem fired. McGraw set the all-time ejection record (131), which stood until Bobby Cox eclipsed the mark in 2007.*

5429 I don't shock easily. I read the umpires' reports.—*Phyllis Merhige, AL public relations director, on listening to some off-color remarks made at a baseball banquet, 1985.*

5430 When he called me a blankety-blank, I decided to ignore it. But when he called me a blinkety-blank, he was gone.—*Pam Postema, Pacific Coast League umpire, on why she ejected Las Vegas Stars manager Larry Bowa, 1986.*

5431 Hey, I just ran Yogi. You might as well go with him and wash his back.—*Frank Umont, AL umpire, to Yankees manager Casey Stengel following the ejection of catcher Yogi Berra, 1954.*

5432 He said the strike zone changes at 3 A.M.—*Darryl Strawberry, Mets outfielder, on being thrown out during the 17th inning of a 19-inning game against Atlanta, 1985. Strawberry argued a third-strike call by umpire Terry Tata. The Mets won the game 16–13, just before 4 A.M.*

5433 There you are. Now you've got it in black and white.—*Umpire Tom Gorman to Orioles third baseman Brooks Robinson after umpire Emmett Ashford confirmed Gorman's call, 1966. Ashford was the first African-American umpire in the major leagues.*

5434 I'd rather live on a dollar a day than withstand the blackguarding which every umpire is subject to.—*Tom York, former outfielder, on giving up his brief umpiring career, 1886.*

5435 When parents and kids began arguing with me as I walked to my car, I knew $7.50 wasn't enough.—*Dick Enberg, sportscaster, on his days as a Little League umpire, 1987.*

5436 Ed, you're the second best umpire in the league. The other 23 are tied for first.—*Carl Yastrzemski, Red Sox outfielder, to AL umpire Ed Runge.*

5437 Logic? Umpires? If they had any logic, they wouldn't be doing this for a living.—*Doug Rader, Rangers manager.*

5438 Whenever you have a tight situation and there's a close pitch, the umpire gets a squawk no matter how he calls it. You wonder why men take a job in which they get so much abuse.—*Red Barber, Hall of Fame broadcaster.*

5439 I just don't think women should be umpires, period.... I'd kill any player who ever called a daughter of mine the names I've been called by the umpires and the names I've called them.—*Roger Craig, Giants manager, 1988.*

5440 I think I could see the day. Can't you hear it? Kill the umpress.—*Dick Butler, AL supervisor of umpires, on hiring female umpires, 1977.*

5441 What would they do with the chest protectors? Rebuild them all?—*Early Wynn,*

Twins pitching coach, on the possibility of women being hired as umpires, 1968.

5442 In all my years as an umpire, I've never had a person come up to me and say, "Are you Nestor Chylak, the umpire?"—*Nestor Chylak, on his retirement, 1979.*

5443 You go into this business knowing that they'll never build a monument to you.—*Charlie Berry, AL umpire, 1961.*

5444 *George Magerkurth (NL umpire):* Did I hear you call me a blind bat, Durocher?

Leo Durocher (manager): What, you can't hear either, Magerkurth?

5445 I called a lot of "baa-rikes" and "stri-alls." —*Ron Luciano, former umpire.*

5446 Do you think I'd admit to that?—*Augie Donatelli, former NL umpire, when asked if he ever made a bad call, 1974.*

5447 Nothing comes in handy when you're arguing with an umpire.—*Tony LaRussa, Oakland A's manager, when asked if his law degree helped when it came to confrontations with umpires, 1989.*

5448 The first guy who lays a finger on this blind old man is fined fifty bucks.—*Gene Mauch, Expos manager, on disputing an umpire's call.*

5449 Listen, Alex, on a clear day I can see the sun, and that sucker is 93 million miles away!—*Dick Stello, Texas League umpire, to Fort Worth Cats manager Alex Grammas, who accused Stello of not being able to see if a ball was fair or foul 250 feet away, 1964.*

5450 In my heart, I never called one wrong. —*Umpire Bill Klem.*

5451 For anyone who enjoys being screamed and cursed at and occasionally threatened, and having things thrown at them, while living out of a suitcase six or seven months a year for almost no money and absolutely no praise, this is the perfect job.—*Umpire Ron Luciano.*

5452 Umpires are carved from granite and stuffed with microchips. They are supposed to be dispassionate dispensers of Pure Justice, icy islands of emotionless calculation. In short, umpires should be natural Republicans—dead to human feelings.—*George Will, columnist, 1986.*

5453 I've been called everything but my name. —*Umpire Dave Phillips, 1980.*

5454 Being an umpire is a lot like being a king. It prepares you for nothing.—*Ron Luciano, former umpire.*

5455 I'm very glad to receive the Klem Award, but I'll tell you the truth. Klem hated my guts and I hated his.—*Umpire John Reardon on receiving the Bill Klem Award, 1970.*

5456 Any time I got those bang-bang plays at first base, I called 'em out. It made the game go faster.—*Umpire Tom Gorman.*

5457 An umpire is never going to satisfy everybody; I was pleased when I could satisfy somebody.—*Ron Luciano, former umpire.*

5458 The only rule that is simple is the designated hitter rule, because it was written by the umpires. The rest of the rules in baseball are very ambiguous.—*Ron Luciano, former umpire, 1983.*

5459 When I am right, no one remembers. When I am wrong, no one forgets.—*Doug Harvey, NL umpire.*

5460 You guys are just like politicians. You're never right.—*Gerald Ford, former President of the United States, to the umpires at the 1978 All-Star Game.*

5461 Let me tell you something, son
Before you get much older.
You cannot hit the ball, my friend
With the bat upon your shoulder.
—*Bill Byron, a.k.a. "The Singing Umpire," whenever a batter argued a called third strike, 1913–1919.*

5462 Umpires are most vigorous when defending their miscalls.—*Jim Brosnan, Reds reliever.*

5463 The bigger the guy, the less he argues. You never heard a word out of Stan Musial, Willie Mays or Roberto Clemente. They never tried to make you look bad.—*Umpire Tom Gorman, 1975.*

5464 I don't understand why fans boo an umpire. I know it's part of the game. But why is it?—*Umpire Jocko Conlan.*

5465 It ain't nothing till I call it.—*Umpire Bill Klem.*

5466 Well, I blew it the way I saw it.—*Ralph DeLeonardis, minor league umpire, 1966.*

5467 If you don't think you're out, read the morning paper.—*Umpire Bill McGowan.*

5468 An umpire's vision must be at least 20–400 or, failing that, adequate enough to look at a police lineup of Heather Locklear, Meat Loaf and a parking meter and successfully identify the one most likely to wear heels. That pretty much eliminates American League ump Gary Cederstrom, who didn't happen to notice that the Kansas City Royals' Greg Gagne was out by only a par–5 on a bunt attempt last Thursday, thus ruining the Oakland A's Bobby Witt's perfect game. The blind moron.—*Rick Reilly, sportswriter, 1994. Witt settled for a one-hit shutout, June 23, 1994.*

5469 He had a chance to become famous as the umpire in the 12th perfect game in baseball history, and he blew it.—*Milt Pappas, Cubs pitcher, on umpire Bruce Froemming, who called ball four on a full count with two outs in the top of the ninth in an 8–0 no-hitter against San Diego, September 2, 1972.*

5470 It was the biggest call of my career, and I kicked the shit out of it.—*Umpire Jim Joyce, admitting that he blew a call at first base on what would have been the final out of a perfect game tossed by Tigers pitcher Armando Galarraga, June 2, 2010.*

5471 I've never met a perfect man, and I know I'm going to miss one now and then. You just pray it doesn't happen in a big moment. The umpire who makes a bad call to blow a no-hitter is going to cry himself to sleep for the next 30 nights.—*Ron Luciano, former umpire.*

5472 The umpires stay the same. Only the names of the managers change.—*Umpire Jerry Neudecker, 1983.*

5473 I'm getting restless. An umpire watching a baseball game is like a mailman taking a walk on his day off.—*Umpire Ken Kaiser on the 1979 umpires' strike.*

5474 Don't fight with the umpires. You can't expect them to be as perfect as you are.—*Joe McCarthy, Yankees manager.*

5475 Jerry Dale is a great umpire. He's got 20–20 ears.—*Danny Ozark, Phillies manager, 1974.*

5476 No manager ever thinks he got a break. I call them like I see them, and I don't care what team it is. If I'm right only half the time, I'm batting .500—and I never saw a ballplayer bat .500.—*Umpire Jim Odom.*

5477 Sometimes I have this fantasy: The manager's been popping off all day and his team's just blown a big lead. I call time and walk over to the dugout and say very politely, "Excuse me, sir. Your second baseman just booted one with the bases loaded."—*Umpire Nestor Chylak.*

5478 I've got to remind myself that I'm the only guy in the ballpark who is there to root for the umpire.—*NL President Chub Feeney, 1970.*

5479 I told Luciano I wasn't out to get him fined. I'm out to get him fired.—*Billy Martin, Rangers manager, on AL umpire Ron Luciano, 1975.*

5480 I cussed him out in Spanish and he threw me out in English.—*Lou Piniella, Yankees outfielder, on an argument with umpire Armando Rodriguez, 1975.*

5481 He didn't have a good view of the game, so I gave him a chance to watch the end of it on television.—*Umpire Stan Landes on ejecting Dodgers second baseman Maury Wills, 1971.*

5482 How could he be doing his job when he didn't throw me out of the game after the things I called him?—*Mark Belanger, Orioles shortstop, on umpire Russ Goetz.*

5483 The toughest call an umpire has to make is not the half-swing; the toughest call is throwing a guy out of the game after you blew the hell out of the play.—*Umpire Johnny Rice.*

5484 We've got the worst in this league. Earl Weaver, Billy Martin, Ralph Houk, Gene Mauch, you name them, they're all maniacs. You can't reason with those guys. You don't try. —*Jim McKean, AL umpire, 1977.*

5485 Baseball regards umpires as a necessary evil. If they could play games without umpires, I'm sure the majority would vote to do so.—*Umpire Harry Wendelstedt.*

5486 I don't say the umpiring is bad in our league, but we'd be better off playing on the honor system.—*Dick Williams, Oakland A's manager, 1973.*

5487 It will never happen, because when you do that you've taken away all the alibis. Who can the managers blame losses on? Who can pitchers and hitters blame their troubles on? Believe me, the umpire will always be with us.—*Former umpire Beans Reardon on the possibility of replacing umpires, 1969.*

5488 Listen, I'm with the umpires on this. I think sportswriters should be able to punctuate and use capitals any way we damn please. if i want to write all lower case with no punctuation at all like ee cummings the poet then thats what i should be able to do just like frank pulli has a strike zone the size of rhode island and eric greggs outside corner used to be wider than the tires on a monster truck.—*Bill Conlin, sportswriter, on claims by umpires that they should be free to interpret the strike zone individually, 1999.*

5489 If a manager doesn't do his job, he gets fired. If a player doesn't do his job, he is sent to the minors. If umpires don't do their job, they just pack their bags and go to the next city.—*Joe Torre, Yankees manager, 1997.*

5490 *Larry King:* Are there such things, Ron, as natural umpires?

Ron Luciano: Yeah, there really are, but nobody starts out that way. (1984)

5491 I couldn't see well enough to play when I was a boy, so they gave me a special job—they made me the umpire.—*Harry S Truman, 33rd President of the United States.*

5492 I occasionally get birthday cards from fans. But it's often the same message: they hope it's my last—*Umpire Al Forman.*

5493 Many fans look upon the umpire as sort of a necessary evil to the luxury of baseball, like the odor that follows an automobile.—*Christy Mathewson, New York Giants pitcher.*

5494 My favorite umpire is a dead one.—*Johnny Evers, Cubs second baseman.*

5495 Umpire's heaven is a place where he works third base every game. Home is where the heartache is.—*Umpire Ron Luciano.*

5496 I made a game effort to argue, but two things were against me: the umpires and the rules.—*Manager Leo Durocher.*

5497 You argue with the umpire because there is nothing else you can do about it.—*Manager Leo Durocher.*

5498 That's either a threat to be ignored or an offer to be accepted.—*Sandy Alderson, major league baseball executive vice president of operations, on hearing the umpires might walk off the job, 1999.*

5499 Call 'em fast and walk away tough.—*Umpire Tim Hurst on how to be an ump. From 1891 to 1909, Hurst was an umpire, but in 1898 he spent one season as manager of the St. Louis Browns, finishing 39–111. Hurst returned to umpiring the next season.*

5500 Maybe, but I wouldn't have if I had a bat.—*Umpire Bill Klem to Cubs outfielder Hack Wilson who complained that Klem had missed a pitch.*

5501 I've been thinking about going to umpiring school. Hopefully, I can get more hitters out as an ump than I can as a pitcher.—*Tommy John, Dodgers pitcher, 1977.*

5502 Umpire school is sort of like military basic training, but without the fun.—*Umpire Ken Kaiser.*

5503 Something like 4,000 bottles have been thrown at me in my day, but only about 20 ever hit me. That does not speak very well for the accuracy of the fans' throwing.—*Southern League umpire Harry "Steamboat" Johnson.*

5504 The best umpired game is the game in which the fans cannot recall the umpires who worked it.—*Umpire Bill Klem.*

5505 Umpiring is the only profession in the world where you have to be perfect when you start and continue to improve.—*Attributed to every umpire who ever lived.*

Winning

5506 Winning is better than the next worst thing.—*Bill Lee, Red Sox pitcher.*

5507 Losing feels worse than winning feels good.—*Vin Scully, Dodgers announcer.*

5508 Winning isn't the only thing, but wanting to is.—*Catfish Hunter, Yankees pitcher, 1975.*

5509 When you win, you eat better, sleep better and your beer tastes better. And your wife looks like Gina Lollobrigida.—*Johnny Pesky, Red Sox manager, 1963.*

5510 Everything looks nicer when you win. The girls are prettier. The cigars taste better. The trees are greener.—*Billy Martin, Yankees manager, 1975.*

5511 When we lose I can't sleep at night. When we win I can't sleep at night. But when you win you wake up feeling better.—*Joe Torre, Mets manager.*

5512 Somebody's gotta win and somebody's gotta lose—and I believe in letting the other guy lose.—*Pete Rose, Reds third baseman.*

5513 You can't win any game unless you're ready to win.—*Connie Mack, Philadelphia A's owner-manager.*

5514 There is no room in baseball for sentiment if you want to win.—*Frankie Frisch, Cardinals player-manager.*

5515 Winning is the most important thing in my life, after breathing. Breathing first, winning next—*George Steinbrenner, Yankees owner, 1997.*

5516 *Reporter:* How many games did you win, Mr. Young?

Cy Young (age 88): Son, I won more games (511) than you'll ever see.

5517 When we got to the ball park we knew we were going to win. That's all there was to it. We weren't cocky. I wouldn't call it confidence either. We just knew. Like when you go to sleep and you know the sun is going to come up in the morning.—*George Pipgras, Yankees pitcher, on the 1927 team.*

5518 These are the days when the Yanks are leading both leagues—the American and the Pacific.—*Bob Addie, sportswriter, during World War II. New York won the World Series in 1941 and 1943.*

5519 We're not cocky, we shouldn't get cocky and we won't get cocky. But with this team, if we want to be cocky, we can be cocky.—*Wally Backman, Mets second baseman, on the 1986 World Series champions.*

5520 You can tell a team wants to win when guys spend more time looking at the won-and-lost statistics than they do at their own statistics.—*Catfish Hunter, Yankees pitcher, 1976.*

5521 It's like love. There are a lot of ways to describe it, but you can never explain the full meaning.—*J.R. Richard, Astros pitcher, on winning.*

5522 You never get used to the feeling of winning. It's like a new bride every night.—*Bob Lemon, Royals manager, 1971.*

5523 You may go a long time without winning, but you never forget that scent.—*Steve Busby, Royals pitcher, 1979.*

5524 There is no such thing as second place. Either you're first or you're nothing.—*George Weiss, Yankees executive.*

5525 There are two places to be in this league:

first place and no place.—*Tom Seaver, Mets pitcher.*

5526 Be in a hurry to win. Don't be in a hurry to lose.—*John McGraw, New York Giants manager.*

5527 In playing or managing, the game of ball is only fun for me when I'm out in front and winning. I don't care a bag of peanuts for the rest of the game.—*John McGraw, New York Giants manager.*

5528 You can't win them all.—*Connie Mack, Philadelphia A's manager, after losing 117 games, 1916.*

5529 Look at Mel Ott over there. He's a nice guy, and he finishes second. Now look at The Brat. He can't hit, can't run, can't field. He's no nice guy, but all the little SOB can do is win.—*Leo Durocher, Brooklyn Dodgers manager, on second baseman Eddie Stanky. This is the diatribe that has been misquoted as* "Nice guys finish last."

5530 I never posed as a choirboy. I was just a guy who wanted to win, and I would have taken your teeth to do it.—*Leo Durocher, Dodgers coach, 1960.*

5531 What are we at the park for except to win? I'd trip my mother. I'll help her up, brush her off, tell her I'm sorry. But mother don't make it to third.—*Shortstop Leo Durocher.*

5532 Win any way you can as long as you can get away with it.—*Manager Leo Durocher.*

5533 Another club can be beating you for six innings, but for some reason the good ball clubs get tough and win in the last three.—*Billy Martin, Rangers manager, 1974.*

5534 Let's be honest. We're losing by eight runs (11–3), and all I'm thinking about at that point is getting back to the hotel by midnight because that's when room service closes. All of a sudden we start getting hits and more hits, and I'm saying, "I'm not going to make it." If you're not going to get room service, you might as well win.—*John Kruk, Phillies outfielder-first baseman, on scoring nine runs in the ninth inning to beat the Dodgers 12–11, August 27, 1990.*

5535 Cincinnati is nuts with baseball! They ought to call this town Cincinnutty!—*Bugs Baer, sportswriter, on the Reds winning the 1919 World Series over the White Sox.*

5536 When the astronauts walked on the moon, I figured we had a chance to win. Nothing seemed impossible after that.—*Tug McGraw, Mets reliever, on winning the 1969 World Series.*

5537 The guys on the field had to run for their lives. There were 57,000 people pouring out onto the field to offer congratulations.—*Tom Seaver, Mets pitcher, on the celebration at Shea Stadium after winning the 1969 World Series.*

5538 Fifteen minutes after the Mets clinched their championship, their followers had torn up the Shea Stadium surface.... And, being true Mets fans with their roots in 1962, they missed first base.—*Leonard Koppett, sportswriter, on New York winning the 1969 World Series.*

5539 It's hard to win a pennant, but it's harder losing one.—*Chuck Tanner, Pirates manager.*

5540 A win in April is just as important as a win in September.—*Dave Bristol, Reds manager.*

5541 I just won the Nobel Prize of baseball.—*Elston Howard, Yankees catcher, on being named the 1963 AL MVP.*

5542 If there was nobody else pitching, they still wouldn't give it to me.—*Joaquin Andujar, Cardinals pitcher, on consecutive 20-win seasons in which he finished fourth in the Cy Young voting, 1985.*

5543 I had such a good year. I didn't want to forget it.—*Dick Stuart, Red Sox first baseman, on why he didn't change his expired license plates, 1964. Stuart led the AL with a career-best 118 RBI in 1963.*

5544 If you don't play to win, why keep score? —*Vernon Law, Pirates pitcher.*

5545 This might be a game of inches, but the Tigers have all the inches right now. They own the yardstick.—*Bob Kearney, Mariners catcher, on the record-setting 35–5 start by the Tigers, 1984. Detroit finished 104–58 and defeated the Padres in the World Series.*

5546 It's the most exciting day I've ever had with my clothes on.—*Jane Fonda, actress and wife of Braves owner Ted Turner, on Atlanta winning the 1995 World Series.*

5547 This is the greatest day for Cleveland sports fans since the invention of the polyester bowling shirt.—*Jay Leno, talk show host, on the Indians victory over the defending World Series champion Yankees in the 1997 Division Series.*

5548 I wouldn't be at all unhappy if this baseball team never did win. Second place now and then would be nice. Second place. Give 'em something to look forward to, you know. But win and you'll spoil 'em. Win and they'll expect you to win all the time—and nobody can do that.—*Roy Hofheinz, Astros owner.*

5549 Baseball is a game where you gotta have fun. You do that by winning.—*Dave Bristol, Reds manager, 1967. Bristol didn't have much fun after leading the Cincinnati to a third-place finish in 1969. He was fired after the season, and Sparky Anderson subsequently led the Reds to the 1970 World Series. In seven more seasons as a manager, Bristol's teams never had a winning record.*

5550 The motto of the team I played for was "win or else." I don't know what the "else" part meant, and I never wanted to learn.—*Chuck Cary, White Sox pitcher, on playing in Japan, 1993.*

5551 The only bad thing about winning the pennant is that you have to manage the All-Star Game the next year. I'd rather go fishing for three days.—*Whitey Herzog, Cardinals manager.*

5552 There's a couple of clowns in our market, where if I win the World Series, they're going to say that I didn't sweep. And if we sweep, they'll figure out a reason why we didn't shut anybody out. It's petty ridiculous.—*Bobby Valentine, Mets manager, on making the playoffs as a wild card team, 2000. The Mets did make the World Series but lost to the Yankees.*

5553 Realistically, we know to get back into the race with them some extraordinary things have to happen—like the earth stops rotating.—*Mike Magnante, A's reliever, on the possibility of catching Seattle in the AL West, July 2001. At the All-Star break, Seattle led the division by 19 games, yet Oakland finished with 102 wins—14 games behind the Mariners—and made the postseason as the wild card.*

5554 We know next year was supposed to be our year, but we didn't feel like waiting.—*Paul Konerko, White Sox first baseman, September 2000. The Sox won 95 games but were swept by Seattle in the ALDS.*

5555 It took them 42 years to win the World Series, or as the Boston Red Sox call it, "beginner's luck."—*David Letterman, talk show host, on the Anaheim Angels winning the 2002 World Series.*

5556 Today at Disneyland, they celebrated by having a parade down Main Street. That's something that doesn't happen every day! Boy, how unusual!—*Jay Leno, talk show host, on the victory celebration for the 2002 World Series Champion Anaheim Angels.*

5557 Mystique and aura? Those are dancers at a nightclub.—*Curt Schilling, Diamondbacks pitcher, on the prospect of facing the vaunted Yankees in the 2001 World Series. Arizona defeated New York in a dramatic seven-game series.*

5558 The good news for the Red Sox is, tonight's weather definitely favors the Red Sox. The forecast is breezy—with about a 60 percent chance of hell freezing over.—*David Letterman, talk show host (and former weatherman), on the forecast for Game 7 of the 2004 ALCS between the Yankees and Red Sox. Boston became the first team to come back from losing the first three games of a series.*

5559 You know, a lot of people say they didn't want to die until the Red Sox won the World Series.... Well, there could be a lot of busy ambulances tomorrow.—*Johnny Damon, Red Sox outfielder, on the eve of winning the 2004 World Series, Boston's first since 1918.*

5560 When I go eat with my wife, it'll be dinner for three. I'm going to name it and give it its own plate.—*Todd Jones, Detroit reliever, on receiving his 2006 AL championship ring.*

5561 We are not the new Yankees, the old Yankees, any kind of Yankees. We're the Boston Red Sox. We're not your father's Red Sox, but we ain't ever going to be no Yankees.—*Larry Lucchino, Red Sox president, on winning the World Series in 2004 and 2007 after not winning one for almost a century.*

5562 Congratulations to the New York Yankees. Clinched their playoff berth. It just goes to show you what grit, hustle and a half a billion dollars will do.—*David Letterman, talk show host, 2009.*

5563 The L.A. Dodgers signed former base-stealing champion Maury Wills as their new base running and bunting coordinator. You know, the Yankees have a "bunting coordinator" too. He's the guy who hangs all the red, white and blue banners around Yankee Stadium every year for their postseason games.—*Jerry Perisho, comedy writer, 2000.*

5564 If you do everything right, you'll still lose 40 percent of your games—but you'll also end up in the World Series.—*Thomas Boswell, writer.*

5565 Always root for the winner. That way you won't be disappointed.—*Tug McGraw, Phillies reliever.*

INDIVIDUALS

Kinerisms: The Best of Ralph Kiner

During an amazing six-year run with the Pirates, Ralph Kiner led the majors in homers and made six All-Star teams, finishing in the top ten of the MVP voting five times. After two trades and a back injury, Kiner retired at the age of 32 following the 1955 season. He became an announcer for the White Sox in 1961, but he is best known as one of the original broadcasters for the New York Mets—a position he held ever since their inception in 1962. Kiner was inducted into the Hall of Fame in 1975.

5566 I'm Ralph Kiner along with Tim ... and Tim, what's your last name?—*Ralph Kiner, Hall of Fame outfielder and Mets broadcaster, to partner Tim McCarver.*

5567 All his saves have come during relief appearances.—*On Phillies reliever Steve Bedrosian, 1989.*

5568 You have really solidified the Mets centerfield problem.—*To outfielder Daryl Boston, 1990.*

5569 The reason the Mets have played so well at Shea this season is that they have the best home record in baseball.

5570 The Mets have the best record in baseball. In both leagues.—*1988.*

5571 The Mets will be returning to Stay Shea-dium.

5572 Rookie Wilson was a candidate for Mookie of the Year.—*On Mets outfielder Mookie Wilson.*

5573 Now up to bat for the Mets is Gary Cooper.—*On catcher Gary Carter.*

5574 In the hunt to buy the San Francisco Giants was George Shinn, owner of the Charlotte Harlots.—*Meaning to say Hornets, 1992.*

5575 This is Ralph Kiner, along with Frank Cashen, general manager of the San Diego Padres.—*Cashen was GM of the Mets, 1990.*

5576 The Mets just had their first .500-or-better April since July of 1992.—*1994.*

5577 The Hall of Fame ceremonies are on the 31st and 32nd of July.

5578 Rick Sutcliffe was the Rookie of the Year in his first year.

5579 Jim Gott can slow down a game as fast as anybody.—*1994.*

5580 [Don] Sutton lost 13 games in a row without winning a ball game.

5581 Jones allowed four earned runs—three of them unearned.—*1994.*

5582 There's a base hit into center field as Santana can't get to it. But he gets there and makes the catch.

5583 It's going, it's going, it's going ... to be caught.

5584 Kevin McReynolds stops at third; he scores.—*1989.*

5585 So [Dave] Magadan hit a sinking liner to left, but it went right into the glove of Murphy in right.—*1991.*

5586 There's a curveball. [Tug] McGraw seldom throws the curve. He probably throws it more now than ever before.

5587 Darryl Strawberry with the grand slam home run. And it comes on the anniversary of his last grand slam home run—by Kevin McReynolds.—*1990.*

5588 They will surpass the father-son tandem of Buddy Bell and Yogi Berra.—*On Barry and Bobby Bonds becoming the career father-son home run leaders, 1989. The father-son tandems of Gus and Buddy Bell and Yogi and Dale Berra had combined for 407 home runs each. In 1995, the Bonds duo also surpassed Maury and Bump Wills on the all-time father-son stolen base list.*

5589 The Mets have gotten their leadoff hitter on base only once this inning.—*1987.*

5590 They have been thrown out only one less time than the last place team has been thrown out the most.—*On the base-stealing of the 1989 Expos.*

5591 We'll be back with a recrap right after this message.—*1993.*

5592 [Mike] Scioscia's taken the onyx off [Darryl] Strawberry's back.—*1990.*

5593 We'll be back to wrap things up and talk about David Cone's 19-strikeout performance after this word from Bud Black.—*Meaning to say Bud Light, 1991.*

5594 We'll be back after this word from Manufacturer's Hangover.—*1988.*

5595 We're experiencing audio technicalities.

5596 He's been released by four different countries: The United States, Mexico, Japan and Valenzuela.—*On Padres reliever Keith Comstock, 1988.*

5597 Baseball began right here in this very stadium back in 1869.—*On Cincinnati's Riverfront Stadium, which was built in 1969.*

5598 This time he grounds it on the ground. —*1994.*

5599 Right down the middle for ball one.—*1989.*

5600 The game will start at 5 P.M. Pacific Coast League Daylight time.—*1987.*

5601 And the first pitch to [Kevin] Mitchell, lined into right field, deep to right field. It's out of here! Off the wall.

5602 He calls more balks than any other pitcher in the National League.—*On umpire Bob Davidson, 1994.*

5603 Leading off for the Mets will be Walter Johnson. Make that Howard Johnson. Well, Walter was a good hitter, too.

5604 Scott Sanderson was traded from Montreal on Pearl Harbor Day, June 7, 1983. —*1985. In 1988, President George H.W. Bush would make a similar mistake by referring to Pearl Harbor Day as September 7, 1941.*

5605 Third base is certainly a reactionary position.—*1988.*

5606 Some quiet guys are inwardly outgoing.—*1991.*

5607 Wagner simply played the game without the fanfare Cobb and Wagner generated.—*On Hall of Famers Honus Wagner and Ty Cobb, 1996.*

5608 All the Mets road wins against Los Angeles this year have been at Dodger Stadium.—*1989.*

5609 The Pirates won eight of their 102 losses against the Mets last year.

5610 He's going to be out of action the rest of his career.—*On an injury to Braves reliever Bruce Sutter, 1989.*

5611 Andy Van Slyke is 0 for his last 17 in his last 17 at bats.—*1995.*

5612 That was Johnnie LeMaster's first hit of the year against the Mets after 19 at-bats in which he went 0 for 19.

5613 Jay Bell is 0 for 6 in the series, with 10 homers and 52 RBIs—*1991.*

5614 Solo homers usually come with no one on base.

5615 Plesac is trying to pick up his first save of the year—and he can't do that.—*On reliever Dan Plesac who entered a game in a non-save situation, May 1996.*

5616 David Cone is the only Mets pitcher who has a pinch hit as a pinch-hitter.—*1991.*

5617 The right-hander is Charlie Lea and the left-hander is Bill Lee. One of them comes from another country, and the other one comes from another world.

5618 Today is Father's Day, so everybody out there, happy birthday.—*1987.*

5619 Tony Gwynn was named Player of the Year for April.

5620 It's a nice day for baseball if it doesn't rain.

5621 Santiago in Spanish means San Francisco. No. Santiago in San Diego means St. James.—*Translating the name of Padres catcher Benito Santiago, 1990.*

5622 If Casey Stengel were alive today, he'd be spinning in his grave.

5623 That's the great thing about baseball: You never know what's going on.

5624 Half of Jeff King's extra-base hits last year were extra base hits.

5625 Down the left-field and right-field lines, it's 99 liters.—*On the dimensions at Olympic Stadium in Montreal, which were marked using the metric system.*

5626 In every game that the Mets have taken an early lead they have scored first.

5627 He once called ex–Reds catcher Dann Bilardello "Don Bordello."—*Tim Kurkjian, sportswriter, on Ralph Kiner, 1988.*

5628 Would you intentionally throw a game to avoid appearing on the Mets postgame show, *Kiner's Korner*?—*David Letterman, talk show host, to Mets pitcher David Cone, 1989.*

Maverick Owner: Bill Veeck

Bill Veeck was the last of his kind—an owner who was not independently wealthy and did whatever he could to promote the game. Many of his antics annoyed his fellow owners, but Veeck's legacy of passion and innovation are beyond compare. As owner of the Cleveland Indians, St. Louis Browns and Chicago White Sox, he instituted a multitude of fan-friendly promotions, integrated the AL by signing Larry Doby and Satchel Paige, and—yes—he once sent a midget up to bat. Veeck was posthumously inducted into the Hall of Fame in 1991.

5629 Anything you do to enhance sales is a promotion.

5630 Baseball is a game to be savored rather than taken in gulps.

5631 Baseball is the only game left for people. To play basketball you have to be 7-feet, 6-inches. To play football, you have to be the same width.—*1973.*

5632 Baseball is the only orderly thing in a very unorderly world. If you get three strikes, even Edward Bennett Williams can't get you off.—*1975.*

5633 Baseball is the only thing besides the paper clip that hasn't changed.

5634 Baseball is the working man's game. A baseball crowd is a beer-drinking crowd, not a mixed drink crowd.

5635 The career operators, the lifelong baseball men, are like dinosaurs. Our time is past. Calvin [Griffith] and I are the last. There won't be any more.

5636 I'll have a long-range shotgun. If you swing the bat, you're gone.—*As St. Louis Browns owner, to 3'7" pinch hitter Eddie Gaedel, who became the shortest man ever to play in the major leagues. In the second game of a doubleheader, Gaedel walked on four pitches in his only at-bat, August 19, 1951.*

5637 He'd have been great in a short series.—*On Eddie Gaedel, 1981. Gaedel's uniform number was ⅛.*

5638 How can you be a sage if you're pretty? You can't get your wizard papers without wrinkles.

5639 I can't see as well as I could and I have to wear glasses. Watching this team, non-vision eases the pain.—*On the White Sox, 1976.*

5640 I'm shocked, amazed and chagrined.—*On the forfeiture of the second game of a doubleheader against Detroit, July 12, 1979. The ruling occurred after Chicago fans stormed the Comiskey Park field during Disco Demolition Night, a promotion concocted by his son Mike.*

5641 I'm the only person who invested every dime he had in a bad ball club that has the oldest ball park in either league. And I have no tax write-offs. Nobody else in baseball can make that claim.—*1977.*

5642 I try not to break the rules, but merely to test their elasticity.

5643 I used to pick my night spots so I'd never run into any of the players. But I kept my eye on them in my own way. Like, Ken Keltner was a free spirit, but it never seemed to affect his playing, and I worked out a deal with the bartender of his favorite spot, the Mickey Mouse bar. I told the bartender I'd give him $20 every time he put Keltner in a cab and sent him home at night. By the end of the season it cost me $600, but it was worth every penny.—*As owner of the 1948 Indians, 1976.*

5644 I was in the game for love. After all, what else can an old-timer like me with one leg, who can't hear or see, live like a king while doing the only thing I wanted to do?—*On selling the White Sox, 1981.*

5645 In a confused and confusing world in which the underpinnings are less stable than the shifting sand, more like a quagmire, baseball is an island of stability.—*1977.*

5646 The Browns are unable to beat their way out of a paper bag with a crowbar.—*As St. Louis Browns owner.*

5647 Many critics were surprised to know that the Browns could be bought, because they didn't know that the Browns were owned.—*John Lardner, sportswriter, on the purchase of the St. Louis Browns by Bill Veeck, 1951.*

5648 Sometime, somewhere, there will be a club nobody wants. And then Ole Will will come wandering along to laugh some more. Look for me under the arc lights, boys. I'll be back.—*On selling the White Sox, 1961. Veeck reclaimed the team in 1976.*

5649 Of all the things I've never wanted, this is it.—*On being offered the Washington franchise in the proposed World Baseball League, 1974.*

5650 We hope to bring a small degree of honor to Chicago, and a small degree of cash to ourselves.—*On heading a group of investors seeking to buy the White Sox, 1975.*

5651 It isn't the high price of stars that is expensive, it's the high price of mediocrity.—*On why he had to sell the White Sox, 1980.*

5652 People identify with the swashbuckling individuals, not polite little men who field their positions well. Sir Galahad had a big following, but I'll bet Lancelot had more.—*1971.*

5653 The season starts too early and finishes too late and there are too many games in between.—*1976.*

5654 It never ceases to amaze me how many of baseball's wounds are self-inflicted.

5655 That's the true harbinger of spring, not crocuses or swallows returning to Capistrano, but the sound of a bat on a ball.

5656 To compare baseball with other games is to say the Hope Diamond is a nice chunk of carbon. The endless variety of physical and mental skills demanded by baseball is both uncomparable and incomparable.

5657 We can't always guarantee the ball game is going to be good; but we can guarantee the fan will have fun.

5658 We can't catch the ball very well. We hit a little. We get hit a lot.—*On the White Sox, 1977.*

5659 We had a wirewalker once that we didn't pay because he fell behind the scoreboard. Nobody could see him. Any showman would have fallen in front of the scoreboard.—*1980.*

5660 We're doing this whole thing backward. Attorneys should wear numbers on their backs, and box scores should have entries for writs, depositions and appeals.—*1976.*

5661 We will scheme, connive, steal and do everything possible to win the pennant—except pay big salaries.—*1979.*

5662 When the Supreme Court says baseball isn't run like a business, everybody jumps up and down with joy. When I say the same thing, everybody throws pointy objects at me.—*1965.*

5663 Whatever I said over the years, the owners have looked at me as though I were a little boy trying to run fast so the propeller on my beanie would spin.

5664 What I will really be remembered for is sending a midget up to bat.... As a matter of fact, I don't mind if they put on my tombstone, "He helped the little people."—*1981.*

5665 My time is past, the way P.T. Barnum's time is past. I'm an individualist. Baseball has become a syndicate business.—*As White Sox owner, 1976.*

5666 All I ever said is that you can draw more people with a losing team, plus bread and circuses, than with a losing team and a long, still silence.

5667 Every innovation in baseball except a couple of kookie things that Charlie Finley tried—like orange baseballs and silly uniforms—originated with Veeck. Electric scoreboards, giveaways, fan days, concerts, and a pinch hitting midget.—*Hank Greenberg, Hall of Fame first baseman, 1981.*

5668 Bill Veeck belongs in the Hall of Fame down here. As for where he's headed, we can only caution folks up there to be ready. Nobody will be getting much sleep anymore.—*Bob Verdi, sportswriter, on Bill Veeck's death, 1986. Veeck was posthumously inducted to the Hall of Fame in 1991.*

5669 If James Brown is the "Godfather of Soul," Veeck was the "Godfather of the Diamond." He was a little irreverent; he had fun. Everything he did had heart. Now baseball takes itself too seriously. We've got a lot of "suits" in the game who have the passion of a mackerel.—*Mike Veeck, son of Bill Veeck.*

5670 They give away a bat or ball and it's called a promotion. To me, that's not a promotion, it's a giveaway. A promotion is something you generate out of thin air and make fly.—*Rudie Schaffer, baseball executive for all of Bill Veeck's teams, on the genius of Veeck's promotions.*

The Old Professor Speaks: The Words of Casey Stengel

He debuted as an outfielder with the Brooklyn Dodgers in 1912, and he went on to play fourteen seasons in the majors. He retired from baseball at 75 years old after managing the expansion New York Mets for their first four years—all in last place. And in between, he was manager during the greatest era in Yankees history, winning ten pennants and seven World Series titles in just twelve years. Inducted into the Hall of Fame in 1966, Charles Dillon "Casey" Stengel was one of the most colorful characters in the game, possessing a speech pattern and sense of humor all his own.

5671 Sometimes I get a little hard-of-speaking.

5672 I was pitching batting practice and they told me not to throw hard. I wanted to impress the manager, so I threw as hard as I could. Them hitters commenced hitting balls over buildings. I threw harder and they hit the ball further. Then I told the manager I was really an outfielder.—*On a tryout with Kansas City of the American Association, 1910.*

5673 I broke in with four base hits, and the writers promptly decided they had seen the new Ty Cobb. It took me only a few days to correct that assumption.—*On his debut with the Brooklyn Dodgers, 1912.*

5674 They brought me up to the Brooklyn Dodgers, which at that time was in Brooklyn.—*On his debut as an outfielder, 1912.*

5675 I was a left-handed dentist who made people cry.—*On his career before baseball.*

5676 Wake up, muscles! We're in New York now.—*On arriving at the Polo Grounds after being traded from the Phillies to the New York Giants, 1921.*

5677 When you're losing, everyone commences to play stupid.

5678 If anyone is going to be a clown on this club, it's going to be me.—*As Brooklyn Dodgers manager to outfielder Frenchy Bordagary, who showed up for spring training sporting a mustache and goatee, 1936.*

5679 A shave please, but don't cut my throat. I may want to do it later myself.—*As Brooklyn Dodgers manager to his barber after losing a doubleheader, 1935.*

5680 Managing the team back then was a tough business. Whenever I decided to release a guy, I always had his room searched for a gun. You couldn't take any chances with some of them birds.—*On managing the Brooklyn Dodgers of the 1930s.*

5681 I like the idea of bridges. Everywhere I go they throw in a bridge as part of the service. Every manager wants to jump off a bridge sooner or later, and it's very nice for an old man to know he doesn't have to walk fifty miles to find one.—*As manager of the Oakland Oaks of the Pacific Coast League, on the Golden Gate Bridge, 1946.*

5682 Ain't it funny, Bill, how all of a sudden I got so smart and you got so dumb.—*As Yankees manager to Pirates manager Billy Meyer after Stengel was named Manager of the Year, 1949. Meyer won the award the previous year.*

5683 He thinks I was born at the age of 62 and started managing immediately.—*As Yankees manager, on rookie outfielder Mickey Mantle, 1951.*

5684 You couldn't fool Casey because he'd pulled every stunt that ever was thought up, and he did it fifty years before we ever got there.—*Mickey Mantle, Yankees outfielder.*

5685 I don't play cards, I don't play golf, and I don't go to the picture show. All that's left is baseball.

5686 If you're playing baseball and thinking about managing, you're crazy. You'd be better off thinking about being an owner.—*As Yankees manager.*

5687 The Yankees don't pay me to win every day—just two out of three.

5688 I couldn't have done it without my players—*On winning his fifth consecutive World Series, 1953.*

5689 *Casey Stengel:* I won't trade my left fielder.
Reporter: Who's your left fielder?
Stengel: I don't know, but if it isn't him, I'll keep him anyway.

5690 Nobody knows this, but one of us has just been traded to Kansas City.—*As Yankees manager to outfielder Bob Cerv, 1956.*

5691 Son, we'd like to keep you around this season, but we're going to try to win a pennant. —*As Mets manager to pitcher Aubrey Gatewood, 1962.*

5692 Do you choke on your fucking microphone?—*When asked by a TV reporter if the Yankees "choked" after losing the seventh game of the 1957 World Series to the Milwaukee Braves.*

5693 If you're gonna pitch in the majors, you're gonna have to learn to catch 'em in your mouth.—*As Yankees manager to rookie pitcher Mark Freeman, who was called for a bases-loaded balk because a bug flew into his eye during the windup, 1959.*

5694 Always keep your eye on a fly ball. Don't look where you're running. We got grounds keepers to see that there's no ditches in the park.

5695 Well, we've got this Johnny Lewis in the outfield. They hit a ball to him yesterday, and he turned left, then turned right, then he went straight back and caught the ball. He made three good plays in one.—*As Mets manager, 1965.*

5696 About this autograph business. Once someone in Washington sent this picture up to me and I wrote, "Do good in school." I look up; this guy is 78 years old.—*As Yankees manager.*

5697 I love signing autographs. I'll sign anything but veal cutlets. My ball-point pen slips on veal cutlets.

5698 Well, the feller I got on there is hitting pretty good and I know he can make the throw and if he don't make it, that other feller I got coming up has shown me a lot and he if can't, I have my guy and I know what he can do. On the other hand, the guy's not around now. Ah well, this guy may be able to do it against left-handers if my guy isn't strong enough. But I know one of my guys is going to do it.

5699 Well, I made up my mind, but I made it up both ways.—*As Yankees manager on whether he would retire if the Yankees lost the 1960 World Series. Pittsburgh defeated New York in seven games and Stengel was let go by the Yankees days later.*

5700 I'll never make the mistake of being 70 years old again.—*On not having his contract renewed by the Yankees after losing the 1960 World Series to Pittsburgh.*

5701 It's great to be back at the Polar Grounds again with the New York Knickerbockers.—*On being hired as the first manager of the expansion New York Mets, 1962.*

5702 My health is good enough above the shoulders.—*On becoming Mets manager, 1962.*

5703 Everybody keeps saying how good I'm looking. Well, maybe I do. But they should see me inside. I look terrible inside.—*On returning to baseball as manager of the 1962 Mets.*

5704 Too bad we can't win a few games for that nice owner of ours over in Europe. What's her name?—*As Mets manager on owner Joan Payson, 1962.*

5705 The way our luck has been lately, our fellows have been hurt on days off.—*As Mets manager, 1962.*

5706 If any writers want to talk to me, tell 'em I'm being embalmed.—*As Mets manager, 1962.*

5707 They're amazing. Can't anyone here play this game?—*As Mets manager, 1962.*

5708 When one of them guys hits a single to you, throw the ball to third. That way we can hold them to a double.—*To the Mets outfielders, 1962.*

5709 You have to have a catcher, because if you don't, you're likely to have a lot of passed balls.—*As Mets manager, on why New York selected catcher Hobie Landrith as the first player in the 1961 expansion draft.*

5710 And I want to thank the tremendous fans. We appreciate every boys' group, girls' group, poem and song. And keep goin' to see the Mets play.—*At his Hall of Fame induction, 1966.*

5711 I want to thank all my players for giving me the honor of being what I was.—*On being named "Baseball's Greatest Living Manager" at baseball's 100th birthday party, 1969.*

5712 You have to remember that this team came up slow, but fast.—*On the Mets, who went from 120 losses in 1962 to a World Series victory in 1969.*

5713 It's wonderful to meet so many friends that I didn't use to like.—*At an old-timers' game in Cincinnati, 1971.*

5714 Old-timers' weekends and airplane landings are alike. If you can walk away from them, they're successful.—*1975.*

5715 Me manage again? If I do it'll be a girls' team.—*1971.*

5716 Edna Lawson. Best catch I ever made.—*On his wife of 51 years.*

5717 It used to be that you had to catch the ball two-handed because the glove was so small. Why, when I got married I couldn't afford dress gloves, so I wore my baseball mitt to my wedding and nobody even noticed. That took care of my right hand, and I was smart enough to keep my left hand in my pocket.—*1972.*

5718 I feel greatly honored to have a ball park named after me, especially since I've been thrown out of so many.—*On a ballpark dedication ceremony in Glendale, California, 1973.*

5719 Well, I'll tell you, young fella, to be truthful and honest and frank about it, I'm 83 years old, which ain't bad. To be truthful and honest and frank about it, the thing I'd like to be right now is an astronaut.—*When asked if he would like to manage again, 1973.*

5720 The Mets have been paying me for the past 10 years, and people ask me what I do for them. I don't bother them, that's what.—*1974.*

5721 There comes a time in every man's life—and I've had plenty of them.—*1974.*

5722 There were a lot of people who could play ball that I saw, and [Joe] DiMaggio could be as good as any of them, but I can't tell you who was best because the others would all get angry and some of them are dead at the present time.—*1975.*

5723 I was the best manager I ever saw, but I tell people that to shut them up quickly and because I also believe it.

5724 Baseball is very big at the present time. This makes me think baseball will live longer than Casey Stengel or anybody else.

5725 The way he's going, I'd be better off if he was hurt.—*As Yankees manager on first baseman Bill "Moose" Skowron.*

5726 He can write a book on why a curveball curves, but he can't show you.—*On Mets pitcher Jay Hook, 1962. Hook, who earned a master's degree in thermodynamics, was credited with the first Mets victory on April 23, 1962—after New York lost the first nine games of the season.*

5727 The best thing wrong with Jack Fisher is nothing.—*1966.*

5728 He has wonderful stuff and wonderful control and throws strikes, which shows he's educated. But say you're educated and you can't throw strikes; then they don't have you in too long.—*On Dodgers pitcher Mike Marshall, 1974.*

5729 Because then there'd be two languages I couldn't speak—French and English.—*On why he never visited Montreal.*

5730 You done splendid.—*His favorite compliment.*

5731 You could look it up.—*One of his favorite sayings.*

5732 Some people say they have trouble understanding me. I don't know why. I understand myself.

5733 Mr. Stengel can talk all day and all night on any kind of track, wet or dry.—*John Lardner, sportswriter.*

5734 He used the double-talk as a ploy to avoid answering questions he didn't want to answer. You could be listening to Casey when he was in that mood, go away, come back three hours later and he'd still be talking, unaware you had ever gone.—*Sparky Anderson, Tigers manager, 1985.*

5735 Casey knew his baseball. He only made it look like he was fooling around. He knew every move that was ever invented and some that we haven't even caught on to yet.—*Manager Sparky Anderson.*

5736 The hiring of Stengel was a masterstroke because Casey could have given PR lessons to FDR. Having been fired by the Yankees for becoming the oldest living manager ever to win ten pennants in twelve years, he was returning to New York as a beloved and somewhat ill-used figure, full of years, honors, and sympathy. [...] He created a feeling, I suppose, that if he could come out of retirement in his old age and suffer through a Met ball game every day, the least the rest of the subway commuters could do was to come on out and suffer along with him.—*Bill Veeck, former owner, 1965.*

5737 If he ever turned pro, he'd put us all out of work.—*George Gobel, comedian, on Casey Stengel.*

5738 Casey Stengel just can't keep from being Casey Stengel.—*Commissioner Kenesaw Mountain Landis.*

5739 I'm probably the only guy who worked for Stengel before and after he was a genius.—*Warren Spahn, Hall of Fame pitcher, on playing for Stengel's 1942 Milwaukee Braves and 1965 New York Mets, 1983.*

5740 Everybody knows that Casey Stengel has forgotten more baseball than I'll ever know. That's the trouble, he's forgotten it.—*Jimmy Piersall, Mets outfielder, 1963.*

5741 Casey's memory is legendary. It is also inaccurate.—*Edward Linn, sportswriter.*

5742 It is fashionable to say that successful people, in any field, could have been whatever they wanted, but you could not picture Casey Stengel being anything else but what he was, the greatest showman baseball ever knew.—*Mickey Herskowitz, sportswriter.*

5743 Casey Stengel is a white American male with a speech pattern that ranges somewhere between the sound a porpoise makes underwater and an Abyssinian rug merchant.—*Jim Murray, sportswriter.*

5744 Excuse me, Casey, now I have to throw this upstairs to our translators.—*Tony Kubek, broadcaster, during an interview with Stengel at the 1970 World Series.*

5745 I looked at film clips of Casey and listened to tapes, and I couldn't understand how he did it. He never seemed to stop for commas or periods. When I tried it, I hyperventilated. I had to find my cadence or die.—*Actor Paul Dooley on the challenge of portraying Stengel on stage in* The Amazin' Casey Stengel or Can't Anybody Here Speak This Game? *1981.*

5746 It's the first role I've ever played in a foreign language.—*Charles Durning, actor, on talking over for Paul Dooley to portray Stengel on stage.*

5747 I always understood everything Casey Stengel said, which sometimes worried me.—*Rod Dedeaux, University of Southern California coach.*

5748 When I was young and smart, I couldn't understand him. Now that I'm older and dumber, he makes sense to me.—*Sandy Koufax, Dodgers pitcher, 1966.*

5749 Casey could fool you. When he wanted to make sense he could. But he usually preferred to make you laugh.—*Yogi Berra, former Yankees catcher.*

5750 He is gone and I am supposed to cry, but I laugh. Every time I saw the man, every time I heard his voice, every time his name was mentioned, the creases in my mouth would give way and a smile would come to my face.—*Maury Allen, sportswriter, on the death of Casey Stengel, September 29, 1975.*

5751 Well, God is certainly getting an earful tonight.—*Jim Murray, sportswriter, on the death of Casey Stengel, September 29, 1975.*

Yogi-isms: The Wisdom of Yogi Berra

He played in the World Series fourteen times, winning ten championships. He won three AL MVP awards, finishing in the top 15 of the voting twelve times. He was a fifteen-time All-Star, and when his playing days were over, he won the pennant as manager of the 1964 Yankees and 1973 Mets. And he was inducted into the Hall of Fame in 1972. But beyond all his baseball accomplishments, Lawrence Peter "Yogi" Berra is best know for simply being Yogi—a catcher from St. Louis who became a New York icon and a purveyor of homespun philosophy and twisted logic. He is as beloved a figure as the sport has ever known, and easily the most quotable.

5752 What's a Yogi-ism?

5753 If the world was perfect, it wouldn't be.

5754 You can see a lot just by observing.

5755 Baseball is 90 percent mental and the other half is physical.

5756 This ain't work. Geez, you're only out there three hours.—*As Yankees manager, 1984.*

5757 Baseball is the champ of them all. Like somebody said, the pay is good and the hours are short.

5758 Bill Dickey learned me all his experience.—*On the catcher he succeeded, 1946.*

5759 There's no stopping the future.

5760 A home opener is always exciting, no matter whether it's at home or on the road.

5761 How can I hit and think at the same time?

5762 I had a bad year last year, and maybe the reason was I tried to hit too many good pitches.

5763 I want to thank everyone who made this day necessary.—*At Yogi Berra Day in St. Louis, 1947.*

5764 I wish I had an answer to that because I'm getting tired of answering that question.—*As Yankees manager, 1984.*

5765 If people don't come out to the ballpark, who's going to stop them?

5766 *Casey Stengel (Yankees manager):* What would you do if you found a million dollars?

Yogi Berra (Yankees catcher): If the guy was poor, I would give it back.

5767 If you can't imitate him, don't copy him.

5768 If you come to a fork in the road, take it.

5769 Never answer an anonymous letter.

5770 If you don't catch the ball, you catch the bus.

5771 It ain't over till it's over.—*1973.*

5772 It gets late early out there.—*On left field in Yankee Stadium.*

5773 Nobody goes there anymore. It's too crowded.—*On a popular restaurant.*

5774 It was hard to have a conversation with anyone, there were so many people talking.—*At a White House dinner, 1985.*

5775 Just when you think you know baseball, you don't.

5776 Listen up, because I've got nothing to say and I'm only going to say it once.—*1984.*

5777 A nickel ain't worth a dime anymore.

5778 The other teams could make trouble for us if they win.—*As Yankees manager, 1964.*

5779 This is the earliest we've ever arrived late.

5780 Uniforms are all the same. Some are just hotter than others.—*On becoming a coach for the Astros, 1986.*

5781 We made too many wrong mistakes.—*On the Yankees losing the 1960 World Series to Pittsburgh.*

5782 We may lose again tomorrow, but not with the same guys.—*As Yankees manager after a lopsided loss, 1984.*

5783 Only the scary parts.—*As Astros coach and a part-time movie critic, when asked if* Fatal Attraction *had frightened him, 1987.*

5784 Oh, what's the matter with you now?—*After his wife Carmen told him she had just seen* Dr. Zhivago.

5785 We have a good time together, even when we're not together—*On his wife Carmen.*

5786 *Mayor's wife:* You look nice and cool, Yogi.
Yogi: You don't look so hot yourself.

5787 *Lady:* Yoo-hoo? Is that hyphenated?
Yogi: Lady, it ain't even carbonated.—*On a chocolate drink Yogi promoted.*

5788 *Mickey Mantle*: I just wanted to wish you a happy birthday.
Yogi: Thank you. The same to you.

5789 You mean now?—*When asked what time it was.*

5790 You've got to be very careful if you don't know where you are going, because you might not get there.

5791 You've got to say Pittsburgh's the team to beat in our division. I'm not worried about the Yankees. We don't have to play them.—*As Mets manager, 1975.*

5792 Bobby Avila had a good year for them. He got the MVP that year, I think. 1954? I'm pretty sure. Didn't he?—*Yogi won the 1954 AL MVP; Avila finished third.*

5793 Hey, Jack, you've known me all these years. And you still don't know how to spell my name?—*As Yankees catcher to broadcaster Jack Buck, after receiving a check that read,* "Pay to Bearer."

5794 Why buy good luggage? You only use it when you travel.

5795 That's because they have to import those English muffins.—*On why a hotel coffee shop charged $8.95 for juice, coffee and an English muffin.*

5796 I knew I was going to take the wrong train, so I left early.

5797 It's not too far, it just seems like it is.—*Giving directions.*

5798 We're lost, but we're making good time.—*On driving to his Hall of Fame induction, 1972.*

5799 Don't look a good thing in the eye.

5800 I get up at 6 A.M., no matter what time it is.

5801 I ain't gonna sleep standing up.—*On staying in a residential hotel room with a Murphy bed, 1956.*

5802 We have deep depth.—*As Yankees manager, 1984.*

5803 You wouldn't have won if we had beaten you.—*As Yankees catcher to Dodgers executive Al Campanis, after losing the 1963 World Series to Los Angeles.*

5804 Third ain't so bad if nothing is hit to you. —*As Yankees catcher on experimenting with playing third base, 1960.*

5805 A three-game series at the beginning of the season is longer than a three-game series in July.

5806 No, but he did a lot better than I thought he would.—*As Yankees manager when asked if rookie first baseman Don Mattingly had exceeded expectations, 1984.*

5807 He has exceeded my expectations and done even better.—*As Yankees manager on rookie first baseman Don Mattingly, 1984.*

5808 *Reporter:* Yogi, have you made up your mind yet?
Yogi: Not that I know of.

5809 The only color I don't have is navy brown.—*On his sweater collection.*

5810 It reminds me of being in the Army, even though I was in the Navy.—*On seeing a Broadway production of Neil Simon's* Biloxi Blues.

5811 When you're struggling, the way to win is to play a team that's also struggling.—*As Yankees manager, 1985.*

5812 I'd rather be the Yankees catcher than the President, and that makes me pretty lucky, I guess, because I could never be the President.—*As Yankees catcher.*

5813 *Yogi Berra (Yankees catcher):* Henry, you'd better turn the trademark around so you can read it. Otherwise you'll break your bat.

Henry Aaron (Braves outfielder): Yogi, I came up here to hit, not to read.—*Conversation at home plate during the 1958 World Series. Aaron hit .333 for the Series, but the Yankees won in seven games.*

5814 It was pretty good. Even the music was nice.—*After seeing the opera* Tosca *with his parents in Milan, Italy, 1961.*

5815 No, but I saw him.—*When asked if he had an audience with the Pope while in Italy.*

5816 Always go to other people's funerals, otherwise they won't come to yours.

5817 Anybody who can't hear the difference between a ball hitting concrete and a ball hitting wood must be blind.—*As Yankees catcher, arguing with an umpire that a hit to the outfield should have been a home run but was erroneously ruled a double because the umpire thought the ball hit the wooden outfield wall, not the concrete facade of the stadium.*

5818 Come over here and show me how to work this thing.—*To a teammate on his new piano.*

5819 It's nothing but rooms.—*On his new house.*

5820 Don't know, they were wearing a bag over their head.—*When asked if a streaker was male or female.*

5821 Well, who's in it?—*When asked by a reporter if he wanted to see a pornographic movie.*

5822 My little son can't wait to shave so he can grow a beard.

5823 I'm not going to buy my kids an encyclopedia. Let them walk to school like I did.

5824 *Radio host:* We've got Yogi Berra of the New York Yankees here, and he and I are going to do some free associating. I'm going to say a name, and Yogi's going to say the first thing that pops into his mind ... Mickey Mantle.

Yogi: What about him?

5825 It's never happened in the World Series competition, and it still hasn't.—*On teammate Don Larsen's perfect game in the 1956 World Series, 1990.*

5826 I prefer to remember Mickey as he is.—*When asked if he ever looked at Mickey Mantle's 1952 baseball card.*

5827 *Yogi Berra (Yankees coach):* Don't look now, Fish, but there's someone famous at the table behind you.

Catfish Hunter (Yankees pitcher): Yeah, Yogi, who is it?

Yogi: Well, I'm not sure. See, he's one of two brothers, but one of them is dead. I can't remember which one died, so I can't figure out which that one is—the one that's alive or the one that's dead.

5828 *Yogi Berra (during a game of 20 Questions):* Is he living?

Del Webb (Yankees part-owner): Yes.

Yogi: Is he living now?

5829 You dead yet?—*In a phone call to former teammate Whitey Ford who had a recurrence of cancer, May 2000. Ford's reply: "I'm still here."*

5830 Boy, I hope I never see my name up there.—*To former teammate Whitey Ford, on a list of deceased Yankees players that appeared on the scoreboard at Old Timers' Day, 2004.*

5831 *Carmen Berra:* Yogi, you are from St. Louis, we live in New Jersey, and you played ball in New York. If you go before I do, where would you like me to have you buried?

Yogi Berra: Surprise me.

5832 *Larry Berra:* Dad, the guy is here for the venetian blinds.

Yogi Berra: Look in my pants pocket and give him five bucks.

5833 Nobody never hit nobody nohow.—*As Yankees catcher after a brawl involving several players at the Copacabana night club, 1957.*

5834 Every time I see him, he's not there.—*When asked by a writer during spring training if Yogi had seen Yankees announcer Phil Rizzuto lately, 2000.*

5835 It ain't hard. We agree different.—*As Yankees manager on how he was able to get along with owner George Steinbrenner.*

5836 He was so popular, no one could stand him.—*On a high school classmate.*

5837 I say a lot of things I don't remember.

5838 I don't care. They don't mean bad and they're making me famous.—*As Yankees manager on reporters who make up quotations and attribute them to him, 1984.*

5839 I didn't really say everything I said.

5840 It's like what Yogi said.... What did Yogi say?—*George Bell, White Sox outfielder, 1992.*

5841 He told the pitchers to pair off in threes. —*Mickey Mantle, former Yankees outfielder, on the first spring practice in 1964 under manager Yogi Berra.*

5842 You can pitch a gem and still lose, but you can't lose when you win.... Wait, don't quote me on that. I sound like Yogi Berra.—*Eric Show, Padres pitcher, 1988.*

5843 As Yogi Bear once said, "A thing is not done until it is done."—*Robert Maxwell, British press magnate, attempting to paraphrase Yogi while in New York to buy the* Daily News.

5844 You may not understand his words, but you always understand his meaning.—*Larry Andersen, Astros reliever, on coach Yogi Berra, 1989.*

5845 No one feels baseball better than Yogi Berra, no one relishes the excitement of its competition more, no one reacts more quickly to its constant challenge. He is a masterpiece of a ballplayer.—*Robert Creamer, sportswriter.*

5846 The decision to make Yogi Berra, of all people, the manager of the Yankees was admittedly one of the more moonstruck episodes in baseball.—*Bill Veeck, former baseball owner. After winning the pennant in his first year as manager in 1964, Berra was fired.*

5847 Yogi Berra is a completely manufactured product. He is a case study of this country's unlimited ability to gull itself and be gulled.—*Jim Bouton, former Yankees pitcher.*

5848 Yogi's supposed to have said a lot of funny things, but I don't know how anyone hears all the funny things he says, because he doesn't talk.—*Sparky Lyle, Yankees reliever, 1978.*

5849 They say he's funny. Well, he has a lovely wife and family, a beautiful home, money in the bank, and he plays golf with millionaires. What's so funny about that? —*Casey Stengel, former Yankees manager, on Yogi.*

5850 He'd fall in a sewer and come up with a gold watch.—*Casey Stengel.*

5851 He was a peculiar fellow with amazing ability.—*Casey Stengel.*

5852 Yogi has been an inspiration to me—not only because of his baseball skills—but of course for his enduring mark he left on the English language. Some of the press corps even think he might be my speech writer.—*President George W. Bush at a luncheon for Hall of Famers, including Yogi, March 2001.*

5853 If I hadn't woken up, I'd still be asleep.—*Yogi's wife Carmen, on receiving a Pinnacle of Achievement Award from the Salvation Army, 2000.*

5854 Our similarities are different.—*Dale Berra, Pirates infielder, on his father Yogi, 1982.*

Appendix: Rank by Number of Quotations (7 or more)

Stengel, Casey	142
Berra, Yogi	136
Coleman, Jerry	94
Kiner, Ralph	73
Veeck, Bill	59
Letterman, David	55
Rose, Pete	54
Lee, Bill	52
Jackson, Reggie	49
Dean, Dizzy	48
Anderson, Sparky	42
Van Slyke, Andy	42
Lasorda, Tommy	39
Leno, Jay	39
Murray, Jim	38
Quisenberry, Dan	38
Uecker, Bob	38
Martin, Billy	37
Durocher, Leo	32
Ostler, Scott	32
Bouton, Jim	31
Bridges, Rocky	30
Weaver, Earl	30
Garagiola, Joe	28
Gomez, Lefty	28
Piniella, Lou	28
Andersen, Larry	26
Herzog, Whitey	26
Rickey, Branch	24
Mauch, Gene	23
McCarver, Tim	23
Caray, Harry	22
Guillen, Ozzie	22
Mantle, Mickey	22
Torre, Joe	22
Turner, Ted	22
Kruk, John	21
Paige, Satchel	21
Rizzuto, Phil	21
Scully, Vin	20
Williams, Mitch	20
Boswell, Thomas	19
Donnelly, Rich	19
Luciano, Ron	19
Ruth, Babe	19
Williams, Ted	19
Finley, Charlie	18
Armsatrong, Jim	17
Feller, Bob	17
Leyland, Jim	17
Nettles, Graig	17
Rivers, Mickey	17
Steinbrenner, George	17
Andujar, Joaquin	16
Griffith, Calvin	16
Henderson, Rickey	16
Smith, Red	16
Sutton, Don	16
Robinson, Frank	15
Cobb, Ty	14
DiMaggio, Joe	14
Greenwald, Hank	14
Koufax, Sandy	14
Lincicome, Bernie	14
Mack, Connie	14
Aaron, Henry	13
Ashburn, Richie	13
Brett, George	13
Grace, Mark	13
Perisho, Jerry	13
Hough, Charlie	12
McGraw, Tug	12
Chandler, Happy	11
Drysdale, Don	11
Fairly, Ron	11
Lemon, Bob	11
Stone, Steve	11
McGraw, John	11
Suzuki, Ichiro	11
Hornsby, Rogers	10
Hunter, Catfish	10
Jackson, Bo	10
Palmer, Jim	10
Richards, Paul	10
Simmons, Lon	10
Thompson, Fresco	10
Will, George	10
Winfield, Dave	10
Zimmer, Don	10
Belinski, Bo	9
Bench, Johnny	9
Bowa, Larry	9
Clary, Ellis	9
Dark, Alvin	9
Fregosi, Jim	9
Gibson, Bob	9
Logan, Johnny	9
Magrane, Joe	9
Mays, Willie	9
McKeon, Jack	9
Musial, Stan	9
Parker, Dave	9
Perry, Gaylord	9
Rader, Doug	9
Robinson, Brooks	9
Ryan, Nolan	9
Stargell, Willie	9
Stark, Jayson	9
Baer, Bugs	8
Bavasi, Buzzie	8
Brenly, Bob	8

Buck, Jack	8
Deshaies, Jim	8
FitzGerald, Tom	8
Gammons, Peter	8
Gibson, Bob	9
Hoyt, Waite	8
Kahn, Roger	8
Monday, Rick	8
Nash, Ogden	8
Olbermann, Keith	8
Shaughnessy, Dan	8
Young, Cy	8
Young, Dick	8
Alderson, Sandy	7
Allen, Dick	7
Banks, Ernie	7
Bonds, Barry	7
Brock, Lou	7
Brosnan, Jim	7
Canseco, Jose	7
Caray, Skip	7
Clemens, Roger	7
Conlin, Bill	7
Costas, Bob	7
Craig, Roger	7
Eckersley, Dennis	7
Frey, Jim	7
Gwynn, Tony	7
Hurdle, Clint	7
John, Tommy	7
Johnson, Davey	7
Kaat, Jim	7
Kearney, Bob	7
Kerfeld, Charlie	7
Kern, Jim	7
Klem, Bill	7
LaPoint, Dave	7
Lardner, Ring	7
LaRussa, Tony	7
Maddon, Joe	7
Manuel, Charlie	7
Mitchell, Kevin	7
Ozark, Danny	7
Paul, Gabe	7
Ray, Alan	7
Seaver, Tom	7
Torborg, Jeff	7
Trebelhorn, Tom	7

Name Index

Subject Index